E ROUGH GUIDE TO

PARIS

ROUGH GUIDES

This sixteenth edi
Ruth Blackm

Contents

OPPOSITE RUE NORVINS, MONTMARTRE **PREVIOUS PAGE** VIEW OF THE EIFFEL TOWER FROM MONTMARTRE

Introduction to
Paris

Paris captivates and charms in equal measure. Heartbreakingly beautiful, impeccably stylish and unashamedly romantic, it is also a city of immense cultural importance, having spent much of the last thousand years at the centre of European artistic and literary life. And for all its magnificent monuments – the iconic industrial chic of the Eiffel Tower, the grandeur of the Panthéon, the jaw-dropping glasswork of the Louvre pyramid – the real Paris operates on a very human scale. Some of the most memorable moments come when stumbling across exquisite, secret little nooks or village-like neighbourhoods that revolve around the local boulangerie and café. Even as the capital's culture has been radically transformed by its large immigrant populations, even as extravagant new buildings are commissioned and erected, Paris never feels anything but timeless. Traditional and cosmopolitan, nostalgic and forward-looking – a dynamic combination that gives this unique city its profound emotional pull.

In the great local tradition of the *flâneur*, or thoughtful urban wanderer, Paris is a wonderful city for aimless exploration. Quarters such as the charming Marais, elegant St-Germain and romantic Montmartre are ideal for strolling, browsing the shops and **relaxing in cafés**, while the centre boasts some beautiful formal gardens and **landscaped promenades** that run beside the River Seine.

There are nearly 150 **art galleries** and **museums** on offer, and barely any of them are duds. Places to **eat and drink** line the streets and boulevards, ranging from chic temples of gastronomy and grandly mirrored brasseries down to tiny, chef-owned neo-bistros and steamy Vietnamese diners. After dark, the city's theatres, concert halls and churches host world-leading productions of drama, **dance and classical music**, and there is no better place in the world for **cinema**. There are also plenty of great places to enjoy clubbing and **live gigs** – not least jazz, world music and the home-grown singer-songwriter genre of *chanson*.

ABOVE TAXI PARISIEN

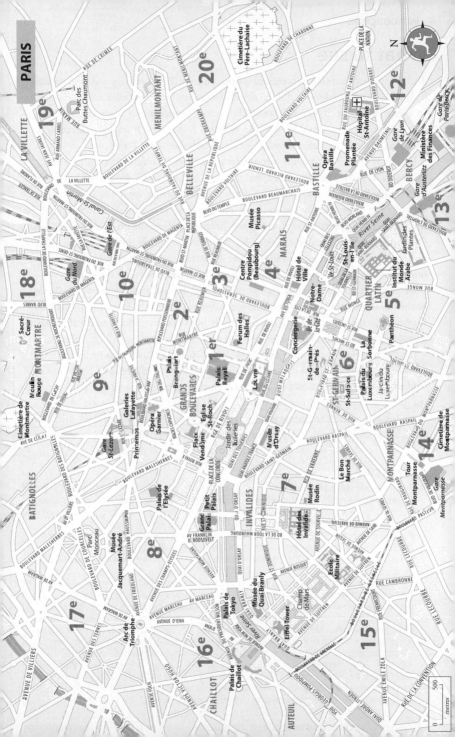

What to see

The now-demolished ring of fortifications that once encircled the city and was replaced by the *boulevard périphérique* still defines the boundary between Paris and its suburbs. At its widest point, the city is only about 12km across – roughly two hours' walk. At the hub of the circle, in the middle of the **River Seine**, is the island from which all the rest grew: the **Ile de la Cité**, defined by its Gothic cathedral of **Notre-Dame**.

The city is divided into twenty **arrondissements**. Centred on the royal palace and mighty gallery of the **Louvre**, they spiral outwards in a clockwise direction. On the north or **Right Bank** (Rive Droite) of the Seine, which is the smarter, more business-focused of the city's two halves, the longest and grandest vista in all Paris runs west from the Louvre: this is **La Voie Triomphale** – comprising the Tuileries gardens, the grand avenue of the **Champs-Elysées** and the Arc de Triomphe. North of the Louvre is the commercial and financial quarter, where you can shop in the department stores on the broad **Grands Boulevards**, in the little boutiques of the glass-roofed **passages** or in the giant, underground mall of **Les Halles**. East of the Louvre, the enchanting **Marais** and vibrant **Bastille** quarters are alive with trendy shops, cafés and bars. Further east, cool Parisians from all over the city gravitate to the once seedy but rapidly regenerating **Canal St-Martin** and **Ménilmontant** for cutting-edge bars and nightlife.

The south bank of the river, or **Left Bank** (Rive Gauche), is quieter and a tad more raffish. The **Quartier Latin** is the traditional domain of the intelligentsia – from artists to students – along with **St-Germain**, which becomes progressively more chichi until it hits the grand district of ministries and museums that surrounds the **Eiffel Tower**. As you move south towards **Montparnasse** and the southern swathe of the Left Bank, high-rise flats start to alternate with charming bourgeois neighbourhoods.

THE SEINE

Referred to by some as Paris's main avenue, or its 21st arrondissement – and by others as a murky, polluted waterway – the **Seine** is integral to the capital, sashaying through its centre in a broad arc and taking in all the grandest monuments. It even makes its way into the city's coat of arms, which depicts a ship sailing on choppy waters accompanied by the words *fluctuat nec mergitur* – "it is tossed about but does not sink", a singularly apt motto for a place that has weathered turbulent events from the French Revolution and the Commune to the terror attacks in November 2015, when the phrase was taken up by many Parisians as a sort of rallying cry of resistance.

The Seine brought the city into being and was for centuries its lifeblood, a major conduit of **trade** and **commerce**. Floods, however, have always been a regular hazard, sometimes sweeping away bridges, houses and lives. One of the worst recorded was in 1176, when the city was almost completely engulfed; the water also reached dangerously high levels in 2016. Largely, however, the construction of the **quais** in the nineteenth century helped to alleviate the problem, and these tree-lined walkways have today become one of Paris's major assets – attractive, leafy havens away from the urban clatter. Meanwhile, more and more of the riverbank is being **reclaimed** for pedestrians and cyclists; cars are banned from the **Parc Rives de Seine**, a loop that takes in stretches of both the Left and Right banks, while in summer, during **Paris Plages**, tonnes of sand are imported to create a kind of Paris-sur-Mer for overheated urbanites, complete with palm trees and deckchairs.

CLOCKWISE FROM TOP LEFT CHEESE STALL, MARCHÉ BIO; *THE KISS*, MUSÉE RODIN; ALONG THE CHAMPS-ELYSÉES

WALLACE'S FOUNTAINS

Moved by the suffering that Parisians had endured during the Siege of Paris in 1870–71 (see box, p.186), which had deprived the citizens of running water, a wealthy British resident called **Richard Wallace** came up with the perfect gift. In 1872, Wallace gave the city fifty cast-iron **drinking fountains**, each topped with a kind of miniature temple designed by the sculptor Charles-Auguste Lebourg, its roof supported by four caryatids representing Simplicity, Temperance, Charity and Goodness. More fountains were added in later years, and today some 67 still stand. Painted in lustrous green, their usefulness is limited these days by the loss of the cups once permanently attached to them, but they still work (from mid-March to mid-Nov only, because of the risk of damage from ice in winter) and the water's good to drink – it's the same water that flows through all the city's taps, although a recent study showed that only around thirty percent of Parisians actually drink from them. All the same, **les fontaines Wallace** remain quintessential symbols of Paris. Curiously, they have an unusual status in the French language, too, being one of the few Gallic words to begin with "w"; like *le whisky, le weekend* and *le wi-fi, les fontaines Wallace* are something of a linguistic collector's item.

Back on the Right Bank, many of the outer arrondissements were once outlying villages. Hilly **Montmartre**, with its rich artistic and bohemian associations, is the most picturesque, but the residential districts of **Belleville** and **Passy** have also retained distinct neighbourhood identities – working-class in the east, wealthy in the west.

Central Paris abounds in wonderful gardens, notably the **Jardin du Luxembourg**, **Jardin des Tuileries** and **Jardin des Plantes**, all of them well used by the city's inhabitants. For something a little wilder and more expansive, the best big parks are the **Bois de Vincennes** and the **Bois de Boulogne**, at the eastern and western edges of the city, respectively. Smaller pockets of green crop up all over Paris: not least at any number of museums, including the Petit Palais, Musée Rodin, Musée du Quai Branly, Musée de Montmartre and Musée de l'Histoire de France.

The region surrounding the capital, beyond the **boulevard périphérique** ring road, is known as the **Ile-de-France**, and is dotted with cathedrals and châteaux. Sights such as the Gothic cathedral at **St-Denis** and the astonishing royal palace at **Versailles** are easy to reach, while full day-trip destinations include the stunning cathedral town of **Chartres** and Monet's lovely garden at **Giverny**. An equally accessible outing from the capital is that most un-French of French attractions, **Disneyland Paris**.

When to go

In terms of climate (see p.33), **spring** is deservedly the classic time to visit, with bright days balanced by refreshing rain showers. Paris in high **summer** is usually hot and can be uncomfortably humid, especially between mid-July and the end of August, when many Parisians flee south, leaving the city to the tourists. In **autumn**, things can be pleasingly mild and gratifyingly uncrowded (except during the autumn fashion show and trade-fair season, when hotels fill up early), but on overcast days – all too common – it can feel somewhat melancholy. **Winter** can be harsh, with icy winds cutting down the boulevards and snow not uncommon; the winter sun, on the other hand, is the city's most flattering light.

Author picks

Our authors have explored every corner of Paris in order to uncover the very best it has to offer. Here are some of their favourite things to see, do, sip and savour.

Divine boulangerie It's futile to resist anything made at *Des Gateaux et Du Pain* (see p.336), *Du Pain et Des Idées* (p.335) – try the rosewater and green tea croissants – or *Le Grenier à Pain* (p.336).

People-watching The quintessential Parisian pastime. Try the *terrasses* at *Les Philosophes* (p.279), *Bar du Marché* (p.299) or *Café Fluctuat* (p.292); you could also simply head for the Jardin du Luxembourg (p.144) or the Parc Rives de Seine (p.91).

Foodie heaven How to choose? Our favourite places to pile our baskets high with crusty baguettes and fresh produce include the Marché d'Aligre (p.114) and Marché Edgar-Quinet (p.340), rue des Martyrs (p.188) and the many fine delis in St-Germain (p.134).

Quirky buys For a unique keepsake, check out the fossils, butterflies and stuffed beasts at Deyrolle (p.340) and the one-off French artisan ceramics from Empreintes (see p.340).

Perfect apéros Sipping a *pastis* or a *kir* in a Paris bar – life doesn't get much better. Try *Aux Deux Amis* (p.294), *Chez Camille* (p.300), *Maison Maison* (p.272), *La Palette* (p.283) or *Rosa Bonheur sur Seine* (p.285).

Blissful sunsets You're spoilt for choice. It's fun to go the whole tourist hog at the top of the Arc de Triomphe (p.63) or the Eiffel Tower (p.149), or to join the crowds on the Sacré-Coeur steps (p.185). For an alternative, head for the the roof terrace of *Le Perchoir* (p.302).

Live music We love Hungarian gypsy music at *La Bellevilloise* (p.304), *chanson* at *Au Limonaire* (p.306) and *Au Lapin Agile* (p.308), world music on the *Batofar* barge (p.303), gypsy jazz at *Lou Pascalou* (p.302) and grand symphonic concerts at the Philharmonie de Paris (p.319).

> Our author recommendations don't end here. We've flagged up our favourite places – a perfectly sited hotel, an atmospheric café, a special restaurant – throughout the Guide, highlighted with the ★ symbol.

FROM TOP BREAKFAST PARISIAN STYLE; JARDIN DU LUXEMBOURG; *BAR DU MARCHÉ*

20

things not to miss

It's not possible to take in everything Paris has to offer on a short trip – and we don't suggest you try. What follows is a subjective selection of the city's highlights, in no particular order, ranging from big monuments to intimate moments, which will help you find the very best things to see, do and experience. All highlights are colour-coded by chapter and have a page reference to take you straight to the Guide, where you can find out more.

1 **JARDIN DU LUXEMBOURG**
The oasis of the Left Bank: students hang out on the lawns, old men play chess under the trees and children sail toy yachts across the pond.

2 **MUSÉE RODIN**
Elegance matched with passion: Rodin's powerful works are shown off to their best advantage in the sculptor's beautiful eighteenth-century mansion and garden.

3 **CENTRE POMPIDOU**
The Pompidou's radical "inside-out" architecture looks just as ground breaking as when it was built in the 1970s; the main draw, however, is the fine modern art museum inside.

4 EIFFEL TOWER

The closer you get to the Eiffel Tower, the less familiar and the more exhilarating it becomes.

5 PUCES DE ST-OUEN

It's easy to lose track of an entire weekend morning browsing the acres of fine antiques, covetable curios and general bric-a-brac at St-Ouen, the mother of Paris's flea markets.

6 LEFT BANK CAFÉS

The cafés of St-Germain and Montparnasse remain gloriously Parisian institutions.

7 NOTRE-DAME

A superb, early Gothic cathedral, Notre-Dame rises majestically from its island in the middle of the Seine.

8 PÈRE-LACHAISE

Pay homage to Edith Piaf, Oscar Wilde and Jim Morrison – just some of the notables buried in one of the world's most famous cemeteries.

9 BRASSERIES

Belle époque interiors, perfect steaks and white-aproned waiters: the city's brasseries offer a nostalgic slice of Parisian life.

4

5

13

14

15

18

19

20

Itineraries

Paris is made for exploring on foot. The following itineraries take in some of the capital's most famous sights as well as a few lesser-known districts.

TWO DAYS IN PARIS

Day 1

Ile de la Cité Begin at the beginning, on the island where Paris was founded by early Celtic tribes. See p.43

Notre-Dame Visit the magnificent Gothic cathedral of Notre-Dame, which graces the very centre of Paris. See p.46

Pont-Neuf Walk across the oldest bridge in the city to the Left Bank and the fashionable St-Germain *quartier*. See p.43

Lunch Enjoy amazing small plates and seafood tapas at Yves Cambeborde's lively *L'Avant Comptoir/L'Avant Comptoir de la Mer*. See p.283

Jardin du Luxembourg Stroll through elegant place St-Sulpice to the Jardin du Luxembourg, the green heart of the Left Bank, and linger awhile on its iconic green chairs. See p.144

Musée d'Orsay The world-beating collection includes provocative works such as Manet's *Le déjeuner sur l'Herbe*. See p.135

The Eiffel Tower Do as other tourists do and take a sunset visit to the Eiffel Tower. See p.149

Dinner For a deliciously traditional French meal, served on red checked tablecloths, head to *Les Marches*, near the Palais de Tokyo. See p.286

Nightlife Wander across to the Palais itself, where *Les Grands Verres* is a cool new bar serving craft cocktails and good food,

with a stunning view of the Eiffel Tower to boot. See p.286

Day 2

Centre Pompidou This radical building is home to one of the world's best collections of modern art. See p.87

The Marais Amble through the delightful Marais *quartier*, full of handsome Renaissance mansions and fascinating museums. See p.94

Musée Picasso The Picasso museum displays an extraordinary collection of works by this restlessly inventive artist. See p.102

Lunch The Marché des Enfants Rouges is an excellent place for street food; sit at one of the communal tables or get a takeaway and head for the nearby Square du Temple. See p.104

Place des Vosges Take a break in arguably the city's most beautiful square, with galleries and cafés under the arches, and buskers playing jazz and classical favourites. See p.95

Canal St-Martin Enjoy a stroll along the tree-lined canal, with its iron-work bridges, arty shops and cafés. See p.197

Dinner and drinks Soak up the canalside vibe at locals' favourite *Chez Prune*, then head for dinner at *Le Verre Volé*. See p.292 & p.294

Nightlife Drinking and dancing at *Le Comptoir Général*, a unique flea market-cum-museum-cum-bar-cum-music venue, is an exhilarating way to end the night. See p.301

ABOVE ILE ST-LOUIS

PARIS ON A BUDGET

Despite Paris's reputation as an expensive city, there are many treats to be enjoyed for free – and even some restaurants where you can sample wonderful food without breaking the bank.

Galeries du Panthéon Bouddhique Start the day with a short spell relaxing in the Japanese garden at this free gallery of Buddhist art. **See p.159**

Musée d'Art Moderne de la Ville de Paris, Palais de Tokyo Move on to enjoy a choice – and free – collection of modern art, including works by Chagall and Matisse, without the crowds and queues of the Centre Pompidou. **See p.160**

Bus ride Hop on the #63 near the Pont de l'Alma and enjoy an inexpensive sightseeing ride along the Left Bank, taking in Les Invalides and the Musée d'Orsay. **See p.26**

Lunch Alight at the Maubert-Mutualité métro stop in the Quartier Latin and head down rue Mouffetard to *Le Verre à Pied*, an old market bar where you'll get a good, simple *formule* for just €15. **See p.284**

Centre Pompidou Check out the centre's Galerie de Photographies, which stages free photography exhibitions taken from its extensive archive. **See p.87**

Vintage buys Wander through the Marais, browsing for bargains in the many vintage and secondhand clothes shops **See p.327**

Dinner *Chez Hanna*, in the Marais, is a favourite with locals, who come for its reasonably priced Middle Eastern and Jewish delicacies. **See p.279**

Drinks Head north to Montmartre, strolling its romantic streets and enjoying an *apéro* or two in its laidback neighbourhood bars. **See p.300**

Nightlife As the night draws in the cool set moves on to SoPi, where hip DJ bars offer free music and club nights. **See p.303**

RIVERSIDE PARIS

The elegant riverbanks and bridges of the Seine provide some of Paris's finest vistas. Spend a waterside day enjoying some of the city's most memorable experiences.

Boat ride The classic way to enjoy the Seine is from the water. The popular Bateaux-Mouches leave from and return to the Pont de l'Alma. **See p.27**

Parc Rives de Seine Check out what's happening on this landscaped riverfront promenade; there are frequent events, food festivals and activities, and it's a great place simply to linger. **See p.91**

Lunch Enjoy a drink, tapas or a half-dozen oysters at the quirky floating barge *Rosa Bonheur sur Seine*. **See p.285**

Musée d'Orsay Walk along the riverbank to the Musée d'Orsay and track down paintings of the Seine by the Impressionists Renoir, Sisley, Pissarro and Monet. Don't forget to take a peek through the huge clock window. **See p.135**

Bouquinistes All along the riverbank from the Musée d'Orsay to the Quai de la Tournelle you'll see the distinctive green stalls of the *bouquinistes*; selling secondhand books, posters and postcards, they're always good for a browse. **See p.122**

Pont des Arts The pedestrian Pont des Arts enjoys classic views of the Ile de la Cité and the Louvre. **See p.140**

River islands The graceful Pont-Neuf will take you across to the Ile de la Cité and the Ile St-Louis, which with its tranquil, leafy quais is especially good for a riverside stroll. Further south, the slender Ile aux Cygnes offers a leafy river promenade that culminates in a mini Statue of Liberty. **See p.43, p.48 & p.174**

Dinner Just a couple of streets inland from Ile St-Louis, the neo-bistro *Métropolitain* offers adventurous cuisine in lovely, métro-themed surroundings. **See p.279**

Drinks At *Le Marcounet*, a canal barge moored on the Quai de l'Hôtel de Ville by the Pont Marie, you can enjoy an *apéritif* on deck and a jazz or blues concert down below. **See p.307**

Nightlife If you're up for more, head south to *Batofar* or any other of the quirky club/live music barges near the Gare d'Austerlitz. **See p.303**

CANAL DE L'OURCQ, PARC DE LA VILLETTE

Basics

Getting there

Paris's main international airports – Roissy-Charles de Gaulle (CDG) and Orly – along with the smaller, and less convenient, Paris Beauvais, offer direct connections with airports all over the world. Meanwhile, high-speed rail links mean that London can be as little as 2hr 20min away on the Eurostar.

By Eurostar from the UK and Ireland

The most enjoyable way to reach Paris from Britain is the **Eurostar** train service (☎03432 186186, ⓦeurostar.com). It's competitively priced, and can be far quicker than the plane if you live in the southeast: flying time from London is around 1hr 10min, but once you've added travel to and from airports, extended check-in times and ever more frequent delays, any journey time saved is negligible. The train is far less carbon-intensive, too. The Eurostar takes 2hr 20min–2hr 45min from London St Pancras to **Paris Gare du Nord**, with a few services stopping at Ebbsfleet International or Ashford International stations, in Kent.

Tickets can be bought online or over the phone. If you're coming from outside London, it usually pays to buy a through ticket – available from any mainline station. **Prices** depend on how far in advance you book and how much flexibility you need. The lowest fares are almost always for early-morning trains, especially those departing midweek, but that is by no means set in stone. The key is to book early – it is possible to find tickets for as little as £36 single, but you could pay more than three times that for last-minute or holiday-period bookings. Fares for children aged 4–11 start at £28 single, children under 4 travel free, but don't get an allocated seat. Note, too, that Eurostar services are now covered by **InterRail** and **Eurail** passes.

If you are booking within thirty to seven days of travel, and have flexibility, head first for the **Eurostar Snap** site – you have to sign in with Facebook or Twitter – where you will be offered a range of non-exchangeable, non-refundable cheap morning or "afternoon" (stretching into the evening) fares. You may well end up on a very early or very late service, but you'll only be informed of your exact train 48 hours before travel.

For excellent and detailed advice on train travel to France, check the excellent **Man in Seat 61** (ⓦseat61.com).

Flights from the UK and Ireland

The flight from London to Paris is around an hour shorter than the train journey – though bear in mind the caveats outlined in "By Eurostar from the UK and Ireland" – and travellers using regional airports may find flying is the best bet. **Airfares** usually depend on the season, with the highest being around early June to the end of August; the lowest prices are available from November to March (excluding Christmas and New Year). Using a flight comparison site such as Skyscanner (ⓦskyscanner.net) will help you navigate the maze of fares: the most competitive prices from the UK and Ireland tend to be with **no-frills airlines** such as **easyJet** (ⓦeasyjet.com), as well as a number of other operators on regional routes – **Flybe** (ⓦflybe.com) offers direct flights to Paris CDG from London City, Belfast, Birmingham, Cardiff, Doncaster-Sheffield, Edinburgh, Exeter, Glasgow, Manchester and Southampton (from where you can also fly to Orly), for example, while **Jet2** (ⓦjet2.com) flies to CDG from East Midlands and Leeds Bradford. Once you've added airport tax, **fares** typically work out at around £90–120 return in high season, though you can pick up tickets for much less if you book well in advance and travel off-peak. National carriers **British Airways** (ⓦbritishairways.com), **Air France** (ⓦairfrance.com), **KLM** (ⓦklm.com) and **Aer Lingus** (ⓦaerlingus.com) are sometimes no more expensive than the low-cost airlines, with flights from regional airports, and they may have special offers; students and people under 26 should ask about discounts on scheduled flights. **Ryanair**

(**W**ryanair.com) flights from Dublin land at **Beauvais airport**, inconveniently located around 80km northwest of Paris; again, high-season return fares can go for around €90.

Flights from the US and Canada

From the US, the widest choice of flights to Paris (around 7hr 30min from New York, 11hr from the west coast) is offered by **Air France**, with regular nonstop scheduled services to Paris CDG. American Airlines (**W**aa.com) may be slightly cheaper, as may non-French European carriers, including British Airways and Lufthansa (**W**lufthansa.com), though you'll probably have to change flights in their hub city within Europe. With all the airlines you should be able to find deals from New York from around US$500 return, but more typical midweek **fares** range from around US$700 in low season to US$1200 in high season, and higher, of course, the further west you depart from.

Air France, Air Canada (**W**aircanada.com) and Air Transat (**W**airtransat.ca) fly nonstop to Paris from all the major cities in **Canada**. Return flights from Montréal, Québec and Toronto take between 6hr 30min and 7hr 30min and generally start at around Can$750 in low season; high-season **fares** can top Can$2000, but with a little flexibility over dates it's usually possible to pay around half that. Equivalent fares from Vancouver (10hr) are generally about Can$250 higher.

Flights from Australia, New Zealand and South Africa

Airlines including Cathay Pacific (**W**cathaypacific .com) and Malaysia Airlines (**W**malaysiaairlines .com) offer flights to Paris from **Auckland**, **Brisbane**, **Cairns**, **Melbourne**, **Perth** and **Sydney**, usually with a transfer or overnight stop in Asia or the Middle East, but you can find a wider range of options by flying to another European capital – often London – and making a connection from there. Flights via the US are generally slightly more expensive. From Australia, you should be able to find **fares** to Paris for around Aus$1500–1700 in low season (roughly Nov–March, excluding Christmas and New Year), and Aus$1900–2200 in high season. **From New Zealand** you might pay from NZ$2000 right up to NZ$3000-plus in peak season. Flight times vary considerably depending on the route, but it's roughly 24hr from Sydney or Auckland to Paris.

From **South Africa**, Johannesburg is the best place to start, with Air France flying direct to Paris from around ZAR9000 return and BA, flying via London, from around ZAR10,000; fares rise by ZAR2000–3000 in high season. The flight from Johannesburg to Paris takes about 11hr.

By car, ferry and coach from the UK and Ireland

The most convenient way to take a **car** across to France is to drive down to the Channel Tunnel, load it on the frequent **Eurotunnel** (**W**euro tunnel.com) "Le shuttle" train service, and be whisked under the Channel in 35min to Sangatte, just outside Calais, on the French side. The British tunnel entrance is off the M20 at junction 11A, just outside Folkestone. You can simply buy a ticket at one of the booths and drive straight on, as there are departures roughly every 15min (or hourly midnight–6am), but it's cheaper to book in advance. Expect to pay in the region of £50–200 per car each way, depending on the time of year and how far ahead you book, and how much flexibility you need. In summer and around Easter you should definitely book in advance to avoid queues and higher tariffs – don't worry if you miss your departure, though, as you can usually just roll onto the next available train. Once on the French side, it's little more than a 3hr drive to Paris on the fast autoroutes A26 and A1 (tolls payable).

The **car ferries** from Dover to Calais (1hr 30min) or Dunkerque (2hr) – the drive to Paris from either takes just over 3hr – are slower but less expensive than the Eurotunnel. **P&O** (**W**poferries.com) runs regular services on the former route, **DFDS** (**W**dfdsseaways.com) on both; DFDS also offers ferries from Newhaven to Dieppe (4hr; 2hr 30min drive to Paris), while **Brittany Ferries** travels from Portsmouth to Cherbourg (3hr; 4hr drive to Paris), Caen (5hr 45min; 3hr drive to Paris), Le Havre (8hr; 2hr 30min drive to Paris) and St Malo (11hr; 4hr drive to Paris), from Poole to Cherbourg (4hr 15min) and from Plymouth to Roscoff (5hr 30min; 5hr drive to Paris) and St Malo (10hr 30min). **Fares** vary according to season (school and bank holidays being the most expensive), and, on certain routes, depending on how many passengers there are. Lower fares are usually available if you can avoid travelling out on Fridays and Saturdays. While you can find deals for as little as £50 return on a ferry, you should normally expect to pay £80–200. It can be cheaper to book through a **discount agent** – check out Eurodrive

(Ⓦeurodrive.co.uk) or Ferrysavers (Ⓦferrysavers .co.uk).

Given the competitive prices and relative speed of the Eurostar, it is generally not worth the hassle to travel from the UK to Paris by **coach**, though it can be cheaper in high season. **Eurolines** (Ⓦeurolines.co.uk) runs **bus-and-ferry** services from London's Victoria Coach Station to Paris's CDG Airport and the *gare routière* in Bagnolet in eastern Paris (see p.25). Off-peak return fares can be as low as £30, if you book well in advance, but it's usually more like £40–45, and the journey takes a tedious 9hr. **Megabus** (Ⓦuk.megabus.com) runs a similar service, for similar prices, stopping at CDG and in Paris at Porte Maillot, a couple of métro stops from the Arc de Triomphe. **Ouibus** (Ⓦuk .ouibus.com), part of the French national train company, SNCF, runs coaches from London to CDG and the Paris-Bercy train station; single fares vary between £20 and £60, but it's always worth comparing prices between all companies.

AGENTS AND OPERATORS

Even if you're not interested in a package tour, if you're aiming to stay in three- or four-star hotels it's worth considering booking a **hotel-and-flight package**, as these can save you considerable

sums. The drawback is that the hotels on offer tend to lack character, and of course you're more restricted in your choice than if you book independently.

Abercrombie & Kent US ☎ 1 800 554 7016, Ⓦ abercrombiekent .com. An upmarket travel agency running a variety of guided tours to France, some of which include days in Paris. An eleven-day river cruise taking in Paris, Burgundy and the South of France, for example, starts at US$7695.

Eurostar UK ☎ 0800 408 0772, Ⓦ eurostar.com. The website puts together rail-and-hotel packages which can represent significant savings on doing it yourself – though its choice of hotels is relatively limited.

French Travel Connection Australia ☎ 1300 858 304, Ⓦ frenchtravel.com.au. Specialists in French travel, with a good selection of Paris packages (four nights from Aus$1050).

Martin Randall Travel UK ☎ 020 8742 3355, Ⓦ martinrandall .com. A regularly changing roster of high-quality, small-group cultural tours, led by experts in their field. On subjects such as "Versailles" (£1680 for four days) or "Paintings in Paris" (£1790 for four days), city tours concentrate on a specific detail of the capital and its environs; accommodation and all travel is included, but you can opt to make your own way to Paris for a reduced price.

North South Travel UK ☎ 01245 608291, Ⓦ northsouthtravel .co.uk. Friendly travel agency, offering discounted air fares – profits are used to support projects in the developing world, especially the promotion of sustainable tourism.

PERFECT PARIS VIEWS

Few cities present such a harmonious skyscape as Paris. Looking down on the ranks of seven-storey apartment buildings from above, it's easy to imagine the city as a lead-roofed plateau split by the leafy canyons of the boulevards and avenues. Spires, towers and parks – not to mention multi-coloured art museums and glass pyramids – stand out all the more against the solemn grey backdrop. Fortunately, many of Paris's tall buildings provide access to wonderful rooftop views. The following are some of the best in town:

Arc de Triomphe Look out over an ocean of traffic and enjoy impressive vistas of the Voie Triomphale. See p.63

Eiffel Tower It's worth battling the queues for the unrivalled panorama of the city. Best at night. See p.149

Institut du Monde Arabe The ninth floor has a panoramic view overlooking the Seine, plus a Middle Eastern restaurant if you want to dine while you gaze. See p.133

Notre-Dame Perch among the gargoyles for a spot of waterside contemplation and a clear view of the Panthéon dome. See p.46

Nüba, Cité de la Mode et du Design Kick back and enjoy a cocktail – or a daytime coffee – at *Nüba*, where the huge rooftop

deck offers amazing views of the river and the Right Bank. See p.303

Parc André-Citroën A tethered balloon rises 150m above this modern park. See p.174

Parc de Belleville Verdant and peaceful little park where you can watch the sun set over the city's skyline. See p.208

Pompidou Centre An arty backdrop for rooftop ogling. See p.87

Sacré-Coeur Paris's second-highest point, where on a clear day you can sit on the basilica steps and marvel at an unobstructed view of the city. Be warned – it's a popular spot at sunset. See p.185

Tour Montparnasse The only panoramic view in Paris that takes in the Eiffel Tower too. Stunning. See p.163

STA Travel UK ☎ 0333 321 0099, Ⓦ statravel.co.uk; US ☎ 1 800 781 4040, Ⓦ statravel.com; Australia ☎ 134 782, Ⓦ statravel .com.au; New Zealand Ⓦ 0800 474 400, Ⓦ statravel.co.nz; South Africa ☎ 0861 781 781, Ⓦ statravel.co.za. Worldwide specialists in low-cost flights and tours for students and under-26s.
Trailfinders UK ☎ 020 7368 1200, Ⓦ trailfinders.com. One of the best-informed and most efficient agents for independent travellers.

Visas

Citizens of EU countries do not need any sort of visa to enter France for a stay of up to ninety days. Currently, visitors from the US, Canada, Australia and New Zealand enjoy visa-free access, but it's best to check on the current situation; as this Guide went to press, for example, there was talk of introducing mandatory visas for US citizens. British citizens are also likely to face more red tape after leaving the EU. Citizens of all other countries must obtain a visa before arrival.

Two types of tourist **visa** are currently issued. A short-stay visa ("*Schengen* visa") is valid for multiple stays of up to ninety days in a six-month period. All non-EU citizens who wish to remain **longer than ninety days** must apply for a long-stay (*long séjour*) visa, for which you'll have to show proof of – among other things – a regular income, or sufficient funds to support yourself, and medical insurance. Note that you can't change your visa to long-stay if you've already arrived in France on a short-stay visa. Always check the current regulations with your embassy or consulate well in advance of travelling. A complete list of all French government websites, including **embassies** and **consulates**, can be found at Ⓦ gksoft.com/govt /en/fr.html.

FOREIGN EMBASSIES AND CONSULATES IN PARIS

Australia 4 rue Jean-Rey, 15ᵉ; Ⓜ Bir-Hakeim (☎ 01 40 59 33 00, Ⓦ france.embassy.gov.au).
Canada 35 av Montaigne, 8ᵉ; Ⓜ Franklin-D.-Roosevelt (☎ 01 44 43 29 00, Ⓦ canadainternational.gc.ca).
Ireland 4 rue Rude, 16ᵉ; Ⓜ Charles-de-Gaulle-Etoile (☎ 01 44 17 67 00, Ⓦ dfa.ie/irish-embassy/france).
New Zealand 103 rue de Grenelle, 7ᵉ; Ⓜ Varenne (☎ 01 45 01 43 43, Ⓦ bit.ly/nzembassy).
South Africa 59 quai d'Orsay, 7ᵉ; Ⓜ Invalides (☎ 01 53 59 23 23, Ⓦ afriquesud.net).
UK 35 rue du Faubourg-St-Honoré, 8ᵉ; Ⓜ Concorde (☎ 01 44 51 31 00, Ⓦ www.gov.uk/government/world/organisations/ british-embassy-paris).
US 2 av Gabriel, 1ᵉʳ; Ⓜ Concorde (☎ 01 43 12 22 22, Ⓦ fr.usembassy .gov).

Arrival

Many British travellers to Paris arrive by Eurostar at the central Gare du Nord train station, while visitors from more far-flung starting points are likely to land at one of Paris's airports: Roissy-Charles de Gaulle, Orly or Beauvais. Trains from other parts of France or continental Europe draw in at one of the six central mainline stations (Ⓦ gares-sncf.com).

By train

The **Eurostar** (see p.21) terminates at **Gare du Nord**, rue Dunkerque, in the 10ᵉ. Also welcoming trains from Calais and other north European countries, this is a bustling convergence of international, long-distance and suburban services, plus the métro, RER and several bus routes. Coming off the train, turn left for the métro and the RER, right for the taxi rank (a sample price would be €11–18 to a hotel in the 4ᵉ) – ignore the touts who approach you directly and wait in line in the specified spot. The station has a **tourist office** welcome centre (daily 8am–6pm; Ⓦ parisinfo.com), **left luggage** facilities (*consignes*; daily 6.15am–11.15pm; €5.50– 9.50 for the first 24hr, depending on locker size, and then €5/24hr after that), and **public toilets** (daily 6am–midnight; €0.70) at the bottom of the escalators down to the métro. The station isn't dangerous but keep your wits about you, and avoid scammers offering to "help" with tickets or taxis.

Nearby, **Gare de l'Est** (place du 11-Novembre-1918, 10ᵉ) serves eastern France and central and eastern Europe. **Gare St-Lazare** (place du Havre, 8ᵉ), serving the Normandy coast and Dieppe, is the most central station, close to the Madeleine and the Opéra Garnier. Still on the Right Bank but towards the southeast corner is **Gare de Lyon** (place Louis-Armand, 12ᵉ), with trains from Italy and Switzerland and TGV lines from southeast France. South of the river, **Gare Montparnasse** on boulevard de Vaugirard, 15ᵉ, is the terminus for Chartres, Brittany, the Atlantic coast and TGV lines from southwest France. **Gare d'Austerlitz**, on boulevard de l'Hôpital, 13ᵉ, serves the Loire Valley and the Dordogne; at the time of writing, it was undergoing a major expansion, due for completion in 2020. The motorail station, **Gare de Paris-Bercy**, is down the tracks from the Gare de Lyon on boulevard de Bercy, 12ᵉ.

All the stations have cafés and/or restaurants, *tabacs*, ATMs and bureaux de change, and all are connected with the métro system. Secure, but limited, **left luggage** facilities are available at all except St-Lazare and Paris-Bercy.

By plane

The city's two main international **airports**, Roissy-Charles de Gaulle and Orly, are well connected to the centre; **Paris Beauvais** (BVA), meanwhile, served by Ryanair, is quite a trek.

Roissy-Charles de Gaulle airport

Roissy-Charles de Gaulle airport (Ⓦparisaeroport .fr), usually referred to as **Charles de Gaulle** and abbreviated to CDG or Paris CDG, is 26km northeast of the city. The airport has three terminals: CDG 1, CDG 2 and CDG 3.

The quickest and easiest way to get into town is on the **Roissyrail** train link that runs on **RER line B** (daily 4.50am–11.50pm; every 10–20min; 25–50min; €10 one way). The train stops at Gare du Nord, Châtelet-Les Halles, St-Michel and Denfert-Rochereau, all of which have métro stations for onward travel. A number of regular **RER stopping trains** also serve the airport; these only take about five minutes more than the Roissyrail to get to the centre, though they aren't designed to accommodate luggage.

Various bus companies provide services from Charles de Gaulle direct to a number of city-centre locations, but they're slightly more expensive than Roissyrail and may take longer. The **Roissybus**, for instance, connects the three terminals with the Opéra Garnier (corner of rues Auber and Scribe in the 9ᵉ; Ⓜ Opéra/RER Auber; daily 6am–12.30am; every 15–20min; 1hr; €11.50). **Le Bus Direct** buses (daily; every 30min; €17 one way, €30 return; Ⓦlebusdirect .com) run from CDG 1 and 2: the green-coded line 2 runs to Av de Suffren, near the Eiffel Tower, stopping near the Champs-Elysées and at the Trocadéro on the way (5.45am–11pm; 1hr 10min to the Eiffel Tower), while the orange-coded line 4 stops at Gare de Lyon before terminating near Gare Montparnasse (6am–10.30pm; 1hr 15min to Montparnasse).

Taxis into central Paris from CDG cost around €50–70, more at night, and should take about 1hr. Slightly less expensive is the **minibus door-to-door service**, Paris Blue, which costs from €40 for two people, with no extra charge for luggage. It operates around the clock but bookings must be made at least 24hr in advance on ☎01 30 11 13 00 or via Ⓦparis-blue-airport-shuttle.fr.

If your flight gets in after 12.30am, you could also use the Noctilien #N140 bus, which links the airport to Gare de l'Est every 30min until 4.30am (€8).

Orly airport

Orly airport (Ⓦparisaeroport.fr), 14km south of Paris, has two terminals, Orly Sud (south, for international flights) and Orly Ouest (west, for domestic flights), linked by shuttle buses but walkable. One of the easiest ways into the centre is the fast **Orlyval train shuttle** link to the RER line B station Antony (daily 6am–11.35pm; every 5–7min; €9.30 to Antony, €12.05 into central Paris; Ⓦorlyval.com), followed by métro connection stops at Denfert-Rochereau, Châtelet-Les Halles and Gare du Nord.

Two other services are also worth considering: the **Orlybus**, which runs to Denfert-Rochereau RER/métro station in the 14ᵉ (daily 6am–12.30pm; every 10–20min; around 30min; €8); and **tram T7**, which runs to métro Villejuif Louis Aragon, on line 7 (daily 5.30am–12.30am; every 8–15min; 30min; €1.90). Finally, the **Bus Direct** line 1 (purple) service runs to Etoile/Champs-Elysées, stopping at Gare Montparnasse, the Eiffel Tower and Trocadéro on the way (6am–11.40pm; every 20min; about 1hr to Etoile/Champs-Elysées; €12 one way, €20 return; Ⓦlebusdirect.com).

Taxis take about 35min to reach the centre of Paris and cost around €40.

Beauvais airport

Beauvals airport (sometimes called Paris Beauvais-Tillé; Ⓦaeroportbeauvais.com), 80km northwest of Paris, is served by Ryanair flights. **Coaches** (€17 one way, €15.90 if reserved online; 1hr 15min) shuttle between the airport and Porte Maillot in the 17ᵉ arrondissement, where you can pick up métro line 1 to the centre. The coach leaves around 20min after the flight has arrived; on the way back to the airport it sets off 3hr before the flight departs. Tickets can be bought online, at Arrivals, or, in Paris, at the Pershing car park where the bus sets off.

By bus and car

Almost all the **buses** coming into Paris – whether international or domestic – arrive at the main **gare routière** at 28 av du Général-de-Gaulle, Bagnolet, at the eastern edge of the city in the 20ᵉ; métro Gallieni (line 3) links it to the centre. If you're **driving** into Paris yourself, don't try to go straight across the city to your destination unless you know what you're doing. Use the ring road – the **boulevard périphérique** – to get around to the nearest "porte". Apart from during rush hour, it's very quick – sometimes frighteningly so – and relatively easy to navigate.

Getting around

A combination of walking, cycling and public transport is undoubtedly the best way to discover Paris. The bike rental service, Vélib', is hugely useful for visitors, and the city's integrated public transport system of bus, métro and RER trains – the RATP (Régie Autonome des Transports Parisiens) – is cheap, fast and meticulously signposted. There are various tickets and passes available.

Free **maps** of varying sizes and detail are available at most métro stations: the largest and most useful is the *Grand Plan de Paris avec rues (numéro 2)*, which overlays the métro, RER and bus routes on a city plan so you can see exactly how transport lines and streets match up; you may find these on the walls of the stations, along with interactive touchscreens to aid journey planning, but it can be difficult to get a hard copy from the ticket offices, who are far more likely to hand you a *Plan des lignes (numéro 1)*, a simplified but useful pocket-sized métro/RER/bus map showing all the routes. Some RATP information leaflets, available at stations, do include the *Grand Plan*, and you can view it online (Ⓦ ratp.fr). If you have a smart phone, it's also worth downloading the RATP app, Next Stop Paris, useful for planning your journey across Paris.

By métro and RER

The **métro** (underground) combined with the five **RER** (Réseau Express Régional) suburban express lines, is the simplest way of moving around the city and also one of the cheapest – €1.90 for a single journey anywhere in the centre (children aged 4–10 travel half-price; kids under 4 travel free). Both the métro and the RER run from 5.30am to around 1am (the métro runs until 2.15am on Fridays and Saturdays, with fewer services on Sundays).

Many of the métro lines follow the streets that run above them; line 1, for example, shadows the Champs-Elysées and rue de Rivoli. **Stations** (abbreviated in this guide as: Ⓜ Concorde, RER Luxembourg, etc) are evenly spaced and you'll rarely find yourself more than 500m from one in the centre, though the interchanges at big stations can involve a lot of legwork. Train lines are colour-coded and designated by numbers for the métro and by letters (A–E) for the RER. You also need to know the **direction in which you want to travel** – signposted using the names of the terminus: for example, travelling from Montparnasse to Gare du Nord on métro line 4, you follow the sign "Direction Porte de Clignancourt"; from Gare d'Austerlitz to Maubert Mutualité on line 10 you follow "Direction Boulogne–Pont de St-Cloud". The numerous interchanges (*correspondances*) make it possible to cover most of the city in a more or less straight line.

For RER journeys beyond the city, make sure that the station you want is illuminated on the platform display board.

By bus and tram

Buses are often rather neglected in favour of the métro, but can be very useful where the métro journey doesn't quite work. They aren't difficult to use and naturally you see much more, with bus lanes making journeys relatively unproblematic. Generally, buses run from Monday to Saturday from 7am to 8.30pm with some services continuing to 12.30am, and a restricted night bus service, Noctilien, taking over between 12.30 and 5.30am. Around half the lines also operate on Sundays and holidays – bus maps list those that do. Every bus stop displays the numbers of the buses that stop

---

SEEING THE CITY BY BUS

One good way to take in the city sights is to hop on a public **bus**. Bus #20 from the Gare de Lyon follows the Grands Boulevards and does a loop through the 1er and 2e arrondissements. Bus #24 between Bercy and Gare St-Lazare follows the left bank of the Seine from the Gare d'Austerlitz to the Pont de la Concorde. Bus #29 is one of the best routes for taking in the city: it ventures from the Gare St-Lazare past the Opéra Garnier, the Bourse and the Centre Pompidou, through the heart of the Marais and past the Bastille to the Gare de Lyon. For the Champs-Elysées, take a trip on bus #73 between La Défense and the Assemblée Nationale, while bus #63 drives a scenic route along the Seine from the Assemblée Nationale on the Rive Gauche, then crosses the river and heads up to Trocadéro, where there are some wonderful views of the Eiffel Tower. Many more bus journeys – outside rush hours – are worthwhile trips in themselves: take a look online at Ⓦ ratp.fr or get hold of a map from a métro station and check out routes #38, #42, #48, #64, #67, #68, #69, #73, #82, #87 and #95.

there, a map showing all the stops on the route, and some form of timetable; you need to hail the driver if you want the bus to stop. You can buy a single **ticket** (€1.90) from the driver, or use a pre-purchased **carnet** of ten tickets or a pass (see below). Press the red button to request a stop. All Paris bus lines are accessible for wheelchairs and prams.

Paris's **tram** lines are mostly concentrated in the outer reaches of town – however, the T3a line, from Pont du Garigliano in the west to Porte de Vincennes in the east, is useful for getting from east to west in the south of the city, and convenient for Parc Montsouris (see Ⓦ ratp.fr for maps and schedules).

Tickets and passes

Greater Paris's integrated transport system (Ⓦ ratp. fr) is divided into five **zones**; the métro system more or less fits into zones 1 and 2. The same **tickets** are valid for bus, métro and, within the city limits and immediate suburbs (zones 1 and 2), the RER express rail lines, which also extend far out into the Ile-de-France. Only one ticket is ever needed on the métro system, and within zones 1 and 2 for any RER or bus journey, but you can't switch between bus and métro/RER on the same ticket. For **RER journeys** beyond zones 1 and 2 you must buy an RER ticket; visitors often get caught out, for instance, when they take the RER to La Défense using a métro ticket. Be sure to keep your ticket until the end of the journey as you'll be fined on the spot if you can't produce one; you'll also need it to exit the RER.

Individual **tickets** cost €1.90, so for a short stay it saves money (and time) to buy a **carnet** of ten tickets (€14.50), available from self-service machines and ticket offices at the stations or from any *tabac*. (**Eurostar** travellers can also buy *carnets* from the information desk in the St Pancras International departure lounge, or from the buffet car on the train.) If you're making a number of journeys in one day, it might be worth getting a **Mobilis day-pass** (from €7.30 for zones 1 and 2 to €17.30 for zones 1 to 5), which offers unlimited access to the métro, buses and, depending on which zones you choose, the RER – note that this is a day- rather than a 24hr pass, so it pays to buy it in the morning.

BOAT TRIPS

Seeing Paris from a **boat** is one of the city's most enduring experiences – and a lot of fun. The **Batobus** river bus (see p.28) is the easiest option, but there are a number of alternatives if you want to enjoy a more leisurely cruise.

BATEAUX-MOUCHES

Bateaux-Mouches Trips start from the Embarcadère du Pont de l'Alma, on the Right Bank in the 8° ⓣ Ⓤ I 42 25 96 10, Ⓦ bateaux-mouches.fr; Ⓜ Alma–Marceau. Many a romantic evening stroll along the quais has been rudely interrupted by the sudden appearance of a Bateau-Mouche, with its dazzling floodlights and blaring commentaries. One way of avoiding the annoyance is to get on one yourself. You may not be able to escape the noisy narration, but you'll certainly get a glamorous close-up view of the classic buildings along the Seine (daily: April–Sept every 20–45min 10.15am–10.30pm; Oct–March 10.15am–9.20pm; €13.50, children 4–12 €6). You're probably best off avoiding the overpriced lunch and dinner trips, for which "correct" dress is mandatory (€60 for lunch, from €75 for dinner).

OTHER RIVER-BOAT TRIPS

River cruise companies The main competitors to the Bateaux-Mouches are: Bateaux Parisiens, from the Eiffel Tower all year round, or Notre-Dame from April to October (Ⓦ bateauxparisiens. com); Vedettes de Paris, from the Eiffel Tower (Ⓦ vedettesdeparis.fr); and Bateaux-Vedettes du Pont-Neuf, from the Pont-Neuf (Ⓦ vedettesdupontneuf.com). They're all much the same, with hour-long cruises at around €10–15.

CANAL TRIPS

Canauxrama ⓣ 01 42 39 15 00, Ⓦ canauxrama.com. Less overtly touristy than the river trips, Canauxrama boats offer a number of narrated cruises on the St-Martin, Ourcq and St-Denis canals, the Seine and the River Marne. Options include a romantic 2hr 30min trip between the Port de l'Arsenal and Bassin de La Villette; at the Bastille end is a long, spooky tunnel, complete with light installation (reservations essential; 9.45am & 2.30/2.45pm departures in summer, fewer at other times; €18, under-12s €9, under-4s free).

Paris-Canal ⓣ 01 42 40 96 97, Ⓦ en.pariscanal.com. Catamaran tours of the Canal St-Martin, between the Musée d'Orsay (quai Anatole-France by the Pont Solférino, 7°; Ⓜ Solférino) and the Parc de la Villette (La Folie des Visites du Parc, on the canal by the bridge between the Grande Salle and the Cité des Sciences, 19°; Ⓜ Porte de Pantin). Cruises last 2hr 30min and run from February to mid-November (from Musée d'Orsay 9.45am & 2.25pm; from Parc de la Villette 10.15am & 2.30pm; €20, 12–25-year-olds and over-65s €17, 4–11s €13).

Marin d'Eau Douce Bassin de la Villette, 37 quai de la Seine; ⓣ 01 42 09 54 10, Ⓦ marindeaudouce.fr. For a bit more independence, you can hire your own electric boat to explore the canal. There are three sizes of craft, with the smallest accommodating up to five people (€40/hr, €90/3hr). You can even order a picnic hamper too (or take your own). Phone or book online. Daily 9.30am–10pm.

If you've arrived early in the week, are staying more than three days and plan to use public transport a lot, it might be more economical to buy a swipeable **Navigo Découverte** pass (🌐 navigo.fr). A weekly pass costs €22.15 for zones 1 and 2, and is valid for an unlimited number of journeys on all modes of transport from Monday morning to Sunday evening. You can only buy a ticket for the current week until Wednesday; from Thursday you can buy a ticket to begin the following Monday. Monthly passes are also available (€70 for zones 1 and 2). You need to factor in the initial one-off purchase of the Navigo swipe card itself (€5, nonrefundable); you'll also need a passport photo.

Paris Visites, passes that cover one, two, three or five consecutive days, either in the central zones or extending as far as the suburbs and the airports (€11.65–63.90), are not as good value as the Navigo and Mobilis passes, but they do give reductions on certain tourist attractions.

By taxi

The best place to get a **taxi** is at a rank (arrêt taxi) – which is usually more effective than hailing from the street. Bear in mind that finding a taxi at lunchtime, during rush hour or after 7pm can be difficult; give yourself time if you're aiming to get somewhere punctually. The green light on top of the vehicle signals the taxi is free and the red light means it's in use. If there are no taxis waiting at the rank you can call for one on ☎01 45 30 30 30. You can also call a company such as Taxis G7 (☎01 41 27 66 99 for an English-speaking operator, 🌐 taxisg7.fr), Taxis Bleus (☎3609, 🌐 taxis-bleus.com) or Alpha Taxis (☎01 45 85 85 85, 🌐 alphataxis.fr) – note, though, that calling a taxi out will cost more than picking one up on the street.

Taxis are metered and **charges** are fairly reasonable: between €8 and €17 for a central daytime journey if you hail one on the street. Rates vary from €1.06/km to €1.56/km depending on when you travel and whether you are in the centre or outside the périphérique. There's a minimum charge of €7 and a pick-up charge of €2.60. Taxis can take up to four passengers. A **tip** of ten percent, while optional, is generally expected.

Despite angry protest from regular taxi drivers, use of the app-based taxi service **Uber** (🌐 uber .com) has become very popular in Paris. In an attempt to challenge this competition, the French government recently launched eight free "official" taxi apps; you can find a list on 🌐 le.taxi.

By boat

The **Batobus** river bus (Jan–March, Nov & Dec every 40min: Mon–Thurs 10am–5pm; Fri–Sun 10am–7pm; April, Sept & Oct daily 10am–7pm every 30min; May–Aug daily 10am–9.30pm every 25min; 🌐 batobus.com) provides a thrilling way to get around Paris, stopping at nine points along the Seine, completing a loop from the Eiffel Tower at Port de la Bourdonnais (🎻 Bir Hakeim/Trocadéro) to Beaugrenelle at Port de Javel (🎻 Bir Hakeim/Charles-Michel). The total journey time for a one-way, straight-through trip is around 2hr. A hop-on, hop-off day-pass costs €17 and a two-day (consecutive) pass €19. You can buy tickets online, at Batobus stops and at the tourist offices (see p.40).

By car

Travelling around **by car** – in the daytime at least – is hardly worth it, not least because of the difficulty of finding parking spaces. Drivers are better off finding a motel-style place on the edge of the city and using public transport to get around. But if you're determined to use the pay-and-display parking system, note that the meters don't take cash. If you have a smartphone you can pay via the app P Mobile or PayByPhone, or you can pop into a tabac and buy a **Paris Carte**, worth €15 or €40; you then look for the blue "P" signs alongside grey parking meters, introduce the card into the meter and it gives you a ticket while automatically deducting the appropriate value from the card – €2.40–4 an hour depending on location, for a maximum of two hours. Parking is generally free on Sundays and from 7pm to 9am.

Alternatively, make for one of the many underground **car parks**, which cost up to €3.50 per hour, or from around €24 for 24 hours. Whatever you do, don't park in a bus lane or the Axe Rouge express routes (marked with a red square). Should you be

---

PEDESTRIAN CROSSINGS

Pedestrian/zebra crossings, marked with horizontal white stripes on the road, have a different meaning from those back home: they're simply there to suggest a good place to cross, but certainly won't give you priority over cars. It's very dangerous to step out onto one and assume drivers will stop. Take just as much care as you would crossing at any other point.

CHAUFFEUR-DRIVEN TOURS: PARISIAN STYLE

A number of companies now offer tours in the nimble little **Citroën 2CV**. The classic, open-top "deux chevaux" was originally designed as an economy vehicle for farmers, but has since become a beloved symbol of French identity. The original and still most adaptable company is **4 Roues Sous 1 Parapluie** ("4 Wheels under an Umbrella"), which offers a range of tours, from a thirty-minute zip around Montmartre, with an English-speaking driver suggesting places to which you might want to return, to a three-hour Paris gardens tour or a ninety-minute trip focused on the Impressionists or on André Citroën, the car's inventor (from €20; maximum of three people in each car; ☎ 01 58 59 27 82, ⓦ 4roues-sous-1parapluie.com).

towed away, you'll find your car in the pound (*fourrière*) belonging to that particular arrondissement. The website ⓦ parkingsdeparis.com locates dozens of public car parks and lets you pre-book discounted spaces. The associated book *Parkings de Paris*, handy to keep in the car, has even more information on the city's 215 car parks – it's available at bookshops for €15.

The French **drive on the right** – if your car is right-hand drive, you must (by law) adjust your headlights to dip to the right before you go; this is most easily done by sticking on black glare deflectors. Remember also that you have to be 18 to drive in France, regardless of whether you hold a licence in your own country.

In the event of a **breakdown**, call Dan Dépann (☎ 01 40 06 09 64, ⓦ dandepann.fr) or ask the police (see p.35) for advice. For **traffic conditions** in Paris tune in to 105.1 FM (FIP).

Car rental

If you're intending to rent a car for a short time in Paris, your cheapest option is the city's pioneering **electric car rental scheme**, Autolib' (ⓦ autolib .eu), which operates on a similar model to the successful bike rental scheme Vélib'. Around four thousand electric cars are currently available to rent from around a thousand stands (700 in central Paris itself) dotted all over the greater Paris region. Cars can be picked up at one station and deposited at another. Users need to buy a subscription card first, either online, from one of the subscription kiosks around central Paris, or in the Autolib' showroom at 5 rue Edouard VII, 9ᵉ (ⓜ Opéra). You will simply need your driving licence, a valid ID and a credit card. There are two kinds of subscription. The Prêt à Rouler will suit most visitors who just want one-off use; there is no subscription charge, you just pay €9.50 for the first 30min and then €6.33 per each extra 20min. There is also a yearly subscription, where you pay €10 a month; each trip costs €7 for the first 30min, €4.66 for each subsequent 20min. You can reserve a car up to 30min beforehand online, via the Autolib' app, or directly from one of the car rental points.

The big international rental companies, including Avis (ⓦ avis.co.uk), Budget (ⓦ budget.co.uk), Europcar (ⓦ europcar.co.uk) and Hertz (ⓦ hertz .co.uk), have offices at the airports and at several locations in the city; the best deals will be found online, particularly if you're renting for several days. One **local company** worth checking out is Locabest (ⓦ locabest.fr).

North Americans and Australians in particular should be aware that it's difficult to rent a car with automatic transmission in France; if you can't drive a manual/stickshift, try and book an **automatic** (*voiture à transmission automatique*) well in advance, and be prepared to pay a much higher price for it.

By bike

Paris is becoming ever more cycle-friendly: it currently has 700km of **cycle lanes**, with plans to double this by 2020, including lanes along the Champs Elysées and the major east–west artery, rue de Rivoli. You can pick up a free **map** of the routes, *Paris à Vélo*, from the tourist office or bike-rental outlets, or download it from ⓦ paris.fr/velo.

Renting a bike is very easy in Paris thanks to the city's pioneering Vélib' bike-rental scheme (ⓦ velib. paris.fr), which has been going some ten years now – and, at the time of writing, was about to get even better. The fleet of 20,000 bikes is due to be upgraded at the beginning of 2018 and will be run by new operator Smoovengo. The improved bikes will be lighter and stronger and a third of them will be electric (handy for those hilly climbs up to Montmartre). The 18,000 docking stations will also be replaced. As before, these municipal bikes will be available to anyone over 14, can be picked up from any one of the docking stations and deposited at any other. It's best to check on the website for the latest information on fees and different subscription options; what is certain is

BIKE TOURS

Zipping around on a Vélib' is a splendid way to take a short hop around Paris, but if you want to go deeper, it is well worth considering a **cycling tour**. Here is a selection of the best.

Blue Bike Tours (Blue Fox Travel) Ⓦ bluefox.travel/paris. Small-group cycle tours, setting off from place St-Michel in St Germain (6ᵉ), with local, English-speaking guides. Options include an evening tour, a trip to Versailles and a "hidden secrets" tour that takes you beyond the major sights. Prices start at €35/person and reservations are required – book well in advance if you can.

Fat Tire Bike Tours 24 rue Edgar Faure, 15ᵉ ☎ 01 82 88 80 96, Ⓦ fattiretours.com/paris; Ⓜ Dupleix. Friendly, Anglo-run agency offering 3–4hr 30min guided bicycle trips in English, with a choice of day and night tours (€34), and full-day tours to Versailles (including train travel). Also offers electric Segway tours (€70). Reservations are recommended for the standard tours, especially from June to August, and required for Versailles; online deals can cut costs.

Paris à Vélo C'est Sympa 22 rue Alphonse Baudin, 11ᵉ ☎ 01 48 87 60 01, Ⓦ parisvelosympa.com; Ⓜ Richard Lenoir. One of the least expensive (€25 for a weekend, or €65 for a tandem) and most

helpful bike rental companies. Their excellent 3hr tours of Paris, run on weekends only, take a different angle – including "Unusual Paris" and "Paris Contrasts", combining modern architecture with green spaces. €35, €29 for under-26s. Reservations required.

Paris Bike Tour 13 rue Brantôme, 3ᵉ ☎ 01 42 74 22 14, Ⓦ parisbiketour.net; Ⓜ Rambuteau/Hôtel de Ville. Bike rental (€15/day, €16 at the weekend, €30 for a whole weekend; bike delivery and pick-up extra) and a range of relaxed tours (from €34), including a "tasting tour" with a stop at a covered market. Reservations required.

Paris Charms and Secrets Place Vendôme, 1ᵉʳ ☎ 01 40 29 00 00, Ⓦ parischarmssecrets.com. Something different – an electric bike tour (covering a lot of ground and taking the effort out of pedalling) that explores the city's little corners and secret places, as well as its major sights – raincoats and gloves are provided in bad weather, and they can even rent you a heated jacket (Mon–Sat 9.30am, 2.30pm & 8pm, Sun 8.30am, 2.30pm & 8pm; 3–4hr; reservations required; €49).

---

that the first thirty minutes will be free and that you will be able to pay by card or mobile phone; the Navigo pass (see p.28) will also be valid. The city's **P'tit Vélib'** scheme, offering bike rental for kids, will no doubt continue to be available, too.

Many **bike tour** operators (see box, above) also rent bikes, which may work out cheaper if you want a whole day of cycling. Prices depend on the type of bike; you have to leave a variable *caution* (deposit) or your credit card details.

Note that during the so-called **Paris Respire** scheme, on Sundays and public holidays from 9am to 5pm, all the riverside expressways and many other city streets are **closed to cars**. If you want a bike on one of those days, when it feels like all of Paris takes to the *quais*, it's best to book in advance.

For more on **recreational cycling**, turn to the "Activities and sports" chapter (see p.343).

By scooter

In 2016, it was the scooter's turn to get its own rental sharing scheme – Cityscoot (Ⓦ cityscoot.eu). There are currently around 1000 electric scooters available to rent in central Paris, with plans to extend the scheme to Greater Paris. To join, you'll need a smartphone, as all bookings are made via the Cityscoot app. It works on a pay-as-you-go basis, with no subscriptions required. You register your card online and just pay for the minutes you use – the basic rate is €0.28/min, or you can buy a

"pack" of 100 minutes, for example, for €25. The scooters can be picked up and deposited in any valid parking space – there are no fixed docking stations. The Cityscoot app allows you to locate the nearest scooter and then sends you a pin code to "unlock" the bike. A driver's licence is only required if you were born after 1987, and for the novice scooter-rider a free "initiation" session can be arranged first.

You can also of course rent a scooter from a number of standard rental outlets. Freescoot (Ⓦ scooter-rental-paris.com) has 50ccs from €55/ day, while Paris by Scooter (Ⓦ parisbyscooter.com), which rents Vespas from €69/day, also offers customizable private scooter tours, ranging from three hours to a full day – including an *Amélie* movie-themed jaunt, and a trip to Versailles – from €149. Costs include the bike being delivered and picked up from your hotel.

The media

Despite hefty state subsidies the traditional French press is currently in something of a crisis – circulation is low and print costs some of the highest in Europe. Meanwhile many believe that the fact that the majority stakeholders of practically all the major newspapers now come from big business is inevitably compromising political neutrality. As for

television, there is plenty of interesting output – though some of it will look pretty familiar, as many stations depend as heavily on American imports as British channels do.

Newspapers and magazines

British newspapers, as well as the *Washington Post*, *New York Times* and the *International Herald Tribune*, are widely on sale in the city on the day after publication.

Of the quality **French daily papers**, the centre-left *Le Monde* (Ⓦlemonde.fr) is the most intellectual; it is widely respected, though somewhat austere. *Libération* (Ⓦliberation.fr), founded by Jean-Paul Sartre in the 1960s, is slightly more colloquial and choosy in its coverage – while not as radical as in Sartre's day, it retains a leftist stance. *Le Figaro* (Ⓦlefigaro.fr) is a highly respected centre-right national, the oldest daily paper in France. The best-selling tabloid is *Le Parisien* (Ⓦleparisien.fr; published as *Aujourd'hui en France* outside Paris), good on local news and events, while for sports news the paper of choice is *L'Equipe* (Ⓦlequipe.fr).

News weeklies include the wide-ranging, in-depth and left-leaning *L'Obs* (Ⓦtempsreel.nouvelobs.com; formerly *Le Nouvel Observateur*), the right-centrist *L'Express* (Ⓦexpress.fr) and staunchly republican *Marianne* (Ⓦmarianne.net). The best investigative journalism is to be found in the satirical weekly *Le Canard Enchaîné* (Ⓦlecanardenchaine.fr), a sort of *Private Eye* equivalent. *Charlie Hebdo* (Ⓦcharliehebdo.fr), meanwhile, which hit the world's headlines in January 2015 (see p.377), continues to publish its transgressive and often outrageous cartoons, poking fun at everything from religion to politicians.

TV and radio

The main public television channels are **France 2** (Ⓦfrance2.fr), with lots of light entertainment and imports, the slightly more highbrow **France 3** (Ⓦfrance3.fr), which serves up drama, documentaries, news and arts programmes, and the even loftier **France 5** (Ⓦwww.france5.fr), composed entirely of factual programmes. **Arte** (Ⓦarte-tv.com) is a cultural channel, with lots of documentaries and subtitled films. The two major commercial channels are **TF1** (Ⓦtf1.fr) and **M6** (Ⓦ6play.fr), both heavy on the American imports and reality shows. The chief French **news broadcasts** are at 8pm on France 2 and TF1. The main cable channel is C8 **Canal Plus** (Ⓦcanalplus.fr), good for films, drama and sports. France also has its own rolling news station, **France 24** (Ⓦfrance24.com), which puts across a French outlook on world affairs and covers politics, arts and culture. It broadcasts in English, French, Arabic and Spanish.

PARIS WALKING TOURS

Walking tours can be a great way to get to know the city, whether you're a first-time sightseer wanting to get an overall feel for the city or a regular visitor wanting to delve a bit further under the surface. Some tours focus on a particular theme, such as food and wine or a specific period of history, and customized private tours are often available too. One or two walking-tour companies advertise their walks as free, though in practice you're expected to give a tip.

Discover Paris Walks ☎ 09 70 44 97 24, Ⓦ discoverwalks.com/city/paris-walking-tours. Ninety-minute "free" (tips only) walking tours, conducted by English-speaking locals every day apart from Dec 24 and 25. You can book online or just turn up, though numbers are limited to eight. Walks range from the major landmarks to "hidden gems". They also run some interesting "speciality tours", such as street art (€25) and Paris food and wine (€75).

Localers ☎ 01 83 64 92 01, Ⓦ localers.com/our-tours-in-Paris. Themed tours run by local experts such as photographers, historians and food connoisseurs, aiming to give you an insider's view of Paris. The fascinating World War II tour takes you to places like the Marais' Jewish quarter, the Mémorial de la Shoah and Notre Dame, while the Sweet Side Food tour has you sampling eight different pastries in the best pâtisseries in Saint Germain-des-Prés. Some tours are tailored to families. Prices start at around €55/person.

Paris Walks ☎ 01 48 09 21 40, Ⓦ paris-walks.com. One of the city's longest-established walking-tour companies, staffed mostly by native English-speakers, long resident in Paris. Daily walks are available on a wide variety of interesting themes, including Hemingway's Paris, Art Nouveau and the French Revolution. You can just turn up for most walks, or book ahead online. Tours cost around €15 a head (€10 for children).

Sandemans New Europe Tours Ⓦ neweuropetours.eu. If you're a first-time visitor to Paris, the three-hour overview of Paris tour ("free", tips only) can be a good way to get your bearings and see some of the city's highlights. The tour runs several times daily; you can either book online or just turn up. Other tours focus on a particular area, such as the Latin Quarter or Montmartre (€16), and there are also tours to Versailles and a "Paris pub crawl".

For **radio news** in French, there's the state-run France Inter (Ⓦfranceinter.fr; 87.8FM), Europe 1 (Ⓦeurope1.fr; 104.7FM), or round-the-clock news on France Info (Ⓦfranceinfo.fr; 105.5FM).

Living in Paris

Work

Although EU nationals and Swiss citizens are free to move to France without a special permit, and can look for work on the same basis as French citizens, it's worth noting that casual work in Paris is hard to come by and generally poorly paid. It was unclear at the time of writing what arrangements will be in place after Brexit for UK nationals seeking work in France, while, for visitors from North America or Australasia arriving without a prearranged job offer, the chance of finding legal paid employment is practically nil. Most nationalities need authorization from a prospective employer in order to apply for a visa/residency permit or, if the work period is less than ninety days, for a short-stay work visa. There are a number of different permits available; check with the French consulate in your home country as to the latest regulations.

EU nationals are legally entitled to the same pay, conditions and union rights as French nationals. The French **minimum wage** (SMIC – *Salaire Minimum Interprofessionnel de Croissance*), indexed to the cost of living, is currently around €9.80 an hour (for a maximum 152-hour month). Employers, however, are likely to pay lower wages to temporary foreign workers who don't have easy access to legal resources, and may make them work longer hours.

If you're looking for secure employment, it's important to begin planning before you leave home. A **book** that might be worth consulting is *Work Your Way Around the World* by Susan Griffith. The website Ⓦexpatica.com/fr also has some useful advice on finding work in France, as does Ⓦangloinfo.com.

For **temporary work** check the ads in *FUSAC* (Ⓦfusac.fr). You could also try the notice boards at CIDJ (see opposite), a youth information agency that advertises some temporary jobs for foreigners. Job-seekers with professional qualifications and experience should check out Ⓦjobsinparis.fr. The national employment agency, **Pôle Emploi** (Ⓦpole-emploi.fr), advertises jobs in all fields and, in theory, offers a whole range of services to

job-seekers; though it's open to all EU citizens, it is not renowned for its helpfulness to foreigners. If your French is up to par, take a look at Keljob (Ⓦkeljob.com), an informative site that can help with your CV, interview questions and other job-seeking issues.

Other possible sources include the English-language French news website Ⓦthelocal.fr and notice boards at English bookshops, the American Church in Paris and the American Library. The American/Irish/British **bars and restaurants** sometimes have vacancies. You'll need to speak French, look smart and be prepared to work very long hours. Obviously, the better your French, the better your chances are of finding work.

Teaching

Finding a **teaching job** is best done in advance, usually in late summer. In Britain, jobs are often advertised in the *Times Educational Supplement* (Ⓦtes.com). You don't need fluent French to get a post, but a degree and a TEFL (Teaching English as a Foreign Language) qualification are usually required. The TEFL site (Ⓦtefl.org.uk) is a useful resource, as is the British Council's website (Ⓦbritishcouncil.org), which has a list of English-teaching vacancies. If you apply for jobs from home, most schools will fix up the necessary papers for you. EU nationals don't need a work permit, but getting social security can still be tricky should employers refuse to help. For addresses of schools, look under "Cours de langues" in the *Yellow Pages* (Ⓦpagesjaunes.fr). If you offer **private lessons** (via university notice boards or classified ads), you'll have lots of competition.

Au pair work

Although **working as an au pair** can be set up online via dedicated sites such as Ⓦaupair.com, this sort of work can be misery if you end up with an unpleasant employer. If you're determined to try – and it can be a very good way of learning the language – it's better to apply once in France, where you can at least meet the family first and check things out. Again, FUSAC (Ⓦfusac.fr) is a good resource, with a classified ads section dedicated to childcare. Conditions vary, but you should expect board, lodging and pocket money, along with some sort of travel pass. Working hours are officially capped at 30hr a week, plus two or three evenings' babysitting.

Claiming benefit

Any EU citizen who has been signing on for **unemployment benefit** at home, and intends to try and continue doing so in Paris, needs a letter of introduction from their own social security office, plus a U2 certificate of authorization (be sure to give them plenty of warning to prepare this). You must pre-register with the Pôle Emploi office (see opposite) within seven days of your arrival in France – either online or by phone (❶ 39 49) – to make an appointment to register at their offices.

It's possible to claim benefit for up to three months while you look for work, but it can often take that amount of time for the paperwork to be processed. Pensioners can arrange for their **pensions** to be paid in France, but cannot receive French state pensions.

Study

It's relatively easy to be a **student** in Paris. Foreigners pay no more than French nationals to enrol on a course, and the only problem then is how to support yourself, though you'll be eligible for subsidized accommodation, meals and all the student reductions. Few people want to do undergraduate degrees abroad, but for higher degrees or other diplomas, the range of options is enormous. Strict entry requirements, including an exam in French, apply only for undergraduate degrees. For a comprehensive rundown on studying in France, including a list of programmes and courses, information on how to apply and possible grants, check ⓦ campusfrance .org.

Courses at the non-profit **Alliance Française** (101 bd Raspail, 6ᵉ; ⓦ alliancefr.org; ⓜ St Placide) are quite reasonably priced (from €100/week for 9hr of classes) and well regarded, while the **Sorbonne** (ⓦ ccfs-sorbonne.fr) has special short courses aimed at foreigners.

STUDY AND WORK PROGRAMS

American Institute for Foreign Study US +1 (617) 236 2051 or 1800 888 2247, UK ❶ +44 020 7581 7300; Australia ❶ +61 2 8235 7000; France ❶ +33 1 4439 0424; Germany ❶ +49 228 957 300; Poland ❶ +48 22 826 7147, ⓦ aifs.com. Language study and cultural immersion.

Council on International Educational Exchange (CIEE) US ❶ 1207 553 4000, ⓦ ciee.org. Leading NGO offering study programs and volunteer projects around the world.

STUDENT/YOUTH ORGANIZATIONS

Student information (CROUS) (Le Centre régional des oeuvres universitaires et scolaires de Paris) 39 av Georges-Bernanos, 5ᵉ ⓦ www.crous-paris.fr; RER Port-Royal. The University of Paris student organization, providing help with student accommodation and other services.

Youth information (CIDJ) (Centre d'Information et de Documentation de la Jeunesse) 101 quai Branly, 15ᵉ ⓦ cidj.com; ⓜ Bir-Hakeim. Provides all sorts of information for young people and students, for example on studying in France and finding somewhere to live. Tues–Fri 1–6pm, Sat 1–5pm.

Travel essentials

Addresses

Paris is divided into twenty districts, or **arrondissements**. The first arrondissement, or "1ᵉʳ", is centred on the Louvre, in the heart of the city. The rest wind outward in a clockwise direction something like a snail's shell: the 2ᵉ, 3ᵉ and 4ᵉ are central; the 5ᵉ, 6ᵉ and 7ᵉ lie on the inner part of the Left (south) Bank; and the 8ᵉ–20ᵉ make up the outer districts. Parisian addresses generally quote the arrondissement, often with the nearest métro station, or stations, too. The **postcode** in Parisian addresses consists of the generic 750 plus the number of the arrondissement: so, for example, the 14ᵉ becomes 75014 Paris. Bis and ter (as in 4bis rue de la Fontaine, for example) are the equivalent of "a" and "b".

PARIS CLIMATE	Jan	Feb	Mar	Apr	May	Jun	Jul	Aug	Sep	Oct	Nov	Dec
AVERAGE DAILY TEMPERATURE												
Max/min (°F)	43/34	45/34	54/40	61/43	68/50	72/55	77/59	75/57	70/54	61/46	50/41	45/36
Max/min (°C)	6/1	7/1	12/4	16/6	20/10	23/13	25/15	24/14	21/12	16/8	10/5	7/2
AVERAGE RAINFALL												
mm	56	46	35	42	57	54	59	64	55	50	51	50

Climate

Paris's **climate** is fairly stable, with longish stretches of sunshine (or rain) year-round. Summer can get hot, with temperatures occasionally reaching as high as 38ºC (100ºF), and humidity high. It can rain at any time of year: summer sees fewer downpours, while at other times there's a tendency to drizzle. Spring sees its fair share of showers, but is characterized by bright, sunny days, and autumn can be very rewarding, weather-wise. Winter can be cold, but the light is beautiful.

Costs

Paris has the potential to be very expensive, certainly more so than the rest of France, particularly for visitors from outside the Eurozone. However, transport prices (see p.27) compare favourably with other north European capitals, and although accommodation prices are high, if you are one of two people sharing a comfortable central hotel room, you can get by happily on around €125 per person per day. At the bottom line, by watching the pennies, staying at a hostel and visiting monuments and museums on free entry days (see box, below), you could survive on as little as €70 a day, including one restaurant meal.

In budget **hotels**, simple doubles with shower can be had from as little as €70 in high season (around €10–15 less without shower), but for more comfort, prices start at around €100. At most hotels breakfast costs an extra €7–14; it will invariably be cheaper to eat in a local café.

Eating out in restaurants can be expensive. Prices vary of course, but even in the cheaper places a three-course dinner could easily set you back €30. The lunchtime *menu* will be cheaper (from around €15) and you can generally get a filling midday *plat du jour* (hot dish of the day) for around €12.

PARIS ON A BUDGET

Paris is a pricey destination, but there are a few tips to bear in mind that will make it easier to keep control of your spending.

MUSEUM ENTRY

The permanent collections at the following municipal museums are **free year-round**: Musée d'Art Moderne de la Ville de Paris (see p.160); Maison de Balzac (see p.218); Musée Bourdelle (see p.163); Musée Carnavalet (see p.97); Musée Cernuschi (see p.68); Musée Cognacq-Jay (see p.98); Musée du Général Leclerc de Hauteclocque et de la Libération de Paris/Musée Jean Moulin (see p.165); Petit Palais/Musée des Beaux-Arts de la Ville de Paris (see p.67); Maison de Victor Hugo (see p.95); and Musée de la Vie Romantique (see p.190).

In addition, the national museums are **free on the first Sunday of the month**: Cité de l'Architecture et du Patrimoine (see p.158); Musée National d'Art Moderne at the Pompidou (see p.87); Musée National des Arts Asiatiques Guimet (see p.158); Musée des Arts et Métiers (see p.105); Musee de la Chasse et de la Nature (see p.100); Musée National Eugène Delacroix (see p.142); Musée National Gustave Moreau (see p.191); Cité National de l'Histoire de l'Immigration (see p.119); Musée National du Moyen Age (see p.123); Musée de l'Orangerie (see p.72); Musée d'Orsay (see p.135); Musée Picasso (see p.102); and Musée du Quai Branly (see p.151).

Note too that **Eurostar travellers** can get two-for-one admission at a few of the big museums, including the Orsay and the Louvre – these deals change regularly, so check the pages at the back of the in-train magazine.

FREE ATTRACTIONS

Churches, **cemeteries** and, of course, **markets** (except for some specialist annual antique and book markets) are free. Most **parks** are free but some gardens within have small entry charges, usually around €1.50. **Libraries** and the cultural centres of different countries often put on films, shows and exhibitions for next to nothing – check details in the listings magazines (see p.40).

ENTERTAINMENT

Discounted theatre tickets are available online at Ⓦ billetreduc.com. Cinema tickets will be much cheaper at the smaller independent cinemas, particularly those around the student area in the 5ᵉ. Regular **free festivals** (see p.321) and **cultural offerings**, from bands in the streets to firework shows, come courtesy of the Mairie de Paris and are publicized throughout the city. It's well worth checking out what's on before you arrive (Ⓦ parisinfo.com).

EMERGENCY NUMBERS

Fire brigade/Paramedics (sapeurs-pompiers) ☎ 18
Medical emergencies See box, below
Police ☎ 17
Rape crisis ☎ 08 00 05 95 95

Drinks in cafés and bars can easily mount up; in many cafés it's cheaper to stand at the bar than sit at a table, and some places charge a premium for outside seating on the *terrasse*. A black espresso coffee (*un café*) is the cheapest drink (around €2); a *café crème* ranges from around €2.60 at the bar to anything up to €9 on a *terrasse* in the more touristy areas. Glasses of wine cost from around €4, but draught lager tends to be a bit more expensive. Mixed drinks or cocktails generally cost €8–16.

Discounts

Institutions have different policies, but at the time of writing, all **national museums** are free for under-18s, plus EU nationals (as well as students studying in the EU who can prove it) under the age of 26, and are also free to all on the first Sunday of the month (see box, opposite). All public monuments are free for under-12s, Under-4s are usually let in free everywhere, under-8s less often. Privately owned sights usually offer half price or reduced admission to 5- to 18-year-olds, though more commercial places charge adult rates for anyone aged 12 upwards.

If you are a full-time **student**, it's worth carrying the **ISIC** (International Student Identity Card; ⓦ isic .org) to gain reductions on museum admissions (usually about a third off) and at some restaurants. The card is universally accepted as ID, while the student card from your home institution is not. Travellers aged 30 or younger qualify for the **International Youth Travel Card** – these offer similar discounts to the ISIC and are available via ⓦ isic.org. For anyone over 60 or 65 (depending on the institution), reductions are only patchily available; carry your passport with you as proof of age.

Whatever your age, if you are going to visit a lot of museums, it's worth considering the **Paris Museum Pass** (€48 two-day, €62 four-day, €74 six-day; ⓦ parismuseumpass.com). Available online and from the tourist offices, Fnac stores and museums, the pass is valid for more than thirty museums and monuments, including the main ones (though not special exhibitions), in Paris, and twenty in the surrounding area. It also allows you to bypass ticket queues (though not the security checkpoints).

Crime and personal safety

On high alert since the terrorist attacks of 2015, Parisian attractions have upped their **security** – it's best not to carry large bags to the bigger museums, for example, and you might encounter longer waits than usual in most places as all bags are checked. Travellers of North African or Arab appearance may occasionally encounter excessive police interest; carrying your passport at all times is a good idea (everyone is legally required to have identification on them in any case). That said, although there are occasional reports of hotels or restaurants claiming to be fully booked, or clubs refusing entry, racist incidents involving tourists are fairly rare.

Meanwhile, petty **theft** is as common in the crowded hangouts of the capital as in most major cities; take the usual precautions, especially on the métro and in the train stations. If you need to report a theft, go immediately to the *commissariat de police* of the arrondissement in which the crime took place – you can find a list, organized by arron-dissement, on ⓦ www.prefecturedepolice.interieur .gouv.fr. The officers will fill out a *constat de vol*; the first thing they'll ask for is your passport – keep a copy and vehicle documents if relevant. Although the police are not always as co-operative as they might be, it is their duty to assist you if you've lost your passport or all your money – if you've lost something less serious, try the **lost property office** (see p.37).

The two main types of **police** (in popular slang, *les flics*) that you see on the streets – the Police Nationale and the Gendarmerie Nationale – are for all practical purposes indistinguishable. The CRS (Compagnies Républicaines de Sécurité), on the other hand, are an entirely different proposition, used to guard sensitive embassies, control

MEDICAL EMERGENCY NUMBERS

Europe-wide emergency number (English-speaking operators available)
☎ 112
Paramedics/Fire brigade (sapeurs-pompiers) ☎ 18
SAMU (Service d'Aide Médicale d'Urgence) Serious medical emergencies/ambulance ☎ 15
SOS Dentaire Emergency dental care
☎ 01 43 37 51 00
SOS Médecins Doctor call-out
☎ 01 47 07 77 77

demonstrations and keep the peace during highly sensitive situations – following the Charlie Hebdo attacks in 2015, for example.

Should you have the misfortune to be **arrested**, you have the right to contact your consulate, which you should do immediately – you can find a list, organized alphabetically by country, on Ⓦen .parisinfo.com.

Electricity

France uses double, round-pin wall sockets that supply 220V. If you haven't bought the appropriate adaptor (*adapteur*) or transformer (*transformateur* – for US appliances) before leaving home, try the electrical section of a large department store like BHV (see p.325).

Health

Citizens of all EU countries are entitled to take advantage of French health services under the same terms as residents, provided they have the correct documentation. At the time of writing, British citizens were still covered by the European Health Insurance Card (**EHIC**), which can be applied for, free of charge, at UK post offices or online at Ⓦnhs.uk. It's unclear whether this benefit will still be available after the UK leaves the EU – checking the situation via Ⓦehic.org.uk before you travel is advisable. Non-EU citizens have to pay for most medical attention and are strongly advised to take out some form of travel insurance.

Under the French Social Security system, every hospital visit, doctor's consultation and prescribed medicine incurs a charge, which you have to pay upfront. Although all EU citizens with the correct documents are entitled to a **refund** of around 70–80 percent of the standard fee for medical and dental expenses (the refund is lower when it comes to the cost of prescribed medicines) – providing the

doctor is a *médecin conventionné* (government-registered and providing state rather than private care) – this can still leave a hefty shortfall, especially after a stay in hospital. Present your EHIC when dealing with any medical service, and keep the treatment form (*feuille de soins*), plus all receipts, prescriptions and any paperwork, in order to claim any reimbursements. Reimbursements should be claimed from the local CPAM (Caisse Primaire d'Assurance Maladie) office in Paris; you will need to present your bank details, including IBAN and BIC.

In **emergencies** you will always be admitted to the nearest hospital (*hôpital*), either under your own power or by ambulance, which even French citizens must pay for. Far better to call the fire brigade (*sapeurs-pompiers*) instead; acting as paramedics, they are equipped to deal with medical emergencies and are the fastest and most reliable emergency service.

The Hôtel Dieu, at 7 Ile de la Cité, is the most centrally located **hospital** and has a 24hr Accident and Emergency department. If you prefer to go private you could try one of two English-speaking **private hospitals**: the American Hospital of Paris at 63 bd Victor-Hugo, Neuilly-sur-Seine (☎01 46 41 25 25, Ⓦamerican-hospital.org; Ⓜ Porte Maillot), and the Hertford British Hospital at 4 rue Kléber (☎01 47 59 59 59, Ⓦbritish-hospital.org; ⓂKléber). Note that any costs incurred for private health care are not refundable.

To find a **doctor**, ask at any *pharmacie*, local police station, tourist office or your hotel. Alternatively, look under "Médecins" in the *Yellow Pages* or search for healthcare providers near you on Ⓦannuairesante.ameli.fr. An average consultation fee should be between €20 and €30. You will be given a *feuille de soins* for later insurance claims. Prescriptions (*ordonnances*) should be taken to a *pharmacie* and must be paid for; the medicines will have little stickers (*vignettes*) attached to them, which you should remove and stick to your *feuille de soins*, together with the prescription itself.

Pharmacies, signalled by an illuminated green cross, can give advice on minor complaints and are also equipped to provide first aid on request (for a fee). Most pharmacies will have at least one chemist who speaks English. They tend to open from Monday to Saturday – many are closed on Sundays, though there are plenty in central areas such as the Marais that open – from roughly 8am to 8pm; at night, details of the nearest open pharmacy are posted in the windows. To find your closest duty pharmacy call ☎ 32 37 or search on Ⓦ www.3237.fr (though note that not all of the city's pharmacies are listed here).

For a list of pharmacies that are open on particular nights, check Ⓦ pharmaciesdegarde.fr.

Insurance

Even though EU healthcare privileges apply in France, you'd do well to take out an **insurance policy** before travelling to cover against theft, loss, emergency repatriation or injury. Many policies can be chopped and changed to exclude coverage you don't need – for example, sickness and accident benefits can often be excluded or included at will. If you do take **medical coverage**, check whether benefits will be paid as treatment proceeds or only after you return home, and whether there is a 24hr medical emergency number. When securing **baggage cover**, make sure that the per-article limit – typically under £500 – will cover your most valuable possession. If you need to make a claim, you should keep **receipts** for medicines and medical treatment (see opposite), and in the event that you have anything stolen you must obtain an official statement from the police (called a *constat de vol*).

Internet

Though most hotels have free **wi-fi** (with variable reception), US and UK visitors will find that automatic free access in cafés and bars is not generally as widespread as in their home countries. In the centre of town the international coffee chains are a safe bet, or you could follow the bobo (bourgeois-bohemian) trail to the cool haunts of the Marais, Montmartre, Belleville and the Canal St-Martin – though note that some of the hipper coffee houses actively ban computers and tablets. You can also connect to the city's free wi-fi network from more than 260 **parks, museums and libraries** – these are all clearly marked with a "Paris Wi-Fi" logo, and are listed on the municipal website,

Ⓦ paris.fr/wifi. **Internet cafés** are becoming harder to find. *Milk* has two branches (both daily 24hr; Ⓦ milklub.com): the most central is near Les Halles at 31 bd Sébastopol, 1ᵉʳ (€3.90/hr), and the other is in Montparnasse at 5 rue d'Odessa, 14ᵉ (€4/hr). Both also offer printing, photocopying and scanning services.

Laundry

You shouldn't have any trouble finding a **laundry** in Paris, especially in the more residential areas such as Montmartre and the Canal St-Martin. They're often unattended, so bring small change with you. Hours vary, but generally self-service laundries open at 7am and close around 10pm; prices vary, too, but you could reckon on paying around €4 for a 7kg load, and €1 for 8min in the dryer. The alternative *blanchisserie*, or pressing services, are likely to be expensive, and hotels in particular charge high rates. If you're doing your own washing in hotels, keep quantities small and be discreet, as most places forbid doing laundry in your room.

Lost property

The **lost property office** (Bureau des Objets Trouvés) is in the Préfecture de Police, 36 rue des Morillons, 15ᵉ (Mon–Thurs 8.30am–4.30pm; ☎ 3430; Ⓜ Convention). For property lost on public transport, phone the RATP on ☎ 3246. If you lose your passport, report it at a police station immediately (see p.35).

Mail

Most French **post offices** (*bureaux de poste* or *PTTs*; Ⓦ laposte.fr) – look for bright yellow-and-blue La Poste signs – also offer money exchange, photocopying and phone services. They are generally open 9am until 7pm Monday to Friday, and 9am till noon on Saturdays. At the time of writing, **Paris's main office**, at 52 rue du Louvre, 1ᵉʳ (Ⓜ Etienne Marcel), was closed for renovations until 2018; until then the nearby office at 16 rue Etienne Marcel is taking over its duties, offering postal services Monday to Saturday from midnight till 6am and from 8am until midnight, and from 10am until midnight on Sundays (the other services are daytime only, as in all post offices).

Standard airmail letters (20g or less) and postcards within France and to European Union countries cost €0.85 and to North America, Australia and New Zealand €1.30. Remember that you can also buy **stamps** from *tabacs*.

To post your letter on the street, look for the bright yellow **post boxes**.

Maps

The **maps** in this Guide and the free *Paris Map* available from the tourist offices (see p.40) should be adequate for a short sightseeing stay, but for a more detailed map your best bet is the pocket-sized *L'Indispensable Plan de Paris* 1:15,000, published by Atlas Indispensable; it comes in a robust plastic cover, and gives full A–Z street listings.

Money

France's currency is the euro (€), which is split into 100 cents. There are seven euro notes – in denominations of 500, 200, 100, 50, 20, 10 and 5 (though many vendors are reluctant to accept the 500 and 200 euro notes) – and eight different coin denominations, from 2 euros down to 1 cent. For the most up-to-date exchange rates, consult the currency converter website ⓦoanda.com.

The easiest way to access your funds while away is with a **debit or credit card** – but it's not necessarily the cheapest option, with many UK banks levying charges totalling around 5 percent on foreign withdrawals. Added to the French bank's transaction charges, these can really add up. Depending on your bank, it may be necessary to contact them before leaving to let them know you'll be abroad, so they won't block your funds for security reasons. Most foreign cards will work in a French ATM/cash machine (called a *distributeur* or *point argent*). Credit cards are widely accepted but it's always worth checking first that restaurants and hotels will accept your card – American Express cards can sometimes be a bit tricky, and some smaller places won't accept them, even if they have a sign suggesting that they do. And note that some machines don't recognize foreign cards at all – transport vending machines and automatic petrol pumps, especially those at major supermarkets, are particularly problematic, but it can happen in restaurants and hotels, too. North American credit cards, for example, are not accepted at RATP/SNCF machines. French cards use the **chip-and-pin system**.

To cancel **lost or stolen** cards, call the following 24hr numbers: American Express

ⓣ+44 1273 696 933; MasterCard ⓣ0800 96 4767; Visa ⓣ0800 89 1725.

Changing money and banking hours

Exchange rates and **commission fees** charged by banks and bureaux de change vary considerably. On the whole, the best exchange rates are offered by **banks**, though there's always a commission charge on top (a 2–4 percent commission on cash). **Bureaux de change** can give terrible rates, though the ones at the airports and those on the Champs-Elysées, near *McDonald's*, are usually pretty reputable.

Standard **banking hours** are Monday to Friday or Tuesday to Saturday from 9am till 5pm. Some banks close at lunchtime (usually 12.30–2pm). All are closed on Sunday and public holidays. Money-exchange bureaux stay open longer, tend not to close for lunch and may even open on Sundays in the more touristy areas.

Avoid the **automatic exchange machines** at the airports and train stations and outside many money-exchange bureaux, except in emergencies. They offer a very poor rate of exchange.

Opening hours and public holidays

Most shops, businesses, information services, museums and banks in Paris stay open all day. The exceptions are the smaller shops and enterprises, which may close for lunch sometime between noon and 2.30pm. Although France recently eased its Sunday trading restrictions, with shops in the more touristy areas allowed to stay open (see p.325), basic **hours of business** are from 9am to 7pm Monday to Saturday. Big department stores will also have a *"nocturne"* each week – a night where they stay open late, and supermarkets often stay open until 9 or 10pm. You can always find boulangeries and food shops that stay open on days when others close – on Sunday normally until noon (but note that many boulangeries also have a day or a couple of days each week when they close). Most shops – large and small – open on Sundays in December.

Museums generally open at 9/10am and close at 5/6pm. Summer hours may differ from winter hours. Don't be caught out by museum **closing days** – usually Monday or Tuesday and sometimes both. A number of museums stay open late one night a week, usually until 9 or 10pm.

Many restaurants and smaller shops take a **holiday** between the middle of July and the end of August (see below) and over Easter and Christmas.

France celebrates eleven **national holidays** (*jours fériés* or j.f.) – not counting the two that fall on a Sunday anyway. Throughout the Guide, opening hours given for Sundays also apply to public holidays. With three, and sometimes four, holidays, **May** is a particularly festive month. It makes a peaceful time to visit, as people clear out of town over several weekends, but many businesses will have erratic opening hours. Just about everything, including museums, will be closed on May 1. July 14 heralds the beginning of the French holiday season and people leave town en masse between then and the end of August.

NATIONAL HOLIDAYS

January 1 (New Year's Day) Le Jour de l'an
Easter Sunday Pâques
Easter Monday Lundi de Pâques
May 1 (May Day) La Fête du travail
May 8 (VE Day) La Fête de la Victoire 1945
Ascension Day (40 days after Easter: mid-May to early June) L'Ascension
Whitsun (7th Sun after Easter: mid-May to early June) La Pentecôte
Whit Monday (7th Mon after Easter: mid-May to early June) Lundi de Pentecôte
July 14 (Bastille Day) La Fête nationale
August 15 (Feast of the Assumption) l'Assomption
November 1 (All Saints' Day) La Toussaint
November 11 (Armistice Day) L'Armistice 1918
December 25 (Christmas Day) Noël

Phones

Most foreign mobile/cell phones automatically connect to a local provider as soon as you arrive in France. Data roaming charges, which used to be extortionate, have now been scrapped within the EU, though British travellers may face high charges again post-Brexit; check with your provider before you travel.

France operates on the European GSM standard, so US **cell phones** won't work unless you've got a tri-band phone. If you're making a lot of calls, consider buying a local SIM card or a prepaid SIM card (*carte prépayée sans engagement*) once in Paris. These are sold in mobile phone shops, Fnac stores (see p.334) and some supermarkets. Note that some devices, particularly smartphones, need to be unlocked in order to switch SIMs. Check with your provider about this process.

For **calls within France** – local or long distance – dial all ten digits of the number. Paris and

INTERNATIONAL CALLS

To **call France from abroad**, use the international dialling code for your country (00 or 011 in most cases) followed by the French country code (33), then the local number minus the initial "0". So to call Paris from the UK, Ireland and New Zealand dial ☎00 33 then the nine-digit number; from the US, Canada and Australia, dial ☎011 33.

CALLING HOME FROM PARIS

UK 00 + 44 + area code (minus initial zero) + number
US & Canada 00 + 1 + area code + number
Ireland 00 + 353 + area code (minus initial zero) + number
Australia 00 + 61+ area code (minus initial zero) + number
New Zealand 00 + 64 + area code (minus initial zero) + number
South Africa 00 + 27 + area code + number

Ile-de-France numbers start with ☎01. Numbers beginning with ☎080 up to ☎08 05, ☎30 and ☎31 are free to call; ☎081 is charged at local rates, no matter where you're calling from; all other ☎08 numbers, and ☎118 numbers, are premium rate and can't be accessed from outside France. Numbers beginning with ☎06 or ☎07 are **mobile** and therefore expensive to call.

Sales tax

VAT (Value Added Tax) is referred to as **TVA** in France (*taxe sur la valeur ajoutée*). The standard rate in France is currently 20 percent; it's lower for books, food and health products, but there are no exemptions. Non-EU residents who are visiting the country for less than six months are entitled to a refund (*détaxe*) of some or all of this amount (usually around twelve percent) if you spend at least €175 in a single trip to one shop. Though department stores and luxury boutiques tend to participate, not all stores do – ask first. To be eligible for the refund you must present your passport when you pay and ask for the *bordereau de vente à l'exportation* form, which needs to be signed by both you and the seller. The procedure for then claiming the refund – upon leaving the country, and within three months of the relevant purchase – is complicated; check the latest regulations on ◉douane.gouv.fr.

Smoking

Smoking is officially banned in public places in France, including train stations, but don't be surprised to find yourself occasionally surrounded by cigarette smoke if you're dining on a *terrasse* – even if it's covered.

Time

Paris, and all of France, is in the Central European Time Zone (GMT+1): 1hr ahead of the UK, 6hr ahead of Eastern Standard Time and 9hr ahead of Pacific Standard Time. France is 8hr behind all of eastern Australia and 10hr behind New Zealand from April to October (but 10hr behind south-eastern Australia and 12hr behind New Zealand from November to March).

Toilets

Paris's automatic public toilets, known as "*sanisettes*", are free to use. Elsewhere, ask for *les toilettes* or look for signs for the WC (pronounced "vay say"); when reading the details of facilities outside hotels, don't confuse *lavabo*, which means washbasin, with lavatory. French toilets in some of the cheapest and most old-fashioned bars are still occasionally of the hole-in-the-ground variety, and might lack toilet paper. Toilets in railway stations (for which there is a charge) and department stores are commonly staffed by attendants who will expect a bit of spare change.

Tourist information

The main **Paris tourist office** is at 25 rue des Pyramides, 1ᵉʳ (daily: May–Oct 9am–7pm; Nov–April 10am–7pm; Ⓦ parisinfo.com; Ⓜ Pyramides/RER Auber); there is a smaller **welcome centre** at Gare du Nord (daily 8am–6pm). In addition to giving out general information and maps, the offices can help with booking accommodation and sell public transport tickets, tour tickets and museum passes (see p.35). The website has a **hotel booking service**, and also allows you to buy tickets online for some of the most popular sights, such as the Louvre and the Musée d'Orsay, enabling you to bypass long queues.

For information on attractions and activities in Paris and the **surrounding area**, Ⓦ visitparisregion .com is another handy resource. **LGBT visitors** should check out Ⓦ parisgayvillage.com, which offers a free information and welcome service (see

p.358). *FUSAC* (France USA Contacts; Ⓦ fusac.fr) is useful for flats, jobs and entertainment news.

For detailed **what's-on information** check Paris's weekly **listings magazine** *L'Officiel des Spectacles* (Ⓦ offi.fr; €1), available from all newsagents and kiosks. *Pariscope* (online only; Ⓦ pariscope.fr) has details of concerts, dance performances, theatre and exhibitions, but no longer includes the cinema listings for which it was once famed. Keep a lookout, too, for the free weekly lifestyle and listings paper, *A nous Paris* (Ⓦ anousparis.fr), which comes out on Mondays and is available from métro stations. In addition, a number of free pocket independent nightlife guides (*Lylo* is a good one; Ⓦ lylo.fr) can be picked up in bars, cafés and the cooler stores.

Travellers with disabilities

Paris has never had a particularly good reputation for **access facilities**, though there have been significant improvements, especially to the bus network, and the city's public toilets (*sanisettes*) are fully accessible to wheelchair users.

The tourist board website, Ⓦ parisinfo.com, includes a section dedicated to disabled travellers. In addition to featuring possible itineraries, their *Accessible Paris* guide lists museums that are either accessible or offer **guided visits and activities** for disabled people. Meanwhile, Ⓦ accesculture.org has a list of **theatres** where audio descriptions or surtitles are provided for the visually impaired or deaf/hard-of-hearing. Admission to most **museums** is free for blue badge holders and one companion.

The **Eurostar** offers a good deal for wheelchair users. There are two spaces in the first-class carriages for wheelchairs, each with an accompanying seat for a companion. Fares for all four are fixed at the lowest standard-class fare (with semi-flexible conditions), and you will normally get the first-class meal as well. You need to reserve well in advance and arrange the special assistance that Eurostar offers at either end. Companions travelling on the Eurostar with visually and hearing impaired travellers – who pay the normal fare – can travel at the same price as a wheelchair user's companion by calling ☎ 08432 186 186.

Getting around

G7 Access (☎ 01 47 39 00 91, Ⓦ g7.fr) offers fully adapted **taxis** and drivers trained to take care of physically disabled and sight-impaired travellers. Fares are the same as for classic taxis; you just need to reserve four hours in advance.

Bus lines are accessible for wheelchairs, with mechanical ramps for getting on and off and a designated wheelchair space in the bus. Not all **RER** stations are accessible, however, and most require an official to work the lift for you. The Météor **métro** line (14), and the RER line E are designed to be easily accessible by all.

For travel on the buses, métro or RER, the RATP offers **accompanied journeys** for disabled people – *Les compagnons du voyage* (W compagnons.com) – which costs €32.30 an hour (€22 for over-60s) and is available round the clock. You have to book online or on ☎01 58 76 08 33 (Mon–Fri 7am–7pm) at least a day in advance.

Information in English and French on disabled access on the bus, métro and RER is available on W infomobi.com, or you can download a guide (in French only) at W ratp.fr.

Cars with hand controls can be rented from Hertz, usually with 24 hours' advance notice.

RESOURCES FOR DISABLED TRAVELLERS

W **accessinparis.org** Thoroughly researched and nicely put together guide which, although last updated in 2008, still has a lot of good detail on what it is like to travel in Paris, with sections on transport, accommodation and toilets, among others.

APF (Association des Paralysés de France) W apf.asso.fr. National organization providing information and support for disabled people.

Handitourisme One of the best sources of information for travellers with disabilities in France (with a large section on Paris), published by Petit Futé (W petitfute.fr; available in digital format too). Written in French, and regularly updated, the guide lists hundreds of sites, museums, hotels and restaurants with full accessibility to handicapped travellers.

W **infomobi.com** Useful source of information on getting around Paris, with English translations and a helpline.

W **jaccede.com** Handy website (in French only) giving a list of museums, monuments and other public places in Paris that are wheelchair accessible.

PONT-NEUF

The islands

There's no better place to start a tour of Paris than the two river islands at its centre, the Ile de la Cité and the Ile St-Louis. The former is the core from which the rest of Paris grew and harbours the cathedral of Notre-Dame, a superb example of Gothic grandeur and harmony, and the stunning Sainte-Chapelle, preserved within the precincts of the Palais de Justice. Linked to the Ile de la Cité by a footbridge, the smaller Ile St-Louis has no heavyweight sights, but possesses a beguiling charm of its own, with its tall, austerely beautiful houses on single-lane streets, tree-lined *quais*, a church and assorted restaurants, cafés and shops. The island feels removed from the rest of Paris, an oasis little touched by the city's turbulent years of revolution and upheaval. Inhabitants of the island even have their own name: "Louisiens".

Ile de la Cité

Ⓜ Cité/St-Michel/Pont-Neuf

The **Ile de la Cité** is where Paris began. It was settled in around 300 BC by a Celtic tribe, the Parisii, and in 52 BC was overrun by the Romans, who built a palace-fortress at the western end of the island. In the tenth century, the Frankish kings transformed this into a splendid palace, of which the **Sainte-Chapelle** and the **Conciergerie** prison survive today. At the other end of the island they erected the great cathedral of **Notre-Dame**. By the twelfth century the small Ile de la Cité teemed with life, somehow managing to accommodate twelve parishes plus numerous chapels and monasteries. It was all too much for the monks at St-Magloire, who moved out in 1138 to quieter premises on the Right Bank.

It takes some imagination today – or a visit to the **Crypte Archéologique** near Notre-Dame (see p.47) – to picture what the medieval city must have looked like, as most of it was erased in the nineteenth century by Baron Haussmann, Napoléon III's Préfet de la Seine (equivalent to mayor of Paris). This act displaced 25,000 people and destroyed ninety streets – which had, admittedly, become squalid and dangerous. In their place were raised four imposing Neoclassical edifices, largely given over to housing the law and police. The few corners of the island untouched by Haussmann include the tranquil **square du Vert-Galant**, **place Dauphine** and the medieval streets **rues Chanoinesse**, **des Ursins** and **de la Colombe**, north of the cathedral.

Pont-Neuf

Ⓜ Pont-Neuf

A popular approach to the Ile de la Cité is via the graceful, twelve-arched **Pont-Neuf**, which, despite its name ("New Bridge"), is Paris's oldest surviving bridge; it was built by Henri IV, who is commemorated with a statue halfway across. Made of stone and free of the usual medieval complement of houses, it was a radical departure from previous structures, hence its name. Henri IV, one of the capital's first great town planners, took much interest in Pont-Neuf's progress and would sometimes come to inspect it, delighting the workmen on one occasion by taking a flying leap over an incomplete arch.

So impressive was the bridge in scale and length that it soon became symbolic of the city itself, drawing large crowds; peddlers, secondhand book- and flower-sellers, dog-barbers and tooth-pullers set up stalls, while acrobats and actors entertained passers-by.

Square du Vert-Galant

Ⓜ Pont-Neuf

The **square du Vert-Galant** is enclosed within the triangular stern of the island, and reached via steps leading down behind the statue of Henri IV on the Pont-Neuf. "Vert-Galant", meaning a "green" or "lusty" gentleman, is a reference to the king's legendary amorous exploits, and he would no doubt have approved of this tranquil, tree-lined garden, a popular haunt of lovers – the prime spot to occupy is the knoll dotted with trees at the extreme point of the island. From here you can also hop onto one of the river boats that dock on the north side of the square (see p.27).

Place Dauphine

Ⓜ Pont-Neuf

On the eastern side of Pont-Neuf, across the street from the Henri IV statue, red-brick seventeenth-century houses flank the entrance to **place Dauphine**, one of the city's most secluded and attractive squares. The traffic noise recedes, often replaced by nothing more intrusive than the gentle tap of boules being played in the shade of the chestnuts. At the eastern end is the hulking facade of the **Palais de Justice**, which swallowed up the palace that was home to the French kings until Etienne Marcel's bloody revolt in 1358 frightened them off to the greater security of the Louvre.

Sainte-Chapelle

Palais de Justice, 4 bd du Palais, 1ᵉʳ · Daily: April to mid-May & mid-Sept to end Sept 9am–7pm; mid-May to mid-Sept 9am–9.30pm; Oct–March 9am–5pm · €10, combined admission with the Conciergerie €15 · ☎ 01 53 40 60 80, ⓦ sainte-chapelle.fr · Ⓜ Cité

The only part of the Ile de la Cité's old palace that remains in its entirety is the **Sainte-Chapelle**, its fragile-looking spire soaring above the Palais buildings and its excessive height in relation to its length giving it the appearance of a lopped-off cathedral choir. Though damaged in the Revolution, during which it was used as a flour warehouse, it was sensitively restored in the mid-nineteenth century, and remains one of the finest achievements of French High Gothic, renowned for its exquisite stained-glass windows. It was built by Louis IX in 1242–48 to house a collection of holy relics bought at an extortionate price – far more than it cost to build the Sainte-Chapelle – from the bankrupt Byzantine Empire. The relics, supposedly Christ's crown of thorns plus fragments of the True Cross and a nail of the Crucifixion, are now in Notre-Dame's treasury, displayed only on certain days, including Good Friday.

The upper and lower chapels

The Sainte-Chapelle actually consists of two chapels: the simple **lower chapel** was intended for the servants, and the **upper chapel**, reached via a spiral staircase, was reserved for the court. The latter is dazzling, its walls made almost entirely of **stained glass** held up by powerful supports, which the medieval builders cleverly crafted to appear delicate and fragile by dividing them into clusters of pencil-thin columns. When the sun streams through, the glowing blues and reds of the stained glass dapple the interior and you feel like you're surrounded by myriad brilliant butterflies. There are 1113 glass panels, two-thirds of which are original (the others date from the nineteenth-century restoration); they tell virtually the entire story of the Bible, beginning on the north side with Genesis, continuing with the Passion of Christ (east end) and the history of the Sainte-Chapelle relics (on the south side), and ending with the Apocalypse in the rose window. The chapel is used for classical **concerts** almost daily – you can buy tickets a day or so in advance on the door or online (ⓦclassictic.com).

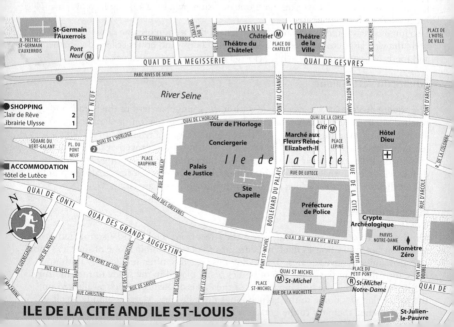

ILE DE LA CITÉ AND ILE ST-LOUIS

Conciergerie

Palais de Justice, 2 bd du Palais, 1ᵉʳ • Daily 9.30am–6pm • €9, combined ticket with Sainte-Chapelle €15 • ☎ 01 53 40 60 80, ⓦ paris-conciergerie.fr • Ⓜ Cité

The **Conciergerie** is one of the few remaining vestiges of the old medieval Palais de Justice and is Paris's oldest prison, where Marie Antoinette and the leading figures of the Revolution were incarcerated before execution. Inside are several splendid, vaulted Gothic halls, including the Salle des Gens d'Armes, built in 1301–15. The far end is separated off by an iron grille; during the Revolution this area was reserved for the *pailleux*, prisoners who couldn't afford to bribe a guard for their own cell and had to sleep on straw (*paille*).

Beyond is a corridor where prisoners were allowed to wander freely. There are a number of reconstructed rooms here, such as the "salle de toilette", where the condemned had their hair cropped and shirt collars ripped in preparation for the guillotine. On the upper storey is a mock-up of **Marie Antoinette's cell** in which the condemned queen's crucifix hangs forlornly against peeling fleur-de-lys wallpaper.

Tour de l'Horloge

Ⓜ Cité

Outside the Conciergerie is the **Tour de l'Horloge**, a tower built around 1350, and so-called because it displayed Paris's first public clock. The ornate face, set against a background of vivid blue and gold, is flanked with statues representing Law and Justice, added in 1585. The clock tower's bell, which would once have rung out to mark special royal occasions, and which was sounded during the St Bartholomew's Day massacre (see p.365), was melted down during the Commune (see p.186).

Place Lépine

Ⓜ Cité

East from the Conciergerie is **place Lépine**, named after the police boss who gave Paris's coppers their white truncheons and whistles. The **Préfecture de Police**, or police

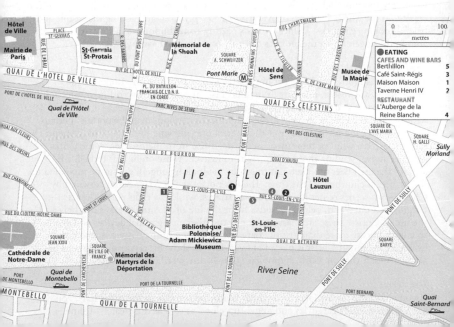

headquarters, known popularly as the Quai des Orfèvres (as readers of Georges Simenon's Maigret novels will know), stands on one side of the square, though the police are set to move to new modern offices before long. Livening up the square on the other side is a daily **flower market**, which is augmented by a chirruping bird market on Sundays. Following a state visit by the British queen in 2014, the market officially changed its name to Marché aux Fleurs Reine-Elizabeth-II, but nobody uses its full name.

Cathédrale de Notre-Dame

Parvis Notre-Dame, 4ᵉ • **Cathedral** Mon–Fri 8am–6.45pm, Sat & Sun 8am–7.15pm; guided tours 1hr–1hr 30min in English (Wed, Thurs & Fri 2pm, Mon, Tues & Sat 2.30pm) and French (Mon–Fri – though not first Fri of the month or any Fri during Lent – 2pm & 3pm, Sat & Sun 2.30pm) • Free • ☎ 01 42 34 56 10, ⓦ cathedraledeparis.com • **Towers** daily: April–Sept 10am–6.30pm; Oct–March 10am–5.30pm • €10 • ⓦ tours-notre-dame-de-paris.fr • **Trésor** Daily 9.30am–6pm • €3 • Ⓜ St-Michel/Cité

A Gothic masterpiece, the **Cathédrale de Notre-Dame** rears up from the Ile de la Cité like a great ship moored by huge flying buttresses. Built on the site of the Merovingian cathedral of St-Etienne, itself sited on the old Roman temple to Jupiter, Notre-Dame was begun in 1160 under the auspices of Bishop de Sully and completed around 1345. The cathedral's seminaries became an ecclesiastical powerhouse, churning out six popes during the thirteenth and fourteenth centuries, though it subsequently lost some of its pre-eminence to other sees, such as Rheims and St-Denis. The building later fell into decline, and during the Revolution the frieze of Old Testament kings on the facade was damaged by enthusiasts who mistook them for the kings of France. Napoleon restored some of the cathedral's prestige, crowning himself emperor here in 1804, though the walls were so dilapidated they had to be covered with drapes to provide a sufficiently grand backdrop.

In the 1820s Notre-Dame was given a much-needed **restoration**, largely thanks to a petition drawn up by Victor Hugo. Hugo had stirred public interest through his novel *Notre-Dame de Paris*, in which he lamented the building's sorry state (Gothic architecture was particularly favoured by Romantic novelists, who deemed the soaring naves of the great cathedrals singularly suited to sheltering "tormented souls"). The task was given to architect **Viollet-le-Duc**, who carried out an extensive and thorough renovation, some would say too thorough, remaking much of the statuary on the facade – the originals can be seen in the Musée National du Moyen Age (see p.123) – and adding the steeple and baleful-looking gargoyles. Viollet-le-Duc's parting contribution was a statue of himself among the angels lining the roof: it's the only one looking heavenwards.

The facade

The **facade** is Notre-Dame's most impressive exterior feature; the Romanesque influence is still visible, not least in its solid H-shape, but the overriding impression is one of lightness and grace, created in part by the filigree work of the central rose window and the gallery above. Of the magnificent **carvings over the portals**, perhaps the most arresting is the scene over the central one showing the Day of Judgement: the lower frieze is a whirl of movement as the dead rise from their graves, while Christ presides above, sending those on his right to heaven, those on his left to hell. All around the arch peer out alert and mischievous-looking angels, said to be modelled on the cathedral choirboys of the time. The left portal shows Mary being crowned by Christ, with scenes of her life in the lower friezes, while the right portal depicts the Virgin enthroned and, below, episodes from the life of St Anne (Mary's mother) and the life of Christ. These are masterfully put together, using visual devices and symbols to communicate more than just the bare-bones story – in the nativity scene, for example, the infant Christ is placed above Mary to show his elevated status and lies on an altar rather than in a crib, symbolizing his future sacrifice.

The towers

If you climb the **towers** (access to which is around the side of the cathedral), you can see Viollet-le-Duc's gargoyles and angels up close, as well as the great 13-tonne

Emmanuel Bell in the south tower. One of the largest and oldest bells in Europe, the Emmanuel Bell was forged in 1685 and spared during the 1789 Revolution (unlike Marie, the large bell in the north tower, which was destroyed and melted down). It is only rung at Christmas and on other special occasions, or in times of mourning, such as after the terrorist attacks in November 2015. The cathedral's other nine bells, which had become badly out of tune, were replaced in 2013. Note that there are 387 **steps** to the top of the South Tower. It's possible to skip the notoriously long queues to access the towers by downloading the app Jefile, which allows you to choose a time slot, though it only works on the actual day of your visit (from 7.30am) and within 25km of the site.

The interior

Inside Notre-Dame, you're struck immediately by the dramatic contrast between the darkness of the nave and the light falling on the first great clustered pillars of the choir. It is the end walls of the transepts, nearly two-thirds glass, including two magnificent rose windows coloured in imperial purple, that admit all this light. These, the vaulting and the soaring shafts reaching to the springs of the vaults, are all definite Gothic elements, while there remains a strong influence of Romanesque in the stout round pillars of the nave and the general sense of four-squareness. The **trésor** is unlikely to appeal unless ornate nineteenth-century monstrances and chalices are your thing.

Your best bet if you want to avoid the crowds is to visit between 8 and 9am or in the evening. To join a free **tour**, meet at the back of the cathedral, near the organ; free audioguides are also available (Mon–Sat 9.30am–6pm, Sun 1–6pm). Free **organ recitals** are held regularly; the instrument, crafted by the great nineteenth-century organ-maker Aristide Cavaillé-Coll, is one of France's finest, with more than six thousand pipes.

Kilomètre zéro

Ⓜ Cité

Notre-Dame, at the heart of Paris, is also the symbolic heart of France: outside on the pavement by the cathedral's west side is a bronze star, known as **kilomètre zéro**, from where all main-road distances in France are calculated. The large square in front of the cathedral, built by Haussmann in the 1860s, is known as the **Parvis** (from "paradise") **Notre-Dame**. Paving stones show the outlines of the small streets and buildings that stood here in medieval times.

Crypte Archéologique

Parvis Notre-Dame, 4ᵉ • Tues–Sun 10am–6pm • €8 • ☎ 01 55 42 50 10, Ⓦ crypte.paris.fr • Ⓜ Cité/St-Michel

At the far end of the Parvis Notre-Dame is the entrance to the **Crypte Archéologique**. This large, well-presented excavated area holds the remains of the original cathedral (St-Étienne) plus vestiges of the streets and houses that once clustered around Notre-Dame; most are medieval, but some date as far back as Gallo-Roman times and

---

SCHOOL FOR SCANDAL

On rue Chanoinesse, the cathedral school of Notre-Dame, forerunner of the Sorbonne, once flourished. Around the year 1200, one of the teachers was **Peter Abélard**. A philosophical whiz kid and cocker of snooks at establishment intellectuals, he was very popular with students but not with the authorities, who thought they caught a distinct whiff of heresy. Forced to leave the school, he set up shop on the Left Bank with his disciples, in effect founding the University of Paris. Less successful was the story of his love life. While living near the rue Chanoinesse, he fell passionately in love with his landlord's niece, **Héloïse**, and she with him. She gave birth to a baby, her uncle had Abélard castrated, and the story ended in convents, lifelong separation and lengthy correspondence. They were reunited in death, however, and lie side by side in Père-Lachaise cemetery (see p.209).

include parts of the city's Roman quay and its thermal baths. Digital technology, including touchscreens on which you can explore the cathedral – and the city – from every angle during four stages of its development, give context to what might otherwise be little more than an evocative set of stones, while excellent captions go deeper into the history of everything from Paris's lost topography to the many myths that have gone into writing about Lutetia, the Roman city.

Mémorial des Martyrs de la Déportation

Square de l'Ile de France, 4ᵉ • Tues–Sun: April–Sept 10am–7pm; Oct–March 10am–5pm • Free • ☎ 01 46 33 87 56 • ⓂSt-Paul/Maubert Mutualité

At the eastern tip of the Ile de la Cité is the stark and moving symbolic tomb of the 200,000 French who died in Nazi concentration camps – among them Resistance fighters, Jews and forced labourers. The **Mémorial des Martyrs de la Déportation** is easily missed and barely visible above ground; stairs hardly shoulder-wide descend into a claustrophobic underworld reminiscent of a prison yard, and off here is a stifling, narrow crypt, its walls lined with thousands of illuminated quartz pebbles representing the dead. Barred cells sit on either side, and it ends in a dark, raw space with a single naked bulb hanging in the middle. Above the exit are the words "Pardonne. N'oublie pas" ("Forgive. Do not forget").

Ile St-Louis

Museums: Wed–Sat 2.15–6pm; closed Aug • €5 • ☎ 01 55 42 83 83 • Ⓜ Pont Marie/Sully Morland

The **Ile St-Louis** is arguably the most romantic part of Paris. For centuries this was nothing but swampy pastureland, a haunt of lovers, duellists and miscreants on the run, until in the seventeenth century developer Christophe Marie chose to fill it with elegant mansions; by 1660 the island was transformed. Unlike its larger neighbour, the Ile St-Louis has no sights as such, save for three tiny "**museums**" in the Bibliothèque Polonaise at 6 quai d'Orléans: a room devoted to Frédéric Chopin, another to Boleslas Biegas – sculptor, painter, playwright of the Viennese Secession – and one to Romantic Polish poet **Adam Mickiewicz**.

Hôtel Lauzun

17 quai d'Anjou, 4ᵉ • Not open to the public • Ⓜ Pont Marie/Sully Morland

One of the most elegant mansions on Ile St-Louis, the **Hôtel Lauzun** was built in 1657 by Versailles architect Le Vau. Its most famous inhabitant was the poet **Baudelaire** who lived in a small apartment on the second floor from 1843 to 1845. He wrote much of *Les Fleurs du mal* here and hosted meetings of the Hashischins club, attended by bohemian writers and artists, including Manet, Balzac and Delacroix. During these meetings, and as the name suggests, hashish was handed round – apparently in the form of a green jelly. Flutes of champagne are probably as heady as things get these days, as the mansion is often used for government receptions.

Southern quais

A visit to the island wouldn't be complete without a stop at *Berthillon* on rue St-Louis-en-l'Ile (see p.270); eating one of its exquisite ice creams while strolling the streets is a tradition. For seclusion, head for the **southern quais** (quai de Béthune and quai d'Orléans), or to the garden across boulevard Henri-IV to reach Paris's best sunbathing spot. Ile-St-Louis is particularly atmospheric in the evening, when an arm-in-arm stroll along the *quais* is a must on any lovers' itinerary.

The Louvre

The Louvre – a catch-all term for the palace and the museum it houses – cuts a grand Classical swathe through the centre of the city, running west along the right bank of the Seine from the Ile de la Cité towards the Champs-Elysées. Even if you don't venture inside, the sheer bravado of the architectural ensemble is thrilling. If you do, you'll find a truly astonishing museum. Its paintings, sculptures and decorative arts cover everything from the Middle Ages to the beginnings of Impressionism, while the collection of antiquities from Egypt, the Middle East, Greece and Rome is unrivalled. The hoard of Italian Renaissance paintings is priceless, and the French collection acts as the gold standard of the nation's artistic tradition. Separate from the Louvre proper, but still within the palace, is the Musée des Arts Décoratifs, which is dedicated to fashion and textiles, decorative arts and advertising.

The original **Palais du Louvre** was little more than a feudal fortress, begun by Philippe-Auguste in the 1190s. Charles V was the first French king to make the castle his residence, in the 1360s (the ground plan of his new palace can be seen traced on the pavement of the **Cour Carrée**). It wasn't until 1546, the year before the death of François I, that the first stones of the Louvre we see today were laid by the architect Pierre Lescot. Henri II continued François I's plans, building the two graceful wings that now form the southwestern corner of the Cour Carrée. It's still possible to imagine how extraordinary the building would have looked, a gleaming example of the new Renaissance style surrounded by the late Gothic of Charles V's day.

When Henri IV took charge in 1594, he set about linking the Louvre with Catherine de Médicis' Palais des Tuileries (see box, p.72), building the long, riverside Grande Galerie. Louis XIII and Louis XIV contented themselves with merely completing the Cour Carrée in a style copied from Lescot's original facade, and the only architectural intrusion of this era was Claude Perrault's sober **Classical colonnade** facing rue de l'Amiral de Coligny, which tragically beat Bernini's stunning Baroque design (occasionally on display in the collection of Prints and Drawings) for the same contract. Napoléon III's main contributions – the courtyard facades of the nineteenth-century Richelieu and Denon wings – repeated the basic theme of the Cour Carrée, with typical conservatism.

Brief history of the collections

The **Musée du Louvre** began as the personal art collection of François I who, in 1516, summoned Leonardo da Vinci from Milan. Leonardo brought his greatest works with him across the Alps, and later kings set up "cabinets" of artworks and antiquities in the Louvre, but these were all very much private collections. Artists and academics – as well

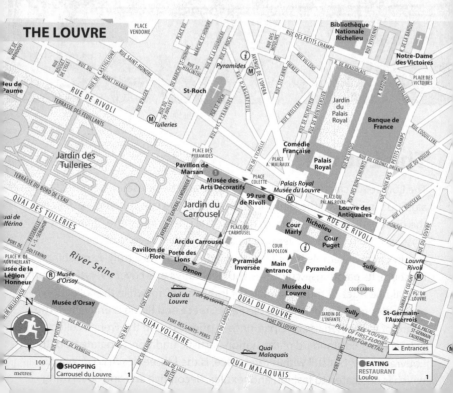

as prostitutes – lived in the palace under Louis XIV, and a royal arts academy mounted exhibitions here, known as *salons*, as early as 1725. But the plan for a public museum was only conceived in the 1740s, and it wasn't until 1793, the year of Louis XVI's execution, that the gallery actually opened. Within a decade, Napoleon's wagonloads of war booty – not all of which has been returned – transformed the Louvre's art collection into the world's largest. Since then, various projects, notably the Grand Louvre project in the 1980s (see p.51), have concentrated on expanding the museum's exhibition space and exporting the Louvre to other sites. In 2012, the Musée du Louvre-Lens was opened in the former coal-mining town of Lens, in northern France, while 2017 saw the opening of the "Louvre Abu Dhabi" annexe, which borrows works from the main collection.

The great 1980s makeover

For all its many additions and alterations, the palace remained a surprisingly harmonious building, its grandeur and symmetry soberly suited to this most historic of Parisian landmarks. Then, in 1989, I.M. Pei's controversial glass **Pyramide** erupted from the centre of the Cour Napoléon like a visitor from another architectural planet. (Just for the record, the pyramid has 673 panes of glass, not the fabled 666.) It was the centrepiece of President Mitterrand's **"Grand Louvre"** makeover, along with the basement Carrousel du Louvre shopping complex and fashion arena, the weird, downward-pointing **Pyramide Inversée** (which later found a starring role in *The Da Vinci Code*) and the dramatic glazing over of the courtyards of the Richelieu wing – from which the Finance Ministry was ejected. The Pyramide has since found a place in the hearts of most Parisians, surpassing even Napoleon's pink marble **Arc du Carrousel**. Emboldened by this success, the Louvre completed another daring project in 2012 when a stunning metal-and-glass roof – by the Franco-Milanese architectural team of Mario Bellini and Rudy Ricciotti – was installed in the **Cour Visconti** (home of the new Islamic art collection).

INFORMATION

Opening hours Permanent collection: Mon & Wed–Sun 9am–6pm, Wed & Fri till 9.45pm; closed Jan 1, May 1 and Dec 25. Doors shut 30min before the museum closes. Almost a quarter of the museum's rooms are closed one day a week on a rotating basis, so if you're interested in one of the less popular sections it's worth checking the schedule online.

Admission €15; free to all under-18s and EU residents aged 18–26; free to under-26s from any country on Fri after 6pm; free to all on the first Sun of each month Oct–March, as well as July 14. Your ticket is also valid for a same-day visit to the Musée National Eugène Delacroix (see p.142). Tickets can be bought at the museum, or online in advance (€17); for temporary exhibitions you usually have to book online. Tickets bought in advance are time-stamped and you're expected to arrive within 30min of the time shown.

Contact details ☎ 01 40 20 53 17, ⊕ louvre.fr.

Métro ⓜ Palais Royal Musée du Louvre.

Access The main entrance is via the Pyramide, but you'll find shorter queues at two different entrances: the one near the Arc du Carrousel (which can also be accessed from 99 rue de Rivoli and from the line #1 platform of the Palais Royal Musée du Louvre métro stop); and at the Porte des Lions entrance, just east of the Pont Royal (though this is sometimes closed, so it's best to phone ahead to check). If you've already got a ticket or a museum pass (see p.35) you can join a fast-track queue at the Pyramide. Disabled access is via the futuristic sinking column in the middle of the Pyramide; entry is free to registered disabled visitors plus one companion. Once you've entered the museum, you'll then need to queue to have your bags checked, and if you haven't already got a ticket, you'll also need to queue at a machine or ticket desk; it sounds daunting, but things usually move pretty quickly.

Maps Free maps, from information booths in the Hall Napoléon under the Pyramide, show exactly what is where.

Tours and guides Ninety-minute guided tours in English of the masterpieces run every day (except public hols and free-admission days; see p.34) at 11am and 2pm (€12; not bookable in advance). Nintendo 3DS audioguides, with an interactive map, can be rented for €5 (ID required). Thematic trails for adults and children are available on request or can be downloaded and printed in advance from the website. Another option worth considering, especially if you're visiting with children, is a "treasure hunt" run by THATLou (⊕ thatmuse.com), which involves hunting down different paintings in the museum to find the answers to a list of questions; there are various themes to choose from, the most popular one being "Beauty & the Bestiary", which includes Egyptian sphinxes, Greek centaurs and other mythical creatures. It's not cheap at €25/person (children under 5 free), plus the cost of the Louvre ticket, but it can be a fun way to experience the museum.

LOUVRE SURVIVAL TIPS

Tales of **queues** outside the Pyramide, miles of corridors and paparazzi-style jostles in front of the *Mona Lisa* can leave you feeling somewhat intimidated by the Louvre before you've even set foot in the place. Don't attempt to see too much – even if you spend the entire day here you'll only see a fraction of the collection. Arrive early or come for the evening openings; Thursday tends to be relatively quiet, though more sections than usual often close on this day. If you want to avoid the crowds, stay away from the busy Denon wing; after all, the Louvre is much more than just the Italian Renaissance and the *Mona Lisa*. Note also that **pickpocketing** is a significant problem, so be careful about how you carry your money and watch out for people trying to distract you, especially at the ticket machines.

Eating The elegant *Café Richelieu* (first floor, Richelieu) has a wonderful summer-only terrace with a view of the Pyramide. *Café Mollien* (first floor, Denon) is the busiest and also has a summer terrace. *Café Denon* (lower ground floor, Denon) is cosy and classy.

ORIENTATION

The Louvre has **three named wings**, each accessible from under the great Pyramide: Denon (south), Richelieu (north) and Sully (east, around the giant quadrangle of the Cour Carrée). The exhibits are arranged in **themed sections**: Antiquities (Near Eastern, Egyptian and Greek/Roman); Painting; Sculpture; Decorative arts; Prints and drawings (exhibited on a temporary, rotational basis); Islamic art; and the Medieval Louvre. Some sections spread across two wings, or two floors of the same wing. Most visitors head straight to the **Denon wing**, whose first floor contains the *Mona Lisa* and Italian paintings, plus the great French nineteenth-century canvases and the stunning, gilded Galerie d'Apollon; its lower floors house the sublime Classical sculpture collection. Denon is the busiest part of the museum; a relatively peaceful alternative would be to focus on the grand chronologies of French painting and sculpture in the **Richelieu wing**, starting on the second floor. It's in Richelieu, too, that you'll find the dramatic, glazed-over courtyards, and the superb Decorative arts section (first floor). Few visitors begin with the **Sully wing**, though it's well worth seeing the foundations of Philippe-Auguste's twelfth-century fortress on the lower ground floor, and there are also some rooms preserved from the original palace (see box, p.54).

Painting

The largest section by far is **Painting**. The Richelieu side of the museum houses the main French and Northern European painting collections, while the Italian, Spanish and large-scale nineteenth-century French works are found in Denon. Interspersed throughout are rooms dedicated to the Louvre's impressive collection of **prints and drawings**; these are exhibited in rotation, because of their vulnerability to the light.

French painting

The main chronological circuit of **French painting** begins on the second floor of the Richelieu wing, and continues right round the Cour Carrée in the Sully wing. It traces the extraordinary development of French painting from its edgy, pre-Renaissance beginnings through to Corot, whose airy landscapes anticipate Impressionism.

Medieval and Renaissance

Surprisingly few works predate the Renaissance. There are some intriguing portraits of French kings, notably the Sienese-style *Portrait of John the Good*, Jean Fouquet's pinched-looking *Charles VII* and Jean Clouet's two noble portraits of *François I*, the king who attracted numerous Italian artists to his court. Look out for the strange atmosphere of the two **Schools of Fontainebleau** (rooms 9 and 10), which were heavily influenced by Italian Mannerist painting. Two portraits of royal mistresses are provocatively erotic: from the First School of Fontainebleau (1530s), Henri II's mistress, Diane de Poitiers, is depicted semi-nude as the huntress Diana, while in a Second School piece from the 1590s, Gabrielle d'Estrées, the favourite of Henri IV, is shown sharing a bath with her sister, pinching her nipple as if plucking a cherry.

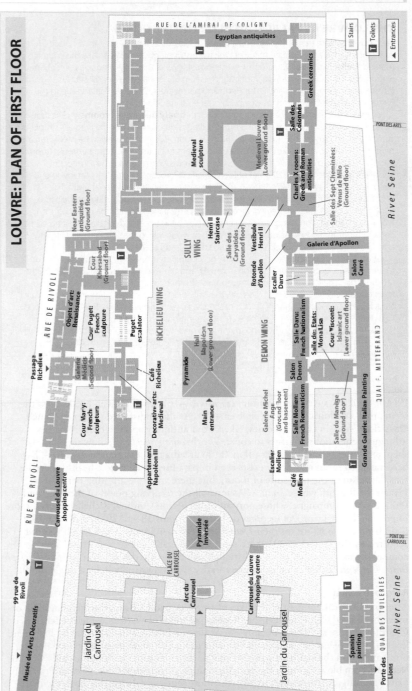

LOUVRE: PLAN OF FIRST FLOOR

RUE DE L'AMIRAL DE COLIGNY

Egyptian antiquities

Greek ceramics

Salle des Colonnes

Medieval Louvre (Lower ground floor)

Medieval sculpture

Salle des Sept Cheminées: **Venus de Milo** (Ground floor)

Charles X rooms: Greek and Roman antiquities

Henri II Staircase

Salle des **Caryatides** (Ground floor)

Vestibule **Henri II**

SULLY WING

Rotonde **d'Apollon**

Galerie d'Apollon

Escalier **Daru**

PONT DES ARTS

River Seine

Near Eastern antiquities (Ground floor)

Obets d'art: Renaissance

Cour **Khorsabad** (Ground floor)

Cour Puget: **French sculpture**

Puget escalator

RICHELIEU WING

Galerie **Médicis** (Second floor)

Passage **Richelieu**

Café **Richelieu**

Decorative arts: Medieval

Salon Carré

Hall **Napoléon** (Lower ground floor)

Pyramide

Main entrance

DENON WING

Salle Daru: **French Nationalism**

Cour **Visconti:** Islamic art (Lower ground floor)

Salle des États: Mona Lisa

Salon Denon

Galerie Michel **Ange** (Ground floor and basement)

Salle Mollien: **French Romanticism**

Salle du Manège (Ground floor)

Escalier **Mollien**

Café **Mollien**

Grande Galerie: Italian Painting

QUAI F. MITTERAND

RUE DE RIVOLI

Cour Mary: **French sculpture**

Appartements Napoléon III

Carrousel du Louvre shopping centre

99 rue de Rivoli

Musée des Arts Décoratifs

Jardin du Carrousel

PLACE DU CARROUSEL

Pyramide Inversée

Arc du Carrousel

Carrousel du Louvre shopping centre

Jardin du Carrousel

Spanish painting

Porte des Lions

QUAI DES TUILERIES

River Seine

PONT DU CARROUSEL

River Seine

Stairs

T Toilets

▲ Entrances

THE LOUVRE AS PALACE: AN ALTERNATIVE GUIDE

The Louvre is more than an art gallery: it is one of the greatest of France's royal palaces. To tour its historic rooms and galleries, many of which are stunningly decorated, take the entrance marked "**Sully**" in the Hall Napoléon. On the lowest level of the Sully wing you can continue through to the Louvre's medieval foundations (see p.50), or take the Henri II staircase – with its intertwined monograms H and D, for Henri and his mistress, Diane de Poitiers – up to the Renaissance Salle des Caryatides (see p.58) on the ground floor.

Up again, on the first floor, there's a succession of **finely decorated rooms**: the Vestibule Henri II, where the gilded, sixteenth-century ceiling is graced with George Braque's simple but stirring *The Birds* (room 33); the Salle des Bronzes (room 32), its huge ceiling painted a dazzling blue by Cy Twombly in 2010; the Salle des Sept Cheminées, once the royal bedroom (room 74); and the Rotonde d'Apollon (off room 34), built for Louis XIV by Le Vau, the architect of Versailles. Most stunning of all is the golden Galerie d'Apollon (room 66), its utterly splendid decor conceived by Charles Le Brun in 1661; it's particularly atmospheric at night. The decoration represents Louis XIV (the Sun King) as Apollo (the sun god); Eugène Delacroix added his *Apollo Slaying the Serpent Python* to the central medallion of the ceiling in 1851. From here you can skirt the grand Escalier Daru (see p.58) to enter the Italian painting section, passing through the lofty Salon Carré (see p.55) on your way to the Grande Galerie (rooms 5, 8 and 12), which was originally built to link the Louvre and Tuileries palaces.

For **architectural gems** from the grand Third Empire remodelling, seek out the Salle du Manège on the ground floor of Denon (room A), and the Appartements Napoléon III on the first floor of Richelieu. For the lavish museum established for Charles X in the 1820s, visit the first floor of Sully (rooms 33–44); room 40, the Salle des Colonnes, has a fine mosaic floor and Neoclassical ceiling paintings of French monarchs by Antoine-Jean Gros. The highlights of I.M. Pei's 1980s makeover are the Pyramide and its strange twin, the Pyramide Inversée in the Carrousel du Louvre shopping complex; the two glazed-over courtyards of the Richelieu wing; and the magnificent escalator climbing alongside the Cour Puget. Don't miss the Cour Visconti, either, with its sinuous, new glass roof.

Classicism

It's not until the seventeenth century (rooms 12–16), when Poussin breaks onto the scene, that a definitively French style emerges. As the undisputed master of **French Classicism**, Poussin's grand themes, taken from antiquity and the Bible, were to influence generations of artists to come. *The Arcadian Shepherds*, showing four shepherds interpreting the inscription "Et in arcadia ego" ("I, too, in Arcadia"), has been taken to mean that death exists even in paradise. You'll need a healthy appetite for Classicism in the next suite of rooms, but there are some arresting portraits by Hyacinthe Rigaud, whose *Louis XIV* shows all the terrifying power of the king, and Philippe de Champaigne, whose portrait of his patron Cardinal Richelieu is even more imposing. The paintings of Georges de la Tour (rooms 28 and 29) and the three Le Nain brothers (look out for their *Denial of St Peter*, an intense work which was only acquired by the Louvre in 2010) are more idiosyncratic. De la Tour's *Card Sharp* is compelling for its uneasy poise and strange lack of depth, though his *Christ with Joseph in the Carpenter's Shop* is a more representative work, mystically lit by a single candle.

Rococo to Realist

After the Classical bombast of the likes of Le Sueur and Le Brun, the more intimate or movement-filled eighteenth-century **Rococo** paintings of Watteau come as a relief, as do Chardin's intense still lifes – notably *The Skate* – and the inspired sketches by Fragonard known as the *Figures of Fantasy*, traditionally thought to have been completed in just one hour. From the southern wing of Sully to the end of this section, the chilly wind of **Neoclassicism** blows through the post-Revolution paintings of Gros, Gérard, Prud'hon, David and Ingres. These contrast with the more sentimental style that begins with Greuze and continues into the **Romanticism** of Géricault and Delacroix, which largely supplanted the Neoclassical style from the 1820s onwards. Ingres' glassily exquisite portraits were understandably much in demand in his day, but modern visitors are much taken with his nudes: the bathers from 1808 and 1828, and the *Turkish Bath* (room 60), a painting at once sensuous and abstracted. The final set of rooms takes in Millet, Corot and the **Barbizon School** of painting, the precursor of Impressionism. For anything later than 1848, you'll have to head over to the Musée d'Orsay (see p.135).

Northern European painting

The western end of Richelieu's second floor is given over to a relatively selective collection of **German, Flemish** and **Dutch** paintings, though the seventeenth-century Dutch suite is strong, with no fewer than twelve paintings by Rembrandt – look out for *Bathsheba* and *The Supper at Emmaus* in room 31 – and two serene canvases from Vermeer, *The Astronomer* and *The Lacemaker*, in room 37. An awesome set of two dozen works by Rubens can be found in the **Galerie Médicis** (room 18), a stripped-down modern replica of a room originally in the Palais du Luxembourg (see p.144). These works, known as the Cycle de Marie de Médicis, were commissioned by the eponymous queen herself and are dedicated to her glory. Rubens painted the entire 300 square metres of canvas himself, and his swirling colours and swathes of flapping cloth were to influence French painters from Fragonard to Delacroix.

Italian painting

The staggering **Italian collection** spreads across the first floor of the Denon wing, at the head of the Escalier Daru. Things begin well with two exquisite Botticelli frescoes painted for the Villa Lemmi near Florence. Next, the high-ceilinged **Salon Carré** (room 3) was used to exhibit contemporary paintings from the first exhibition or "salon" of the Académie Royale in 1725; it now displays the so-called Primitives, with thirteenth- to fifteenth-century works from Italian painters such as Giotto, Cimabue and Fra Angelico, as well as one of Uccello's bizarrely theoretical panels of the Battle of San Romano.

To the west of the Salon, the **Grande Galerie** stretches into the distance, a ribbon of pale, perfect parquet. On its walls, it parades all the great names of the Italian Renaissance, kicking off with Mantegna's opulent *Madonna of Victory* and his meticulous miniature of the Crucifixion, and continuing through Giovanni Bellini, Filippo Lippi, Raphael, Coreggio and Titian, in the first part of the gallery alone. Leonardo da Vinci's *Virgin of the Rocks*, *St John the Baptist* and *Virgin and Child with St Anne* are on display just after the first set of pillars, normally untroubled by crowds. The restored **Salle des Etats** (room 6) is the noisy, bustling setting for Leonardo da Vinci's **Mona Lisa** (see box, p.56), as well as Paolo Veronese's vast *Marriage at Cana*, which once hung in the refectory of Venice's island monastery of San Giorgio Maggiore. Sadly, there's little chance to enjoy the other Venetian works nearby in peace, but you can walk through to the twin galleries of French Nationalism and Romanticism. A little further down the Grande Galerie, the Mannerists make their entrance with a wonderfully weird *St Anne with Four Saints* by Pontormo and a Rosso Fiorentino *Pietà*. From here on, the quality falls off.

Spanish painting

The relatively small **Spanish collection** is relegated to the far end of the Grande Galerie. There are a few gems, however, notably Murillo's tender *Beggar Boy*, and the *Marquise de Santa Cruz* among the Goya portraits. Zurbarán's *St Bonaventure Lying in State* splendidly betrays the artist's obsession with cloth, and it's hard not to be beguiled by De Ribera's bittersweet portrait of *The Clubfoot*; the overwrought genius of El Greco's *Crucifixion*, meanwhile, is simply mind-blowing.

French Nationalism

Running parallel to the Grande Galerie are two giant rooms dedicated to post-Revolution **French Nationalism** and early to mid-nineteenth-century Romanticism. The museum plan

THE MONA LISA

The **Mona Lisa** receives some six million visitors per year. Reason enough to smile, maybe, but how did a small, rather dark sixteenth-century portrait acquire such unparalleled celebrity? It can't be **Leonardo da Vinci**'s sheer excellence, as other virtuoso works of his hang nearby, largely ignored. Nor the painting's famously seductive air – Napoleon was so captivated by it that he had the picture hung in his bedroom in the Tuileries, but there are other, far sexier, portraits in the Louvre. (Sadly, the nude version Leonardo apparently painted has been lost for centuries, and is known only from early copies.) Instead, the answer lies in the painting's own story.

The English title is a corruption of *Monna* ("milady") *Lisa*, the title of the painting's (probable) subject, **Lisa Gherardini**. She was the wife of one Francesco del Giocondo. It's from his surname that the Italians get their name for the painting, *La Gioconda*, and the French their *La Joconde*, and it may even explain the *Mona Lisa*'s "smile", as *giocondo* means "light-hearted" in Italian. It is said that Lisa smiled because Leonardo employed singers and jesters to keep her happy while he painted.

The *Mona Lisa* probably came to France along with Leonardo himself, when he joined the service of François I. It remained largely neglected, however, until the mid-nineteenth century, when the poet Théophile Gautier described how the painting "mocks the viewer with such sweetness, grace and superiority that we feel timid, like schoolboys in the presence of a duchess". Then the English critic **Walter Pater** famously gushed that she is "expressive of what in the ways of a thousand years men had come to desire… She is older than the rocks among which she sits; like the vampire, she has been dead many times, and learned the secrets of the grave; and has been a diver in deep seas, and keeps their fallen day about her; and trafficked for strange webs with Eastern merchants … and all this has been to her but as the sound of lyres and flutes, and lives only in the delicacy with which it has moulded the changing lineaments, and tinged the eyelids and hands".

Pater made her famous, but the *Mona Lisa* only really went stellar when she was **stolen** by an Italian chancer and self-professed nationalist in August 1911. By the time the painting was recovered, in December 1913, that face had graced the pages of countless newspapers. Since then, celebrity has fed on itself, despite the complaints of art critics. Bernard Berenson, for example, decided she was "watchful, sly, secure, with a smile of anticipated satisfaction and a pervading air of hostile superiority"; Roberto Longhi called her a "wan fusspot". Still, she now faces more cameras every day than a well-dressed starlet on Oscar night.

Visitors today are sometimes unimpressed. The painting is surprisingly small (53x76cm, or 21x30 inches, to be exact) and fogged by filth – no art restorer has yet dared to propose actually working on the picture. Eventually, time may force the museum's hand, as the thin poplar panel the image is painted on is reported to be slowly warping. The new, air-conditioned glass frame – designed, appropriately, by a Milanese firm – may help. Meanwhile, if you can struggle past the crowds, the patina of fame and the dirt of centuries, you might just discover a strange and beautiful painting. If not, try the Leonardo portrait known as *La Belle Jardinière*, in the Grande Galerie, adjacent.

labels this section "large-format French paintings", and it features some of the best-known French works. The Salle Daru (room 75) boasts David's epic *Coronation of Napoleon I*, in which Napoleon is shown crowning himself with a rather crestfallen clergy in the background; almost unbelievably, David conceived this work as part of a much larger composition. Nearby are some fine portraits of women, including Prud'hon's Leonardo-like *Josephine in the Park at Malmaison*, and some compellingly perfect canvases by Ingres.

Romanticism

Géricault's dramatic *Raft of the Medusa*, based on a notorious incident off the coast of Senegal in 1816, heralds **Romanticism** in the Salle Mollien (room 77). The survivors are seen despairing as a ship disappears over the horizon – as one described it, "from the delirium of joy we fell into profound despondency and grief". The fifteen shown here were the last of 150 shipwrecked sailors who had escaped on the raft – thirst, murder and cannibalism having carried off the rest. The dead figure lying face down with his arm extended was modelled by Delacroix, whose *Liberty Leading the People* also hangs in this room; Delacroix's work is a famous icon of revolution, though you can tell by the hats that it depicts the 1830 revolution, which brought in the "bourgeois king" Louis-Philippe, rather than that of 1789. On seeing the painting, Louis-Philippe promptly ordered it to be kept out of sight so as not to give anyone dangerous ideas.

Sculpture

French sculpture fills the lowest two levels of the Richelieu wing, including the twin, glass-roofed courtyards. Cour Marly shelters the four triumphal Marly Horses, which once stood in the park at Marly-le-Roi: two were done by Coysevox for Louis XIV (the ones at the top of the stairs), and two by Costou for Louis XV. Cour Puget has Pierre Puget's dynamic *Milon de Crotone* as its agonizing centrepiece, the lion's claws tearing into Milon's apparently soft flesh.

The surrounding rooms trace French sculpture from painful Romanesque Crucifixions through to the lofty nineteenth-century works of David d'Angers. Don't miss the Burgundian *Tomb of Philippe Pot*, borne by hooded mourners known as *pleurants*, Michel Colombe's Italianate relief of *St George Slaying the Dragon*, or the distinctively French and strangely liquid bas-reliefs sculpted by Jean Goujon in the 1540s, at around the same time as he was working on Lescot's facade for the Cour Carrée. After a while, however, you may find yourself crying out for an end to all the gracefully perfect nudes and grandiose busts of noblemen. François Rude's charming *Neapolitan Fisherboy* provides some respite, but really the best antidote to all this is Rodin – and, unfortunately, his career postdates the Louvre's self-imposed 1848 cut-off, so you'll have to visit the Musée d'Orsay (see p.135) or Musée Rodin (see p.156) to explore his work.

Italian sculpture

The small, intense **Italian sculpture** section fills the long Galerie Michel Ange (room 4), on the ground and basement floors of Denon. Here you'll find such bold masterpieces as two of Michelangelo's torturedly erotic *Slaves*, Giambologna's airy *Flying Mercury*, the anonymous *Veiled Woman* and Canova's irresistible *Cupid and Psyche*. At the gallery's western end, the grand Escalier Mollien leads up towards the main Painting section (see p.52) while, immediately below, in the old stables on the lower ground floor (room 1), you'll find early Italian sculpture, notably Duccio's virtuoso *Virgin and Child Surrounded by Angels*, and the **Tactile Gallery**, where you can run your hands over copies of some of the most important sculptures from the collection. In the small adjacent rooms A to C you can seek out some severe but impressive **Gothic Virgins** from Flanders and Germany.

Decorative arts

The vast **Decorative arts** section (not to be confused with the separate **Les Arts Décoratifs** museum in the Louvre's westernmost wing; see p.60), on the first floor of the Richelieu wing, presents the finest tapestries, ceramics, jewellery and furniture commissioned by France's most wealthy and influential patrons, beginning with an exquisite little equestrian sculpture of Charlemagne (or possibly Charles the Bald) and continuing through 81 relentlessly superb rooms to a salon decorated in the style of Louis-Philippe, the last king of France. Walking through the entire chronology gives a powerful sense of the evolution of aesthetic taste at its most refined and opulent, and numerous rooms have been partially re-created in the style of a particular epoch, so it's not hard to imagine yourself strutting through a Renaissance chamber or gracing an eighteenth-century salon, especially as whole suites are often devoid of other visitors. Towards the end, the circuit passes through the breathtaking **apartments** of Napoléon III's Minister of State (room 87), full of plush upholstery, immense chandeliers and dramatic ceiling frescoes, in true Second Empire style.

Antiquities

The enormous **Antiquities** collection offers an embarrassment of riches. The superb Egyptian and Near Eastern collections reflect the long-standing French fascination with both regions, while the outstanding Greek and Roman collections date back to the eager acquisitions of François I, Richelieu and Mazarin.

Near Eastern antiquities

Covering the Mesopotamian, Sumerian, Babylonian, Assyrian and Phoenician civilizations, plus the art of ancient Persia, the **Near Eastern antiquities** collection is on the ground floor of Richelieu. The highlight is the boldly sculpted stonework, much of it in relief. Watch out for the statues and busts depicting the young Sumerian prince Gudea, and the black, 2m-high Mesopotamian Code of Hammurabi, which dates from around 1800 BC. Standing erect like a warning finger, a series of royal precepts (the "code") is crowned with a stern depiction of the king meeting the sun god Shamash, dispenser of justice. The Cour Khorsabad, adjacent, is dominated by two giant Assyrian winged bulls (one is a reproduction) that once acted as guardians to the palace of Sargon II, from which many treasures were brought to the Louvre.

Egyptian antiquities

Jean-François Champollion, who translated the hieroglyphics of the Rosetta Stone, began collecting **Egyptian antiquities** for France, and the collection is now second only to Cairo's. Starting on the ground floor of the Sully wing, the thematic circuit leads up from the atmospheric crypt of the Sphinx (room 1) to the Nile, source of all life in Egypt, and takes the visitor through the everyday life of Pharaonic Egypt by way of cooking utensils, jewellery, the principles of hieroglyphics, musical instruments, sarcophagi and a host of mummified cats. Upstairs, on the first floor, the chronological circuit keeps the masterpieces on the right-hand side, while pots and statuettes of more specialist interest are displayed to the left. Look out for the *Great Sphinx*, carved from a single block of pink granite; the polychrome statue *Seated Scribe*; the striking, life-size wooden statue of Chancellor Nakhti; a bust of Amenophis IV; and a low-relief sculpture of Sethi I and the goddess Hathor.

Greek and Roman antiquities

The magnificent collection of **Greek and Roman antiquities** brings together everything from the stylized Cycladic *Woman's Head* of around 2700–2300 BC, to the finest Roman marbles. On the ground floor of Denon, the handsomely vaulted **Salle du Manège** (room A) was built as a riding school for the short-lived son of Napoléon III, but now houses Italian Renaissance copies and restorations of antique sculptures. To the east of the adjoining vestibule, the grand **Galerie Daru** (room B) kicks off with the poised energy of Lysippos's *Borghese Gladiator*. At the eastern end of the gallery, Lefuel's imperial **Escalier Daru** rises triumphantly under the billowing, famous feathers of the recently restored *Winged Victory of Samothrace* towards the Italian painting section and the Grande Galerie. Skirting the staircase will take you to the **Etruscan and Roman** collections, with their beautiful mosaics and stunning, naturalistic frescoes.

Beyond, in the Sully wing, you enter Pierre Lescot's original sixteenth-century palace. In the **Salle des Caryatides** (room 17), which houses Roman copies of Greek works, the musicians' balcony is supported by four giant caryatids, sculpted in 1550 by Jean Goujon. Beyond, in the main Greek section of Sully, you'll find the graceful marble head known as the *Tête Kaufmann* (room 16) and the delightful *Venus of Arles* – both early copies of the work of the great sculptor Praxiteles. Up on the first floor, the gorgeous marble-and-gilt decor of rooms 32 to 44 dates from a museum created here for Charles X (see box, p.54). The works are primarily a daunting run of terracotta and ceramics.

Islamic art

In 2012, an entirely new section of the museum was opened in the central Cour Visconti – the **Islamic art collection**, the Louvre's eighth department, partly funded by Prince Alwaleed bin Talal of Saudi Arabia. In the museum's most daring architectural project since I.M. Pei's pyramid, the Cour Visconti was covered over with an undulating, gold-filigree glass roof that seems to float in midair (it is supported by just eight slender columns). Suggesting for some the shimmering wings of an insect, for others a bedouin tent, a flying carpet or sand dunes, the roof is a fittingly stunning "crown" to the beautiful artworks below. Some three thousand objects are on display (out of an archive of eighteen thousand), ranging from early Islamic inscriptions to intricate Moorish ivories, and from ninth-century Iraqi moulded glass to exquisite miniature paintings from the courts of Mughal India.

The collection is arranged on **two floors**: the ground floor, directly under the roof, which covers the seventh to eleventh centuries, and the rather darker lower floor ("*parterre*"), which continues up to the nineteenth century. Some of the objects challenge the usual clichés about Islamic art: for example, an exquisite ivory box, from tenth-century Spain, carved with hunting scenes and people collecting eggs and picking dates, disproves the popular belief that figurative depictions are forbidden in Islamic art, as do a nearby copper peacock vase from the same period and an elegant, twelfth-century bronze lion that would have served as a fountainhead in an Andalusian palace garden. Elsewhere there is evidence of the diversity of cultures that co-existed under Islamic rule: a wooden portal from Cairo, for example, bears Hebrew inscriptions, while a flabellum, or ceremonial fan, from twelfth-century Egypt depicting the Virgin and Child, would have been used by a Christian congregation.

The Medieval Louvre

For a complete change of scene, descend to the **Medieval Louvre** section, on the lower ground floor of Sully. The dramatic stump of Philippe-Auguste's keep soars up towards the enormous concrete ceiling like a pillar holding up the entire modern edifice, while vestiges of Charles V's medieval palace walls buttress the edges of the vast chamber. A similar but more intimate effect can be felt in the adjacent Salle St-Louis, with its carved pillars and vaults cut short by the modern roof.

Musée des Arts Décoratifs

107 rue de Rivoli, 1ᵉʳ • Tues, Wed & Fri–Sun 11am–6pm, Thurs 11am–9pm (late opening during exhibitions only) • €11; free to all under-18s and under-26s from (or studying in) most European countries • ☎ 01 44 55 57 50, ⓦ www.lesartsdecoratifs.fr

The westernmost wing of the Palais du Louvre, on the north side, houses a second, entirely separate, museum, the **Musée des Arts Décoratifs**, which is devoted to "the art of design" or, more prosaically, the "applied arts". You could easily spend a whole day here, taking in the extraordinarily rich **permanent collection** of decorative arts and design from medieval times to the present day, as well as the popular **temporary exhibitions** which draw on the museum's extensive holdings of advertising, graphic arts, fashion and textiles. The entry ticket is valid all day, so you could choose to break up your visit – perhaps with lunch at the museum's stylish new restaurant, *Loulou* (see p.272).

The museum centres on its grand "nave" on the first floor – an original feature of the building, which dates from the 1870s, and which is used for temporary exhibitions. The second floor of the museum is occupied by a quartet of themed galleries. The **toys gallery** runs from wooden soldiers and china dolls to *Star Wars* figures and (playable) computer games. **Jewellery** focuses on twentieth-century designs, notably from the Art Nouveau jeweller René Lalique. A third gallery contains paintings by the "outsider" artist **Jean Dubuffet** (1901–85), while the **Galerie d'Etudes** houses clever, themed exhibitions – recent shows have included the use of trompe l'oeil in paintings, and an unlikely exhibition of wallpaper (the museum has the largest collection in the world – more than 400,000 samples).

The permanent collection: Medieval to nineteenth century

At the museum's heart is a grand chronology of French furnishings, which begins on the third floor; it's worth picking up the free audioguide in English here, particularly if you don't read French. You may well find that you have the whole collection more or less to yourself – it's curiously overlooked by visitors. The **Middle Ages** and **Renaissance** rooms are full of beautifully sculpted chests, tapestries, ceramic ware and paintings. The highlight is a reconstruction of a late fifteenth-century bedchamber, complete with original wall panelling, canopied bed, chairs and benches – even the door, fireplace and windows date from the period. The rooms covering the **seventeenth, eighteenth and nineteenth centuries** represent the glory years of French interior and furniture design. If you start to feel you've seen enough Rococo clocks, gilt consoles and chinoiserie, look out for the reconstructed rooms. One of these rooms shows off panelling installed in the Hôtel de Verrüe in the 1720s, when the fashion for *singeries*, or frescoes themed around monkeys dressed in human clothing, was in full swing. Another, found on the terrace level overlooking the nave, is a reconstruction of the splendid panelling from the aptly named "golden study" of the Hôtel de Rochegude, at Avignon.

The permanent collection: Art Nouveau to Philippe Starck

In the early twentieth century, French designers shaped the tastes of the world, and in this section of the museum (first, third and fourth floors, at the far end of the nave) it's easy to see why. There's a complete 1903 bedroom by Hector Guimard (the Art Nouveau designer behind the original Paris métro stations), a 1925 study by Pierre Chareau and an entire apartment created in the early 1920s by Armand-Albert Rateau for the *couturière* Jeanne Lanvin. On the first floor, the **Salon des Boiseries** shows off the best in French wood panelling; check out, too, the **Salon du Bois**, a huge drawing room made for the 1900 Universal Exhibition by Georges Hoentschel.

The final part of the chronology takes you through a suite of interlinked rooms stacked inside the lofty **Pavillon Marsan** (with stunning views down the rue de Rivoli and over the Tuileries). You begin on the ninth floor with the 1940s, and end many, many designer chairs later on the fifth floor, with the contemporary collections. On the sixth floor, you'll find the original carriage design for the TGV high-speed train and various podiums devoted to individual designers of the 1980s and 90s. **Philippe Starck**, for instance, is represented by five hyper-cool chairs, a stool, a mirror and a lampshade.

Temporary exhibitions

The eastern half of the museum, to the left of the main entrance, puts on exhibitions dedicated to fashion and advertising. These can be among the city's most innovative, as most shows are curated by industry professionals rather than state museum administrators. On the first and second floors, the **department of fashion and textiles** holds high-quality temporary exhibitions drawn from the large permanent collection. Recent shows have included one on the Bauhaus movement and another on Barbie-doll fashion. On the third floor, directly above, the **department of advertising and graphic arts** shows off its collection of advertising posters and video through cleverly themed, temporary exhibitions, which might feature, for example, Henri de Toulouse-Lautrec's posters of Montmartre nightlife. The space is appropriately trendy – exposed brickwork and steel panelling meets crumbling Louvre finery – and you can access the digital archive too.

CHAMPS-ELYSÉES

The Champs-Elysées and around

Synonymous with glitz and glamour and studded with luxury hotels and high-end fashion boutiques, the Champs-Elysées sweeps through one of the city's most exclusive districts. The avenue in turn forms part of a grand 9km axis, extending from the Louvre at the heart of Paris to the business district of La Défense in the west. With impressive vistas along its length, this axis, sometimes referred to as the Voie Triomphale (Triumphal Way), incorporates some of the city's most famous landmarks – the place de la Concorde, Tuileries gardens and the Arc de Triomphe. The whole ensemble is so regular and geometrical it looks as if it were laid out by a single town planner rather than successive kings, emperors and presidents, all keen to add their stamp and promote French power and prestige.

Last to join the list was President Mitterrand (whose *grands projets* for the city outdid even Napoleon's) – his glass pyramid entrance to the Louvre (see p.51) and immense marble-clad cubic arch at La Défense (see p.228) effectively mark each end of the historic axis. The two great constructions echo each other in scale and geometry, with both aligned at the same slight angle away from the axis; certainly in the case of the Grande Arche, this was more pragmatic than aesthetic, its foundations having to be laid in an area riddled with tunnels for the métro and RER.

The Arc de Triomphe

Daily: April–Sept 10am–11pm; Oct–March 10am–10.30pm • €12 • Ⓦ paris-arc-de-triomphe.fr; Ⓜ Charles-de-Gaulle-Etoile

The **Arc de Triomphe** towers up in the middle of place Charles de Gaulle, better known as place de l'Etoile, essentially a giant roundabout. The arch is modelled on the ancient Roman triumphal arches and is impressive in scale, memorably likened by Guy de Maupassant in his novel *Bel Ami* to "a shapeless giant on two monstrously large legs, that looks as if it's about to stride off down the Champs-Elysées". Begun by Napoleon in 1806 in homage to his Grande Armée, the monument was only completed in 1836 by Louis-Philippe, who dedicated it to the French army in general. Later, victorious German armies would make a point of marching through the arch to compound French humiliation. After the Prussians' triumphal march in 1871, Parisians lit bonfires beneath the arch and down the Champs-Elysées to eradicate the "stain" of German boots. Still a potent symbol of the country's military might, the arch is the starting point for the annual Bastille Day procession, a bombastic march-past of tanks, guns and flags.

Access to the arch is via underground stairs on the north corner of the Champs-Elysées. The names of 660 generals and numerous French battles are engraved on its inside, while reliefs adorn the exterior; the best is François Rude's extraordinarily dramatic *Marseillaise*, in which an Amazon-type figure personifying the Revolution charges forward with a sword, her face contorted in a fierce rallying cry. Climbing the 280 twisty, narrow steps to the top (there is a lift you can ask to use) rewards you with panoramic views, at their best towards dusk on a sunny day when the marble of the Grande Arche de la Défense sparkles in the distance in the setting sun and the Louvre is bathed in warm light. A **mini-museum** at the top of the arch screens relevant historical footage, including extraordinary images of Victor Hugo's funeral in 1885, when more than half the population of Paris turned out to pay their respects to the poet, his coffin mounted on a huge bier beneath the arch, draped in black velvet for the occasion.

The Champs-Elysées

Twelve avenues radiate out from place de l'Etoile (étoile meaning "star"), of which the best known is the **Champs-Elysées** ("Elysian Fields"). Tree-lined and broad, it sweeps down from the Arc de Triomphe towards the place de la Concorde. Close up it can be a

---

THE TOMB OF THE UNKNOWN SOLDIER

A poignant ceremony is conducted every evening to 6.30pm at the foot of the Arc de Triomphe, when war veterans stoke up the flame at the **Tomb of the Unknown Soldier**, killed in the Great War. Not even the Nazi occupation of Paris on June 14, 1940, could interrupt this sacred act. At 6.30pm that day, German troops gathering around the Arc de Triomphe were astonished to see two elderly French soldiers marching towards them in full dress uniform. The Germans instinctively stood to attention while Edmond Ferrand, the guardian of the **Eternal Flame**, and André Gaudin, a member of the flame's committee, solemnly saluted the tomb; the Germans, somewhat disconcerted, apparently followed suit.

little disappointing, with its constant stream of traffic, its fast-food outlets and chain stores, though it has recently regained something of its former cachet. The avenue's renaissance started with a facelift in the mid-1990s, when the rows of trees the Nazis removed during World War II were replanted and pavements were refurbished. Luxury hotels subsequently moved in, and formerly dowdy shops underwent stylish makeovers. Now major fashion brands have their flagship stores on the avenue. The southern side, where Louis Vuitton, Lanvin and the like flaunt their wares, is more sought-after than the northern side. On account of its high concentration of luxury hotels and flagship designer stores, the area bounded by the Champs-Elysées and, to the south, avenue Montaigne and rue François 1er, is nicknamed the **Triangle d'Or** (Golden Triangle). Every first Sunday of the month, the avenue closes to traffic.

Brief history

The Champs-Elysées began life as a leafy promenade, an extension of the Tuileries gardens. It became fashionable during the Second Empire when the *haute bourgeoisie* built splendid mansions along its length and high society came to stroll and frequent the cafés and theatres. Most of the mansions finally gave way to office blocks and the *beau monde* moved elsewhere, but remnants of the avenue's heyday live on: at the *Lido* cabaret; *Fouquet's* café-restaurant (see p.271); the perfumier Guerlain's shop, occupying an exquisite 1913 building; and the former *Claridges* hotel, now a swanky shopping arcade, the Galerie du Claridge. One of the most opulent of the mid-nineteenth-century mansions also survives: the restaurant at no. 25 (*Bistro 25*) was once home to the famous courtesan, La Païva, whose bathroom alone, it is said, was worthy of a Sultana in the *Arabian Nights*.

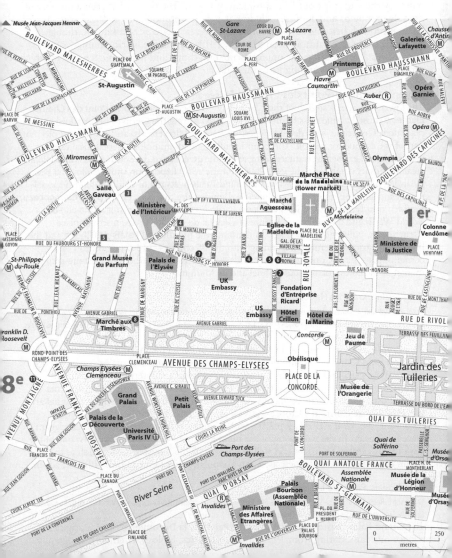

The Champs-Elysées occupies an important place in the national psyche and is a rallying point at times of crisis and celebration; crowds thronged here to greet Général de Gaulle as he walked down the avenue just after the Liberation in May 1944, and many turned out to support him again in 1968 in the wake of the student riots, while around a million Parisians congregated here in 1998 after France won the football World Cup.

Théâtre des Champs-Elysées
15 av Montaigne • ☎ 01 49 52 50 50, ⓦ theatrechampselysees.fr • Ⓜ Alma–Marceau

At the bottom of avenue Montaigne is the **Théâtre des Champs-Elysées**, one of the city's premier concert halls (see p.317). Erected in 1913, it was among the first buildings in Paris to be made of reinforced concrete, its exterior softened with marble reliefs by the sculptor Bourdelle, a student of Rodin. The theatre has seen a number of **notable premieres and debuts**, including that of Josephine Baker in 1925, who created a sensation with her sensual, abandoned dancing. It's perhaps best known, though, for being the scene of great uproar on May 29, 1913, during the world premiere of Stravinsky's *Rite of Spring*, the unprecedented rhythmic and harmonic ferocity of which provoked loud catcalls and fights in the stalls.

Beyond the Rond-Point des Champs-Elysées

The lower – eastern – stretch of the Champs-Elysées between the **Rond-Point des Champs-Elysées** (whose Lalique glass fountains disappeared during the German occupation) and place de la Concorde is bordered by chestnut trees and flowerbeds, and is the most pleasant part of the avenue for a stroll. The gigantic building with grandiose Neoclassical exterior, glass roofs and exuberant statuary rising above the greenery to the south is the **Grand Palais**, created with its neighbour, the **Petit Palais**, for the 1900 **Exposition Universelle**. The Petit Palais has a fine arts museum, while the Grand Palais hosts major exhibitions and special events and also contains a science museum. Between the two palaces lies **place Clemenceau**, presided over by statues of Georges Clemenceau, French prime minister at the end of World War I, and a more recent bronze of Général de Gaulle. To the north of place Clemenceau, police guard the high walls around the presidential **Palais de l'Elysée** and the line of ministries and embassies, ending with the **US embassy** in prime position on the corner of place de la Concorde. On Thursdays and at weekends there's a **postage-stamp market** at the corner of avenues Gabriel and de Marigny.

Grand Palais: Galeries Nationales
Av Winston Churchill, 8ᵉ, Galeries Nationales entrance at 3 av du Général-Eisenhower • Opening times vary, but usually Mon, Thurs, Sat & Sun 10am–8pm, Wed & Fri 10am–10pm • Usually €13–14, though prices vary • ☎ 01 44 13 17 17, ⓦ grandpalais.fr • Ⓜ Champs Elysées Clemenceau

The 45m-high glass cupola of the **Grand Palais** can be seen from most of the city's viewpoints and forms the centrepiece of the nef (nave), a huge, impressive exhibition space, whose glass-and-steel ceiling allows light to flood the interior. After a lengthy restoration project, the palais has resumed its role as the city's premier special-events venue, hosting music festivals and art exhibitions – including the prestigious annual art fair, **FIAC** (ⓦ fiac.com), in October – as well as trade fairs and fashion shows. Its restaurant, the *Mini Palais* (see p.271), with its grand colonnaded terrace, is an elegant place for dinner. In the west wing of the building are the **Galeries Nationales**, one of the city's major exhibition spaces and well known for its blockbuster shows, such as the Rodin exhibition in 2017; these are always popular, so it's best to book online in advance.

Grand Palais: Palais de la Découverte
Av Franklin D. Roosevelt, 8ᵉ • Tues–Sat 9.30am–6pm, Sun 10am–7pm • €9, combined ticket with planetarium €12 • ☎ 01 56 43 20 20, ⓦ palais-decouverte.fr • Ⓜ Champs Elysées Clemenceau/Franklin D. Roosevelt

The Grand Palais' eastern wing houses the **Palais de la Découverte**, Paris's original science museum, dating from 1937. It covers physics, biology, chemistry, geography, mathematics and astronomy. The emphasis is, as the name suggests, very much on discovery and experiment; there are plenty of interactive exhibits and working models to help you explore the properties of electromagnets, for example, or find out how ants and spiders communicate, and around forty live experiments are conducted throughout the day. There are also engaging temporary exhibitions on subjects as diverse as dinosaurs, clay and climate change, as well as an excellent **planetarium**.

Petit Palais: Musée des Beaux-Arts de la Ville de Paris

Av Winston Churchill, 8ᵉ • Tues–Sun 10am–6pm; concerts 12.30pm (arrive 30min beforehand to collect your free ticket) • Free •
☎ 01 53 43 40 00, ⓦ petitpalais.paris.fr • Ⓜ Champs Elysées Clemenceau

The **Petit Palais**, facing the Grand Palais on avenue Winston Churchill, holds the **Musée des Beaux-Arts de la Ville de Paris**. It's hardly "petit", but it's certainly palatial, with its highly decorated Neoclassical exterior, interior garden with Tuscan colonnade, beautiful spiral wrought-iron staircases and a grand gallery on the lines of Versailles' Hall of Mirrors. The museum's extensive holdings of paintings, sculpture and decorative artworks are displayed on two floors and range from the ancient Greek and Roman period up to the early twentieth century. At first sight it looks like it's mopped up the leftovers after the city's other galleries have taken their pick, but there are some real gems here, such as Monet's *Soleil couchant sur la Seine à Lavacourt*, Courbet's provocative *Demoiselles du bord de la Seine* and Pissarro's delicate *Le Pont Royal et le Pavillon de Flore*, painted a few months before he died. Decorative arts feature strongly, especially eighteenth-century furniture and porcelain, including a whimsical clock decorated with a monkey orchestra in Meissen china. There's also fantasy Art Nouveau jewellery, an elegant pear-wood dining room designed by Hector Guimard (who designed the original Paris métro stations), Russian icons and a fine collection of seventeenth-century Dutch landscape painting. Changing exhibitions allow the museum to display works from its vast reserves. There's a smart **café** that opens out onto the lovely interior garden, plus free classical music **concerts**, often on a Thursday lunchtime (see website).

Grand Musée du Parfum

73 rue du Faubourg St-Honoré, 8ᵉ • Tues–Sun 10.30am–7pm, Fri till 10pm • €14.50 • ☎ 01 42 65 25 44, ⓦ grandmuseeduparfum.fr •
Ⓜ Miromesnil/Franklin D. Roosevelt

Set over the four floors of an elegant mansion just off the rue du Faubourg St-Honoré, the newly opened **Grand Musée du Parfum** is entirely dedicated to **perfume** and all things olfactory. Using high-tech interactive displays, the museum introduces you to the art of perfume-making and looks at the sense of smell more generally. There's an engaging section on the history of perfume, charting its use from ancient Egypt onwards. The second section of the museum explores the link between smell, emotion and memory; in the "Garden of Scents" giant diffusers dispense evocative fragrances such as basil, cinnamon, Coca-Cola and wood smoke. In the final part of the museum, you can find out about the art of the perfumier and smell the raw ingredients that make up a perfume.

South of the Arc de Triomphe

Heading **south of the Arc de Triomphe** down avenues Kléber or d'Iéna, both lined with imposing mansion blocks, will take you to the Trocadéro quarter (see p.157). En route you could take in one or two smaller sights such as the **Musée Dapper**, the glitzy **Galerie-Musée Baccarat** or the newly opened **Musée Yves Saint Laurent**.

Musée Dapper

35 rue Paul-Valéry, 16ᵉ • Usually mid-Oct to mid-July Mon, Wed & Fri–Sun 11am–7pm (the museum is closed between exhibitions) • €6 •
☎ 01 45 00 91 75, ⓦ dapper.fr • Ⓜ Victor Hugo/Kléber

The small and intimate **Musée Dapper**, specializing in tribal art from sub-Saharan Africa, puts on well-thought-out and fascinating exhibitions on themes such as initiation ceremonies, carnivals, and rites and traditions associated with eating and drinking. Masks, wooden sculptures and other artefacts, usually accompanied by videos, are well displayed in darkened rooms. The downstairs café and bookshop are also worth a detour.

Galerie-Musée Baccarat

11 place des Etats-Unis, 16ᵉ • Tues–Sat 10am–6pm • €10 • ☎ 01 40 22 11 00, ⓦ baccarat.fr • ⓜ Boissière

The **Galerie-Musée Baccarat** is a small museum displaying some exquisite examples of Baccarat crystal glassware. It occupies the first floor of a grand mansion, once owned by Vicomtesse de Noailles, renowned patron of the Surrealists, and is now the headquarters of the Maison Baccarat. An air of opulence reigns in the red-carpeted entrance hall and upstairs rooms, redesigned by Philippe Starck in neo-Rococo style. The items on display include Art Deco perfume bottles, ornate glassware commissioned for Tsar Nicholas II, sketches of designs for elaborate candelabras and chandeliers, and items made for the Universal Exhibitions of the 1860s and 70s, such as an elephant-shaped decanter. You can also peek into the adjoining restaurant, *Le Cristal Room*, to admire the lavish decor.

Musée Yves Saint Laurent

5 av Marceau, 16ᵉ • Check website for opening times and admission fee • ☎ 01 44 31 64 00, ⓦ fondation-pb-ysl.net • ⓜ Monceau

At the time of writing, a new museum dedicated to Yves Saint Laurent was due to open its doors at the end of 2017. The building on avenue Marceau, currently the Fondation Pierre Bergé-Yves Saint Laurent, was where the designer worked and created his couture pieces for almost thirty years. You'll be able to visit Saint Laurent's atelier and the haute couture salons, as well as exhibitions drawing on the museum's rich collection of clothes, accessories, sketches and photographs.

Quartier Monceau

North of the Arc de Triomphe, the 16ᵉ and 17ᵉ arrondissements are somewhat cold and soulless, their huge, fortified apartments empty much of the time. Further east, however, the **Quartier Monceau** has more to offer, with its attractive park and honey-coloured stone mansions, ornamented with pilasters, caryatids and elaborate mouldings. These aristocratic buildings are the legacy of the building boom in the 1860s; for the Second Empire's newly rich financiers and property developers, the ultimate status symbol was a mansion on the plaine de Monceau. As much money was lavished on the interiors, with many amassing fine collections of furniture and art – some of these collections have been preserved and now make for rewarding museums: the **Musée Cernuschi**, **Musée Nissim de Camondo**, **Musée Jean-Jacques Henner** and, most magnificent of all, the **Musée Jacquemart-André**.

Parc Monceau

Daily: May–Aug 7am–10pm; Sept–April 7am–8pm • ⓜ Monceau

Surrounded by grand houses, **Parc Monceau** is an informal, English-style park, with undulating lawns, rock gardens, a moss-grown, mock-Classical colonnade and statues of brooding French musicians and writers such as Maupassant and Gounod. Perhaps there should be a statue of Marcel Proust, as he came here often as a child and lived nearby for much of his life. It's very much a locals' park, with children coming to play here after school and picknickers lolling on the grass in fine weather.

Musée Cernuschi

7 av Velásquez, 8ᵉ • Tues–Sun 10am–6pm • Free • ☎ 01 53 96 21 50, ⓦ cernuschi.paris.fr • ⓜ Monceau/Villiers

The **Musée Cernuschi** houses a small collection of Far Eastern art, mainly ancient Chinese, bequeathed to the state by the banker Cernuschi, who nearly lost his life for giving money to the insurrectionary Commune of 1871, and in whose elegant mansion the museum is housed. A grand staircase takes you up to the permanent collection on the first floor, where there are some exquisite pieces, including a selection of ceremonial jade objects dating from 3000 BC, highly worked bronzes from the Shang era (1550–1005 BC) and some unique ceramics detailing everyday life in ancient China. On the mezzanine, among a collection of Buddhas and other statuary, a beautiful, sinuous figure playing a lute, dating from the Wei dynasty, stands out.

Musée Nissim de Camondo

63 rue de Monceau, 8ᵉ • Wed–Sun 10am–5.30pm • €9 • ☎ 01 45 63 26 32, ⓦ www.lesartsdecoratifs.fr • Ⓜ Monceau/Villiers

Beside the Musée Cernuschi, the **Musée Nissim de Camondo** has an impressive collection of eighteenth-century decorative art and painting, built up by Count Moïse de Camondo, son of a wealthy Sephardic Jewish banker who emigrated from Istanbul to Paris in the late nineteenth century. To provide a showcase for his treasures, the count commissioned a mansion in eighteenth-century style, modelled on Versailles' Petit Trianon (see p.233). The **ground-floor rooms** overflow with Gobelin tapestries, paintings of pastoral scenes by Huet and Vigée-Lebrun, gilded furniture and delicate Sèvres porcelain; an excellent free audioguide helps you get the most out of the exhibits. On the **upper floor**, where the family spent most of their time, the rooms are more homely; here and there some of the anachronistic mod-cons of an early twentieth-century aristocratic home surface, such as the count's well-appointed bathroom. These rooms take on a progressively melancholy air, however, as you learn more about the Camondos and their fate: after a few years of marriage Moïse's wife left him for the head groom; his beloved son, Nissim, after whom the museum is named, died on a flying mission in World War I; while his remaining child, Béatrice, perished together with her children in the concentration camps in World War II. The house and its contents, preserved exactly as Moïse left them, are a poignant memorial to an extinguished family.

Musée Jean-Jacques Henner

43 av de Villiers, 17ᵉ • Mon & Wed–Sun 11am–6pm • €6 • ☎ 01 47 63 42 73, ⓦ musee-henner.fr • Ⓜ Villiers

Housed in a slender nineteenth-century townhouse is a museum dedicated to the artist **Jean-Jacques Henner** (1829–1905). Although hardly a household name, Henner was much celebrated in his day and is well worth discovering, if only to see what an "establishment painter" was producing at the same time as the Impressionists were bursting on to the scene. The selection of Henner's two-thousand-odd paintings and sketches, displayed over the three floors of the house, ranges from tender, intimate portraits of family members from his native Alsace to epic works on mythical and biblical themes; among the paintings that stand out are a portrait of a flaming-red-haired Salome holding the head of John the Baptist and numerous paintings of the dead Christ, a subject the artist returned to again and again. His rendering of the body of Christ is very striking – strangely sensual and spiritual at the same time.

The house itself is a delight. Although Henner never actually lived here, it was owned by an acquaintance of his, fellow artist Guillaume Dubufe, and has been faithfully restored, giving you some idea of how a successful artist lived at the time, and of the rich cultural and artistic life in general of the Monceau *quartier* in the 1870–90 period. Reflecting the tastes of the time, the decor is a mix of different styles; there's a neo-Renaissance salon with coffered ceiling and Doric columns, carved Arabian latticework and an Oriental-inspired winter garden.

Musée Jacquemart-André

158 bd Haussmann, 8ᵉ • Daily 10am–6pm (Mon until 8.30pm during exhibitions) • €13.50; tickets can be bought in advance online •
☎ 01 45 62 11 59, ⓦ musee-jacquemart-andre.com • Ⓜ Miromesnil/St-Philippe-du-Roule

A few blocks south of the Parc Monceau stands the lavishly ornamented palace of the nineteenth-century banker and art-lover Edouard André and his wife, society portraitist Nélie Jacquemart. Built in 1870 to grace Baron Haussmann's grand new boulevard, the Hôtel André is now the **Musée Jacquemart-André**, housing the couple's impressive art collection and a fabulous salon de thé (see p.270). Bequeathed to the Institut de France by

Edouard's widow, the museum deploys the couple's collection exactly as they ordained. Nélie painted Edouard's portrait in 1872 – on display in what were their private apartments on the ground floor – and nine years later they were married, after which Nélie gave up her painting career and the pair devoted their spare time to collecting art. Their preference for **Italian art** is evident in the stunning collection of fifteenth- and sixteenth-century genius, including the works of Tiepolo, Botticelli, Donatello, Mantegna and Uccello, which form the core of the collection. Almost as compelling as the interior and art collection is the insight gleaned into an extraordinary marriage and grand nineteenth-century lifestyle, which are brought to life by the fascinating narration on the free audioguide.

Ground floor

In Room 1, mostly eighteenth-century French paintings are displayed, including several portraits by **Boucher**, in addition to two lively paintings of Venice by Canaletto. The reception area (room 2) has specially constructed folding doors which, when opened, transformed the space into a ballroom large enough to hold a thousand guests. Room 3 contains three huge tapestries depicting Russian scenes that capture the fashion for Slav exoticism of the mid-eighteenth century, while Dutch and Flemish paintings, including three by Van Dyck and two by Rembrandt, adorn the walls of room 6, formerly the library. One of the most striking rooms is the Salon de Musique (the other half of the ballroom), its dramatic high ceiling decorated with a mural by Pierre Victor Galant; the musicians would play from the gallery, and you're treated to a mini-concert on the audioguide as you gaze at the ceiling. In Room 8, a huge, animated fresco by **Tiepolo**, depicting the French king Henri III being received by Federico Contarini in Venice, graces the extraordinary marble, bronze and wrought-iron, double spiral staircase that leads from an **interior garden** of palm trees up to the musicians' gallery. Room 9, which was once the smoking room, where the men would retreat after dinner, is hung with the work of eighteenth-century English portraitists, among them **Joshua Reynolds**.

First floor

Leading off the music gallery, on the **first floor**, are the rooms in which the couple displayed their **early Italian Renaissance collection**. The first, a sculpture gallery, its walls covered in low-relief carvings, includes three bronzes by **Donatello**. The Florentine room next door includes a wonderful, brightly coloured *Saint George Slaying the Dragon* (1440) by **Uccello**, a **Botticelli** *Virgin and Child* (1470) depicted with touching fragility, and an exquisite, sixteenth-century inlaid choir-stall. Adjacent is the Venetian room, with paintings by **Bellini** and **Mantegna** among others.

Place de la Concorde

At the eastern end of the Champs-Elysées lies the grand, pleasingly harmonious **place de la Concorde**, marred only by its constant stream of traffic. Its centrepiece is a **gold-tipped obelisk** from the temple of Ramses at Luxor, given by Muhammad Ali of Egypt to Louis-Philippe in 1831, and flanked by two ornate bronze fountains, modelled on those in St Peter's Square, Rome. The square's history is much less harmonious than its name "Concorde" suggests. The equestrian statue of Louis XV that formerly stood at the centre of the square was toppled in 1792, and between 1793 and 1795, 1300 people died here beneath the revolutionary guillotine, including Louis XVI, Marie Antoinette, Danton and Robespierre. When deciding later what to put in place of Louis XV's statue, Louis-Philippe thought the obelisk would be ideal – having no political message, it wasn't likely ever to be demolished or become the focus of popular discontent. It was erected with much pomp in October 1836 in the presence of 200,000 spectators, while an orchestra played tunes from Bellini's *I Puritani*.

From the centre of the square there are magnificent views of the Champs-Elysées and Tuileries, and you can admire the symmetry of the Assemblée Nationale, on the far side of the Seine, with the Eglise de la Madeleine at the end of rue Royale to the north. An even better way to take it all in is to ride on the giant Ferris wheel, **la Grande Roue** (mid-Nov to mid-May Mon–Thurs & Sun 10.30am–midnight, Fri & Sat 10am–1am; €12, children under 10 €6), which is erected in the winter months on the Tuileries gardens side of the square.

Hôtel de la Marine

Two vast, colonnaded eighteenth-century buildings flank the rue Royale, forming a splendid backdrop to the place de la Concorde. One, the luxury Hôtel Crillon, has just emerged from a sumptuous restoration, while the other, the **Hôtel de la Marine**, was about to be restored at the time of writing. Originally the royal storehouse and then the ministry of naval affairs, this grand edifice will reopen in 2019 as a museum. You'll be able to visit a number of lavishly decorated rooms and apartments and enjoy the stunning panoramic views from the first-floor veranda.

Fondation d'Entreprise Ricard

12 rue Boissy d'Anglas, 8ᵉ • Tues–Sat 11am–7pm • ☎ 01 53 30 88 00, Ⓦ www.fondation-entreprise-ricard.com • Ⓜ Concorde/Madeleine

Located just off the place de la Concorde, this prestigious art foundation is a good place to discover emerging French artists. It organizes around five or six exhibitions a year of contemporary art, and also hosts the **Fondation d'Entreprise Ricard** prize (roughly equivalent to the Turner Prize).

Jardin des Tuileries

Extending for around 1km from the place de la Concorde to the Louvre, the **Jardin des Tuileries** is the formal French garden *par excellence*. The grand central alley is lined with clipped chestnut trees and manicured lawns, and framed by ornamental ponds. Surrounding these is an impressive gallery of statues (by the likes of Rodin, Coustou and Coysevox), many brought here from Versailles and Marly (Louis XIV's retreat from Versailles, no longer in existence), though a number are copies, with the originals in the Louvre. Elsewhere in the gardens are sculptures by artists such as Louise Bourgeois and Giacometti; a handy app, pARTcours, put together by the Louvre and the Centre National des Arts Plastiques, offers three different walking tours of the artworks.

The much-sought-after chairs strewn around the ponds make good bases for admiring the surroundings, and there are also a number of cafés nestling among the trees. Flanking the garden at the western Concorde end are two Neoclassical buildings: the **Musée de l'Orangerie** art gallery, by the river, and the **Jeu de Paume**, the city's premier photographic exhibition space, by the rue de Rivoli. At the eastern end of the gardens in front of the Louvre is the **Jardin du Carrousel**, a raised terrace where the **Palais des Tuileries**, burnt down by the Communards in 1871, once stood (see box, p.72). It's now planted with yew hedges, interspersed with bronzes of buxom female nudes by Maillol.

Brief history

The garden originated in the 1570s when **Catherine de Médicis** had the site cleared of the medieval warren of tile manufacturers (*tuileries*) that stood here to make way for a palace and grounds (see box, p.72). The Palais des Tuileries, as it became known, was surrounded by formal vegetable gardens, a labyrinth and a chequerboard of flowerbeds. The present layout, however, is largely the work of the landscape architect **Le Nôtre**, who was commissioned by Louis XIV a hundred years later to redesign the gardens on a grander scale. Employing techniques he went on to perfect at Versailles, Le Nôtre took the opportunity to indulge his passion for symmetry, straight avenues, formal flowerbeds and splendid vistas. During the eighteenth century, the gardens were where chic Parisians came to preen and party, and in 1783 the Montgolfier brothers, Joseph and Etienne, launched the first successful hot-air balloon here. Serious replanting was

3

THE LOST PALAIS DES TUILERIES

For much of its life, the Louvre stood facing a twin sister, the **Palais des Tuileries**. Built in 1559 for **Catherine de Médicis** shortly after the accidental death of her husband, Henri II, it was a place where she could maintain her political independence while wielding power on behalf of her sickly son, François II. It was apparently Catherine herself who conceived the idea of linking the two palaces with a *grande galerie* running along the right bank of the Seine, but in 1572 she abandoned the entire project. Tradition has it that she was warned by a soothsayer to "beware of St-Germain" if she wanted to live into old age – and the Tuileries lay in the parish of St-Germain l'Auxerrois. It's more likely that the palace's location just outside the protection of the city walls was the problem, as 1572 was a dangerous year: on August 24, the bells of St-Germain l'Auxerrois rang out according to a prearranged signal, whereupon radical Catholics set about the murder of some three thousand Parisian Protestants, possibly under the secret orders of Catherine herself.

It wasn't until forty years after the St Bartholomew's Day Massacre that the two palaces were finally linked, in the reign of Henri IV. Louis XIV moved across from the Louvre in 1667, but the court soon departed for Versailles, and the Tuileries remained largely empty until the Revolution, when Louis XVI was kept under virtual house arrest there by the revolutionary mob until the *sans-culottes* finally lost patience on June 20, 1792, breaking in and forcing the king to don the revolutionary red bonnet. The Tuileries was revived under Napoleon, who built the **Arc de Triomphe du Carrousel** facing its central pavilion, and its status grew still greater under his nephew, Napoléon III, who finally united both royal palaces around a single gigantic courtyard, the whole complex being dubbed the Cité Impériale. This glorious perfection didn't last long: the Tuileries was set alight by the revolutionary Communards as they lost control of the city in May 1871 (see p.371). The ruins of the Tuileries were cleared away and replaced by the **Jardin du Carrousel**.

---

carried out after the Revolution, and in the nineteenth century rare species were added to the garden, which was by now dominated by chestnut trees.

Jeu de Paume

1 place de la Concorde, 1ᵉʳ • Tues 11am–9pm, Wed–Sun 11am–7pm • €10; tickets can be booked online in advance • ☎ 01 47 03 12 50, Ⓦ www.jeudepaume.org • Ⓜ Concorde

The **Jeu de Paume** was once a royal (indoor) tennis court and the place where French Impressionist paintings were displayed before being transferred to the Musée d'Orsay. Since 2004 it's been a major exhibition space dedicated to photography and video art. The building is not as well lit as you might expect from the soaring, light-filled foyer, but it's one of the top venues for major retrospectives of photographers such as Martin Parr and Edward Steichen. There's also a small café and a good bookshop.

Musée de l'Orangerie

Jardin des Tuileries, 1ᵉʳ • Mon & Wed–Sun 9am–6pm • €9; book in advance as queues can be long • ☎ 01 44 77 80 07, Ⓦ www.musee-orangerie.fr • Ⓜ Concorde

Opposite the Jeu de Paume is the **Musée de l'Orangerie**, an elegant, Neoclassical-style building, originally designed to protect the Tuileries' orange trees, and now housing a private art collection including eight of **Monet**'s giant water lily paintings. Displayed in two oval rooms, flooded with natural light, these vast canvases were executed in the last years of the artist's life, when he almost obsessively painted the pond in his garden at Giverny, attempting to capture the fleeting light and changing colours.

On the lower floor is a rather fine collection of paintings by Monet's contemporaries. Highlights include still lifes, portraits and landscapes by **Cézanne**. **Renoir** is represented by some sensuous nudes and touching studies of children, such as *Jeunes filles au piano*, the two girls' rapt concentration on the music wonderfully conveyed. There are works by **Picasso** and **Matisse**; the latter's *Les Trois Soeurs* stands out for its striking portrayal of three women, the simplicity of line and colour reminiscent of a Japanese print. Space is also devoted to **Derain**, including a number of iridescent nudes and vibrant landscapes, and **Soutine**'s more expressionistic canvases.

GALERIE VIVIENNE

The Grands Boulevards and *passages*

Built on the site of the city's old ramparts, the Grands Boulevards stretch from the Madeleine in the west to the Bastille in the east. Once fashionable thoroughfares where "le tout Paris" came to seek entertainment, they're still a vibrant part of the city, with their brasseries, theatres and cinemas. The streets off the Grands Boulevards constitute the city's main commercial and financial district, incorporating the solid institutions of the Banque de France and the Bourse, while to the northwest is the glittering Opéra Garnier. Well-heeled shopping is concentrated on rue St-Honoré and around place Vendôme, and to the south, the Palais Royal gardens provide a retreat from the traffic. Threading their way throughout the district are the *passages* – delightful shopping arcades, full of old-fashioned charm.

The Grands Boulevards

The **Grands Boulevards** is the collective name given to the eight busy streets that form one continuous thoroughfare running from the Madeleine to République (see p.197), then down to the Bastille (see p.110). With their Haussmann-era blocks, shops and imposing banks, they seem pretty unremarkable nowadays, but in the nineteenth century these were the most fashionable streets in Paris. Even as recently as the 1950s, a visitor to Paris would, as a matter of course, have gone for a stroll along the Grands Boulevards to see "*Paris vivant*". Something of this tradition still survives in the brasseries, cafés, theatres and cinemas, including the Max Linder and Grand Rex, the latter an extraordinary building inside and out (see p.311).

Brief history

The **western section** of the Grands Boulevards, from the Madeleine to Porte St-Denis, follows the rampart built by Charles V in the mid-fourteenth century. When its defensive purpose became redundant with the offensive foreign policy of Louis XIV in the seventeenth century, the walls were pulled down and the ditches filled in, leaving a wide promenade. However, it wasn't until the nineteenth century that the boulevards became a fashionable place to stroll and be seen; the cafés on the west-end **boulevard des Italiens** were a hotbed of intellectual debate and ferment, their chic customers setting the trends for all of Paris in terms of manners, dress and conversation.

The **eastern section** developed a more colourful reputation, derived from its association with street theatre, mime artists, jugglers, puppet shows and cafés of ill repute, earning itself the nickname the "*boulevard du Crime*", immortalized in the 1945 film *Les Enfants du Paradis*. Some of this area was swept away in the latter half of the nineteenth century by Baron Haussmann's huge place de la République (see p.197).

It was at **14 boulevard des Capucines**, in the *Grand Café* (now the *Hôtel Scribe*), in 1895, that Paris saw its first film, or animated photography, as the **Lumière brothers'** invention was called. Some years earlier, in 1874, another artistic revolution had taken place at **no. 35** in the former studio of photographer Félix Nadar – the first **Impressionist exhibition**, which was greeted with outrage by the art world; one critic said of Monet's *Impression, soleil levant* ("Impression: sunrise"), "it was worse than anyone had hitherto dared to paint".

Musée Grévin

10 bd Montmartre, 9e • Hours vary, but usually Mon–Fri 10am–6pm, Sat & Sun 9.30am–7pm; last admission 1hr before closing • €22.50, children €17.50; see website for special offers • ☏ 01 47 70 85 05, ⓦ grevin-paris.com • Ⓜ Grands Boulevards

A remnant from the fun-loving times on the Grands Boulevards is the waxworks museum, the **Musée Grévin**. You can have your photo taken next to Isabelle Adjani, Omar Sy, Zlatan Ibrahimovic and many other French and international celebrities, but perhaps the best thing about the museum is its rooms: the magical Palais des Mirages (Hall of Mirrors), built for the Exposition Universelle in 1900; the theatre with its sculptures by Bourdelle; and the 1882 Baroque-style Hall of Columns.

Opéra Garnier

8 rue Scribe, at rue Auber, 9e • **Interior** Available for visits daily 10am–5pm • €11; bookable online • **Performances** See p.316 • Ⓦ operadeparis.fr • Ⓜ Opéra

Set back from boulevard des Capucines is the dazzling Opéra de Paris – usually referred to as the **Opéra Garnier** to distinguish it from the newer opera house at the Bastille (see p.110). Constructed between 1865 and 1872 as part of Napoléon III's vision for Paris, it crowns the long, rather monotonous avenue de l'Opéra. The architect, Charles Garnier, whose golden bust by Carpeaux can be seen on the rue Auber side, drew on a number of existing styles and succeeded in creating a fantastically ornate building the like of which Paris had never seen before – when the Empress Eugénie asked in bewilderment what style it was, Garnier replied that it was "Napoléon III style". Certainly, if any building can be said to exemplify the Second Empire, it is this – in its show of wealth, ambition and hint of vulgarity. In the event, however, it was only completed in 1875 after the Empire had been swept away by the Third Republic, and even Garnier had to pay for his ticket on the opening night. Part of the reason construction took so long – fourteen years in all – was the discovery of a water table which had to be drained and replaced by a huge concrete well, giving rise to the legend of an underground lake, popularized by Gaston Leroux's 1910 novel *Phantom of the Opera*.

The theatre's **facade** is a fairy-tale concoction of white, pink and green marble, colonnades, rearing horses, winged angels and gleaming gold busts of composers. The group sculpture on the right of the entrance, Carpeaux's *La Danse* (the original is now in the Musée d'Orsay), caused a stir upon unveiling for its frank sensuality; one outraged protestor went as far as to throw black ink over the fleshy thighs of the two female nude dancers. Perhaps more audacious to modern eyes is the recently added **restaurant** on the rue Halévy side, featuring shocking-red decor and a sinuous glass structure that encloses the Rotonde du Glacier, up which patrons would once have driven in their carriages.

The interior

You can **visit** the opulent **interior**, including the auditorium, as long as there are no rehearsals; your best chance is between 1 and 2pm. With its spacious gilded-marble and mirrored lobbies, the building was intended to give Second Empire society suitably grand spaces in which to meet and be seen. The auditorium itself is all red velvet and gold leaf, hung with a six-tonne chandelier; the colourful ceiling was painted by Chagall in 1964 and depicts scenes from well-known operas and ballets jumbled up with famous Parisian landmarks. Entry tickets include the **Bibliothèque-Musée de l'Opéra**, which contains exquisite model sets, dreadful nineteenth-century paintings and rather better temporary exhibitions on operatic themes. Amid the postcards and memorabilia in the **shop** is one of the city's most unusual souvenirs – honey collected from hives on the vast copper and zinc roof of the opera house; some 125,000 bees seek out nectar from parks, cemeteries and window boxes and produce up to 300kg of honey a year.

Musée du Parfum Fragonard

3–5 square de l'Opéra Louis Jouvet, 9ᵉ • Mon–Sat 9am–6pm • Free, guided visits only • ☎ 01 40 06 10 09, ⊚ musee-parfum-paris
.fragonard.com • ⓜ Opéra/Auber

Transferred to smart new premises near the opera house in 2016, the *parfumerie* Fragonard's **Musée du Parfum** gives you a chance to find out everything you ever wanted to know about perfume and the perfume-making process. Even if you've only a passing interest in perfume, you'll probably find this quite an engaging museum. Visits are with a guide (English-speaking available) who explains, with the help of a few exhibits and short videos, the history of perfume and how it is made. It quickly becomes apparent why perfume was so important in earlier times when you learn that Louis XIV, for example, had only five baths in his entire life. There's also the chance to

---

BEAUTIFUL BANKS

Following in the wake of the Printemps and Galeries Lafayette department stores on boulevard Haussmann, a number of **imposing banks** were built in the area. The Crédit Lyonnais at 19 boulevard des Italiens, south of boulevard Haussmann, is perhaps the most impressive, its grand pavilion echoing that of the Louvre and its huge gold clock flanked by gigantic caryatids. Across the road at no. 20 the Banque Nationale de Paris occupies another striking building, with gilded wrought-iron balconies and finely sculpted friezes depicting hunting scenes. It used to be the *Maison Dorée*, a restaurant from the 1840s, where on any given evening you might have bumped into Balzac, Hugo, Flaubert and Nerval, among other literary figures. At no. 16 is the bank's main building – a sleek 1930s Art Deco edifice. As you cross over rue Laffitte to reach it, you get a wonderful view of Notre-Dame de Lorette, with the Sacré Coeur rearing up in the background.

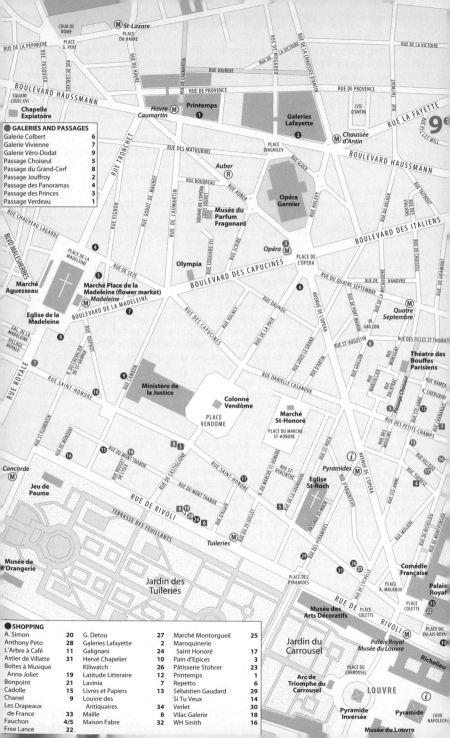

THE GRANDS BOULEVARDS AND PASSAGES

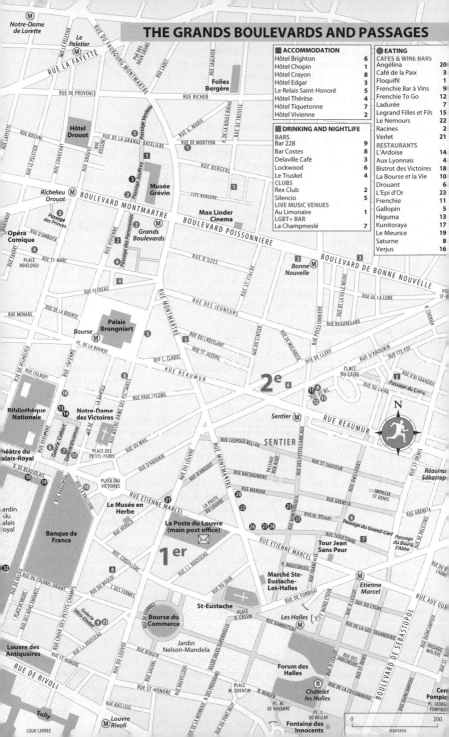

■ ACCOMMODATION
Hôtel Brighton	6
Hôtel Chopin	1
Hôtel Crayon	8
Hôtel Edgar	3
Le Relais Saint-Honoré	5
Hôtel Thérèse	4
Hôtel Tiquetonne	7
Hôtel Vivienne	2

■ DRINKING AND NIGHTLIFE
BARS
Bar 228	9
Bar Costes	1
Delaville Café	3
Lockwood	6
Le Truskel	4

CLUBS
Rex Club	2
Silencio	5

LIVE MUSIC VENUES
Au Limonaire	1

LGBT+ BAR
La Champmeslé	7

● EATING
CAFÉS & WINE BARS
Angélina	20
Café de la Paix	3
Floquifil	1
Frenchie Bar à Vins	9
Frenchie To Go	12
Ladurée	7
Legrand Filles et Fils	15
Le Nemours	22
Racines	2
Verlet	21

RESTAURANTS
L'Ardoise	14
Aux Lyonnais	4
Bistrot des Victoires	18
La Bourse et la Vie	10
Drouant	6
L'Epi d'Or	23
Frenchie	11
Gallopin	5
Higuma	13
Kunitoraya	17
Le Meurice	19
Saturne	8
Verjus	16

test out how good you are at identifying different scents and find out if you'd make a good "nose" (it takes up to six years to train to be a *parfumeur*). The 45-minute tour inevitably ends in the gift shop, but there's no pressure to buy.

Printemps and Galeries Lafayette
Bd Haussmann, 9ᵉ • Ⓜ Chausée d'Antin/Havre Caumartin

Just to the north of the Opéra you'll find two of the city's big department stores, **Printemps** and **Galeries Lafayette** (see p.326). Built at the beginning of the twentieth century, they may have lost their grand central staircases, but they still sport their proud Art Nouveau stained-glass domes. Printemps' dome is particularly splendid, in glowing hues of green and blue, best appreciated from the brasserie beneath.

Chapelle Expiatoire
29 rue Pasquier, 9ᵉ • Tues–Fri 10am–12.30pm & 1.30–6.30pm • €6 • Ⓜ Madeleine/St-Augustin

A rather overlooked monument, set in a peaceful garden, the austere Neoclassical **Chapelle Expiatoire** stands on the spot where Louis XVI, Marie Antoinette and many other victims of the guillotine were buried. It was commissioned in 1815 by Louis XVIII as a memorial to the executed king and queen, and their bodies were transferred to the Basilique de St Denis (see p.225). Inside are marble statues of King Louis XVI being borne away by an angel to heaven, and Marie Antoinette embracing Religion. Die-hard royalists and aristocrats gather here for the annual Mass held on January 21.

Eglise de la Madeleine and around
Place de la Madeleine, 8ᵉ • Ⓜ Madeleine

South of boulevard Haussmann, occupying nearly the whole of the place de la Madeleine, is the imperious-looking **Eglise de la Madeleine**, a favourite venue for society weddings. Modelled on the Parthenon, the building is surrounded by 52 Corinthian columns and fronted by a huge pediment depicting the Last Judgement; its facade is a near mirror image of the Assemblée Nationale, which lies directly opposite, just across the river, on the far side of the place de la Concorde – a fine vista best appreciated from the top of the Madeleine steps. Originally intended as a monument to Napoleon's army – a plan abandoned after the French were defeated by the Russians in 1812 – the building was nearly turned into a railway station before finally being consecrated to Mary Magdalene in 1845.

Inside, a theatrical stone sculpture of the Magdalene being swept up to heaven by two angels draws your eye to the high altar. The half-dome above is decorated with a fresco by Jules-Claude Ziegler (1804–56), a student of Ingres; entitled *The History of Christianity*, it commemorates the concordat signed between the Church and State after the end of the Revolution, and shows all the key figures in Christendom, with Napoleon centre stage, naturally. The church's interior is otherwise rather gloomy and heavy with gilt-edged marble. If you're lucky, the sombre atmosphere may be broken by the sound of the organ, reckoned to be one of Paris's best – the church is a regular venue for recitals and choral concerts. Illustrious former organists include Saint-Saëns and Fauré, whose famous *Requiem* was premiered at the Madeleine in 1888 – to be heard here again at the composer's own funeral 36 years later.

Place de la Madeleine
Ⓜ Madeleine

If the Madeleine church feeds the soul, the square in which it sits is given over to nourishment of an earthier kind, for this is where some of Paris's top **gourmet food stores** are located: among them are Fauchon (see p.337), with its eye-catching window displays, the Maison de la Truffe and Maille mustard shop. East of the church is one of the city's oldest flower markets, dating back to 1832, and open every day except Monday, while nearby some rather fine Art Nouveau public toilets, built in 1905, are definitely worth inspecting.

Place Vendôme and around
Ⓜ Pyramides/Opéra

A short walk east of place de la Madeleine lies **place Vendôme**, one of the city's most impressive set pieces, built by Versailles architect Hardouin-Mansart during the final years of Louis XIV's reign. It's a pleasingly symmetrical, eight-sided *place*, enclosed by a harmonious ensemble of elegant mansions graced with Corinthian pilasters, mascarons and steeply pitched roofs. Once the grand residences of tax collectors and financiers, they now house such luxury establishments as the *Ritz* hotel, the legendary watering hole of Ernest Hemingway, F. Scott Fitzgerald and Cole Porter in the 1920s (and from where Di and Dodi set off on their last journey in 1997), Cartier, Bulgari and other top-flight jewellers, lending the square a decidedly exclusive air. The **Ministière de la Justice** (Ministry of Justice) is also sited here, on the west side; its facade still has the marble plaque showing a standard metre that was put here in 1795 in order to familiarize Parisians with the new unit of measure. No. 12, on the opposite side, now occupied by Chaumet jewellers, is where Chopin died, in 1849.

Colonne Vendôme

Somewhat out of proportion with the rest of place Vendôme, the centrepiece is the **Colonne Vendôme**, a towering triumphal column modelled on Trajan's column in Rome, and surmounted by a statue of Napoleon dressed as Caesar. It was raised in 1806 to celebrate the Battle of Austerlitz – bronze reliefs of scenes of the battle, cast from 1200 recycled Austro-Russian cannons, spiral their way up the monument. The structure that stands here today is actually a replica of the original, which was brought crashing down during the Commune in 1871 – the main instigator behind this act was the artist Gustave Courbet, who was imprisoned and ordered to pay for the column's restoration; he was financially ruined and lived the rest of his life in exile in Switzerland.

Rue St-Honoré
Ⓜ Pyramides/Madeleine/Palais Royal Musée du Louvre

You'll need a healthy bank balance if you intend to do more than window-shop in the streets around place Vendôme, especially ancient **rue St-Honoré**, the preserve of top fashion designers and art galleries. All the classic designers such as Hermès, Yves Saint Laurent and Christian Lacroix are here.

East of place Vendôme, on rues **St-Roch** and **Ste-Anne**, in particular, the Japanese community has established a mini-enclave; you'll find some good noodle and sushi bars here, such as *Higuma* and *Kunitoraya* (see p.275).

Eglise St-Roch
296 rue St-Honoré, 1ᵉʳ • Ⓜ Pyramides

On the corner of rue St-Roch and rue St-Honoré stands the **Eglise St-Roch**, which was begun in 1653 but not completed until 1740, as money kept running out. Its handsome honey-coloured Classical facade has been scrubbed clean and shows little sign of the battering it received in 1795 when the young Napoleon dispersed a Royalist uprising with cannon (or a "whiff of grapeshot", as he famously put it), and was rewarded with promotion to the rank of general. The St-Roch *quartier* used to be much more densely populated than it is now and boasted many illustrious parishioners, some of whom – Corneille, Diderot and Le Nôtre (who landscaped the Versailles and Tuileries gardens) among them – are buried in the church. The nave is very long, filled with light and flanked with numerous chapels that are richly decorated with paintings and sculpture by Coysevox and Coustou, and other leading artists of the day. There is some labelling in English, and a free leaflet detailing the works is available from the welcome desk. The church is also a venue for evening concerts, and holds free lunchtime song and chamber music recitals most Tuesdays from 12.30 to 1.15pm.

Palais Royal
Place du Palais Royal, 1ᵉʳ • Ⓜ Palais Royal Musée du Louvre

There are two main parts to the handsome **Palais Royal** complex: the palace itself and, beyond it, galleries surrounding gardens on three sides. The palace, a fine colonnaded building, dates back to 1624, though it has been much modified and renovated since. It was built for Cardinal Richelieu, who left it to the king, Louis XIV, then just a boy; he and his mother lived here for a time. The building later passed to his brother, the duc d'Orléans, and provided sanctuary to Henrietta Maria, the widow of executed English king, Charles I. It is now occupied by various government departments; an annexe to the side houses the **Comédie Française**, a long-standing venue for the classics of French theatre (see p.315).

The gardens and arcades
Beyond the palace lie sedate **gardens** lined with stately **arcaded buildings**, which were put up in the 1780s by Philippe-Egalité, a descendant of the duc d'Orléans. Desperate to pay off his debts, he let out the spaces under the arcades to shops. Among the **exclusive boutiques** that have sought shelter under the arcades today remain one or two fascinating relics of earlier times, such as Bacqueville, which has produced Légion d'Honneur medals since 1790, and A l'Oriental, 19 Galerie de Chartres, dating from 1818 and selling an extraordinary collection of smokers' pipes, many of them beautifully decorated. Two other quirky shops worth seeking out are the the Boîtes à Musique Anna Joliet (see p.340), which specializes in exquisite music boxes, and Les Drapeaux de France (see p.340) with its extraordinary collection of tin soldiers.

Former residents of the desirable flats above the arcades include Jean Cocteau and Colette – the latter enjoyed looking out over the gardens when she was too crippled with arthritis to walk. It's certainly an attractive and peaceful oasis, with avenues of lime trees, fountains and flowerbeds. You'd hardly guess that for many years this was a site of gambling dens, funfair attractions and brothels (it was to a prostitute here that Napoleon lost his virginity in 1787). The clearing of Paris's brothels in 1829–31 and the prohibition on public gambling in 1838, however, put an end to the fun; later, the Grands Boulevards took up the baton. Folly, some might say, has returned – in the form of Daniel Buren's black-and-white-striped **pillars**, rather like sticks of Brighton rock, all of varying heights, dotted about the main courtyard in front of the palace. Installed in 1986, they're rather disconcerting, but certainly popular with children and rollerbladers, who treat them as an adventure playground and obstacle course respectively.

The *passages* and around
The 2ᵉ arrondissement is scattered with around twenty **passages**, or shopping arcades, that have survived from the early nineteenth century. In 1840, more than a hundred existed, but most were later destroyed to make way for Haussmann's boulevards. After decades of neglect, some have now been restored, with a number of chic boutiques moving in. The overall atmosphere, however, is one of charm and nostalgia, as many of the shops, selling old-fashioned toys, prints, secondhand books, postcards and stamps, hark back to another age. Their entrances are easy to miss and where you emerge at the other end can be quite a surprise. Most are closed at night and on Sundays.

Galerie Véro-Dodat
Between rues Croix-des-Petits-Champs and Jean-Jacques Rousseau, 1ᵉʳ • Ⓜ Palais Royal Musée du Louvre

The most homogeneous and aristocratic of the *passages*, with painted ceilings and panelled mahogany shop fronts divided by faux marble columns, is the elegant **Galerie Véro-Dodat**, which was named after the two butchers who set it up in 1824. It's been largely colonized by design shops, fashion boutiques (including Christian Louboutin) and art galleries, though some older businesses, such as R.F. Charle, at no. 17, specializing in the repair and sale of vintage stringed instruments, remain.

The **Banque de France** lies a short way northwest. Rather than negotiating its massive bulk to reach the *passages* further north, it's more pleasant to walk through the garden of the Palais Royal via place de Valois. Rue de Montpensier, running alongside the gardens to the west, is connected to rue de Richelieu by several tiny *passages*, of which **Hulot** brings you out at the statue of Molière on the junction of rues Richelieu and Molière. A certain charm also lingers about rue de Beaujolais, bordering the northern end of the gardens, with its corner café looking out on the Théâtre du Palais-Royal, and with glimpses into the venerable *Le Grand Véfour* restaurant, plus more short arcades leading up to rue des Petits-Champs.

Galerie Vivienne

Ⓦ galerie-vivienne.com • Ⓜ Bourse

The flamboyant Grecian and marine motifs in elegant **Galerie Vivienne**, which links rue Vivienne with rue des Petits-Champs, create the perfect ambience in which to buy Jean Paul Gaultier gear. Alternatively, you could browse in the atmospheric secondhand bookshop, Librairie Jousseaume, once frequented by Balzac, Dumas and Hugo, or check out the delightful wooden toys at Si Tu Veux toyshop (see p.356). Close by is **Galerie Colbert**; owned by the Institut National d'Histoire d'Art, it has no shops, but is worth seeing for its elegant decor and beautiful glass rotunda, with a statue of Eurydice beneath it.

Place des Victoires and place des Petits-Pères

At the eastern end of rue des Petits-Champs rears up a grand equestrian statue of Louis XIV; it's at the centre of circular, Italianate **place des Victoires**, which was designed by Hardouin-Mansart. The elegant seventeenth-century townhouses lining the square are occupied by designer fashion boutiques, such as Kenzo and Cacharel. Adjoining the square to the north is the appealingly asymmetrical **place des Petits-Pères**, once the courtyard of the monastery of the Petits-Pères, closed during the Revolution. Its church, **Notre-Dame des Victoires** (daily 8.30am–7.30pm), survives, and is notable for its collection of paintings by Carl Van Loo, as well as the extraordinary number of "ex-votos" (marble plaques and offerings of thanksgiving for prayers answered) – some 37,000 cover the walls from floor to ceiling. Across the street at no. 10 is *Le Moulin de la Vierge*, a lovely Art Nouveau boulangerie-café dating from 1896. The large isolated building on the west side of the square (no. 1) once housed, as a plaque testifies, the notorious French Commissariat for Jewish Affairs (1941–44), which more than willingly collaborated in rounding up the city's Jews for deportation to German concentration camps.

Bibliothèque Nationale

58 rue de Richelieu, 2ᵉ • Mon–Sat 9am–8pm, but times vary for temporary exhibitions • Admission prices vary, depending on the exhibition • ☎ 01 53 79 59 59, Ⓦ bnf.fr • Ⓜ Bourse

Across from the Palais Royal, on the other side of rue des Petits-Champs, looms the forbidding wall of the **Bibliothèque Nationale**, part of whose enormous collection was transferred to the new François Mitterrand site (see p.178) in 1996. At the time of writing, it was undergoing major renovation work, due for completion in 2020, to improve the conditions in which the library's remaining twenty million documents are kept, and to open up more of the building to the public. Included in the renovation work (and thus also closed until 2020) is the Cabinet des Monnaies, Médailles et Antiques, a collection of coins, Etruscan bronzes, ancient Greek jewellery and other ancient treasures built up by successive kings from Philippe-Auguste onwards. Parts of the library may remain open during this period for exhibitions, though it's best to check the website for the latest updates.

The library's origins go back to the 1660s, when Louis XIV's finance minister Colbert deposited a collection of royal manuscripts here, and it was first opened to the public in 1692. It's well known for its atmospheric reading rooms, such as the huge Salle Ovale and the Salle Labrouste, with its slender iron columns supporting nine domes, a fine example of the early use of iron frame construction.

Passage Choiseul

Ⓜ Pyramides/Quatre-Septembre

West of Galerie Vivienne along rue des Petits-Champs lies one of the longest of the arcades, **passage Choiseul**. This once dark and dingy arcade is now flooded with light once more after its glass roof was repaired in 2003 and the ugly netting removed. It was here, in the early 1900s, that the author Louis-Ferdinand Céline lived as a boy, and judging by his account of it in his autobiographical *Death on Credit*, it was none too salubrious: "The gas lamps stank so badly in the stagnant air of the *passage* that towards evening some women would start to feel unwell, added to which there was the stench of dogs' urine to contend with." Nowadays the only aromas likely to assail you come from the takeaway food shops, which keep company with discount clothes and shoe stores, jewellers, galleries and well-known supplier of artists' materials, Lavrut (no. 52). Also here is an entrance to the Théâtre des Bouffes Parisiens, where in 1858 Offenbach conducted the first performance of *Orpheus in the Underworld*.

Palais Brongniart and rue Réaumur

Rue Notre-Dame des Victoires, 2ᵉ • Ⓜ Bourse

A little to the north of the Bibliothèque Nationale stands the **Palais Brongniart**, the former Paris stock exchange, or *bourse*, an imposing Neoclassical edifice built under Napoleon in 1808 and enlarged in 1903 with the addition of two side wings. With trading taking place online these days, the building is now chiefly used for conferences and trade fairs. Overshadowing the *bourse* from the south is the antennae-topped building of Agence France-Press (AFP), the French news agency.

Rue Réaumur, running east from here, used to be the Fleet Street of Paris, but all the newspapers (as in London) have now moved elsewhere. The building at no. 124, once the offices of the newspaper *Le Parisien*, is a striking Art Nouveau structure whose facade is almost entirely made of glass and metal. The street is notable in fact for its Art Nouveau architecture: other fine examples include nos. 118 and 130, as well as no. 39, with its impressive caryatids modelled on the American dancer Loïe Fuller.

Passage des Panoramas

Ⓜ Grands Boulevards/Bourse

The grid of arcades north of Palais Brongniart, just off rue Vivienne, is known as the **passage des Panoramas**, and was named after two large rotundas that once stood here showing huge panoramic paintings of cities and battle scenes. It was also around here, in 1817, that the first Parisian gas lamps were tried out. The atmosphere of the arcade during its Second Empire heyday, with its brightly glowing lamps and garish colours, cheap knick-knacks and jewellery, is vividly evoked in Emile Zola's *Nana*. Nowadays, a little shabby, but still full of charm, the *passage* combines old-fashioned chic and workaday ambience. It's long been a favourite with philatelists, who frequent the many stamp dealers, and has also become a foodie destination, with a number of delis and popular wine *bistrots*, such as *Racines* (see p.275), elbowing in among the Vietnamese and Indian takeaways. The restaurant *Canard & Champagne* at no. 57 is worth a peek for its beautiful carved-wood ornamentation dating from the 1900s, as is the shop at no. 47, which used to house the print shop Stern and has preserved its original 1834 decor.

Passages Jouffroy and Verdeau

Ⓜ Grands Boulevards

On the other side of boulevard Montmartre from the passage des Panoramas, **passage Jouffroy** is also a delight, though the recent arrival of a Marks and Spencer food shop strikes a somewhat incongruous note. Among the more appealing traditional shops are M & G Segas, selling eccentric walking canes and theatrical antiques, and Pain d'Epices (see p.356), which stocks exquisite dolls' house furnishings and fittings. Near the romantic *Hôtel Chopin* (see p.257), La Librairie du Passage's fine art books occupy three floors and spill out into the arcade, while La Maison du Roy (no. 24) has everything you might need to kit out your house in Marie Antoinette style. Crossing rue de la Grange-Batelière, you enter equally enchanting **passage Verdeau**, sheltering vintage comic books, antiquarian tomes, old prints, postcards, galleries and the embroidery shop *Le Bonheur des Dames*.

Passage des Princes

Ⓜ Richelieu Drouot

At the top of rue de Richelieu, near Richelieu Drouot métro, the tiny **passage des Princes**, with its beautiful glass ceiling, stained-glass decoration and elegant globe lamps, has been taken over by the toy emporium JouéClub. Its erstwhile neighbour, the passage de l'Opéra, described in Surrealist detail by Louis Aragon in his 1926 *Paris Peasant*, was eaten up with the completion of Haussmann's boulevards.

Hôtel Drouot

9 rue Drouot • Viewing possible 11am–6pm on the eve of the sale, 11am–noon on the day of the sale • Ⓦ drouot.com • Ⓜ Le Peletier/
Richelieu-Drouot

While in the area of the passage des Princes, you could take a look at what's up for sale at auction house **Hôtel Drouot**. It's possible simply to wander around looking at the goods before the action starts – auctions are announced in the press, under "Ventes aux Enchères". You'll find details, including photos of pieces, online at Ⓦ gazette-drouot.com.

Sentier and around

Ⓜ Sentier/Etienne Marcel

At the heart of the 2ᵉ arrondissement lies the **Sentier** *quartier*, a network of narrow streets lined with modest townhouses that are fronted by sober Classical facades. Until fairly recently, the area was the centre of Paris's rag trade, and there are still a fair number of fabric and clothes outlets, though inevitably some of the former shops have given way to trendy loft apartments. Just to the northeast of Sentier métro lies **place du Caire**; here, beneath an extraordinary pseudo-Egyptian facade of grotesque Pharaonic heads (a celebration of Napoleon's conquest of Egypt), an archway opens onto a series of arcades, the **passage du Caire**. Entirely monopolized by wholesale clothes shops (not open to the public), it is very dilapidated and little frequented these days, though it's actually the oldest (and longest) of the *passages*, built in 1798.

LE CROISSANT

Just east of Palais Brongniart, on the corner of rue du Croissant and rue Montmartre, **Le Croissant**, now a *bistrot* but once a popular drinking den, was the scene of the assassination of Socialist leader **Jean Jaurès** on July 31, 1914. He was shot by young French nationalist Raul Vilain, protesting at Jaurès' pacifism. Even if he had survived it seems unlikely that Jaurès could have held back the slide to war: just three days later Germany declared war on France. The table at which Jaurès was drinking when he was shot can still be seen.

Tour Jean Sans Peur

20 rue Etienne Marcel • Wed–Sun 1.30–6pm • €5 • ☎ 01 40 26 20 28, ⓦ tourjeansanspeur.com • Ⓜ Etienne Marcel

Bordering the Sentier district to the south is rue Etienne Marcel, which is roughly where the old medieval city wall used to run. At no. 20, a rare vestige from this period survives: the **Tour Jean Sans Peur**, a fine Gothic tower, the sole remnant of a grand townhouse that used to straddle the old wall. It was built by Jean Sans Peur, the duc de Bourgogne, who had the tower erected as a place of refuge; he feared reprisal after having assassinated Louis d'Orléans, the king's brother in 1407 – a murder that kicked off a thirty-year war between the Armagnacs and Burgundys. A spiral stone staircase (138 steps) inside the tower ends with a beautiful vaulted roof decorated with stone carvings of oak leaves, hawthorn and hops – symbols of the Burgundy family. The rooms off the staircase contain information (in English) on the tower, while temporary exhibitions focus on aspects of medieval life.

Passage du Grand-Cerf

Ⓜ Etienne Marcel

Between rue St-Denis and rue Dussoubs arches the lofty, three-storey **passage du Grand-Cerf**, one of the most attractive of all the arcades. The wrought-iron work, glass roof and plain-wood shop fronts have all been restored, attracting chic arts, craft and design shops. There's always something quirky and original on display in the window of Le Labo (no. 4), specializing in lamps and other lighting fixtures made from recycled objects, while As'Art, opposite, is a treasure-trove of home furnishings and objects from Africa.

Rue St-Denis

Ⓜ Etienne Marcel

The northern stretch of **rue St-Denis**, beyond rue Etienne Marcel, is the city's centuries-old red light area, where weary women still wait in doorways between strip clubs and sex shops. The area is changing, however, and some of the older outlets are closing down, partly because sex megastores have taken some of their business and partly because the 2ᵉ arrondissement *mairie* is attempting to clean up the area by encouraging new businesses to move in.

Rue Montorgueil and around

Ⓜ Etienne Marcel

The emphasis on rues Montmartre, Montorgueil and de Turbigo, all south of rue Réaumur, is firmly on food as they approach the Les Halles complex. Worth lingering over in particular is the picturesque, pedestrianized market street **rue Montorgueil**, where grocers, delicatessens and fishmongers ply their trade alongside cafés and traditional restaurants, such as *L'Escargot*, serving snails since 1832, and *Au Rocher du Cancale*, famous for its oysters in the nineteenth century and featured in a number of Balzac's novels. Don't miss Stohrer's pâtisserie, in business since 1730, with its exquisite cakes, and beautiful decor by Paul Baudry (1864).

Rue Montmartre is characterized by excellent kitchenware shops, such as A. Simon (see p.338), MORA and Bovida, stocking all the essential utensils for rustling up a perfect *tarte tatin* or *coq au vin*.

Beaubourg and Les Halles

Straddling the third and fourth arrondissements, the Beaubourg *quartier* hums with cafés, shops and galleries, and has the popular Pompidou Centre at its heart. Celebrating its fortieth anniversary in 2017, this iconic arts centre provoked a storm of controversy when it opened on account of its groundbreaking architecture, but has since won over critics and the public alike, becoming one of the city's most recognizable landmarks and drawing large numbers to its modern art museum and high-profile exhibitions. By contrast, nearby Les Halles, an underground shopping complex built at around the same time as the Pompidou Centre, was probably the least inspired of all the capital's late twentieth-century developments, though a recent makeover has attempted to salvage it and make it a more inviting space.

Centre Pompidou

Rue St-Martin, 4ᵉ • ⓦ centrepompidou.fr • **Centre Pompidou** Free • Mon & Wed–Sun 11am–10pm • ☎ 01 44 78 12 33 **BPI** Separate entrance 19 rue Beaubourg • Mon & Wed–Fri noon–10pm, Sat & Sun 11am–10pm • Free • ☎ 01 44 78 12 75, ⓦ www.bpi.fr • Ⓜ Rambuteau/Hôtel de Ville

Attracting more than five million visitors a year to its blockbuster art exhibitions, dance performances, films and concerts, the **Centre Pompidou**, known locally as Beaubourg, would seem to have fulfilled its founder Georges Pompidou's vision of a world-class modern art museum and multi-disciplinary arts centre. To mark its fortieth anniversary in 2017, the centre announced major renovations for 2018–20, including replacing the snake-like escalators on the outside of the building. The building is set to remain open throughout the work, but it might be advisable to check online before visiting.

When the centre first opened, it met with a very mixed reception, with one critic dubbing it an oil refinery. The building's design is certainly radical. The architects, the then unknown Renzo Piano and Richard Rogers, wanted to move away from the idea of galleries as closed treasure-chests to create something more open and accessible, so they stripped the "skin" off the building and made all the "bones" visible. The infrastructure was put on the outside: escalator tubes and utility pipes, colour-coded according to their function, climb around the exterior, giving the building its crazy snakes-and-ladders appearance.

The centre's main draw is its outstanding modern art museum, the **Musée National d'Art Moderne**, the largest in Europe, with some 120,000 works. Only a tiny fraction of the artworks can be displayed at any one time, though with the opening in 2010 of its sister gallery, the Pompidou Metz, and a new "pop-up" gallery in Málaga, Spain, many more can now be enjoyed by the public. The collection is displayed on the fourth and fifth floors, with cutting-edge temporary exhibitions on the sixth and first levels. One of the added treats of visiting the upper levels is that you get to ascend the transparent escalator on the outside of the building, affording superb views over the city. Equally good is the vista from the sleek sixth-floor restaurant *Georges*. It's possible to just go up the escalator and see the **view**; you can buy a "Vue de Paris" ticket for €5 on the ground floor.

On the lower floors there are cinemas, a performance space, café, a bookshop, design boutique and the BPI, or **Bibliothèque publique d'information**, a public reference library, which has an impressive collection of periodicals, including international press, an extensive sound and film archive and free internet access. Also worth checking out is the **Galerie de Photographies** (free) on the basement level, which organizes three exhibitions a year drawn from the centre's archive of photographs, particularly strong on the 1920s and 30s and including Man Ray and Brassaï.

If you're travelling with children you should see what's going on at the excellent **Galerie des enfants** (children must be accompanied by an adult; children's admission is free, adults need a museum ticket) on the first floor, which stages regular exhibitions and workshops.

Musée National d'Art Moderne

Pompidou Centre • Daily except Tues 11am–9pm (last entry 8pm; on Thurs temporary exhibitions open till 11pm) • Museum and exhibitions €14; under-18s free; museum (but not temporary exhibitions) free to EU residents aged 18–25, and to all first Sun of the month; tickets can be bought online or from the ticket office; audioguides are available from the ticket office, €5; guided tours take place Saturdays at noon, €4.50 • ☎ 01 53 67 40 00, ⓦ mam.paris.fr • Ⓜ Rambuteau/Hôtel de Ville

Thanks to an astute acquisitions policy and some generous gifts, the **Musée National d'Art Moderne** is a near-complete visual essay on the history of twentieth-century art. The fifth floor covers 1905 to roughly 1965, while the fourth floor takes up where the fifth floor leaves off and concentrates on contemporary art. Although works are frequently rotated, the fifth-floor layout doesn't tend to change much. The fourth-floor collection is much more fluid and undergoes a major rehang every two years (often entailing a few weeks' closure). You might consider downloading the museum's free app, which includes tours and commentaries on some of the works.

Your museum ticket is valid for a single visit only; you can't, for example, pop out for a break in one of the centre's cafés and re-enter. The collection is densely and efficiently organized, so, unlike many of the more unwieldy museums in Paris, half a day is probably enough. Queues to get in can be long; it's worth booking ahead online or going later in the day when it's a little quieter.

Fauvism

The collection on floor five is organized more or less chronologically and starts in a blaze of colour with the **Fauvists – Braque, Derain, Vlaminck** and **Matisse**. Their vibrant works

reflect the movement's desire to create form rather than imitate nature. Colour becomes a way of composing and structuring a picture, as in Braque's *L'Estaque* (1906), where trees and sky are broken down into blocks of vivid reds and greens. Matisse's series of *Luxe* paintings also stands out, the colourful nudes recalling the primitive figures of Gauguin.

Cubism

After the Fauvists, shape is broken down even further in Picasso's and Braque's early **Cubist paintings**. Highlights include **Picasso**'s portrait of his lover, Fernande (*Femme assise dans un fauteuil*; 1910), in which different angles of the figure are shown all at once, giving rise to complex patterns and creating the effect of movement. Hung alongside Picasso's works, and almost indistinguishable from them, are a number of **Braque**'s works, such as *Nature morte au violon* (1911) and *Femme à la guitare* (1913). The juxtaposition of these paintings illustrates the intellectual and artistic dialogue that went on between the two artists, who lived next door to each other at the Bateau-Lavoir in Montmartre.

Another artist heavily influenced by the new Cubism was **Fernand Léger**. In paintings such as *Femme en rouge et vert* (1914) and *Contraste de formes* (1913) Léger creates his own distinctive form of Cubism based on tubular shapes, inspired by the modern machinery of World War I, in which he fought.

Dadaism

Reaction to the horror of the 1914–18 war gave rise to the nihilistic **Dada movement**; leading members included **Marcel Duchamp**, who selected everyday objects ("ready-mades") such as the *Hat Rack* (1917), and elevated them, without modification, to the rank of works of art, simply by taking them out of their ordinary context and putting them on display. As well as the *Hat Rack*, you can inspect Duchamp's most notorious ready-made – a urinal that he called *Fontaine* and first exhibited in New York in 1917.

Abstract art

The museum holds a particularly rich collection of **Kandinsky's abstract paintings**. His series entitled *Impressions, Improvisations and Compositions* consists of non-figurative shapes and swathes of colour, and heralds a move away from an obsession with subject towards a passion for the creative process itself. Fellow pioneering abstract artists **Sonia and Robert Delaunay** set the walls ablaze with their characteristically colourful paintings. In Sonia Delaunay's wonderfully vibrant *Marché de Minho* (1916), the juxtaposition of colours makes some appear to recede and others come forward, creating a shimmering effect.

Surrealism and abstract expressionism

Surrealism, an offshoot of the Dada movement, dominates in later rooms with works by Magritte, Dalí and Ernst. Typical of the movement's exploration of the darker recesses of the mind, **Ernst**'s disturbing *Ubu Imperator* (1923) depicts a figure that is part man, part Tower of Pisa and part spinning top, and would seem to symbolize the perversion of male authority. A more ethereal, floating world of abstract associations is depicted in **Joan Miró**'s and **Jean Arp**'s canvases. **Matisse**'s later experiments with form and colour are usually on display. His technique of *découpage* (creating a picture from cut-out coloured pieces of paper) is perfected in his masterpiece *La Tristesse du roi* (1952), in which a woman dances while an elderly king plays a guitar, mourning his lost youth.

American **abstract expressionists** are also represented, including **Jackson Pollock** and **Mark Rothko**. In Pollock's splattery *No. 26A, Black and White* (1948), the two colours seem to struggle for domination; the dark bands of colour in Rothko's large canvas *No. 14 (Browns over Dark)*, in contrast, draw the viewer in.

Contemporary art

The fourth floor is given over to **contemporary art**, featuring installations, photography and video art, as well as displays of architectural models and contemporary design. Established

5

French artists such as Annette Messager, Sophie Calle, Christian Boltanski, Daniel Buren and Dominique Gonzalez-Foerster often feature, alongside newer arrivals such as Anri Sala.

Atelier Brancusi

Pompidou Centre piazza (Place Georges Pompidou) • Mon & Wed–Sun 2–6pm • Free • ☎ 01 44 78 12 33, ⓦ centrepompidou.fr • Ⓜ Rambuteau/Métro Hôtel de Ville

On the northern edge of the Pompidou Centre, down some steps off the piazza in a small, separate one-storey building, is the **Atelier Brancusi**. Upon his death in 1956, the sculptor **Constantin Brancusi** bequeathed the contents of his 15ᵉ arrondissement studio to the state, on the condition that it be reconstructed exactly as it was found. The artist had become obsessed with the spatial relationship of the sculptures in his studio, going so far as to supplant each sold work with a plaster copy, and the four interconnected rooms of the studio faithfully adhere to his arrangements. Studios one and two are crowded with fluid sculptures of highly polished brass and marble, his trademark abstract bird and column shapes, stylized busts and objects poised as though they're about to take flight. Unfortunately, the rooms are behind glass, adding a feeling of sterility and distance. Perhaps the most satisfying rooms are ateliers three and four, his private quarters, where his tools are displayed on one wall almost like works of art themselves.

Quartier Beaubourg

Ⓜ Rambuteau/Hôtel de Ville

The lively **quartier Beaubourg** around the Pompidou Centre offers much in the way of visual art. The colourful moving sculptures and fountains in the pool in front of Eglise St-Merri on **place Igor Stravinsky**, on the south side of the Pompidou Centre, were created by Jean Tinguely and Niki de Saint Phalle; the squirting waterworks pay homage to Stravinsky – each fountain corresponds to one of his compositions (*The Firebird, The Rite of Spring*, and so on) – but show scant respect for passers-by. Stravinsky's music in many ways paved the way for the pioneering work of **IRCAM** (Institut de la Recherche et de la Coordination Acoustique/Musique), whose entrance is on the west side of the square. Founded by the composer Pierre Boulez and now under the umbrella of the Pompidou Centre, it's a research centre for contemporary music and a concert venue (see p.319), much of it underground, with an overground extension by Renzo Piano. To the north of the Pompidou Centre numerous commercial art galleries and the odd bookshop and *salon de thé* occupy the attractive *hôtels particuliers* (mansions) of narrow, pedestrianized **rue Quincampoix**. Towards the bottom of the street on the east side is the charming, cobbled **passage Molière**, with some unusual shops such as Librairie Scaramouche, specializing in rare cinema posters.

Musée de la Poupée

Impasse Berthaud, 3ᵉ • **Museum** Tues–Sat 1–6pm • €8; children €4 • **Workshops** Wed 2.30pm • €14; book in advance • ☎ 01 42 72 73 11, ⓦ museedelapoupeeparis.com • Ⓜ Rambuteau

Off rue Beaubourg is the **Musée de la Poupée**, a doll museum certain to appeal to small children. In addition to the impressive collection of antique dolls, there are displays of finely detailed tiny irons and sewing machines, furniture, pots and pans, plus other minuscule accessories. There are fun **workshops** for children, such as making outfits for Barbie dolls, on Wednesday afternoons.

Hôtel de Ville

Place de l'Hôtel de Ville, 4ᵉ • **Guided tours** Once a week (days and times vary); book well ahead via email (ⓔ visites.hdv@paris.fr), or at Paris Rendez-vous • **Exhibitions** Entrance at 5 rue de Lobau • Mon–Sat 10am–6.30pm • Free • ⓦ paris.fr • **Paris Rendez-vous** 29 rue de Rivoli • ⓦ rendezvous.paris.fr • Ⓜ Hôtel de Ville

South of the Pompidou Centre, rue du Renard runs down to the **Hôtel de Ville**, the seat of the city's government and a mansion of gargantuan proportions in florid

THE PARC RIVES DE SEINE

The Parc Rives de Seine, a **riverside promenade** at the heart of Paris, was opened in 2017. Following up on the success of the Left Bank **Berges de Seine** (see p.154) a comparable section on the Right Bank riverside has now also been opened up to pedestrians and cyclists. Covering 3.3km, it extends from the Tuileries to the bassin de l'Arsenal, near the Bastille. At the time of writing, the Right Bank stretch still had a little way to go to catch up with the Left, but soon there should be a similar range of leisure **activities** on offer, such as pétanque courts, childrens' playgrounds, cafés where you can sit out and play board games, food trucks and a bike-repair station. You can walk the entire Parc Rives de Seine promenade as one continuous 5.5km stretch, starting at the Bastille, crossing over the passerelle L.S. Senghor and joining up with the promenade on the Left Bank extending nearly as far as the Eiffel tower.

neo-Renaissance style. It was built in 1882 and modelled pretty much on the previous building, which was burned down in the Commune in 1871. Weekly guided tours allow you to see some of the lavish reception rooms, decorated with murals by the leading artists of the day, such as Puvis de Chavannes and Henri Gervex. The Hôtel de Ville also stages regular free, highly popular **exhibitions** on Parisian themes, such as a recent one on the history of Les Pompiers, Paris's fire brigade. Smaller-scale exhibitions are held at **Paris Rendez-vous**, a souvenir shop and gallery within the Hôtel de Ville.

An illustrated history of the Hôtel de Ville is displayed along the platform of Châtelet métro station on the Neuilly–Vincennes line. Those opposed to the establishments of kings and emperors created their alternative municipal governments in this building: the Revolutionaries installed themselves in 1789, the poet Lamartine proclaimed the Second Republic here in 1848 and Gambetta launched the Third Republic in 1870. But, with the defeat of the Commune in 1871, the conservatives, in control once again, concluded that the Parisian municipal authority had to go if order was to be maintained and the people kept in their place. Thereafter Paris was ruled directly by the ministry of the interior until eventually, in 1977, the city was allowed to run its own affairs and Jacques Chirac was elected mayor.

Place de l'Hôtel de Ville

The **Place de l'Hôtel de Ville**, the large square in front of the Hôtel de Ville, stages occasional open-air concerts and screens live sporting events. It's also traditionally the location of a popular **ice rink** in winter (Dec–Feb Mon–Thurs noon–10pm, Fri & Sat 10am–midnight, Sun 10am–10pm; skate rental €6), though in 2016 and 2017 this was suspended; check the website ⓦparis.fr for updates. Formerly known as place de la Grève, the square used to be a shingly beach (*grève*), where boats bringing in food and supplies for the city would have docked. It was also a notorious execution site from the Middle Ages up to 1830, and witnessed many a guillotining during the Revolution.

Les Halles

ⓂLes Halles/Châtelet/RER Châtelet-Les-Halles

Located right at the heart of the city is the sprawling underground shopping and leisure complex, gardens and métro interchange of **Les Halles** (pronounced "lay al"), which has just been given a much-needed revamp. The most striking feature of the facelift is the **Canopée** ("canopy") – a vast, undulating, metal-and-glass roof, suspended over the entrance to the complex, which has allowed more light to flood into the underground **Forum des Halles** shopping mall. The roof itself, though, feels anything but light – its sheer size and weight feel oppressive as you walk under – a far cry from the original, elegant glass structures created by Victor Baltard in response to Napoléon III's request for "a covering as light as an umbrella".

THE BELLY OF PARIS

Described by Zola as *le ventre de Paris* ("the **belly of Paris**"), the original Les Halles was Paris's main **food market** for more than eight hundred years until it was moved out to Rungis in the suburbs in 1969. Victor Baltard's elegant nineteenth-century iron pavilions were largely destroyed (two were saved – one is in Nogent-sur-Marne, the other in Yokohama, Japan) to make way for the ugly **Forum des Halles** glass-and-steel shopping mall plus the huge suburban rail and métro station, the biggest in Europe. The working-class quarter, with its night bars and *bistrots* for market traders, was largely swept away, and the area developed an unsavoury reputation for petty drug dealing. This "urban catastrophe", as Mayor Anne Hidalgo once described it, has been a source of much shame and regret on the part of the Paris authorities ever since; the attempt to retrieve it is a welcome step, but for many Parisians the destruction of Les Halles is an act of self-sabotage that can never be repaired.

The redevelopment also includes newly landscaped gardens (the Jardin Nelson-Mandela), a library, a music and arts conservatoire and, perhaps most significantly, a **hip-hop** performance and workshop space, La Place ⓦ laplace.paris, the first of its kind in the capital and in part an acknowledgement of the popularity of Les Halles with the *banlieusards* – the young people who come in from the housing estates in the suburbs.

Forum des Halles

ⓦ forumdeshalles.com **Forum des Images** Tues–Fri 12.30–9pm, Sat & Sun 2–9pm • ☎ 01 44 76 63 00, ⓦ forumdesimages.fr • Ⓜ Les Halles/Châtelet/Châtelet/RER Châtelet Les Halles

The **Forum des Halles** is spread over four levels. On the bottom level is the métro/RER station, where five métro lines and three suburban lines intersect, used by some 750,000 commuters a day. The other levels accommodate numerous shops, mostly high-street fashion chains (H&M, Zara, Muji and Gap, to name a few), though there's also a decent Fnac bookshop. Leisure facilities include a swimming pool (see p.346) and a number of cinemas, including the **Forum des Images**, which houses five screens, a café (*Le 7e Bar*) and an archive of some nine thousand films, many connected with Paris and any of which you can watch in your own private booth in the Salle des Collections (Wed–Sun 2–9pm; €6 for up to 2hr).

St-Eustache

2 impasse St-Eustache, 1ᵉʳ • Ⓜ Les Halles

For an antidote to the Forum des Halles' steel-and-glass troglodytism, head for the soaring vaults of the beautiful church of **St-Eustache**, on the north side of the gardens. Built between 1532 and 1637, the church is Gothic in structure, with lofty naves and graceful flying buttresses, and Renaissance in decoration – all Corinthian columns and arcades. Molière, Richelieu and Madame de Pompadour were baptized here, while Rameau and Marivaux were buried in the building. The side chapels contain some minor works of art, including, in the tenth chapel in the ambulatory, an early Rubens (*The Pilgrims at Emmaus*) and, in the sixth chapel on the north side, Coysevox's marble sculpture over the tomb of Colbert, Louis XIV's finance minister. In the Chapelle St-Joseph there is a naive relief by British artist Raymond Mason, *The Departure of Fruit and Vegetables from the Heart of Paris, 28 February 1969*, showing a procession of market traders, resembling a funeral cortege, leaving Les Halles for the last time. The church has a long and venerable musical tradition and is a popular venue for **concerts** and **organ recitals** (Sun 5.30–6pm; free); the *grand orgue* is reputedly the largest in France, with eight thousand pipes.

Bourse de Commerce

2 rue de Viarmes, 1ᵉʳ • Ⓜ Louvre Rivoli

Facing the Canopée at the western end of Les Halles gardens stands the striking **Bourse de Commerce**, the city's former corn market, an eighteenth-century circular building under a glass cupola, which is being converted into a museum of contemporary art, the **Paris Collection Pinault**, due to open at the end of 2018. The artworks, including pieces by Damien Hirst and Mark Rothko, will come from the huge collection built up by the luxury goods billionaire François Pinault, who already has an art museum in Venice and has long been seeking a Paris outlet for his collection. It is hoped by the Paris authorities that the new museum will further help to revitalize the Les Halles quarter.

Fontaine des Innocents

Place Joachim du Bellay, 1ᵉʳ • Ⓜ Les Halles/Châtelet

Looking slightly marooned amid the fast-food joints, tattoo parlours and shoe shops of place Joachim du Bellay is the perfectly proportioned Renaissance **Fontaine des Innocents** (1549), adorned with reliefs of water nymphs. On warm days shoppers sit on its steps, drawn to the coolness of its cascading waters. The fountain takes its name from the cemetery that used to occupy this site, the Cimetière des Innocents, which was closed in 1786 and its contents transferred to the catacombs in Denfert-Rochereau.

Châtelet and around

Ⓜ Châtelet

The labyrinth of tiny streets heading southeast from Les Halles to **place du Châtelet** teems with jazz bars, clubs and restaurants, and is far more crowded at 2am than at 2pm. One of these streets, narrow little rue de la Ferronnerie, was the scene of Henri IV's assassination in 1610. A plaque at no. 11 marks the spot where Henri's carriage came to a standstill, caught in the seventeenth-century equivalent of a traffic jam, giving his assassin, religious fanatic Ravaillac, the chance to plunge his dagger into the king's breast.

Théâtre du Châtelet and Théâtre de la Ville

Place du Châtelet, 1ᵉʳ • Ⓜ Châtelet

Place du Châtelet was once the site of a notorious fortress prison and is now a maelstrom of traffic overlooked by two of the city's most prestigious theatres, the **Théâtre du Châtelet** (see p.320) and the **Théâtre de la Ville** (see p.317), built in the 1860s during Haussmann's *grands travaux*. The latter was formerly known as the Théâtre Sarah Bernhardt (changed to Théâtre des Nations during the German occupation on account of Bernhardt's Jewish origins) after the great actress bought it and regularly performed on stage here until her death in 1923.

Tour St-Jacques

Rue de Rivoli, 1ᵉʳ • **Guided tours** July & Aug Mon & Fri–Sun 10am–5pm, Sept & Oct Fri–Sun 10am–5pm • €10 • Ⓦ desmotsetdesarts .com • Ⓜ Châtelet

One block north of the place du Châtelet stands the **Tour St-Jacques**. Built in Flamboyant style and dating from the early sixteenth century, it's all that remains of the Eglise St-Jacques-de-la-Boucherie, which was built by butchers from nearby Les Halles and destroyed in the Revolution. The church used to be an important stopping point for pilgrims on their way to Santiago de Compostela. At the base of the tower a statue commemorates Blaise Pascal, who carried out experiments on atmospheric pressure here in the seventeenth century. The tower is now used as a weather station and monitors pollution and air quality. Organized visits of the tower are held in summer; book online in advance.

The Marais

The Marais is one of the most seductive areas of central Paris, known for its sophistication and artsy leanings, and for being the neighbourhood of choice for LGBT+ Parisians. Largely untouched by Baron Haussmann and modern development, it preserves its enchanting narrow streets and magnificent Renaissance *hôtels particuliers* (mansions). Some of these mansions have become chic flats, boutiques and commercial art galleries, while others provide grand settings for a number of excellent museums, not least among them the splendidly revamped Musée Picasso, the Musée Carnavalet history museum and the Musée d'Art et d'Histoire du Judaïsme. As the Marais is one of the few areas of the city where places open on a Sunday, many Parisians come here for brunch and a leisurely afternoon's shopping.

The area was little more than a riverside swamp (*marais*) up until the thirteenth century, when the Knights Templar (see p.104) moved into its northern section and began to drain the land. It became a magnet for the aristocracy in the early 1600s after the construction of the place des Vosges by Henri IV in 1605. This golden age was relatively short-lived, however, for the aristocracy began to move away after the king took his court to Versailles in the latter part of the seventeenth century, leaving their grand houses to the trading classes, who were in turn displaced during the Revolution. From this point on, the mansions became slum tenements and the streets degenerated into squalor. It was only in the 1960s, with its designation as a *secteur sauvegardé* (a conservation area), that efforts were made to smarten up the neighbourhood and improve living conditions.

The main artery running through the Marais, dividing it roughly north and south, is the busy **rue de Rivoli** and its continuation to the Bastille, rue St-Antoine. South of this line is the quieter **quartier St-Paul**, with its antique shops and atmospheric backstreets. To the north lies the beautiful **place des Vosges**; the old **Jewish quarter** centred on rue des Rosiers; and the Marais' other main street, **rue des Francs-Bourgeois**, lined with aristocratic mansions and chic fashion and interior-design boutiques. Other streets worth exploring are rue Vieille du Temple, with its terraced cafés and bars, and the streets further north in the trendy **Haut Marais**, home to young designers and contemporary art galleries.

Place des Vosges and around

Ⓜ Bastille/Chemin Vert/St-Paul

Whether you approach via the narrow streets from Bastille or from the north or west, nothing quite prepares you for the size and grandeur of the **place des Vosges**, a magnificent square bordered by arcaded pink-brick and stone mansions, with a **formal garden** at its centre. A masterpiece of aristocratic elegance and the first example of planned development in the history of Paris, the square was commissioned in 1605 by Henri IV, and was inaugurated in 1612 for the wedding of Louis XIII and Anne of Austria; it is Louis' statue – or, rather, a replica of it – that stands hidden by chestnut trees in the middle of the gardens. Originally called place Royale, it was renamed Vosges in 1800 in honour of the *département*, the first to pay its share of the expenses of the revolutionary wars.

A royal palace, the Hôtel des Tournelles, stood on what is now the north side of the square until 1559, when it was demolished by Catherine de Médicis after her husband Henri II was killed here during a joust. The vacant space became a huge weekly horse market, trading between one and two thousand horses. So it remained until Henri IV decided on the construction of his place Royale.

Through all the vicissitudes of history, the *place* has never lost its cachet as a smart address. Today, the **arcades** harbour upmarket art, antique and fashion shops, as well as a number of restaurants and cafés. Buskers play classical music and jazz, and in the garden toddlers play in the sandpits and families picnic on the grass; this is one of the few Parisian gardens where the grass is not out of bounds.

Maison de Victor Hugo

6 place des Vosges, 4ᵉ • Tues–Sun 10am–6pm; closed hols • Free • ☎ 01 42 72 10 16, ⓦ maisonsvictorhugo.paris.fr • Ⓜ Bastille

Among the many celebrities who made their homes in the place des Vosges was Victor Hugo; the second-floor apartment at no. 6, where he lived from 1832 to 1848 and wrote much of *Les Misérables*, is now a museum, the **Maison de Victor Hugo**. Hugo's life, including his nineteen years of exile in Jersey and Guernsey, is evoked through a somewhat sparse collection of memorabilia, portraits, photographs and first editions of his works. What you do get, though, is an idea of the writer's prodigious creativity: as well as being a prolific author, he drew – a number of his ink drawings are exhibited –

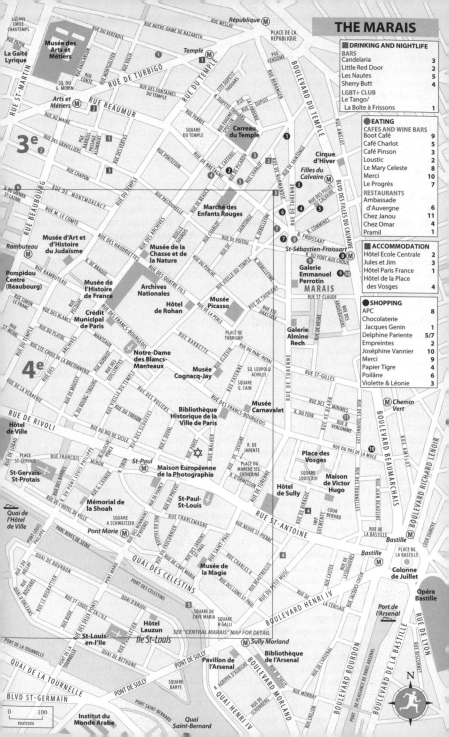

and designed his own Gothic-style furniture, in which he let his imagination run riot, as seen in some of the pieces displayed. He even put together the extraordinary Chinese-style dining room, originally designed for the house of his lover, Juliette Drouet, in Guernsey, re-created in its entirety here. Among the family portraits is one by Auguste de Châtillon of Hugo's daughter, Léopoldine, shown holding a Book of Hours open at the Dormition of the Virgin – a poignant detail, given that eight years later at the age of 19 she drowned, along with her husband of just six months. Her loss inspired some of Hugo's most moving poetry, including the well-known *Demain dès l'aube*.

Hôtel de Sully

62 rue St-Antoine, 4ᵉ • Ⓦ hotel-de-sully.fr • Ⓜ St-Paul/Bastille

From the southwest corner of the place des Vosges, a door leads through to the formal château garden, orangerie and exquisite Renaissance facade of the **Hôtel de Sully**. The garden (daily 9am–7pm), with its park benches, makes for a peaceful rest stop; it's also a handy shortcut through to rue St-Antoine. The *hôtel* is the headquarters of the Centre des Monuments Nationaux, which manages more than a hundred national monuments and publishes numerous books and guides, many of which are on sale in the excellent ground-floor bookshop near the rue St-Antoine entrance; it's also worth a look for its fine seventeenth-century painted beamed ceiling.

A short distance to the west along rue St-Antoine, almost opposite the sixteenth-century **church of St-Paul-St-Louis**, which was inaugurated by Cardinal Richelieu, you'll find another square. A complete contrast to the imposing formality of the place des Vosges, the tiny **place du Marché Ste-Catherine**, with its trees and little restaurant terraces, is intimate and irresistibly charming.

Rue des Francs-Bourgeois and around

Ⓜ St-Paul/Rambuteau

Running west from the place des Vosges, the main lateral street of the northern part of the Marais is the narrow **rue des Francs-Bourgeois**. Beatnik Jack Kerouac translated it as "the street of the outspoken middle classes", which is a fair description of the contemporary residents, though the name in fact means "people exempt from tax", referring to the penurious inmates of a medieval almshouse that once stood on the site of no. 34.

Along and just off this street lie some of the Marais' finest mansions, such as the superb **Musée Carnavalet**, which traces the history of Paris; the bijou **Musée Cognacq-Jay**, devoted to eighteenth-century art and decorative arts; the engaging **Musée d'Art et d'Histoire du Judaïsme**; and the **Musée de l'Histoire de France**, the state archives museum, housed in one of the grandest mansions of all.

Musée Carnavalet

23 rue de Sévigné, 4ᵉ • ☎ 01 44 59 58 58, Ⓦ carnavalet.paris.fr • Ⓜ St-Paul

The **Musée Carnavalet**, the fascinating museum of Paris's history, is currently closed for an extensive revamp and will reopen at the beginning of 2020. The two beautiful Renaissance mansions (Hôtel Carnavalet and Hôtel Le Peletier) that house the museum will be renovated, and its extraordinary collection of works from the early Neolithic beginnings of Paris to the modern day, including paintings, original interior decors, furnishings, sculptures and artefacts from the French Revolution, will be reorganized and made more accessible to visitors.

La Galerie des Bibliothèques and around

22 rue Mahler • Tues–Sun 1–7pm, Thurs till 9pm • €16 • ☎ 01 72 63 40 74, Ⓦ bibliocite.fr • Ⓜ St-Paul

The **Galerie des Bibliothèques** is an exhibition space that draws on documents and artefacts from the city's libraries. Past shows have included Charles Trenet, Paris during the war years and the great flood of 1910. Much of the material for these exhibitions is drawn from the huge archives of the nearby **Bibliothèque Historique de la Ville de Paris** (Mon–Sat 10am–6pm; ☎01 44 59 29 40, ⊕bibliotheques-specialisees.paris.fr), housed in the splendid sixteenth-century Hôtel Lamoignon on rue des Francs-Bourgeois. Next to the Lamoignon on rue Pavée – so-called because it was among the first of Paris's streets to be paved, in 1450 – was the site of **La Force prison**, where many of the Revolution's victims were incarcerated, including the Princesse de Lamballe, who was lynched in the massacres of September 1792; her head was presented on a stake to her friend Marie Antoinette.

Musée Cognacq-Jay

8 rue Elzévir, 4ᵉ • Tues–Sun 10am–6pm • Free • ☎ 01 40 27 07 21, ⊕ museecognacjay.paris.fr • Ⓜ St-Paul/Chemin Vert

One block west of the Musée Carnavalet lies the intimate **Musée Cognacq-Jay**, occupying the fine Hôtel Donon. The Cognacq-Jay family built the Samaritaine department store, and were noted philanthropists, as well as lovers of eighteenth-century European art. Their small collection of pieces on show includes a handful of works by Canaletto, Fragonard, Rubens and Quentin de la Tour, as well as an early Rembrandt and an exquisite still life by Chardin, displayed in beautifully carved wood-panelled rooms filled with Sèvres porcelain and Louis XV furniture.

Musée de l'Histoire de France

60 rue des Francs-Bourgeois, 4ᵉ • Mon, Wed–Fri 10am–5.30pm, Sat & Sun 2–5.30pm • €3–6 • ☎ 01 40 27 60 96, ⊕ www.archives-nationales.culture.gouv.fr • **Gardens** Daily: April–Oct 8am–8pm; Sept–March 8am–5pm • Free • Ⓜ Rambuteau/St-Paul

At the western end of the rue des Francs-Bourgeois there once stood a magnificent, early eighteenth-century palace complex, filling the entire block from rue des Archives to rue des Quatre Fils, and from rue Vieille-du-Temple to rue des Francs-Bourgeois. Only half remains today, but it is utterly splendid, especially the grand colonnaded courtyard of the **Hôtel de Soubise**, with its fabulous Rococo interiors, paintings by Boucher and vestigial fourteenth-century towers on rue des Quatre Fils. A stroll through the adjoining, rather charming **gardens** allows you to admire the setting all the more.

The Hôtel de Soubise houses a large number of the city archives, dating from the period before 1790, and the **Musée de l'Histoire de France**, which mounts changing exhibitions drawn from its extensive holdings; the museum's fascinating haul includes Joan of Arc's trial proceedings, with a doodled impression of her in the margin, and a Revolutionary calendar, where "J" stands for Jean-Jacques Rousseau and "L" for "labourer". The *hôtel's* ground-floor Chambre du Prince is the scene of **chamber music recitals** (€14), held here most Saturdays, usually at 7pm, and sometimes Wednesday lunchtimes (often free).

The **Hôtel de Rohan**, near the Musée de l'Histoire de France, is part of the archives complex and is sometimes used when there are large exhibitions. Its fine interiors include the Chinese-inspired Cabinet des Singes, whose walls are painted with monkeys acting out various aristocratic scenes.

Crédit Municipal de Paris

55 rue des Francs-Bourgeois, 4ᵉ • La Galerie du Crédit Municipal: Mon–Fri 9am–6pm, Sat 9am–5pm, closed between exhibitions • Free • ☎ 01 44 61 64 00, ⊕ creditmunicipal.fr • Ⓜ Rambuteau/St-Paul

Opposite the Hôtel de Soubise stands the **Crédit Municipal de Paris**, formerly the Mont-de-Piété, a kind of state-run pawn shop (now with normal banking facilities too), in existence since 1637; any items that are not redeemed are sold at auction. It's started hosting free exhibitions on a range of interesting themes, such as a recent one on Paris street art. It's also worth peeking at the building's fine courtyard, which bears traces of the old medieval wall that used to encircle Paris; for the past two years it has hosted a pop-up café/bar during the summer months (June–Sept) and seems set to make it an annual event.

CENTRAL MARAIS

ACCOMMODATION

Hôtel Bourg Tibourg	3	Hôtel de Nice	4
Hôtel de la Bretonnerie	7	Hôtel du Petit Moulin	1
Caron de Beaumarchais	5	Hôtel St-Louis Marais	10
Le Fauconnier	9		
Le Fourcy	8		
Hôtel Jeanne d'Arc	6		
Maubuisson	7		

DRINKING AND NIGHTLIFE

BARS

La Belle Hortense	8
La Perle	3
Stolly's	11

LGBT+ BARS AND CLUBS

3W-Kafé	10
Café Cox	7
CUD	2
Le Duplex	1
Le Free DJ	5
L'Open Café	6
Le Raidd	4
Le So What	12
Les Souffleurs	9

LIVE MUSIC

Péniche le Marcounet	13

SHOPPING

Antoine et Lili	7	La Fausse Boutique	20
Aubade	14	Free "P" Star	26
Autour du Monde	19	French Trotters	3
Ba&sh	12	K Jacques	24
Le BHV Marais	18	Lemaire	2
CSAO	8	Maje	10
Delphine Pariente	25	Mamz'Elle Swing	23
Dominique Picquier	4	Marché des Enfants Rouges	1
L'Eclaireur	16	Mariage Frères	13
Entrée des Fournisseurs	21		

Matières à Réflexion	5		
Mélodies Graphiques	29		
Les Mots à la Bouche	11		
Papier Plus	28		
Petit Pan	27		
Sacha Finkelsztajn/ Boutique Jaune	15		
Sandro	9/22		
Vanessa Bruno	6		
Zadig & Voltaire	17		

EATING

CAFES AND WINE BARS

L'As du Fallafel	7
La Caféothèque	13
L'Ebouillanté	11
Le Loir dans la Théière	10
Marché des Enfants Rouges	1
Les Philosophes	8
Pozzetto	9

RESTAURANTS

Breizh Café	3
Chez Hanna	6
Grand Coeur	5
Métropolitain	12
La Petite Maison dans la Cour	14
Pink Flamingo	4
Le Potager du Marais	2

0 ___ 100 metres

Further east, beyond several more imposing facades, you can admire the delicate filigree ironwork of the balcony above the main entrance to the **Hôtel d'Albret** (no. 31), built in 1740, its stately courtyard a delightful setting for occasional concerts in summer.

Musée de la Chasse et de la Nature

62 rue des Archives, 3ᵉ • Tues–Sun 11am–6pm, Wed till 9.30pm • €8, free for under-18s and to everyone first Sun of the month • ☎ 01 53 01 92 40, ⓦ chassenature.org • Ⓜ Rambuteau

Housed in the beautiful Hôtel Guénégaud and the neighbouring Hôtel Mongelas, the **Musée de la Chasse et de la Nature** largely explores the theme of hunting, especially animals of the hunt. The museum starts with a series of rooms, each of which is devoted to a particular animal, such as the wild boar, wolf and dog. A "cabinet of curiosities" invites you to pull open drawers and discover miscellaneous bits and bobs, such as paw prints, animal droppings and drawings, and you can look through eyeglasses and watch a video of each animal in its natural habitat – all quite appealing to children in particular. The rest of the collection includes a formidable array of stuffed animals, including a giant polar bear, weapons ranging from prehistoric stone arrowheads to highly decorative crossbows and guns, and paintings by French artists, such as Desportes, romanticizing the chase.

Musée d'Art et d'Histoire du Judaïsme

71 rue du Temple, 3ᵉ • Tues–Fri 11am–6pm, Sat & Sun 10am–6pm (open Wed till 9pm during temporary exhibitions) • €9, under-18s free • ☎ 01 53 01 86 53, ⓦ mahj.org • Ⓜ Rambuteau

One block west of the Musée de la Chasse et de la Nature stands the attractively restored Hôtel de St-Aignan, home to the **Musée d'Art et d'Histoire du Judaïsme**. The museum traces the culture, history and artistic endeavours mainly of the **Jews in France**, though there are also many artefacts from the rest of Europe and North Africa. The result is a very comprehensive collection, as educational as it is beautiful. Free audioguides in English are available and worth picking up if you want to get the most out of the museum.

The medieval period to the nineteenth century

Highlights of the museum's holdings from the **medieval period to the nineteenth century** include a Gothic-style Hanukkah lamp, one of the very few French-Jewish artefacts to survive from the period before the expulsion of the Jews from France in 1394; an Italian gilded circumcision chair from the seventeenth century; and a completely intact, late nineteenth-century Austrian *sukkah*, "a temporary dwelling built for the celebration of the Harvest, decorated with paintings of Jerusalem and the Mount of Olives". Other artefacts include Moroccan wedding garments, highly decorated marriage contracts from eighteenth-century Modena and gorgeous, almost whimsical, spice containers.

The Dreyfus archives

The **Dreyfus archives**, donated to the museum by Dreyfus's grandchildren, document the notorious **Dreyfus affair** (see box, opposite) through letters, photographs and press clippings; you can read Emile Zola's famous letter *J'accuse…!* in which the novelist defends Dreyfus's innocence, as well as the letters Dreyfus sent to his wife from prison on Devil's Island in which he talks of *épouvantable* ("terrible") suffering and loneliness.

The twentieth century

The museum also hosts a significant collection of paintings and sculpture by **Jewish artists** – Marc Chagall, Samuel Hirszenberg, Chaïm Soutine and Jacques Lipchitz – who came to live in Paris at the beginning of the twentieth century. The Holocaust is only briefly touched on, since it's dealt with in depth by the Musée de la Shoah (see p.107). The main reference is an installation by contemporary artist Christian Boltanski: one of the exterior walls of a small courtyard is covered with black-bordered death announcements printed with the names of the Jewish artisans who once lived in the building, a number of whom were deported.

THE DREYFUS AFFAIR

The **Dreyfus Affair** was one of the biggest crises to rock the Third Republic. It centred on Alfred Dreyfus, a captain in the French army and a Jew, who was arrested and **convicted of spying** for the Germans in 1894 on the flimsiest of evidence – his handwriting was said to resemble that on documents detailing French armaments found in the German embassy. In a humiliating public ceremony of "*dégradation*" in the courtyard of the Ecole Militaire, his epaulettes were torn from his uniform and his sword broken, while anti-Semitic slogans were chanted by crowds outside. He was then sent to the notorious penal colony of Devil's Island, off Guyana. His family, convinced of his innocence, began campaigning for a retrial. Two newspapers, *L'Eclair* and *Le Matin*, questioned the evidence, and in 1897 Colonel Georges Picquart, the new head of the Statistical Section, discovered a document which suggested that the true culprit was Major Ferdinand Walsin-Esterhazy. Esterhazy was perfunctorily tried by the Ministry of War, and let off. The government, keen to uphold the army's authority and reputation, acquiesced to the verdict, and Colonel Picquart was packed off to Tunisia.

However, a storm broke out when shortly afterwards writer **Emile Zola** published his famous open letter, titled *J'accuse…!*, to the President of the Republic in the *Aurore* newspaper on January 13, 1898. In it he denounced the army and authorities and accused them of a cover-up. Zola was convicted for libel and sentenced to a year's imprisonment, which he avoided by fleeing to England. The article triggered a major outcry and suddenly the *affaire* was the chief topic of conversation in every café in France. French society divided into two camps: Dreyfusards and anti-Dreyfusards. The former, convinced the army was guilty of a cover-up, comprised republicans committed to equal rights and the primacy of parliament and included many prominent intellectuals and left-wing figures such as Jean Jaurès, Anatole France, Léon Blum, Georges Clemenceau and Marcel Proust. Ranked among the anti-Dreyfusards were clerics, anti-Semitic newspapers such as *La Libre Parole*, monarchists and conservatives, all suspecting a Jewish conspiracy to tarnish the army's reputation. The former clamoured for justice, while the latter called for respect and order.

In June 1897, the secret dossier that convicted Dreyfus was finally re-examined; there was a retrial and, again, Dreyfus was convicted of treason, but was quickly pardoned by President Loubet, desperate to draw a line under the whole affair. Finally, in 1906, Dreyfus, his health broken by hard labour, was granted a **full pardon** and awarded the *Légion d'honneur*. The matter was formally closed, but the repercussions of the affair were deep and long-lasting; it had revealed fundamental divisions in French society, and split the country along lines that would determine France's development in the twentieth century.

The Jewish quarter: rue des Rosiers

Ⓜ St-Paul

One block south of the rue des Francs-Bourgeois, the area around narrow, pedestrianized **rue des Rosiers** has traditionally been the **Jewish quarter** of the city since the twelfth century. However, soaring property prices and the area's burgeoning popularity with tourists have forced many of the traditional grocers, bakers, bookshops and cafés to close, and the area is in real danger of losing its identity. The hammam (no. 4) now houses a clothing store, as does *Jo Goldenberg* (no. 7), once the city's most famous Jewish restaurant. Despite these changes, the area still retains a Jewish flavour, with a number of kosher food shops and a Hebrew bookshop. There's also a distinctly Mediterranean feel in the *quartier*; on Sunday lunchtimes the street fills with people who come to pick up a falafel wrap from one of the handful of Middle Eastern cafés. This development is testimony to the influence of the **North African Sephardim**, who, since the end of World War II, have sought refuge here from the uncertainties of life in the French ex-colonies. They have replenished Paris's Jewish population, depleted when its Ashkenazim, having escaped the pogroms of Eastern Europe, were rounded up by the Nazis and the French police and transported back east to concentration camps. Another vestige of the strong Yiddish community that once lived here is the lovely Art Nouveau **synagogue** designed by Hector Guimard on nearby rue Pavée.

6

The Haut Marais

Ⓜ Filles du Calvaire/St-Sebastien-Froissart

The northern part of the Marais, known as the **Haut Marais** ("upper Marais"), encompasses the old **Quartier du Temple**, named after the Knights Templar's stronghold that once stood at its heart, and the city's original **Chinatown**, concentrated on the upper end of rue du Temple and the streets to the west. Here the aristocratic stone facades of the lower Marais give way to the more humble, though no less attractive, stucco, paint and thick-slatted shutters of seventeenth- and eighteenth-century streets. Some bear the names of old rural French provinces: Beauce, Perche, Saintonge, Picardie. Formerly a quiet backwater, the area now attracts an arty crowd who come to browse the many contemporary art galleries (see box, below), interior design shops and boutiques of young fashion designers concentrated on **rue Charlot**, rue de Poitou, rue Vieille-du-Temple and around. The area's chief visitor attractions are the revamped **Musée Picasso**, the absorbing **Musée des Arts et Métiers** and the state-of-the-art **La Gaîté Lyrique** digital arts centre.

Musée Picasso

5 rue de Thorigny, 3ᵉ • Tues–Fri 10.30am–6pm, Sat & Sun 9.30am–6pm, last entry 5.15pm • €12.50; free to under-18s and under-26s from (or studying in) the EU; free to everyone first Sun of the month • ☏ 01 85 56 00 36, ⓦ museepicassoparis.fr • Ⓜ Chemin Vert/St-Paul

On the northern side of rue des Francs-Bourgeois, rue Payenne leads up to the lovely gardens and houses of **rue du Parc-Royal** and on to **rue de Thorigny**. Here, at no. 5, the magnificent classical facade of the seventeenth-century **Hôtel Salé**, built for a rich salt-tax collector, conceals the **Musée Picasso**, which in 2014 emerged from a major five-year renovation. The museum now has three times as much exhibition space available to display its five thousand paintings, drawings, ceramics, sculptures and photographs – one of the largest collections of Picasso's work anywhere, representing

---

PRIVATE ART GALLERIES IN THE MARAIS

The Marais, and the Haut Marais in particular, is where most of the city's private **commercial art galleries** are concentrated. Many occupy handsome old mansions, which are set back from the road and reached via cobbled courtyards. Below are some of the highlights; all are free to visit. A handy **guide** to the best galleries is the *Galeries mode d'emploi*, usually available in the galleries themselves, and downloadable online from ⓦ fondation-entreprise-ricard.com or available as an app.

Galerie Almine Rech 64 rue de Turenne, 3ᵉ ☏ 01 45 83 71 90, ⓦ alminerech.com; Ⓜ St-Sébastien-Froissart; map p.96. Installed in an elegant gallery, Rech represents around fifty artists, including Ugo Rondinone and Jeff Koons. Tues–Sat 11am–7pm.

Galerie Chantal Crousel 10 rue Charlot, 3ᵉ ☏ 01 42 77 38 87, ⓦ crousel.com; Ⓜ Filles du Calvaire; map p.99. Around since 1980, this gallery (which also has an annexe in the 10ᵉ at 11F rue Léon Jouhaux) represents mostly foreign and some French artists, such as Thomas Hirschhorn and Mona Hatoum, working in a variety of media. It also promotes the work of video artists, such as Pierre Huyghe. Tues–Sat 11am–1pm & 2–7pm.

Galerie Emmanuel Perrotin 76 rue de Turenne, 3ᵉ ☏ 01 42 16 79 79, ⓦ perrotin.com; Ⓜ St-Sébastien-Froissart; map p.96. One of the most influential galleries on the French contemporary art scene, Perrotin has exhibited French artists like Sophie Calle as well as international names such as Takashi Murakami and Maurizio Cattelan. Tues–Sat 11am–7pm.

Galerie Marian Goodman 79 rue du Temple, 3ᵉ ☏ 01 48 04 70 50, ⓦ mariangoodman.com; Ⓜ Rambuteau; map p.99. This offshoot of the famed New York gallery exhibits the works of renowned artists such as Tacita Dean, Steve McQueen and Rineke Dijkstra. Tues–Sat 11am–7pm.

Galerie Thaddeus Ropac 7 rue Debelleyme, 3ᵉ ☏ 01 42 72 99 00, ⓦ ropac.net; Ⓜ Filles du Calvaire; map p.99. Recent exhibitions at this well-established gallery have included Robert Rauschenberg and Robert Mapplethorpe. Also well worth a visit is Ropac's enormous outpost just outside the city in Pantin, near La Villette, sited in a former factory and ideal for showing large-scale installations and sculptures by the likes of Anselm Kiefer and Georg Baselitz. Tues–Sat 10am–7pm.

almost all the major periods of the artist's life from 1905 onwards. Many of the pieces were owned by Picasso and, on his death in 1973, were donated to the state by his family in lieu of taxes owed. The result is an unedited body of work, which, although not including the most recognizable of Picasso's masterpieces, nevertheless provides a sense of the artist's development and an insight into the person behind the myth.

As the museum is very popular, it's worth reserving tickets in advance to avoid long queues. The free museum map provides a fair amount of information on the works displayed, but to really get the most out of your visit you might want to reserve a "visioguide" (€5) with your ticket online or download the same as an app. The small *Café sur le Toit*, with an outside terrace, is a nice spot for a restorative cuppa.

The collection

The **collection**, spread over four floors, from level −1 to floor 2, includes **paintings** from the artist's Blue Period, studies for the *Demoiselles d'Avignon*, experiments with Cubism and Surrealism, as well as larger-scale works on themes of war and peace (eg the chilling *Massacre in Korea*, 1951) and his later preoccupations with love and death, which are reflected in his Minotaur and bullfighting paintings. Among the works that stand out are the more personal paintings – the portraits of the artist's lovers, Dora Maar and Marie-Thérèse, show how the two women inspired him in different ways: Dora Maar is painted with strong lines and vibrant colours, suggesting a vivacious personality, while Marie-Thérèse's muted colours and soft contours convey serenity and peace.

The numerous **engravings**, **ceramics** and **sculpture** on display reflect the remarkable ease with which the artist moved from one medium to another. Some of the most arresting sculptures are those Picasso created from recycled household objects, such as the endearing *La Chèvre* (The Goat), whose stomach is made from a basket, its udders from terracotta pots; and the *Tête de taureau*, an ingenious pairing of a bicycle seat and handlebars. Also fascinating to see are the paintings Picasso bought or was given by contemporaries such as Matisse and Cézanne; his collection of African masks and sculptures; and photographs taken by Dora Maar and Brassaï of Picasso in his studio, including one of him painting *Guernica*, cigarette in one hand, paintbrush in the other.

Marché des Enfants Rouges

39 rue de Bretagne, 3e • Tues–Sat 8.30am–2pm & 4–7.30pm, Sun 8.30am–2pm • Ⓜ Filles du Calvaire

Just west of rue Charlot, a little short of the vibrant rue de Bretagne, is the easily missed entrance to the **Marché des Enfants Rouges**, one of the smallest and oldest food markets in Paris, dating back to 1616, its name a reference to the red uniforms once worn by children at the orphanage that stood nearby. It has a very lively atmosphere and outdoor tables where you can eat takeaway soups, couscous, sushi and much else (see p.279). **Rue de Bretagne** itself is full of traditional food shops including cheesemongers, bakeries and coffee merchants, as well as some popular cafés such as *Café Charlot* (see p.276) and *Le Progrès* (see p.278).

Carreau du Temple

4 rue Eugène Spuller, 3e • ☎ 01 83 81 93 30, ⓦ carreaudutemple.eu • Ⓜ Temple

A former market pavilion, the **Carreau du Temple** was converted in 2014 into an arts and sports centre. The shell of the nineteenth-century brick, glass and iron-frame structure has been preserved to create a wonderfully light and elegant space for all kinds of events from cocktail-tasting to jazz concerts, salons, plays and fashion shows. The lower floor has dance studios and a gym, and there's also a stylish bar-restaurant, *Le Jules*. On the lower floor you can see vestiges of the old **Temple keep**, a 50m-high turreted building that used to stand on this site; this was where Louis XVI and the royal family were imprisoned before their execution (see box, opposite).

The Carreau and the nearby **Square du Temple** gardens stand on what was once the Enclos du Temple, or Temple precinct, the stronghold of the **Knights Templar**, a

THE TEMPLE AND LOUIS XVII

Louis XVI, Marie Antoinette, their two children and immediate family were all **imprisoned** in the keep of the Knights Templar's ancient fortress in August 1792 by the revolutionary government. By the end of 1794, when all the adults had been executed, the two children – the teenage Marie-Thérèse and the 9- or 10-year-old Dauphin, now, in the eyes of royalists, **Louis XVII** – remained there alone, in the charge of a family called Simon. Louis XVII was literally walled up, allowed no communication with other human beings, not even his sister, who was living on the floor above (Marie-Thérèse, incidentally, survived, went into exile in 1775, and returned to France in 1814 with the Bourbon restoration). He died of tuberculosis in 1795, a half-crazed imbecile, and was buried in a public grave.

For many years afterwards, however, **rumours** circulated that Louis XVII was in fact alive. The doctor, for example, who certified the child's death kept a lock of his hair, but it was later found not to correspond with the colour of the young Louis XVII's hair, as remembered by his sister. Furthermore, Mme Simon confessed on her deathbed that she had substituted another child for Louis XVII, giving rise to the theory that the real Louis had died early in 1794 and been replaced with another child, in order to provide Robespierre with a hostage he could use against internal and foreign royalist enemies.

Taking advantage of this atmosphere of uncertainty, 43 different people subsequently claimed to be Louis XVII. After nearly two centuries of speculation, all rumours were put to rest in 2000 when **DNA** from the child who died of TB was found to match samples obtained from locks of Marie Antoinette's hair, and also that of several other maternal relatives.

military order established in Jerusalem at the time of the Crusades to protect pilgrims to the Holy Land. Its members were exceedingly rich and powerful, with some nine thousand commands spread across Europe. They came to a sticky end early in the fourteenth century, however, when King Philippe le Bel, alarmed at their growing power, and in alliance with Pope Clement V, had them tried for sacrilege, blasphemy and sodomy. Fifty-four of the order's members were burnt, and the order abolished. The Temple buildings survived until they were demolished in 1808 by Napoleon.

Rue du Temple

Ⓜ Arts et Métiers/Temple

A couple of blocks to the west of the Carreau du Temple, on and around the top end of **rue du Temple**, lies Paris's original **Chinatown**. The area was settled during World War I when Chinese immigrants came over to fill the gap in the workforce left by the departure of French troops for the front. Rue du Temple, lined with many beautiful houses dating back to the seventeenth century, is full of Chinese-run wholesale businesses trading in leather and fashion accessories, as well as jewellers' shops, a hangover from the times when this formed part of the Temple precinct, the inhabitants of which were accorded special privileges such as tax exemption and the exclusive right to make costume jewellery.

The streets to the west of rue du Temple are narrow, dark and riddled with passages, the houses half-timbered and bulging with age. No. 51 rue de Montmorency is Paris's oldest house, built in 1407 for the alchemist Nicolas Flamel, whose name will ring a bell with *Harry Potter* fans; the building is now a restaurant, *Auberge Nicolas Flamel*.

Musée des Arts et Métiers

60 rue de Réaumur, 3ᵉ • Tues–Sun 10am–6pm, Thurs till 9.30pm • €8 • ☎ 01 53 01 82 00, Ⓦ arts-et-metiers.net • Ⓜ Arts et Métiers

The **Musée des Arts et Métiers** is a fascinating museum of technological innovation. It's part of the Conservatoire des Arts et Métiers and incorporates the former Benedictine priory of St-Martin-des-Champs, its original chapel dating from the fourth century. The most important exhibit is **Foucault's pendulum**, which the scientist used to demonstrate the rotation of the earth in 1851, a sensational event held at the Panthéon in Rome and attended by a huge crowd eager to "see the earth go round". The orb itself, a hollow brass sphere, is under glass in the chapel, and there's a working model set up nearby.

Other exhibits include the laboratory of Lavoisier, the French chemist who first showed that water is a combination of oxygen and hydrogen, and, hanging as if in mid-flight above the grand staircase, the elegant "Avion 3", a flying machine complete with feathered propellers, which was donated to the Conservatoire after several ill-fated attempts to fly it.

La Gaîté Lyrique

3bis rue Papin, 3ᵉ • Tues–Sat 2–8pm, Sun 2–6pm • ☎ 01 53 01 51 51, Ⓦ gaite-lyrique.net • Ⓜ Réaumur-Sébastopol/Arts et Métiers

The **Gaîté Lyrique** is a dynamic centre for digital arts and electronic music. This venerable Italian-style theatre, built in 1862, was once renowned as a venue for operettas under such illustrious directors as Jacques Offenbach, and hosted the Ballets Russes in the 1920s. The facade, entrance hall and splendid first-floor marble foyer (a wonderful setting for the café) have been restored, and the interior has been opened up to accommodate a state-of-the-art concert hall, exhibition spaces, artists' studios and a free video-games room. The busy programme of events includes regular concerts, film, dance and theatre performances, art installations and exhibitions on contemporary themes; its recent exhibition "Aéroport: Ville-Monde" saw the creation of a virtual "airport" using music, robotics and digital art.

Quartier St-Paul

Ⓜ St-Paul/Sully-Morland/Pont Marie

The southern part of the Marais, the **Quartier St-Paul**, between the rue de Rivoli, rue de St-Antoine and the Seine, is less buzzy than the rest of the district, its quiet, atmospheric streets lined with attractive old houses. The chief sights are the moving **Mémorial de la Shoah**, with its museum documenting the fate of French Jews in World War II; the **Maison Européenne de la Photographie**, which hosts exhibitions by contemporary photographers; and the **Pavillon de l'Arsenal**, a showcase for the city's current architectural projects. The area is also a good hunting ground for antiques, concentrated mostly in the **Village St-Paul** and rue St-Paul.

St-Gervais-St-Protais

Place St-Gervais, 4ᵉ • Ⓜ Hôtel-de-Ville

There's been a church on the site of **St-Gervais-St-Protais** since the sixth century; the current building was started in 1494, though not completed until the seventeenth century, which explains the mismatched late Gothic interior and Classical exterior. There's some lovely stained glass inside, sixteenth-century carved misericords and a seventeenth-century organ; it's one of Paris's oldest and has been played by eight generations of the Couperin family, including the famous François Couperin. The third chapel down on the right commemorates the 88 victims of a German shell that hit the church on Good Friday 1918 and caused part of the nave to collapse.

Exiting the church round the altar at the back, you enter cobbled **rue des Barres**, a picturesque little street, filled with the scent of roses from nearby gardens in summer, and a nice setting for the outdoor terrace of *L'Ebouillanté* café (see p.278).

Mémorial de la Shoah

17 rue Geoffroy l'Asnier, 4ᵉ • Mon–Fri & Sun 10am–6pm, Thurs till 10pm • Free • Every second Sun of the month at 3pm there's a free guided visit in English • ☎ 01 42 77 44 72, Ⓦ memorialdelashoah.org • Ⓜ St-Paul/Pont Marie

The grim fate of French Jews in World War II is commemorated at the **Mémorial de la Shoah**, within the Centre de Documentation Juive Contemporaine. President Chirac opened a new museum here in 2005 and, alongside the sombre **Mémorial du Martyr Juif Inconnu** (Memorial to the Unknown Jewish Martyr), unveiled a Wall of Names; ten researchers spent two and a half years trawling Gestapo documents and interviewing French families to compile the list of the 76,000 Jews – around a quarter of the wartime population – sent to death camps from 1942 to 1944. In 2006, the **Mur des Justes** was added, a wall listing the names of French people who aided Jews at this time.

Chirac, in 1995, was the first French president to acknowledge that France was involved in systematically persecuting Jews during World War II. In most instances, it was the French police, not the Nazi occupiers, who rounded up the Jews for deportation. The most notorious case was in July 1942, when 13,152 Jews (including more than 4000 children) were rounded up in the Vel d'Hiv bicycle stadium in Paris and sent to concentration camps.

The museum

The Vel d'Hiv incident, along with much else, is documented in the excellent **museum**, with plenty of information in English. The main focus is events in France leading up to and during World War II, but there is also lots of background on the history of Jews in France and in Europe as a whole. Individual stories are illustrated with photos, ID cards, letters and other documents. You learn about model citizens such as the Javel family, who were all deported and died in the camps, their long-established residence in France and distinguished record of military service counting for naught in the relentless Nazi drive to exterminate all Jews. Others, such as the Lifchitz family, who fled pogroms in Russia and settled in France in 1909, managed to survive the war – in this case by going into hiding and obtaining false ID as Orthodox Christians. The collection also features drawings and letters from Drancy, the holding station outside Paris, from which French Jews were sent on to camps in Germany. The museum ends with the **Mémorial des Enfants**, an overwhelming collection of photos, almost unbearable to look at, of 2500 French children, each image marked with the date of their birth and the date of their deportation.

Maison Européenne de la Photographie

4 rue de Fourcy, 4ᵉ • Wed–Sun 11am–7.45pm • €8 • ☎ 01 44 78 75 00, ⓦ mep-fr.org • Ⓜ St-Paul/Pont Marie

Between rues de Fourcy and François-Miron, a gorgeous Marais mansion, the early eighteenth-century Hôtel Hénault de Cantobre, houses the **Maison Européenne de la Photographie**, dedicated to the art of contemporary photography. Temporary shows combine with a revolving exhibition of the permanent collection; young photographers and photojournalists get a look-in, as well as artists using photography in multi-media creations or installation art. There's also a library, *vidéothèque* (video library) and stylish café.

Hôtel de Sens

1 rue de Figuier, 4ᵉ • Ⓜ St-Paul/Pont Marie

Standing in isolation on the rue du Figuier, the turreted **Hôtel de Sens**, dating back to the fifteenth century, has been nearly completely reconstructed – perhaps too much so, as it jars somewhat with the rest of its surroundings. The public library that it now houses, the **Bibliothèque Forney**, filled with volumes on fine and applied arts, frequently hosts excellent, free exhibitions (Tues–Sat 1–7pm), such as a recent one on women's fashion during World War I.

Village St-Paul

Ⓜ St-Paul/Pont-Marie

East of the Maison Européenne de la Photographie is **Village St-Paul**, a network of courtyards and streets housing around a hundred antique, interior-design and art shops. This part of the Marais suffered a postwar hatchet job, and, although seventeenth- and eighteenth-century magnificence is still in evidence (there's even a stretch of the city's defensive wall dating from the early thirteenth century in the *lycée* playground on rue des Jardins St-Paul), it lacks the architectural cohesion of the Marais to the north.

Musée de la Magie

11 rue St-Paul, 4ᵉ • Wed, Sat & Sun 2–7pm; live magic show every 30min 2.30–6pm • €13, children €10 • ☎ 01 42 72 13 26, Ⓦ museedelamagie.com • Ⓜ St-Paul/Sully-Morland

Set amid the antique shops on rue St-Paul is the **Musée de la Magie**, a delightful museum of magic and illusion. Automata, distorting mirrors and optical illusions, objects that float on thin air, plus a box for sawing people in half – they're all on view, with examples from the eighteenth and nineteenth centuries, as well as contemporary magicians' tools and hands-on exhibits for children. Most fun is a live magician's demonstration. The museum shop sells books on conjuring, plus magic cards, wands, boxes, scarves and the like. School groups tend to visit on Wednesdays, so it's better to visit at weekends.

Pavillon de l'Arsenal

21 bd Morland, 4ᵉ • Tues–Sat 10.30am–6.30pm, Sun 11am–7pm • Free • ☎ 01 42 76 33 97, Ⓦ pavillon-arsenal.com • Ⓜ Sully-Morland

The **Pavillon de l'Arsenal** is an exhibition centre that presents the capital's current **architectural projects** to the public. There's also a permanent exhibition on Paris's architectural development, centring on a huge interactive screen on the floor showing Google Earth images of Paris; superimposed on it are all the major construction projects planned over the next twenty years, so you can bring up a projected image of what, for example, the Clichy-Batignolles district will look like when the new development is complete.

Bastille and around

A symbol of revolution since the toppling of the Bastille prison in 1789, the Bastille quarter used to belong in spirit and style to the working-class districts of eastern Paris. After the construction of the opera house in the 1980s, however, it became a magnet for artists, fashion folk and young people, who brought with them over the years stylish shops and an energetic nightlife. Much of the action takes place around rues Amelot, de Charonne and de Lappe, where cocktail lounges and theme bars have edged out the old tool shops, cobblers and ironmongers. However, some of the working-class flavour lingers on, especially along rue de la Roquette and in the furniture workshops off rue du Faubourg-St-Antoine, testimony to a long tradition of cabinet making and woodworking in the district.

South of Bastille, the relatively unsung **twelfth arrondissement** offers an authentic slice of Paris, with its neighbourhood shops and bars, plus traditional markets, such as the lively Marché d'Aligre. Attractions include the **Promenade Plantée**, an ex-railway line turned into an elevated walkway running from Bastille to the green expanse of the **Bois de Vincennes**, and **Bercy Village**'s appealing cafés and shops set in old wine warehouses.

Place de la Bastille

Ⓜ Bastille

The vast **Place de la Bastille**, its centre marked by a green-bronze commemorative column, is indissolubly linked with the events of July 14, 1789, when the Bastille prison fortress was stormed, triggering the **French Revolution** and the end of feudalism in Europe. **Bastille Day** (July 14) is celebrated throughout France and the square is the scene of dancing and partying on the evening of July 13; it still has strong symbolic value and is often the starting point for rallies and demos. The prison itself no longer stands – paving stones set into the cobbles between boulevard Henri-IV and rue Sainte-Antoine show the outline of the fortress, and its only visible remains have been transported to square Henri-Galli at the end of boulevard Henri-IV. The constant hurly-burly of the traffic around the place de la Bastille hardly invites you to linger and ponder its historical significance, though at the time of writing, work was under way to give it a major facelift over the next couple of years, part of a city-wide project to revamp Paris's landmark squares, including the place de la Nation (see p.114). There are plans to reduce the volume of traffic and make it more pedestrian-friendly, with the addition of benches, trees and plants.

Opéra Bastille

Place de la Bastille, 11ᵉ · ☎ 08 92 89 90 90 (from within France), ☎ 01 71 25 24 23 (from abroad), ⓦ operadeparis.fr · Ⓜ Bastille

The Bicentennial of the French Revolution in 1989 was marked by the inauguration of a new opera house on place de la Bastille, the **Opéra Bastille**, one of François Mitterrand's pet projects. It fills almost the entire block between rues de Lyon, de Charenton and Moreau. One critic described it as a "hippopotamus in a bathtub", and you can see his point. The architect, Uruguayan Carlos Ott, was concerned that his design should not bring an overbearing monumentalism to place de la Bastille. The different depths and layers of the semi-circular facade do give a certain sense of the building stepping back, but self-effacing it is not. With time, use and familiarity, Parisians became reconciled to it, and today people happily sit on its steps, wander into its shops and libraries, and camp out all night for the free performance on July 14. Guided tours are available in French only (1hr 30min; book online at ⓦ operadeparis.fr; €15).

THE COLONNE DE JUILLET

A gleaming gold statue, a winged figure of Liberty, stands atop the bronze **Colonne de Juillet** at the centre of place de la Bastille. The plinth on which it stands was once intended to hold quite a different monument – **Napoleon** had wanted a giant elephant fountain to stand here, with a spiral staircase inside one leg and a viewing platform on top. The project never came to fruition, but the full-scale model that was made became a curiosity in its own right and stood for a while near the Gare de Vincennes (Gavroche in Victor Hugo's *Les Misérables* sought shelter in it). After 35 years it was sold for 3833 francs. The same architect (Jean-Antoine Alavoine) who had worked on the elephant built the present column, which was erected to commemorate the **July Revolution of 1830**, replacing the autocratic Charles X with the "Citizen King" Louis-Philippe. When Louis-Philippe fled in the more significant 1848 Revolution, his throne was burnt beside the column and a new inscription was added. Four months later, the workers again took to the streets. All of eastern Paris was barricaded, with the fiercest fighting on rue du Faubourg-St-Antoine (see p.369), until the rebellion was quelled with the usual massacres and deportation of survivors.

Port de l'Arsenal

Ⓜ Bastille

Just south of the place de la Bastille is the **Port de l'Arsenal** marina, occupying part of what was once the moat around the Bastille. The Canal St-Martin starts here, flowing underneath the square and emerging much further north, just past place de la République, a route plied by canal pleasure-boats run by Canauxrama (see p.27). Some two hundred boats are moored up in the marina, and the landscaped banks, with children's playgrounds, make it quite a pleasant spot for a wander.

Maison Rouge

10 bd de la Bastille, 11ᵉ • During exhibitions Wed–Sun 11am–7pm, Thurs till 9pm • €10 • ☎ 01 40 01 08 81, ⓦ lamaisonrouge.org •
Ⓜ Bastille/Quai de la Rapée

One of the former industrial spaces bordering the port de l'Arsenal has been converted into a light and spacious contemporary art gallery, called the **Maison Rouge – Fondation Antoine de Galbert**. Founded in 2004 by collector Antoine de Galbert, the Maison Rouge, which takes its name from the bright-red pavilion at the centre of the building, has become a major player on the contemporary art scene, hosting quality exhibitions, either devoted to an individual artist or a private collection. The presence of a branch of *Rose Bakery* here also makes it a nice place for a bite to eat. The whole place closes between exhibitions; check online before visiting.

East of place de la Bastille

Northeast of place de la Bastille, off rue de la Roquette, narrow, cobbled **rue de Lappe** is a lively place at night, crammed with bars drawing a largely teenage and out-of-town crowd. At no. 32, *Balajo* is one remnant of a very Parisian tradition: the *bals musettes*, or music halls of 1930s *gai Paris*, established by the area's large Auvergnat population and frequented between the wars by such luminaries as Edith Piaf, Jean Gabin and Rita Hayworth. It was founded by one Jo de France, who introduced glitter and spectacle into what were then seedy gangster dives, enticing Parisians from the other side of the city to drink absinthe and savour the rue de Lappe lowlife. Parisians are still drawn here and to the bars on neighbouring streets, such as **rue Daval** to the north.

Off rue Daval, on the left as you walk up from rue de Lappe, is charming little pedestrianized **cour Damoye**, a narrow cobbled street formerly lined with furniture workshops and now mostly inhabited by architects' studios and design shops. Other streets worth exploring are the nearby section of **rue de Charonne**, home to fashion boutiques and wacky interior designers, and **rue Keller**, clustered with alternative, hippie outfits, indie record stores and young fashion designers.

Rue de la Roquette

Ⓜ Bastille/Voltaire

Parallel to rue de Charonne is buzzy **rue de la Roquette**, which is home to cheap and cheerful shops, Turkish restaurants and local bars. Towards its eastern end is **square de la Roquette**, the site of an old prison, where four thousand members of the Resistance were incarcerated in 1944. The low, forbidding gateway on rue de la Roquette has been preserved in their memory.

Rue du Faubourg-St-Antoine

Ⓜ Bastille/Ledru-Rollin/Faidherbe-Chaligny

After Louis XI licensed the establishment of craftsmen in the fifteenth century, the **rue du Faubourg-St-Antoine**, running east from place de la Bastille, became the principal working-class *quartier* of Paris, cradle of revolutions and mother of street-fighters. From its beginnings, the principal trade associated with it has been **furniture making**,

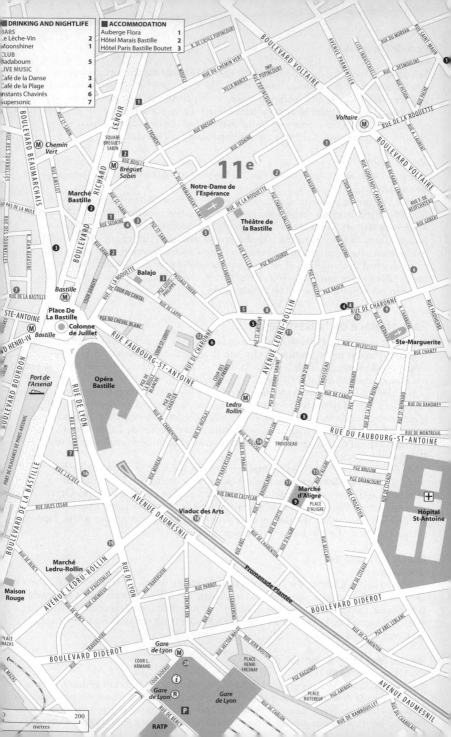

11ᵉ

Notre-Dame de l'Espérance

Théâtre de la Bastille

Balajo

Place De La Bastille

Colonne de Juillet

Bastille

Marché Bastille

Chemin Vert

Bréguet Sabin

Square Bréguet-Sabin

Voltaire

Ste-Marguerite

Port de l'Arsenal

Opéra Bastille

Ledru Rollin

Marché d'Aligre

Place d'Aligre

Viaduc des Arts

Marché Ledru-Rollin

Maison Rouge

Hôpital St-Antoine

Promenade Plantée

Gare de Lyon

Gare de Lyon

Place Henri Fresnay

RATP

metres   200

BASTILLE AND EAST

Empire – were developed. There are still quite a few furniture shops on the street, and a number of workshops, as well as related trades such as inlayers, stainers and polishers, continue to inhabit the maze of interconnecting yards and *passages* that run off the faubourg, especially at the western end. One of the most attractive courtyards is at no. 56, the cour du Bel Air, with its lemon trees and ivy- and rose-covered buildings.

Place de la Nation
Ⓜ Nation

Rue du Faubourg-St-Antoine leads eastwards to the huge **place de la Nation**, which is currently undergoing major work to make it a more attractive and pedestrian-friendly green space. At the centre of the *place* stands a monumental bronze group, the *Triumph of the Republic*, topped with a stately female figure personifying the Republic. To the east, framing the avenue du Trône, are two tall Doric columns, surmounted by statues of medieval monarchs, which look very small and insignificant. During the Revolution, when the old name of place du Trône became place du Trône-Renversé ("the overturned throne"), more people were guillotined here in six weeks than on the more notorious execution site of place de la Concorde (see p.70). The bodies of the victims were buried in communal graves at the nearby **Cimetière de Picpus** (35 rue de Picpus; Mon–Sat 2–5pm; €2; ☎01 43 44 18 54); even today, only those descended from victims of the Terror are allowed to be interred here. One descendant, Adrienne de Noailles, lies buried next to her husband, General Lafayette, whose tomb is visited by the American ambassador in a special ceremony every July 4.

Marché d'Aligre
Ⓜ Ledru-Rollin

South of rue du Faubourg-St-Antoine is the **Marché d'Aligre**, a lively, raucous market, held every morning except Monday, and particularly animated on Saturdays and Sundays. The square itself is given over to clothes and bric-a-brac stalls, selling anything from old gramophone players to odd bits of crockery. There's also a covered food market with traditional *fromageries* and charcuteries, plus more unusual stalls such as Sur les Quais, selling numerous varieties of olive oil. It's along the adjoining **rue d'Aligre**, however, where the market really comes to life, with the vendors, many of Algerian origin, doing a frenetic trade in fruit and veg. As the market winds down, you could follow the locals to the old-fashioned *Le Baron Rouge* wine bar (see p.280) for a glass of wine and some *saucisson*, or drink in the North African atmosphere at the *Ruche à Miel* café (see p.280) at 19 rue d'Aligre and order some mint tea with sticky cakes.

The Promenade Plantée and around
Ⓜ Bastille/Ledru-Rollin

The **Promenade Plantée**, also known as the Coulée Verte, is an excellent way to see a little-visited part of the city – and from an unusual angle. This disused railway viaduct, part of the old Paris–Cherbourg line, has been ingeniously converted into an **elevated walkway**, similar to New York's High Line, and planted with a profusion of trees and flowers – cherry trees, maples, limes, roses and lavender.

The walkway starts near the beginning of **avenue Daumesnil**, just south of the Opéra Bastille, and is reached via a flight of stone steps – or lifts (though these are frequently out of order) – with a number of similar access points further along. It takes you to the Jardin de Reuilly, then descends to ground level and continues as far as the *boulevard périphérique*, from where you can walk to the Bois de Vincennes. The whole route is around 4.5km long, but if you don't feel like doing the entire thing you could just complete the first part, along the viaduct – a twenty-minute stroll – which also happens to be the most attractive stretch, running past venerable old mansion blocks and giving you a bird's-eye view of the street below. Small architectural details such as decorative mouldings and elaborate wrought-iron balconies (not to mention elegant interiors) that you wouldn't normally notice at street level come to light – the oddest sight is the series of caryatids adorning the police station at the end of avenue Daumesnil.

Viaduc des Arts
Ⓜ Bastille/Gare de Lyon/Ledru-Rollin
Underneath the Promenade Plantée, the red-brick arches of the viaduct itself have been converted into attractive spaces for artisans' studios and craft shops, collectively known as the **Viaduc des Arts**. The workshops house a wealth of creativity: furniture and tapestry restorers, interior designers, cabinet-makers, violin- and flute-makers, embroiderers, plus fashion and jewellery designers.

Jardin de Reuilly
Ⓜ Montgallet/Dugommier
The Viaduc des Arts ends around halfway down avenue Daumesnil, but the Promenade Plantée continues, taking you to the **Jardin de Reuilly**, an old freight station that is now an inviting, circular expanse of lawn, popular with picnickers on sunny days and bordered by terraces and arbours. The open-air café here makes a good refreshment stop if you're walking the length of the *promenade*. You can also choose to bypass the park altogether by taking the gracefully arching wooden footbridge that spans it.

Allée Vivaldi to the boulevard périphérique
Towards the eastern end of the Promenade Plantée walkway is the nondescript **allée Vivaldi**, which is lined with modern blocks. Next, you go through a tunnel to emerge in the old railway cutting, a delightful stretch that meanders through a canopy of trees and flowers below street level. At this point the path divides into two – one for pedestrians, the other for cyclists – landscaped all along, taking you through a series of ivy-draped ex-railway tunnels and shadowing the rue du Sahel for most of the way. The walk ends at the *boulevard périphérique*. From here you're not far from the Porte Dorée métro station and the Porte Dorée entrance to the **Bois de Vincennes**. A pathway to the right takes you behind a sports stadium (with the *périphérique* on your left) before turning into rue Edouard Lartet, then rue du Général Archinard. At the end of this turn left into avenue du Général Messimy, which leads into the main avenue Daumesnil; the métro station is to the right, and the entrance to the *bois* is to the left.

Bercy
Ⓜ Bercy
The former warehouse district of **Bercy**, along the Seine east of the Gare de Lyon, was transformed in the late 1990s by a series of ambitious and ultramodern developments designed to complement the grand-scale "Paris Rive Gauche" project (see p.178) on the opposite bank.

Ministère des Finances
139 rue de Bercy, 12e • Ⓜ Bercy
As you emerge from Bercy métro station, the first thing you notice is the imposing bulk of the **Ministère des Finances**, constructed in 1990 to house the treasury staff after they had finally agreed to move out of the Richelieu wing of the Louvre. Housing some 4700 employees, it stretches like a giant loading bridge from above the river (where higher bureaucrats and ministers arrive by boat) to rue de Bercy, a distance of around 400m.

Parc de Bercy

Parc Mon–Fri 8am–sunset, Sat & Sun 9am–sunset • Free • **Maison du Jardinage** April–Sept Tues–Fri 1.30–5.30pm, Sat & Sun 1.30–6.30pm; Oct–March Tues–Sat 1.30–5pm • Free • Ⓜ Bercy

Southeast of the Ministère des Finances squats the charmless **AccorHotels Arena**. Built in 1983, its concrete bunker frame, clad with grass, covers a vast space used for sporting and cultural events (see p.346). Beyond it, the area that used to house the old Bercy warehouses, where for centuries the capital's wine supplies were unloaded from river barges, is now the extensive **Parc de Bercy**. Here, the French formal garden has been given a modern twist with geometric lines and grid-like flowerbeds, but it also cleverly incorporates elements of the old warehouse site such as disused railway tracks and cobbled

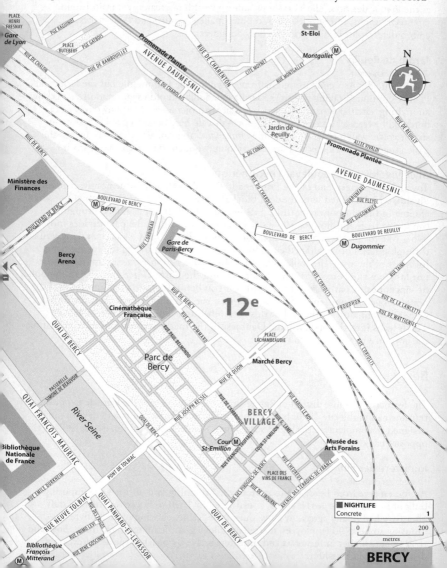

lanes. The western section of the park is a fairly unexciting expanse of grass with a huge stepped fountain (popular with children) set into one of the grassy banks, but the area to the east is attractively landscaped with arbours, rose gardens, lily ponds and an orangerie. There's also a **Maison du Jardinage**, a garden exhibition centre, where you can consult gardening books and magazines and visit the adjoining greenhouse and vegetable garden.

Cinémathèque Française

51 rue de Bercy, 12ᵉ • **Museum** Mon & Wed–Sun noon–7pm • €5, free Sun 10am–1pm • ☎ 01 71 19 33 33, ⓦ cinematheque.fr • Ⓜ Bercy

Of the new buildings surrounding the Parc de Bercy, the most striking, on the north side, is the **Cinémathèque**. Designed by Guggenheim architect Frank Gehry, it's constructed from zinc, glass and limestone and resembles a falling pack of cards – according to Gehry, the inspiration was Matisse's collages, created "with a simple pair of scissors". Its huge archive of films dates back to the earliest days of cinema, and regular retrospectives of French and foreign films are screened in its four cinemas (see p.310). It also has an engaging **museum**, tracing the history of cinema, with lots of early cinematic equipment, magic lanterns, silent-film clips and costumes, including outfits from Eisenstein's *Ivan the Terrible*. On the upper floor, the **Galerie des Donateurs** stages exhibitions on the work of various film directors such as François Truffaut, or on other cinema-related themes.

Cour St-Emilion

Ⓜ Cour St-Emilion

A little east of the Cinémathèque, arched footbridges take you over the busy rue Joseph Kessel into the eastern extension of the park and the adjoining **Bercy Village**, the hub of which is the **Cour St-Emilion**, a pedestrianized, cobbled street lined with former wine warehouses that have been stylishly converted into shops, restaurants and wine bars. These are popular places to come before or after a film at the giant Bercy multiplex at the eastern end of the street, particularly on Sundays when shops in many other areas of Paris are closed.

Musée des Arts Forains

53 av des Terroirs-de France, 12ᵉ • Daily tours (1hr 30min) to be booked in advance by phone or online (visits are at 11am, 2.30pm & 4.30pm) • €16, children €8 • ☎ 01 43 40 16 15, ⓦ arts-forains.com • Ⓜ Cour St-Emilion

A set of old stone wine warehouses contains the privately owned funfair museum, the **Musée des Arts Forains**, with its collection of nineteenth- and early twentieth-century funfair rides (which you can try out), fairground music and Venetian carnival rooms. It's only open to groups, though individuals can join a tour if they book in advance; tours are in French, but you can ask for a leaflet in English.

Vincennes

Ⓜ Porte Dorée/Porte de Charenton/Château-de-Vincennes

Beyond the 12ᵉ arrondissement, across the *boulevard périphérique*, lies the **Bois de Vincennes**, the largest green space the city has to offer aside from the Bois de Boulogne in the west. The main draws are the **Parc Floral**, an attractive park with an adventure playground, and the **zoo**. To the east the **Cartoucherie de Vincennes**, an old munitions factory, is home to four theatre companies, including the radical Théâtre du Soleil (see p.315), while bordering the Bois to the north stands the **Château de Vincennes**, the country's only surviving medieval royal residence. West of the Bois de Vincennes is the **Cité Nationale de l'Histoire de l'Immigration**, devoted to the history of immigration in France.

Bois de Vincennes

Ⓜ Porte Dorée/Porte de Charenton/Château de Vincennes; buses #46 and #86

The extensive **Bois de Vincennes** was once a royal hunting ground roamed by deer; nowadays, unfortunately, it's crisscrossed with roads, but it does have some pleasant corners, including the Parc Floral and the two lakes. The sights are quite a long distance from each other, so you may want to target one or two, or you could pick up a Vélib' bike (see p.29) from near the entrance to the Parc Floral or near Lac Daumesnil.

Parc Floral

Bois de Vincennes • Daily 9.30am–8pm, winter till dusk • Free except June–Sept Wed, Sat & Sun, when entry is €5.50 • ☎ 01 49 57 24 84, Ⓦ www.parcfloraldeparis.com • Ⓜ Château de Vincennes, then bus #112 or a short walk

If you've only got a limited amount of time in the Bois de Vincennes, first make for the **Parc Floral**, just behind the Château de Vincennes. This is one of the best gardens in Paris – flowers are always in bloom in the Jardin des Quatre Saisons, and you can picnic beneath pines, then wander through camellias, rhododendrons, cacti, ferns, irises and bonsai trees. Between April and September there are art and horticultural exhibitions in several pavilions, free jazz and classical concerts, and numerous activities for children including a mini-golf course studded with miniature Parisian monuments and an adventure playground (see p.351).

The lakes and around

For a lazy afternoon in the park, you could go boating on the **Lac Daumesnil**, near the Porte Dorée entrance, or feed the ducks on the **Lac des Minimes** (bus #112 from Vincennes métro), on the other side of the wood.

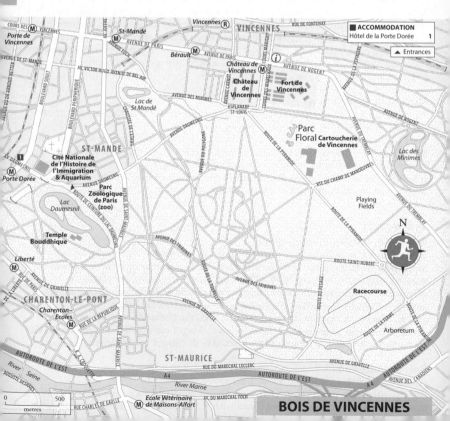

Parc Zoologique de Paris

Junction of av Daumesnil and route de Ceinture du Lac Daumesnil, 12ᵉ • April, Sept & Oct Mon–Fri 10am–6pm, Sat, Sun & hols daily 9.30am–7.30pm; May–Aug daily 10am–8.30pm (till 10.30pm on Thurs in June & July); Nov to mid-March daily except Tues 10am–5pm • €22, 3–11-year-olds €14, 12–25-year-olds €16.50 • ☎ 08 11 22 41 22, ⓦ parczoologiquedeparis.fr • Ⓜ Porte Dorée

North of the Lac Daumesnil lies the **Parc Zoologique de Paris**, the city's main **zoo**, reopened in 2014 after a six-year closure. Its landmark Grand Rocher, an extraordinary 65m-high fake boulder, built in 1934 when the zoo first opened, is still here, but just about everything else has been completely rebuilt. The zoo has tried to improve conditions for its one thousand-odd animals (representing 180 species) by re-creating as far as possible their natural habitats. Animals are grouped by region rather than by type: Patagonia, Sahel-Sudan, Europe, Guyana and Madagascar. As well as the more usual lions and zebras, there are less well known and endangered species such as manatees, wolverines, anteaters and white rhino. Highlights include the giant tropical hothouse harbouring tortoises, iguanas, caimans and other reptiles; and the giraffe house, where you get a great view of the leggy beasts from the glass viewing balcony. Plenty of information is provided on the animals and their habitats in French only, though you can buy an English-language leaflet for €3 from the ticket office. There are picnic areas, two restaurants and plenty of snack stands.

Château de Vincennes

Donjon Daily: mid-May to mid-Sept 10am–6pm; rest of year 10am–5pm • **Sainte-Chapelle** Daily: mid-May to mid-Sept 10.30am–1pm & 2–5.15pm; rest of year 10.30am–1pm & 2–6.15pm • €9, under-18s free • ☎ 01 48 08 31 20, ⓦ chateau-vincennes.fr • Ⓜ Château de Vincennes

On the northern edge of the Bois de Vincennes stands the **Château de Vincennes**, which is enclosed by an impressive defensive wall and surrounded by a (now empty) moat. It was built by Charles V, and subsequently by turns transformed into a state prison, porcelain factory, weapons dump and military training school. It presents a rather austere aspect on first sight, but is worth visiting for its beautiful Flamboyant Gothic **Sainte-Chapelle**, completed in the mid-sixteenth century and decorated with superb Renaissance stained-glass windows. Nearby, in the impressive fourteenth-century **donjon** (keep), you can see some fine vaulted ceilings and Charles V's bedchamber, as well as graffiti left by prisoners, whose number included the Marquis de Sade. The château fell into the hands of the English in the fifteenth century and it was in Charles V's bedchamber that Henry V of England died of dysentery.

Cité Nationale de l'Histoire de l'Immigration

293 av Daumesnil, 12ᵉ • Tues–Fri 10am–5 30pm, Sat & Sun 10am–7pm • €4.50–6, free for under-26s and for all on the first Sun of the month; aquarium €5–7, children €3.50–5 • ☎ 01 53 59 58 60, ⓦ histoire-immigration.fr • Ⓜ Porte Dorée

Just outside the Bois de Vincennes, across the way from the Porte Dorée entrance, a huge Art Deco building, the Palais de la Porte Dorée, houses the **Cité Nationale de l'Histoire de l'Immigration**, which examines the history of immigration to France over the last two centuries (around fifteen million French citizens have foreign roots) through photos, artwork, multi-media displays and audio installations. The museum is located in a building erected for the 1931 Colonial Exhibition and sports a vast, somewhat dubious bas-relief illustrating the former French colonies. Artworks themed around immigrants' struggles to integrate into French society and images of vehicles loaded with possessions arriving at the border are among the thought-provoking exhibits. Perhaps the most poignant items on display, though, are the suitcases brought over by immigrants, containing photos of loved ones, religious texts and teddy bears. There are also regular temporary exhibitions, such as a recent one on the history of Italian immigration to France. On the lower ground floor is an **aquarium** with a collection of tropical fish and a crocodile pit, left over from the *palais'* previous incarnation as the Musée des Arts Africains et Océaniens, whose exhibits have been transferred to the Musée du Quai Branly.

The Quartier Latin

The traditional heartland of the Quartier Latin lies between the Seine and the Montagne Ste-Geneviève, a hill once crowded with medieval colleges and now proudly crowned by the giant dome of the Panthéon. In medieval times, the name "Latin quarter" was probably a simple description, as this was the area whose inhabitants – clergymen and university scholars for the most part – ordinarily spoke Latin. It's still a scholarly area, home to the famous Sorbonne and Jussieu campuses, plus two of France's most elite lycées and a cluster of stellar academic institutes. Few students can afford the rents these days, but they still maintain the quarter's traditions in the cheaper bars, cafés and *bistrots*, decamping to the Luxembourg gardens, over in the 6e arrondissement (see p.144), on sunny afternoons.

The term Quartier Latin is often used, as here, as shorthand for the entire 5e arrondissement. It's one of the city's more palpably ancient districts, retaining some of the medieval lanes, venerable churches and hidden corners that, elsewhere in Paris, were so often "improved" in later centuries. The antiquated thoroughfare of the **rue Mouffetard** still snakes its way south to the boundary of the 13e arrondissement, while Roman and sixteenth-century buildings house the **Musée National du Moyen Age** – a splendid medieval museum worth visiting for the sublime tapestry series, *The Lady and the Unicorn*, alone. The churches of **St-Séverin** and **St-Etienne-du-Mont** are among the most atmospheric in the city, too. The giant domed **Panthéon**, meanwhile, provides a touch of splendour atop the Left Bank's highest point. Out towards the eastern flank of the 5e, beside the Seine, the theme is more Arabic than Latin, what with the **Institut du Monde Arabe** and the **Mosquée de Paris** (Paris Mosque). Nearby, the verdant **Jardin des Plantes** stretches down to the river, a lovely swathe of lawns and flowerbeds with splendid hothouses, natural history museums and a small zoo.

Place St-Michel and the riverside

Ⓜ St-Michel

The pivotal point of the Quartier Latin is **place St-Michel**, where the tree-lined boulevard St-Michel or "boul' Mich" begins. The once-famous student chic has these days given way to commercialization, but the cafés around the square are still lively haunts. A favourite meeting place is by the fountain, which spills down magnificently from a statue of the archangel Michael stamping on the devil. Just east of the square, rue de la Huchette and the surrounding huddle of streets – notably the tight-squeezed rue du Chat-qui-Pêche – are rare vestiges of the medieval city's pinched footprint. Sadly, the ubiquitous kebab joints and sports pubs, and the crowds of tourists, rather strip the zone of its atmosphere. There's a single relic of the era when **rue de la Huchette** was a hub for postwar Beat poets and Absurdists, too: the pocket-sized **Théâtre de la Huchette**, at no. 23 (see p.316). Since 1957 it's been showing two Ionesco plays nightly – well worth a trip if your French is up to it.

St-Séverin

1 rue des Prêtres St-Séverin, 5e • Mon–Sat 11am–7.30pm, Sun 9am–8pm • ☎ 01 42 34 93 50 • Ⓜ St-Michel/Cluny La Sorbonne

The mainly fifteenth-century church of **St-Séverin** is one of the city's more intense churches, its interior seemingly focused on the single, twisting, central pillar of the Flamboyant choir. The effect is heightened by deeply coloured stained glass designed by the modern French painter Jean Bazaine. The flame-like carving that gave the *flamboyant* ("flaming") style its name flickers in the window arch above the entrance while, inside, the first three pillars of the nave betray the earlier, thirteenth-century origins of the church. Outside, on the south side of the building, you can see the remains of what looks like a cloister enclosing a modest courtyard garden on two sides; this was in fact a **charnel house** for the mortal remains of fifteenth-century parishioners. Today, it's the last surviving one anywhere in the city.

One block south of the church, **rue de la Parcheminerie** is where medieval scribes and parchment sellers used to congregate. Take a look at the decorations on the facades, including that of no. 29, where you'll find the Canadian-run Abbey Bookshop (see p.334).

St-Julien-le-Pauvre

79 rue Galande, 5e • Tues–Sat 9.30am–1pm & 2.30–6pm, Sun 9.30am–1pm • ☎ 01 43 54 52 16, Ⓦ sjlpmelkites.com • Ⓜ St-Michel/ Maubert Mutualité

The much-mutilated church of **St-Julien-le-Pauvre** is almost exactly the same age as Notre-Dame. It used to be the venue for university assemblies until rumbustious students tore it apart in 1524. For the last hundred years it has belonged to an Arabic-speaking Greek Catholic sect, the Melchites, hence the unexpected iconostasis

RIVE GAUCHE

In French, **Rive Gauche** means much more than just the "left bank" of the Seine. Technically, all Paris south of the river is the Left Bank (imagine you're looking downstream), but to Parisian ears the name conjures up the cerebral, creative, sometimes anarchic spirit that once flourished in the two central arrondissements, the 5e and 6e, in vigorous opposition – supposedly – to the more conformist, commercial and conservative *rive droite*. In the **Quartier Latin**, around the 5e, a distinctively alternative ambience has long been sustained by the powerful and independent-minded Sorbonne university, while for much of the twentieth century any painter, writer or musician worth their bohemian salt would have lived or worked in or around **St-Germain** and the 6e arrondissement. Between the wars you could find the painters Picasso and Modigliani in the cafés of **Montparnasse**, hobnobbing with writers such as Guillaume Apollinaire, André Breton, Jean Cocteau and Anaïs Nin, and expat wannabes like Henry Miller and Ernest Hemingway. After World War II the glitterati moved on to the cafés and jazz clubs of St-Germain, which became second homes to writers and musicians such as Jacques Prévert, Boris Vian, Sidney Bechet and Juliette Gréco – and, most famously, to the existentialists Jean-Paul Sartre and Simone de Beauvoir.

But what really defined the Rive Gauche's reputation for turbulence and innovation were *les événements*, the political "events" of **May 1968** (see box, p.126). Escalating from leftist student demonstrations to factory occupations and massive national strikes, they culminated in the near-overthrow of De Gaulle's presidency. Since that infamous summer, however, conservatives have certainly had their vengeance on the spirit of the Left Bank. The streets that saw revolution now house expensive apartments, art galleries and high-end fashion boutiques, while the cafés once frequented by penniless intellectuals and struggling artists are filled with designers, media and political magnates, as well as scores of well-heeled foreign residents.

screening the sanctuary, and the liturgy of St John Chrysostom sung in Greek and Arabic (Sun 11am & 6pm, Tues & Thurs 12.15pm). It's also a popular venue for classical music and gospel concerts.

Outside, look for a hefty slab of brownish stone by the well, to the right of the entrance; it is all that remains of the paving of the Roman thoroughfare now replaced by rue St-Jacques. The adjacent pocket of worn grass that is **square Viviani** provides a perfect view of Notre-Dame. The three-quarters-dead tree propped on a couple of concrete pillars is reputed to be Paris's oldest, a false acacia planted in 1601.

Shakespeare and Company

37 rue de la Bûcherie, 5e • Daily 10am–11pm; antiquarian section Tues–Sat 11am–7pm • ☎ 01 43 25 40 93, ⓦ shakespeareandcompany .com • Ⓜ St-Michel

A few steps from square Viviani is the home of the American-run English-language bookshop **Shakespeare and Company**. The original store, owned by the American Sylvia Beach, the long-suffering publisher of James Joyce's *Ulysses*, was on rue de l'Odéon, over in St-Germain, but this "new" incarnation has played host to plenty of literati since it opened in 1951. In 1957, when Allen Ginsberg, William Burroughs and Gregory Corso were living in the so-called Beat Hotel, over on rue Gît-le-Cœur, they'd read their poems on the street outside the store. It still has a lively roster of literary events and has just opened a – pricey – café in an adjacent building. Some of the staff are "Tumbleweeds": young would-be Hemingways who bunk up upstairs in the first-floor library and pay their rent by helping out. More books, postcards and prints are on sale from the nearby **bouquinistes**, who display their wares in green padlocked boxes hooked onto the parapet of the riverside *quais*.

The University quarter

Ⓜ Cluny La Sorbonne/RER Luxembourg

Rue des Ecoles – the appropriately named "street of schools" – marks the beginning of the student quarter. It's here, just outside Square Paul Painlevé, that you'll find a bronze statue of the great Renaissance essayist, **Michel de Montaigne**, his toe rubbed shiny by generations of students seeking good luck in their exams. Above stretch the slopes of the Montagne Ste-Geneviève, clustered with the modern heirs of the colleges that once attracted the finest scholars from all over medieval Europe. Paris doesn't have quite the same world-beating status now, but the **Lycée Louis-le-Grand** attracts the cream of France's schoolchildren, the **Sorbonne** remains one of France's top universities for the arts, and the **Collège de France** is the leading research institution for the humanities. For visitors, the chief draw of this area is the **Musée National du Moyen Age**, an astoundingly rich storehouse of medieval art housed in an early Renaissance palace.

Musée National du Moyen Age

6 place Paul Painlevé, 5ᵉ • Daily except Tues 9.15am–5.45pm • €8, €9 including temporary exhibitions, free first Sun of the month; free audioguide in English (bring ID as a deposit) • ☎ 01 53 73 78 16, ⓦ musee-moyenage.fr • Ⓜ Cluny La Sorbonne

The best-preserved Roman remains in all Paris, the third-century **baths**, front onto the busy boulevard St-Michel. Behind them, on rue du Sommerard, stands the sixteenth-century **Hôtel de Cluny**. It's a beautiful Renaissance mansion, as befits the Paris pied-à-terre of the abbots of Burgundy's powerful Cluny monastery, and provides a fine setting for the superb **Musée National du Moyen Age**. While there is an astonishing wealth of artefacts on display in this treasure house of medieval art, it is the **tapestries** that form the highlight, and in particular the series **La Dame à la licorne** ("*The Lady and the Unicorn*"), one of the great masterpieces of European art. The museum also puts on an excellent programme of medieval music **concerts**; look out especially for the regular "concerts-rencontres", held on Monday lunchtimes (12.30pm) and Sunday afternoons (4pm), with tickets at just €6.

At the time of writing, the Musée National du Moyen Age was undergoing an extensive **restoration** programme, slated to continue until 2020, which will open up new areas to the public and improve existing tourist facilities – including a new reception area on boulevard St-Michel. In the meantime, some spaces may be closed when you visit, if only for an hour or so at a time.

The exhibits

On the **ground floor**, room 5 holds attractively naive wood and alabaster **altarpiece plaques** found in homes and churches all over Europe. In room 6, there are some wonderful backlit panels of **stained glass** from the Sainte-Chapelle. It's fascinating to see the jewel-bright artistry so close up, and to feel the storytelling urge behind scenes, such as one of Samson having his eyes gouged out.

Down the steps, in the modern structure built around the old baths, you'll find the melancholy array of 21 thirteenth-century heads – or parts of heads – of the **Kings of Judah**. Lopped off the west front of Notre-Dame during the Revolution, they were only discovered in a 1977 excavation. Arching over the frigidarium, the cold room of the **Gallo-Roman baths**, the magnificent brick-and-stone vaults are preserved intact. They shelter some beautifully carved pieces of first- and second-century columns, notably the so-called *Seine Boatmen's Pillar*, inscribed with the legend "Boatmen of the city of the Parisii", and the *Pillar of St-Landry*, which has gods and musicians animating three of its faces.

The **first floor** offers an amazing ragbag of carved choir stalls, altarpieces, ivories, Limoges enamels, stained glass, illuminated Books of Hours, games, brassware and all manner of precious objets d'art, including the stunning **Golden Rose of Basel**, a papal gift dating from 1330. In the main Hôtel de Cluny section, the building itself – all creaking parquet floors, heavy beams and vast, carved fireplaces – is as fascinating as the exhibits, with stunning tapestries adorning nearly every wall. The *hôtel*'s light-bathed, Flamboyant **chapel** is worth a look, with its remarkable vault splaying out from a central pillar, but the real big hitter up here is the room devoted to the huge **Lady and the Unicorn** tapestries.

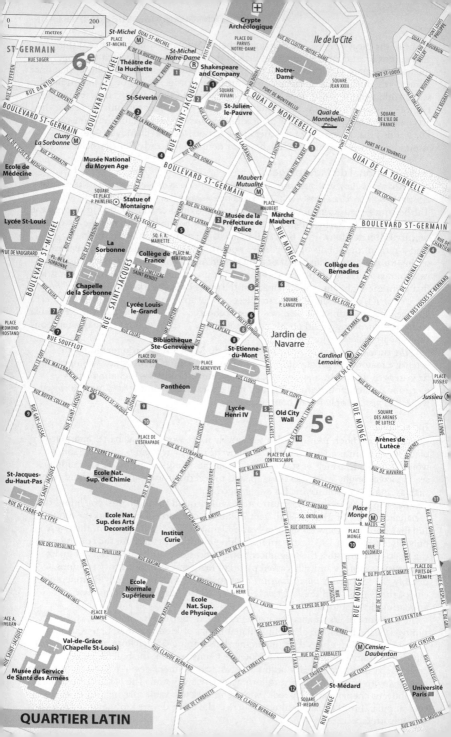

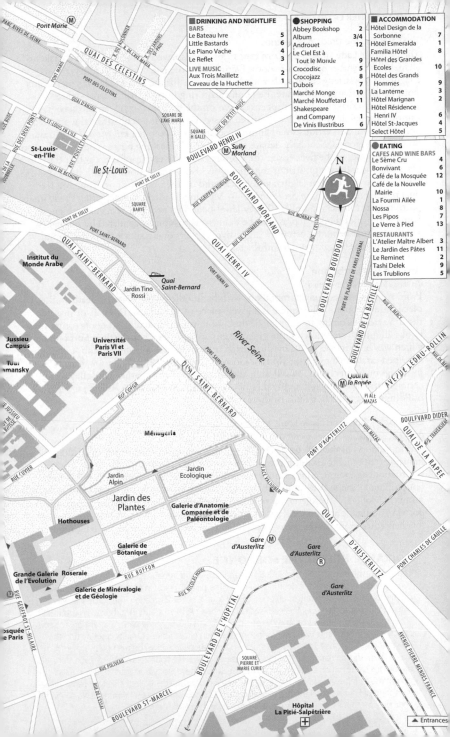

The Lady and the Unicorn tapestries

The exquisite **Lady and the Unicorn tapestries** are displayed by themselves in a darkened, chapel-like chamber on the first floor. Dating from the late fifteenth century, the six allegorical tapestries were probably made in Brussels for the Le Viste family, merchants from Lyon, perhaps to celebrate the family acquiring its own coat of arms – three crescents on a diagonal blue stripe, as shown on the flags floating in various scenes. Each sumptuous, poetic and highly evocative tapestry centres on a richly dressed woman, a lion, a unicorn and various small animals, set against a deep red *millefleurs* or "thousand-flower" background. Scholarly debate rages over their meaning but, at one level, they are clearly allegories of the five senses: the woman takes a sweetmeat from a goblet (taste); plays the organ (hearing); strings together a necklace of carnations (smell); holds a mirror up to the unicorn (sight); and lays a hand on the unicorn's horn (touch). The final panel, entitled *A Mon Seul Désir* ("To My Only Desire") and depicting the woman putting away (or picking up) her heavy jewel-bedecked necklace, remains ambiguous. Some authorities think it represents the dangerous passions engendered by sensuality – the open tent behind is certainly suggestive – others that it shows the sixth "moral sense" that guards against such sinfulness.

Around the Sorbonne

Ⓜ Cluny La Sorbonne/RER Luxembourg

From rue des Ecoles, **rue Champollion**, with its huddle of arty cinemas, leads to the **place de la Sorbonne**. The square is a lovely place to sit and rest, in a café or just under the lime trees, listening to the play of the fountains and watching students toting their books about. Overshadowing the graceful ensemble is the **Chapelle de la Sorbonne**, which was built in the 1640s by the great Cardinal Richelieu, whose tomb it contains. It helped establish a trend for Roman Counter-Reformation-style domes, which mushroomed over the city's skyline in the latter part of the century. The chapel is certainly the most architecturally distinctive part of the **Sorbonne**, as the university buildings were entirely rebuilt in the 1880s.

Collège de France and Lycée Louis-le-Grand

Ⓜ Maubert Mutualité

The foundation of the **Collège de France** was first mooted by the Renaissance king François I, in order to establish the study of Greek and Hebrew in France. Its modern incarnation, as a research institution, has attracted intellectual giants such as Michel Foucault and Claude Lévi-Strauss. Behind it, on rue St-Jacques, the **Lycée Louis-le-Grand** numbers Molière, Robespierre, Sartre and Victor Hugo among its former pupils. It's a portal to academic and political success, hothousing some of France's brightest students for their entry exams to the *grandes écoles*, France's elite colleges of higher education.

SOIXANTE-HUIT AT THE SORBONNE

The **Sorbonne** is much more to Parisians than just a world-famous educational institution. It's a living memorial to one of the defining events of the postwar era. On **May 3, 1968**, a riot broke out here after police violently intervened to break up a political meeting. The Sorbonne wasn't actually the first to flare up – the lead was taken in March, by students in suburban Nanterre – but it was the university's central, historical location that caught the nation's attention. To send police into the Sorbonne was a flagrant contravention of centuries of tradition separating the university and civic authorities. To see students fighting police down on the boulevard St-Michel – as millions did, on national television – aroused powerful national memories of revolution, and the unions came out on strike in sympathy. The Sorbonne's faculty buildings were occupied by a potent mix of left-wing radicals, poseurs and intellectuals, and the college briefly became the flashpoint of France's **student-led rebellion** against institutional stagnation, housing a vibrant, anarchic commune before finally being stormed by the police on June 16.

Musée de la Préfecture de Police

4 rue de la Montagne-Ste-Geneviève, 5ᵉ • Mon–Fri 9.30am–5pm, third Sat of the month 10.30am–5.30pm • Free • ☎ 01 44 41 52 50, ⓦ www.prefecturedepolice.interieur.gouv.fr • Ⓜ Maubert Mutualité

The **Musée de la Préfecture de Police**, housed in a brutally ugly police station, offers a surprisingly intriguing and varied collection of memorabilia, stitching together the city's criminal history from the establishment of the police force in 1667. There's too much to see here – photos, clippings, original documents, equipment, uniforms, memorabilia – for a casual visit, but there are plenty of oddities, from a guillotine blade used during the Revolution to an ivory plug hidden internally by prisoners to store their escape tools. There are cabinets on early serial killers and gruesome murder tools, on female criminals and the Paris Commune, with displays pretty much winding up with the *évenements* of 1968.

Collège des Bernardins

20 rue de Poissy, 5ᵉ • Mon–Sat 10am–6pm, Sun 2–6pm; French-language guided tours daily 4pm • Free; guided tours €6 • ☎ 01 53 10 74 44, ⓦ collegedesbernardins.fr • Ⓜ Cardinal Lemoine

In 1300, at the height of Paris's medieval Renaissance, there were some three thousand students living in colleges dotted all over the Left Bank. One of the few remaining vestiges of this period is the beautifully restored **Collège des Bernardins**, founded by the English monk Etienne de Lexington in 1247. It provided lodgings for Cistercian monks from all over Europe until it was confiscated during the Revolution. The building was subsequently put to a variety of uses, including as a police barracks and fire station. Purchased and restored by the Diocese of Paris in 2001–8, it has returned to its teaching tradition and is now a theological conference and research centre. Visitors can enter for free the lengthy Gothic vaulted nave (the former monks' refectory), as well as the lofty sacristy, which once adjoined the long-demolished church and now hosts contemporary art installations. The rest of the building, including its vaulted cellars and upper floor, can be visited as part of a guided tour (in French only).

The Panthéon

Place du Panthéon, 5ᵉ • Daily: Jan–March & Oct–Dec 10am–6pm; April–Sept 10am–6.30pm; last entry 45min before closing • €9; audioguides €4.50 • ☎ 01 44 32 18 00, ⓦ paris-pantheon.fr • Ⓜ Cardinal Lemoine/RER Luxembourg

The towering hulk of the **Panthéon** squats under its vast dome atop the Montagne Ste-Geneviève. It was originally built as a church by Louis XV, on the site of the ruined Ste-Geneviève abbey, to thank the saint for curing him of illness and to emphasize the unity of the church and state, which were troubled at the time by growing divisions between Jesuits and Jansenists. Not only had the original abbey church entombed Geneviève, Paris's patron saint, but it had been founded by Clovis, France's first Christian king. The building was only completed in 1789, whereupon the revolutionary state promptly turned it into a secular **mausoleum**, adding the words *Aux grands hommes la patrie reconnaissante* ("The nation honours its great men") underneath the pediment of the giant portico. The remains of **French heroes** such as Voltaire, Rousseau, Hugo and Zola are now entombed in the vast crypt below. Of the 77 interred, only five are **women**: Sophie Berthelot (1907), whose husband, chemist Marcellin Berthelot, asked that she should be buried with him; Marie Curie (1995); and Germaine Tillion and Geneviève de Gaulle-Anthonioz (2015), Resistance fighters who were captured and sent to Ravensbrück concentration camp during World War II; and Simone Veil (2017), who survived the holocaust to become one of France's most respected politicians, instrumental in legalizing abortion in France. Other recent arrivals include Alexandre Dumas (2002), who arrived in a coffin covered with a cloth embroidered with the phrase "All for one, one for all", from his novel *The Three Musketeers*. There's also a plaque to Antoine de Saint-Exupéry, author of the much-loved *Le Petit Prince*. He'd have a full-scale monument, but because his plane was lost at sea he fell foul of the rule that, without a body part to inter, you cannot be *panthéonizé*.

The interior and dome

The Panthéon's **interior** is bleak and chilly, and its muscular frescoes and sculptures do little to lift the spirits. The **dome**, however, is pretty impressive – it was from here, in 1851, that French physicist Léon Foucault suspended a pendulum to demonstrate vividly the rotation of the earth. While the pendulum appeared to rotate over a 24-hour period, it was in fact the earth beneath it turning. The demonstration wowed the scientific establishment and the public alike, with huge crowds turning up to watch the ground move beneath their feet. The pendulum you see today is a working model – the original is now in the Musée des Arts et Métiers (see p.105).

St-Etienne-du-Mont

Place Ste-Geneviève, 5ᵉ • July & Aug Tues–Sat 10am–noon & 4–7.45pm, Sun 10am–12.45pm & 4–6.45pm; Sept–June Mon 6.30–7.30pm, Tues, Thurs & Fri 8.45am–7.45pm, Wed 8.45am–10pm, Sat 8.45am–12.15pm & 2–7.45pm, Sun 8.45am–12.15pm & 2.30–7.45pm • ☎ 01 43 54 11 79, ⓦ saintetiennedumont.fr • Ⓜ Cardinal Lemoine/RER Luxembourg

Sloping downhill from the main portico of the Panthéon, broad rue Soufflot entices you west towards the Luxembourg gardens. On the east side of the Panthéon, a lone Gothic tower is all that remains of the earlier church of Ste-Geneviève. The saint's remains, and those of two seventeenth-century literary greats who didn't make the Panthéon, Pascal and Racine, lie close at hand in the church of **St-Etienne-du-Mont**. The church's facade is a splendidly mad seventeenth-century dog's dinner, its three levels stacking Gothic atop Renaissance atop neo-Grecian. The interior is no less startling, the transition from Flamboyant Gothic choir to sixteenth-century nave smoothed by a strange high-level catwalk which springs from pillar to pillar before transforming itself into a rood screen that arches across the width of the nave. This last feature is highly unusual in itself, as most French rood screens were destroyed by Protestant iconoclasts, reformers or revolutionaries. Tall windows flood the church with light, while an elaborately carved organ-loft crams itself into the west end of the nave. In the fifth chapel along, on the south side of the nave, there's a finely sculpted, sixteenth-century Entombment scene – life-size, as was long the custom in France.

Val-de-Grâce

1 place Alphonse Laveran, 5ᵉ • Tues–Thurs, Sat & Sun noon–6pm; closed Aug • €5 • ☎ 01 40 51 51 92, ⓦ bit.ly/museeval-de-grace • Ⓜ Les Gobelins/RER Port Royal

The southern half of the student quarter is lorded over by the elite Institut Curie and the **Ecole Normale Supérieure**, on rue d'Ulm, which grooms its *normaliens* for the top arts jobs in the country. It's a closed world to outsiders, however, and the only sight as such is the magnificent church of **Val-de-Grâce**, set just back from rue St-Jacques. Built by Anne of Austria as an act of pious gratitude following the birth of her first son in 1638, the church is a suitably awesome monument to the young prince who went on to reign as Louis XIV.

You can only enter Val-de-Grâce via the **Musée du Service de Santé des Armées**, a thorough history of military medicine that probably isn't for non-French-speakers – though the mock-ups of field hospitals, prosthetic limbs and reconstructive plastic surgery exert a gruesome fascination. The church, properly known as the **Chapelle St-Louis**, is reached via a curved iron grille behind which the Benedictine nuns once attended Mass. Inside, Roman Baroque extravagance is tempered by cool French Classicism. In the dome, Pierre Mignard's trompe l'oeil fresco of Paradise depicts Anne of Austria offering a model of the church to the Virgin.

The Mouffetard quarter

Ⓜ Place Monge/Censier–Daubenton

Medieval travellers heading south would leave Paris along the narrow, ancient incline of **rue Descartes** and its continuation, **rue Mouffetard**, following the line of the old

Roman road to Italy. Today the quarter's cheap restaurants and bars draw crowds of students and tourists alike.

Place de la Contrescarpe

Ⓜ Place Monge

Just south of the church of St-Etienne-du-Mont, you pass the medieval city limits – a giant stump of Philippe-Auguste's early thirteenth-century **city wall** still protrudes into rue Clovis, a few steps short of rue du Cardinal-Lemoine. Rue Descartes climbs briefly from here, past a landmark blue **mural** of a tree by the Belgian artist Pierre Alechinsky, before suddenly arriving at **place de la Contrescarpe**. The little square has been a dubious watering hole for centuries: the medieval poet-outlaw François Villon drank at taverns here, as did the scurrilous sixteenth-century writer François Rabelais; and the modern-day *Café Delmas*, on the square's sunny side, was once the run-down café *La a Chope*, as described by Ernest Hemingway in *A Moveable Feast*. Hemingway lived just around the corner on the fourth floor of 74 rue du Cardinal-Lemoine, in a miserable flat paid for by his wife Hadley's inheritance.

Rue Mouffetard

Ⓜ Place Monge

"La Mouffe", as the **rue Mouffetard** is known to locals, was for generations one of the great **market streets** of Paris. Some traces of the past can be found on the old shop fronts near place de la Contrescarpe, most obviously the two cows adorning a former butcher's at no. 6, and no. 16's hand-painted sign depicting a black man in striped trousers waiting on his mistress, with the unconvincing – and often vandalized – legend, "Au Nègre Joyeux". Mouffetard's market traditions cling on at the southern end of the street, where you'll find fruit and veg stalls in the mornings, classy delis and a couple of old-fashioned market cafés, notably *Le Verre à Pied* (see p.282). There are more old shop signs, too: no. 69 features a sturdy carved oak tree, while no. 122, labelled *"A la Bonne Source"* ("The Good Spring"), advertises either the fresh water or the produce that was once available there.

St-Médard

141 rue Mouffetard, 5ᵉ • Tues–Sat 8am–12.30pm & 2.30–7.30pm, Sun 9am–12.30pm & 4–8.30pm • Free • ☎ 01 44 08 87 00, Ⓦ saintmedard.org • Ⓜ Censier–Daubenton

Opposite the beautiful painted facade at 134 rue Mouffetard sits **St-Médard**. Once a country parish church, and only brought within the city walls during the reign of Louis XV, the church twice achieved notoriety: in 1561, when it was sacked by Protestant rioters in the so-called Tumult of St-Médard, and again in 1727, when fanatical supporters of François de Paris – a leading light in the reforming Jansenist movement, which had been condemned by pope and king alike but drew massive popular support in Paris – gathered at his fresh grave. Rumours of miracles led crowds of *"convulsionnaires"* into collective hysteria, rolling on the ground around their saint's tomb, eating the earth and even wounding or crucifying themselves. These excesses helped split the Jansenist movement, and led the authorities to post armed guards at the church gates in 1732, beside a sign reading *"De par le roi, défense à Dieu/De faire miracle en ce lieu"* ("By order of the king, God is forbidden to work miracles in this place"). The church today preserves its simple, narrow Gothic nave and more elaborate late sixteenth-century choir. A fine Zurbarán painting of *The Promenade of St Joseph and the Child Jesus* lurks in the right transept, while statues carved by the great Renaissance sculptor Germain Pilon in the 1640s top the outstanding organ loft.

Arènes de Lutèce

Entrances on rue de Navarre, rue des Arènes and through a passage on rue Monge • Daily dawn–dusk • Free • Ⓜ Jussieu

The surprisingly large – and remarkably well hidden – open space of the **Arènes de Lutèce** lies east of rue Mouffetard. A few ghostly rows of stone seats are all that's left of the Roman amphitheatre that once amused ten thousand here; the entertainment is now provided by the old men playing boules, or the children playing football, in the sand below. Benches, gardens and a kids' playground stand behind.

Jardin des Plantes

Rues Cuvier, Buffon & Geoffroy St-Hilaire, 5ᵉ • Daily: Feb & mid-Oct to late Oct 8am–6.30pm; early to mid-March 7.30am–7pm; mid- to end March 7.30am–7.30pm; April to mid-Sept 7.30am–8pm; mid-Sept to end Sept 8am–7.30pm; early Oct to mid-Oct 8am–7pm; Nov– Jan 8am–5.30pm • Free • ☎ 01 40 79 56 01, ⓦ jardindesplantes.net • Ⓜ Gare d'Austerlitz/Censier–Daubenton/Place Monge/Jussieu

The **Jardin des Plantes** is one of Paris's finest green spaces, complete with **hothouses** and a **zoo**. Founded as a medicinal herb garden in 1635, it has long retained a scientific role. Its great eighteenth-century director, the Comte de Buffon, is rightly regarded as the father of natural history, while Henri Becquerel stumbled upon radioactivity in the physics labs overlooking the gardens, in 1896, and the Curies cooked up radium here two years later. The gardens still host a suite of very popular **natural history museums**.

The gardens

There are **entrances** to the Jardin des Plantes on all sides except around the northern corner. The southwesternmost entrance, on the corner of rues Buffon and Geoffroy St-Hilaire, takes you past a sophora tree planted by Buffon in 1747 and to the **roseraie**, which contains 170 varieties of rose and is at its glorious best in June. If you enter by the rue Cuvier/rue Lacépède gate, at the northwest corner, and climb the little hillock on the right up to an elegant gazebo (it actually predates the Revolution, making it the oldest ironwork structure in Paris), you can then descend along shaded paths, past a stately cedar of Lebanon planted in 1734, to the central area of lawns and flowerbeds. If you're here in spring, don't miss the flowering of the two Japanese cherries – one white, one pink – two-thirds of the way down. Other highlights include the iris and peony gardens, the vegetable plot and the **Jardin Ecologique**, which shelters the natural flora of the Parisian basin. The **Jardin Alpin** (March–Dec only), meanwhile, a sheltered, sunken space filled with mountain plants from all over the world, is particularly popular among Parisians.

The hothouses

57 rue Cuvier, 5ᵉ • Daily except Tues: March–Sept 10am–6pm; Oct–Feb 10am–5pm • €7 including Galerie de Botanique • ☎ 01 40 79 56 01, ⓦ bit.ly/grandesserres • Ⓜ Jussieu/Place Monge

The *serres*, or **hothouses**, are one of the glories of the Jardin des Plantes. Entrance is via the Art Deco *serre tropicale*, with its graceful, vegetal-themed facade; it's hot, humid, overgrown and splendidly lush, with a three-storey grotto that you can climb as far as the canopy level, and a section, on the sunny side, of desert plants. From the *serre tropicale* you pass into the elegant twin hothouses, revolutionary structures when they were built in the 1830s. The first is home to an amazing diversity of plants from Nouvelle-Calédonie, in the Pacific; the second is a kind of living exhibition on the evolution of plant life. Occasional temporary exhibits – on orchids, for example – are hugely popular, so be prepared to queue.

Grande Galerie de l'Evolution

36 rue Geoffroy St-Hilaire, 5ᵉ • Daily except Tues 10am–6pm • €9, €11 with Galerie des Enfants (see p.355) • ☎ 01 40 79 56 01, ⓦ grandegaleriedelevolution.fr • Ⓜ Censier–Daubenton/Place Monge

Beside the Jardin des Plantes' southwestern entrance, the **Grande Galerie de l'Evolution** tells the story of evolution using **stuffed animals** rescued from the dusty old zoology museum, and given new life with clever lighting and ambient sounds. On the lower level, submarine light suffuses the space where the murkiest deep-ocean creatures are displayed. Above, glass lifts rise silently from the savannah, where a closely packed line

of huge African animals looks as if they're stepping onto Noah's ark. It's great fun for children, who have a small interactive area to themselves, the Galerie des Enfants, on the first floor (see p.355).

Galerie de Minéralogie et de Géologie

Daily except Tues: April–Sept 10am–6pm; Oct–March 10am–5pm • €6 • ☎ 01 40 79 56 01, ⓦ galeriedemineralogieetgeologie.fr •
Ⓜ Censier–Daubenton/Place Monge

The **Galerie de Minéralogie et de Géologie** was undergoing lengthy restoration at the time of writing, though recently reopened one of its rooms for an exhibition (ongoing till 2018) entitled "Trésors de la Terre", drawing on its splendid collection of giant rock crystals, meteorites and precious gems.

Galerie de Botanique

18 rue Buffon, 5ᵉ • Daily except Tues: March–Sept 10am–6pm; Oct–Feb 10am–5pm • €7 including hothouses (see p.130) •
☎ 01 40 79 56 01, ⓦ mnhn.fr/fr/visitez/lieux/galerie-botanique • Ⓜ Gare d'Austerlitz

As an add-on to a visit to the hothouses, the **Galerie de Botanique**, home to France's national herbarium, offers mild interest in its one corridor of glass cabinets – a few wonders of nature, plant samples and fossils, historic botanical drawings and curious old scientific implements – but if time is short you could easily give it a miss.

Galerie d'Anatomie Comparée et de Paléontologie

2 rue Buffon, 5ᵉ • Daily except Tues 10am–6pm • €7 • ☎ 01 40 79 56 01, ⓦ bit.ly/galeriedanatomie • Ⓜ Gare d'Austerlitz

Unchanged since it was laid out in 1900 for the Universal Exhibition, the **Galerie d'Anatomie Comparée et de Paléontologie** has a real old-fashioned charm, full of strange beasts and ancient creatures that need no touch-screens or interactive gizmos to thrill. As you enter the ground floor of the vast, vaulted hall, you're immediately faced by serried thousands of **animal skeletons** that seemingly evolve in well-marshalled order, with a colossal giraffe towering over them all. On the first floor, dinosaurs (some plastercast, some real) are arranged by era. Don't miss – well, you can't miss – the huge glyptodon, with its armadillo-like carapace; the fearsome, 10m-long *Sarcosuchus imperator*, giant ancestor of the crocodile; the aptly named *Triceratops horridus*; and, largest of the lot, the mighty diplodocus.

Ménagerie

Jardin des Plantes, 5ᵉ • Feb daily 9am–5.30pm; March to mid-Oct Mon–Sat 9am–6pm, Sun 9am–6.30pm; mid- to late Oct daily 9am–
5.30pm; Nov–Jan daily 9am–5pm • €13; children and under-26s €9 • ☎ 01 40 79 56 01, ⓦ zoodujardindesplantes.fr • Ⓜ Gare d'Austerlitz

The small **ménagerie** in the Jardin des Plantes was founded just after the Revolution; it is France's oldest **zoo** – and in many ways feels like it. The old-fashioned iron cage housing the Chinese panthers and the glazed-in primate house are not exactly uplifting for modern sensibilities, even if they are historic Art Deco structures. Thankfully, most of the rest of the zoo is pleasantly park-like and given over to deer, tapir, red pandas, flamingos and other beasts that seem happy enough in their outdoor enclosures, and it is usually possible to see the animals up close.

Mosquée de Paris

2bis place du Puits de l'Ermite, 5ᵉ • Daily except Fri & Muslim holidays 9am–noon & 2–6pm • €3 • ☎ 01 45 35 97 33, ⓦ mosqueedeparis
.net • Ⓜ Jussieu

The **Mosquée de Paris** (Paris Mosque) stands behind crenellated walls west of the Jardin des Plantes. Built by Moroccan craftsmen in the early 1920s, in a style influenced by Moorish Spain, it feels oddly repro in style, though the artisanship of tiles and woodcarvings is very fine, and the cloistered gardens are deliciously peaceful. You can stroll freely, but non-Muslims are asked not to enter the prayer room. Towards the back of the building, on the rue Geoffroy St-Hilaire side, lies a simple monument to the

Algerian scholar and national hero Abd el-Kader, who led the resistance against French invasion before finally being forced to surrender in 1847. The gate on the southeast corner of the mosque complex, on rue Daubenton, leads into a lovely courtyard **tearoom** (see p.282), and an atmospheric **hammam** (see p.344).

Institut du Monde Arabe

1 rue des Fossés-St-Bernard, 5ᵉ • **Institut** Tues–Fri 10am–6pm, Sat & Sun 10am–7pm • Free; fees charged for temporary exhibitions • **Museum** Tues–Fri 10am–6pm, Sat & Sun 10am–7pm • €8 • ☎ 01 40 51 38 38, ⓦ imarabe.org • Ⓜ Jussieu/Cardinal Lemoine

North of the Jardin des Plantes stands the loathed **Jussieu campus**, an uncompromising complex built around the brutal skyscraper of the Tour Zamansky. Built to house the baby-boomers coming of university age in the late 1960s – and, they say, to thwart any unseemly outbreaks of student rebellion with its single entrance **gate** – its population has since outgrown it and partly decamped upstream (see p.178).

The campus hides a vastly more successful piece of modern metal-and-glass architecture. Conceived by the Mitterrand government in collaboration with the Arab League, the **Institut du Monde Arabe** is a radical piece of architectural engineering, designed by a team including Jean Nouvel, who subsequently built the Musée du Quai Branly (see p.151) and the Philharmonie (see p.203). Its broad southern facade comprises thousands of tiny light-sensitive shutters that were designed to modulate light levels inside while also mimicking a *moucharabiyah*, the traditional Arab latticework balcony – unfortunately, the computer system operating the little steel diaphragms has a habit of crashing.

Inside the institute – a tangle of glass walls and elevators, mirrors, stairs and narrow corridors – the ground-breaking design can feel less inspiring than enervating. There is lots to see, however: high-profile and high-tech **temporary exhibitions**, films and concerts by leading artists from the Arab world pull in the intelligentsia, while a permanent **museum** aims to illuminate the complexity and diversity of Arab cultures. Scholars have use of a library and multi-media centre, and there's a good **bookshop** with some English-language titles and a fine selection of Arab music. Up on the ninth floor, the **terrace** (Tues–Sun 10am–6pm) offers fabulous views of the city, especially downriver towards the apse of Notre-Dame. The Lebanese **restaurant** here, *Le Ziryab*, has some alfresco terrace seating, but it's expensive (€39 for a two-course lunch; Tues–Sun noon–midnight; ☎ 01 55 42 55 42). On the same floor you can nibble sweet cakes and Middle Eastern snacks without the views at the *Le Moucharabié* **café** (Tues–Sun 11.30am–3.30pm), while *Café littéraire*, on the ground floor (Tues–Sun 10am–7pm), does a nice line in Arabic sweets.

The museum

A sprawling affair, winding down from the seventh floor to the fourth, the institute's **museum** loosely covers five themes – the body, self and others; Arabian identity; the sacred; towns and cities; and concepts of beauty – via a wealth of exquisite ceramics, metal- and glasswork, musical instruments, carpets, tiles and textiles, some going back as far as prehistoric times. Look out for the bronze incense burner in the shape of a horse from eleventh-century Khorasan, the exquisite hammam accessories from Turkey and Tunisia, and the oldest exhibit, a statuette of an earth goddess from Jordan, dating from the seventh century BC. The objects are undeniably exquisite, but the layout, in floating glass cases under bright lighting, with much of its captioning in pale (usually French) text printed on glass, can be challenging.

TOY BOATS IN THE JARDIN DU LUXEMBOURG

St-Germain

Encompassing the 6ᵉ arrondissement and the eastern fringe of the 7ᵉ, St-Germain has all the sophistication of the Right Bank combined with an easy-going chic that makes it uniquely appealing. The *quartier* has moved ever further upmarket since the postwar era, when it was the natural home of arty mould-breakers and trendsetters, but it clings to its offbeat charm. Among the designer boutiques and fashionable *bistrots*, you can still find the cafés that made the quarter famous, and left-wing media types and intellectuals continue to rub shoulders along with crowds of well-dressed Parisians and international visitors. The quarter also preserves its two landmark attractions: the lovely Jardin du Luxembourg and the Musée d'Orsay.

Historically, St-Germain has stood outside the city proper for most of its life. From the sixth century onwards, its fields and riverine meadows fell under the sway of the giant Benedictine abbey of St-Germain-des-Prés. Marie de Médicis built the Palais du Luxembourg in the early seventeenth century, but the area only became urbanized a hundred years later, as aristocrats migrated across the Seine from the Marais in search of spacious plots of land for their mansions. The Faubourg St-Germain soon became one of Europe's most fashionable districts.

The now-celebrated **boulevard St-Germain** was driven right through the heart of the quarter by Baron Haussmann in the mid-nineteenth century, but it became famous in its own right after World War II, when the cafés **Flore** and **Les Deux Magots** attracted the resurgent Parisian avant-garde – Sartre debated existentialism with de Beauvoir and Boris Vian sang in smoky cellar jazz bars. As Guy Béart and, later, Juliette Gréco sang, "*Il n y a plus d'après à Saint-Germain-des-Prés*" – there's no tomorrow in St-Germain.

Of course, there was – even if an older Juliette Gréco tried to fight it with her movement "SOS St-Germain" in the late 1990s. Though the quarter maintains its cool credentials, high-rolling publishers, designers and politicians have long since shouldered out boho intellectuals and musicians. **Fashion**, now, is king; the streets around the carrefour de la Croix Rouge and place St-Sulpice, in particular, swarm with high-end boutiques, while a little further west the historic **Bon Marché** department store stocks an ever-classier range. Towards the river, on the other hand, antique shops and **art dealers** dominate. Though St-Germain can boast a number of excellent markets and cafés, the **restaurant** scene as a whole is distinctly chichi, with well-heeled foodies flocking to the gastronomic palaces of celebrity chefs like Hélène Darroze and Joël Robuchon, and foreign visitors filling the pricey *bistrots* around Mabillon.

There are some fine buildings to enjoy – from the domed **Institut de France**, by the river, to the churches of **St-Germain-des-Prés** and majestic **St-Sulpice**. Two small museums, the **Musée Maillol** and **Musée National Eugène Delacroix**, make intimate antidotes to the grand Right Bank institutions, while the exhibitions at the **Musée du Luxembourg** are regularly among the city's most exciting. And of course there's the **Musée d'Orsay**, at the western edge of the quarter, loved as much for its stunning railway-station setting as its jaw dropping Impressionist collection. Meanwhile, in the southeastern corner of the quarter, hard against the Quartier Latin, the romantic **Jardin du Luxembourg** is one of the largest green spaces in Paris – and surely the loveliest.

Musée d'Orsay

62 rue de Lille, 7ᵉ, entrance at 1 rue de la Légion d'Honneur • Tues, Wed & Fri–Sun 9.30am–6pm, Thurs 9.30am–9.45pm • €12; free to under-26s from the EU, and to all first Sun of the month; combined ticket with Musée de l'Orangerie (see p.72) €16, combined ticket with Musée Rodin (see p.156) €18 (both valid for three months); admission ticket also gets reduced entry to the Opéra Garnier (see p.74) and the Musée National Gustave Moreau (see p.191) for up to one week; it's worth booking tickets in advance at busy times to avoid long queues • ☎ 01 40 49 48 14, ⓦ musee-orsay.fr • Ⓜ Solférino/RER Musée d'Orsay

Facing the Tuileries gardens across the River Seine, the **Musée d'Orsay** is one of the city's unmissable attractions. The museum's staggering collection of the electrifying works of the **Impressionists** and **Post-Impressionists** has made it one of Paris's most-visited attractions. There's more to it than Monet and Renoir, however. The collection spans the artistically revolutionary era between 1848 and 1914 – between the end of the Louvre's Classical traditions and the start of the modern era, as represented in the Pompidou Centre (see p.87).

Though the museum covers a lot, it's easy to confine your visit to a specific **section**. Chronologically, the collection begins on the ground floor, under the huge vault of steel and glass, and continues up on the fifth floor with the Impressionists, accessed via the Pavillon Amont, the station's former engine room, which is devoted to decorative arts. It then continues down to the Post-Impressionists, displayed on the terraces and galleries of the middle level (level two), overlooking the main "nave" chamber.

Given the huge scope of its collection, and its many masterpieces, the Orsay occasionally **rearranges rooms** and swaps paintings to make space for new acquisitions. While you can be sure of seeing the big hitters, for precise locations of particular artworks you should treat the account here – and even the museum's printed map – as a loose guide.

The building

The building itself was inaugurated as a **railway station** for the 1900 World Fair. It spans the worlds of nineteenth-century Classicism and industrial modernity brilliantly, the elegant, formal stone facade cunningly disguising the steel-and-glass construction of the railway arch within. The Gare d'Orsay continued to serve the stations of southwest France until 1939, but its platforms became too short for postwar trains and it fell into disuse.

De Gaulle made the station the backdrop for the announcement of his coup d'état of May 19, 1958, but such was the site's degradation by the 1960s that Orson Welles thought it the perfect location for his film of Kafka's nightmarish *The Trial*. Despite this illustrious history, the station was only saved from destruction by the backlash of public opinion that followed the demolition of Les Halles. In 1986, the job of redesigning the interior as a museum was given to the fashionable Milanese architect Gae Aulenti.

The ground floor

The ground floor sets off with works by **Gérôme**, **Ingres** and **Delacroix** – the bulk of whose work is in the Louvre – and the serious-minded artworks of the "academic" painters, which were acceptable to the mid-nineteenth-century salons. The influential **Barbizon School**, some of the first to break with the established norms of moralism and idealization of the past, is represented with canvases by Millet, among others – the soft-toned landscapes and quickly executed scenes were highly influential on later, avowed Impressionists. A number of galleries are given over to **symbolism**, displaying the relatively wacky works of artists such as Gustave Moreau and Odilon Redon, with some unsettlingly dream-like paintings from Edward Burne-Jones and a rather alarming late portrait of Sarah Bernhardt by her friend Georges Clairin.

Don't miss the **Neo-Impressionists**, featuring the vibrant works of Seurat and Signac, their tiny daubs (sometimes called pointillism) creating ground-breaking effects of colour and light – Seurat's exuberant *Cirque* practically shimmers off the canvas. Also on show is a collection of paintings by the likes of Vuillard, Vallotton and Bonnard, who began their careers as part of an Art Nouveau group known as the **Nabis**, who turned their back on naturalism and Impressionism to focus on simple lines and colour blocks – for the bulk of the Vuillard and Bonnard collection, however, you should head up to level five.

The seedy glamour of the fin-de-siècle Paris *demi-monde* is brought to life with some breathtaking paintings by **Toulouse-Lautrec** – his tenderly intimate *Le Lit* and Picasso's haunted absinthe drinker, *La Buveuse d'Absinthe*, hang in the same room. There are also some early **Degas** (pre-1870), a few religious works by **Cézanne** and two rooms of **Orientalist** works. A display of **early photographs** leads to a room of canvases by **Courbet**, including his *L'Origine du Monde*, which still has the power to shock even contemporary audiences – many of whom simply pretend it's not there. The nude female torso – effectively a close-up of female genitalia – was acquired by the Orsay from psychoanalyst Jacques Lacan, who concealed it behind a decorative panel in his offices.

Level five: Impressionism
To continue chronologically, proceed via the Pavillon Amont straight to level five, where you'll find the **Impressionists' collection**. In a series of large, warmly lit rooms, well-spaced paintings hang against walls of charcoal grey. The result is stunning: the vibrant colours and vigorous brushstrokes of even the almost-too-familiar Monets and Renoirs strike you afresh. The first room is dominated by Manet's scandalous **Le déjeuner sur l'herbe** and **Olympia**, both held to have announced the arrival of Impressionism (see box, below). Thereafter follows masterpiece after masterpiece: Degas' *Dans un Café (L'Absinthe)*; Renoir's *Bal du Moulin de la Galette*; Cézanne's *Les Joueurs de Cartes*; Monet's *Coquelicots* ("Poppies") and his two radiant versions of *Femme à l'Ombrelle* … the list is endless.

A host of small-scale landscapes and outdoor scenes by Renoir, Sisley, Pissarro and Monet is owed to the novel practice of setting up easels in the open – often as not, on the banks of the Seine. Less typical works include **Degas' ballet dancers**, which demonstrate his principal interest in movement and line as opposed to the more common Impressionist concern with light – his stunning bronze sculpture *Petite Danseuse de quatorze ans*, with wrinkled stockings and a real, ragged tutu, is poignant in its naturalism. In one room, a selection of Monet's waterlily paintings and works from his **Rouen cathedral series**, each painted in different light conditions, face Renoir's pneumatic nudes – a wonderful counterpoint that illuminates the dizzying scope of this artistic revolution. Renoir's joyous pairing *Danse à la Ville/Danse à la Campagne* has a wall to itself, as does Manet's smaller *Sur la Plage*, which shows distinct Japanese influence in its lack of depth and its flattened planes. **Berthe Morisot**, the first woman to join the early Impressionists, is represented by her famous *Le Berceau*, among others.

Level two
On **level two**, the flow of the painting section continues with the various offspring of Impressionism – you can feel an edgier, more modern sensibility emerging, with a much greater emphasis on psychology. There's a large collection of **Van Goghs**, transfixing with their fervid colours and disturbing rhythms, and an intriguing **Gauguin** selection – not only his Tahitian paintings but also less familiar works from his period in Brittany. A suite of rooms devoted to the **Nabis** artists **Bonnard** and **Vuillard** includes their distinctively intimate portraits, nudes and Parisian street scenes, rendered with breathtaking spontaneity, naturalism and emotion.

On the **sculpture terraces**, amid works by Maillol, Bourdelle and others, it is pieces by **Rodin** that stand out, not least his exceptionally grim *Ugolin*. The painful imagery of *L'Age Mûr*, a heartbreaking appeal to Rodin from his pupil and lover **Camille Claudel**, shows the exceptional skill of this lesser-known artist. If you still have any energy, seek out the rooms dedicated to **Art Nouveau** furniture and objets d'art by designers such as Hector Guimard, Victor Horta, Emile Gallé and Antoni Gaudí.

THE SHOCKING SALON OF 1863
Manet's painting *Le déjeuner sur l'herbe*, or *The Picnic*, which hangs in the Musée d'Orsay, caused outrage at the **1863 Salon des Refusés**. This was a deliberately confrontational show of works (a "salon") that had been rejected by the judges of the official Salon of 1863. It has often been said to mark the beginning of the **Impressionist** movement. The problem with Manet's picnic scene wasn't so much the nakedness of its female figure – female nudity was absolutely standard in French Classical art. It was rather the fact that Manet had juxtaposed her with male figures in modern dress, making her look not like an idealized representation of womanhood so much as a common harlot. Manet had shifted his interest away from the ideal and towards the everyday, and this was regarded as amoral at best. Also hanging in the Orsay, Manet's provocative *Olympia*, with its brash and sensual surfaces, appeared at the same salon. No less shocking, it portrays Olympia as a high-class whore who returns the stares of her audience with a look of insolent defiance.

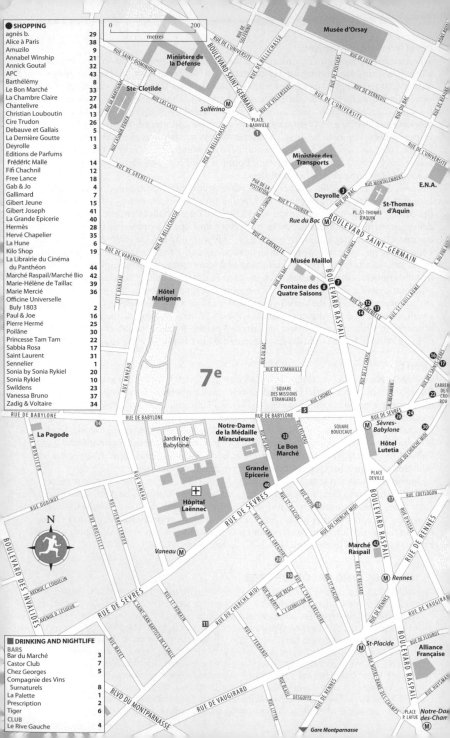

● SHOPPING

agnès b.	29
Alice à Paris	38
Amuzilo	9
Annabel Winship	21
Annick Goutal	32
APC	43
Barthélémy	8
Le Bon Marché	33
La Chambre Claire	27
Chantelivre	24
Christian Louboutin	13
Cire Trudon	26
Debauve et Gallais	5
La Dernière Goutte	11
Deyrolle	3
Editions de Parfums Frédéric Malle	14
Fifi Chachnil	12
Free Lance	18
Gab & Jo	4
Gallimard	7
Gibert Jeune	15
Gibert Joseph	41
La Grande Epicerie	40
Hermès	28
Hervé Chapelier	35
La Hune	6
Kilo Shop	19
La Librairie du Cinéma du Panthéon	44
Marché Raspail/Marché Bio	42
Marie-Hélène de Taillac	39
Marie Mercié	36
Officine Universelle Buly 1803	2
Paul & Joe	16
Pierre Hermé	25
Poilâne	30
Princesse Tam Tam	22
Sabbia Rosa	17
Saint Laurent	31
Sennelier	1
Sonia by Sonia Rykiel	20
Sonia Rykiel	10
Swildens	23
Vanessa Bruno	37
Zadig & Voltaire	34

■ DRINKING AND NIGHTLIFE

BARS
Bar du Marché	3
Castor Club	7
Chez Georges	5
Compagnie des Vins Surnaturels	8
La Palette	1
Prescription	2
Tiger	6

CLUB
Le Rive Gauche	4

7ᵉ

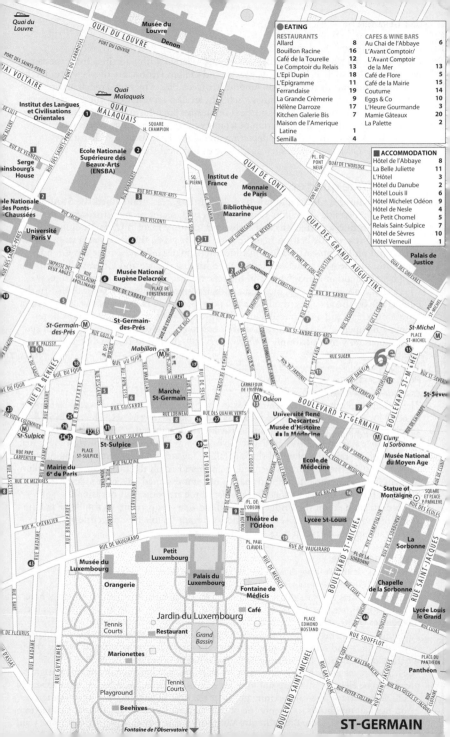

● EATING

RESTAURANTS		CAFES & WINE BARS	
Allard	8	Au Chai de l'Abbaye	6
Bouillon Racine	16	L'Avant Comptoir/	
Café de la Tourelle	12	L'Avant Comptoir	
Le Comptoir du Relais	13	de la Mer	13
L'Epi Dupin	18	Café de Flore	5
L'Epigramme	11	Café de la Mairie	15
Ferrandaise	19	Coutume	14
La Grande Crèmerie	9	Eggs & Co	10
Hélène Darroze	17	L'Heure Gourmande	3
Kitchen Galerie Bis	7	Mamie Gâteaux	20
Maison de l'Amerique		La Palette	2
Latine	1		
Semilla	4		

■ ACCOMMODATION

Hôtel de l'Abbaye	8
La Belle Juliette	11
L'Hôtel	3
Hôtel du Danube	2
Hôtel Louis II	6
Hôtel Michelet Odéon	9
Hôtel de Nesle	4
Le Petit Chomel	5
Relais Saint-Sulpice	7
Hôtel de Sèvres	10
Hôtel Verneuil	1

ST-GERMAIN

9

Pavillon Amont

More superb **Art Nouveau** furniture and objets, together with paintings from the same period by artists such as Vuillard, Rousseau and Odilon Redon, are displayed on levels two, three and four of the **Pavillon Amont**. Art Deco pieces by non-French artists, notably from the Vienna and Glasgow schools, are also represented. The ground level of the *pavillon* is dominated by Courbet's impressive large-format paintings, including *A Burial at Ornans*, a stark depiction of a family funeral; these huge works were ground-breaking in their day for depicting everyday scenarios on a scale usually reserved for "noble" subjects, such as historic or mythical scenes.

The riverside quarter

East of the Musée d'Orsay, and north of the bustling, restaurant-lined rue **St-André-des-Arts**, the **riverside** slice of St-Germain feels both secretive and aristocratic. Studded with fine seventeenth- and eighteenth-century mansions, concealing private gardens and courtyards behind massive *porte cochère* gates, the area is also strewn with artistic and philosophical associations. Picasso painted *Guernica* in rue des Grands-Augustins; on rue Mazarine, Molière opened his first theatre and Champollion finally deciphered Egyptian hieroglyphics in his attic rooms. Rue Visconti, meanwhile, was where Delacroix painted, Racine died and Balzac's printing business went bust. In the parallel rue des Beaux-Arts, the Romantic poet Gérard de Nerval went walking with a lobster on a lead and a disgraced Oscar Wilde died "fighting a duel" with his hotel room's wallpaper – "One or the other of us has to go," he remarked. You can still stay in the hotel, now named simply *L'Hôtel* (see p.260), or call in for a drink at its theatrical bar.

Pont des Arts

Ⓜ St-Germain-des-Prés/Louvre–Rivoli

The pedestrian **Pont des Arts**, which crosses the Seine to the Louvre, became as famous recently for its controversial "love locks" as for its classic river views. The tradition of attaching a **padlock** to the bridge and throwing the key into the Seine to express undying love started in 2008; by 2014 the bridge was so weighed down with locks that a section of the railings collapsed (luckily falling inwards and not onto passing boats below). In 2015 the authorities stepped in and removed all the locks (around a million of them), replacing the railings with panels of commissioned street art as an interim solution. Today plain glass panels have replaced the artworks, but occasional exhibitions are held on the bridge itself, and the views – upstream to the Ile de la Cité and across to the Louvre, screened behind its elegant double row of gentle white poplars and muscular plane trees – remain as beguiling as ever.

Institut de France

23 quai de Conti, 6ᵉ • **Institut de France** Ⓦ institut-de-france.fr • **Bibliothèque Mazarine** Mon–Fri 10am–6pm • Free • ☎ 01 44 41 44 06, Ⓦ bibliotheque-mazarine.fr • Ⓜ Pont-Neuf/St-Michel

The Pont des Arts owes its name not to the artists who have long sold their work here but to the institute that sits under the elegant dome on the St-Germain side. This is the **Collège des Quatre-Nations**, seat of the **Institut de France**. Of the Institut's five academies of arts and sciences, the most famous is the **Académie Française**, an august body of writers and scholars whose mission is to award literary prizes and defend the integrity of the French language against Anglo-Saxon invasion. The chosen few are known as *Immortels* – though ironically, by the time they have accumulated enough prestige to be elected, most are not long for this world. That said, the list has evolved in recent years: among the forty-strong group at the time of writing, five were women.

You need an invitation to attend one of the Institut's lectures, but visitors are free to look around the exquisite **Bibliothèque Mazarine**, where scholars of religious history sit in hushed contemplation of some of the 200,000 sixteenth- and seventeenth-century volumes, surrounded by *rocaille* chandeliers, marble busts and Corinthian columns.

Monnaie de Paris

11 quai de Conti, 6ᵉ • Tues, Wed & Fri–Sun 11am–7pm, Thurs 11am–9pm • Temporary exhibitions €10 • ☎ 01 40 46 56 66,
ⓦ monnaiedeparis.fr • Ⓜ Pont-Neuf/St-Michel

The **Monnaie de Paris**, the French Mint, is housed in an imposing eighteenth-century palace complex, the **Hôtel des Monnaies**, which has one of the largest facades fronting the Seine. Traditionally, the Monnaie's museum of coinage – which hosts regular contemporary art exhibitions – was the only part of this grand Neoclassical building that was open to visitors, but after major renovation work, the entire site, including three interior courtyards and a newly landscaped garden, is open to the public. It is possible to pay to follow a behind-the-scenes circuit taking in the ateliers – collector's coins and medals are made in the workshops here, while everyday euros are minted at the sister site in the Gironde. The Monnaie is also home to Michelin-starred *Restaurant Guy Savoy* – diners can enjoy superb views of the river and the Louvre from the huge windows.

Ecole Nationale Supérieure des Beaux-Arts (ENSBA)

Campus 14 rue Bonaparte, 6ᵉ • Mon–Fri 8am–10pm • Free • **Palais des Beaux-Arts** 13 quai Malaquais • Tues–Sun 1–7pm • €7.50 •
☎ 01 47 03 50 00, ⓦ beauxartsparis.com • Ⓜ St-Germain-des-Prés

To the west of the Institut de France lies the **Ecole Nationale Supérieure des Beaux-Arts (ENSBA)**, the School of Fine Art, whose glory days gave its name to an entire epoch. It's worth taking a look around the rather lovely courtyard. The elaborate, three-storey facade of the chapel on the right actually came from the sixteenth-century château d'Anet, which was built by Henri II for his lover, Diane de Poitiers – you can see their intertwined initials above the doors. On the left is what the French call a *mur renard* – a false or "fox" facade, built to mask a neighbour's blank gable end. But the centrepiece is the grand Italianate building at the end of the courtyard, Félix Duban's **Palais des Etudes**, which dates to the 1830s. You can enter the serene covered court, with its polychrome decoration and immense conservatory roof – added by the architect in 1863 – but the gardens, Duban's Cour du Mûrier (a lovely cloister set around a mulberry tree) and the remnants of the sixteenth-century Hôtel de Chimay are out of bounds. Regular exhibitions are held at the **Palais des Beaux-Arts**, displaying work from its collections and past and current students.

Serge Gainsbourg's House

5bis rue de Verneuil, 6ᵉ • Ⓜ St-Germain-des-Prés

West of the Ecole des Beaux-Arts is the house where iconoclastic pop legend **Serge Gainsbourg** lived until his death in 1991 – it's now owned by his film-star daughter Charlotte. Over the years, the garden wall was steadily covered by layer upon layer of graffiti quoting famous lyrics like "God smokes Havanas" and aerosol-sprayed versions of *Gainsbarre*'s distinctive silhouette. Ever since a catastrophic day in April 2000, however, the **Mur de Gainsbourg** has received regular coats of whitewash. It hasn't deterred the fans in the slightest, but to get the full effect you'll have to hope you don't visit just after the decorators – the official decorators, that is – have been.

Around St-Germain-des-Prés and Odéon

Ⓜ St-Germain-des-Prés/Odéon

The **boulevard St-Germain** was bulldozed right through the Left Bank under Baron Haussmann (see p.370), and is a fairly undistinguished thoroughfare for much of its length. One short stretch around **place St-Germain-des-Prés**, however, comprises one of Paris's most celebrated micro-neighbourhoods. The **Deux Magots** café stands on one corner of the square, while the equally celebrated **Café de Flore** (see p.283) lies a few steps further along the boulevard. Both are chiefly renowned for the postwar writers and philosophers who drank and debated there – most famously, the philosopher-novelist Simone de Beauvoir and her existentialist lover, Jean-Paul Sartre. Although the two cafés charge high prices and attract plenty of tourists, they're still genuine St-Germain institutions – albeit patronized by moneyed professionals rather than penniless writers these days. The cognoscenti judge *Flore* to have maintained an edge of authenticity.

At the eastern edge of St-Germain, around the **Odéon** junction, you feel the gravitational pull of the university; indeed, this area is sometimes considered to be part of the Quartier Latin.

Church of St-Germain-des-Prés

Place St-Germain-des-Prés, 6ᵉ • Daily 8am–7.45pm • Free • ☎ 01 55 42 81 18, ⓦ eglise-saintgermaindespres.fr • Ⓜ St-Germain-des-Prés

The powerful tower dominating place St-Germain-des-Prés belongs to the church of **St-Germain-des-Prés**, and is all that remains of an enormous Benedictine monastery whose lands once stretched right across the Left Bank. Having survived a post-Revolution stint as a saltpetre factory, the church itself is one of Paris's oldest surviving buildings, a rare Romanesque structure that dates back to the late tenth and early eleventh centuries. The choir, however, was rebuilt in the fashionable Gothic style in the mid-twelfth century – work that's just about visible under the decorative greens, golds and reds of nineteenth-century paintwork. The marble columns of its middle triforium level date from an even earlier church on this site, erected in the sixth century, which housed the remains of the Merovingian kings.

Outside the church, on the corner of rue de l'Abbaye and rue Bonaparte, there's a pretty little **garden** with some strange fragments of Gothic stonework. These, along with a single stained-glass window in the apse of the main church, are the melancholy last remains of a thirteenth-century chapel. They make a perfect backdrop to the **Picasso sculpture** of a woman's head that also stands here, dedicated to the memory of the poet Apollinaire.

Musée National Eugène Delacroix

6 rue de Furstenberg, 6ᵉ • Daily except Tues 9.30am–5pm • €7; €15 with the Louvre (see p.49) • ☎ 01 44 41 86 50, ⓦ musee-delacroix.fr • Ⓜ Mabillon/St-Germain-des-Prés

Hidden away round the back of St-Germain-des-Prés, **place de Furstenberg** is one of Paris's most lovable small squares, huddling round its quartet of Paulownia trees and candelabra-like street lamp. Tucked into a courtyard off its northwest corner is the pocket-sized **Musée National Eugène Delacroix**, in the apartment where the painter lived and worked from 1857 until his death in 1863, accompanied by Jenny Le Guillou, who'd been his servant since 1835. Three small rooms in the main building display some relatively minor works by Delacroix and his contemporaries – most interesting are Delacroix's portrait of Jenny (1840) and the intense *La Madeleine dans le désert* (1845) – along with a few of the painter's personal effects. More paintings, alongside temporary exhibitions, can be seen in Delacroix's studio outside, overlooking a peaceful walled garden where you are free to sit after your visit. It's all quite charming, but for Delacroix's major work you'll have to visit the Louvre (see p.49) and Musée d'Orsay (see p.135), or head over to the murals at nearby St-Sulpice (see opposite).

Rue de Buci

Ⓜ Mabillon/Odéon

Rue de Buci was once a proper street market, and still preserves a brash and faintly chaotic air. That said, the morning-only greengrocers' stalls are known locally as jewellery shops – for their prices rather than the colour of the fruit. The entire street is now ringed by delis, sandwich shops and restaurants – as well as some of the livelier bars on the Left Bank.

Cour du Commerce St-André
Ⓜ Odéon

A few steps east of the main rue de Buci crossroads on rue de Seine, the little semi-covered *passage* of the **cour du Commerce St-André** cuts through enticingly from rue St-André-des-Arts to the boulevard St-Germain. Marat had a printing press here, and Dr Guillotin honed his fabled scientific execution device by practising on sheep's heads. Backing onto the street is *Le Procope* – Paris's first coffee house, which opened its doors in 1686. It was the favourite watering hole and talking shop of Voltaire and Rousseau, among others, and the Enlightenment's great project, the *Encyclopédie*, was dreamed up here in a fug of caffeine. *Le Procope* is still open for business, but as a rather touristy restaurant rather than a philosopher's lair. A couple of smaller courtyards open off the alleyway, revealing another stretch of Philippe-Auguste's twelfth-century city wall.

Marché St-Germain
Rue Lobineau • Ⓜ Mabillon

The **Marché St-Germain** is a modern reconstruction of a covered market that was one of the few architectural legacies left to the city by Napoleon. The site is more ancient still, having been the venue for the raucous St-Germain fair, which was held at the gates of the abbey in medieval times. Sadly, upmarket international chains – including the only Apple store on the Left Bank – have replaced the old market stalls. The area around the Marché, on rues Princesse, Lobineau, Guisarde and des Canettes, is known collectively as **rue de la soif**, or the "street of thirst", and it heaves with diners and drinkers of an evening. There are plenty of passable (and very popular) "pubs", but few really good addresses – though the wine bar *Chez Georges* (see p.299) is a classic.

The Odéon quarter
Ⓜ Odéon

The defining landmark of the **Odéon quarter** is the restored **Théâtre de l'Odéon** (Ⓦ theatre-odeon.eu), its proud Doric facade fronting a handsome semi-circular plaza. This was one of the learned Louis XVI's last projects before the Revolution, and had a then-unheard-of capacity of 1900.

Musée d'Histoire de la Médecine
Université René Descartes, 12 rue de l'Ecole de Médecine, 6ᵉ • Mon–Wed, Fri & Sat 2–5.30pm • €3.50 • ☎ 01 76 53 16 93, Ⓦ www .parisdescartes.fr • Ⓜ Odéon

Hidden away on the third floor of the eighteenth-century Ecole de Chirurgie building – a Neoclassical behemoth, now home to the Descartes University – the **Musée d'Histoire de la Médecine** is a quirky delight, if perhaps not for the squeamish. Climb sweeping marble staircases and head down lofty corridors to find this glorious, skylit, wood-panelled hall, its collection of surgical instruments beautifully presented in wooden cabinets. Starting with ancient implements – many unearthed from Pompeii – and moving through every area of medicine from asthma to gynaecology, the entire collection is fascinating. Highlights include early prosthetics and anatomical mannequins, the kit used for Napoleon's autopsy and Etruscan false teeth made of hippopotamus bone. Many of the instruments are oddly exquisite, delicately and artistically wrought – less lovely is the table mosaicked with petrified blood, bile, liver, lungs and vertebrae, topped with four human ears and a foot, generously gifted by an Italian doctor to Napoleon III in 1866.

St-Sulpice
Ⓜ St-Sulpice

The fact that the actor Catherine Deneuve has an apartment on **place St-Sulpice** is a good clue to its character. This is a classy yet still faintly arty corner of the city, and architecturally the square is enchanting, with its lion fountain and chestnut trees overlooked by the not-quite-twin towers of the **church**: the south tower has long waited in sculptural limbo – you can see uncut masonry blocks at the top, still awaiting the sculptor's chisel.

Church of St-Sulpice
Place St-Sulpice, 6ᵉ • Daily 7.30am–7.30pm • Free • ☎ 06 59 92 59 68, ⓦ pss75.fr/saint-sulpice-paris, ⓦ stsulpice.com for details of organ recitals • Ⓜ St-Sulpice

The church of St-Sulpice, the largest in Paris, is a muscular Neoclassical edifice erected either side of 1700. For decades, the gloomy **interior** was best known for three **Delacroix murals**, in the first chapel on the right, and a huge, 101-stop, five-manual, part-eighteenth-century **organ**, which is among the finest in the world and is used at frequent recitals. St-Sulpice also acquired brief notoriety after the publication of *The Da Vinci Code*, in which Dan Brown attributed the church's **solar observatory** – or gnomon – with mystical powers. The truth is more pedestrian – the observatory was an astronomical clock, created to ascertain the exact moment of noon and determine proper dates for the church's moveable feasts. A lens in the south transept window, long since removed, focused the sun's rays on a narrow brass strip, or meridiana, which still runs right across the floor of the nave and up a stone pillar on the north side. At its winter low, the sun would exactly crown the obelisk at noon; at its summer height, it would burn down on the start of the brass line. Originally designed in 1727 by an English clockmaker called Henry Sully, the instrument as it survives now is the remnant of a 1740s scientific attempt to measure the exact time of the winter and summer solstices.

Jardin du Luxembourg
Entrances on place Edmond Rostand, rue Guynemer and rue de Vaugirard, 6ᵉ • Roughly dawn–dusk • ☎ 01 42 64 33 99, ⓦ senat.fr/visite/jardin • Ⓜ Odéon/Mabillon/RER Luxembourg

Ernest Hemingway liked to claim he fed himself in Paris by shooting pigeons in the **Jardin du Luxembourg**. These lovely gardens belong to the **Palais du Luxembourg**, which now houses the French Senate, but was originally built for Marie de Médicis, Henri IV's widow. They get fantastically crowded on summer days, especially the shady **Fontaine Médicis** in the northeast corner and the southern tail of the gardens – the latter being the only place where you're allowed to sit out on the **lawns**. Everywhere else you'll have to settle yourself on the heavy, green metal chairs, which are liberally distributed around the gravel paths. Alternatively, there's a tree-shaded (and not exorbitantly priced) **café**, *Pavillon de la Fontaine*, near the Fontaine Médicis, and a more upmarket restaurant, *La Table du Luxembourg*, on the gardens' western side.

Exploring the gardens
Children rent toy yachts to sail on the octagonal pond, the **Grand Bassin**, but the western side of the gardens, beside the **tennis courts** (see p.345), is the more active area: there are pony rides, a marionette show (see p.350) and playgrounds for children, plus the inevitable sandy area for boules. More than one hundred **sculptures** are scattered around the park, including an 1890 monument to the painter Delacroix by Jules Dalou and a suitably mischievous homage to the Surrealist poet Paul Eluard by the sculptor Ossip Zadkine (see p.166). In the quieter, far western section you can also find one of Paris's miniature versions of the Statue of Liberty, just bigger than human size, and a cluster of well-tended **beehives**. The southwest corner ends in a fabulous orchard of heritage apple and pear trees whose fruit graces the tables of senators or, if surplus to requirements, is given to organizations for the homeless.

The north–south spine of the gardens extends down into a tail pointing towards the Paris observatory, following the line of the old Paris meridian (see p.170). At the extreme southern end of the gardens, the **Fontaine de l'Observatoire** symbolizes Paris's historic self-conception as the very navel of the world, with Jean-Baptiste Carpeaux's fine sculptures of the four continents supporting a mighty iron globe.

Orangerie

Jardin du Luxembourg • W senat.fr/evenement/ete_du_senat/2006/orangerie.html • M St-Sulpice/RER Luxembourg

For two or three weeks in late September, the half-glazed **Orangerie** is the venue for the annual **Exposition d'Automne**, which shows off the garden's finest fruits and floral decorations. It's closed for the rest of the winter, sheltering scores of exotic trees – palms, bitter oranges, oleanders and pomegranates, some of them more than two hundred years old. All are wheeled back outside, in their giant wooden containers, every spring.

Musée du Luxembourg

19 rue de Vaugirard, 6ᵉ, Jardin du Luxembourg • Daily 10.30am–7pm • €12 • T 01 40 13 62 00, W en.museeduluxembourg.fr • M St-Sulpice/Mabillon/RER Luxembourg

Immediately behind the Orangerie, but with its entrance on rue de Vaugirard – Paris's longest street – stands the **Musée du Luxembourg**. Some of the city's biggest and most exciting art exhibitions are held here, often causing long queues to form alongside the giant railings of the Jardin du Luxembourg. Recent successes have included the Tudors and an exhibition focusing on Pissarro.

The western fringe of St-Germain

The broad, ugly gash of **rue de Rennes** signals the western boundary of the core St-Germain neighbourhood, but the 6ᵉ arrondissement continues officially as far west as rue des Sts-Pères – and, in feel, this quarter extends well into the 7ᵉ arrondissement, or at least as far as rue du Bac. The whole area, certainly, is stuffed to bursting with swanky shops, and it's here that you'll find the landmark Left Bank department store, Le Bon Marché. On Sunday mornings, meanwhile, the celebrated **Marché Raspail** food market (see p.341) lines the boulevard Raspail between the Sèvres–Babylone and Rennes métro stations.

The carrefour de la Croix Rouge and around

M St-Sulpice/Sèvres–Babylone

You might not find the most exclusive Right Bank designers or the more alternative-minded Marais boutiques here, but rues Bonaparte, Madame, de Sèvres, de Grenelle, du Vieux-Colombier, du Dragon, du Four and des Sts-Pères are lined with the big names in Parisian clothes and accessories, from agnès b. (see p.326) to Zadig et Voltaire (see p.328). It's hard to imagine now, but smack in the middle of all this, at the **carrefour de la Croix Rouge**, there was a major barricade in 1871, during the Paris Commune (see box, p.186). These days you're more likely to be suffering from till-shock than shell shock, though César's 5m bronze statue of a **Centaur**, cast in homage to Picasso in 1983, is distinctly alarming. It surveys the crossroads with ferocity, with two sets of genitals and a shovel and rake for a tail. Hovering above its face – which is a César self-portrait – is a mask representing a likeness of Picasso.

Hôtel Lutetia

45 bd Raspail, 6ᵉ • W lutetia-paris.com • M Sèvres–Babylone

Facing the Bon Marché department store across square Boucicaut is the monumental **Hôtel Lutetia**, a notorious St-Germain address famed for its gorgeous Art Deco interiors. At the outbreak of World War II, scores of artists and writers fled here, seeking sanctuary of a kind – the hotel itself was requisitioned by the Germans during the Occupation. One guest had been James Joyce – peeved, it's said, that the growing conflict had overshadowed the publication of his novel, *Finnegans Wake*.

Le Bon Marché

Le Bon Marché 24 rue de Sèvres, 7ᵉ • Mon–Wed & Sat 10am–8pm, Thurs & Fri 10am–8.45pm • ☎ 01 44 39 80 00, ⓦ lebonmarche.com • **Grande Epicerie** 38 rue de Sèvres, 7ᵉ • Mon–Sat 8.30am–9pm • ☎ 01 44 39 80 00, ⓦ lagrandeepicerie.com • Ⓜ Sèvres–Babylone

Just across the boundary with the 7ᵉ arrondissement, at the far side of the green square Boucicaut, stands the grand department store, **Le Bon Marché** (see p.326). One of the great institutions of the nineteenth century (and the setting for Zola's novel *Au Bonheur des Dames*), its name means "inexpensive", but these days it's one of Paris's most upmarket shopping spaces. A 1920s annexe on the west side of rue du Bac now houses the luxurious **Grande Epicerie**, or "big grocer's" (see p.337).

Notre-Dame de la Médaille Miraculeuse

140 rue du Bac, 7ᵉ • Mon & Wed–Sun 7.45am–1 & 2.30–7pm, Tues 7.45am–7pm • Free • ☎ 01 49 54 78 88, ⓦ chapellenotredamedelamedaillemiraculeuse.com • Ⓜ Sèvres–Babylone

If you stand outside Le Bon Marché, especially on a Sunday, you'll notice that a surprisingly large proportion of people among the crowds isn't here for the shopping. The reason lies down an alley hidden behind 140 rue du Bac, just north of the aerial bridge joining the two wings of the department store. Tucked away at its end is a little chapel with the unwieldy name of **Notre-Dame de la Médaille Miraculeuse**. It was here, in 1830, that a 24-year-old nun called Catherine Labouré had visions of the Virgin Mary dressed in silk, with her feet resting on a globe. A voice told Catherine to "have a medal struck like this – those who wear it will receive great graces". The nuns duly obeyed, and have been quite literally coining it ever since. You can buy a souvenir medal and visit the chapel, which was rebuilt in 1930 to accommodate huge pilgrim congregations.

Musée Maillol and around

61 rue de Grenelle, 7ᵉ • Mon–Thurs, Sat & Sun 10.30am–6.30pm, Fri 10.30am–9.30pm • €13 • ☎ 01 42 22 59 58, ⓦ museemaillol.com • Ⓜ Rue du Bac

The bijou **Musée Maillol** shares its space between post-Impressionist sculptor Aristide Maillol's buxom female nudes – represented in paintings, drawings, tapestries and sculptures – and temporary exhibitions on contemporary and modern art. Recent shows have featured the maverick street artist Ben and the French art scene of the 1960s. Note that the museum is only open during temporary exhibitions – check the website for dates.

A few steps east of the museum stands the **Fontaine des Quatre-Saisons**, less a fountain than a piece of early eighteenth-century architectural theatre. At the centre of the curved stone arcade sits the City of Paris herself, flanked by two sinuous figures representing the rivers Seine and Marne.

Deyrolle

46 rue du Bac, 7ᵉ • Mon 10am–1pm & 2–7pm, Tues–Sat 10am–7pm • Free • ☎ 01 42 22 30 07, ⓦ deyrolle.com • Ⓜ Rue du Bac

You might not normally go out of your way to visit a **taxidermist's**, but **Deyrolle** should be an exception. The fancy garden/homeware shop below is a mere front for the real business upstairs, in a room perfumed with the sharp, coal-tar smell of taxidermy. Giant, antique wooden display cases are stuffed with pinned butterflies and shards of prehistoric trilobites, while above and all around them are scores of stuffed rabbits, ducks, sheep, boar, bears and even big cats. Astonishingly, this isn't a museum: the entire stock (apart from a billy goat and a donkey) was replaced from scratch after a disastrous fire in 2008, and all the pieces on view are for sale. A lion could be yours for around €10,000, or you can pick up a fossil for about €10.

THE EIFFEL TOWER

The Eiffel Tower quarter

The Eiffel Tower, standing sentinel over a great bend in the Seine as it flows out of Paris, towers above the city like some glorious monumental flagpole. It surveys the most relentlessly splendid of all Paris's districts, embracing the palatial heights of the Trocadéro on the Right Bank and the wealthy, western swathe of the 7e arrondissement on the Left. These are street vistas planned for sheer magnificence: as you look out across the river from the terrace of the Palais de Chaillot to the Eiffel Tower and the huge Ecole Militaire, or let your gaze run from the ornate Pont Alexandre III past the parliament building to the vast Hôtel des Invalides, you are experiencing city design on a truly monumental scale.

The quarter is home chiefly to diplomats, government officials and aristocrats, both old-school and new. Unsurprisingly, it's pretty dead in terms of shops and restaurants, but it is studded with some compelling **museums**, from the stunningly designed gallery of "primitive" art at **quai Branly** to an offbeat attraction dedicated to Paris's **sewers**. In the heart of the 7e (septième), the imposing **Hôtel des Invalides** houses the French army's vast **war museum**, centred on the tomb of Napoleon. The splendid **Musée Rodin**, nearby, shows off the revolutionary sculptor's works in the intimate surroundings of a handsome private *hôtel*, or mansion house. Just across the river, in the **Trocadéro** quarter of the 16e arrondissement, you'll find a pocket of fine museums specializing in Asian Buddhist art, fashion and architecture, along with two of the most exciting art museums in the city: the **Palais de Tokyo**'s galleries of Parisian modern art and contemporary French artworks.

Note that the easternmost end of the 7e – including the Musée d'Orsay and the shopping area around rue du Bac and the Sèvres-Babylone métro – belongs more in feel to St-Germain and is thus covered in our St-Germain chapter (see p.134).

The Eiffel Tower and around

Daily: mid-June to Aug 9am–12.45pm; Sept to mid-June 9.30am–11.45pm • €17 (for the top), €11 (second level); you can climb the stairs (not as gruelling as it might sound if you're reasonably fit) as far as the second level for €7 and buy a "supplément ascenseur" ticket to the top for a further €6; save queueing time by buying tickets online (well in advance), or, to beat the worst of the queues, turn up on the day early in the morning (around 1–2hr before the tower opens for the lift, around 20min in advance for the stairs) • ☎ 0892 701 239, Ⓦ toureiffel.paris • Ⓜ Trocadéro/Bir-Hakeim/Pont de l'Alma/RER Champs de Mars-Tour Eiffel

Despite being one of the most familiar landmarks in the world, the **Eiffel Tower** – the quintessential symbol of Paris – has lost none of its power to dazzle, both from a distance and up close. The city looks surreally microscopic from the top and the **views** are arguably better from the second level, especially on hazier days. But there's something irresistible about taking the lift all the way up. At the very top, you can peer through a window into a re-creation of Gustave Eiffel's airy little study, or splash out on a glass of fizz at the champagne bar, while at the second level is Alain Ducassse's gastronomic restaurant, *Jules Verne* (see p.286). On the first level, meanwhile, a **glass floor** affords dizzying views of the ground (and long queues) below, and there's another, less formal, restaurant, *58 Tour Eiffel*. Note that since 2016 heightened **security measures** (see p.377) mean that queues are longer and slower than they ever were, with bag searches even to enter the area below the tower; make sure to give yourself plenty of time, whether or not you have booked in advance.

Outside daylight hours, sodium **lights** illuminate the main structure, while twin xenon arc-lamps, added for the millennium celebrations, have turned the tower into an oversized urban lighthouse. There's also a third lighting system: for the first five minutes of every hour (until 1am) thousands of bulbs scramble about the structure, defining the famous silhouette in luminescent champagne.

Brief history

It's hard to believe that this brilliant feat of industrial engineering was designed to be a **temporary structure** for a fair. Late nineteenth-century Europe had a taste for giant-scale, colonialist-capitalist extravaganzas, but Paris's 1889 **Exposition Universelle** was particularly ambitious: at 300m, its tower was the tallest building ever yet built. Outraged critics protested against this "grimy factory chimney". "Is Paris", they asked, "going to be associated with the grotesque, mercantile imaginings of a constructor of machines?" Eiffel believed it was a piece of perfectly utilitarian architecture. "The basic lines of a structure must correspond precisely to its specified use," he said. "To a certain extent the tower was formed by the wind itself."

Curiously, this most celebrated of landmarks was only saved from demolition by the sudden need for "wireless telegraphy" aerials in the first decade of the twentieth

---

MODERN ARCHITECTURE IN THE SEPTIÈME

The septième is renowned for its grand state monuments and extravagant aristocratic mansions, which mostly date from the seventeenth and eighteenth centuries, but you can also seek out a trio of the city's most exciting **Art Nouveau** apartment buildings, the work of Jules Lavirotte at the turn of the nineteenth century. From the **contemporary era**, the Musée du Quai Branly (see opposite) is the most trumpeted representative, but hidden away nearby is a fascinating example of the postmodernist architecture of Christian de Portzamparc.

29 avenue Rapp (RER Pont de l'Alma). Art Nouveau to the extreme, with colourful, glazed ceramic tiles and an extravagant doorway representing an inverted phallus inside a vulval arch. Designed by Jules Lavirotte in 1901.

3 square Rapp Off avenue Rapp (RER Pont de l'Alma). More of Lavirotte's extravagant Art Nouveau work, dating from 1900 and tucked behind a decorative iron fence. There's also a fine trellis trompe l'oeil on the wall alongside.

12 rue Sédillot (RER Pont de l'Alma). From the studio of Lavirotte in 1899, featuring Art Nouveau and Art Deco elements, with superb dormers and curvaceous wrought-iron balconies.

Conservatoire de Musique Erik Satie 7 rue Jean-Nicot (Ⓜ Invalides). This early structure from stellar architect Christian de Portzamparc (1984) shows typical postmodern exuberance, with a distinctive half-peeled tube of a tower.

---

century, and nowadays the original crown is masked by an efflorescence of antennae. The tower's **colour scheme** has changed too: the early coats of deep red then canary-yellow paint have been covered with a sober, dusty brown since the late 1960s. The only structural maintenance it has ever needed was carried out in the 1980s, when one thousand tonnes of metal were removed to make the tower ten percent lighter, and the frame was readjusted to remove a slight warp. In 2017, it was announced that the tower's system of temporary railings and checkpoints – raised in the wave of increased citywide **security** following the terrorist attacks two years earlier – was to be replaced by a bulletproof **glass wall** around the base of the structure with bag checks for anyone wanting to get into the area below the tower and then again for those waiting to access the north *pilier* and ascend to the top.

Champ de Mars

Stretching back from the Eiffel Tower, the **Champ de Mars** has been an open field ever since it was used as a mustering ground for royal troops – hence the name "Martial Field". After 1789 it became the venue for the great revolutionary fairs, including Robespierre's vast "Fête of the Supreme Being" in 1794, while the Second Empire turned it into a giant industrial exhibition area, which explains the location of the Eiffel Tower. It's now a popular place for sunbathing on hot days. At the far southern end lie the eighteenth-century buildings of the **Ecole Militaire**, founded in 1751 by Louis XV for the training of aristocratic army officers – including the "little corporal", Napoleon Bonaparte.

UNESCO headquarters

7 place de Fontenoy, 7ᵉ • ☎ 01 45 68 10 00, Ⓦ unesco.org/fr/cultural-events • Ⓜ Ecole Militaire

The *quartier* surrounding the Ecole Militaire is expensive, elegant and classic, and the Y-shaped **UNESCO building** is the controversial exception. Built in reinforced concrete in 1958 by, appropriately, an international team, it houses artworks by Giacometti, Calder, Miró and Picasso, as well as the so-called "Nagasaki angel" – a rare survivor of the atomic atrocities of August 1945. The public is welcome at various exhibitions and concerts, ranging from "Colours and Impressions of Albania" to Lebanese chamber music – book in advance.

Behind UNESCO, the avenue de Saxe continues the grand line southeast towards the giant Necker hospital, passing through the **place de Breteuil**, a huge roundabout – even by Parisian standards – centred on a **monument to Louis Pasteur**, the much-loved inventor of pasteurization. His role as a hero who saved millions of lives is represented by the Grim Reaper cowering beneath him, while a healthy shepherd and cowherd attest to his pioneering work in the field of vaccinations.

Musée du Quai Branly

37 quai Branly, 7ᵉ • Tues, Wed & Sun 11am–7pm, Thurs–Sat 11am–9pm • €10; €8 upon presentation of a ticket for the Musée de l'Homme (see p.158); temporary exhibitions €10; permanent collection and temporary exhibitions €12; free on first Sun of the month • ☎ 01 56 61 70 00, Ⓦ quaibranly.fr • Ⓜ léna/RER Pont de l'Alma

A short distance upstream from the Eiffel Tower, the **Musée du Quai Branly** – the brainchild of President Chirac, whose passion for **non-Western art** helped secure funding – cuts a postmodern swathe along the riverbank. It's worth visiting for Jean Nouvel's architectural **design** alone, which plays with the divide between structure and outside world. Hidden within a surprisingly unruly garden, cut off from the riverbank by a tall glass wall, the building unfurls in a long glazed curve, its brightly coloured panels revealing sudden cavities or box-like swellings that pop outwards. The museum has in its collection hundreds of thousands of non-European objects bought or purloined by France over the centuries, displayed on rotation in a high-concept space that involves quite a bit of walking. A long, winding stroll from the ticket desk brings you to areas devoted to the Pacific ("Oceania"), Asia, Africa and the Americas, snaking through dimly lit rooms lined by curving "mud" walls in brown leather; the desired effect – to create a mysterious, dream-like environment, in which non-Western art is seen in terms of the exotic "other" – can feel slightly uncomfortable. However, the artefacts themselves – ancient Hawaiian feather helmets, Kii appaat masks from Greenland, Christian paintings from Ethiopia, a straw funerary coat from Papua New Guinea, contemporary Aboriginal dot paintings, Oruro carnival costumes – are as fascinating as they are beautiful, with an especially amazing collection of textiles and masks. The sheer amount of stuff can be overwhelming – if you are short of time, concentrate on **Oceania**, which has some particularly unusual pieces. Note that artefacts at this museum are presented largely as works of art; for a more "scientific" approach to anthropology, head to the Musée de l'Homme (see p.158).

Musée des Egouts de Paris

Quai d'Orsay, 7ᵉ, entrance on northeast side of place de la Résistance • Mon–Wed & Sat: May–Sept 11am–6pm; Oct–April 11am–5pm • €4.40 • ☎ 01 53 68 27 81 • Ⓜ Alma–Marceau/RER Pont de l'Alma

The chief attraction of the **Musée des Egouts de Paris**, or **Sewers Museum**, is that it's actually in the sewers. The main part of the visit runs along a gantry walk poised alarmingly above a main sewer. It's dark, damp and noisy with gushing water, but not quite as smelly as you might fear. A good companion guide might be Victor Hugo's *Les Misérables*: the author turns the history of the sewer system – "a dread sink-hole which bears the traces of the revolutions of the globe as of the revolutions of man, and where are to be found vestiges of all cataclysms from the shells of the Deluge to the rag of Marat" – into a magnificent lecture.

The museum is more than half a publicity exercise by the sewage board. Bilingual displays of photographs, engravings, dredging tools, lamps and other flotsam and jetsam render the history of the city's water supply and waste management surprisingly interesting, revealing how the natural water cycle was disrupted by the city's dense population, then slowly controlled by increasingly good management. What it doesn't say is that the work isn't quite finished. Almost all the effluent from the sewers goes to the Achèves treatment plant, northwest of Paris, but in particularly heavy storms the system can get overloaded with rainwater, and excess – waste and all – has to be emptied straight into the Seine.

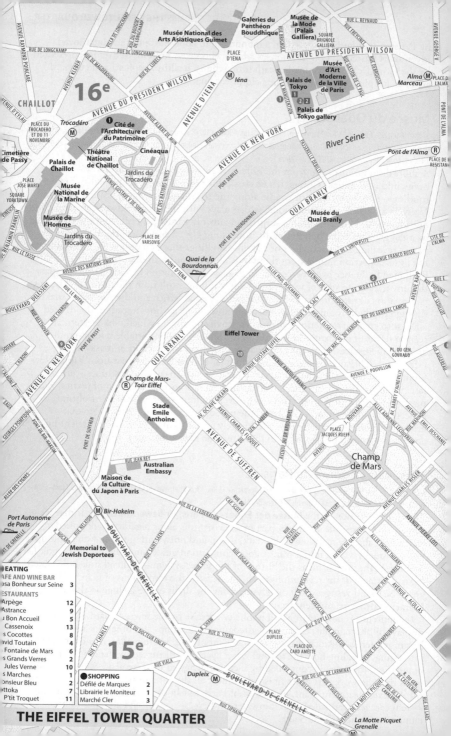

THE EIFFEL TOWER QUARTER

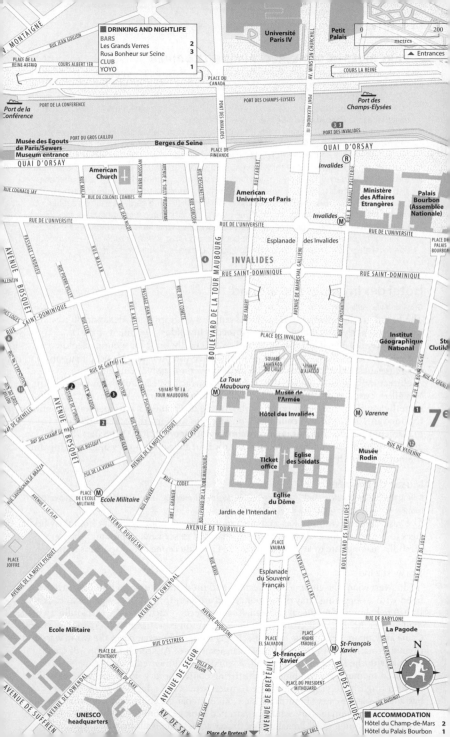

10

> ## PARC RIVES DE SEINE: RECLAIMING THE RIVER
>
> In 2013, what was once a noisy, traffic-choked highway between the pont d'Alma and Musée d'Orsay was re-created as the Berges de Seine, a pedestrianized **promenade** running for 2.3km along the river. The Berges proved so successful that in 2017 a similar promenade was established on the Right Bank (see box, p.91); it's possible to combine the two, now known together as the **Parc Rives de Seine**, in one 5.5km walk.
>
> The Left Bank riverside is particularly lively on weekends in the warmer months, where you can eat out on a sunny terrace, listen to concerts, take part in a sporting event, play a game of chess over a cup of coffee or simply relax in a deckchair and enjoy the river **views**. One of the features of the design is that, with its clever use of shipping containers and railway sleepers, in the event of a flood warning everything can be dismantled within 24 hours. The promenade also has an athletics track and a fitness course, Vélib' bikes and a small adventure playground for young children. Near the Pont de l'Alma are five small floating gardens, each on a different theme, with plenty of space for picnics: one is an "orchard" planted with apple trees, for example, while another is planted with meadow grasses. Picnic tables and benches are dotted all along the promenade, while restaurant-bars such as *Faust*, *Bistrot Alexandre III*, *Flow* and *Rosa Bonheur* (see p.285) – the last three on huge floating barges – offer food and drink.

Hôtel des Invalides and around

Ⓜ La Tour-Maubourg/Invalides/Varenne/RER Invalides

The broad green **Esplanade des Invalides** runs down from **Pont Alexandre III** towards the resplendently gilded dome of the **Hôtel des Invalides**. Despite its palatial appearance, Les Invalides, as it is known, was actually built for wounded soldiers in the reign of Louis XIV – whose foreign wars gave the building a constant supply of residents and whose equestrian statue lords it over a massive central arch. Architecturally, the building evokes a kind of barracks version of the awesome spirit of Versailles, stripped of finer flourishes – other than the dome – but crushingly grand nonetheless. The complex is home to the **Musée de l'Armée**, a national war museum founded in 1905, and two **churches** – one for the soldiers, the other intended as a mausoleum for the king but now containing **Napoleon's tomb**. Note that the grassed-in moat around the Invalides complex means you can only approach it from the north or south sides.

Musée de l'Armée

Daily: April–Oct 10am–6pm; Nov–March 10am–5pm; closed first Mon of each month Oct–June • €11 including Eglise du Dôme (see opposite) • Ⓦ musee-armee.fr • Ⓜ La Tour-Maubourg/Varenne

The vast **Musée de l'Armée** plots a course through French military history from the Middle Ages to the end of the Cold War; there's a great deal to see here, so pick and choose carefully, making sure to leave time to see the **Eglise du Dôme** and Napoleon's tomb.

The west wing

In the **west wing**, the gloomy old refectory and modernized arsenal building have been filled with a staggering array of **weaponry and armour**, from Bronze Age spearheads and Iron Age helmets to **medieval** and **Renaissance** pieces – including the extraordinary mail made for François I, a big man for his time – and some beautifully worked swords from **China** and **Japan**. Perhaps the most affecting galleries, however, cover the **world wars** and their aftermath, beginning with Prussia's annexation of Alsace-Lorraine in 1871 and ending with the fall of the Berlin Wall. Events are documented through imaginatively displayed memorabilia combined with stirring contemporary newsreels, most of which have an English-language option. The simplest artefacts – a rag doll found on a battlefield, plaster casts of mutilated faces, an overcoat caked in mud from the trenches – tell a stirring human story, while un-narrated footage, from the Somme, Dunkirk and a bomb attack on a small French town, flicker across bare walls in grim silence.

The east wing

The **Extraordinary Cabinets** in the **east wing** display historical figurines, artillery models and **military musical instruments**, among them some wonderful, serpent-like wind instruments. The floor above, covering the years from 1643 to 1870, has a number of intriguing **Napoleon** exhibits – a glossy Ingres portrait of the little emperor on his throne; personal effects including his campaign bed, trademark bicorne hat and coat; and even, somewhat surprisingly, his horse Vizir (now stuffed).

On the top floor, the **Musée des Plans-Reliefs** (Ⓦ museedesplansreliefs.culture.fr), a collection of around 25 super-scale models of French ports, fortified cities and islands, is surprisingly engaging. Essentially giant three-dimensional maps, these were created from the seventeenth century onwards to plan defences, plot potential artillery positions and mark successful campaigns. With the eerie green glow of their landscapes only just illuminating the long, tunnel-like attic, the effect is rather chilling.

You could easily skip the **Charles de Gaulle Historial** (closed Mon), in the basement, a sequence of hagiographic displays that leaves you with the distinct impression that de Gaulle was personally responsible for the liberation of France.

Eglise du Dôme

April–Sept daily 7.30am–6.45pm, Tues till 8.45pm; Oct–March daily 7.30am–6.45pm • €11 including Musée de l'Armée (see opposite) • Ⓦ musee-armee.fr • Ⓜ La Tour-Maubourg/Varenne

The **Eglise du Dôme**, on the south side of the complex, was formerly the Eglise Royale, intended for the private worship of Louis XIV and the royal family. The big draw here is **Napoleon's tomb**, a mighty sarcophagus of deep red porphyry, without any name or inscription, entombed in a giant circular pit and overlooked by guardian statues that represent his military victories. Friezes on the surrounding gallery parade the emperor's civic triumphs, along with quotations of gigantic (and largely accurate) conceit such as "Wherever the shadow of my rule has fallen, it has left lasting traces of its value". Napoleon was finally laid to rest in Paris on December 14, 1840, when his remains, freshly returned from St Helena – where he had died nineteen years earlier – were carried through the streets from the newly completed Arc de Triomphe to Invalides. Even though Louis-Philippe, a Bourbon, was on the throne, and Napoleon's nephew, Louis-Napoléon, had been imprisoned for attempting a coup four months earlier, the Bonapartists came out in force – half a million of them – to watch the emperor's last journey; Victor Hugo wrote that "it felt as if the whole of Paris had been poured to one side of the city, like liquid in a vase which has been tilted".

Perhaps more affecting than Napoleon's tomb is the memorial to **Maréchal Foch**, commander-in-chief of the allied forces at the end of World War I, which stands in the side chapel by the stairs leading down to the crypt. The marshal's effigy is borne by a phalanx of bronze infantrymen displaying a soldierly grief – particularly poignant when kissed by blue light from the stained-glass windows.

BONAPARTE'S BONES

In 2002 a French historian asked for **Napoleon's ashes** to be exhumed for DNA testing, claiming that the remains had been swapped for those of his *maître d'hôtel* on St Helena, one Jean-Baptiste Cipriani. Apparently, a witness at the original 1821 burial observed that the great man's teeth were "most villainous", whereas at the exhumation it was reported that they were "exceptionally white". There was some reason for suspicion, as the last round of tests – on a lock of the emperor's hair – suggested he had died of **arsenic poisoning**, not cancer, as the British claimed. Some said the traces were caused by the green – and therefore arsenic-laced – pigment in the imperial wallpaper, others that he was murdered by his captors. In 2008, however, the latter conspiracy theory was rebutted. Italian researchers found hairs from Napoleon's boyhood home and compared them with others taken on Elba and on St Helena. The arsenic levels were found to be consistently high, not just in the final sample; the British, it seems, were not as perfidious as all that.

Eglise des Soldats

The relatively spartan **Eglise des Soldats** (or **Soldiers' Church**) was – and remains – separated from the Eglise du Dôme by a glass wall, a design innovation that allowed worshippers on either side to share the same high altar without the risk of coming into social contact. Inside it's bright, airy and simply adorned, the high walls lined with almost a hundred enemy standards captured on the battlefield by the French army over the centuries. A commemorative Mass is still said here on May 5, the anniversary of the emperor's death.

Pont Alexandre III

Ⓜ/RER Invalides

North of the Invalides complex, the eastern end of the quai d'Orsay opens out into a grand esplanade. Extending across the river towards the giant conservatories of the Grand and Petit Palais is the **Pont Alexandre III**. The vista here was so cherished that when this bridge was built it was set as low as possible above the water so as not to get in the way of the view. That said, it's surely the most extravagant bridge in the city, its single-span metal arch stretching 109m across the river. It was unveiled in 1900, just in time for the Exposition Universelle, its name and elaborate decoration symbolizing Franco-Russian friendship – an ever more important alliance in the face of fast-growing German power. The nymphs stretching out downstream represent the Seine; those facing upstream signify St Petersburg's River Neva.

Quai d'Orsay

Ⓜ Alma–Marceau/Pont de l'Alma

To the west of the Pont Alexandre III, the pale neo-Gothic tower and copper spire of the **American Church** (Ⓦacparis.org) stand out on the **quai d'Orsay**. Together with the private **American University of Paris** nearby at 5 boulevard de la Tour-Maubourg, it plays a key role in the busy life of the city's large expat American community. News stories on French foreign policy use "the quai d'Orsay" to refer to the **Ministère des Affaires Etrangères** (Ministry of Foreign Affairs), which sits next to the Esplanade des Invalides and the **Palais Bourbon**, home of the **Assemblée Nationale**.

Rue Cler

Ⓜ La Tour-Maubourg/Ecole Militaire

An attractive, villagey wedge of early nineteenth-century streets huddles between avenue Bosquet and the Invalides, contrasting starkly with the grand austerity of much of the rest of the septième. At its heart is the market street **rue Cler**, lined with brasseries, food stores and fruit stalls on barrows – and the cross-streets, rue de Grenelle and rue St-Dominique, are full of classy boutiques, posh *bistrots* and little hotels.

Musée Rodin

77 rue de Varenne, 7ᵉ • Tues–Sun 10am–5.45pm • Museum and gardens €10; gardens €4 • ☎ 01 44 18 61 10, Ⓦ musee-rodin.fr • Ⓜ Varenne

Quite apart from its jaw-dropping collection, the **Musée Rodin** must have the loveliest setting of all Paris's museums: a gracious eighteenth-century mansion that the sculptor leased from the state in return for gifting them all his work upon his death. The generous **gardens** are an attraction in themselves, dotted with bronze versions of major projects like *The Burghers of Calais*, *The Thinker*, *The Gate of Hell* and *Ugolini and his Sons* – the last forming the centrepiece of the ornamental pond. There's a nice café, too.

Inside, the passionate intensity of the sculptures contrasts with the graceful wooden panelling, parquet and chandeliers, while the many age-tarnished mirrors make the perfect foil for Rodin's theory of profiles, in which each sculpture is formed from a collection of views from different standpoints. The collection is sensitively arranged in

---

LA PAGODE

The Japanese-style **La Pagode**, overlooking the corner of rue Monsieur at 57bis rue de Babylone, was built in 1895 for the wife of a director of the Bon Marché department store (see p.147), and later turned into an **historic cinema** – in 1959 it premiered Cocteau's extraordinary *Le Testament d'Orphée* and, a year later, was one of the first cinemas to screen the movies of the Nouvelle Vague. With its glorious Art Deco interior and pretty Japanese garden, it remained a leading light on the city's art-house movie circuit until 2015, when a long-running dispute between tenants and owner led to its closure. The building, in a parlous condition, was being restored at the time of writing, but its future remains uncertain.

10

---

chronological order, spotlighting major works and an intriguing range of lesser-known pieces to create a rounded picture of an extraordinary artist.

Many people are here, of course, to see much-loved works like **The Kiss**, which portrays Paolo and Francesca da Rimini, from Dante's *Divine Comedy*, in the moment before they were discovered and murdered by Francesca's husband. Contemporaries were scandalized by Francesca's distinctly active engagement; art critics today like to think of it as the last masterwork of figurative sculpture before the whole art form was reinvented – largely by Rodin himself. Paris's *Kiss* is one of only four marble versions of the work.

However, the *Kiss*, while breathtaking, is perhaps almost too familiar – the museum's great strength is on placing the big hitters (the **Burghers of Calais** and **The Thinker** are also here) into context. Most of the works on display are actually in clay or plaster, as these are considered to be Rodin's finest achievements. Vigorous, impressionistic **studies**, taken from life, reveal the human form in all its poignant vulnerability – a particularly striking and unidealized monument to Victor Hugo (1889) shows the great writer in a surprisingly collapsed, naked pose, while a number of dynamic busts of **Balzac** (in fact modelled by a cart driver, whom Rodin felt was the spitting image of the writer) reveal every human emotion. A plaster study for Balzac's dressing gown is touching and surreal in equal measure, a combination also repeated in a fascinating set of **assemblages** that meld different forms together to create bizarre amalgams – female nudes creeping out of antique vases, for example, or a mask of Camille Claudel melded with a male hand. Rodin's ability to shock is perhaps nowhere better displayed – literally – than in the vibrant **Iris**, whose pose, as she leaps through the air, is particularly explicit.

One room is devoted to **Camille Claudel**, Rodin's pupil, model and lover. Among her works is the painfully allegorical *L'Âge Mûr* (*The Age of Maturity*), symbolizing her ultimate rejection by the sculptor – you can see here an early plaster version and the far more heartbreaking final result. There's also an intimate bust of Rodin himself – Claudel's perception of her teacher was so akin to his own that he considered it his self-portrait.

Finally, don't forget to look at Rodin's collection of personal **artworks**, from quirky walls of ancient (sculpted) hands and feet to the paintings of his contemporaries. Dotted throughout the galleries, these range from Eugène Carrière's ghostly sepia portraits to the Van Gogh masterpiece *Le Père Tanguy*.

The Trocadéro quarter

Ⓜ Trocadéro

On the western side of the Eiffel Tower area, the **Trocadéro quarter** lies on the elevated northern bank of the Seine – a picturesque above-ground métro line (line 6) crosses the river on the Pont de Bir-Hakeim, offering excellent views of the Tower. The *quartier* is also connected to the septième by three fine bridges: the businesslike Pont de l'Alma, the graceful Passerelle Debilly and the handsome Pont d'Iéna, which thrusts north as if from under the very legs of the Tower into the embrace of the **Palais de Chaillot**.

10

Palais de Chaillot

1 place du Trocadéro et du 11 Novembre, 16ᵉ • Ⓜ Trocadéro

From behind its elaborate park and fountains, the sweeping arcs of the **Palais de Chaillot** seem designed to embrace the view of the Eiffel Tower across the river. The Modernist-Classical architecture dates the palace to 1937, when it was built as the showpiece of the Exposition Universelle, one of Paris's regular trade and culture jamborees. The central terrace between the two curving wings provides a perfect platform for photo opportunities, curio-sellers and skateboarders.

The *palais* houses several museums, including the revamped **Musée de l'Homme**, which charts human evolution, and the outstanding **Cité de l'Architecture et du Patrimoine**, an architectural treasure trove. The **Musée National de la Marine**, which explores French naval history, shipping and marine exploration, is closed for renovations until 2022. Beneath the central terrace lies the superb **Théâtre National de Chaillot**, which stages diverse and usually radical productions (see p.317); enter via the northern wing.

Musée de l'Homme

Palais de Chaillot, 17 place du Trocadéro, 16ᵉ • Mon & Wed–Sun 10am–6pm • €10, under-26s free; €8 upon presentation of a ticket for the Musée du Quai Branly (see p.151) • ☎ 01 44 05 72 72, ⓦ museedelhomme.fr • Ⓜ Trocadéro

The **Musée de l'Homme**, recently updated to re-present its vast, and historic, ethnography collection for modern audiences, asks many questions about what it means to be human. Long philosophical captions ponder three key themes – Who are we? Where do we come from? Where are we headed? – and, unlike the city's other ethnographical museum, Musée du Quai Branly (see p.151), which presents its objects as works of art, the Musée de l'Homme is clearly on the side of science. That's not to say it's dry – there's a genuine attempt to outline connections and contexts between the exhibits, which range from old-fashioned stuffed animals and skeletons to high-tech digital touchscreens. Look for the history of **waxworking**, particularly the bizarre eighteenth-century pieces – including a model of a newborn as seen only by its arteries, veins and organs – and the jars of brains, ranging in size from tiny (crocodile) to enormous (elephant). Exhibited in Paris in 1882, the Peruvian **mummy** displayed here, coiled like a foetus, is said to have inspired Edvard Munch's *The Scream*. Not all the exhibits are quite so gruesome; **carnival costumes** and masks from eastern Europe, for example, are suffused with strange playfulness. Things do peter out a little as you head upstairs, when the focus shifts towards the prehistoric era before bringing things up to date with features on the effects of globalization.

There's a fancy **restaurant**, *Café de l'Homme* (daily noon–2am), on the ground floor; its terrace has a fabulous view of the Eiffel Tower, which you can also gaze upon from the museum's **snack bar**, *Café Lucy*, on the second floor.

Cité de l'Architecture et du Patrimoine

Palais de Chaillot, 16ᵉ • Wed–Sun 11am–7pm, Thurs till 9pm • €8; temporary exhibitions €5; combination ticket €12; free first Sun of the month • ☎ 01 58 51 52 00, ⓦ citechaillot.fr • Ⓜ Trocadéro/Iéna

The splendid **Cité de l'Architecture et du Patrimoine**, a combined institute, library and **museum of architecture**, occupies the eastern wing of the Palais de Chaillot. The bedrock of the museum, the long **Galerie des Moulages**, on the loftily vaulted ground floor, displays giant plaster casts of sections of great French buildings. Seen here as crisp and clean as they were before age dulled their detail, these vibrant casts vividly display the development of national (mainly church) architecture from the Middle Ages through to the nineteenth century. There are entire portals from Romanesque cathedrals, Gothic windows, Renaissance tombs and exact reproductions of the finest statuary in France. The casts date from an earlier, nineteenth-century museum, and to see French architecture laid out as a kind of grand historical panorama is as eye-opening now as it was for the original curiosity-seekers.

On the second floor, the **Galerie d'Architecture Moderne et Contemporaine** showcases the nineteenth and twentieth centuries with some stunning, original architectural models, and a full-size – and distinctly poky – reconstruction of an "E2 superior" apartment from Le Corbusier's Cité Radieuse in Marseille, which you can actually walk through. This gallery offers a fascinating lesson in the evolution of modern design, but more wondrous still is the **Galerie des Peintures Murales et des Vitraux**, which occupies the central pavilion on the second and third floors. In the same spirit as the *moulages* gallery, it displays life-size copies of French wall paintings, frescoes and stained glass. Its stunning centrepiece is the lofty, Byzantine-style cupola from Cahors cathedral, but it's worth penetrating deeper into the maze-like sequence of rooms as far as the claustrophobic reconstruction of the Romanesque crypt of the church of Tavant, in the Loire region, and heading up to the third floor for the terrifying sequence of medieval Passions and Last Judgements. The **library** on the first floor is also well worth a look for its copy of a Romanesque vault mural from the church of St-Savin-sur-Gartempe, and the **temporary exhibitions** – on subjects from Art Deco to beach architecture – are generally excellent.

Cinéaqua

5 av Albert de Mun, 16e • Daily 10am–7pm • €20.50, children aged 3–12 €13, aged 13–17 €16; it's best to book online to avoid queues • ☎ 01 40 69 23 23, ⓦ cineaqua.com • Ⓜ Trocadéro/Iéna

Paris's aquarium, **Cinéaqua**, accessed from a ramp on the riverfront side of the Palais de Chaillot, features hundreds of tropical fish, including sharks, as well as the more humble specimens found in the River Seine. Children will particularly enjoy the *bassin caresses*, where you can feed and touch tame koi carp, and the mermaid shows at weekends. The two cinemas regularly screen fishy-themed cartoons and documentaries.

Musée National des Arts Asiatiques Guimet

6 place d'Iéna, 16e • Mon & Wed–Sun 10am–6pm • €7.50, €9.50 with temporary exhibitions, free first Sun of the month • ☎ 01 56 52 53 00, ⓦ guimet.fr • Ⓜ Iéna

The **Musée National des Arts Asiatiques Guimet** winds round four floors groaning under the weight of statues of Buddhas and gods, some fierce, some meditative, and all of them dramatically displayed alongside ceramics, paintings and other objets d'art. Each room is devoted to a different country of origin, stretching from the Greek-influenced Buddhist statues of the Gandhara civilization, on the first floor, to fierce demons from Nepal and pot-bellied Chinese Buddhas. The highlight, however, is the breathtaking roofed-in **courtyard**: it's a perfectly airy space in which to show off the museum's world-renowned collection of **Khmer sculpture** – from the civilization that produced Cambodia's Angkor Wat. On the third floor is a rotunda that was used by the collection's founder, **Emile Guimet**, for the first Buddhist ceremony ever held in France.

Galeries du Panthéon Bouddhique

19 av d'Iéna, 16e • Mon & Wed–Sun 10am–5.45pm • Free • ☎ 01 40 73 88 00, ⓦ guimet.fr • Ⓜ Iéna

Emile Guimet's original collection, which he brought back from his travels in Japan in 1876, is exhibited near the Musée Guimet in the **Galeries du Panthéon Bouddhique**. While far smaller, in some ways it's a more satisfying affair than the larger museum, as the gilded ranks of Buddhas are presented with a Buddhist's eye rather than an art collector's. At the back is a Japanese garden, its ranks of bamboo and pussy willow reflected in still pools.

Musée de la Mode

10 av Pierre 1er de Serbie, 16e • Tues, Wed & Fri–Sun 10am–6pm • Thurs 10am–9pm • Admission varies • ☎ 01 56 52 86 00, ⓦ palaisgalliera.paris.fr • Ⓜ Iéna/Alma–Marceau

The rather exquisite bijoux box of the **Palais Galliera** was built in the 1880s by the Duchesse de Galliera to house her private art collection. It now belongs to the city, and is the home of the **Musée de la Mode**. The museum's unrivalled collection of some seventy thousand garments and accessories from the eighteenth century to the present day is rotated through two or three shows a year, with themes such as "Creating the Myth of Marlene Dietrich" or focusing on single designers such as Jeanne Lanvin or Balenciaga. During changeovers the museum is closed.

Palais de Tokyo

13 av du Président-Wilson, 16ᵉ • Ⓜ Iéna/Alma–Marceau

10

The **Palais de Tokyo** houses two galleries of modern art, both of which are among the most rewarding in Paris, though they see fewer visitors than the Pompidou Centre. The entrance to the palace is on its north side, but most people arrive across the Seine via the pedestrian **Passerelle Debilly**. Rather surprisingly, given its modern looks, this bridge is a contemporary of its near neighbour, the profoundly more ornate Pont Alexandre III – both were opened in 1900, in time for the Exposition Universelle.

The Palais de Tokyo dates from a later exhibition, the tension-filled 1937 World Fair, at which the German and Russian pavilions faced each other across the Seine in an architectural standoff. **Antoine Bourdelle**'s bronze statue of "France", which surveys the terrace, is a living reminder of the fervid nationalism of those times. The palace was always intended to be a gallery of **modern art**, however, and most of its decoration takes a more consciously artistic theme. Alfred Auguste Janniot's vast Art Deco bas-reliefs, which frame the central staircase, represent the nine muses, and the colonnaded building itself is simple and beautiful. The terrace, meanwhile, is also a suntrap, much favoured by skateboarders and graffiti artists.

On Wednesday and Saturday mornings, a bustling **food market** takes over avenue du Président-Wilson, from Iéna métro station down to the palace.

Palais de Tokyo gallery

Palais de Tokyo • Mon & Wed–Sun noon–midnight • €12 • ☎ 01 81 97 35 88, Ⓦ palaisdetokyo.com • Ⓜ Iéna/Alma–Marceau

In the west wing of the Palais de Tokyo building, the **Palais de Tokyo gallery**, one of Europe's largest and most ambitious contemporary art spaces, has a reputation for exciting avant-garde shows exhibitions. It calls itself "a rebellious wasteland", and some of the space appears deliberately semi-derelict, with industrial-looking concrete walls and exposed piping creating a sense of work in progress. The museum has no permanent exhibits, but instead mounts large-scale exhibitions involving multiple curators. Prominence is given to French work, but many international artists are also represented, ranging from the well established, such as Julio Le Parc, to emerging figures including Taro Izumi. The museum has a good bookshop and two **restaurants**: *Les Grands Verres*, with its cool cocktail bar (see p.286), and classy *Monsieur Bleu* (see p.286), overlooking the Seine.

Musée d'Art Moderne de la Ville de Paris

Palais de Tokyo • Tues–Sun 10am–6pm, Thurs till 10pm • Free; varying charges for temporary exhibitions • ☎ 01 53 67 40 80, Ⓦ mam.paris.fr • Ⓜ Iéna/Alma–Marceau

The east wing of the Palais de Tokyo building houses the **Musée d'Art Moderne de la Ville de Paris**. The collection can't rival the Pompidou Centre's, but it's free, relatively uncrowded and the environment is far more contemplative – and architecturally more fitting when it comes to works by early twentieth-century artists. The ground floor, by the entrance – actually level 4 – is given over to temporary exhibitions, as is level 6. There's a small **café**, too, with seating on the Palais de Tokyo's sunny central terrace and great Eiffel Tower views.

Dufy and Matisse

The gallery received unwelcome publicity in 2010 when a lone thief made off with five priceless canvases by Picasso, Matisse, Modigliani, Braque and Léger, but it still has its marvellous (and entirely untransportable) centrepieces. On level 5 a vast, curving chamber provides wall-space for Raoul Dufy's giant fresco **La Fée Electricité** ("The Electricity Fairy"). Originally designed for the Light and Electricity Pavilion in the 1937 Exposition Universelle, its 250 vivid panels tell the story of electricity from the earliest experimenters to the triumph of industrialization that was the power station. On level 3 the chapel-like **salle Matisse** is devoted to two versions of Matisse's balletic and heart-lifting *La Danse de Paris* (1931–33) – an incomplete early version and a later work which, although Matisse was satisfied with it, proved to be the wrong size for the building for which it was designed. Daniel Buren's *Mur de Peintures* (1995–2006), in his trademark stripes, is displayed in the same room.

10

The permanent collection

The main **permanent collection** spreads across levels 1 and 2. It's chronologically themed, starting with Fauvism and Cubism, and progressing through to Dada and the Ecole de Paris, and beyond. Most artists working in France – Braque, Chagall, Robert and Sonia Delaunay, Derain, Duchamp, Dufy, Klein, Léger, Modigliani, Picasso and others – are represented, and there is a Parisian theme to many of the works. The collection is kept up to the minute by an active buying policy, and some bold acquisitions of sculpture, painting and video by contemporary artists are displayed in the final suite of rooms. Look out in particular for **Christian Boltanski**'s photographs and installations of children's clothing and phone books; their unsettling existentialism stands in dramatic contrast to the works of Eva & Adele nearby – kitsch narcissism dressed up as performance art.

Place de l'Alma and around

Ⓜ Alma Marceau

A few steps upstream of the Palais de Tokyo, on **place de l'Alma**, stands a full-scale, golden replica of the flame from the Statue of Liberty. Given to France in 1987 as a symbol of Franco–American relations, a decade later the flame became an unofficial memorial to **Princess Diana**, who died after her Mercedes crashed in the underpass beneath; you may still see the odd bunch of withered flowers or heartfelt message left as tribute. More recently, however, since the practice was banned at the Pont des Arts (see p.140), the monument has been strewn with padlocks – the work of young lovers convinced that the only way to prove their passion is to hang a "love lock" from a Paris landmark.

Pont de l'Alma

Ⓜ Alma–Marceau

The **Pont de l'Alma**, which crosses the Seine to arrive on the Left Bank a little west of the Sewers Museum (see p.151), is a rather brutal 1970s steel-and-concrete affair. It's worth taking a peek at its celebrated **zouave** statue, however, which hides away by the waterline, on the upstream side. The name comes from the North African soldiers who fought in the French army during the Crimean War, and it was one of four military statues that adorned the previous Alma bridge. It has long served as Parisians' yardstick for measuring the Seine's flooding. In 1910, the water came up to the zouave's shoulders, a record that has yet to be broken. On the new bridge, however, he actually stands slightly higher than he used to, so even a knee-high flood is a fairly serious event; during the dramatic floods of June 2016 the waters came to just below his waist.

MUSÉE BOURDELLE

Montparnasse and southern Paris

The parade of cafés, brasseries and cinemas that runs through the heart of modern Montparnasse has historically been a honeypot for pleasure-seekers, as well as a kind of border dividing well-heeled St-Germain from the amorphous populations of the three arrondissements of southern Paris, the 13e, 14e and 15e. Overscale developments from the 1950s to the present day have scarred parts of this side of the city, but there are three great parks – André-Citroën (with its very own tethered balloon), Georges-Brassens and Montsouris – and some enticing pockets that have been allowed to evolve in a happily patchy way. The old Butte-aux-Cailles neighbourhood in the 13e, for example, is a delight – and a complete contrast in atmosphere to the slick riverside complex known as Paris Rive Gauche.

Montparnasse and the 14ᵉ

The story goes that, before it was levelled in the early eighteenth century, students used to drink and declaim poetry from the top of a pile of spoil deposited from the Denfert-Rochereau quarries, calling the mound "Mount Parnassus" after the legendary home of the muses of poetry and song, and of drunken Bacchus. That may or may not be true, but the image of **Montparnasse** as a neighbourhood for carousing really stems from the construction of the Mur des Fermiers Généraux in 1784, or "Customs Wall", which split the high-taxed city from the poorer, less-regulated township areas beyond. In the nineteenth century, left-leaning intellectuals and poets such as Verlaine and Baudelaire abandoned the city centre for Montparnasse, drawn by the inexpensive cafés and lively nightlife. The quarter's lasting fame, however, rests on its role as the **birthplace of Modernism**, following the artistic exodus from Montmartre. In the *années folles*, or "Mad Years" following World War I, artists such as Picasso, Matisse, Brancusi, Kandinsky, Modigliani, Giacometti and Chagall were all habitués of the celebrated cafés around **place Vavin**. They were soon joined by a self-professed "lost generation" of bohemia-hunting and Prohibition-fleeing Americans – Hemingway, Pound, Man Ray and Dos Passos among them. Many were buried in **Montparnasse cemetery**, and still more bones lie nearby in the grim **catacombs**.

The area immediately around Montparnasse's railway station is dominated by the gigantic **Tour Montparnasse**, which you can ascend for a superb view of the city. North of Montparnasse station are two beguiling **artists' museums**, recalling the area's heyday, while the nearby **Fondation Cartier** showcases contemporary art and architecture. South of the station, the **14ᵉ** is one of the most characterful of the outer arrondissements, with a wonderful green space in the **Parc Montsouris**. An old-fashioned network of streets still exists in the **Pernety** and **Plaisance** *quartiers*, where many artists chose to live in the affordable *villas* (similar to mews) built in the 1920s and 1930s.

Musée Bourdelle

18 rue Antoine Bourdelle, 15ᵉ • Tues–Sun 10am–6pm • Free; charge for temporary exhibitions • ☎ 01 49 54 73 73, ⓦ bourdelle.paris.fr • ⓜ Montparnasse Bienvenüe/Falguière

The **Musée Bourdelle** is built around the artist's former studio and garden. As Rodin's pupil and Giacometti's teacher, Antoine Bourdelle bridged the period between naturalism and a more geometrically conceived style; he was arguably the first Modernist. Huge plaster models of mythological subjects such as *Hercules the Archer* and *The Dying Centaur* take pride of place in the skylit Modernist **Great Hall**, along with the imposing *Monument to General Alvear* and *France*; asked why the centaur was dying, Bourdelle replied that he dies, like all the gods, "because no-one believes in him any more". You can see small marble, wood and bronze sculptures and another plaster *Dying Centaur* in the sculptor's atmospheric old **studio**, which looks almost as if he has just stepped out, plus bronze versions of the major monumental works in the charming, leafy **gardens**. His **living quarters**, complete with day bed and original stove, hold paintings and small sculptures from his own collection. You can also see a sequence of studios displaying his works – including paintings – in **chronological order**, from 1883 to his death in 1929; the highlight here is a wonderful series of tumultuous **Beethoven** busts and masks, sculpted between 1887 and 1929. Bourdelle was all but obsessed with the composer, and portrayed him in sculptural form more than eighty times.

Tour Montparnasse

Rue de l'Arrivée, 15ᵉ • Observation deck/viewing terrace daily: April–Sept 9.30am–11.30pm; Oct–March 9.30am–10.30pm • €15 • ☎ 01 45 38 52 56, ⓦ tourmontparnasse56.com • ⓜ Montparnasse Bienvenüe

Montparnasse station's arch gives onto a broad concrete esplanade surrounded by traffic, the prospect of the city blocked by the brown glass face of the **Tour Montparnasse**. At the time of its deeply controversial construction in 1973, this was one of Paris's first skyscrapers, defying the problem of the city's quarried-out limestone bedrock with 56 massive piles driven into a chalk layer more than 40m below ground. Few Parisians have a good word to say for this ugly monolith, but the panoramic **views** from the open-air, often windy **rooftop platform** (210m high) are arguably better than from the Eiffel Tower – you can see the Eiffel Tower from here, after all, and on a (very) clear day visibility extends to 40km. There's another, glassed-in, observation deck (196m) on the 56th floor, where you'll also find a café and a few interactive exhibits – the super-speedy elevator ride up is a thrill in itself.

Jardin Atlantique

Place des Cinq Martyrs du Lycée Buffon, behind Montparnasse train station, 15e; access from bd Pasteur or by the stairs alongside platform #3 • Mon–Fri 8am–7pm/9.30pm, Sat & Sun 9am–7pm/9.30pm (depending on season) • Free • ⓜ Montparnasse Bienvenüe

Montparnasse was once the great arrival and departure point for boat travellers across the Atlantic and Bretons seeking work in the capital. Brittany's influence is

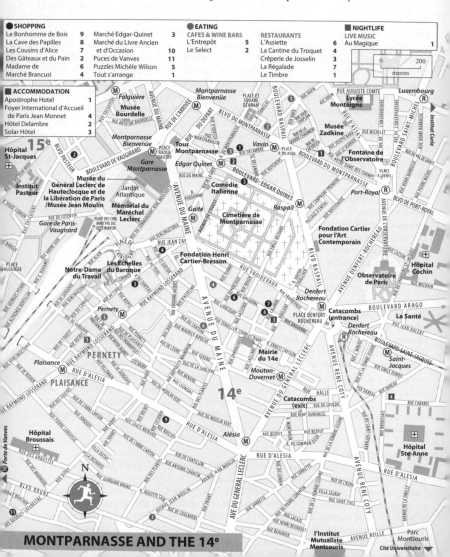

● SHOPPING			
Le Bonhomme de Bois	9	Marché Edgar-Quinet	3
La Cave des Papilles	8	Marché du Livre Ancien	
Les Cousins d'Alice	7	et d'Occasion	10
Des Gâteaux et du Pain	2	Puces de Vanves	11
Madame de	6	Puzzles Michèle Wilson	5
Marché Brancusi	4	Tout s'arrange	1

● EATING		
CAFÉS & WINE BARS		
L'Entrepôt	5	
Le Select	2	
RESTAURANTS		
L'Assiette	6	
La Cantine du Troquet	4	
Crêperie de Josselin	3	
La Régalade	7	
Le Timbre	1	

■ NIGHTLIFE	
LIVE MUSIC	
Au Magique	1

● ACCOMMODATION	
Apostrophe Hotel	1
Foyer International d'Accueil	
de Paris Jean Monnet	4
Hôtel Delambre	2
Solar Hôtel	3

MONTPARNASSE AND THE 14e

still evident in the abundance of **crêperies** in the area, but the connection is also evoked by the **Jardin Atlantique**, a public park on the station roof. Completed in 1994, between cliff-like glass walls of high-rise blocks, it was lauded as a remarkable piece of design, and though it feels a little dated today it is still a very welcome green space in this part of town, with tennis courts and a children's playground. Lawns – some planted with long coastal grasses – rise and fall in symbolic waves, while a double line of trees (those on the eastern side are of American origin, those on the West, European) runs from the station end to the central **Ile des Hespérides** water-jet fountain. The fountain, with its giant thermometer and rain gauge, is a favourite spot for children on sunny days. Ventilation shafts dotted around the grass mean you can clearly hear the trains rumbling below, and at the southern end of the park, huge canopied ventilation holes reveal glimpses – if you crane your neck – of TGV roofs and rail sleepers.

Musée du Général Leclerc de Hauteclocque et de la Libération de Paris/Musée Jean Moulin

Jardin Atlantique, 15ᵉ • Tues–Sun 10am–6pm • Free • ☎ 01 40 64 39 44 , ⓦ museesleclercmoulin.paris.fr • Ⓜ Montparnasse Bienvenüe

Facing out onto the Jardin Atlantique, the double museum **Musée du Général Leclerc de Hauteclocque et de la Libération de Paris/Musée Jean Moulin** may be worth a stop if you're waiting for a train to Chartres. The Musée Moulin is the most interesting of the two, giving a wordy potted history of the Resistance (with English captioning) illustrated by photos, posters, news footage and newspapers. The central display focuses on Jean Moulin, hero of the Resistance (see p.244). The second museum, focusing on the Free French, with a central display on Général Leclerc, is perhaps a little too detailed for a general-interest visitor.

Rue de la Gaîté

Ⓜ Edgar Quinet/Gaîté

East of the train station, **Rue de la Gaîté**, where Trotsky once lived, may be peppered with sex shops and takeaways today, but it also offers a slice of turn-of-the-twentieth-century theatreland. The Théâtre Montparnasse and the Théâtre Gaîté-Montparnasse are close together at the bottom of the street, while at the northern end, the little **Comédie Italienne** theatre advertises its diet of Goldoni and the like with a wonderfully camp, blue-and-gold exterior – all swags and garlands, commedia dell'arte figures and ornate gilt frames.

Marché Edgar Quinet

Bd Edgar Quinet • Wed & Sat mornings, Sun roughly 10am–dusk • Ⓜ Edgar Quinet

Boulevard Edgar Quinet is entirely consumed by a lively food **market** on Wednesday and Saturday mornings (see p.341), while on Sundays more than a hundred craftworkers take over; photographers jostle with potters, clothes designers with painters, and it's a great place to browse away the day.

Cimetière de Montparnasse

3 bd Edgar Quinet, 14ᵉ • March 16–Nov 5 Mon–Fri 8am–6pm, Sat 8.30am–6pm, Sun 9am–6pm; Nov 6–March 15 closes 5.30pm • Free • ☎ 01 44 10 86 50 • Ⓜ Raspail/Gaîté/Edgar Quinet

The last resting place of many illustrious artistic names, **Montparnasse cemetery**, opened in 1824, is second in size to Père-Lachaise (see p.209), and a long way behind it in celebrity. It's an impressive space, nonetheless, sheltering behind high walls in the lee of the Tour Montparnasse. In the southwest corner, the sailless **windmill**, built in the mid-seventeenth century by local monks, was converted into a tavern after the French revolution and used as a caretaker's lodge when the cemetery opened. It's not open to the public.

To track down the cemetery's illustrious residents, pick up a map from the guardhouse by each entrance. The unembellished joint grave of **Jean-Paul Sartre** and **Simone de Beauvoir** lies right of the main entrance on boulevard Edgar Quinet – Sartre lived out the last few decades of his life just a few metres away on boulevard Raspail. Down avenue de l'Ouest, which follows the inside western wall of the cemetery, you'll find the tombs of **Baudelaire** (who also has a more arresting cenotaph by rue Emile-Richard, on the cemetery's avenue Transversale), the sculptor **Ossip Zadkine** and the Fascist **Pierre Laval** – once the country's prime minister – who was executed in 1945 for treason. You can pay homage to **Proudhon**, the anarchist who coined the phrase "Property is theft!"; he lies in Division 2, by the central roundabout, near the great photographer of Paris, **Brassaï**. In the adjacent Division 1, the tomb of singer **Serge Gainsbourg** is regularly festooned with métro tickets – the "lilacs" of his ticket-punching song *Le Poinçonneur des Lilas* – along with flowers, wine bottles and packets of Gitanes cigarettes.

Monuments and sculptures

Grave-hunting aside, it's worth seeking out some of the cemetery's finer **monuments**. Horace Daillion's 1889 winged bronze, **Le Génie du Sommeil éternel**, dominates the central roundabout, but far more moving is the tragic sculptural scene **La Séparation du Couple**, which stands a short distance below the windmill (in Division 4, beside the allée des Sergeants de la Rochelle). A giant bird created by the sculptor **Niki de Saint Phalle** in mirrored mosaic hovers in the northeast corner of Division 18, next to the avenue de l'Est; the title reads "To my friend Jean-Jacques: a bird which has flown too soon". Perhaps the most poignant monument of all lies in the eastern angle of the cemetery, on the other side of rue Emile-Richard; in the far northern corner of this section, a tomb dedicated to Tania Rachevskaia, a young anarchist, stands crowned with a version of Brancusi's Cubist sculpture **The Kiss**. This gentle, intimate work was commissioned by Rachevskaia's lover, for whom she committed suicide.

Boulevard du Montparnasse
Ⓜ Vavin

Most of the life of the Montparnasse *quartier* is concentrated on **boulevard du Montparnasse**. In the stretch near Vavin métro you'll find Rodin's **Balzac** ruminating over the crossroads, and a cluster of celebrated **cafés**: the *Select* (see p.286), *Coupole*, *Dôme* and *Rotonde*. Their heyday was in the 1910s and 1920s, when artists and poets such as Apollinaire, Chagall, Léger, Modigliani, Picasso and Zadkine rubbed shoulders with exiled revolutionaries, including Lenin and Trotsky, paying a few centimes to occupy tables for hours on end. Even by the 1930s, the fashionable intelligentsia were moving on to St-Germain, but the brasseries remain proudly Parisian classics – if no longer bohemian haunts.

Still trading on their historical cachet, all the cafés have moved steadily upmarket; the swankiest by far is the **Closerie des Lilas**, with its fabled (and now largely glazed-in) *terrasse* on the corner of the tree-lined avenue de l'Observatoire. In the days when it was a cheap café, Hemingway wrote most of *The Sun Also Rises* here. An even more stirring historical association, however, is with Napoleon's Marshal Ney, the "bravest of the brave", as his master called him. His sword-wielding statue – admired from the terrace by everyone from Auguste Rodin to George Orwell, as well as Hemingway – now marks the spot on the pavement outside where he died at the hands of a royalist firing squad.

Musée Zadkine
100bis rue d'Assas, 6ᵉ • Tues–Sun 10am–6pm • Free • ☎ 01 55 42 77 20, ⓦ zadkine.paris.fr • Ⓜ Vavin/RER Port-Royal

The diminutive **Musée Zadkine** occupies the Russian-born sculptor **Ossip Zadkine**'s studio-house, where he lived and worked from 1928 until his death in 1967. Airy and beautifully composed, it has the feel of a private contemporary gallery, with little contextual detail and more focus on the works themselves. The small garden, enclosed by ivy-covered studios and dwarfed by tall buildings, is as important as the interior. Here, dotted among the greenery, are angular Cubist bronzes such as the compelling *Orphée* and a study for *La Ville détruite*, whose twisted, agonized torso was intended to

MONTPARNASSE ARCHITECTURE

Dominated as it is by the skyscraping blade of its tower, the busy boulevards, and the large-scale developments around the station, Montparnasse can feel a little inhuman and over-modernized. Wandering down the backstreets, however, you can find some kindlier examples of **architecture**, ranging from the playful lines of early **Art Deco** to the diaphanous **contemporary** glasswork of Jean Nouvel's Fondation Cartier.

26 rue Vavin 6e; Ⓜ Vavin. Decked in white and blue tiles, the terraced balconies of this elegant apartment block are stepped back, allowing greenery and plants to flourish in the light. Built by Henri Sauvage in 1912.

Rue Schoelcher and rue Froidevaux 14e; Ⓜ Raspail/Denfert-Rochereau. A parade of varied nineteenth- and early twentieth-century styles. Check out 5 rue Schoelcher, especially, for its early Art Deco balconies and windows, dating from 1911 – Picasso had his studio at 5bis for a short time in 1916. The apartments at 11 rue Schoelcher are just sixteen years younger, but the transformation to modernity is complete. (Simone de Beauvoir lived at 11bis from 1955 until her death in 1986.) Also worth seeing is 23 rue Froidevaux, a 1929 block of artists' studios with huge windows for northern light and decorated with stunning floral mosaics.

266 bd Raspail 14e; Ⓜ Raspail/Denfert-Rochereau. The building of this private architecture and design academy dates from 1988 and displays a marked Beaubourg influence, notably the external stairs and blue pipe columns in front. The original Ecole Spéciale d'Architecture building nearby, at no. 254, dates from 1904, and is dreary in comparison.

31 rue Campagne-Première 14e; Ⓜ Raspail. Myriad shell-like, earthenware tiles by Alexandre Bigot encrust the concrete structure of André Arfvidson's desirable 1912 *appartements*, with their huge, iron-framed studio windows. Man Ray had a studio here in the early 1920s.

Fondation Cartier pour l'Art Contemporain 261 bd Raspail, 14e; Ⓜ Raspail. One of Jean Nouvel's most successful, airy, postmodern steel-and-glass structures. See below.

Passage d'Enfer 14e; Ⓜ Raspail. Parallel to rue Campagne-Première, this narrow cobblestone street – whose name translates as "Hell Alley" – was once a Cité Ouvrière, or cul-de-sac of nineteenth-century workers' housing. The narrow, terraced buildings are now extremely covetable.

express the horror of aerial bombing. In the house and studio you can see a collection of gentler, elongated wooden torsos, busts and animal figures, along with smaller-scale bronze and stone works – the artist worked with a wide range of materials including granite, volcanic stone, plaster, ebony and acacia.

Fondation Cartier pour l'Art Contemporain

261 bd Raspail, 14e • Tues 11am–10pm, Wed–Sun 11am–8pm • €10.50 • ☎ 01 42 18 56 50, Ⓦ fondation.cartier.com • Ⓜ Raspail

The **Fondation Cartier pour l'Art Contemporain** occupies one of the finest contemporary buildings in Paris, a stunning glass-and-steel construction designed in 1994 by Jean Nouvel. A glass wall follows the line of the street like a false start to the building proper, leaving space for the Tree of Liberty, planted by Chateaubriand during the Revolution, to grow in the garden behind. The glass of the building itself cleverly suggests a kind of fade-out into the air. Inside, all kinds of contemporary art – installations, videos, photography, multi-media, graffiti – often by foreign artists little known in France, are shown in temporary exhibitions that use the light and generous spaces to maximum advantage.

The catacombs

Place Denfert-Rochereau, 14e • Tues–Sun 10am–8.30pm, last entry 7.30pm • €12 • ☎ 01 43 22 47 63, Ⓦ catacombes.paris.fr • Ⓜ Denfert-Rochereau

Unlike in the nearby Montparnasse cemetery, you won't find any celebrity dead in the **catacombs** – just row upon row of anonymous human bones. The entrance is on the square that Parisians have long known as place d'Enfer, or "Hell Square", though the name may derive from nothing more sinister than the Latin Via Inferiora ("The Low Road"); the huge lion in the middle was designed by **Bartholdi**, better known for the

UNDERGROUND PARIS

In September 2004, while on a training exercise in a group of **tunnels** underneath the Palais de Chaillot, the Parisian police stumbled upon a clandestine underground cell. Nothing to do with terrorism, this one, but an actual **subterranean chamber**, 400 square metres in size, which had been fitted out as a cinema by the secretive underground arts organization UX. As the story hit the press, a band of troglodytes emerged blinking into the full beam of the media spotlight. Since the 1980s, it turned out, hundreds of these "*cataphiles*" had been holding anything from underground parties and art exhibitions to festivals and, it was rumoured, orgies. Experienced tunnel-goers talked of elaborate murals and a huge, pillared party room known as "La Plage", overlooked by a graffiti version of Hokusai's *The Wave*.

In fact, the tunnels underneath Chaillot form only a small part of a vast network that dates back to the **medieval era**, when the stone for building Paris was quarried out from its most obvious source, immediately underfoot. Today, more than 300km of underground galleries lie beneath the city, especially on the Left Bank's 5e, 6e, 14e and 15e arrondissements, where the Grand Réseau Sud runs for more than 100km. Another separate network lurks beneath the 13e arrondissement, while in the 16e, it's said that the rock is like Gruyère cheese – full of holes. In 1774, after a cave-in swallowed up whole buildings in what is now avenue Denfert-Rochereau, a **royal commission** was set up to map the old quarries and shore up the most precarious foundations. Great galleries were cut along the lines of the roads and the material used to infill the worst voids. Today, some of these underground "streets" still exist, while those above have disappeared. Some attribute modern Paris's relative lack of skyscrapers to doubts about the quality of the city's foundations.

In the nineteenth century, many tunnels were used for mushroom cultivation (the everyday supermarket variety is still known in France as the *champignon de Paris*), others for growing endives or brewing beer, while Carthusian monks even practised distillation under the modern-day Jardin du Luxembourg. The most creative scheme, however, involved the hygienic storage of human remains. From the 1780s, the contents of Paris's overcrowded cemeteries were slowly transferred underground. In Montparnasse, one bone-lined section of the **catacombs** can still be visited (see p.167) but, otherwise, "penetrating into or circulating within" the network has been **illegal** since 1955. You can get down into the métro, of course, and at the Musée des Egouts de Paris (see p.151) you can descend into a part of the city's 2300km of sewers. But it would be foolish to try anything more adventurous; while cool *cataphiles* still trudge into the bowels of the earth to create art, throw pool parties and even scuba dive, this is very much a clandestine activity, and in 1993, one such urban explorer apparently disappeared into the labyrinth, never to return.

Statue of Liberty. Underneath lies a warren of tunnels, originally part of the gigantic quarry network beneath the city (see box, above). From 1785, a use was found for all that empty space, when it was realized that Paris's overflowing graveyards and charnel houses were poisoning the water supplies and sparking epidemics. For the next eighty years, the stony corridors were gradually filled with **skeletal remains**, and it's estimated that the remains of six million Parisians are interred here – nearly three times the population of the modern city, not counting the suburbs.

The underground passages

There's one claustrophobic passageway to follow. The first turning takes you into the **Galerie de Port-Mahon**, a chamber dominated by a bas-relief of a fortress in Menorca, where its sculptor was once imprisoned. Beyond, passing a door inscribed "*Arrête! C'est ici l'empire de la mort*" ("Stop! This is Death's empire"), the catacombs proper begin. Passages are lined with long thigh bones stacked end-on, forming a wall to keep in the smaller ones heaped higgledy-piggledy behind. These macabre walls are inset with skulls and plaques carrying light-hearted quotations such as "Happy is he who always has the hour of his death in front of his eyes, and readies himself every day to die". Older children often love the whole experience, though there are a good couple of kilometres to walk, and if you're unlucky, you might find yourself in a bottlenecked queue of shrieking

teenagers. It's fairly cold (a constant 14°) and a touch squidgy underfoot, so avoid wearing flip-flops and a T-shirt; you'll be down here for around 45 minutes. Only two hundred people at a time are allowed in, so be prepared to queue or book tickets in advance.

Observatoire de Paris and around

Av de l'Observatoire, 14ᵉ • ⓦ obspm.fr • Ⓜ Denfert-Rochereau/RER Port-Royal

About 500m northeast of the catacombs, the classical **Observatoire de Paris** sat precisely on 0° longitude from the 1660s, when it was built, until 1914, when France finally gave in and agreed to recognize the Greenwich Meridian as the standard. The Observatoire itself is rarely open to visitors, but you can check out a couple of commemorative bronze medallions set in the pavement on either side of the front gate. Similar discs run right through the city, marking the old meridian, now named the **Arago line** after the early nineteenth-century astronomer. The building itself is a graceful structure, and the telescope cupola perched on the east tower adds an exotic touch.

On the other side of the boulevard de Port-Royal, the green avenue de l'Observatoire stretches due north into the Jardin du Luxembourg (see p.144). Curiosity-seekers might want to stroll down to boulevard Arago where, beside the high wall of La Santé prison, a few steps west of rue de la Santé, stands Paris's last remaining **Vespasienne**: an open-air, public urinal. It still works – and still stinks.

Fondation Henri Cartier-Bresson

2 impasse Lebouis, 14ᵉ • Tues, Thurs, Fri & Sun 1–6.30pm, Wed 1–8.30pm, Sat 11am–6.45pm • €8 • ⓣ 01 56 80 27 00, ⓦ henricartierbresson.org • Ⓜ Gaîté

The elegant **Fondation Henri Cartier-Bresson** houses the copious archive of the father of photojournalism and arch-documenter of Paris; he died in 2004, a year after the foundation opened. Fascinating, often intimate temporary shows of the work of Cartier-Bresson and his contemporaries alternate with exhibitions promoting younger photographers, including the winner of the foundation's biennial prize.

Notre-Dame du Travail

36 rue Guilleminot, 14ᵉ • Mon–Fri 7.30am–7.45pm, Sat 9am–7.30pm, Sun 8.30am–7.30pm • Free • ⓦ notredamedutravail.net • Ⓜ Pernety

The name of this unusual church – **Notre-Dame du Travail**, or "Our Lady of Work" – reflects the artisanal and industrial jobs of the men it was built for: the workers who constructed the 1899 Exposition Universelle, including the Eiffel Tower. Its construction is deliberately factory-like too: some of its stone came from the Cloth Pavilion, when it was dismantled after the Exhibition closed, while the exposed steel columns of the nave came from the Palace of Industry. Architecturally, it's a fascinating – and surprisingly successful – industrial take on Gothic, and was way ahead of its time.

Les Echelles du Baroque and around

Ⓜ Gaîté

Immediately north of the church of Notre-Dame du Travail stand the two great wings – one oval, the other squared off – of Ricardo Bofill's postmodern housing development, **Les Echelles du Baroque** (1986). Beyond again is **place de Catalogne**, a plaza filled with a giant, flat disc of a fountain designed by the Israeli artist Shamaï Haber. To the northwest, further up boulevard Pasteur, there's a little-known but striking view down the horse-chestnut-lined slope of the street towards the Eiffel Tower, apparently floating over the city below.

Pernety

Ⓜ Pernety/Plaisance

Around **Pernety** métro station, the 14ᵉ arrondissement takes on a residential feel; a wander along Cité Bauer and rue des Thermopyles reveals adorable houses, secluded courtyards and quiet mews. Cinema has one of its best Parisian venues, meanwhile, at **L'Entrepôt**, 7–9 rue Francis-de-Pressensé (see p.286), with spaces for talks, meals and drinks, an excellent live music programme and a garden.

Puces de Vanves

Avs Marc Sangnier & Georges Lafenestre, 14e • Sat & Sun 7am–2pm • Ⓦ pucesdevanves.fr • Ⓜ Porte de Vanves

At the weekend it's worth heading out to the southern edge of the 14e arrondissement for one of the city's best **flea markets**, the **Puces de Vanves** (see p.341). Starting early, hundreds of vendors spread along the pavements of avenues Marc Sangnier and Georges Lafenestre, petering out at its western end in place de la Porte-de-Vanves, where the city fortifications stood until the 1920s. It's smaller and less formal than the St-Ouen (Clignancourt) market (see p.341), with more bric-a-brac and vintage curiosities, and fewer serious antiques.

Parc Montsouris

Bd Jouran, rue de la Cité Universitaire, rue Gazan, av Reille and rue Nansouty, 14e • Daily 9am–dusk • RER/Tramway Cité Universitaire

With its undulating green contours and its waterfall cascading into a lake – home to turtles and a number of migratory birds – the sizeable **Parc Montsouris** is one of Paris's great city parks, much beloved of students at the nearby Cité Universitaire. Unusual features include a marker of the old meridian line, near boulevard Jourdan; the RER tracks cutting right through the middle; and, by the southwest entrance, a French Astronomy Association office.

Around Parc Montsouris

The area surrounding Parc Montsouris offers some iconic architecture with artistic and historic associations. Le Corbusier's first building in Paris was the **Studio Ozenfant** (1922), at 53 avenue Reille – a typically elegant, minimal structure designed for his co-founder of the Purist movement, Amédée Ozenfant. The intriguing 1920s mews of **Villa Seurat**, off rue de la Tombe-Issoire, was home to many artists and writers, including Chana Orloff, Chaïm Soutine, Jean Lurçat, Henry Miller and Lawrence Durrell – it was here that Miller wrote his notorious *Tropic of Cancer*.

Cité Universitaire

17 bd Jourdan, 14e • Ⓦ www.ciup.fr • RER/Tramway Cité Universitaire

Several thousand students from more than a hundred countries occupy the **Cité Universitaire**, whose buildings follow a kitsch international theme. The central Maison Internationale resembles a traditional French château, while the red brick of the Collège Franco-Britannique all too accurately recalls Britain's institutional buildings. Two of the most remarkable buildings, however, were designed by Le Corbusier: the graceful elevated shoebox of the Fondation Suisse (1931–33) is one of his major works, and still has an original Corbusier fresco inside; the more brutal Maison du Brésil (1957–59) recalls his famous Cité Radieuse in Marseille. The university offers an active programme of theatre, exhibitions and special events.

The 15e

Though it's the largest and most populous of all the arrondissements, the **quinzième** (15e) falls off the agenda for most visitors. Its most distinctive features are the **Île aux Cygnes** – an odd island in the middle of the Seine – and a bristle of miniature skyscrapers on the riverbank, the shabby remainder of a 1960s and 1970s development known as the **Front de Seine**. There's little reason to penetrate this latter maze unless you're a particular fan of postwar architecture, or perhaps raised pedestrian walkways. The 15e does, however, have two lovely and distinctly offbeat parks in its southern corners, the **Parc André-Citroën** and the **Parc Georges-Brassens**. You could also enjoy a

THE 15e

16e

Avenue du
Président Kennedy

Maison de
Radio-France

Port Autonome
de Paris

Bir-Hakeim

Île aux Cygnes

**Statue de la
Liberté**

PLACE
FERNAND FOREST

SQUARE
BELA
BARTOK

PLACE DE BRAZZAVILLE

PLACE ST-
CHARLES

River Seine

❷

SQUARE
HERICART

PLACE
CHARLES
MICHELS

Mirabeau Ⓜ

Javel Ⓡ

Javel–
André Citroën Ⓜ

AVENUE EMILE ZOLA

Charles
Michels Ⓜ

**Imprimerie
Nationale**

N

RUE DE LA CONVENTION

**Hôpital
Boucicaut**

Parc
André-Citroën

**Cimetière
de Grenelle**

Boucicout Ⓜ

⊤
Fountains

Ⓘ Pont du
Garigliano

Lourmel Ⓜ

**Cimetière
de Vaugirard**

BOULEVARD VICTOR

Balard Ⓜ

**Notre Dame
de Nazareth**

PORTE DE VERSAILLES

**Armée de l'Air
(Etat Major)**

**Palais des
Sports**

Paris Expo

● EATING
RESTAURANTS
Le Café du Commerce	1
Le Grand Pan	3
La Véraison	2

● SHOPPING
Centre Commercial Beaugrenelle	2
Marché Convention	4
Marché Saxe-Breteuil	3
Poilâne	1

■ ACCOMMODATION
3 Ducks Hostel	3
Hôtel de l'Avre	1
Splendid Hotel	2

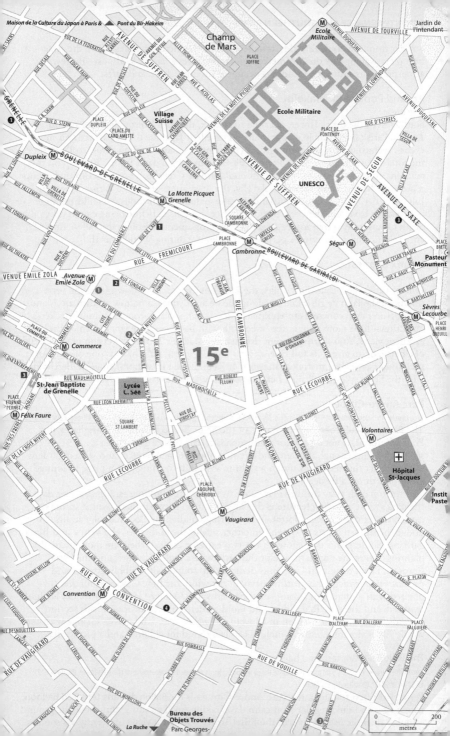

wander from the **boulevard de Grenelle** – where the métro trundles above the street on iron piers – along **Rue du Commerce**, which preserves a laidback, almost villagey, atmosphere, its shuttered buildings occupied by small shops and cafés.

Around Pont de Bir-Hakeim

Ⓜ Bir-Hakeim

Southwest of the Eiffel Tower, near the riverbank, the glass **Maison de la Culture du Japon à Paris** (Ⓦwww.mcjp.asso.fr) puts on excellent Japanese theatre, dance and music events. Immediately south, you can watch the métro trains heading across to Passy on the top level of the two-decker **Pont de Bir-Hakeim**, which dates from 1902. Up on the adjacent raised walkway, at the start of boulevard de Grenelle, a bronze sculptural group represents the notorious **rafle du Vel d'Hiv**, the mass arrest of 13,152 Parisian Jews on July 16 and 17, 1942. Nine thousand people, including four thousand children, were interned for a week at the cycle track that once stood here, before being carted off to the death camps; only thirty adults survived. The monument is dedicated to all victims of anti-Semitic and racist crimes perpetrated in France during World War II.

Île aux Cygnes

Ⓜ Bir-Hakeim

One of Paris's most charming walks, the **Allée des Cygnes**, leads down from the very middle of the Pont de Bir-Hakeim along the **Île aux Cygnes**, a narrow, midstream island built up on raised concrete embankments. It's a strange place – one of Samuel Beckett's favourites – little more than a tree-lined path with benches where you can enjoy the excellent views. At its furthest point downstream stands a 22m-high version of the **Statue of Liberty**, or, to give it its full title, *Liberty Lighting the World*. This was one of the four preliminary models constructed between 1874 and 1884 by sculptor Auguste Bartholdi, with the help of Gustave Eiffel, before the finished article was presented to New York.

Parc André-Citroën

2 rue Cauchy, 15ᵉ • Daily 8am/9am–7pm/7.30pm/8.30pm/9.30pm (depending on season) • Free • Ⓜ Javel–André Citroën/Balard

The **Parc André-Citroën**, on the banks of the Seine between Pont du Garigliano and Pont Mirabeau, is not a park for traditionalists. The central grassy area is straightforward enough, but around it you'll find concrete terraces and walled gardens with abstract themes. It's as much a sight to visit in its own right as a place to lounge around or throw a frisbee.

At the top end, away from the river, are two large glass **hothouses**. On summer days, the park's most tempting feature is the large platform between them, which sprouts a capricious set of automated **fountain** jets, luring children, and occasionally adults, to dodge the sudden spurts of water. On either side of the hothouses, the White and Black gardens feature plants that show off the two extreme colours; there are more themed plantings along the northern side of the park, where high walls surround the **Serial Gardens**. Here, the Green Garden is dedicated to sound, with bubbling water and *Miscanthus sinensis* grasses rustling dryly in the wind; the Blue Garden is for scent, planted with wisteria and strong-smelling herbs; the Orange Garden, for touch, is highly textured; and there are Red, Silver and Gold gardens too. At the foot of this section, towards the river, is the Garden in Movement, whose semi-wild grasses change with the wind. The park's southern end includes a playground for children and a picnic area.

The Ballon de Paris tethered balloon

Parc André-Citroën, 15ᵉ • Daily 9am to 30min before the park closes; flights are weather-dependent, so check online on the day • €12 • ☏ 01 44 26 20 00, Ⓦ ballondeparis.com

Perhaps the best feature in the Parc André-Citroën is the **Ballon de Paris tethered balloon**, which rises and sinks regularly on calm days, taking small groups 150m above the ground – higher than the second level of the Eiffel Tower – for great views of the city. As soon as the original balloon was installed in 1999 it became one of the chief landmarks of the 15e, but in 2008 it took on a new complexion – quite literally: the balloon now changes colour to reflect levels of air pollution. A strip of LEDs on the south side indicates the air quality near traffic – from green (good) via orange (don't panic) to red (gas masks on).

Parc Georges-Brassens

Entrance on rue des Morillons, 15e • Daily dawn–dusk • Free • Ⓜ Convention/Porte de Vanves

The old Vaugirard abattoir, fish market and horse market was transformed into **Parc Georges-Brassens** in the 1980s, and named after the legendary postwar poet-singer-satirist who lived nearby. In homage to the park's old role, the main entrance is flanked by two bronze bulls, and the fish market's original clock tower stands near the pond. The park is a delight, especially for children, who love the puppet shows (Wed, Sat & Sun), the climbing wall and the merry-go-rounds. Other attractions include a stream, lined with pine and birch trees, plus a beehive, a tiny terraced vineyard and a garden of scented herbs and shrubs (best in late spring). The corrugated pyramid with a helter-skelter-like spiral is Le Monfort theatre.

On Saturdays and Sundays, take a look in the sheds of the old horse market between the park and **rue Brancion**, to the east, where dozens of **book dealers** set out their wares.

La Ruche

2 passage Dantzig, 15e • Ⓦ laruche-artistes.fr • Ⓜ Convention

West of Parc Georges-Brassens, in a secluded, semi-wild garden off rue Dantzig, stands an odd polygonal building known as **La Ruche**. The "Beehive" is named not only for its shape, but also for the buzz of artistic activity that has always existed here. It started life as a Gustave Eiffel-designed pavilion for the 1900 World Fair, showcasing fine wines, after which it was resurrected here as a studio space, becoming home to Fernvand Léger, Modigliani (briefly), Chagall, Soutine, Ossip Zadkine and many other artists, mainly Jewish refugees from pogroms in Poland and Russia. It's still something of a Tower of Babel, with around fifty artists from around the world in residence. A room on the ground floor holds occasional exhibitions – check online.

The 13e

The **treizième arrondissement** (**13e**), in the southeastern corner of Paris, has two faces. North of the mega-roundabout of **place d'Italie**, the genteel neighbourhood around the ancient **Gobelins tapestry workshops** seems to look towards the adjacent Quartier Latin. The southern swathe of the arrondissement, by contrast, has more in common with the suburbs, as it was almost completely cleared in the 1960s, and filled in by tower blocks. Focuses for the visitor include **Chinatown**, with its many Asian restaurants; the minor hillock of the **Butte-aux-Cailles**, its pretty old streets alive with restaurants and bohemian bars; and, along the eastern edge of the 13e, beside the Seine, the developing **Paris Rive Gauche** *quartier*, centred on the flagship **Bibliothèque Nationale de France**.

Place d'Italie

Ⓜ Place d'Italie

One of those Parisian roundabouts that takes half an hour to cross, **Place d'Italie** is the central junction of the 13e. On its north side is the *mairie* of the arrondissement, while to the south is Kenzo Tange's huge **Grand Ecran Italie** building. Its curving glass facade cleverly advertised the giant film screen within – the two were roughly the same size – until the cinema was closed down in 2006. For years outraged cinephiles battled the council to reopen a movie house on the site in the face of encroaching malls; in 2016, the Quebecois company Juste pour Rire announced that they would be transforming the building into a theatre.

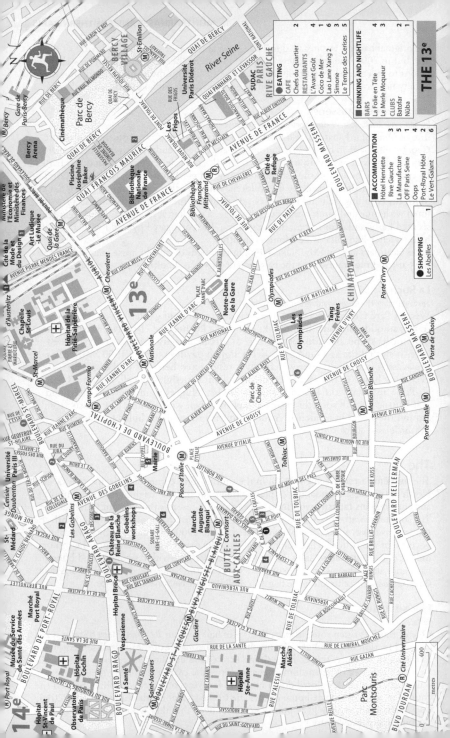

THE 13e

RIVE GAUCHE PARIS

■ **EATING**

CAFÉ	2
Chefs du Quartier	2
RESTAURANTS	
L'Avant Goût	4
Coco de Mer	1
Lao Lane Xang 2	6
Simone	3
Le Temps des Cerises	5

■ **DRINKING AND NIGHTLIFE**

BARS	
La Folie en Tête	4
Le Merle Moqueur	3
CLUBS	
Batofar	2
Nüba	1

■ **ACCOMMODATION**

Hôtel Henriette	3
Rive Gauche	5
La Manufacture	4
OFF Paris Seine	7
Oops	2
Port-Royal Hôtel	6
Le Vert-Galant	1

● **SHOPPING**

Les Abeilles	1

ALONG THE VANISHED RIVER BIÈVRE

The site of the Gobelins tapestry works owes everything to the hidden presence of the **Bièvre**. Once a virtual sewer for tanners and dye-makers, the river was finally covered over in 1910, although its course is still marked by the curves of rues Berbier-du-Mets and Croulebarbe, and by the row of poplars in the green space of the **square René-le-Gall** – a former island once known as the Ile aux Singes for the jugglers' monkeys that lived there. Just off rue Geffroy, which itself turns off rue Berbier-du-Mets, stands the surprising, fairy-tale rump of the **Château de la Reine Blanche**, which once guarded the main medieval route into Paris from the south – along what is today's avenue des Gobelins. The turreted wing (now luxury apartments) was built in the 1520s and 1530s by the aristocratic Gobelins family, but it occupied the site of a much older château torn down after a tragic party in 1393 in which the young Charles VI of France nearly died. Charles and five friends had disguised themselves as tarred-and-feathered savages but one of them brushed against a candle flame; the king was the only survivor of the ensuing conflagration, and never recovered his sanity.

Gobelins workshops

42 av des Gobelins, 13^e · **Gallery** Tues–Sun 11am–6pm; guided tours (1hr 30min; French only) Sat 2.30pm & 4pm · €8, free on last Sun of month; guided tours €14 · **Workshops** Guided tours (1hr 30min; French only) Tues & Wed 1pm; book via FNAC (see p.334) · €15, or €18 including access to gallery · ☎ 01 44 08 53 49, ⊕ www.mobiliernational.culture.gouv.fr · Ⓜ Les Gobelins

The highest-quality **tapestries** have been created in the **Gobelins workshops** for some four hundred years. The **gallery** stages temporary exhibitions of historic and contemporary tapestries, furnishings and textiles, while on the **workshop tour** you can watch the tapestries being made by painfully slow, traditional methods; each weaver completes between one and four square metres a year. The designs are now exactingly specified by contemporary artists, and almost all of the half-a-dozen or so works completed each year are destined for French government offices.

Hôpital de la Pitié-Salpêtrière

47–83 bd de l'Hôpital, 13e · **Chapelle St-Louis** Mon–Sat 10.30am–1.50pm & 3.40–5.40pm, Sun 10.30am–1.50pm · Free · ☎ 01 42 16 00 00 · Ⓜ St-Marcel/RER Austerlitz

East of the Gobelins tapestry workshops, the ornate boulevards St-Marcel and Vincent Auriol are dominated by the immense **Hôpital de la Pitié-Salpêtrière**, built under Louis XIV to house the sick, the disabled and the poor, to jail prostitutes and generally to dispose of the dispossessed. The imprisoned women were released by a revolutionary mob who broke in by force in September 1792. It later became a psychiatric hospital – Jean Charcot staged his theatrical demonstrations of hysteria and hypnosis here, with Freud as one of his fascinated witnesses. Today, it's a leading teaching hospital, but the **Chapelle St-Louis**, at the northern side of the complex, is open to visitors. It's a bleakly beautiful Baroque structure under a modest dome, a fairly typical work by Libéral Bruant, the architect of Les Invalides. It has occasionally been used during the Festival d'Automne (see p.323), staging art installations by the likes of Bill Viola, Jenny Holzer and Tadashi Kawamata.

Butte-aux-Cailles

Ⓜ Corvisart/Place d'Italie

Between boulevard Auguste-Blanqui and rue Bobillot is the **Butte-aux-Cailles**, whose name can be translated picturesquely as the hill (*butte*) of the quails (*cailles*). It's a pleasantly animated little quarter, the sloping, cobbled **rue de la Butte-aux-Cailles** furnished with one of the city's classic, green Art Nouveau drinking fountains (see box, p.8). There are plenty of unpretentious places to eat and drink till the small hours, making it an attractive area for low-key nightlife. If you're coming from métro Corvisart, cross the road and head straight through the passageway in the large apartment building opposite, then climb the steps that lead up through the small Brassaï gardens to rue des Cinq Diamants. Alternatively, it's a short walk up rue Bobillot from place d'Italie.

Chinatown

Ⓜ Olympiades

The area between rue de Tolbiac, avenue de Choisy and boulevard Masséna is known as the **Chinatown** (or the *quartier Chinois*) of Paris, despite the fact that it was actually established by Vietnamese refugees in the late 1970s, and is now home to several East Asian communities. Avenues de Choisy and d'Ivry are full of Vietnamese, Thai, Cambodian, Laotian and indeed Chinese restaurants and food shops. At 48 avenue d'Ivry, you'll find the huge Tang Frères **Chinese supermarket**, a former railway warehouse now stocked with an incredible variety of Asian goods (closed Sun afternoon and Mon). The chief landmark of Chinatown, however, is **Les Olympiades**, a set of 1970s tower blocks – eight of which are named after a city that has hosted the games – with a mall below and a pedestrian area strangely suspended above.

Paris Rive Gauche

Ⓜ Quai de la Gare/Bibliothèque François Mitterrand

Stretching from the Gare d'Austerlitz right down to the *boulevard périphérique*, the once-isolated, desolate, industrial strip between rail tracks and river has been transformed into the modern **Paris Rive Gauche** district. A fine pedestrian footbridge, the **Passerelle Simone de Beauvoir**, crosses the Seine in a futuristic double-ribbon strip; the old docks have become "**Docks en Seine**", incorporating a fashion institute; and Austerlitz station is undergoing a major makeover (it's being connected to a new TGV line to Bordeaux, slated for 2020). The flagship of the quarter is the handsome **Bibliothèque Nationale de France**; tethered nearby is a floating swimming pool, the **Piscine Josephine Baker** (see p.346), and a set of **barges** that have made the area a nightlife attraction in its own right.

In the south of the quarter, the old industrial buildings Grands Moulins de Paris and Halle aux Farines have been rebuilt for the **Université Paris Diderot**, aka "Paris 7", an annexe of the Jussieu site (see p.133), while, just short of the *périphérique*, another early twentieth-century industrial-era site, the handsomely arched **SUDAC** compressed-air building, is now home to a new school of architecture. In addition to these large-scale structures is a scatter of small **private galleries** – west of the library, near métro Chevaleret, a clutch of cutting-edge galleries can be found on **rue Louise Weiss** and rue du Chevaleret. **Le Corbusier** fans might want to head across to rue Cantagrel, where the architect's colourful, if brutal, **Cité de Refuge** (1933), or Salvation Army building, stands at no. 12.

Bibliothèque Nationale de France

Quai François-Mauriac, 13e • **Exhibitions** Tues–Sat 10am–7pm, Sun 1–7pm • €9 • **Public reading rooms** Tues–Sat 10am–8pm, Sun 1–7pm • €3.90 for a day-pass, bring ID • ☎ 01 53 79 59 59, Ⓦ bnf.fr • Ⓜ Quai de la Gare/Bibliothèque François Mitterrand

The architectural star of the **Paris Rive Gauche** development, which Mitterrand managed to inaugurate, though not open, just before his death in 1996, is the **Bibliothèque Nationale de France**. There are regular exhibitions – typically serious, arty and high quality – and the **reading rooms** on the "haut-jardin" level, along with their unrivalled collection of foreign newspapers, are open to anyone aged over 16. The garden level, below, is reserved for accredited researchers only, while the garden itself is out of bounds.

The four enormous L-shaped towers at the corners of the site were intended to look like open books, but attracted widespread derision after shutters had to be added behind the glazing in order to protect the collections from sunlight. Once you mount the dramatic wooden steps surrounding the library, however, the perspective changes utterly. From here you look down into a huge sunken pine wood, with glass walls that filter dappled light into the floors below your feet; it's like standing at the edge of a secret ravine. The concept is original, and almost fulfils architect Dominique Perrault's intention to combine "rigour and emotion", to "generate a sense of dignity, a well-tempered soul for the buildings of the French Republic".

Les Frigos

19 rue des Frigos, 13e • Open to the public during events only • Ⓦ les-frigos.com, Ⓦ lesvoutes.org and Ⓦ aiguillagegalerie.com • Ⓜ Quai de la Gare/Bibliothèque François Mitterrand

On the south side of rue de Tolbiac, opposite the library, the giant, decaying cold-storage warehouse of **Les Frigos** has been occupied by artists and musicians since the 1980s, when it was an infamous squat. It's now an officially sanctioned home to around two hundred workshops, which hold open-door exhibitions once or twice a year. There's often a gig or an event going on in the space known as **Les Voûtes** ("The Vaults"), plus a couple of galleries, including **L'Aiguillage**, which hosts regular shows. Though it's officially only for the artists, the bar/restaurant is usually open to visitors during events.

Les Docks/Cité de la Mode et du Design

34 quai d'Austerlitz, 13e • Daily 10am–midnight • ☎ 01 76 77 25 30, Ⓦ citemodedesign.fr • Ⓜ Gare d'Austerlitz/Quai de la Gare

Sitting on the quai d'Austerlitz upstream of the Pont de Bercy, the ugly concrete warehouses that once belonged to Paris's central port have been rebuilt as **Les Docks/ Cité de la Mode et du Design**, whose intrusive design of twisting, lime-green tubes, by Dominique Jacob and Brendan MacFarlane, is – rather bafflingly – supposed to recall the sinuous shape of the river.

The complex houses a fashion school, the **Institut Français de la Mode** (Ⓦ ifm-paris .com), an **animation museum** and a number of places to eat. It also hosts occasional **exhibitions**, but perhaps the biggest draws are the bars and clubs, among them rooftop *Nüba* (see p.303). You can stroll along the riverbank on a pedestrian promenade, perhaps admiring the giant Bercy development across the river (see p.115). If you start to tire of post-industrial mega-design you could choose to walk just a little further north, beyond the Gare d'Austerlitz, to the historic green space of the Jardin des Plantes (see p.130).

Art Ludique-Le Musée

34 quai d'Austerlitz, 13e • Mon, Wed & Fri 11am–7pm, Thurs 11am–10pm, Sat & Sun 10am–8pm • €16.50, children aged 4–12 €11; includes free audioguide • ☎ 01 45 70 09 49, Ⓦ artludique.com • Ⓜ Gare d'Austerlitz/Quai de la Gare

Art Ludique-Le Musée is a museum entirely dedicated to the art of animation, manga, comics and video games. Its permanent collection, which looks at the first creators of comics as well as contemporary artists, is interesting enough, but the main attraction is its hugely popular exhibitions, which have recently focused on Aardman Animations, Studio Ghibli, Pixar and Disney.

Montmartre and northern Paris

Stacked on its hilltop in the 18e arrondissement of Paris, Montmartre sets itself apart from the city at its feet. Its chief landmark, visible from all over the city, is the church of Sacré-Coeur, crowning the Butte as if an over-enthusiastic pâtissier had run riot with an icing gun. The slopes below, around Abbesses métro, preserve something of the spirit of the village that once basked here, but unlike most villages Montmartre has a diverse population, by turns lefty, trendy and seedy. Between Montmartre and the Grands Boulevards, which define the edge of the city centre proper, stretch the 9e and 10e arrondissements, whose stolid nineteenth-century architecture and lack of green space make them look quite similar. Yet where the 9^e arrondissement is largely genteel, the 10^e is more rough-edged – and fast becoming one of the city's most vibrant areas, as young, hip Parisians move in, attracted by the low rents.

While traditional sights as such are thin on the ground below the Butte of Montmartre, the 9ᵉ arrondissement has two museums devoted to its nineteenth-century artistic heyday, the **Musée National Gustave Moreau** and **Musée de la Vie Romantique**. The northern fringe of the arrondissement around **Pigalle** – traditionally famous for its cabarets and sex shows – is building a reputation for its cool nightlife and restaurant scene. Similarly, the main interest of the gritty 10ᵉ lies in its burgeoning culinary scene, with a rash of "neo-bistros" (see p.278) helmed by young, dynamic chefs. **Batignolles**, meanwhile, a relatively moneyed residential enclave, can give a different taste of Parisian life.

Montmartre

Ⓜ Abbesses/Anvers/Lamarck Caulaincourt

At once a major tourist honeypot and one of the most appealing residential districts in Paris, picturesque **Montmartre** is an unusually proud and tight-knit neighbourhood. Tall, shuttered buildings line the steep cobbled streets that clamber up the Butte, and with many roads linked by staircases, or barely touched by cars, it is easy to find peace and quiet. Incorporated into the city only in the mid-nineteenth century, Montmartre's bohemian heyday was from the last years of the nineteenth century to World War I, when its villagey appeal and low rents attracted crowds of **artists**. Since then, the *quartier's* physical appearance has changed little, thanks largely to the warren of **plaster-of-Paris quarries** that perforate its bowels and render the ground too unstable for new building. Minuscule squares still give way to sudden vistas south over the rooftops of central Paris, and the occasional atelier window is a tangible reminder of its illustrious artistic past.

In the second half of the twentieth century, Montmartre slumped into a half-life of porn shows and semi-genteel poverty, but has undergone radical gentrification in recent years. Today, though it still has an artsy vibe beyond the tourist hotspots, that is – and retains a relatively healthy ethnic mix, the neighbourhood is primarily the domain of the young and moneyed rather than impoverished artists and sex workers. The liveliest section is around **Abbesses** métro, with its many bijou bars and restaurants, getting scruffier – and hipper – as it extends down to Pigalle, where the old sleazy edge has not yet quite been cleaned away.

When it comes to sightseeing, most visitors make straight for the landmark church of **Sacré-Coeur** via the steps or **funicular** (covered by ordinary métro tickets) immediately below. For a less touristy approach, and to truly get the feel of this lively, charming pocket of the city, head up via place des Abbesses.

Abbesses

Ⓜ Abbesses

You could almost be persuaded that pretty, tree-shaded **place des Abbesses** was a village square – were it not for its centrepiece, one of Guimard's rare, canopied Art

---

MONTMARTROBUS

The diminutive **Montmartrobus** (which looks like a miniature version of a regular Paris bus) is designed to be able to negotiate the twisting streets of the Butte, and its determinedly ecological electric engine also makes it fit right in with the *quartier's* spirit. If you don't want to walk, taking this bus is probably the best way of doing a Montmartre tour, and **normal métro/bus tickets** are valid. Starting at place Pigalle, the route heads up rue des Martyrs and west along rue des Abbesses and rue Durantin, then follows the curve of rue Lepic to rue des Saules and rue Caulaincourt, before jinking up to Jules-Joffrin métro. On the return leg it heads down rues Ramey, Custine and Lamarck, curling round the foot of Sacré-Coeur and the *funiculaire* and heading back up to place du Tertre. It then winds back towards place des Abbesses via rues Cortot, Girardon and Gabrielle, before finally running down rues Chappe, Yvonne Le Tac and Houdon back to place Pigalle.

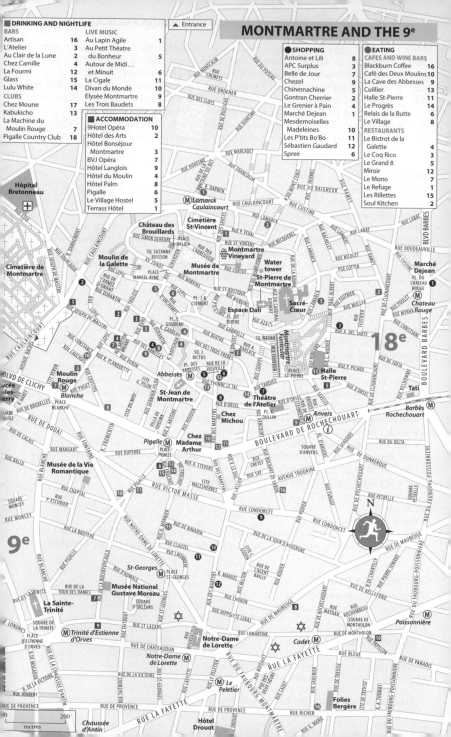

MONTMARTRE AND THE 9e

DRINKING AND NIGHTLIFE

BARS
Artisan	16
L'Atelier	3
Au Clair de la Lune	2
Chez Camille	4
La Fourmi	12
Glass	15
Lulu White	14

CLUBS
Chez Moune	17
Kabukicho	13
La Machine du Moulin Rouge	7
Pigalle Country Club	18

LIVE MUSIC
Au Lapin Agile	1
Au Petit Théatre du Bonheur	5
Autour de Midi… et Minuit	6
La Cigale	11
Divan du Monde	10
Elysée Montmartre	9
Les Trois Baudets	8

ACCOMMODATION
9Hotel Opéra	10
Hôtel des Arts	2
Hôtel Bonséjour Montmartre	3
BVJ Opéra	7
Hôtel Langlois	9
Hôtel du Moulin	4
Hôtel Palm	8
Pigalle	6
Le Village Hostel	5
Terrass Hôtel	1

SHOPPING
Antoine et Lili	8
APC Surplus	3
Belle de Jour	7
Chezel	3
Chinemachine	5
Gontran Cherrier	4
Le Grenier à Pain	4
Marché Dejean	1
Mesdemoiselles Madeleines	9
Les P'tits Bo'Bo	11
Sébastien Gaudard	12
Spree	6

EATING

CAFES AND WINE BARS
Blackburn Coffee	16
Café des Deux Moulins	10
La Cave des Abbesses	9
Cuillier	13
Halle St-Pierre	14
Le Progrès	14
Relais de la Butte	6
Le Village	8

RESTAURANTS
Le Bistrot de la Galette	4
Le Coq Rico	3
Le Grand 8	5
Miroir	12
Le Mono	7
Le Refuge	1
Les Rillettes	15
Soul Kitchen	2

▲ Entrance

Nouveau métro entrances; there are only two others in the city (see box, below). The métro canopy isn't in fact an authentic Abbesses sight, as it was transferred from the Hôtel de Ville, complete with its glass porch, tendril-like railings and lascivious-looking lanterns – but it looks perfectly at home here in the square. At the north end of the *place*, in the tiny Square Jehan Rictus, **Le mur des je t'aime** is a tiled wall inscribed with the words for "I love you", handwritten in some three hundred languages from Malayalam to Navajo.

St-Jean de Montmartre

19 rue des Abbesses, 18ᵉ • Mon–Sat 9am–7pm, Sun 9.30am–6pm • Free • ☎ 01 46 06 43 96, ⓦ saintjeandemontmartre.com • Ⓜ Abbesses

Opposite place des Abbesses stands the eye-catching red-brick church of **St-Jean de Montmartre**, dating from 1904. Pass through the portal, mosaicked with ceramic lozenges of bronze, blue and gold, to take a look at its radical construction. The slender pillars, elegant gallery and broad vaulting were only made possible by the experimental use of reinforced cement, a material that was, as the church's architect Anatole de Baudot claimed, both the bones and the skin. With its rich mosaic-work and decorative details the overall effect is at once modern, startling and warmly welcoming.

THE MÉTRO: AN OVERVIEW OF THE UNDERGROUND

When you descend into the **métro** network, Paris's true ethnic and social mix is revealed. The city centre may be flush with the white and wealthy, but the *franciliens* who live beyond the *périphérique* ring road – women in Islamic veils, streetwise kids from the housing projects, working men in overalls – mostly travel to and from work underground. And every new immigrant group sends a wave of buskers down the tunnels, filling the air with anything from gypsy rap to old fashioned *chanson*. The métro also has its own **culture**. When it gets crowded everyone knows not to use the *strapontins*, the folding seats by the doors, and it's understood that only someone really pushy walks up or down an escalator. There's a certain style about the way Parisians travel, too, notably the casual upward flick of the wrist that turns the door handle just before the train stops moving.

Internationally, however, the métro is best known for its beautiful Art Nouveau signs and entrances, designed by **Hector Guimard** in 1900. (As usual when confronted with cutting-edge design, Parisians were initially less than impressed, comparing Guimard's sinewy green railings and lantern holders to threatening tentacles.) The last three complete Guimard stations, with their glazed roofs intact, can be found at **Abbesses**, below Montmartre; at the **Porte Dauphine**, on the edge of the Bois de Boulogne; and at **Châtelet**'s place St-Opportune entrance. Not far away from the last, at the Palais Royal Musée du Louvre métro entrance on place Colette, you can see a different take on Guimard's design: arching over the entrance are two colourful "crowns" made of glass and aluminium designed by artist Jean-Michel Othoniel and known as the "Kiosque des Noctambules". Some stations have distinct characters below ground, too: check out the sci-fi copper-submarine styling of Arts et Métiers; the historic cartoons at Bastille; the funky multi-coloured lamps at Bonne Nouvelle; the hanging globe lights at Cité; the mosaicked giant autographs from artists, poets and kings emblazoning the ceiling at Cluny La Sorbonne; the one-letter-per-tile decor of Concorde (which spells out the Revolutionary Declaration of the Rights of Man); the museum cabinets and jewelled entrance at Palais Royal Musée du Louvre; St-Germain-des-Prés' sleek comic-book projections; and Varennes' massive Rodin sculptures.

Technologically, the métro is one of the finest underground systems in the world, though its famous rubber tyres are actually restricted to lines 1, 4, 6, 11 and 14. Lines 1 and 14 – soon to be joined by line 4 – have the latest in air-conditioned, articulated, driverless trains (sitting right in the front carriage offers exciting views down the tunnels). There are more elevated métro pastimes than playing train drivers, too. The writer Jacques Jouet and the avant-garde literary group, Oulipo, invented a system for composing **métro poems**; you have to write a line every time the train is still, and think up the next while the train is moving.

Butte Montmartre

At 130m, the "Mound", or **Butte Montmartre**, is the highest point in Paris. The various theories as to the origin of its name all have a Roman connection: it could be a corruption of *Mons Martyrum* – "the Martyrs' hill", the martyrs being St Denis and his companions; on the other hand, it might have been named *Mons Mercurii*, in honour of a Roman shrine to Mercury; or possibly *Mons Martis*, after a shrine to Mars.

If you're in any doubt about finding your way **up the Butte**, just keep heading uphill – there's no such thing as a wrong turn. One of the quietest and most attractive routes begins at place des Abbesses, climbing **rue de la Vieuville** and the stairs in rue Drevet to the minuscule **place du Calvaire**, which has a lovely view back over the city. Perhaps the most historic route up the Butte, however, is via **rue Lepic**, which owes its winding contours to the requirements of the slow wagons that carried plaster of Paris down from the quarries. The street begins at the seedy place Blanche (near Moulin Rouge métro); above rue des Abbesses, however, it becomes progressively more elegant.

Moulin de la Galette and Moulin Radet

Rue Lepic, 18e • Ⓜ Abbesses

Just off rue Lepic, the **Moulin de la Galette** windmill looks down from its modest patch of green – the last remnant of Montmartre's *maquis*, the scrub that once covered the Butte. The joyous dances here were immortalized by Renoir in his *Bal du Moulin de la Galette*, now hanging in the Musée d'Orsay. Today, the windmill is one of just two survivors of the many that once spun atop Montmartre. The other, the **Moulin Radet**, stands a little further along on rue Lepic itself, and is now the site of the misleadingly named – and rather smart – *Moulin de la Galette* restaurant. If you're approaching from place des Abbesses, you can cut straight up to the windmills via rues Ravignan, Durantin and Tholozé.

Place Marcel Aymé to place Dalida

Beyond the rue Lepic windmills, rue Girardon climbs up to little **place Marcel Aymé** where a quirky statue celebrates Aymé's best-loved short story: *Le Passe-Muraille* or *The Man Who Could Walk Through Walls*. Sweeping west, the exclusive **Avenue Junot** is lined with desirable residences, many of which stand behind digicoded gates. Don't miss the house of Dadaist poet Tristan Tzara at no. 15; built by Adolf Loos in 1926, it's a Cubist masterpiece. A few steps north of place Marcel Aymé, **square Suzanne-Buisson** provides a quiet haven, with a sunken boules pitch and fountains overlooked by a statue of St Denis clutching his head to his breast. Just north again, tiny **place Dalida** has as its centrepiece a distinctly busty bust of the cult singer and gay icon Dalida. She is overlooked by the elegant **Château des Brouillards**, or "Fog House" (1772), where Auguste Renoir once had an atelier. The mansion gets its romantic name from the plumes of steam that used to rise around the Butte from the local hot springs.

BATEAU-LAVOIR

With its graceful Wallace fountain (see box, p.8), its steps, its shady benches and its view down the hill, the tiny **place Emile-Goudeau** is a classic Montmartre square. Here too stands a building that encapsulates Montmartre's rich artistic history: a former piano factory known as the **Bateau-Lavoir**. In 1904 Picasso took up a studio here, and he stayed for the best part of a decade, painting *Les Demoiselles d'Avignon* and sharing loves, quarrels and opium trips with Braque, Juan Gris, Modigliani, Max Jacob, Apollinaire and others, both famous and obscure. It was on the place Emile-Goudeau that he had his first encounter with the beautiful Fernande Olivier, thrusting a kitten into her hand as she passed by. "I laughed," she said, "and he took me to see his studio." Fernande became his model and lover. Although the original building burned down some years ago, the modern reconstruction still provides studio space for artists.

Espace Dalí

9–11 rue Poulbot, 18ᵉ • Daily: July & Aug 10am–8pm; Sept–June 10am–6pm • €11.50 • ☎ 01 42 64 40 10, ⓦ daliparis.com • Ⓜ Abbesses

Set on a typically pretty cobbled Montmartre street, **Espace Dalí** is filled largely with reproduced engravings and wacky sculptures made by others to the Surrealist artist's designs. There's a certain interest in seeing this, less familiar, side of his work, but it's really more of a souvenir shop than a museum, and perhaps lives up to the anagram that André Breton made of Dalí's name: Avida Dollars.

Place du Tertre

Ⓜ Abbesses/Lamarck Caulaincourt

If you want to preserve romantic, sepia-toned memories of the Butte, you'd do best to stop short of the top. What was once a pretty, tree-shaded square at Montmartre's crown, **place du Tertre** has completely fallen victim to its own fame. Today, it's jammed with tour groups, souvenir stalls, overpriced restaurants and jaded street artists knocking out lurid oils of Paris landmarks from memory or offering to paint your portrait. There's even a Starbucks, which opened in 2013 despite passionate opposition from Montmartre locals.

St-Pierre de Montmartre

2 rue du Mont-Cenis, 18ᵉ • Daily 8.30am–7.30pm • Free • ☎ 01 46 06 57 63, ⓦ saintpierredemontmartre.net • Ⓜ Abbesses/Lamarck Caulaincourt

The church of **St-Pierre de Montmartre**, between place du Tertre and the Sacré-Coeur, offers sanctuary from the tourist bustle. It once served a Benedictine convent that occupied the Butte Montmartre from the twelfth century onwards, and now rivals St-Germain-des-Prés for the title of oldest church in Paris. Though much altered, with modern stained glass by Max Ingrand throughout, it still retains its Romanesque and early Gothic structures. More ancient still are four columns inside the church, two by the main entrance and two in the choir; they probably date from a Roman shrine that stood on the hill, though their capitals were carved in Merovingian times.

Sacré-Coeur

Parvis du Sacré-Coeur, 18ᵉ • **Church** Daily 6am–10.30pm • Free • **Dome** Daily: May–Sept 8.30am–8pm; Oct–April 10am–5.30pm • €6 • ⓦ sacre-coeur-montmartre.com • Ⓜ Abbesses/Anvers

Parisian poet Jacques Roubaud compared the **Sacré-Coeur** to a big baby's bottle for the angels to suck. Certainly, it's a sickly sweet confection of French and Byzantine architecture, yet its pimpled tower and white ice-cream-scoop dome have become icons on the Paris skyline. The site has been sacred since the Romans venerated Mars and Mercury here, but today's structure dates from the 1870s, after the Catholic Church raised a public subscription to atone for the "crimes" of the revolutionary Commune (see box, p.186). The thwarted opposition, which included Clemenceau, eventually got its revenge when the space at the foot of the monumental staircase was named **square Willette**, after the local artist who turned out on inauguration day to shout "Long live the devil!" Today the staircase is the territory of tourists enjoying the view, munching on picnics and wielding selfie sticks; the crowds, and the guitar-strumming street entertainers, only increase as night falls.

The interior is neo-Byzantine, and even taking into account its carillon of bells – the largest bell in France, the Savoyarde, at nineteen tonnes, is here – and collection of holy relics from all over France, the most exciting thing about the Sacré-Coeur is undoubtedly the **view from the dome**. The gateway to the stairs – with three hundred steps, it's a steep and claustrophobic climb – is outside the church, on the west side. Once at the top, you're almost as high as the Eiffel Tower, and you can see the layout of the whole city – a wide, flat basin ringed by low hills, with stands of high-rise blocks in the corners.

THE PARIS COMMUNE

In March 1871, **Montmartre** saw the first sparks fly in what would become the great conflagration of the **Paris Commune**. After Napoléon III's disastrous campaign against the Prussians in the summer of 1870, and the declaration of the Third Republic in September of the same year, Paris finally fell to the Prussian army on January 28, 1871, after a four-month siege. Peace terms were agreed by the end of February, and the Prussians withdrew, leaving the new Republic in the hands of a shaky conservative administration. Paris's situation was least secure of all, as the city's workers – and their armed representatives in the National Guard – had been disenfranchised by the February settlement, and were not inclined to respect it. The new Prime Minister, **Adolphe Thiers**, dispatched a body of regular troops under General Lecomte to take possession of 170 guns which the National Guard controlled on the high ground of the Butte Montmartre. Although the troops seized the guns easily in the darkness before dawn, they had failed to bring any horses to tow them away. That gave the revolutionary Louise Michel time to raise the alarm.

An angry crowd of workers and National Guard members quickly gathered. They persuaded the troops to take no action and arrested General Lecomte, along with another general, Clément Thomas, who was notorious for the part he had played in the brutal repression of the 1848 republican uprising. The two generals were shot and mutilated in the garden of no. 36 rue du Chevalier-de-la-Barre, behind the Sacré-Coeur. Across the city, soldiers and National Guard members joined the rebellion, and, by the following morning, a panicking government had decamped to Versailles, leaving the Hôtel de Ville and the whole of the city in the hands of the National Guard. The rebels quickly proclaimed a **revolutionary Commune**, decreeing the separation of Church and state, the enfranchisement of women and numerous measures to protect workers' rights.

By the beginning of April, the Communards were under attack from Thiers' army, its numbers newly swelled by prisoners of war helpfully released by the Prussians. Isolated and ill-equipped, the Communards didn't stand a chance. In the notorious **semaine sanglante** of May 21–28, around 25,000 of their number died – no-one knows the exact figure – with some ten thousannd executed or deported. The cost to Paris was also severe; the Hôtel de Ville and Tuileries palace (see box, p.72) were reduced to smouldering ashes. Today the Communards are commemorated in Père-Lachaise cemetery (see p.209).

Montmartre vineyard

Rue des Saules/rue St-Vincent, 18ᵉ • ⓦ fetedesvendangesdemontmartre.com • Ⓜ Lamarck Caulaincourt

Rue des Saules tips steeply down the northern slopes of the Butte past the terraces of the tiny **Clos Montmartre**, or **Montmartre vineyard**, established in the 1930s as an attempt by locals to prevent rampant development in what was then still a de facto village. Sadly, the actual pressing is no longer down on place du Tertre, as it was in the 1940s – it's now done in a basement of the arrondissement's town hall. The annual harvest yields around 450 bottles of wine, blended from Siebel 54-55, Gamay and Pineau; the results can be rough, but as the profits go to various local charities, few wine buffs would be hard-hearted enough to resist having at least one bottle in the cellar. A raucous **festival** marks the *vendange*, or wine harvest, in early October – a celebration of Montmartre's free-wheeling spirit, it's become a big event. Along with tastings, parades and vineyard tours, it includes the Cérémonie des Non-Demandés en Mariage, at which ardently secular, republican couples publicly state that they "have the honour not to ask your hand in marriage" – as the singer Georges Brassens famously put it.

The picturesque, rose-pink old house standing just north of the vineyard is the cabaret club **Au Lapin Agile**, made famous by the Montmartre artists who drank there in the 1900s. Among them was Picasso, whose famous self-portrait, *Au Lapin Agile*, features the artist as a harlequin, his lover Germaine Pichot and a cabaret guitarist. Today the "nimble rabbit" is alive and well, and still stages classic French *chanson* (see p.306).

Musée de Montmartre

12 rue Cortot, 18ᵉ • Daily. April–Sept 10am–7pm; Oct   March 10am–6pm • €9.50, occasionally more during temporary exhibitions •
⓪ 01 49 25 89 39, ⓦ museedemontmartre.fr • Ⓜ Lamarck Caulaincourt

Standing on one of Montmartre's loveliest cobbled streets, the **Musée de Montmartre**
occupies two fine buildings in pretty gardens. The elegant Maison du Bel Air, which
houses the **permanent collection**, is particularly rich in artistic associations: the oldest
building in Montmartre, it was home, at various times, to Auguste Renoir, Raoul Dufy,
Suzanne Valadon and Maurice Utrillo. Today the atmosphere of Montmartre's heyday is
re-created within its mocked-up period rooms, with a low-key selection of Toulouse-
Lautrec posters, plus paintings and photos of the old neighbourhood and its denizens.
Generally more engaging are the **temporary exhibitions** on themes such as the *Chat Noir*
cabaret or Montmartre in the movies, held in the Hôtel Demarne. This also gives access
to Suzanne Valadon's studio-apartment, where the artist lived with her troubled son
Maurice Utrillo and partner André Utter from 1912 to 1926 – their turbulent life and
frequent rows earned them the nickname the "trio infernal". The apartment's cramped
living quarters contrast with the spacious, light-bathed **studio**, convincingly re-created
from old photos. The bold, confident lines of the drawings on display reveal Valadon's
strong character; she was the first woman to exhibit at the Société Nationale des Beaux
Arts. You get a fine view from the back garden over the hilly northern reaches of the city
and the vineyard, and there's also a café – the *Renoir* – in the grounds.

Rue Cortot is overlooked by a lighthouse-like white **water tower**, which, while
lacking the romance of other Montmartre buildings, is one of the landmarks of the
city's skyline.

Halle St-Pierre

2 rue Ronsard, 18ᵉ • Mon–Fri 11am 6pm, Sat 11am 7pm, Sun noon–6pm • €9 • ⓪ 01 42 58 72 89,
ⓦ hallesaintpierre.org • Ⓜ Anvers/Abbesses

To the south and east of Sacré-Cœur, the **slopes of the Butte** drop steeply down
towards boulevard Barbès and the Goutte d'Or quarter (see p.193). Surrounded by
bustling shops selling cheap fabrics by the metre, the nineteenth-century market
building **Halle St-Pierre** is now an exhibition space dedicated to Art Brut, or works by
artists – often autodidacts – who operate outside the mainstream. The lofty, pavilion-
like space, with its huge windows, benefits from its glorious proportions, and the shows
themselves are frequently visionary. The Halle is energetically run, with concerts,
workshops, readings, a superb art and design bookshop and an excellent café (see
p.289). From here, it's a short walk to the busy, multi-ethnic crossroads around Barbès
Rochechouart métro station, with its edgy street hubbub.

Cimetière de Montmartre

Entrance on av Rachel, 18ᵉ, underneath the bridge section of rue Caulaincourt • March 16–Nov 5 Mon–Fri 8am–6pm, Sat 8.30am–6pm,
Sun 9am–6pm; Nov 6–March 15 closes 5.30pm • Free • Ⓜ Blanche/Place de Clichy

West of the Butte, near the start of rue Caulaincourt in place de Clichy, lies the
Montmartre cemetery. Tucked down below street level in the hollow of an old quarry,
it's a tangle of trees and funerary stone, more intimate and less melancholy than
Père-Lachaise or Montparnasse. A few metres inside the gates, watch out for the
antique cast-iron poor-box (marked "Tronc pour les Pauvres").

The illustrious dead at rest here include Stendhal, Berlioz, Degas, Feydeau,
Offenbach, Nijinsky and François Truffaut, as well as La Goulue, the *Moulin Rouge*
dancer immortalized by Toulouse-Lautrec. Emile Zola's grave stands beside the
roundabout, near the entrance, though his actual remains were transferred to the
Panthéon in 1912 (see p.126). In division 15, left of the entrance, lies Alphonsine
Plessis, the real-life model for the consumptive courtesan Marguerite, the "Dame aux
Camélias" of Alexandre Dumas' novel and, later, the original "Traviata". Franz Liszt,
who became her lover after Dumas, called her "the most absolute incarnation of

Woman who has ever existed". Dumas himself lies on the other side of the cemetery, in division 21. Nearby, in division 22, beside avenue Samson, Vaslav Nijinsky's tomb is adorned with a bronze statue of the dancer as Petrushka in the Ballets Russes' production of the same name. Tucked away behind him, the tomb marked "Marie Taglioni" is usually strewn with rotting ballet shoes, left there by dancers from the Paris ballet in honour of the first woman to dance on pointes – in fact this is the grave of Marie's mother, who was also a ballerina. A large Jewish section lies by the east wall.

The 9ᵉ

Ⓜ St-Georges/Blanche/Notre-Dame-de-Lorette

Immediately south of Montmartre, the **9e arrondissement** isn't much visited by tourists. Yet lurking inside the limits of the broad east–west boulevards that frame it is a handsome, distinctly urban residential district with a powerful nineteenth-century atmosphere, especially around place St-Georges. The once-seedy northern fringe has now been rebranded as the trendy **SoPi**, or "South of Pigalle" district; it still has its gritty elements, though stylish shops, restaurants and bars have moved in, especially in the streets around rue des Martyrs. The wealthier, more commercial, southernmost strip of the arrondissement, next to the Opéra and Grands Boulevards, is covered in Chapter 4.

Blanche and Pigalle

From place de Clichy in the west to Barbès Rochechouart métro in the east, the southern slopes of Montmartre are bordered by the **boulevards de Clichy** and **de Rochechouart**. The pedestrianized centre of the boulevards was occupied by dodgem cars and other tacky sideshows for most of the twentieth century, but Montmartre's upward mobility is now dragging its shabby hem along with it; the traffic-choked roads have been "civilized", as the Paris planners put it, with bus and cycle lanes and lots more greenery. It remains to be seen whether or not they will be recolonized by the sophisticated strollers, or *flâneurs*, who defined them in the late nineteenth century. At the eastern **Barbès** end, where the métro clatters by on iron trestles, the crowds teem round the Tati department store, the cheapest in the city, while the pavements are chock-a-block with Arab and African street vendors hawking watches, trinkets and textiles.

At the **place de Clichy** end, tour buses from all over Europe spill their contents into massive hotels. A few steps east, the photogenic **Moulin Rouge** cabaret – literally a red windmill – still thrives on place Blanche; once Toulouse-Lautrec's inspiration, it's now a shadow of its former self (see box, p.190). The stretch between **place Blanche** and **place Pigalle** has long been a byword for sauce and sleaze, with sex shows, sex shops and prostitutes – male and female – vying for the custom of *solitaires* and couples alike, but in the adjacent streets the character of the area is changing, with hostess clubs and grotty bars being gradually joined, or replaced, by trendy cocktail bars, *bistrots* and organic grocers. East of place Pigalle, **Rue des Martyrs** in particular is one of Paris's most enjoyable gastro-streets, lined with fancy food and flower shops as it descends southwards from the Butte.

Avenue Frochot

Ⓜ Pigalle

One of the city's most elegant *villas* (private streets), **avenue Frochot**, leads off place Pigalle. Ordinary mortals are kept out by a digicoded gate, so you'll never get to see the former residences of such greats as Toulouse-Lautrec, Django Reinhardt and Jean Renoir. Still, the facade of the house beside the gate at the south end is worth a look: it's a giant, Art Deco, stained-glass take on Hokusai's famous woodblock print *The Great Wave*, which depitcts a tidal wave dwarfing Mount Fuji. The window owes its

PARIS CABARETS

For many foreigners, entertainment in Paris is still synonymous with cabaret, especially that mythical name, Pigalle's **Moulin Rouge**, at 82 bd de Clichy, 18ᵉ (☎01 53 09 82 82, ⓦmoulinrouge.fr). Unlike the equally renowned **Folies Bergère**, further south at 32 rue Richer, 9ᵉ ⓦfoliesbergere.com), which has moved into the twenty-first century with a mixed programme of mainstream musicals, the *Moulin Rouge* still trades on the saucy glamour of its cancanning "Doriss Girls". The shows are as glitzy and kitsch as you'd expect, full of high-tech special effects and bobbing feathers, and audiences are mainly made up of package tourists whose deal includes a ticket (otherwise around €90, or from €190 with dinner). For similar alternatives, try the **Lido** (116bis av des Champs-Elysées, 8ᵉ; ☎01 40 76 56 10, ⓦlido.fr), best known for its bare-breasted "Bluebell Girls" – and, these days, its "Lido Boys" too – and its high-tech, high-concept Vegas-style shows (around €75–200). At the **Crazy Horse** (12 av George V, 8ᵉ; ☎01 47 23 32 32, ⓦlecrazyhorseparis.com), performances are relatively arty, with a contemporary burlesque edge (from €85, or €40 at the bar).

The crowds are thinner, and a little cooler, at the pair of tiny **transvestite cabarets** on rue des Martyrs, just up from Pigalle métro. At its best, *Chez Michou*, at no. 80 (☎01 46 06 16 04, ⓦmichou.com), is like a scene from an Almodóvar film, with singing transvestites masquerading as various female celebrities, but you'll need to know French pop culture to get much out of it (from €60, or €45 at the bar). *Chez Madame Arthur*, at no. 75bis (☎01 40 05 08 10, ⓦmadamearthur.fr), provides a cheaper alternative (from €10).

existence to a cabaret that stood here in the 1920s, *Le Shanghaï*, and looks particularly splendid when it's illuminated after dark.

Nouvelle Athènes
Ⓜ St-Georges

The heart of the 9ᵉ arrondissement was first developed in the early nineteenth century as a fashionable suburb. It was soon dubbed **Nouvelle Athènes**, or New Athens, after the Romantic artists and writers who came to live here made it the centre of a minor artistic boom. **Rues Clauzel**, **Milton** and **Rodier** are especially striking for their elegantly ornamented facades. A short distance southwest of St-Georges, a passageway off rue Taitbout leads through to the serene **square d'Orléans**, an 1829 development which aped Regency London and attracted Chopin, Alexandre Dumas *fils* and George Sand as early residents. Some of the fine townhouses of the original Nouvelle Athènes scheme can still be spotted just to the west, along **rue de la Tour des Dames**.

Musée de la Vie Romantique
16 rue Chaptal, 9ᵉ • Tues–Sun 10am–6pm; tea room mid-March to late Oct 10am–5.30pm • Entry price varies during temporary exhibitions, otherwise by donation • ☎01 55 31 95 67, ⓦvie-romantique.paris.fr • Ⓜ St-Georges/Blanche/Pigalle

To get a flavour of the nineteenth-century heyday of Nouvelle Athènes, make for the **Musée de la Vie Romantique**, which occupies the house of the Dutch-French painter Ary Scheffer (1795–1858). In the 1820s, Scheffer was art tutor to Louis-Philippe's children, but he is better known today for his friendships with the writer George Sand and her lover, Frédéric Chopin, who would give private, improvised concerts here. The shuttered building, standing at the end of a private cobbled alley, is a delightful surprise, with its courtyard and tree-shaded rose garden where you can take tea on sunny days. The interior – itself now rather romantically shabby – preserves the heavy style and dark decor of a typical bourgeois home of the nineteenth century. The first floor is lined with Scheffer's paintings, along with those of his contemporaries – look out for the works of Marie d'Orléans, Louis-Philippe's youngest daughter, who became one of the leading female sculptors in France.

The ground floor is given over to fine furnishings and objets once owned by **George Sand** – whom you could compare with England's George Eliot, though she was still more unconventional, what with her cross-dressing and serial taking of lovers. Her bohemian lifestyle is glossed over in the museum, but you will see family portraits, some rather fabulous jewellery – including a modern-looking necklace composed of wooden scarabs – locks of hair and an exquisite cast of Chopin's delicate left hand.

Musée National Gustave Moreau

14 rue de la Rochefoucauld, 9ᵉ • Mon, Wed & Thurs 10am–12.45pm & 2–5.15pm, Fri–Sun 10am–5.15pm • €6; free first Sun of the month • ☎ 01 48 74 38 50, Ⓦ musee-moreau.fr • Ⓜ St-Georges/Trinité d'Estienne d'Orves

The **Musée National Gustave Moreau** was conceived by the painter himself in 1895, to be carved out of the house he had shared with his parents for many years. You can visit their tiny, stuffy apartment rooms on the first floor, crammed with furniture and trinkets along with artworks given to Moreau by his friends Degas, Chassériau and Fromentin. More interesting are Moreau's fantastical Symbolist paintings, which get a lot more room – packed cheek by jowl throughout the ground floor, which is decorated as it would have been when the artist lived here, and, to jaw-dropping effect, in two huge **studios** connected by a beautiful spiral staircase. Hundreds of canvases cover every wall, alive with decorative swirls, emotive colours, unsettling imagery and provocative symbolism – it's easy to see how big an influence Moreau was on the Surrealists who followed him. There are countless highlights among the relentless roll call of paintings, but for a starting point look out for *Jupiter and Semele* – which is perhaps the museum's *pièce de résistance* – the triumphant *Return of the Argonauts* and the decadent *The Daughters of Thespius*.

Place St-Georges

Ⓜ St-Georges

The handsome **place St-Georges** centres on a fountain topped by a bust of Paul Gavarni, a nineteenth-century cartoonist who made a speciality of lampooning the mistresses who were *de rigueur* for bourgeois males of the time. This was the mistresses' quarter – they were known as *lorettes*, after the nearby church of **Notre-Dame-de-Lorette**, built in the 1820s in the Neoclassical style. On the east side of place St-Georges, the **Hôtel de la Païva** was built in the 1840s in an extravagant French Renaissance style for Thérèse Lachman, a famous Second Empire courtesan who married a marquis. On the west side, the **Hôtel Thiers** was destroyed by the Communards in 1871 but quickly rebuilt; it now houses the **Dosne-Thiers foundation**, with a huge library specializing in nineteenth-century French history (Ⓦ fondation-dosne-thiers.fr).

12

La Sainte-Trinité

Rue de la Trinité, 9ᵉ • July & Aug Mon–Fri 9.15am–8pm, Sat 10am–8pm, Sun 8.30am–8.15pm; Sept–June Mon–Fri 7.15am–8pm, Sat 10am–8pm, Sun 8.30am–8.15pm • ☎ 01 48 74 12 77, Ⓦ latriniteparis.com • Ⓜ Trinité d'Estienne d'Orves

As it cuts its bustling way towards the relatively down-at-heel commuter hub of the Gare St-Lazare, **rue St-Lazare** passes the bulbous church of **La Sainte-Trinité**, where the deeply spiritual composer Olivier Messiaen was organist for the best part of half a century. Its single, oversize French Renaissance-style tower is its most exciting feature; inside, the vast space under the barrel vault feels cold and sterile.

The 10ᵉ

Ⓜ Poissonnière/Gare du Nord/Gare de l'Est/Château d'Eau

The rue du Faubourg-Poissonnière (so-called because it used to be the route along which fish – *poisson* – was brought into the city from the coast) separates the 9ᵉ from its grittier twin, the **10ᵉ arrondissement**. At its upper end the **northern stations** dominate, while to the south lies the fast-changing quarter of the **faubourgs St-Denis** and **St-Martin**, traditionally working class, but increasingly popular with young Parisian bobos (see p.209) priced out of the more affluent areas of the city. In the far north, just inside the 18ᵉ, east of Montmartre, lies the African quarter of the **Goutte d'Or**. The prettier end of the arrondissement is to the east, on the far side of the Canal St-Martin (see p.196).

The northern stations

Ⓜ Gare du Nord/Gare de l'Est

The life of the 10ᵉ is coloured by the presence of the big **northern stations**. Most travellers scarcely give them a glance, intent on hurrying off to more salubrious parts of the city, but the station buildings are in fact very beautiful, closer to Classical orangeries in style than icons of the industrial age. The **Gare du Nord** (serving all places north, including the high-speed train lines to London) was built by the architect Jacques

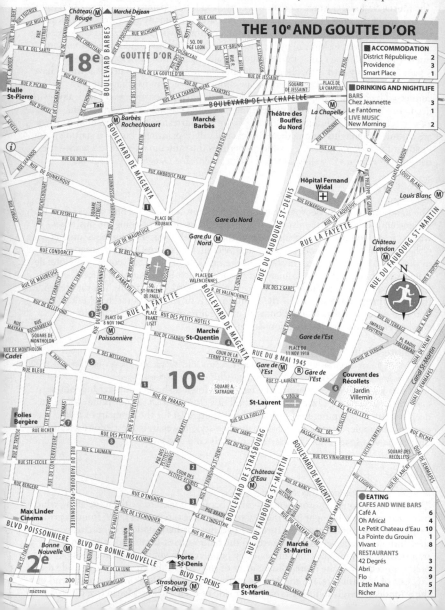

THE 10ᵉ AND GOUTTE D'OR

ACCOMMODATION	
District République	2
Providence	3
Smart Place	1

DRINKING AND NIGHTLIFE	
BARS	
Chez Jeannette	3
Le Fantôme	
LIVE MUSIC	
New Morning	2

● EATING	
CAFES AND WINE BARS	
Café A	6
Oh Africa!	4
Le Petit Chateau d'Eau	10
La Pointe du Grouin	1
Vivant	8
RESTAURANTS	
42 Degrés	3
Abri	2
Flo	9
Little Mana	5
Richer	7

Hittorff in the early 1860s, and is aggressively dominated by its three giant arches, crowned by eight statues representing the original terminus towns, from Amsterdam and Berlin to Vienna and Warsaw. Facing the boulevard de Strasbourg, the slightly earlier **Gare de l'Est** (serving northeastern and eastern France, and Eastern Europe) is more delicate, though when its central arch was open to the elements, as it was when originally built, the steam and smoke billowing out would have had a powerful effect.

The area around the stations is mostly unappealing. Beside the Gare de l'Est, however, a high wall encloses **Jardin Villemin** (entrance on rue des Récollets), which provides a welcome green haven. The garden once belonged to a convent, the **Couvent des Récollets**, one much-restored, seventeenth-century wing of which still stands at 150 rue du Faubourg-St-Martin – it's used as accommodation for academics and artists, and has a wonderful little café (see p.290). Further east again, the **Canal St-Martin** (see p.196) is an even more tranquil place to escape the city hustle. Just south of the Gare de l'Est, the church of **St-Laurent** has a handsome choir dating from the fifteenth century. Thanks to Haussmann, who thought its original facade irritatingly off-centre, the church's Gothic-looking west front actually dates from the same era as the Gare du Nord.

The faubourgs

The southern end of the 10ᵉ arrondissement is its liveliest; it's a gritty, vibrant quarter, home to Indian, black African and Near Eastern communities as well as a growing number of young, trendy Parisians, bringing in their wake a slew of cutting-edge *bistrots*, chic boutiques, delis and cocktail bars. The two main north–south thoroughfares, the **rue du Faubourg-St-Denis** and **rue du Faubourg-St-Martin**, bear the names of the faubourgs, or suburbs, that once stood just outside the town walls. For once, you can still get a vivid sense of the old city limits, as two triumphal arches stand marooned by traffic at either end of the **boulevard St Denis**, which links the two roads in the south. The **Porte St Denis** was erected in 1672 to celebrate Louis XIV's victories on the Rhine – below the giant letters spelling out Ludovico Magno, or "Louis the Great", are the bas-reliefs *The Crossing of the Rhine* (on the south side) and *The Capture of Maastricht* (on the north). With France's northern frontier secured, Louis ordered Charles V's city walls to be demolished and replaced by leafy promenades; they became known as the boulevards after the Germanic word for an earth rampart, a bulwark. Some 200m east, the more graceful **Porte St-Martin** was built two years after its sibling, in celebration of further victories in Limburg and Besançon. Louis planned a veritable parade of these arches, but the military misadventures of the latter part of his reign were hardly worth celebrating.

Rue du Faubourg-St-Denis and around

Near the lower end of **rue du Faubourg-St-Denis**, the historic brasserie *Flo* (see p.291) is tucked away in an attractive old stableyard, the cour des Petites-Ecuries, one of a number of hidden lanes and covered *passages* that riddle this corner of the city – perhaps the best known is the glazed-over **passage Brady**, the hub of Paris's "Little India", lined with Indian barbers, grocers and restaurants. **Rue des Petites-Ecuries**, to the north, has a real buzz about it, with its boutiques, foodie shops and cutting-edge *bistrots*, and is also known for the large jazz and world music club, *New Morning* (see p.308).

The Goutte d'Or

Ⓜ Barbès Rochechouart/Château Rouge

The wide, grotty **boulevard de la Chapelle** forms the northern boundary of the 10ᵉ arrondissement, its only beacon the arty and historic **Théâtre des Bouffes du Nord** (see p.315) and **Marché Barbès**, a busy market held on two mornings a week (Wed and Sat) underneath the métro viaduct. Immediately north of the boulevard, the poetically named **Goutte d'Or** *quartier* stretches between boulevard Barbès and the Gare du Nord rail lines. The setting for Zola's classic novel of gritty realism, *L'Assommoir*, its name – the "Drop of Gold" – comes from a vineyard that stood here in medieval times. After World War I, when large numbers of North Africans were imported to restock the trenches, it became an immigrant ghetto; it is now predominantly the home of West African and Congolese people, along with North African, South Asian, Haitian, Kurdish and other communities.

Marché Dejean and around

Ⓜ Château Rouge

On the rue de la Goutte d'Or you could seek out one of the city's **Wallace fountains** (see box, p.8), on the corner with the rue de Chartres, but the main sight is a few steps north on rue Dejean, where the **Marché Dejean** (daily except Sun afternoon and Mon, roughly 9am–2pm) thrums with shoppers, including many women in brightly coloured West African dress. You can pick up imported African beers and drinks here; if you're self-catering you may want to try vegetables such as plantain, yam and taro root.

Institut des Cultures d'Islam

56 rue Stephenson, 18ᵉ • Tues–Thurs 1–8pm, Fri 4–8pm, Sat & Sun 10am–8pm • Free • ☎ 01 53 09 99 84, ⓦ institut-cultures-islam.org • Ⓜ La Chapelle/Marx Dormoy

The **Institut des Cultures d'Islam** stages exhibitions of contemporary art from the Islamic world. These are usually fascinating and thought-provoking, with recent subjects including Syrian artists responding to the current war and chaos in their country, and female artists depicting domestic life in the Middle East and Iran. On the first floor is a prayer room, while the basement has a hammam with a little tea room. A couple of minutes' walk away, at 19 rue Léon, the institute's smaller, original site is home to a good lunch spot, *Café d'Ici* (Mon–Sat 9am–6pm), which provides employment for local youths. The institute also offers guided **tours** of the Goutte d'Or, focusing on subjects from local beauty shops to popular uprisings and from food-market forays to women's history – contact them via the website for the schedule.

Batignolles

Ⓜ Place de Clichy/Brochant

West of Montmartre cemetery, in a district bounded by the St-Lazare train lines, marshalling yards and avenue de Clichy, lies **Batignolles** "village". Its heart is the attractive **place du Dr Félix Lobligeois**, framing the elegant Neoclassical church of **Ste-Marie-des-Batignolles** – take a look inside to see the extraordinary trompe l'oeil Assumption behind the altar, in which Mary seems to rocket up through the ceiling. On the corners of the *place*, a handful of modern bars and restaurants attracts the neighbourhood's young, bourgeois parents, while, behind, the green **square des Batignolles** is filled with pushchairs and handsome old plane trees. Northeast of the church, the long **rue des Moines** runs past a bustling and covered market, **Marché des Batignolles** (Tues–Sat & Sun afternoon) into an increasingly working-class area. From the market it's a quick stroll northwest to **Parc Martin Luther King**, an ecologically designed public park created on land recovered from the railway. The park is at the centre of a major new redevelopment, the **Clichy-Batignolles** quarter, much of which is scheduled for completion in 2018 (ⓦ clichy-batignolles.fr). As well as apartment blocks, shops and offices, the quarter, covering some 54 acres and built according to green principles, will house in one huge building the new Palais de Justice and Préfecture de Police, due to move out of their central premises on the Ile de la Cité. Designed by Renzo Piano and set to reach 160m, the **Cité Judiciaire** will be the second-tallest building in Paris after the Tour Montparnasse.

The poet Verlaine was brought up on the **rue des Batignolles**, which runs southeast from place du Dr Félix Lobligeois past the **mairie of the 17ᵉ** arrondissement. Just south of the *mairie*, the narrow but lively **rue des Dames** winds its way west to **rue de Lévis** and its food market (Tues–Sun) and east to the avenue de Clichy. Just south lies the traffic- and neon-filled roundabout of **place de Clichy**, dominated by its cinema and a huge, classic old brasserie, *Wepler*.

Cimetière des Chiens

4 Pont de Clichy, Asnières-sur-Seine • Tues–Sun: mid-March to mid-Oct 10am–6pm; mid-Oct to mid-March 10am–4.30pm • €3.50 • ☎ 01 40 86 21 11, ⓦ asnieres-sur-seine.fr • Ⓜ Mairie de Clichy; it's a 15min walk north from the métro along rue Martre, then left at the far end of the Pont de Clichy

The **Cimetière des Chiens**, a **pet cemetery**, is hidden away on a former islet that is now attached to the north bank of the Seine at Asnières – it's outside the city proper but accessible on métro line 13. Most of the tiny graves, some going back as far as 1900, belong to beloved dogs, cats and rabbits, but you'll spot memorials for the odd bird, monkey and horse, too. Photos, plastic flowers and poignant inscriptions abound – "26 years of complicity and shared tenderness"; "Cheated by people; by my dog – NEVER". Some of the more famous furry friends to be interred here include that Hollywood megastar of the 1920s, the German shepherd Rin Tin Tin, while a large memorial is devoted to Barry the St Bernard, who saved the lives of forty snow-disoriented travellers in the Alps. (The dramatic inscription states that he was killed by the 41st, but that is no longer believed to be true.)

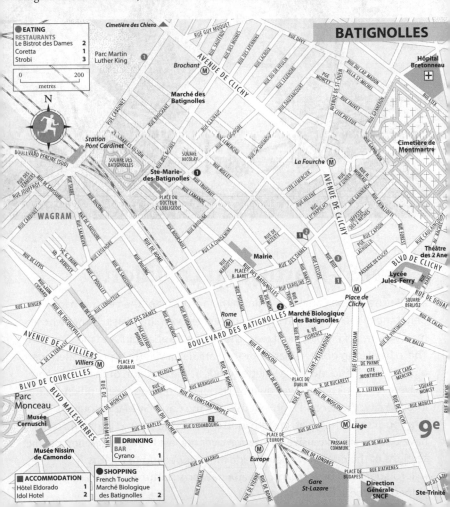

Canal St-Martin and La Villette

La Villette and the Canal St-Martin, in the northeast of the city, were for generations the centre of a densely populated working-class district whose main sources of employment were the La Villette abattoirs and meat market. These have long gone, replaced by the Parc de La Villette, a postmodern park of science, art and music. La Villette stands at the junction of the Ourcq and St-Denis canals. The first was built by Napoleon to bring fresh drinking water into the city; the second is an extension of the Canal St-Martin, built in 1825 as a shortcut to the great western loop of the Seine around Paris. The canals have undergone extensive renovation over the last few decades, and derelict sections of the *quais* have been made more appealing to cyclists, rollerbladers and pedestrians. A major new arts centre, Le 104, has also helped to regenerate the area.

Canal St-Martin and around

13

Ⓜ Jacques-Bonsergent

The **Canal St-Martin** runs underground at the Bastille, emerging after 2.5km near the **place de la République**, and continuing north up to the **place de la Bataille de Stalingrad**. The northern reaches of the exposed canal still have a slightly industrial feel, but the southern part, along the **quai de Jemmapes** and **quai de Valmy**, has a great deal of charm, with plane trees lining the cobbled *quais*, and elegant, high-arched iron footbridges punctuating the spaces between the locks, from where you can still watch the odd barge slowly rising or sinking to the next level. Along this stretch and in the streets just off it, especially **rue des Vinaigriers**, **rue Lucien Sampaix** and **rue de Marseille**, is an ever-growing number of cool cafés and stylish boutiques, the most eye-catching of which is Antoine et Lili (see p.328), with its candy-coloured frontages.

Inevitably, having acquired a certain cachet, the district has attracted property developers, and bland apartment blocks have elbowed in among the traditional, mid-nineteenth-century residences. One of the older buildings, at 102 quai de Jemmapes, is the **Hôtel du Nord**, so named because the barges that once plied the canal came from the north. Made famous by Marcel Carné's film of the same name, starring Arletty and Jean Gabin, it now thrives as a bar-restaurant. Sunday is one of the best days to come for a wander, as the *quais* are closed to traffic and given over to rollerbladers and cyclists. It's especially lively in warmer weather when people hang out along the canal's edge and on the café terraces. Another leisurely way to enjoy the canal is to take a boat trip (see p.27).

Place de la République

Ⓜ République

Just west of the canal, bordering the Marais, lies the **place de la République** (or Répu, as it's affectionately known by locals), one of the city's largest squares, in the centre of which stands an enormous bronze statue of **Marianne**, the female symbol of the Republic, holding an olive branch in one hand, and a tablet inscribed with the words "Droits de l'Homme" in the other. By long-standing tradition, rallies and demonstrations often end in the square; it was here in January 2015 and again in November that year that huge crowds gathered to protest against the massacres carried out by Islamist extremists. The spirit of resilience shown by Parisians in the aftermath of these attacks is paid tribute to by the newly opened café on the square, *Café Fluctuat* (see p.292), a reference to the city's motto, *Fluctuat nec Mergitur* ("it is battered but does not sink"). The café's terrace is a perfect spot for people-watching. The square has become much more inviting since its renovation in 2014, when more trees were planted, fountains and benches installed and traffic (apart from buses) banned from the north side. Skateboarders make the most of the paved expanse and, for much of the year, an open-air "games kiosk", l'R de jeux (May & June Wed, Sat & Sun 2–7pm; July

---

CANAL ST-MARTIN CLEAN-UP OPERATION

The Canal St-Martin is still an important waterway; barges regularly ply up and down, many of them carrying construction materials such as sand and gravel. To maintain the canal in good working order, every fifteen years it is completely drained of water; this allows the nine locks to be restored and the canal cleaned – a costly operation, lasting three to four months. First, some 4.5 tonnes of fish, including perch, carp and crayfish, have to be removed and released upstream. Then, after the water has been drained, a vast clean-up operation begins to take out 10,000 tonnes of mud and rubbish. You never quite know what the canal's depths are going to reveal; past hauls have included two 75mm shells from World War I, gold coins and a human skull. In 2016, the last time the canal was drained, the usual vast quantity of bottles and beer cans was recovered, as well as 104 bikes, 78 Vélib bikes, 23 scooters, 10 pushchairs, washing machines, a pair of ski boots and a pistol.

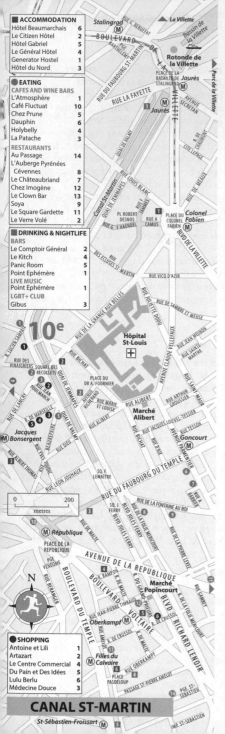

& Aug Wed–Sun 2–8pm; Sept Sat & Sun 2–8pm; Oct to mid-Dec Sat, Sun & Wed 2–6pm), sets up on the eastern side of the square; it has some six hundred toys and games for both adults and children, including construction games, scooters, Monopoly and other board games, any of which you can borrow for free (bring ID).

Boulevard Richard-Lenoir
Ⓜ Oberkampf/Breguet–Sabin/Richard-Lenoir

The wide *boulevard* built over the covered section of the canal, **boulevard Richard-Lenoir**, is attractively landscaped all down its centre, dotted with arched footbridges reminding you of the water flowing underground. It's well worth a wander on Thursday and Sunday mornings in particular, when a big, traditional **food market**, known for its choice range of regional produce, sets up on the lower stretch near the place de la Bastille.

Hôpital St-Louis
Ⓜ Jacques-Bonsergent/Goncourt

On the eastern side of the canal lies the splendid, early seventeenth-century **Hôpital St-Louis** (Mon–Fri 9am–5pm), built in the same style as the elegant place des Vosges in the Marais. Although it still functions as a hospital, you can walk into its quiet central courtyard and admire the fine brick-and-stone facades and steep-pitched roofs that once sheltered Paris's plague victims – the original purpose for which it was built, well away from the city centre.

Le Comptoir Général
80 quai de Jemmapes, 10ᵉ ☎ 01 44 88 24 48, ⓦ lecomptoirgeneral. com • Daily 11am–2am • Free, but donation requested • Ⓜ République/Goncourt

Tucked away off the canal, **Le Comptoir Général** is a vast, rambling space housing a "ghetto museum", an ongoing art and social project that uses found objects, ephemera and vintage domestic bits and bobs to celebrate the creativity of different countries, especially those of west Africa. Little themed areas include a reconstructed photographic studio, a travel agent and a record shop/radio station/dancefloor, all packed with quirky interest and with many items available to buy. There's also a wild garden,

> ## THE MONTFAUCON GALLOWS
>
> Long ago, **rue de la Grange-aux-Belles**, on the north side of the Hôpital St-Louis, was a dusty track leading uphill, past fields, en route to Germany. Where no. 53 now stands, a path led to the top of a small hillock. Here, in 1325, on the king's orders, an enormous **gallows** was built, consisting of a plinth 6m high, on which stood sixteen stone pillars each 10m high. These were joined by chains, from which executed malefactors were hanged in clusters. They were left there until they disintegrated, by way of example, and they stank so badly that when the wind blew from the northeast they reached the nostrils of the still far-off city. The practice continued until the seventeenth century. Bones and other remains from the pit into which they were thrown were found during the building of a garage in 1954.

secondhand books to browse or buy, an African thrift store, a coffee bar and simple world food served at lunchtime, often with live Malian kora music. At night, the whole place transforms into a bar (see p.301).

Rotonde de la Villette
Ⓜ Stalingrad/Jaurès

The Canal St-Martin goes underground at the busy **place de la Bataille de Stalingrad**, dominated by the Neoclassical **Rotonde de la Villette**, a handsome stone rotunda fronted with a portico, inspired by Palladio's Villa La Rotonda in Vicenza. This was one of the toll houses designed by the architect Ledoux as part of Louis XVI's scheme to tax all goods entering the city. At that time, every road out of Paris had a customs post, or *barrière*, linked by a 6m-high wall, known as "Le Mur des Fermiers-Généraux" – a major irritant in the run-up to the Revolution. Cleaned and restored, the *rotonde* is used for occasional exhibitions and has a restaurant with a popular outdoor terrace. Backing the toll house is an elegant aerial stretch of metro, supported by Neoclassical iron-and-stone pillars. The area has a dodgy reputation at night, as it's a known haunt of drug dealers.

Bassin de la Villette
Ⓜ Stalingrad/Riquet/Laumière

Beyond the Rotonde de la Villette the canal widens out into the **Bassin de la Villette**, built in 1808. The recobbled docks area bears few traces of its days as France's premier port, its dockside buildings now offering **canal boat trips** (see p.27) and housing a multiplex cinema, the **MK2** (see p.314), which has screens on both banks, linked by shuttle boat. On weekends and holidays people picnic on the *quais*, jog, cycle, play boules, fish or take a rowing boat out in the dock; in August, as part of the **Paris Plages** scheme (see p.323), you can rent canoes and pedaloes and even swim. Quayside barges such as *Péniche Antipode* (see p.293), a restaurant and live-music venue, add to the general buzz.

At rue de Crimée, the Pont de Crimée, a hydraulic lift bridge with huge pulleys – rather fun to watch in action – marks the end of the dock and the beginning of the **Canal de l'Ourcq**, built in 1802 to bring drinking water to Parisians and to link two branches of the Seine. From the south bank, quai de la Marne, you can cross directly into the Parc de la Villette. On the opposite bank is moored L'Eau et les Rêves (3 quai de l'Oise; Wed–Sun 1–7pm), a bookshop on a barge, specializing in books on maritime themes and hosting occasional exhibitions.

Le Centquatre/Le 104
104 rue d'Aubervilliers, 19ᵉ • Centre: Tues–Fri noon–7pm, Sat & Sun 11am–7pm; La Maison des Petits: Tues–Sun 2.30–6pm • Free entry to the main hall, artists' ateliers & Maison des Petits • ☎ 01 53 35 50 00, ⓦ 104.fr • Ⓜ Riquet

West of the Bassin de la Villette, in one of the poorest parts of the 19ᵉ, is the **Le Centquatre/Le 104**, a huge arts centre. A former grand nineteenth-century funeral parlour, it has two performance spaces and numerous artists' studios, which regularly

13

open their doors to the public. Its main performance space, the central *nef curial*, is an impressive hall, with a high glass roof, grey-painted ironwork and exposed brick walls. After an uncertain start, the centre finally seems to have found its feet, and puts on an exciting programme of contemporary art exhibitions, music, dance and theatre, with an emphasis on the experimental and cutting edge. The complex also houses a good bookshop, café, restaurant, pizza truck and **La Maison des Petits**, a supervised play area for 0- to 5-year-olds with plenty of activities such as painting and crafts. Numbers are limited to thirty at a time, so there can be a wait to get in.

Parc de la Villette

Ⓦ lavillette.com • Ⓜ Porte de la Villette/Porte de Pantin

All the meat for Paris used to come from the slaughterhouses in **La Villette**, an old village that was annexed to the city in the mid-nineteenth century. Slaughtering and butchering, and industries based on the meat markets' by-products, provided plenty of jobs for its dense population, whose recreation time was spent betting on cockfights, skating or swimming, and eating in the numerous local restaurants famed for their fresh meat. In the 1960s, vast sums of money were spent building a huge new abattoir, yet just as it neared completion, the emergence of new

refrigeration techniques rendered the centralized meat industry redundant. The only solution was to switch course entirely; millions continued to be poured into La Villette in the 1980s, with the revised aim of creating an avant-garde **music, art and science complex**.

The end result, the **Parc de la Villette**, which opened in 1986, is enormous in scope and volume. There's so much going on here, most of it stimulating and entertaining (see box, p.203), but it's all so disparate and disconnected, with such a clash of styles, that it can feel more overwhelming than inspiring. According to the park's creators, this is all intentional, and philosophically justified. It was conceived by Bernard Tschumi as a futuristic "activity" park that would dispel the eighteenth- and nineteenth-century notion of parks and gardens as places of gentle and well-ordered relaxation. Instead of unity, meaning and purpose, we're offered a deconstructed landscape: the whole is broken down into its parts. Certainly there's something vaguely disconcerting about the setting. The 900m-long straight **walkway**, with its wavy shelter and complicated metal bridge across the Canal de l'Ourcq, seems to insist that you cover the park from end to end, and there's something too dogmatic about the arrangement of the bright red **follies**, like chopped-off cranes, each slightly different but all spaced exactly 120m apart. Some areas of the park grounds have come to feel rather neglected, with parts of it cordoned off for "repairs". Usually, the liveliest area is the **southern section**, near Porte de Pantin and around the Grande Halle.

Key attractions include the **Cité des Sciences et de l'Industrie**, a huge science museum with a special section for children, an Imax cinema and a decommissioned naval submarine; and the **Philharmonie de Paris**, comprising the city's striking new concert hall and the old Cité de la Musique with its superb **museum of music**. In addition, as well as large expanses of lawn, the park has twelve themed **gardens**, including the Garden of Mirrors, of Shadows and of Dunes (aimed at children; see p.349), all linked by a walkway called the Promenade des Jardins.

Cité des Sciences et de l'Industrie

Tues–Sat 10am–6pm, Sun 10am–7pm • €12 (€9 for under-25s) includes admission to Explora (valid all day, but for four entries only), plus certain temporary exhibitions, the planetarium, the Argonaute submarine and the Louis-Lumière 3D Cinema, subject to availability • ☎ 01 40 05 70 00, Ⓦ cite-sciences.fr • Ⓜ Porte de la Villette

The park's dominant building is the enormous **Cité des Sciences et de l'Industrie**, an abandoned abattoir redesigned by architect Adrien Fainsilber and transformed into a high-tech science museum. Four times the size of the Pompidou Centre, from the outside it appears fortress-like, despite the transparency of its giant glass walls beneath a dark-blue lattice of steel, reinforced by walkways that accelerate out towards the Géode (see p.203) across a moat that is level with the underground floors. Once you're inside, however, the solidity of first impressions is totally reversed by the three themes of water (around the building), vegetation (in the greenhouses) and light – the huge central space is open to the full 40m height of the roof, with light flooding the building from vast skylights and through the glass facade. As well as the permanent exhibition, Explora, the complex includes the brilliant **Cité des Enfants**, specifically designed for children (see p.349). There's a café on the ground floor and a more formal restaurant downstairs, next to a small aquarium.

Explora

Cité des Sciences • Tues–Sat 10am–6pm, Sun 10am–7pm • Included in €12 Cité des Sciences ticket

The **Explora** exhibition space is set across the top two floors of the Cité des Sciences (pick up a plan in English from the welcome desk on level 0) and includes both temporary shows and a permanent exhibition divided into twenty units, many accompanied by English translations. These cover a variety of subjects, among them water, the universe, automobiles, aeronautics, energy, images, genes, sound, mathematics, light and matter, and there's also a section on current scientific

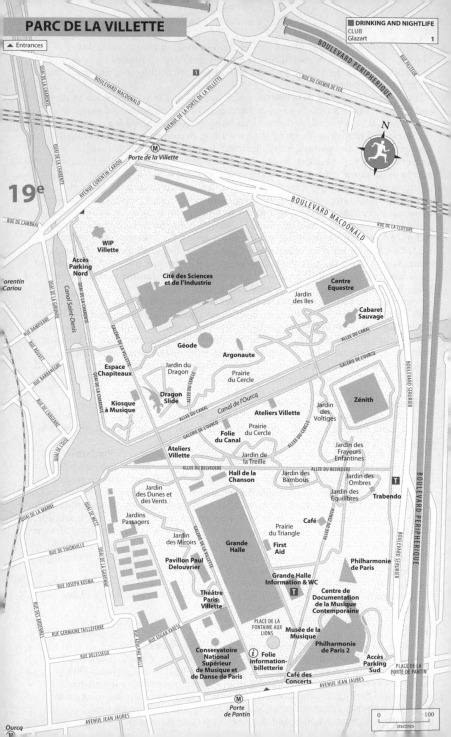

PARC DE LA VILLETTE

▲ Entrances

BOULEVARD PERIPHERIQUE

RUE PASTEUR

AVENUE DE LA PORTE DE LA VILLETTE

RUE DU CHEMIN DE FER

QUAI DE LA CHARENTE

BOULEVARD MACDONALD

QUAI DE LA CHARENTE

1

N

Porte de la Villette

AVENUE CORENTIN CARIOU

19ᵉ

RUE DE CAMBRAI

BOULEVARD MACDONALD

RUE DE LA CLOTURE

Corentin
Cariou

QUAI DE LA GARONNE

Canal Saint-Denis

GALERIE DE LA VILLETTE

QUAI DE LA CHARENTE

WIP
Villette

Accès
Parking
Nord

Cité des Sciences
et de l'Industrie

Centre
Equestre

Jardin
des Iles

RUE DAMPIERRE

RUE BOUDEL

RUE BARBANEGRE

Espace
Chapiteaux

Géode

Argonaute

Cabaret
Sauvage

ALLEE DU CANAL

GALERIE DE L'OURCQ

BOULEVARD SERURIER

Jardin du
Dragon

Prairie
du Cercle

RUE DE L'ARGONNE

QUAI DE L'OISE

Kiosque
à Musique

Dragon
Slide

ALLEE DU CERCLE

Canal de l'Ourcq

ALLEE DU CANAL

Ateliers Villette

Jardin
des
Voltiges

Zénith

GALERIE DE L'OURCQ

Folie
du Canal

Prairie
du Cercle

ALLEE DU CERCLE

Jardin des
Frayeurs
Enfantines

Ateliers
Villette

Jardin de
la Treille

ALLEE DU BELVEDERE

Hall de la
Chanson

Jardin des
Bambous

ALLEE DU BELVEDERE

Jardin des
Ombres

T

Jardin
des Dunes et
des Vents

Jardin des
Equilibres

Trabendo

Jardins
Passagers

QUAI DE LA MARNE

QUAI DE METZ

QUAI DE LA GARONNE

Café

Prairie
du Triangle

ALLEE DU ZENITH

BOULEVARD SERURIER

Jardin
des Miroirs

GALERIE DE LA VILLETTE

Grande
Halle

First
Aid

RUE DE THIONVILLE

Pavillon Paul
Delouvrier

Philharmonie
de Paris

BOULEVARD PERIPHERIQUE

RUE JOSEPH KOSMA

Grande Halle
Information & WC

T

RUE DES ARDENNES

Théâtre
Paris-
Villette

Centre de
Documentation
de la Musique
Contemporaine

RUE GERMAINE TAILLEFERRE

RUE EDGAR VARESE

RUE DELESSEUX

Conservatoire
National
Supérieur
de Musique et
de Danse de Paris

PLACE DE LA
FONTAINE AUX
LIONS

Musée de la
Musique

Philharmonie
de Paris 2

Accès
Parking
Sud

RUE ADOLPHE MILLE

i Folie
information-
billetterie

PLACE DE LA
PORTE DE PANTIN

Café des
Concerts

AVENUE JEAN JAURES

M

Ourcq

Porte
de Pantin

M

AVENUE JEAN JAURES

0   100
metres

PARC DE LA VILLETTE ENTERTAINMENT

The park has a number of distinguished music, arts and theatre venues and festivals.

Cabaret Sauvage Ⓦ cabaretsauvage.com. Live world-music performances.

Espace Chapiteaux Ⓦ lavillette.com. Avant-garde circus venue.

Festival de Cinéma en Plein Air Ⓦ lavillette.com. On summer nights join the crowds lounging on the acres of grass known as "prairies" for an open-air film screening. See p.311.

Grande Halle Ⓦ lavillette.com. The elegant old iron-framed beef market hall hosts art exhibitions and experimental theatre, music and dance performances, and also has a restaurant (*La Petite Halle*) and a bookshop.

Hall de la Chanson Ⓦ lehall.com. Variety shows and *chanson*, held in the old meat market's canteen.

Jazz à la Villette Ⓦ jazzalavillette.com. La Villette's popular jazz festival takes place in September. See p.323.

Philharmonie de Paris Ⓦ philharmoniedeparis.fr. The city's premier classical music venue. See p.203.

Théâtre Paris-Villette Ⓦ theatre-paris-villette.fr. A theatre that encourages young talent and puts on mostly contemporary works.

Trabendo Ⓦ letrabendo.net. A live music venue for jazz and rock.

Zénith Ⓦ le-zenith.com. Rock and pop concerts are staged at this 6000-seat concert hall.

developments. As the name suggests, the emphasis is on exploring, by means of interactive computers, multi-media displays, videos, holograms and games.

On **level 1**, a classic example of chaos theory introduces the **maths section**; La Fontaine Turbulente is a wheel of glasses rotating below a stream of water in which the switch between clockwise and anticlockwise motion is unpredictable beyond two minutes. In **Les Sons** (sounds), you can sit in a cubicle and feel your body tingle with physical sensations as a rainstorm crashes around you, while videos in **L'homme et les gènes** trace the development of an embryo from fertilization to birth, and in **Images** you can use computer simulation to manipulate the *Mona Lisa*'s smile. On **level 2**, the **Jeux de Lumière** offers experiments to do with colour, optical illusions, refraction and the like. You can have your head spun further by a session in the **planetarium** (around six shows daily).

Back on the ground floor, the **Cinéma Louis-Lumière** shows short stereoscopic (3D) films every thirty minutes or so, for which you'll have to queue.

The Géode

Géode Tues–Sun 10.30am–8.30pm; hourly shows • €12 • ☏ 01 40 05 79 99, Ⓦ lageode.fr • **Argonaute** Tues–Sat 10am–5.30pm, Sun till 6.30pm • Included in €12 Cité des Sciences ticket (see p.201)

In front of the Cité des Sciences et de l'Industrie complex floats the **Géode**, a bubble of reflecting steel dropped from an intergalactic boules game into a pool of water that ripples with the mirrored image of the Cité. Inside, the sphere holds a screen for Imax and 3D documentary films on subjects such as the deep sea and the Grand Canyon. Next to the Géode, you can clamber around a real 1957 French military submarine, the **Argonaute**, and view the park through its periscope.

Philharmonie de Paris

221 av Jean-Jaurès, 19ᵉ • ☏ 01 44 84 44 84, Ⓦ philharmoniedeparis.fr • Ⓜ Porte de Pantin

The latest addition to La Villette's collection of futuristic architecture is the **Philharmonie de Paris** concert hall, opened in 2015. Designed by Jean Nouvel (whose other buildings include the Institut du Monde Arabe and Musée du Quai Branly), it's a huge, angular, metal-clad structure. The facade is covered in a pattern of Escher-like, interlocking, bird-shaped aluminium tiles, and a ramp zigzags its way up the facade to the panoramic rooftop; to visit the belvédère (Wed–Sun noon–8pm) take one of the lifts at the entrance and then walk back down the ramp. If the exterior is all jagged and spiky Stravinsky, inside is smooth, seductive Mozart, with soothing cream and ochre colours, rounded balconies and comfy seats. With its

13

state-of the-art acoustics and modular seating and stage, it feels a worthy new venue for grand-scale symphonic concerts.

Concerts (ⓦphilharmoniedeparis.fr) are also held at the smaller hall in the nearby Cité de la Musique, now renamed **Philharmonie 2**. There's a fabulous music museum here too (see below), and a stylish café, the *Café des Concerts*. The building, designed by Christian de Portzamparc in 1995, feels less intimidating than its new twin and conceals a sensual interior; a glass-roofed arcade spirals round the auditorium, the combination of pale blue walls, a subtly sloping floor and the height to the ceiling creating a sense of calm.

To the west, on the other side of the park's main entrance, lies the **Conservatoire National Supérieur de Musique et de Danse de Paris** (also designed by Portzamparc), where regular free recitals and performances are given by the students (see p.319).

Musée de la Musique

Philharmonie 2 • Tues–Sat noon–6pm, Sun 10am–6pm • €7, under-26s free • ⓜ Porte de Pantin

The **Musée de la Musique** presents the history of mainly Western music from the end of the Renaissance to the present day, both visually, exhibiting some one thousand instruments and artefacts, and aurally, via excellent audioguides (available in English, with special ones for children; free) which narrate the history of the instruments, accompanied by extracts of music. It's a truly transporting experience to gaze, for example, at the grouping of harps, made in Paris between 1760 and 1900, and hear an excerpt of music as heavenly as the instruments you're looking at. Other exquisite items include jewel-inlaid crystal flutes, ornately carved theorbos and violas da gamba, a piano that belonged to Chopin and guitars once played by Jacques Brel and Django Reinhardt. Interactive displays can tell you about such subjects as the history of musical notation or the importance of Nuremberg in the manufacture of brass instruments. There's also a small display of instruments from around the world, including Arab ouds and Persian *kamanchehs*. You can hear **live music** too; every afternoon a different instrument is played in the museum, with the chance to meet and talk to the musician.

ARRIVAL AND INFORMATION   PARC DE LA VILLETTE

Access points The Parc de la Villette is accessible from ⓜ Porte de la Villette at the northern end by av Corentin-Cariou and the Cité des Sciences et de l'Industrie; from the Canal de l'Ourcq's quai de la Marne to the west; or from ⓜ Porte de Pantin on av Jean-Jaurès at the southern entrance by the Philharmonie 2.

Information There's an information centre at the southern entrance, which will help you get your bearings, and plenty of restaurants and cafés.

Belleville and Ménilmontant

The old working-class quarters of Belleville and Ménilmontant in the east of Paris are some of the most cosmopolitan in the city, home to North Africans, Malians, Turks, Chinese and many Eastern Europeans. The area is also popular with students and artists, who have done a great deal to create a thriving alternative scene and some of the city's best nightlife. Probably the main reason visitors come to this part of town, though, is to seek out the graves of various famous people – from Modigliani to Jim Morrison – at Père-Lachaise cemetery. A couple of parks, the Buttes-Chaumont and the modern Parc de Belleville, are also worth exploring, not least for their fine views over the city, and there are some rewarding destinations for fans of contemporary art, too.

Belleville and **Ménilmontant** were once villages outside Paris, whose populations were swelled during the Industrial Revolution in the mid-nineteenth century with the arrival of migrants from the countryside. These new arrivals supplied the people-power for the many insurrections in the nineteenth century, including the short-lived Commune of 1871 (see p.186), with the centre and west of Paris battling to preserve the status quo against the oppressed, radical east. Indeed, for much of the nineteenth century, the establishment feared nothing more than the "descente de Belleville" – the descent of the mob from the heights of Belleville. It was in order to contain this threat and be able to swiftly dispatch troops to the eastern districts that so much of the Canal St-Martin (see p.196), a natural line of defence, was covered over by Baron Haussmann in 1860.

Today, only a few reminders of these turbulent times survive, such as the Mur des Fédérés in **Père-Lachaise cemetery** recording the deaths of 147 Communards, and a few streets bearing the names of popular leaders. Some of the old working-class character of the district lives on: narrow streets and artisans' houses survive in places. Much of the area, however, has undergone **redevelopment** over the last few decades. Crumbling, dank and insanitary houses were replaced by shelving-unit apartment blocks in the 1960s and 1970s, giving way in recent years to more imaginative and attractive constructions.

Belleville

Ⓜ Belleville/Pyrénées/Jourdain/Télégraphe

The old village of **Belleville**, only incorporated into the city in 1860, is strung out along the western slopes of a ridge that rises steadily from the Seine at Bercy to an altitude of 128m near the place des Fêtes, the highest point in Paris after Montmartre. "Belle" is not the first adjective that springs to mind when describing Belleville, with its many bland apartment blocks, but there are pockets of charm, especially around the attractive **Parc des Buttes-Chaumont** and **Parc de Belleville**. It's home to what is probably one of the most diverse populations in the city: a mix of traditional working class, various ethnic communities and a good number of students and artists, drawn to the area by the availability of affordable and large spaces, ideal for studios. The best opportunity to view local artists' work is during the **Journées portes ouvertes ateliers d'artistes de Belleville** at the end of May (for dates see ⓦ ateliers-artistes-belleville.fr), when around 250 artists living or working in Belleville open their doors to the public. There's plenty of **street art** too; the best examples can be found on **rue Dénoyez**, off the lower end of rue de Belleville, whose 30m-long wall, dubbed a "*mur d'expression*", is completely covered with graffiti, regularly renewed.

Rue de Belleville and around

Ⓜ Jourdain/Belleville/Pyrénées/Télégraphe

Belleville's main artery is **rue de Belleville**. Its lower, western end is liveliest, with numerous Chinese restaurants and *traiteurs* doing a brisk trade, while adjoining **boulevard de Belleville** is home to Algerian pastry shops, grocers and *shisha* cafés. The boulevard is lined with dramatic new architecture, employing jutting triangles, curves and the occasional reference to the roof lines of nineteenth-century Parisian blocks. Things are particularly vibrant on Tuesday and Friday mornings when the **market** sets up, stretching the whole length of the boulevard. Kosher food shops and cafés, belonging to Sephardic Jews from Tunisia, are also in evidence here and on **rue Ramponeau**, running parallel to rue de Belleville. It was at the junction of rue Ramponeau and rue de Tourtille that the final remaining barricade of the Commune was defended single-handedly for fifteen minutes by the last fighting Communard in 1871.

The upper stretch of rue de Belleville is not as distinctive as its lower end and, with its boulangeries and charcuteries, could be the busy main street of any French provincial town. On the wall of no. 72, a plaque commemorates the birth of the legendary chanteuse **Edith Piaf**; the story goes that she was born under a street lamp

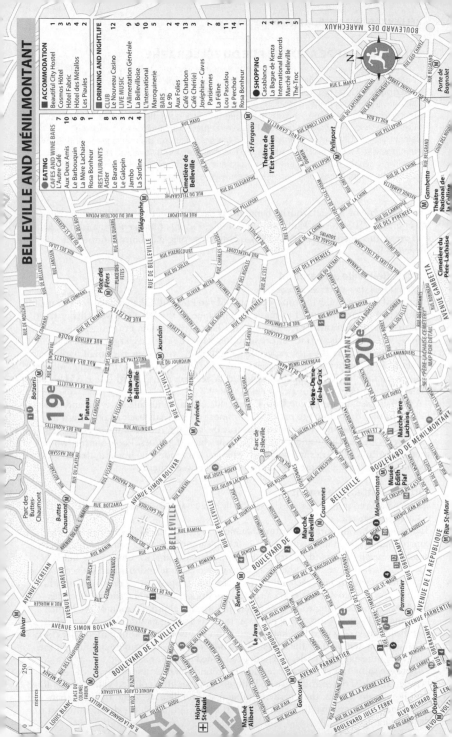

BELLEVILLE AND MÉNILMONTANT

◆ ACCOMMODATION
Beautiful City Hostel	1
Cosmos Hôtel	3
Hôtel Fabric	5
Hôtel des Métallos	4
Les Piaules	2

◆ EATING
CAFÉS AND WINE BARS
L'Autre Café	7
Aux Deux Amis	10
Le Barbouquin	6
La Mère Lachaise	9
Rosa Bonheur	1

RESTAURANTS
Astier	8
Le Baratin	5
Le Galopin	3
Jambo	2
La Sardine	4

◆ DRINKING AND NIGHTLIFE
CLUB
Le Nouveau Casino	12

LIVE MUSIC
L'Alimentation Générale	9
La Bellevilloise	6
L'International	10
Maroquinerie	5

BARS
Le 9b	2
Aux Folies	4
Café Charbon	13
Café Chérie	3
Joséphine – Caves Parisiennes	7
La Féline	8
Lou Pascalou	11
Le Perchoir	14
Rosa Bonheur	1

◆ SHOPPING
Casablanca	2
La Bague de Kenza	4
International Records	3
Marché Belleville	1
Thé-Troc	5

> ## CLAUDE CHAPPE AND THE RUE DU TÉLÉGRAPHE
>
> The rue du Télégraphe, running south off the eastern end of rue de Belleville alongside the Cimetière de Belleville, is named in memory of Claude Chappe's invention of the **optical telegraph**. Chappe first tested his device here in September 1792, in a corner of the cemetery. When word of his activities got out, he was nearly lynched by a mob that assumed he was trying to signal to the king, who was at that time imprisoned in the Temple (see box, p.105). Eventually, two lines were set up, from Belleville to Strasbourg and the east, and from Montmartre to Lille and the north. By 1840, it was possible to send a message to Calais in three minutes, via 27 relays, and to Strasbourg in seven minutes, using 46 relays. Chappe himself did not live to see the fruits of his invention; his patent was contested in 1805 and, distraught, he threw himself into a sewer (his grave is in nearby Père-Lachaise).

just here. One of Piaf's favourite hangouts is back down at rue de Belleville's busy lower end, at 105 rue du Faubourg-du-Temple: *La Java* (Ⓦla-java.fr), a former *bal musette* venue, is still a fixture of Paris nightlife, its original dancehall interior surviving intact.

Parc de Belleville and around
Daily 8/9am till dusk • Free • Ⓜ Pyrénées/Couronnes

A turn off rue de Belleville onto the cobbled **rue Piat** will take you past the beautiful wrought-iron gate that used to mark the entrance to the Villa Ottoz (a little street of houses, long demolished), and on to the **Parc de Belleville**, created in the mid-1990s. From the terrace at the junction with rue des Envierges, there's a fantastic view across the city, especially at sunset. At your feet, the small park descends in a further series of terraces and waterfalls. Families with young children make a beeline for the new state-of-the-art adventure playground (see p.351) that makes clever use of the slopes.

A path crosses the top of the Parc de Belleville past a minuscule vineyard and turns into steps that drop down to **rue des Couronnes** (which leads back to boulevard de Belleville). Some of the adjacent streets – rue de la Mare, rue des Envierges, rue des Cascades – are worth a wander for a feel of the changing times. Look out for two or three beautiful old houses in overgrown gardens, alongside new housing that follows the height and curves of the streets and *passages* between them.

Parc des Buttes-Chaumont
Daily: May & mid-Aug to Sept 7am–9.15pm; June to mid-Aug 7am–10.15pm; Oct–April 7am–8.15pm • Free •
Ⓜ Buttes-Chaumont/Botzaris

The delightful, hilly **Parc des Buttes-Chaumont**, north of the Belleville heights, was constructed under Haussmann in the 1860s to camouflage what until then had been a desolate warren of disused quarries, rubbish dumps and shacks. Out of this unlikely setting, a park was created – there's a grotto with a cascade and artificial stalactites, and a picturesque lake from which a huge rock rises up, topped with a delicate Corinthian temple. You can cross the lake via a suspension bridge, or take the shorter **Pont des Suicides**. This, according to Louis Aragon, the literary grand old man of the French Communist Party, "before metal grilles were erected along its sides, claimed victims even from passers-by who had had no intention whatsoever of killing themselves but were suddenly tempted by the abyss" (*Le Paysan de Paris*). You can go boating on the lake, and, unusually for Paris, you're not cautioned off the grass.

There are some rather desirable residences around the park, especially to the east, between rue de Crimée and place de Rhin-et-Danube; little cobbled **villas** (mews) lined with ivy-strewn houses, their gardens full of roses and lilac trees, can be found here, off rue Miguel-Hidalgo, rue du Général-Brunet, rue de la Liberté, rue de l'Egalité and rue de Mouzaïa.

Le Plateau

33 rue des Alouettes, 19ᵉ • Wed–Sun 2–7pm • Free • ⓦ fracidf-leplateau.com • Ⓜ Jourdain

One block south of the Parc des Buttes-Chaumont is a small contemporary arts centre, **Le Plateau**, set up following a vigorous campaign by local residents who successfully acquired the space after fighting off property developers. Exhibitions tend to focus on experimental, cutting-edge French and international artists.

Ménilmontant

14

Ⓜ Ménilmontant

Like Belleville, much of **Ménilmontant** aligns itself along one straight, steep street, the **rue de Ménilmontant** and its lower extension, rue Oberkampf. Although run-down in parts, its popularity with artists and young professionals, or bobos (*bourgeois-bohémiens*), has helped to revitalize the area. Alternative shops and cool bars and restaurants cluster along **rue Oberkampf** and its parallel street **rue Jean-Pierre-Timbaud**, the city's most vibrant nightlife hub (see p.304). The upper, eastern reaches of rue de Ménilmontant, above rue Sorbier, are quieter, and looking back you find yourself dead in line with the rooftop of the Pompidou Centre, a measure of how high you are above the rest of the city.

Musée Edith Piaf

5 rue Crespin-du-Gast, 11ᵉ • Mon–Wed 1–6pm, Thurs 10am–noon; closed Sept • Donation • Admission by appointment only on
ⓣ 01 43 55 52 72 • Ⓜ Ménilmontant/St-Maur

Sitting very close to the Ménilmontant métro is the **Musée Edith Piaf**. Piaf was not an acquisitive person; the few clothes (yes, including a little black dress), letters, toys, paintings and photographs that she left are almost all here, along with every one of her recordings. The venue is a small flat lived in by her devoted admirer Bernard Marchois, who will show you around and answer any questions (in French).

Père-Lachaise cemetery

Main entrance on bd de Ménilmontant • Mon– Fri 8am–5.30pm, Sat 8.30am–5.30pm, Sun 9am–5.30pm • Free • ⓦ pere-lachaise.com •
Ⓜ Père-Lachaise/Philippe-Auguste

Final resting place of a host of French notables, as well as some illustrious foreigners, **Père-Lachaise** is one of the world's largest and most famous cemeteries. Sited on a hill commanding grand views of Paris, it's a bit like a miniature town, with its grid-like layout, cast-iron signposts and neat cobbled lanes – a veritable "city of the dead". It's surely also one of the world's most atmospheric cemeteries, an eerily beautiful haven, with terraced slopes and magnificent old trees (around six thousand of them) spreading their branches over the moss-grown tombs, as though shading them from the outside world.

Finding individual graves can be a tricky business. Our **map** (see p.211) and the free plans given out at the conservation office near the main entrance will point you in the right direction, though slightly more detailed ones are available to buy from the newsagents or florists near the main entrance.

Père-Lachaise was opened in 1804 and turned out to be an incredibly successful piece of land speculation. Nicolas Frochot, the urban planner who bought the land, persuaded the civil authorities to have **Molière**, **La Fontaine**, **Abélard** (see box, p.212) and **Héloïse** reburied in his new cemetery, and it began to acquire cachet, but it really took off when Balzac set the final scene of his 1835 novel *Le Père Goriot* here. Ironically, Frochot even sold a plot to the original owner for considerably more than the price he had paid for the entire site. Even today, rates are extremely high.

Chopin, Jim Morrison and Oscar Wilde

Among the most visited graves is that of **Chopin** (Division 11), who has a willowy muse mourning his loss and is often attended by groups of Poles laying wreaths and flowers in the red and white colours of the Polish flag.

Swarms also flock to the grave of ex-Doors lead singer **Jim Morrison** (Division 6), who died in Paris in 1971 at the age of 27. Once graffiti-covered and wreathed in marijuana fumes, it has been cleaned up and now has a metal barrier around it, though this hasn't stopped fans scribbling messages in praise of love and drugs on other graves, and trees, nearby. In fact things got so bad some years ago that relatives of undistinguished Frenchmen interred nearby signed a petition asking for the singer's body to be

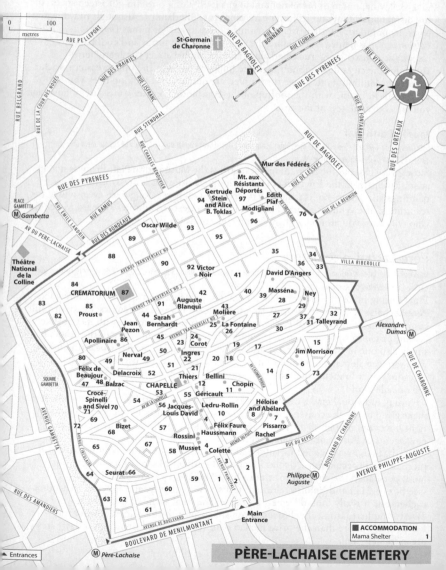

PÈRE-LACHAISE CEMETERY

exhumed and sent home, but the grave, unlike many here, is on a perpetual lease, so the Lizard King is here to stay.

Another tomb that attracts many visitors is **Oscar Wilde**'s (Division 89), topped with a sculpture by Jacob Epstein of a Pharaonic winged messenger (sadly missing its once prominent member, which was last seen being used as a paperweight by the director of the cemetery). The inscription behind is a grim verse from *The Ballad of Reading Gaol*. For many years the tomb was covered in lipstick kisses – it was something of a tradition among Wilde's fans to kiss the tomb and leave their mark. Worried about the damage this was doing to the tomb, the authorities have cleaned it up and installed a surrounding glass barrier.

14

Writers and musicians

Many other **musicians** repose near Chopin, among them Bellini, Cherubini, the violinist Kreutzer, whose commemorative column leans precariously to one side, and the more recently deceased French jazz pianist, Michel Petrucciani. Rossini is honoured with a spot on the *avenue principale*, though in fact his remains have been transferred to his native Italy. Bizet, composer of the opera *Carmen*, lies intact in Division 68; the fine bronze bust that used to adorn his tomb is now kept safely locked away after it was stolen, and then recovered, in 2006.

Most of the celebrated dead have unremarkable tombs. Femme fatale **Colette**'s tomb, close to the main entrance in Division 4, is very plain, though always covered in flowers. The same holds true for the "Divine" **Sarah Bernhardt**'s (Division 44) and the great chanteuse **Edith Piaf**'s (Division 97). **Marcel Proust** lies in his family's conventional, black marble tomb (Division 85). Just across the way is the rather incongruous-looking **Crematorium** (Division 87), crudely modelled on the Aghia Sophia in Istanbul, with domes and minarets. Here among others of equal or lesser renown lie the ashes of Max Ernst, Georges Perec, Stéphane Grappelli and American dancer Isadora Duncan, who was strangled when her scarf got tangled in the rear wheel of her open-top car. Maria Callas has a plaque here, too, though her ashes were removed and scattered in the Aegean.

Artists

Among other eminent representatives of the arts, **Corot** (Division 24) and **Balzac** (Division 48) both have fine busts, as does poet **Alfred de Musset**, near Rossini on the *avenue principale*, and buried, according to his wishes, under a willow tree. **Delacroix** lies in a sombre sarcophagus in Division 49, while **Jacques-Louis David**'s heart rests in Division 56 (the rest of him is buried in Belgium, where he died). His pupil **Ingres** reposes in Division 23. **Géricault** reclines on cushions of stone (Division 12), paint palette in hand, his face taut with concentration; below is a sculpted relief of part of his best-known painting *The Raft of the Medusa*. Close by is the relaxed figure of **Jean Carriès**, a model-maker, in felt hat and overalls, holding a self-portrait in the palm of his hand.

In Division 96, you'll find the grave of **Modigliani** and his lover Jeanne Herbuterne, who killed herself in crazed grief a few days after he died in agony from meningitis. Impressionist painter **Camille Pissarro** lies among the sober, unadorned tombs of the Jewish plot near the main entrance, as does the beautiful nineteenth-century actress **Rachel**, known for one of the briefest love-letter exchanges in history; after seeing her on stage, Prince de Joinville sent her his card with the note "Où? Quand? Combien?", to which Rachel scribbled back, "Chez toi. Ce soir. Pour rien."

Politicians

Notable politicians include **Félix Faure** (on the *avenue principale*, Division 4), French president, who died in the arms of his mistress in the Elysée palace in 1899; draped in a French flag, his head to one side, he cuts rather a romantic figure. **Auguste Blanqui**, after whom so many French streets are named, lies in Division 91. Described by Karl

14

IMMODEST MONUMENTS

In contrast to the many modest monuments marking the tombs of the famous, in Division 48 a now-forgotten French diplomat, **Félix de Beaujour**, is marked with an enormous tower, rather like a lighthouse. To the north in Division 86, one **Jean Pezon**, a lion-tamer, is shown riding the pet lion that ate him. In Division 71, two men lie together hand in hand – **Croce-Spinelli and Sivel**, a pair of balloonists who went so high they died from lack of oxygen. In Division 92, journalist **Victor Noir** – shot at the age of 22 in 1870 by Prince Napoléon for daring to criticize him – is portrayed at the moment of death, flat on his back, fully clothed, his top hat fallen by his feet. However, it's not as a magnet for anti-censorship campaigners that his tomb has become famous, but as a lucky charm – a prominent part of his anatomy has been worn shiny by the touch of infertile women, hoping for a cure.

Marx as the nineteenth century's greatest revolutionary, he served his time in jail – 33 years in all – for political activities that spanned the 1830 Revolution to the Paris Commune. Karl's daughter, **Laura Marx**, and her husband **Paul Lafargue**, who committed suicide together in 1911, lie south from Blanqui's grave, in Division 76.

War memorials and the Mur des Fédérés

Monuments to collective, violent deaths have the power to change a sunny outing to Père-Lachaise into a much more sombre experience. In Division 97, in what's become known as the "coin des martyrs", you'll find memorials to the victims of the Nazi concentration camps, to executed Resistance fighters and to those unaccounted for in the genocide of World War II. The sculptures are relentless in their images of inhumanity, of people forced to collaborate in their own degradation and death.

Marking one of the bloodiest episodes in French history is the **Mur des Fédérés** (Division 76), the wall where the last troops of the Paris Commune were lined up and shot in the final days of the battle in 1871. A total of 147 men were killed, after a frenetic chase through the tombstones, and the remains of around a thousand other Communards were brought here and thrown into a grave-pit. The wall soon became a place of pilgrimage for the Left. The man who ordered the execution, Adolphe Thiers, lies in the centre of the cemetery in Division 55.

Charonne and around

Ⓜ Porte de Bagnolet/Gambetta

Charonne, just south of Père-Lachaise cemetery, retains its village-like atmosphere, with a perfect little Romanesque church and the cobbled street of rue St-Blaise. **St-Germain-de-Charonne**, in place St-Blaise, has changed little, and its Romanesque belfry not at all, since the thirteenth century. It's one of a handful of Paris churches to have its own graveyard; several hundred Communards were buried here after being accidentally disinterred during the construction of a reservoir in 1897. Elsewhere in Paris, charnel houses were the norm, with the bones emptied into the catacombs as more space was required. It was not until the nineteenth century that public cemeteries appeared on the scene, the most famous being Père-Lachaise.

Opposite the church of St-Germain-de-Charonne, the old cobbled village high street, **rue St-Blaise**, pedestrianized to place des Grès, was once one of the most picturesque in Paris, and still has a measure of charm, with its wooden shuttered houses, cafés and artists' ateliers.

FONDATION LOUIS VUITTON

Auteuil and Passy

The affluent districts of Auteuil and Passy, once villages on the outskirts of Paris, were only incorporated into the city in 1860. They soon became the capital's most desirable neighbourhoods, where well-to-do Parisians commissioned new residences. Hector Guimard, designer of the swirly green Art Nouveau métro stations, worked here, and there are also rare Parisian houses by interwar architects Le Corbusier and Mallet-Stevens. The area has an almost provincial air, with its tight knot of streets and charming villas – leafy lanes of attractive old houses, fronted with English-style gardens, full of roses, ivy and wisteria. Flowers, especially waterlilies, feature abundantly in the shimmering Monet canvases displayed in the Musée Marmottan, while contemporary art takes centre stage in the spectacular new Fondation Louis Vuitton in the Bois de Boulogne, Paris's second-largest park after the Bois de Vincennes.

Auteuil

Ⓜ Eglise d'Auteuil

The **Auteuil** district is now completely integrated into the city, but there's still a villagey feel about its streets, and it holds some delightful little *villas* as well as fine specimens of early twentieth-century architecture. The ideal place to start an exploration is the **Eglise d'Auteuil** métro station, close to several of Hector Guimard's **Art Nouveau** buildings.

Rue Boileau to the avenue de Versailles

The house at no. 34 **rue Boileau** (Hôtel Roszé) was one of Guimard's first commissions, in 1891. To reach it from the Eglise d'Auteuil métro, head west along rue d'Auteuil for 200m, then turn left (south) into Boileau. A high fence and wisteria obscure much of the view, but you can see some decorative tile-work under the eaves and around the doors and windows. Further down the street, just before you reach boulevard Exelmans, the Vietnamese embassy at no. 62 successfully combines 1970s Western architecture with the traditional Vietnamese elements of a pagoda roof and earthenware tiles. Continue south for 0.5km along rue Boileau beyond boulevard Exelmans, turn right onto rue Parent de Rosan and you'll find a series of enchanting *villas* off to the right, backing onto the Auteuil cemetery.

Rue Boileau terminates on avenue de Versailles, where you can turn left and head back to the métro via the Guimard apartment block at no. 142 (1905), with its characteristic Art Nouveau flower motifs and sinuous, curling lines. It's just by the Exelmans crossroads (on bus route #72). You can then cut across the **Jardin de Ste-Périne**, once the rural residence of the monks of Ste-Geneviève's abbey, established in 1109, to get back to either Chardon-Lagache or Eglise d'Auteuil métro. Enter the garden opposite 135 avenue de Versailles, or alongside the hospital on rue Mirabeau, just north of the rue Chardon-Lagache junction.

Rue de la Fontaine and around

The old village high street, **rue d'Auteuil**, runs west to **place Lorrain**, which hosts a Saturday market. From here **rue Jean de la Fontaine** runs northeast to the Radio-France building, with Guimard buildings at nos. 14, 17, 19, 21 and 60. No. 14 is the most famous: the "Castel Béranger" (1898), with exuberant Art Nouveau decoration in the bay windows, the roof line and the chimney. At no. 65 there's a huge block of artists' studios by Henri Sauvage (1926) with a fascinating colour scheme, bearing signs of a Cubist influence. Alternatively, head up **rue du Docteur Blanche** for the cool, rectilinear lines of Cubist architects Le Corbusier and Mallet-Stevens (see p.216).

Villa La Roche

8–10 square du Docteur Blanche, 16ᵉ • Mon 1.30–6pm, Tues–Sat 10am–6pm; closed Aug • €8 • ☎ 01 42 88 75 72, Ⓦ fondationlecorbusier.fr • Ⓜ Jasmin; #52 bus

North of place Lorrain, in a cul-de-sac off rue du Docteur Blanche, are **Le Corbusier**'s first private houses (1923), the Villa Jeanneret and the Villa La Roche, now in the care of the Fondation Le Corbusier. You can visit **Villa La Roche**, which was built in strictly Cubist style; it is very plain with strip windows, the only extravagance a curved frontage. The interior, meanwhile, is sparsely furnished, but originally the walls were hung with the outstanding collection of modern art built up by the financier Raoul

---

AUTEUIL BUS ROUTES

Handy **bus routes** for exploring Auteuil are the #52 and the #72. The #52 runs between Ⓜ Opéra in the centre and Ⓜ Boulogne-Pont-de-St-Cloud near the Parc des Princes, stopping at rue Poisson en route, while the #72's route extends between Ⓜ Hôtel-de-Ville in the Marais and Ⓜ Boulogne-Pont-de-St-Cloud, stopping en route by the Exelmans crossroads near some of Guimard's buildings on avenue de Versailles.

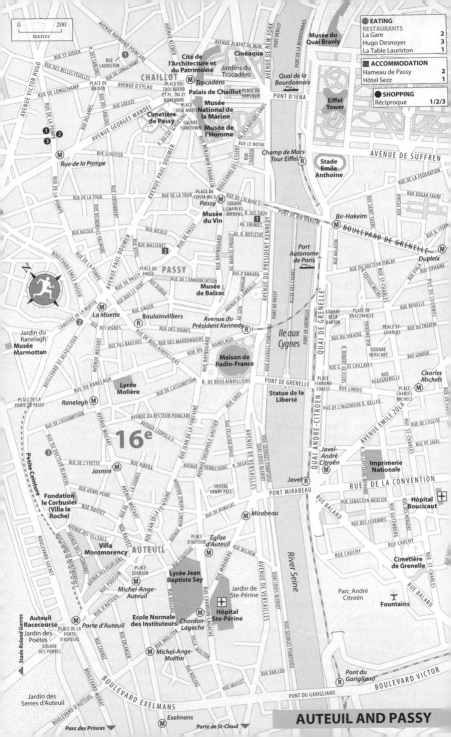

	0		200	
	metres			

EATING

RESTAURANTS
La Gare — 2
Hugo Desnoyer — 3
La Table Lauriston — 1

ACCOMMODATION
Hameau de Passy — 2
Hôtel Sezz — 1

SHOPPING
Réciproque — 1/2/3

AUTEUIL AND PASSY

Albert La Roche, for whom the *villa* was built. The walls are painted in soothing greys, creams and blues, colours that Le Corbusier was fond of using in his easel painting. The two houses look commonplace enough now from the outside, but were a great contrast with anything that had gone before, and once you're inside La Roche, the spatial play still seems ground-breaking.

Rue Mallet-Stevens

Ⓜ Jasmin

Heading north along rue du Dr-Blanche and off to the right, you'll come to the tiny **rue Mallet-Stevens**, built by the architect of the same name in Cubist style. The original proportions of the houses were altered by the addition of three storeys in the 1960s, but you can still see the architectural intention of sculpting the entire street space as a cohesive unit. Continue to the end of rue du Dr-Blanche, turn left and then right onto boulevard de Beauséjour; a shortcut immediately opposite rue du Ranelagh across the disused Petite Ceinture rail line (see box, p.217) takes you to shady avenue Raphaël, which runs alongside the pretty **Jardin du Ranelagh** (featuring a rather engaging sculpture of the fabulist La Fontaine with an eagle and fox) and on to the Musée Marmottan.

Musée Marmottan

2 rue Louis-Boilly, 16ᵉ • Tues–Sun 10am–6pm, Thurs till 9pm • €11 • ☎ 01 44 96 50 33, ⓦ www.marmottan.fr • Ⓜ La Muette

The **Musée Marmottan** is best known for its excellent collection of **Monet paintings**, bequeathed by the artist's son. Among them is *Impression, soleil levant*, a canvas from 1872 of a misty Le Havre morning, whose title the critics usurped to give the Impressionist movement its name. There's also a dazzling selection of canvases from Monet's last years at Giverny, showing the increasingly abstract quality of his later work, including several *Nymphéas* (Water lilies), *Le Pont japonais*, *L'Allée des rosiers* and *Le Saule pleureur*, where rich colours are laid on in thick, excited whorls and lines. The collection also features some of Monet's contemporaries – Manet, Renoir and **Berthe Morisot**. Morisot, who lived most of her life in Passy, is particularly well represented, with two rooms devoted to her work, characterized by vigorous, almost aggressive, brushwork, seen to best effect in paintings such as *Branches d'oranger* (1889) and *Dans le Jardin à Bougival* (1884).

In addition, the museum has a small and beautiful collection of thirteenth- to sixteenth-century **manuscript illuminations** – look out for the decorated capital "R" framing an exquisitely drawn portrait of St Catherine of Alexandria.

West of Auteuil

Attractive gardens west of Auteuil include the **Jardin des Serres d'Auteuil**, the municipal greenhouses and gardens that supply Paris with its plants and flowers, as well as the beautiful **Jardins Albert Kahn**, with pretty French and Japanese gardens and an intriguing museum of early colour photos from around the world.

Jardin des Poètes and Jardin des Serres d'Auteuil

Jardin des Poètes Av du Général Sarrail • Daily 9am–6pm • Free **Jardin des Serres d'Auteuil** 3 av de la Porte d'Auteuil • Daily 10am–6pm, closes 5pm in winter • Free • Ⓜ Porte d'Auteuil

West of place de la Porte d'Auteuil lie two gardens: the **Jardin des Poètes**, with its entrance on avenue du Général Sarrail, and the adjoining **Jardin des Serres d'Auteuil**, entered either at 3 avenue de la Porte d'Auteuil or via the Jardin des Poètes. You can't escape the traffic noise completely, but the Jardin des Poètes is extremely tranquil and very informal. Famous French poets are remembered by verses (mostly of a pastoral nature) engraved on small stones surrounded by little flowerbeds, and a statue of Victor Hugo by **Rodin** stands in the centre.

The Jardin des Serres, known for its elegant *belle époque* metal-frame greenhouses designed by Jean-Camille Formigé, is currently undergoing major redevelopment, due for completion in 2019. Amid much protest, the neighbouring Roland Garros tennis association, with its eye on the Paris 2024 Olympics bid, has been given permission to extend into the gardens and build a new 5000-seater court. It looks as though Formigé's greenhouses, including a palm house and one containing rare flora from New Caledonia, will be preserved, but some of the newer greenhouses will be taken down to make way for a complete re-landscaping of the area.

Jardins et Musée Albert Kahn

10–14 rue du Port, Boulogne-Billancourt • See website for opening hours and admission • ☎ 01 55 19 28 00, Ⓦ albert-kahn.hauts-de-seine .net • Ⓜ Boulogne-Pont-de-St-Cloud/Marcel-Sembat

The **Jardins et Musée Albert Kahn**, in the suburb of Boulogne-Billancourt, consist of a very pretty garden and a **museum** dedicated to temporary exhibitions of *"Les Archives de la Planète"* – photographs, many in colour, and films collected by banker and philanthropist Albert Kahn between 1909 and 1931. Kahn wanted to record human activities and ways of life that he knew would soon disappear forever. His aim in the design of the garden was to combine English, French, Japanese and other styles to demonstrate the possibility of a harmonious, peaceful world. It's an enchanting place, with rhododendrons and camellias under blue cedars, a rose garden, an espaliered orchard, a forest of Moroccan pines, streams with Japanese bridges beside pagoda teahouses, Buddhas and pyramids of pebbles. At the time of writing, the gardens were being restored and a new building was being erected to house Kahn's photographs; there will also be a shop, restaurant and *salon de thé* when work is complete at the beginning of 2018. During renovation work access is restricted to guided tours booked in advance (see website).

Passy

Northeast of Auteuil, the area around the old village of **Passy** offers scope for a good meandering walk. From **La Muette** métro, head east along the old high street, **rue de Passy**, past an eye-catching parade of boutiques, until you reach **place de Passy** and the crowded but leisurely café terrace of *Le Paris Passy*. From the *place*, stroll southeast along cobbled, pedestrianized **rue de l'Annonciation**, a pleasant blend of down-to-earth and genteel well-heeled that gives more of the flavour of old Passy. You may no longer be able to have your Bechstein repaired here or your furniture lacquered, but the food shops that now dominate the street have delectable displays guaranteed to make your mouth water.

THE PETITE CEINTURE

The **Petite Ceinture** ("Little Belt"), a disused railway line, nearly 33km long, that circles the city, was built in the 1850s. Closed in the 1970s and abandoned to nature (and graffiti artists), the line has become overgrown with wild flowers and grasses, and provides a much-needed refuge for birds and butterflies. Seeing the potential of this "green corridor", the city council has opened up one or two stretches to the public and turned them into *sentiers natures*, or **nature trails**. The stretch in the 16e is just over 1km long and extends from boulevard Montmorency (the entrance is opposite no. 37; Ⓜ Porte d'Auteuil) to La Muette métro station (entrance opposite 27 bd de Beauséjour). Open in the daytime only, the path makes a nice getaway from the city, with an appealingly abandoned, rather secretive air. It meanders through trees and bushes, with grand apartment blocks just visible to either side. Another section that has been opened up recently lies in the 15e, between place Balard and rue Olivier de Serres, a stretch of 1.3km linking the Parc André-Citroën and Parc Georges-Brassens. By 2020, a further 6.5km will be open to the public. See Ⓦ paris.fr for more details.

15

Maison de Balzac

47 rue Raynouard, 16ᵉ • Tues–Sun 10am–6pm • Free • ☎ 01 55 74 41 80, ⊛ maisondebalzac.paris.fr • Ⓜ Passy/RER Av-du-Prés-Kennedy
–Maison-de-Radio-France

The **Maison de Balzac** is a delightful little house with pale-green shutters and a decorative iron entrance porch, tucked down some steps in a tree-filled garden. Balzac moved to this secluded spot in 1840 in the hope of evading his creditors. He lived under a pseudonym, and visitors had to give a special password before being admitted. Should any unwelcome callers manage to get past the threshold, Balzac would escape via a back door and go to the river via a network of underground cellars. Well-known works he wrote here include *La Cousine Bette* and *Le Cousin Pons*.

The museum preserves his study, writing desk and monogrammed cafetière (fuelled by coffee, his writing stints could extend up to eighteen hours a day for weeks on end). One room is devoted to the development of ideas for a monument to Balzac, resulting in the famously blobby **Rodin** sculpture of the writer (installed on boulevard du Montparnasse), caricatures of which are on show. Other exhibits include letters to Mme Hanska, whom he eventually married after an eighteen-year courtship, and a complex family tree of around a thousand of the four thousand-plus characters that feature in his *Comédie Humaine*. Outside, the shady, serene, rose-filled **garden** is a pleasant place to dally on wrought-iron seats amid busts of Balzac.

Rue Berton and around

Ⓜ Passy/La Muette

Reached via steps that drop from rue Raynouard behind the Maison de Balzac, **rue Berton** is a cobbled path with gaslights still in place, blocked off by the heavy security of the **Turkish embassy**. The building is an early twentieth-century reconstruction of the seventeenth-century château that stood on this site, the **Hôtel de Lamballe**, which was once home to Marie Antoinette's friend, the Princesse de Lamballe, who met a grisly fate at the hands of revolutionaries in 1792. Later, it became a private asylum where the pioneering Dr Blanche treated patients with nervous disorders. The poet Gérard de Nerval was admitted in 1854, driven insane partly by the task of translating Goethe's *Faust* into French. And in 1892, Guy de Maupassant, suffering serious mental illness brought on by syphilis, was committed; he died here a year later. Get a better view of the building from **rue d'Ankara**, reached by heading down avenue de Lamballe, then left into avenue du Général-Mangin.

Rue des Eaux and the Musée du Vin

Museum: 5 square Charles Dickens, 16ᵉ • Tues–Sat 10am–6pm • €13.90, including glass of wine • ☎ 01 45 25 63 26,
⊛ museeduvinparis.com • Ⓜ Passy

From rue d'Ankara, head northeast along avenue Marcel-Proust, turn right and then left onto rue Charles-Dickens and follow it until it hits rue des Eaux, where fashionable Parisians came in the eighteenth century for the therapeutic benefits of the once-famous, iron-rich Passy waters. Today, the street is enclosed by a canyon of moneyed apartments that dwarf the eighteenth-century houses of **square Charles Dickens**. One of these houses, burrowing back into the cellars of a vanished fourteenth-century monastery that produced wine until the Revolution, holds the **Musée du Vin**, an exhibition of viticultural bits and bobs about as exciting as flat champagne, though the cellar bar is an atmospheric place for a glass of wine or lunch.

Bois de Boulogne

Ⓜ Porte Maillot/Porte Dauphine/bus #244

Designed by Baron Haussmann, the **Bois de Boulogne** was supposedly modelled on London's Hyde Park – though it's a very French interpretation. The *bois*, or "wood", of the name is somewhat deceptive, though the extensive parklands do contain remnants of the once-great Forêt de Rouvray. The Bois was the playground of the wealthy, especially in the nineteenth century, but today the area is a favoured haunt for prostitutes and kerb-crawlers who, despite an obvious police presence and night-time road closures, still do business along its periphery. A certain amount of crime accompanies the sex trade; this is no place for a midnight walk.

By day, however, the Bois de Boulogne is delightful. Entry to the park as a whole is free, but several attractions within it charge entry fees or open for limited times: the new **Fondation Louis Vuitton** contemporary art space; the **Jardin d'Acclimatation**, aimed at children (see p.349); the beautiful floral displays of the **Parc de Bagatelle**; and the **racecourses** at Longchamp and Auteuil. There are 14km of **cycling** routes and **boating** on the Lac Inférieur, while the best, and wildest, part for **walking** is towards the southwest corner.

Fondation Louis Vuitton

8 av du Mahatma-Gandhi, Bois de Boulogne, 16ᵉ • Mon, Wed & Thurs noon–7pm, Fri noon–9pm, Sat & Sun 11am–8pm • €9, under-18s €4 (ticket includes entry to the adjoining Jardin d'Acclimatation) • ☎ 01 40 69 96 00, ⓦ fondationlouisvuitton.fr • Ⓜ Les Sablons; rather than walk from the métro (10–15min) you could take the shuttle minibus (every 10–15min during museum opening hours; 5–10min; €2) from av de Friedland, just off place Charles de Gaulle (aka place de l'Etoile)

Rising amid the trees and greenery of the Bois de Boulogne is the dramatic, Frank Gehry-designed contemporary art centre, the **Fondation Louis Vuitton**, opened in 2014. It houses the collection of France's richest man, Bernard Arnault, head of the luxury goods empire LVMH. From the moment you approach the main entrance, above

15

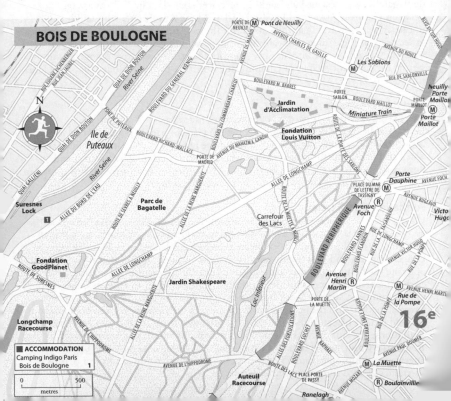

BOIS DE BOULOGNE

ACCOMMODATION
Camping Indigo Paris Bois de Boulogne ... 1

16ᵉ

which gleams a conspicuous silver LV monogram, the impression is of an extravagant building conceived with no expense spared. The huge, abstract structure, dubbed the "cloud of glass", consists of twelve glass "sails", made up of 3600 panels, and sits surrounded by a moat of water. Evoking a ship buffeted by the wind (or possibly a giant insect), the glass sails jut out at odd angles, revealing here and there the dazzling-white inner walls.

Exploring the **interior** is fun; escalators take you down to the moat level (or "grotto") with its striking Olafur Eliasson installation of coloured glass, mirror and sound, while stairways spiral up to several roof terraces revealing unexpected vistas of the Eiffel Tower and La Défense. There are eleven galleries, some vast, some intimate, an auditorium (used for music recitals), a restaurant (*Le Frank*) and a bookshop. The building has an unfinished feel in places and there's a lot of empty space, something which Gehry says is deliberate, seeing it as a work in progress, with opportunities for artists to interact with the space and install their creations. The Fondation mounts acclaimed temporary exhibitions and its **permanent collection** is shown in changing themed displays, including choice works by Rothko, Jeff Koons, Takashi Murakami, Richard Serra and Jean-Michel Basquiat.

Parc de Bagatelle

Bois de Boulogne, 16ᵉ • Daily: May–Sept 9.30am–8pm; Oct–April 9.30am–5.30pm • €6, free Nov–April • Ⓜ Porte Maillot, then bus #244, which takes you to the entrance on allée de Longchamp; there's also an entrance on rte de Sèvres à Neuilly

The **Parc de Bagatelle** comprises garden styles ranging from French and English to Japanese. Its most famous feature, the stunning **rose garden** of the charming Château de Bagatelle, was designed and built in just over sixty days in 1775 as a wager between Comte d'Artois and his sister-in-law Marie Antoinette, who said it could not be achieved in less than three months. The best time for the roses is June, while other parts of the garden see beautiful tulips, hyacinths and daffodils in early April, irises in May and water lilies in early August. The park's attractive orangery is the setting for candlelit recitals of Chopin's music during the Festival de Chopin in late June (see p.322).

Jardin Shakespeare

Bois de Boulogne, 16ᵉ • Daily 2–4pm • Free • Ⓦ jardinshakespeare.com • Ⓜ Porte Maillot

In the middle of the Bois de Boulogne, the Pré Catalan park is famous for its huge two-hundred-year-old copper beech tree and the prestigious *Pré Catalan* restaurant. You'll also find the **Jardin Shakespeare**, where you can study the herbs, trees and flowers referred to in the Bard's plays; from May to September, open-air Shakespearean works, French classics and plays for children are staged here.

Fondation GoodPlanet

1, Carrefour de Longchamp, Domaine de Longchamp, Bois de Boulogne, 16ᵉ • Mid-Feb to mid-Dec Wed–Fri 11am–7pm, Sat & Sun 11am–8pm • Free • ☎ 01 48 42 18 00, Ⓦ goodplanet.org • Ⓜ Porte Maillot & bus #244 (or shuttle bus on Sat & Sun 10.45am–7.45pm; €2)

In spring 2017, the **Fondation GoodPlanet** took up residence in the Domaine de Longchamp, a grand nineteenth-century château, former home of Baron Haussmann, opposite the Longchamp racecourse. Founded in 2005 by renowned photographer and environmentalist Yann Arthus Bertrand, the foundation aims to raise awareness about the environment. Regular workshops, many aimed at families and children, concerts, farmers' markets and themed weekends on subjects such as refugees and organic food, are held in the château and in the extensive grounds. There are also two permanent exhibitions: Passeurs de Sons, a collection of over 2000 musical instruments from around the world, and "Human, l'Exposition", consisting of eight hours of video interviews with people from 65 countries, some of which featured in Yann Arthus Bertrand's 2015 documentary film *Human*.

VERSAILLES

The suburbs

To talk of "the suburbs", in French, doesn't at all have the same connotations as it does in English. In the imagination of those safely ensconced intra-muros, or within the historic centre defined by the old city walls, the banlieue is no sleepily conservative ring of dormitory towns, but a dangerous belt populated by thugs, rioters and gangs. It's true that, politically, ethnically and economically, the outskirts of Paris are almost the reverse of the centre. The architecture of the banlieue is utterly different too, characterized by cités (high-rise housing estates) and industrial estates, with few historic vestiges – and little, at first glance, to attract visitors. The suburbs do have a handful of important sights, however, from opulent palaces to flea markets to gleaming skyscrapers.

Most easily accessible is **St-Ouen market**, a treasure-trove of antiques and curios that sprawls just outside the official city limits north of Montmartre. North of here stands the proud basilica of **St-Denis**, which was the birthplace of the Gothic style and the burial place of almost all the French kings. To the west, meanwhile, the great suburban landmark is the **Grande Arche**, the huge centrepiece of Paris's modern business district, **La Défense**. Perhaps the most visited out-of-town destination, however, is **Versailles**, an overwhelming monument to the reigns of Louis XIV, who built it, and Louis XVI, whose furniture now fills it; the palace sits in its own vast landscaped park on the very edge of the Paris conurbation, southwest of the city. An elegant and far less visited alternative is the **Château de Malmaison**, a little way north, which preserves the exquisite Empire furnishings of Napoleon's wife, Joséphine, along with her delightful gardens. Other than these, whether the various suburban museums deserve your attention will depend on your degree of interest in the subjects they cover: air and space travel or contemporary art at **Le Bourget**; modern art in Vitry-sur-Seine's **Mac/Val**; and the specialist collection of china at **Sèvres**.

Paris has traditionally kept its suburbs at arm's length, keeping its eyes shut and holding its nose, but recently measures have been taken to break down the barriers between the two, including the creation in 2016 of the Métropole du Grand Paris (see box, p.378) and a planned massive expansion of public transport over the next ten to fifteen years. While transport links with central Paris are being improved, and areas like **Pantin** on the northeast edge of the city by the Canal Ourcq are drawing interest from digital and creative businesses, gentrification is a slow – and, as always with urban gentrification, a not uncontroversial – process.

All of the sights listed in this chapter are accessible by RER, métro and bus. Sights further afield, for which you'll need to take a train or have access to a car, are covered in Chapter 17.

St-Ouen flea market

Sat–Mon; different markets keep slightly different hours, but as a rule Mon 11am–5pm, Sat & Sun 10am–5.30pm • ⓦ marcheauxpuces-saintouen.com • ⓜ Porte de Clignancourt, from where it's a 5min walk up the busy av de la Porte-de-Clignancourt, passing under the *périphérique*, or ⓜ Garibaldi, from where you approach the market from the north, along rue Kléber, rue Edgar-Quinet and rue des Rosiers

The vast **St-Ouen market**, sometimes called the Clignancourt market, is located just outside the northern edge of the 18ᵉ arrondissement, in the suburb of St-Ouen. Its popular name of **les puces de St-Ouen**, or the "St-Ouen flea market", dates from the days when secondhand mattresses, clothes and other infested junk were sold here in a free-for-all zone outside the city walls. Nowadays, however, it's predominantly a proper – and generally expensive – **antiques** market, selling mainly furniture, but abounding in all sorts of fashionable odds and ends like old zinc café counters, telephones, traffic lights, posters, vintage record players, jukeboxes and so on. Note that it's quieter on wet days and Mondays.

When walking from the Porte de Clignancourt métro, bear in mind that **rue Jean-Henri-Fabre**, shaded by the flyover, is the market's unofficial fringe area, lined with stalls flogging leather jackets, rip-off DVDs and African souvenirs. Watch your belongings, and don't fall for the guys pulling the three-card monte or cup-and-hidden-ball scams. For a quieter and scarcely slower approach, use Garibaldi station.

The markets

The official complex is a huge, sprawling area, with fourteen separate markets, covered and open air, and some two thousand shops. While you may not find any breathtaking bargains, prices aren't too bad for the smaller items, and the atmosphere provides plenty to enjoy. If time is short, focus on the following four: Marché **Vernaison** is the oldest in the complex, established in around 1920, and its maze-like, creeper-covered alleys are great fun to wander along, threading your way between stalls selling curios

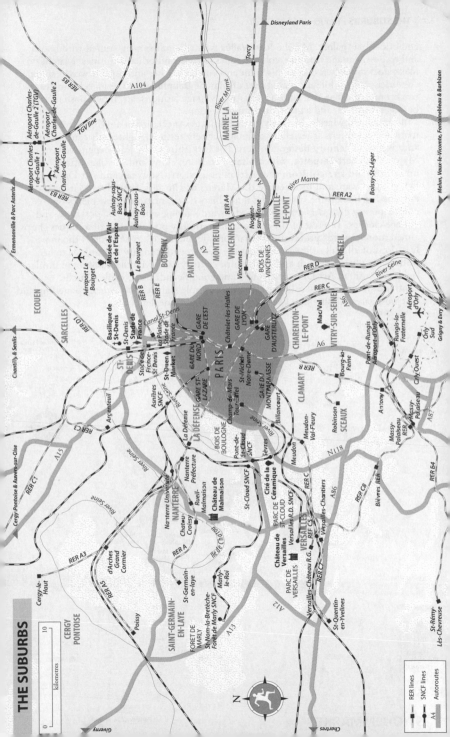

and bric-a-brac galore. Marché **Jules-Vallès** is smaller but similar, stuffed with books and records, vintage clothing, colonial knick-knacks and other curiosities. Marché **Malik** stocks mostly fashion – discount and vintage clothes and bags, as well as some couturier stuff – while the glazed roof of Marché **Dauphine** shelters an eclectic flea market mix of decorative antique furniture, vintage fashions, art, movie posters, rare books and comics, and a great vinyl/music section.

In the domed Marché **Malassis**, little boutiques specialize in anything from maritime ephemera or jewellery to imaginatively restored eighteenth-century pieces and twentieth-century designer objets. For furnishings, the least expensive is Marché **Paul Bert-Serpette**, which offers furniture, china and the like, often unrestored and straight from the auction houses. Art Nouveau and Art Deco light fittings, glassware and bronzes are the Marché **des Rosiers**' speciality. Marché **Le Passage** has lots of fine furnishings and objets d'art, including new pieces by contemporary designers and aged gardenware – along with books, postcards and vintage clothes. The rest of the markets are seriously posh clusters of antiques shops, aimed more towards professionals than private clients. Marché **Biron** is the most luxurious of all, full of treasures from the seventeenth century onward. Marché **Antica** (mainly eighteenth and nineteenth century) and Marché **Cambo** are similar, the latter with an Art Deco area and some good Scandi stuff, while Marché **l'Entrepôt** houses large-scale antiques, from whole staircases to *boiserie* panelling and cast-iron gates. **L'Usine** and **Lécuyer** are restricted to dealers only.

ST-OUEN MARKET

EATING **ST-OUEN MARKET**

Chez Louisette Allée 10, Marché Vernaison, 18ᵉ ☎01 40 12 10 14; ⓜPorte de Clignancourt. An old-school *buvette* buried at the end of Marché Vernaison's Allée 10. The great gypsy jazz guitarist Django Reinhardt sometimes played here, but these days singers belt out Parisian *chanson* with keyboard backing every Sunday afternoon. The food, famously, is nothing special, and the fussed-up ambience won't be to all tastes, but it's a kitsch classic. Mon 10.30am–5.30pm, Sat & Sun 10am–6pm.

Ma Cocotte 106 rue des Rosiers, 18ᵉ ☎01 49 51 70 00, ⓦmacocotte-lespuces.com; ⓜPorte de Clignancourt. Chichi, Philippe Starck-designed and -owned *Ma Cocotte* is a slightly incongruous presence on the shabby rue des Rosiers. The atmosphere is cosy if a little contrived, with an open kitchen, a cocktail bar and diners who want to see and be seen. Mains – bistro staples with modern twists, such as *coquillette* pasta with truffle butter and ham – start at around €22, though there are sharing plates, too, starting at €15. Breakfast only 9am–noon (Sun from 11.30am).

Mon–Thurs 9am–3pm & 7–10.30pm, Fri 9am–3pm & 7–11pm, Sat 9am–4pm & 7–11pm, Sun 9am–9pm.

La Recyclerie 83 bd Ornano, 18ᵉ ☎01 42 57 58 49, ⓦlarecyclerie.com; ⓜPorte de Clignancourt. Where the cool kids off to market hang out, this vast, ramshackle old space, in an abandoned train station right by the métro, has a hint of Berlin or Brooklyn about it with its dilapidated decor and alternative vibe – it's all about recycling here, and yoga classes, plant sales, upcycling workshops and visits to urban farms are just some of the activities on offer. The weekend brunch (€22, €20 for veggies) is a good deal, including locavore dishes such as *pissaladière* or a Basque-style fricassée. Otherwise grab a coffee, fresh juice or evening *apéritif* and settle down by the picture windows overlooking the old railway line, the Petite Ceinture (see box, p.216) – or, on sunny days, head out to the plant-shaded roof terrace. Mon–Wed noon–midnight, Thurs noon–1am, Fri & Sat noon–2am, Sun 11am–10pm.

St-Denis

For most of the twentieth century, **ST-DENIS**, 10km north of the centre of Paris and accessible by métro, was one of the most heavily industrialized communities in France, and a bastion of the Communist party. After the factories closed, unemployment spiralled and immigration radically altered the ethnic mix; for bourgeois Parisians, the political threat of the *banlieue rouge* ("red suburbs") became instead the social threat of what are now dubbed the *banlieue chaude* ("hot [or volatile] suburbs"). Visitors, however, are likely to find a poor but buoyant community, its pride buttressed by the town's twin attractions: the ancient **basilica of St-Denis** and the **Stade de France**, seat of the 1998 World Cup final.

Basilique de St-Denis

1 rue de la Légion-d'Honneur, St-Denis • April–Sept Mon–Sat 10am–6.15pm, Sun noon–6.15pm; Oct–March Mon–Sat 10am–5pm, Sun noon–5.15pm; closed during weddings and funerals, and for extra services on feast days • €9, under-18s free; audioguide €4.50 • ☎01 48 09 83 54, ⓦsaint-denis.monuments-nationaux.fr • ⓜBasilique de St-Denis

The **Basilique de St-Denis** is the most important cathedral in France. This is where the French kings were both crowned (ever since Pepin the Short in 754) and buried (all but three since Hugues Capet, in 996); it is also where the Gothic architectural style was born. The building as it stands today was the twelfth-century masterpiece of unknown masons working under Abbot Suger, friend and adviser to kings. At the cathedral's dedication service, the west front and high, light-filled choir clearly made a deep impression on the bishops who were present – in the next half-century they went on to build most of the great Gothic cathedrals in France on its pattern. The innovative design can still be traced in the lowest storey of the choir, notably the ambulatory space, which allowed pilgrims to process easily around the relics held in the choir. The novel rib vaulting allowed the walls to be no more than an infilling between a stone skeleton, making huge, luminous windows possible. Today, the upper storeys of the choir are still airier than they were in Suger's day, having been rebuilt in the mid-thirteenth century, at the same time as the nave. A good way to appreciate the atmosphere in the basilica is during the **St-Denis Festival** (usually throughout June; ⓦfestival-saint-denis.com), when it plays host to top-flight classical concerts, with an emphasis on choral music.

16

The necropolis

You enter the **necropolis** via a separate entrance in the south portal. Immediately on the left is the bizarre sight of the bare feet of **François 1er** and his wife Claude de France peeking out of their enormous Renaissance memorial. Beside the steps to the ambulatory lies **Charles V**, the first king to have his funeral effigy carved from life, on the day of his coronation in 1364. Alongside him is his wife Jeanne de Bourbon, clutching the sack of her own entrails to her chest – a reminder that royalty was traditionally eviscerated at death, the flesh boiled away from the bones and buried separately.

The **ambulatory** itself is a beautiful double-aisled design raised on the revolutionary pointed or ogival vaults, and richly lit by some of St-Denis' original stained glass, including the famous Tree of Jesse window immediately behind the altar. Just up the south steps and around to the right, a florid Louis XVI and a busty **Marie Antoinette** – often graced by bouquets of flowers – kneel in prayer; the pious scene was sculpted in 1830, long after their execution.

On the north side of the ambulatory you pass the effigy of the sixth-century king **Clovis I**, a canny little German who wiped out Roman Gaul and turned it into France, with Paris for a capital. His effigy was actually executed some six hundred years after his death;

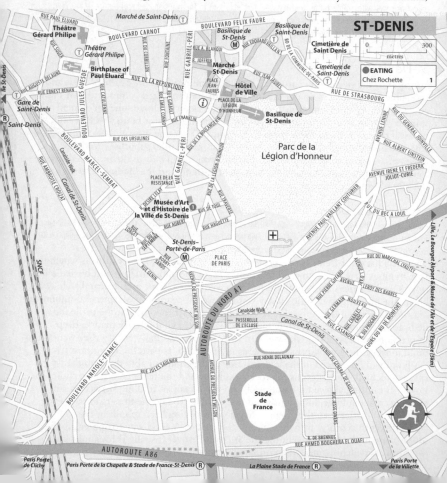

THE LEGEND OF ST DENIS

The first church at St-Denis was probably founded by an early (mid-third-century) Parisian bishop known by the name of St Denis, or **St Dionysius** in English. The legend goes that after he was decapitated for his beliefs at Montmartre – supposedly so-called because it is the "Mount of the Martyr" – he picked up his own head and walked all the way to St-Denis, thereby indicating the exact spot where his abbey should be built. It's not in fact all that far – just over 5km – though as a friend of Edward Gibbon's once remarked, "The distance is nothing, it's the first step that counts".

---

alongside is another Merovingian, Childebert I, whose twelfth-century effigy is the earliest in the basilica. On the right of the northern steps, the tomb of **Henri II** and **Catherine de Médicis** was boldly designed by Primaticcio in the style of a Classical temple: kneeling on top are sculptures by Germain Pilon of the royal couple as living souls; down below, you can just see their soulless, decaying corpses. Just beyond is the memorial to **Louis XII** and **Anne de Bretagne**; again, if you look past the graceful Renaissance structure and allegorical figures you'll see the pain-wracked bodies of the royal couple.

Marché St-Denis

Place Jean-Jaurès • Tues 8am–12.30pm, Fri 8am–1pm, Sun 8am–1.30pm • ⓜ Basilique de St-Denis

The **Marché St-Denis**, held in and around the main place Jean-Jaurès, has hundreds of stalls peddling vegetables at half the price of central Parisian markets, as well as cheap curios, clothes and fabrics. The covered *halles*, near the square just off rue Dupont, are a multi-ethnic affair where the produce on the butchers' stalls – ears, feet, tails and bladders – shows this is not rich folks' territory.

Musée d'Art et d'Histoire de la Ville de St-Denis

22bis rue Gabriel-Péri • Mon, Wed & Fri 10am–5.30pm, Thurs 10am–8pm, Sat & Sun 2–6.30pm • €5, under 16s free • ☏ 01 42 43 05 10, ⓦ musee-saint-denis.fr • ⓜ St-Denis–Porte de Paris

About five minutes' walk south of the St-Denis basilica is the distinctly left-leaning **Musée d'Art et d'Histoire de la Ville de St-Denis**, housed in a former Carmelite convent. The quickest route is along rue de la Légion d'Honneur. The exhibits on display are not of spectacular interest, though the local archeology collection is good, and there are some intriguing paintings of industrial landscapes and an exhibition on the Communist poet Paul Eluard, native son of St-Denis. The one unique collection is of documents relating to the **Commune**: posters, cartoons, broadsheets, paintings, plus an audiovisual presentation.

Stade de France

Rue Francis de Pressensé • April–Aug daily; Sept–March Tues–Sun • Up to two English-language tours a day (1hr; €15) • ☏ 08 92 70 09 00, ⓦ stadefrance.com • ⓜ St-Denis–Porte de Paris

Just beyond the métro stop St-Denis–Porte de Paris (or ten minutes further down rue Gabriel-Péri from the Musée d'Art et d'Histoire), a broad footbridge crosses the motorway and Canal St-Denis to the **Stade de France**, scene of France's first (and so far only) World Cup victory in 1998. On a more sombre note, it was also the first of six sites that were targeted in terror attacks in Paris on November 13, 2015. At least €430 million was spent on the construction of this stadium, whose elliptical structure is best appreciated at night when lit up. If there isn't a match or a mega-event on, you can take a tour that explores the grounds, changing rooms, the VIP stands and a small museum.

INFORMATION

ST-DENIS

Tourist office St-Denis' tourist office is opposite the basilica at 1 rue de la République. It sells tickets for the St-Denis Festival (see p.225) and can provide maps of the town (daily 9.30am–1pm & 2–6pm; ☏ 01 55 87 08 70; ⓦ saint-denis-tourisme.com; ⓜ Basilique de St-Denis).

EATING

Chez Rochette 20 rue Gabriel-Péri ☏ 01 42 43 71 44; Ⓜ St-Denis–Porte de Paris. You'll find nothing fancy at this simple restaurant, near the museum, just good, old-fashioned French cooking – *terrines*, *poulet*, foie gras – at reasonable prices. Tues–Thurs noon–3pm, Fri & Sat noon–3pm & 7–10pm.

La Défense

Ⓜ /RER La Défense/Esplanade de la Défense

A thicket of glass and concrete towers, **La Défense**, just west of the city, is Paris's prestigious **business district**. More than a hundred thousand people commute here daily during the week, and, with its shopping centres and cinemas, it's often a popular and animated place at weekends, too – at least by day. Landmark buildings include the sleek elliptical **Tour EDF**, the **Tour Majunga**, with its radically "flowing" effect, and **Tour First** on the place des Saisons, which, at 231m, is France's tallest skyscraper (though still shorter than the Eiffel Tower). If buildings aren't your thing you may prefer the sixty-odd monumental **outdoor sculptures** – including works by Miró, Alexander Calder and César – scattered throughout the district.

The main artery of La Défense is the pedestrianized **Esplanade du Général de Gaulle**; you can pick up maps at **Info Défense**, an information centre on the main place de la Défense that also has a few exhibits about the development of the district (Mon–Fri 9am–6pm, Sat & Sun 10am–5pm; free; ☏ 01 47 74 84 24, Ⓦ ladefense.fr). The oldest work of art is nearby: Barrias's bronze **La Défense de Paris**, dating from the 1880s and depicting a soldier defending a young, rather powerful-looking woman who symbolizes Paris. It commemorates the defence of the city against the Prussians in 1870 and is the origin of the district's name.

La Grande Arche

Roof daily 9.30am–6.30pm • €15 • ☏ 01 49 07 27 55 • Ⓜ /RER La Défense/Esplanade de la Défense

Built in 1989 to honour the bicentenary of the Revolution, and in conscious tribute to the Arc de Triomphe, **La Grande Arche** is an astounding structure: a 112m, white marble, hollow cube that's large enough to enclose Notre-Dame with ease. It closes the western axis of the Voie Triomphale (see p.62), albeit positioned at a slight angle so as to allow an uninterrupted view from its offices all the way to the Louvre's similarly

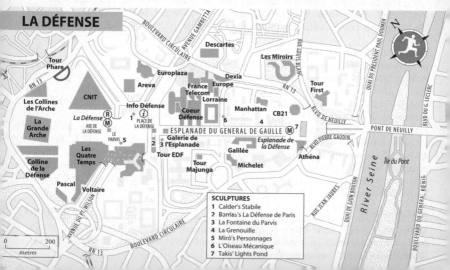

askew Cour Carrée, 8km away. The architect was a little-known Danish professor, Johann Otto von Spreckelsen, who died before the arch's completion. The only thing that slightly mars its perfect form – or softens its brutality, depending on your point of view – is the lift scaffolding and a fibreglass "cloud" canopy, suspended within the hollow. There are excellent **views** from the steps that lead up to the base of the arch: down the Voie Triomphale to the city and along a second axis that leads through the Eiffel Tower and Tour Montparnasse. You can also take the glass elevator to the **roof** of the arch, which has recently reopened after a major renovation; as well as superb views, you'll find a new restaurant (*Les Jardins de Joséphine*) and an exhibition space dedicated to photojournalism.

For the most dramatic approach it's worth getting off a stop before the closest station (La Défense), métro Esplanade de la Défense, from where it's a twenty-minute walk.

Château de Malmaison

Rueil-Malmaison • Château: April–Sept Mon & Wed–Fri 10.30am–12.30pm & 1.30–5.45pm, Sat & Sun 10.30am–12.30pm & 1.30–6.15pm; Oct–March Mon & Wed–Fri 10.30am–12.30pm & 1.30–5.15pm, Sat & Sun 10.30am–12.30pm & 1.30–5.45pm; grounds: daily except Tues 10am–6pm • €6.50 (grounds only €1.50) • ☏ 01 41 29 05 55, ⓦ chateau-malmaison.fr • Ⓜ/RER La Défense, then bus #258 from the bus station at place de l'Iris (every 30min; 25min) towards St-Germain-en-Laye; from Le Château stop, walk 100m back up av Bonaparte, cross over and take the signposted side road (a 10min walk in all)

According to Napoleon's private secretary, the **Château de Malmaison**, 15km west of central Paris, was "the only place next to the battlefield where he was truly himself". It was the home, after all, of his beloved Joséphine de Beauharnais, who shaped it as a perfect example of the grand First Empire style. After their divorce – Joséphine failed to provide the emperor with an heir – she stayed on, receiving just two visits from the emperor there before her death in 1814.

Visitors today can see the stately **official apartments**, on the ground floor, which are preserved almost exactly as they were in Joséphine's day. The design fashions reflect imperial interests in Italy and Egypt – which Napoleon was busy conquering at the time Joséphine first began her interior design works here, in 1799. The cloth-hung Salle du Conseil, where Napoleon had ministerial meetings, feels like a luxurious version of a campaign tent; it's now overlooked by a reproduction of Gérard's heartbreakingly lovely portrait of Joséphine, the original of which hangs in the Hermitage, St Petersburg. The dining room owes its decor to fashionable interest in Pompeii, and still contains the fabulous, eighty-piece gold dinner service used by the Empress. During the Nazi occupation, the imperial chair in the library was rudely violated by the fat buttocks of Reichsmarschall Goering, dreaming perhaps of promotion or the conquest of Egypt. On the top floor, a permanent **exhibition** shows off a more intimate side of the house's history. You can see Joséphine's collections and effects, including the most personal: her slippers, stockings, lace bonnet and petticoats, along with Napoleon's toothbrush.

The park and rose gardens

In Joséphine's time, Malmaison was renowned for its **gardens**, which nurtured scores of exotic species that had never before flowered in France, such as hibiscus, camellia and the heavenly magnolia soulangeana. They are still lovely today. Behind the house extends a fine park in the English style, cut through by a picturesque stream and dotted with landmark trees – including a cedar of Lebanon planted by the imperial couple themselves, in 1800. On either side of the front courtyard stand two **roseries**, a distant echo of Malmaison's legendary collections from the latter half of the nineteenth century. (The question of whether there were roses here in Joséphine's own time, incidentally, is something of a historical mystery, but popular legend has it that the Empress cultivated scores of them herself.) The

Roseraie moderne on the north side features repeat-flowering varieties; the Roseraie ancienne, on the south side, has precious old varieties that flower just once, in June.

Versailles

RER Versailles-Château

Twenty kilometres southwest of Paris, the town of Versailles has grown up around the **Château de Versailles**, the vast palace built for Louis XIV. Consumed with envy of his finance minister's château at Vaux-le-Vicomte (see p.240), the king was determined to outdo him. He recruited the same design team – architect Le Vau, painter Le Brun and gardener Le Nôtre – and ordered something a hundred times the size. With its 700 rooms, 67 staircases and 352 fireplaces, Versailles is the apotheosis of French regal indulgence. While the self-aggrandizing decor of the "Sun King" is astonishing, its park and gardens are also a delight, and shouldn't be overlooked. That said, while it's possible to see the whole complex in one day, it's undeniably tiring, so it's best to pick and choose and plan with care (see p.233).

Château de Versailles

W chateauversailles.fr • RER Versailles-Château

Under its founder and master, Louis XIV, the **Château de Versailles** was the headquarters of every arm of the state, and the entire court of around 3500 nobles lived in the palace – in a state of unhygienic squalor, according to contemporary accounts. Construction began in 1664 and lasted virtually until Louis XIV's death in 1715, after which the château was abandoned for a few years before being reoccupied by Louis XV in 1722. It remained a residence of the royal family until the Revolution of 1789, when the furniture was sold and the paintings dispatched to the Louvre. Thereafter, Versailles fell into ruin until Louis-Philippe established his giant museum of French Glory here; it still exists, though most is mothballed. In 1871, during the Paris Commune, the château became the seat of the nationalist government, and the French parliament continued to meet in Louis XV's opera building until 1879. Restoration only began in earnest between the two world wars, but today it proceeds apace, the château's management scouring the auction houses of the world in the search for original furnishings from Louis XVI's day. Ironically, they have been helped in the task by the efforts of the revolutionaries, who inventoried all the palace's furnishings before they were auctioned off in 1793–94.

Grands Appartements

Tues–Sun: April–Oct 9am–6.30pm; Nov–March 9am–5.30pm • €18 (including audioguide), or included in the Passeport Versailles (see p.233), free for under-18s and EU residents under 26

The rooms you can visit without a guide are known as the **Grands Appartements**, and were used for all the king's official business – which meant all his daily life, as Louis XIV was an institution as much as a private individual. His risings and sittings, comings and goings, were minutely regulated and rigidly encased in ceremony, attendance at which was an honour much sought-after by courtiers. The route leads past the **royal chapel**, a grand structure that ranks among France's finest Baroque creations. From there, a procession of gilded drawing rooms leads to the king's throne room and the dazzling **Galerie des Glaces** (Hall of Mirrors), where the Treaty of Versailles was signed after World War I. Under the golden barrel ceiling, with its paintings by Charles Le Brun showing the glories of Louis XIV, Georges Clemenceau finally won his notorious "war guilt" clause, which blamed the entire conflict on German aggression. The *galerie* is best viewed at the end of the day, when the crowds have departed and the setting sun floods it from the west, across the park. More

LA DÉFENSE (P.228) >

fabulously rich rooms, this time belonging to the **queen's apartments**, line the northern wing, beginning with the queen's bedchamber, which has been restored exactly as it was in its last refit of 1787, with hardly a surface unadorned with gold leaf. At the end of the visit, the staircase leads down to the **Galerie des Batailles**, whose oversized canvases unashamedly blow the trumpet for France's historic military victories; be thankful that most of the rest of Louis-Philippe's historical museum is out of bounds.

The park and gardens

Gardens daily: April–Oct 8am–8.30pm; Nov–March 8am–6pm; park daily: April–Oct 7am–8.30pm; Nov–March 8am–6pm • Free, or €9.50/€8.50/€26 during spectacles (see below) • The petit train (see p.234) shuttles between the terrace in front of the château and the Trianons (€7.50 hop-on hop-off ticket for the full 5km loop); it runs about every 15min in summer

You could spend the whole day just exploring the **gardens** at Versailles. Beyond the great Water Parterres designed by André Le Nôtre, with their statues symbolizing the rivers of France, geometrically planned walks and gardens stretch out on all sides. There are countless statues of nymphs and gods, 50 fountains, 34 pools and of course the cruciform Grand Canal, on which entire naval battles were re-created for the amusement of the court. The outer limits of the estate are known as the **park**, and are made up of woods and fields grazed by sheep; the northernmost area is part of the Domaine de Trianon (see below), and visitable on a separate ticket.

Domaine de Trianon

Château de Versailles park • Tues–Sun: April–Oct noon–6.30pm; Nov–March noon–5.30pm • €12 (buy tickets from the domaine entrance rather than at the palace entrance), or included in the Passeport Versailles, which has to be bought at the palace entrance (see opposite); free for under-18s and EU residents under 26

Hidden away in the northern reaches of the park is the **Domaine de Trianon** (Marie Antoinette's estate), the queen's country retreat, centred on the Petit Trianon palace, where she could find some relief from the stifling atmosphere and etiquette of the court. Here, she commissioned some dozen or so buildings, sparing no expense and imposing her own style and tastes throughout (and gaining herself a reputation for extravagance that wouldn't do her any favours in the long run). She also had a park created in the fashionable English style, and a miniature farm. The Swiss watchmakers Breguet have been responsible for much of the restoration of the estate, reviving a link with the queen that goes back to 1783 when Breguet's founder was commissioned to make her a watch with workings so complex that it was never completed in her lifetime.

VERSAILLES SPECTACLES

On the busiest days of the year, the Versailles gardens play host to what the French call a "*spectacle*": that is, the authorities turn the fountains on while piped classical music booms out all around. The dates are complex, and worth checking online, but broadly the **Grandes Eaux Musicales** run at 9am on Fridays from April to October, with Tuesdays added from July to October. The less exciting **Jardins Musicaux** feature the piped music without the fountains, and generally take place on Tuesdays and Fridays from June to late October (9am). Tickets for the Grandes Eaux Musicales cost €9.50, or €8.50 for the Jardins Musicaux; on days they occur they are included in the Passeports Versailles (see opposite).

For the **Grandes Eaux Nocturnes**, the fountains and gardens are sumptuously lit up with colourful effects and lasers. This event runs on Saturdays from mid-June to mid-September, starting at 8.30pm and with a firework show at 10.50pm; the ticket costs €26. It's preceded by a separate spectacle dubbed **La Sérénade**, in which musicians and dancers perform in the Galerie des Glaces (6.30pm, 6.50pm, 7.10pm, 7.30pm and 7.50pm; €24, €42 combined with the Grandes Eaux Nocturnes).

Petit Trianon

The estate's centrepiece is the elegant and restrained Neoclassical **Petit Trianon** palace, built by Ange-Jacques Gabriel in the 1760s for Louis XV's mistress, Madame de Pompadour, and given to Marie Antoinette by her husband Louis XVI as a wedding gift. The interior boasts a fine stone-and-wrought-iron staircase, sculpted wood panelling, period furniture and the intriguing *cabinet des glaces montantes*, the queen's elegant pale blue salon, fitted with sliding mirrors that could be moved by a sophisticated mechanism to conceal the windows, creating a more intimate space.

Grand Trianon

Included in the ticket for the Domaine de Trianon is the Italianate, pink-marble **Grand Trianon** palace, a little to the west, designed by Hardouin-Mansart in 1687 as a "country retreat" for Louis XIV. Its two wings are linked by a colonnaded portico, with formal gardens to the rear. Napoleon stayed here intermittently between 1805 and 1813 and had the interior refurbished in Empire style. Nowadays it's often used by the French president when entertaining foreign dignitaries.

The formal gardens and Hameau de la Reine

West of the Petit Trianon are the formal gardens (**Jardins à la française**), dotted with pavilions such as the octagonal **Pavillon français** with its gold and marble interior and frieze of sculpted swans, ducks and other wildfowl – which would have been farmed on the estate. More impressive still is the deceptively plain-looking **Petit Théâtre**, built for the queen in 1778–79, where Marie Antoinette would regularly perform, often dressed as a maid or shepherdess, before the king and members of her inner circle. To the east lies the impossibly bucolic **Jardin anglais**, with its little winding stream, grassy banks dotted with forget-me-nots and daisies, classical temple (Le Temple d'Amour), fake waterfall and grotto with belvedere. Further east again lies the equally enchanting, if rather bizarre, **Hameau de la Reine**, a play village and thatch-roofed farm where Marie Antoinette could indulge her fashionable Rousseau-inspired fantasies of returning to the "natural" life.

16

ARRIVAL AND INFORMATION

CHÂTEAU DE VERSAILLES

By train To get to Versailles, take the RER line C5 Champs-de Mars Tour–Eiffel or another Left Bank station to Versailles-Château (40min; €7.10 return); turn right out of the station then take the first left onto av de Paris, which leads to the palace – an 8min walk.

Opening times The château is open throughout the year, except on Mondays, public holidays and during occasional state events. We've given individual opening hours for each attraction within their separate accounts.

Tickets and passes There are several types of ticket available. If you've got limited time, or are not keen on being on your feet for long periods, then you're probably best off buying separate tickets to the Grands Appartements of the château and the Domaine de Trianon according to what you want to see; we've quoted the price details for each attraction within our account. If you've got lots of time, or want to see everything, then it's worth going for a Passeport Versailles, a one- or two-day pass that gives access to all the main sights (€20 one day/€25 two consecutive days; €27/€30 on *spectacle* days). All tickets and passes – except for the *spectacles* (see opposite) – are

free to under-18s and EU residents under 26, year-round; head straight to Entrance A with proof of your status.

Crowds, queues and saving time Whatever the time of year, Versailles can get extremely crowded and the queues can be very long (lasting several hours at peak times – between 10am and 3pm, particularly on weekends and Tuesdays). There are certain things you can do to reduce your queuing time but unfortunately a degree of waiting is inevitable as security is strict. Buying tickets online at ⓦ chateauversailles.fr or ⓦ fnactickets.com is a good option; alternatively, pick them up from any branch of Fnac (see p.334) or at the Versailles town tourist office, near the entrance to the palace at 2bis av de Paris (April–Oct Mon 10am–6pm, Tues–Sun 9am–7pm; Nov–March Sun & Mon 11am–5pm, Tues–Sat 9am–6pm; ☎01 39 24 88 88, ⓦ versailles-tourisme.com). You can then head straight to Entrance A for admission. It's best to avoid the Grands Appartements at the busiest times; being packed in like sardines really diminishes the effect of some of the most popular spaces, such as the Hall of Mirrors. The ideal route to avoid the worst of the crowds would be to head for the gardens and park between 9am and noon, leaving the main palace to the tour buses, following that with the Trianon palaces and Hameau de la Reine, and leaving the palace interior until last, ideally after 4.30pm or so.

Getting around Distances in the park are considerable. Shuttles ("le petit train") run a 5km loop around the complex between the château and the Trianons (every 15min in summer; €7.50 hop-on hop-off ticket), with a soothing background of classical music; these can be a great help on hot or wet days or if you are covering a lot of ground. You can rent bikes (€7.50/hr) at the Grille de la Reine, Porte St-Antoine and by the Grand Canal, and boats (€16/30min) on the Grand Canal, next to a pair of café-restaurants. Electric vehicles are available for rent (€32/hr) for those with reduced mobility.

Guided tours Various guided tours (from €7), including English-language tours, are available, taking you to wings of the palace that can't otherwise be seen; some can be booked online in advance, while still more are bookable in the morning at the information point – turn up reasonably early to be sure of a place – or via the Versailles town tourist office, near the entrance to the palace (see p.233). It's worth taking at least one tour, if only for the guides' well-informed commentaries – though some anecdotes should be taken with a pinch of salt.

Gardens Note that it is possible to visit the gardens only (see p.232).

Refreshments There are a number of snack and drinks carts, cafés and restaurants dotted around the grounds.

Versailles town

The town of **VERSAILLES** (ⓦ versailles-tourisme.com) sits right up against the château gates. Its centrepiece is **place Notre-Dame**, which has a lively food market (Tues, Fri & Sun 7am–2pm). The surrounding streets are full of buzzy cafés, and the little cobbled **rue du Bailliage** and adjoining **passage de la Geôle** are lined with antique shops (ⓦ antiques-versailles.com), selling anything from tin soldiers to books, paintings and ceramics. Versailles is a markedly conservative town, but it does preserve a building dear to the heart of Republicans, the **Salle du Jeu de Paume**, rue du Jeu de Paume. It was at this tennis court, built for the royals in 1686, that the representatives of the Third Estate set the Revolution in progress in 1789, and sealed the fate of the French monarchy; a small museum (April–Oct Tues–Sun 2–5.45pm; free) celebrates the event.

Potager du Roi

10 rue du Maréchal Joffre • Jan–March Tues–Fri 10am–6pm; April–Oct Tues–Sun 10am–6pm; Nov & Dec Tues–Fri 10am–6pm, Sat 10am–1pm • April–Oct Tues–Fri €4.50, Sat & Sun €7; Nov–March €3 • ☏ 01 39 24 62 62, ⓦ www.potager-du-roi.fr • RER Versailles-Château

To reach the **Potager du Roi**, or king's kitchen-garden, turn right as you exit the Château de Versailles' main gate and it's a five-minute signposted walk away. Put aside any thoughts of allotments: this is a walled area the size of a small farm. It was run by Louis XIV's head gardener, Jean-Baptiste La Quintinie, who managed to produce strawberries and melons in March and asparagus in December, and gave the king gardening lessons. Today, a statue of the great man – La Quintinie, that is – stands on the raised terrace watching over his plot, a great sunken square of espaliered fruit trees and geometrically arranged vegetables in the lee of the stately church of St-Louis. Some of the 150 varieties of apples and pears, and fifty types of vegetables, are sold in the little farm shop.

Grande Ecurie du Roy

Av Rockefeller • **Horse shows** Feb–June Sat 6pm, Sun 3pm, July & Aug check website for times • €16–25 • Guided tour of stables Sun 10am (€15; book online), visits without guide Sat & Wed 1.30–4.30pm (€5) • ☏ 01 39 02 62 75, ⓦ bartabas.fr • RER Versailles-Château

Opposite the main entrance to the Château de Versailles, the **Grande Ecurie du Roy**, or royal stables, housed six hundred horses under Louis XIV. It's now the home of the **Académie du Spectacle Equestre**, which puts on highly choreographed theatrical shows of horsemanship. You can also watch the horses being put through their paces at weekly morning **training sessions**.

Sèvres – Cité de la Céramique

2 place de la Manufacture, Sèvres • Daily except Tues 10am–5pm • €6 • ☎ 01 46 29 22 00, ⓦ sevresciteceramique.fr • ⓜ Pont de Sèvres, then cross the bridge and spaghetti junction on foot; the museum is the massive building facing the riverbank on your right – an alternative approach would be to take a métro to ⓜ Boulogne–Pont de St-Cloud and head due south for about 2.5km through the Parc de St-Cloud

Around 10km southwest of Paris, the ceramic factory at **SÈVRES** has been manufacturing some of the world's most renowned **porcelain** since the eighteenth century. The original style, with its painted coloured birds, ornate gilding and rich polychrome enamels, was so beloved by Louis XV's mistress, Madame de Pompadour, that two new colours, *rose Pompadour* and *bleu de roi*, were named after the couple in 1757. The compliment paid off: two years later, when the factory fell into financial trouble, the king bought up all the shares to guarantee its future, and it remained in royal hands until the Revolution. The site is now the **Cité de la Céramique**, which continues to operate as a factory while also housing one of the largest collections of ceramics in the world, with fifty thousand pieces. Inevitably, displays centre on Sèvres ware, but there are also collections of Islamic, Chinese, Italian, German, Dutch and English pieces, and regular temporary exhibitions. Note there is very little information in English, so this is really an attraction for true fans and experts.

Mac/Val

Place de la Libération, Vitry-sur-Seine, 7.5km south of Paris • Tues–Fri 10am–6pm, Sat & Sun noon–7pm • €5 • ☎ 01 43 91 64 20, ⓦ macval.fr • ⓜ Porte de Choisy then bus #183 (the bus stop is right by the métro entrance on av de Choisy) towards Orly Terminal Sud, and get off at the Musée Mac/Val stop (a 15min journey)

The **Musée d'Art Contemporain du Val-de-Marne (Mac/Val)**, south of Paris in Vitry-sur-Seine, is a sleek, icebox-white slice of architectural contemporary cool, incongruously deposited in the suburbs. With its edgy exhibitions of French art since 1950, drawn from a distinguished, two-thousand-piece-strong collection, it consistently lures Parisians away from the centre for their modern art fix. Artists exhibited here include Daniel Buren, Jean Dubuffet, Robert Doisneau, video artists Jean-Luc Vilmouth and Pierre Huyghe, and Christian Boltanski, known for his large-scale installations on themes related to the Holocaust. Temporary exhibitions also showcase international artists, such as the Danish artist Jesper Just, Indian Shilpa Gupta, British Mark Wallinger and Spanish Esther Ferrer. There's a well-stocked bookshop and a restaurant.

Le Bourget airport

7km east of St-Denis • **Museum** Tues–Sun: April–Sept 10am–6pm; Oct–March 10am–5pm • Free, plus an extra €9–21 depending on how many interactive experiences you choose • ☎ 01 49 92 70 00, ⓦ museeairespace.fr • ⓜ La Courneuve/RER Le Bourget (from Gare du Nord); from either métro or RER station, take bus #152 to the museum

Until the development of Orly in the 1950s, **Le Bourget airport**, a short hop up the A1 motorway from St-Denis, was Paris's principal gateway, and is closely associated with the exploits of pioneering aviators – Charles Lindbergh landed here after his epic first flight across the Atlantic. Today Le Bourget is used only for domestic flights, with a museum of powered flight, the **Musée de l'Air et de l'Espace**, occupying some of the older buildings.

Day-trips from Paris

In the further reaches of – and beyond – the boundaries of Ile-de-France lie a number of exceptional towns and sights that are easily accessible as day-trips from the capital. An excursion to Chartres can seem a long way to go for a building; but then you'd have to go a very long way indeed to find a building to beat it, and there are other attractions in the charming town. Of the châteaux that abound in this region, we describe just a select few: Chantilly, with its exceptional art collection and beautiful gardens; Vaux-le-Vicomte, the envy of Louis XIV; and Fontainebleau, the most elegant of Renaissance palaces. Monet's gardens at Giverny, meanwhile, the inspiration for all the artist's water-lily canvases, is perennially popular; it's bright and vibrant in spring, hauntingly melancholy in autumn.

Chantilly

People come to **CHANTILLY**, a small town 40km north of Paris, to watch horse racing and to soak up the superb collection of art in its romantic **château**, which rises from the centre of a lake amid a forested park. Two of the season's classiest flat races are held in the **hippodrome** here – the Prix du Jockey Club and the Prix de Diane, which take place on the first and third Sunday in June respectively.

Domaine de Chantilly

Rue du Connétable • April–Oct daily 10am–6pm (grounds 8pm); Nov–March daily except Tues 10.30am–5pm (grounds 6pm); French-language guided tours of the Duc and Duchesse d'Aumale's private apartments daily (45min; see website for schedule) • Château, grounds, Musée du Cheval (including training session) and equestrian show €30; château, grounds and Musée du Cheval (including training session) €17; Musée du Cheval and equestrian show €21; tours of the Duc and Duchesse d'Aumale's private apartments €3; grounds only €8; mini-train through grounds (April–Oct hourly 11am–6pm) €5 • ☎ 03 44 27 31 80, ⊛ domainedechantilly.com

The **Chantilly estate** was the powerbase of two of the most powerful clans in France: first the Montmorencys, then, through marriage, the **Condés**. It was the château's last private owners, the **Duc and Duchesse d'Aumale**, who, in 1886, donated it to the Institut de France (see p.140), which owns the estate today. The Duc d'Aumale (Henri d'Orléans) had little reason to cling to it, in fact, as he was not actually a Condé at all, but the fifth son of King Louis-Philippe, France's last king. He inherited the château in 1830 – at the tender age of eight – from his godfather, Louis VI Henri de Bourbon-Condé, who had lost all six of his own children (the eldest son was murdered on the orders of Napoleon, in 1804). A great collector, the duke filled it with many of the precious works of art you see here today.

The present, mostly late nineteenth-century **château** replaced a palace, destroyed in the Revolution, which had been built for the Grand Condé (1621–86), who smashed Spanish military power on behalf of the infant king, Louis XIV, in 1643. It's a beautiful structure, surrounded by what's more a lake than a moat, looking out in a romantic manner over a formal arrangement of pools and **gardens** created by André Le Nôtre, the designer of the gardens at Versailles (and indeed at every other seventeenth-century château with pretensions to grandeur). The château has an almost unrivalled **collection** of Classical art, and its **stables**, practically as grand as the main building, house an entertaining **horse museum**.

Chantilly gardens

The **Chantilly gardens** were among Le Nôtre's favourites, and the water features, fountains and statues create a truly elegant ensemble. In addition, there's a rustic **Anglo-Chinese garden**, created in 1773 – with an artful faux-village, including little half-beamed houses, that was said to have inspired Marie Antoinette to create her whimsical Petit Trianon in Versailles – and a romantic nineteenth-century **"English" garden**, created over a part of Le Nôtre's garden that was destroyed during the Revolution.

Cabinet des Livres

Just off an antechamber linking the sixteenth-century wing (the "Petit Château") and the nineteenth-century Grand Château, the Duc d'Aumale's **Cabinet des Livres** holds thirteen thousand volumes and displays a perfect facsimile of the manuscript **Les Très Riches Heures du Duc de Berry**. The original, which is also held here, is the most

GETTING OUT OF PARIS

Within each individual account you'll find information on how to get there from Paris. Return **train tickets** cost €14–36, depending on how far you're going. To check times of specific trains, contact the national train carrier, the SNCF (⊛ sncf-voyages.com), or the transport group for the Paris region, Transilien (⊛ transilien.com); RER and métro routes can be consulted at RATP (⊛ ratp.fr). **Tourist information** on the region surrounding Paris, the Ile-de-France, can be found at ⊛ en.visitparisregion.com.

GETTING YOUR JUST DESSERTS IN CHANTILLY

Chantilly cream, a super-sweet whipped cream flavoured with vanilla, is said to have been invented by chef François Vatel (see box, opposite) as a luxurious component of the Prince de Condé's elaborate banquets. Today you can taste it for yourself in the estate's cosy **Restaurant du Hameau**, in the Anglo-Chinese garden (March & early to mid-Nov daily except Tues noon–6pm; April–Oct daily noon–6pm). Apart from the deliciously rich, cream-festooned desserts (sticky gingerbread with toffee sauce, perhaps), the food is simple (*plats* from €14, *menus* from €22), and the setting is rustic; even without its historic associations, it's a lovely place to take a break.

celebrated of all the medieval Books of Hours, and the museum's single greatest treasure. The illuminated pages illustrating the months of the year with representative scenes from contemporary (early 1400s) rural life – such as harvesting and ploughing, sheep-shearing and pruning – are richly coloured and drawn with a delicate naturalism.

Petit Château

Beyond the Cabinet des Livres, the first floor of the **Petit Château** is filled with the opulent **apartments of the Princes de Condé**, decorated in the seventeenth and eighteenth centuries. A rare treat here is the exquisite *boiseries* (wooden panelling)

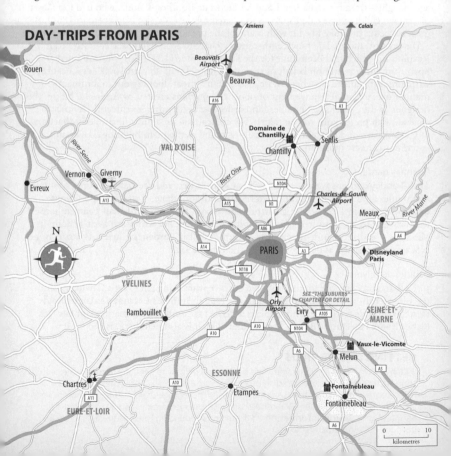

covering the walls of the **Singerie**, or Monkey Gallery, which are wittily painted with allegorical stories, all starring monkeys, in a pseudo-Chinese style.

The nineteenth-century **apartments of the Duc and Duchesse d'Aumale**, on the ground floor – elegant but surprisingly intimate – are visitable on (French-language) guided tours only.

Musée Condé

The **Musée Condé**, which occupies the **Grand Château**, harbours the Duc d'Aumale's art collection, one of the greatest in France. Stipulated to remain exactly as it was when he donated the château to the Institut de France, the arrangement is crowded by modern standards, and immensely satisfying, as the pictures almost seem to spark off each other. Highlights can be found in the skylit **Painting Gallery** and its **Rotunda** – among them Poussin's *Massacre of the Innocents*, Raphael's *Madonna of Loreto*, Philippe de Champaigne's *Portrait of Richelieu* and Piero di Cosimo's allegorical *Simonetta Vespucci* – but the real stunner is the **Sanctuary**, with its three jaw-dropping Italian Renaissance masterpieces: Raphael's diminutive *Three Graces* and the *Orleans Madonna*, as well as Filippino Lippi's *Esther and Assuerus*. The octagonal, red-walled **Tribune**, meanwhile, is astonishing, with Botticelli's resplendently fertile *Autumn* seeming to rival Ingres' astoundingly sexy *Venus Anadyomene*, and works by artists including Delacroix, Poussin, Watteau, Reynolds, Holbein the Younger and Van Dyck crowding in all around.

Musée du Cheval

Five minutes' walk along the drive from the Château de Chantilly towards town stands the colossal stable block, the **Grandes Ecurles**, looking out towards the racetrack. The building was erected at the beginning of the eighteenth century by the incumbent Condé prince, who believed he would be reincarnated as a horse and wished to provide fitting accommodation for 240 of his future relatives. The **Musée du Cheval** here, beyond a row of stables occupied by real-life horses, boasts fifteen rooms devoted to all things equine – from the history of domestication to the evolution of tack over the centuries, the changing depiction of the animal in art and its role in war, hunting and horse racing. Check out the fine ceremonial horses from seventh-century China and nineteenth-century India, the decorative horse cart from Sicily, and early collotypes (1887) created by photographic pioneer Eadweard Muybridge to prove a scientific theory about galloping. In the central ring, a specialist team of riders and trainers puts on spectacular **equestrian shows** combining music, elaborate choreography and horsemanship (April–Nov, 1hr; check website for schedule), and, more frequently, thirty-minute **training sessions** (in French only). A simple **café** serves drinks and snacks.

A MAN OF HONOUR

Chantilly is perhaps most famous as the venue for a single notorious incident: the **suicide of Vatel**. The story is widely retold to illustrate the otherworldly moral code of the *ancien régime*. Maître d' to the nobility at the château, (supposed) inventor of Chantilly cream and orchestrator of financier Fouquet's fateful supper party in 1661 (see p.240), François Vatel was justifiably proud of his status. In April 1671, the Prince de Condé set him to organize a feast for three thousand guests, in honour of Louis XIV. On the opening evening, two tables went without meat thanks to unexpected arrivals. "I cannot endure such a humiliation," Vatel was heard to say, over and over again. At four in the morning, the distraught Vatel was seen wandering the corridors of the palace, where he met a fish supplier with two baskets of fish. The maître d' had sent for supplies from all over France, though these had not yet arrived. "Is that all there is?" he asked, in horror, to which the man replied "Yes". Dishonoured, Vatel played the Roman and ran upon his sword.

7 Vaux-le-Vicomte

50km southeast of Paris • Late March to early Nov daily 10am–7pm (last entry to château 5.15pm, last entry to garden 5.30pm); Dec Sat & Sun 11am–7pm (last entry to château 6pm, last entry to garden 5.45pm); candlelight illumination of state rooms and gardens early May to early Oct Sat 7pm–midnight • €15.50, with candlelight illumination €19.50; gardens only €9.50, with candlelight illumination €15; dome €3 extra • ☎ 01 64 14 41 90, ⊚ vaux-le-vicomte.com

Of all the great mansions within reach of a day's outing from Paris, the Classical château of **Vaux-le-Vicomte** is the most architecturally harmonious, the most aesthetically pleasing and the most human in scale. Standing isolated in the countryside amid fields and woods, the château was built between 1656 and 1661 for **Nicolas Fouquet**, Louis XIV's finance minister, by the finest design team of the day – architect Le Vau, painter-designer Le Brun and landscape gardener Le Nôtre. The result was magnificence and precision in perfect proportion, and a bill that could only be paid by someone who occasionally confused the state's accounts with his own. Fouquet, however, had little chance to enjoy his magnificent residence. On August 17, 1661, he invited the king and his courtiers to a sumptuous housewarming party. Three weeks later he was arrested – by d'Artagnan of Musketeer fame – charged with embezzlement, of which he was certainly guilty, and clapped into jail for the rest of his life. Thereupon, the king stripped the château of most of its furnishings, and carted off the design trio to build his own Versailles.

By 1875, Vaux-le-Vicomte had passed through a series of incompetent aristocratic hands and had fallen into a state of dereliction. It was bought by Alfred Sommier, a French industrialist, who made its restoration and refurbishment his life's work, and was finally opened to the public in 1968.

The château and gardens

Seen from the entrance, the **château** is a rather austerely magnificent pile surrounded by a moat. It's only when you go through to the south side, where the **gardens** decline in measured formal patterns of grass and water, clipped box and yew, fountains and it statuary, that you can look back and appreciate the very harmonious and very French qualities of the building – the combination of steep, tall roof and bulbous central dome with classical pediment and pilasters.

The main artistic interest of the opulent private apartments and state rooms lies in the work of **Le Brun**. He was responsible for the two fine **tapestries** at the entrance, made in the local workshops set up by Fouquet specifically to adorn his house and subsequently removed by Louis XIV to become the famous Gobelins works in Paris (see p.177). Le Brun also painted numerous **ceilings**, notably in Fouquet's bedroom, the Salon des Muses, his *Sleep* in the Cabinet des Jeux, and the so-called "king's bedroom", whose decor is the first example of the ponderously grand style that became known as Louis XIV. Other points of interest are the rather less glamorous **kitchens**, a small **exhibition** on the creation of the gardens and a handsome set of historic **carriages** in the stable block. For an extra fee you can also climb the **dome**, which gives magnificent 360° views over the estate.

On summer Saturday evenings the château and gardens are **illuminated** with two thousand candles, with classical music in the gardens adding to the atmosphere. A fancy restaurant, and an alfresco champagne bar with deckchairs, are both open at this time, along with the standard self-service **restaurant** that's also open during the day. There are two designated **picnic** areas at either end of the gardens.

ARRIVAL AND DEPARTURE   **VAUX-LE-VICOMTE**

By train From Gare de l'Est, take the Provins train (line P) to Verneuil l'Etang (hourly; 35min). From here a frequent "Châteaubus" service (€10 return) covers the 20min journey to the estate (it doesn't meet every train; check ⊚ vaux-le-vicomte.com for up-to-date timetables).

By car Vaux-le-Vicomte is 6km east of Melun, which is itself 46km southeast of Paris; from Paris take the A4 or A6 then N104 and A5 (direction Troyes, exit 15 "Saint-Germain Laxis").

Fontainebleau

The **château of Fontainebleau**, 60km south of Paris, was once a mere hunting lodge in the forest that still surrounds it. Today you can take a lovely walk in the magnificent **Forest of Fontainebleau**, which is crisscrossed with more than 1600km of walking and cycling trails. The main options are marked on Michelin map #106 (*Environs de Paris*; ⓦ travel.michelin.co.uk) and detailed on ⓦ fontainebleau-tourisme.com, which also has information on **rock climbing** in the forest – Fontainebleau's many rocks are a favourite training ground for Paris-based *grimpeurs* (climbers).

Château de Fontainebleau

3km southwest of Fontainebleau-Avon train station • **Château** Daily except Tues: April–Sept 9.30am–6pm; Oct–March 9.30am–5pm • **Grands Appartements and Musée Napoleon 1ᵉʳ** €11; Grands Appartements, Musée Napoleon and Musée Chinois €14; Grands Appartements, Musée Napoleon 1ᵉʳ and 1hr 30min guided tour of Petits Appartements (daily 2.30pm) €16; Grands Appartements, Musée Napoleon 1ᵉʳ and 45min guided tour of Boudoir Turc (daily 4.15pm) €14; Grands Appartements, Musée Napoleon 1ᵉʳ and 30min guided tour of Théâtre Impérial (daily 4.15pm) €14 – book all guided tours in advance online • **Gardens** Daily: March, April & Oct 9am–6pm; May–Sept 9am–7pm; Nov–Feb 9am–5pm • Free • ☎ 01 60 71 50 70, ⓦ musee-chateau-fontainebleau.fr

Starting its days as a medieval hunting lodge, the **Château de Fontainebleau** began its transformation into a luxurious palace in the sixteenth century when François I imported a colony of Italian artists – notably Rosso Fiorentino, Francesco Primaticcio and Niccolò dell'Abate – to carry out the decoration. The palace continued to enjoy royal favour well into the nineteenth century; Napoleon I spent huge amounts of money on it, as did Louis-Philippe. After World War II, when it was liberated from the Germans by General Patton, it served for a while as Allied military HQ in Europe.

The actual buildings, unpretentious and attractive despite their extent, have none of the unity of a purpose-built residence like Vaux-le-Vicomte. In fact, their chief appeal is the gloriously chaotic profusion of styles – a showcase of French architecture from the twelfth to the nineteenth centuries. From the expanse of the **Cour du Cheval Blanc**, built as a humble *basse cour* or working courtyard in the 1530s, you progress up a seventeenth-century horseshoe staircase into a confusion of wings, courtyards and gardens. At the very heart of the palace, the secretive and splendidly asymmetrical **Cour Ovale** conceals a twelfth-century fortress keep, jarringly but pleasingly flanked by fine Renaissance wings on either side.

Take time to wander through the **gardens** – including André Le Nôtre's **Grand Parterre**, the largest formal garden in Europe. With their fountains, statues, winding pathways and exotic plantings, they are quite as splendid as the château itself.

Note that there are no **restaurants** in the château complex.

Grands Appartements and Musée Chinois

The standard admission ticket gets you into the château's **Grands Appartements** – a set of opulent state rooms, private apartments, chapels and galleries. Don't miss the astonishing Renaissance rooms, and in particular the celebrated **Galerie François I**, which is resplendent in gilt, carved, inlaid and polished wood, and adorned down its entire length by intricate stuccowork and painted panels covered in vibrant Mannerist brushwork. The paintings' Classical themes all celebrate or advocate wise kingship and had a seminal influence on the development of French aristocratic art and design. General admission also includes the **Musée Napoléon 1ᵉʳ** – which displays a wide range of Napoleon Bonaparte's furniture, works of art and souvenirs, some of it official and some very personal. For a few euros more you can also take a self-guided tour of the **Musée Chinois**, which shows off the Empress Eugénie's private collection of Chinese and Thai objets d'art in their original Second Empire setting.

Guided tours

Some parts of the château can only be visited on **guided tours**, which it is best to book in advance. Utterly different in style to the Grands Appartements are Napoleon I's

17

elegant **Petits Appartements** – the private rooms of the emperor, his wives and their intimate entourage. The **Boudoir Turc**, meanwhile, an Eastern fantasy designed for Marie Antoinette and later refurbished for Empress Joséphine, is less sober, as is the **Théâtre Imperial**, built between 1853 and 1856 for Napoléon III and Eugénie and based upon Marie Antoinette's little theatre in Versailles (see p.233).

ARRIVAL AND INFORMATION   FONTAINEBLEAU

By train SNCF trains run from the Gare de Lyon to Fontainebleau-Avon station (40min), on the way to Montargis Sens, Montereau or Laroche-Migennes; line 1 bus "Les Lilas" (15min) takes you from the station to the château.
By car Driving to Fontainebleau from Paris is an option; it's

16km from the A6 autoroute (exit "Fontainebleau"). **Tourist office** 4 rue Royale (May–Oct Mon–Sat 10am–6pm, Sun 10am–1pm & 2–5.30pm; Nov–April Mon–Sat 10am–6pm, Sun 10am–1pm; ☎01 60 74 99 99, ⓦ fontainebleau-tourisme.com).

EATING

La Petite Ardoise 16 rue Montebello ☎01 64 24 08 66, ⓦ restaurantlapetiteardoise.fr. A cosy bistro, about 5min walk from the château, serving traditional French dishes – roast camembert, duck, chocolate mousse and the like – at

around €19 for a main course. The lunchtime menu (€18; not Sat) gets you a small plate, a side dish and a dessert. Booking recommended. Tues–Sat noon–2pm & 7–10pm.

Chartres

When King Philippe-Auguste visited **CHARTRES** to mediate between church and townsfolk after the riots of October 1210, the cathedral chapter noted that "he did not wish to stay any longer in the city but, so as to avoid the blasphemous citizens, stayed here only for one hour and hastened to return". Chartres' modern visitors often stay little longer, but if you've come all the way from Paris, a journey of 80km, the modest charms of the little market town at the cathedral's feet may persuade you to linger. One of the world's most astounding buildings, and a UNESCO World Heritage Site, **Chartres cathedral** is best experienced early or late in the day, when the low sun illuminates the stained glass and the quiet scattering of people leaves the acoustics unconfused.

Cathédrale de Chartres

Cloître Notre-Dame • Jan–March, Nov & Dec Mon–Sat 9.30am–12.30pm & 2–5pm, Sun 2–5pm; April–Oct Mon–Sat 9.30am–12.30pm & 2–6pm, Sun 2–6pm • €6 • ☎02 37 21 22 07, ⓦ chartres-cathedrale.fr

Built between 1194 and 1260, Chartres' Gothic **cathedral** was one of the fastest ever constructed and, as a result, preserves a uniquely harmonious design. An earlier Romanesque structure burned down in 1194, but the church's holiest **relic** – the **Sancta Camisia**, reputed to have been the robe Mary wore when she gave birth to Jesus – was discovered three days later, miraculously unharmed. It was a sign that the Virgin wanted her church lavishly rebuilt, at least so said the canny medieval fundraisers. Thereafter, hordes of **pilgrims** stopped here on their way south to the shrine of Santiago de Compostela in Spain, and the church needed to accommodate them with a sizeable crypt, for veneration of the relic, and a nave large enough to sleep hundreds – the sloping floor evident today allowed for it to be washed down more easily.

If those same pilgrims were to see the cathedral today, they might be surprised. An ongoing, and controversial, **refurbishment** – which, at the time of writing, was due to finish in 2018 – is cleaning up the once-gloomy interior in an attempt to restore it to how it is believed it would have originally appeared. Today's gilding and bright, white-painted walls may appear startling – and deeply inauthentic, some claim – but the new (or is it old?) look does help emphasize the rich jewel colours of the stained-glass windows. Sadly, chairs still cover up the **labyrinth** on the floor of the nave, whose diameter is the same size as that of the rose window above the main doors.

The exterior

Outside, hosts of **sculpted figures** stand like guardians at each entrance portal. Along with the south tower and spire which abuts it, the mid-twelfth-century **Royal Portal** actually survives from the earlier Romanesque church, and it's interesting to compare its relatively stylized figures with the more completely Gothic sculptures on the north and south porches, completed half a century later.

The stained glass and choir screen

The geometry of Chartres cathedral is unique in being almost unaltered since its consecration, and virtually all of its magnificent **stained glass** is original – and unsurpassed – thirteenth-century work. Many of the windows in the nave were donated by craft guilds and merchants, whose symbols can often be seen in the bottommost pane. Some of the stories fit the donors' work, such as the carpenters'

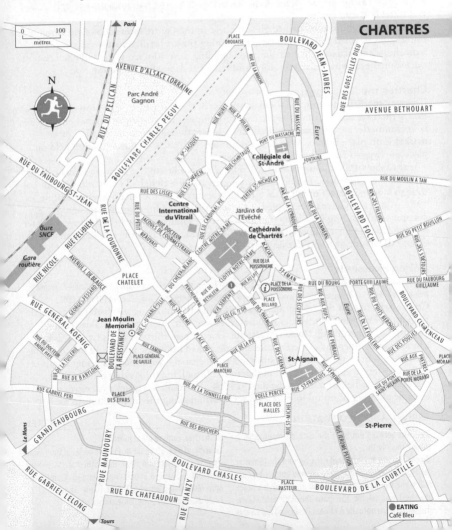

17

window showing Noah's ark. The superb, largely twelfth-century "**Blue Virgin**" window, in the first bay beyond the south transept, is filled with a primal image of the Virgin that has been adored by pilgrims for centuries.

The **choir screen**, which curves around the ambulatory, depicts scenes from the lives of Christ and the Virgin. Its sculptor, Jehan de Beauce, was also responsible for the design of the Flamboyant north tower.

The north tower and gardens

Crowds permitting, you could climb the three hundred steps up the **north tower** for its bird's-eye view of the sculptures and structure of the cathedral. The **gardens** behind the cathedral, meanwhile, are a perfect spot for contemplation of the flying buttresses.

Centre International du Vitrail

5 rue du Cardinal Pie • Mon–Fri 9.30am–12.30pm & 1.30–6pm, Sat 10am–12.30pm & 2.30–6pm, Sun 2.30–6pm • €7 • ☎ 02 37 21 65 72, ⓦ centre-vitrail.org

Occasional exhibitions of stained glass are held in the **Centre International du Vitrail**, a foundation devoted to sustaining and promoting the art form, and also offering workshops and classes. The half-timbered building, just 40m from the cathedral, was once a medieval wine and grain store, and has a handsomely vaulted interior.

Chartres' medieval town

Chartres' **medieval town** spreads out southwest of the cathedral. At the top of rue du Bourg there's a turreted staircase attached to a house, and at the eastern end of place de la Poissonnerie, a carved salmon decorates a sixteenth-century building. The **food market** is on place Billard (Wed & Sat morning), and there's a **flower market** held on place du Cygne (Tues, Thurs & Sat).

At the edge of the old town, on rue Collin-d'Harleville (to the right if you're coming up from the station), a huge broken sword gripped by a clenched fist marks a memorial to **Jean Moulin**, Prefect of Chartres until he was sacked by the Vichy government in 1942. When the Germans occupied the town in 1940, Moulin refused to sign a document attributing Nazi atrocities to Senegalese soldiers in the French army. He later became De Gaulle's number one man on the ground, coordinating the Resistance, and died at the hands of Klaus Barbie in 1943.

Maison Picassiette

22 rue du Repos • April Mon & Wed–Sat 10am–12.30pm & 2–5pm, Sun 2–5pm; May, June & Sept Mon & Wed–Sat 10am–12.30pm & 2–6pm, Sun 2–6pm; July & Aug daily 10am–6pm; Oct Sat 10am–12.30pm & 2–6pm, Sun 2–6pm • €5.60 • ☎ 02 37 90 45 80

Crossing the river at the end of rue de la Tannerie and continuing southwest along rue du Faubourg Guillaume and rue des Rouliers will bring you, after around 1.5km, to the astonishing, idiosyncratic **Maison Picassiette**. Over almost thirty years, Raymond Isidore, a local road-mender and cemetery caretaker, decorated his house inside and out, covering everything – from the walls to the stove to a small chapel – with mosaics, using shards of broken pottery and glass he found in the streets. "I took the things that other people threw away", as he put it, before he died in 1964. The result is a quirky yet moving example of rather beautiful folk art – it's well worth making the small detour to see it.

ARRIVAL AND INFORMATION   CHARTRES

By train Services run from the Gare du Montparnasse (hourly; roughly 1hr).

By car Chartres is 91km from Paris, around 1hr 15min by car. From the *périphérique*, take the A6B autoroute, then follow the signs just after Villejuif and L'Haÿ-les-Roses that lead you via the E50 onto the A10 near Massy. Follow the signs onto the A11 near Orsay, and follow this

to Chartres, coming off at junction 2.

Tourist office 8 rue de la Poissonnerie, a 5min walk from the train station near the cathedral (May–Sept Mon–Sat 9.30am–6.30pm, Sun 10am–5.30pm; Oct–April Mon–Sat 10am–6pm, Sun 10am–5pm; ☎ 02 37 18 26 26, ⓦ chartres-tourisme.com).

EATING

Café Bleu 1 Cloître Notre-Dame ☎ 02 37 36 59 60, ⓦ cafebleu-chartres.com. This buzzy, friendly contemporary bistro has a perfect spot right opposite the cathedral, and it doesn't waste it, with a creative range of dishes from *croques*

monsieur and avocado toast to sea bass with yuzu butter or châteaubriand with Keralan green pepper. Mains €14.50–19; two-course lunchtime *formule* (Mon–Sat) €15.90. Daily except Tues 8am–midnight.

Giverny

Claude Monet considered the **gardens at Giverny** to be his greatest masterpiece. They're out in Normandy, 75km from Paris in the direction of Rouen, but are well worth the trip – though given their fame you certainly shouldn't expect to be alone.

Monet's gardens

84 rue Claude Monet • April–Oct daily 9.30am–6pm • €9.50; €18.50 combined ticket with Musée de l'Orangerie (see p.72); book in advance online to avoid queuing • ☎ 02 32 51 28 21, ⓦ fondation-monet.com

Monet lived in Giverny from 1883 until his death in 1926, painting and repainting the effects of the changing seasonal light on the **gardens** he laid out between his house and the river. Every month has its own appeal, but May and June, when the rhododendrons flower round the lily pond and the wisteria bursts into colour over the famous Japanese bridge, are the prettiest months to visit – though you'll have to contend with crowds photographing the water lilies and posing on the bridge. **Monet's house**, an idyllic, dusky pink building with green shutters, stands at the top of the gardens. Inside, the rooms are all painted different colours, exactly as they were when he lived here, and are packed with family photos and paintings – a pretty blue room features the painter's original collection of Japanese prints, including wonderful works by Hokusai and Hiroshige. Note, though, that you won't see any original Monet paintings.

Musée des Impressionnismes

99 rue Claude Monet • April–Oct daily 10am–6pm • €7 • ☎ 02 32 51 94 65, ⓦ mdig.fr

Just up rue Claude Monet from the artist's gardens is the **Musée des Impressionnismes**. The modern museum owes its existence to the circle of American artists drawn to Giverny by Monet's fame, but it extends its remit beyond Impressionism per se to explore a broad range of artists and themes inspired by the movement. Two major exhibitions are staged each year: shows have included "Brussels, Impressionist Capital" and "Impressionism along the Banks of the Seine". The **brasserie**, in the pretty landscaped garden, is a useful pit stop.

ARRIVAL AND DEPARTURE   GIVERNY

By train Without a car, the easiest approach to Giverny is by train to the small town of Vernon, across the Seine 6km north. Trains leave from St-Lazare (15 daily; 50min). At St-Lazare, follow signs to the mainline "Grandes Lignes" platforms; the Ile-de-France counter is for suburban services only. A bus service, timed to meet the Paris trains, can take you from Vernon to the gardens (€8 return; 20min); there are only four daily services from Vernon to Giverny, so check the website (ⓦ fondation-monet.com) to time your arrival accordingly (they fill up

quickly on busy days). Buses back from the gardens are more frequent. You can also take a taxi (€21), rent a bicycle from *L'Arrivee Giverny*, the café opposite the station (€14 for the day; it's best to reserve in advance on ☎ 02 32 21 16 01), or simply walk (1hr): cross the river and turn right on the D5; make sure as you enter Giverny to follow the left fork, otherwise you'll make a long detour to reach the garden entrance.
By car Giverny is an hour's drive from Paris; take the A13, direction Vernon/Giverny, to exit 16.

EATING

Les Nymphéas Square Gérald et Florence Van der Kemp ☎ 02 32 21 20 31, ⓦ giverny-restaurant-nympheas.fr. Footsteps away from Monet's garden, and popular with tourists, this welcoming restaurant is set in an old farmhouse with a flower-filled garden of its own. The

traditional, home-made food features quiche and hearty salads, plus daily specials such as rabbit leg with cider or potato tart with smoked ham. Mains €10–26. April–Nov daily 9am–6pm.

Disneyland Paris

Children will love Disneyland. What their minders will think of it is another matter, though a cartoon moment is still likely to cadge a smile from most grown-ups – and you can terrify yourself on a roller coaster at any age. Many of the rides are looking better than ever – Disneyland Paris celebrated its twenty-fifth anniversary in 2017 and marked the event by revamping some of its most popular attractions and freshening up others. The complex is divided into three areas: Disneyland Park, the original Magic Kingdom, with most of the big rides; Walt Disney Studios Park, a more technology-based attempt to re-create the world of cartoon film-making, along with a few rides; and the restaurant complex of Disney Village. There's also the vast discount shopping mall – sorry, "village" – of La Vallée (see p.329); regular park shuttles connect it to the Disney hotels.

The **best time to go** is a term-time weekday, when you'll probably get round every ride you want, though queuing for and walking between rides is purgatorial in wet or particularly cold weather. At other times, long waits for the popular rides are common, though most of the very popular attractions offer the "Fastpass" prebooked time-slot scheme (see box, p.251).

If you're doing a lot of planning in advance, the official **website** ⓦdlpguide.com is worth a look. It has videos and reviews of rides, full restaurant listings, up-to-date minimum height regulations, and so on. It's very easy to visit Disneyland on a day-trip from central Paris; it's just forty minutes away on the RER (see p.26) and, if you decide in advance which rides you want to go on and use the Fastpass scheme, you can get to see and do a fair amount. The advantage of staying in the resort for a few days is that you can dip in and out and take things at a more leisurely pace, and you might be able to enjoy some perks such as having access to the park before it officially opens (see p.252).

There's not much that's French at Disneyland – for that, try the Parc Astérix (see p.351) – though Sleeping Beauty's Castle is partly based on an illustration in the medieval manuscript *Les Très Riches Heures du Duc de Berry* (see p.237), and there's the odd crêpe stand – otherwise, the food in the resort is almost always American, and often disappointing. The commentaries or scripts in the more theatrical attractions are usually in French, however, with translated summaries displayed on a board. In the most audience-focused attractions, you'll find an English-language headset to don.

Disneyland Park

The introduction to Disneyland Paris is **Main Street USA**, a mythical vision of a 1900s American town. It leads from Town Square, just beyond the entrance turnstiles, up to **Central Plaza**, the hub of the park. Clockwise from Main Street are Frontierland, Adventureland, Fantasyland and Discoveryland. The **castle**, directly opposite Main Street across Central Plaza, belongs to Fantasyland. A steam-train **Railroad** runs round the park with stations at each "land" and at the main entrance.

This guide reviews all but the most minor rides, with some warnings about suitability, though it's difficult to tell what one child will find exhilarating and another upsetting. For the youngest kids, **Fantasyland** is likely to hold the most thrills. There are no height restrictions here, and rides are mostly gentle. Each of the other three themed areas offers a landmark roller coaster and a theme: **Adventureland** sports tropical, pirate-themed sets; **Frontierland** is divided into the Wild West; while **Discoveryland** emphasizes technology and the Space Age. There aren't many green patches, though Adventureland has a few tree-shaded nooks and crannies, and you could try the seats by the river in Frontierland. Opportunities for afternoon naps, certainly, are limited; renting a pushchair (see p.152) for even an older child might be a good idea.

Main Street USA

Main Street is really just a giant mall for Disney sponsors. See if you can get down it without buying one of the following: a balloon; a hat with your name embroidered on it; an ice cream; silhouette portraits of the kids; the *Wall Street Journal* of 1902; a Donald Duck costume; a bag of muffins; or a complete set of Disney characters in ceramics, metal, plastic, rubber or wool. Leaving Main Street is quickest on foot (crowds permitting), although omnibuses, trams, horse-drawn streetcars and fire trucks are always on hand, plus the Disney *pièce de résistance*, the **Railroad**, for which Main Street Station has the longest queues.

RIDES AND ATTRACTIONS

The symbol ⓕ denotes that the ride uses Fastpass.

DISCOVERYLAND

Autopia Miniature futuristic cars to drive on rails. Good fun, especially for younger children, but there's no possibility of any race-day stratagems. Minimum height to drive is 1.32m.

ⓕ**Buzz Lightyear Laser Blast** An interactive cart ride through a black-light universe, inspired by *Toy Story 2*. You shoot at threatening space creatures, helping Buzz and his friendly three-eyed Martians save the galaxy. Good for little kids.

Les Mystères du Nautilus A stroll through a mock-up of the *Nautilus* submarine – Captain Nemo's vessel in *20,000 Leagues under the Sea*. What's supposed to impress you is the faithfulness of the decor to the original Disney set, though there is a fishy surprise inside.

Orbitron The "rockets" on this ride go round and round fairly slowly and go up (at your control) to a daring thirty degrees above the horizontal. Suitable for small kids and for those who dislike more violent rides.

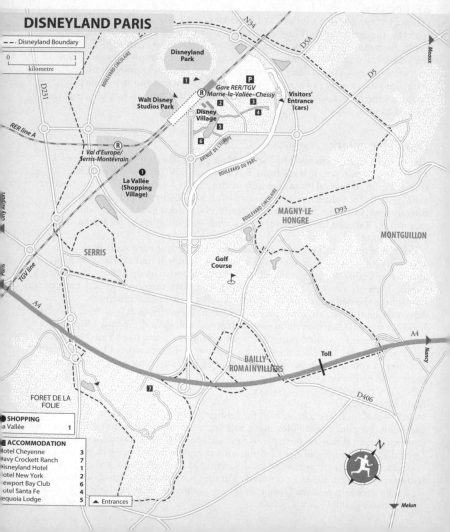

DISNEYLAND PARIS

- - Disneyland Boundary

0 — 1
kilometre

Disneyland Park

N34

D5A

Meaux

D5

BOULEVARD CIRCULAIRE

D231

Walt Disney Studios Park

RER line A

1 ▲

Ⓟ

Gare RER/TGV
Marne-la-Vallée–Chessy

Ⓡ

3

4

Visitors'
Entrance
(cars)

Disney
Village

5

6

Ⓡ *Val d'Europe/*
Serris-Montévrain

AVENUE DE L'EUROPE

1

La Vallée
(Shopping
Village)

BOULEVARD DU PARC

BOULEVARD CIRCULAIRE

MAGNY-LE-
HONGRE

D93

MONTGUILLON

SERRIS

Paris

TGV line

A4

Golf
Course

A4

Nancy

**BAILLY-
ROMAINVILLIERS**

Toll

D406

FORET DE LA
FOLIE

7

N

● SHOPPING
a Vallée   **1**

■ ACCOMMODATION
Hotel Cheyenne	3
Davy Crockett Ranch	7
Disneyland Hotel	1
Hotel New York	2
Newport Bay Club	6
Hotel Santa Fe	4
Sequoia Lodge	5

▲ Entrances

Melun

🕐 **Star Tours – The Adventures Continue** The original Star Tours ride was overhauled in 2016 as part of the twenty-fifth anniversary celebrations. Prepare yourself for a giddy, simulated 3D journey in a spacecraft piloted by friendly, incompetent C-3PO of *Star Wars* fame. Each ride is selected at random from seventy possible voyages, featuring footage from all the Star Wars films, so you're likely to get a different experience every time. Minimum height 1.02m. Pregnant women and those with health problems are advised not to board.

🕐 **Star Wars Hyperspace Mountain** In 2017, the classic Hyperspace Mountain ride was revamped and given a Star Wars spin; this thrilling space ride provides 1.3g of speed and a moment of weightlessness, all in an elaborately lit ambience, with a blaze of red and green blaster fire and a Stars Wars soundtrack. Minimum height 1.32m, and pregnant women and people with health problems are advised not to ride.

FANTASYLAND

Alice's Curious Labyrinth A giant maze with surprises. There are passages that only people under 1m can pass through without ducking and enough false turns and exits to make it a decent enough labyrinth. Takes maybe 10min, with the option to exit at the halfway point.

Blanche-Neige et les Sept Nains This *Snow White and the Seven Dwarfs* ride takes you through lots of menacing, moving trees, swinging doors and cackling witches, re-creating scenes from the classic Disney film. Can frighten smaller kids.

Le Carrousel de Lancelot A stately merry-go-round, whose every horse has its own individual medieval equerry in glittering paint.

Casey Jr – Le Petit Train du Cirque This charming little circus train chugs around rolling landscaped gardens behind Le Pays des Contes de Fées. Not too fast, not too slow, it's just right for little ones.

Dumbo the Flying Elephant Dumbo and his clones provide a safe, slow, aerial ride in which you can regulate the rise and fall of the revolving elephants with a lever. One of the most popular rides in Fantasyland, with queues to match, though it only lasts a measly 20 seconds.

It's a Small World This is a quintessential Disney experience; there's one in every Disneyland, and Walt considered it to be the finest expression of his corporation's philosophy. Your boat rides through a polystyrene and glitter world, where animated dolls in national/ethnic/tribal costumes dance beside their most famous landmarks or landscapes, singing the song *It's a Small World*. Some children seem to enjoy the sugar-coated fantasy.

Mad Hatter's Teacups Great big whirling teacups slide past each other on a chequered floor. Not a whizzy ride, so it suits younger ones, though it's disappointingly short.

Le Pays des Contes de Fée A boat ride through cleverly miniaturized fairy-tale scenes: *Alice in Wonderland*, *Pinocchio*, etc. Fine for little kids.

🕐 **Peter Pan's Flight** Very young children seem to really enjoy this jerky "flight" above Big Ben and the lights of London to Never-Never Land. Very popular.

Sleeping Beauty's Castle The castle stands at the entrance to Fantasyland, just off the Central Plaza at the end of Main Street. There's little to see inside other than a few bits of plasticky vaulting, stained glass and cartoon tapestries, though a huge animated dragon lurks in the dungeon.

Les Voyages de Pinocchio A rattling, swervy wagon ride through a string of beautifully re-created scenes from *Pinocchio*; some are dimly lit and faintly menacing.

ADVENTURELAND

Adventure Isle Not a ride, but a sort of playground of caves, bouncy bridges, huge boulders, trees, tunnels and waterfalls built on two small islands in the middle of Adventureland. Parents of over-tired children and those who need a break from the queues should not underestimate the thrill of just being able to wander around unfettered.

SHOWS AND PARADES

The all-dancing, all-costumed **Shows** and **Parades** in both Disneyland and Walt Disney Studio Park are huge affairs. Timing a visit to a popular ride to coincide with a big show is a clever idea if getting on all the big rides is your priority, though the parades are a memorable part of the Disney experience, especially for kids, so it's worth trying to catch at least one. Timetables are handed out with maps as you enter the park. One of the best parade vantage spots is on the queuing ramp for It's a Small World (see p.249), right by the gates through which the floats appear. From here, the parades progress, very slowly, to Town Square. The best seating is in front of the Fantasyland Castle, one of the points where the floats stop and the characters put on a performance. New parade floats, music and costumes, as well as a giant 7m-high dragon, were introduced in 2017 to celebrate the park's twenty-fifth anniversary. The floats represent all the top box-office Disney movies and characters, from Mickey and Minnie Mouse to the *Toy Story* team and the *Pirates of the Caribbean* crew. Everyone waves and smiles, and characters on foot shake hands with the kids who've managed to get to the front.

18

La Cabane des Robinson The 27m mock banyan tree at the top of Adventure Isle is one of Disneyland Paris's most obsessively detailed and most enjoyable creations, complete with hundreds of thousands of (false) leaves and blossoms. It's reached by walkways and a series of more than 170 steps, so it's best avoided by pram-pushers and toddler-haulers.

Indiana Jones and the Temple of Peril A fast roller coaster along rattling train tracks through a classic Indy landscape. Moderately intense and renowned for its 360-degree loop, though it's no Space Mountain. The minimum height for the ride is 1.40m. Children under around 8 years old, pregnant women and people with health problems should steer clear.

Le Passage Enchanté d'Aladdin A sedate meander on foot through a colourful, Oriental-style passageway takes you past animated scenes from *Aladdin*, featuring the genie, the flying carpet and some truly insistent theme music.

Pirates' Beach The ladders, walkways, climbing ropes and slides at this nautical-themed adventure playground give kids a great chance to run off steam, in the shadow of Captain Hook's pirate ship. It's divided into two different areas: one for 3–6s, the other for 7–9s.

Pirates of the Caribbean This satisfyingly long ride underwent extensive renovation in 2017 and is one of the finest, consisting of an underground ride on water and down waterfalls, past scenes of evil piracy. The animated automata are superb – be warned that they set small children whimpering and crying immediately. Battles are staged across the water, skeletons slide into the deep, parrots squawk, chains rattle and a treasure-trove is revealed.

FRONTIERLAND

Big Thunder Mountain This popular roller coaster, refurbished in 2016, mimics a runaway mine train. As well as wicked twists and turns, sudden tunnels and hairy moments looking down on the water, the new ride also promises an "explosive surprise". No violent upside-down or corkscrew stuff. Minimum height 1.02m; not suitable for small children.

The Chaparral Theater Shows seasonal theatrical spectaculars featuring all the usual Disney suspects. Times are displayed outside and on the programme handed out with the main park map.

Legends of the Wild West A series of models, displays and mocked-up rooms commemorating characters and scenes from the gold-rush days of America's Wild West, all housed in Fort Comstock, a replica log-built stockade.

Phantom Manor *Psycho*-style house on the outside and Hammer Horror Edwardian mansion within. Holographic ghosts appear before cobweb-covered mirrors and ancestral portraits, but nothing actually jumps out and screams at you. Probably too frightening for young children nevertheless.

Pocahontas Indian Village This Native American-themed adventure playground is nicely sited by the water, providing a welcome spot for parents to sit down and recharge their batteries while their offspring play on the slides, bridges, climbing areas and tepees. For children aged 4–8.

Rustler Roundup Shootin' Gallery There's a small extra fee for this attraction, apparently because, without some check, people stay for hours and hours shooting infrared beams at fake cacti.

Thunder Mesa Riverboat Landing A rather pointless cruise around the lake, but the paddleboat steamer is carefully built to offer lots of antique-style curiosities, and it's fun to watch the roller coaster rattle around the rocks of Big Thunder Mountain.

Walt Disney Studios Park

The **Walt Disney Studios Park** complex has fewer mega-rides than its older, larger neighbour, and as a result tends to be less busy: the queues are often shorter and it's easier to meet characters as the area is smaller. And in some ways this side of the park is a more satisfying affair, focusing on what Disney was and is still renowned for – animation. You can try your hand at drawing, there are mock film and TV sets where you can be part of the audience, and the special effects and stunt shows are impressive in their way, although probably not as impressive as just going to the movies. This is also where you'll find one of the park's newer attractions, the family-friendly **Ratatouille** ride, plus three thrilling rides: the corkscrew-looping, heavy metal-playing white-knuckler of the **Rock 'n' Roller Coaster Starring Aerosmith**, the plummeting elevator of the **Twilight Zone Tower of Terror** and the swirling, "undersea" exhilarations of **Crush's Coaster**.

RIDES AND SHOWS

The symbol ⊕ denotes that the ride uses Fastpass.

Animagique Theatre Puts on shows featuring Disney characters, such as Mickey and the Magician.

Armageddon Special Effects Your group of fifty or so is ushered into a circular chamber decked out as a space station. As meteors rush towards the screens on all sides, the whole ship seems about to break up. Less cynical children may find the whole experience overwhelming.

Art of Disney Animation You progress through two mini-theatres, one showing famous moments from Disney cartoons, the next with a "cartoonist" chatting to an on-screen animated creation, explaining to the creature how it came to look as it did. In the lobby area, children are taught to draw Mickey Mouse faces.

Cars Quatre Roues Rallye *Cars*-inspired ride on the lines of a destruction derby. The ride is real enough, though sedate – the hell-raising element is engineered using special effects.

Crush's Coaster The theme of this very popular coaster is taken from *Finding Nemo*. You're taken into a virtual underwater world on the back of a turtle, then into a minute-long roller-coaster section which isn't especially fast but features an unusual spinning mechanism. Minimum height 1.07m. Note that there's limited capacity and it doesn't use Fastpass, so be prepared to queue.

Disney Junior Live on Stage A lively, smiley stage show drawn from the TV series, featuring costumed characters aimed at littler ones: Mickey, the Little Einsteins, Handy Manny. Seating is on the floor.

⊘ Flying Carpets Over Agrabah A good, solid fair-ground ride where the carpet-shaped cars wheel around the central lamp for a disappointingly short time. Very popular with smaller children, especially the lever that makes their carpet rise up and down.

Moteurs...Action! Stunt Show Spectacular Decked out like a Mediterranean village, a big arena is the scene for some spectacular stunts: jumping rally cars, sliding motorbikes, leaping jet skis, stuntmen falling from heights and so on. Various timed shows throughout the day.

⊘ Ratatouille: L'Aventure Totalement Toquée de Rémy Opened in 2014 and costing a record 150 million euros, this ride is based on the 2007 animated film about a rat who dreams of becoming a chef. You're "shrunk" to the size of rats and taken in trackless, GPS-guided ratmobiles on a frantic 3D chase through a kitchen, in which you dodge waiters' feet and falling ladles and experience real physical sensations, such as aromas of food. It's aimed at families, though younger children may find it overwhelming.

RC Racer A half-pipe roller coaster: you're shuttled back and forth and up and down an upended semi-circle till you're begging to get off. Minimum height 1.20m.

⊘ Rock 'n' Roller Coaster Starring Aerosmith A real heart-stopper, reaching 5g here at one point. There are corkscrews, loops and violent lurches, and the whole thing takes place in a neon-lit and hard rock-soundtracked darkness that makes it all the more alarming. It's all over in less than 2min. Minimum height 1.2m; entirely unsuitable for small children.

Slinky Dog Zigzag Spin This fairly gentle ride takes you round and round on an undulating track pulled by said Slinky Dog.

Stitch Live! A theatrical-type experience in which children talk and play with the virtual reality alien Stitch who, despite being on screen, manages to interact with the audience.

Studio Tram Tour: Behind the Magic An electric tram takes you on a circuit of various bits and pieces of film set. The high point is the halt among the Wild West rocks of Catastrophe Canyon – sit on the left for the scariest ride.

Toy Soldiers Parachute Drop Hanging in a group of bucket seats under a giant umbrella, you're repeatedly lifted up and dropped – not all that fast, but from fairly high up. Minimum height 0.81m.

⊘ Twilight Zone Tower of Terror Exciting ride in which you "enjoy" the sensation of free-falling in the lift of a classic, crumbling Hollywood hotel. Not actually physically demanding, though the Twilight Zone video might scare some, and it does turn your stomach upside down. Minimum height 1.02m.

QUEUES AND FASTPASS

Energy-sapping, one-hour waits for the popular rides are pretty standard during school holidays and on summer weekends. Don't be fooled by the length of the visible queues; they often snake for a further 100m or more inside. Realistic **wait times** are posted at the entry to most rides (eg 20 minutes, 50 minutes). The free Disneyland app gives real-time waiting times for attractions but, frustratingly, neither of the parks offers free wi-fi access, and the app requires internet in order to work; the closest free access is available in some of the Disney Village restaurants and most of the hotels. Bring sun hats or umbrellas, and make sure your kids have all been to the toilet recently before you begin to queue as, once you're in, it can be hard to get out; keep snacks and drinks handy, too. A number of rides use the **Fastpass** scheme (free), well worth making use of; all you have to do is insert your entry card into a ticket machine by the entrance to the ride; the machine then spews out a time at which you should come back and join the much shorter Fastpass queue. You're limited to one reservation at a time, unless you have a **VIP Fastpass** (given to guests staying in certain hotel suites) or a **Disney Hotel Fastpass** (available only to guests at selected Disneyland hotels), which both offer unlimited access to all Fastpass lanes.

Disney Village

The **Disney Village** entertainment and restaurant complex, opposite the Marne-la-Vallée–Chessy train station, is basically a street lined with expensive shops and restaurants. The work of architect Frank Gehry, it looks like a circus tent that has had its top carried off by a bomb, with a pedestrian street driven through the middle of it. "Buffalo Bill's Wild West Show" (cowboys and Indians charging round a ring on horseback, with slapstick routines and dancing Disney characters) and rides on the PanoraMagique tethered balloon await you, alongside *Annette's Diner*, *Planet Hollywood*, the *Rainforest Café* and a host of other themed restaurants. You'll find French and Bavarian food at *King Ludwig's Castle* (mains start from around €18). There's live outdoor music on summer nights, IMAX and multiplex cinemas and lots of sideshows.

When you're nearing exhaustion from so much enchantment, you can return to your **hotel** (see opposite) and have a sauna, jacuzzi or whirlpool dip and be in bed in time to feel fresh and fit to meet Mickey and Minnie again over breakfast. In the hotel area of the resort, you can play **golf** (27-hole course) and sail (in summer), though these activities can be expensive.

ARRIVAL AND DEPARTURE
DISNEYLAND PARIS

From London by train There are direct Eurostar trains to Disneyland, but it can sometimes be less expensive to change onto the TGV at Lille; all these trains arrive at Marne-la-Vallée–Chessy station, right outside the main entrance.

From the airports If you're coming straight from the airport, there are shuttle buses from both Charles de Gaulle and Orly, taking 45min from either airport (roughly every 45min 9am–7.30pm; see ⓦ magicalshuttle.fr/uk for timetables and pick-up points). Tickets cost €23 one way, but children under 12 pay €10, and under-3s go free.

From Paris by train Take RER line A – from Châtelet-Les Halles, Gare de Lyon or Nation – to Marne-la-Vallée–Chessy station, which is right next to the train terminal, and opposite the main park gates (40min; €7.60 single, children under 10 half-price, under-4s free). You can get Mobilis travel cards that include Disneyland Paris (see p.27).

By car The park is a 32km drive east of Paris along the A4; take the Porte de Bercy exit off the *périphérique*, then follow "direction Metz/Nancy", leaving at exit 13 for *Davy Crockett Ranch* (see opposite) or exit 14 for Parc Disneyland and the hotels. From Calais follow the A26, changing to the A1, the A104 and finally the A4.

INFORMATION

Opening hours Depending on the season and whether it's a weekend, the parks open from 10am to anywhere between 7pm and 11pm at Disneyland Park, or between 6pm and 7pm at Walt Disney Studios. Staying in one of the Disney hotels might allow you two extra hours in the park in the morning if you come at the right time of year.

Admission One-day one-park costs €32–61 for adults/€32–55 children aged 3–11, depending on the season; one-day two-park tickets start from €44. There are often two-for-one offers in August. See ⓦ dlpguide.com for more information and tips on the best deals.

Contact details UK ☎ 0844 800 8898, France ☎ 01 60 30 60 30, ⓦ dlpguide.com, ⓦ disneylandparis.com.

Tickets To avoid queuing, buy tickets online or from tourist offices (see p.40). The one-day one-park pass allows you to visit either the main Disneyland Park or the Walt Disney Studios Park, but you can't swap between them; you can come and go during the day, however.

Information At Disneyland Park, you enter underneath Main Street Station, on the internal railroad system; information is available at City Hall to the left. Information at Walt Disney Studios Park can be found at Studio Services, by the entrance.

Left luggage Luggage can be left in "Guest Storage" lockers near the park entrances; there are also lockers at Marne-la-Vallée–Chessy station (from €5).

Disabled access The *Disabled Visitors Guide* is available from City Hall in Disneyland Park, or Studio Services in Walt Disney Studios Park; alternatively, visit ⓦ bit.ly/disabledaccess. Staff aren't allowed to lend assistance in getting into and out of the less accessible rides, but all toilets, shops and restaurants are wheelchair accessible. You can rent wheelchairs (€15; €150 deposit) in Town Square, in Disneyland Park – the building on the right as you exit Main Street Station. Given the relative dearth of benches, visitors who can normally manage without a chair might appreciate having one.

Babies and small children You can rent pushchairs (€15; €150 deposit if you move between parks) from the same place as wheelchairs (see above). There are two Baby Care centres: next to *Plaza Gardens* restaurant in Disneyland Park, and beside Studio Services in Walt Disney Studios Park.

OVERNIGHT PACKAGES

If you plan to stay at a Disneyland hotel, it's much cheaper to book a special accommodation and entry package. Visit an agent, or book through Disney, either online or on ☎ 0844 800 8898 in the UK, ☎ 08 25 30 05 00 in France, or ☎ 00 33 1 60 30 60 53 from other countries.

ACCOMMODATION

18

Disney's seven **themed hotels** are a mixed bag of kitsch designed by some of the world's leading architects – Michael Graves, Antoine Predock, Robert Stern and Frank Gehry. For all the dramatically themed exteriors and lobbies, the rooms are much the same inside: comfortable, huge and soulless. **Prices** vary hugely according to season and which package you book (see box, above) – there are almost always offers. The prices we've given below are only a guide to what you might pay in high season for one night for a room accommodating two adults and two children, including entry tickets to the park. It's usually better value to book for two nights or more. All hotels except *Hotel New York* and *Disneyland Hotel* are too far away to walk to comfortably from the entrance with luggage, but free bright-yellow **shuttle buses** run to all the hotels from the bus station in the Central Plaza; the hotel name is shown on the front of each bus. Car drivers can go straight to their hotel (free parking) or to the Disneyland parking areas (€20/day).

HOTELS

Hotel Cheyenne Along with the *Sante Fe*, the *Cheyenne* is broken up into attractively small units: the filmset buildings of a Western frontier town, complete with wagons, cowboys, a hanging tree and scarecrows. With its Wild West theme and bunk beds in all the rooms, this is a good hotel for children – and it's usually relatively inexpensive. **€686**

Davy Crockett Ranch Self-catering bungalows and log cabins (4–6 people) in a wooded, Wild West-themed setting – there's even a high-wire tree-top assault course. The ranch is a 15min drive from the park, with no shuttle service laid on, so you'll need your own transport. **€616**

Disneyland Hotel Situated right over the entrance to the park with wings to either side, the large, frilly, pastel-pink *Disneyland Hotel* is decked out in glitzy Hollywood style. It's the most upmarket and best located by far. **€1196**

Hotel New York Outside, the hotel is a plasticky, post-modern attempt at conjuring up the New York skyline, while the furnishings within are pseudo Art Deco with lots of apples. Comfortable, and towards the top of the range. **€808**

Newport Bay Club The largest of the hotels, with one thousand rooms, this "New England seaside resort circa 1900" spreads like a game of dominoes. Blue-and-white-striped canopies over the balconies fail to give it that cosy guesthouse feel, but some rooms have the benefit of looking out over the lake and the hotel underwent an extensive makeover in 2016. **€808**

Hotel Santa Fe Smooth, mercifully unadorned, imitation sun-baked mud buildings in various shapes and sizes. Between them are tasteful car wrecks, a cactus in a glass case, strange geological formations and other products of the distinctly un-Disney imagination of New Mexican architect Antoine Predock. Usually relatively inexpensive. **€666**

Sequoia Lodge Overlooking the lake and built around the theme of the "mountain lodge" typically found in the national parks of the western United States, but on a giant scale. **€750**

EATING AND DRINKING

There are opportunities to eat throughout both parks, as well as in Disney Village. As you'd expect, there's a lot of pricey American junk food, and although the "all-you-can-eat" buffet-style restaurants are not a bad deal, you can still end up paying three or four times the price of a meal outside the park. Consider booking ahead (at City Hall or Studio Services, or on ☎ 01 60 30 40 50), as all restaurants fill up quickly at lunch and dinner times. Adults can drink wine or beer at any of the park's restaurants. Officially, you're not supposed to bring in full-on picnics, but Goofy won't turn nasty if he sees you eating a sandwich.

L'HÔTEL, ST-GERMAIN

Accommodation

Good-value accommodation is not, on the whole, Paris's strong point, though you can get great deals if you do your research and book well in advance. At the luxury end, things are sumptuous and stylish, and there are a fair few chic boutique hotels. Unless you stumble upon a special promotion, however, prices at the top end are stratospheric, and even in the better three- and four-star establishments, rooms are typically cramped for the price. If you stay at the back of the building – probably overlooking a courtyard – rooms can be dark, too, though at least you're spared potential street noise. There are, however, a few genuine gems, and many places where the welcome, the character or the location – and often, the views – easily outweigh the lack of space.

ESSENTIALS

Reservations The best hotels are typically booked up well in advance, especially in the spring, early summer and autumn. It's wise to reserve a room as early as you can, particularly if you fancy staying in one of the more characterful places. You can generally book online, but if you speak French and have a bit of chutzpah you might consider calling and asking for a discount on the advertised rate; in Aug and Nov–Feb (apart from Christmas, when rates soar) you may be able to negotiate a reduction.

Tourist offices If you find yourself stuck on arrival, the tourist offices (see p.40) can find you a room; this service is free of charge.

Hotel breakfasts Breakfast (*petit déjeuner*) is sometimes included (*compris*) in the room price but is normally extra

(*en supplément*) – around €7–14/person. Always make it clear whether you want breakfast or not when you take the room. Either way, it's usually a continental affair of croissants/baguette, fresh orange juice and coffee.

Stairs and lifts A number of hotels, especially at the cheaper end of the scale, are shoehorned into very old buildings. What you gain in quirky character you lose out on in amenities – many hotels don't have lifts, or have lifts only up to a certain floor – so if you have difficulty walking or carrying luggage, ask for a room on a lower floor.

Wi-fi Free wi-fi access is generally offered as standard in most hotels. The few hotels that do still charge for it should make this clear.

HOTELS

Our hotel recommendations are listed by area, following the same geographical divisions used in the Guide. Most hotels have a selection of rooms – singles, doubles, twins and triples – at prices that can fluctuate widely throughout the year, depending upon occupancy, day of the week, or how far in advance you book. In our listings we quote online **rates for the cheapest double room in high season** – which may have a shared bathroom, and will occasionally involve paying upfront with no refund for cancellation. You'll almost invariably get the best deal by booking direct with the hotel.

THE ISLANDS

Hôtel de Lutèce 65 rue St-Louis-en-l'Île, 4e ☎ 01 43 26 23 52, ⓦ hoteldelutece.com; ⓜ Pont Marie; map p.44. This narrow seventeenth-century townhouse, located on the most desirable island in France, has 23 tiny, pretty wood-beamed en suites. All have been renovated in a contemporary style and come with modern bathrooms. €209

THE CHAMPS-ELYSÉES AND AROUND

Le 123 123 rue du Faubourg St-Honoré, 8e ☎ 01 53 89 01 23, ⓦ astotel.com; ⓜ St-Philippe-du-Roule; map p.64.

Friendly, stylish hotel – one of the generally good *Astotel* chain – a 5min walk from the Champs-Elysées. Rooms are a good size with high ceilings, laminate floors and modern furnishings, plus iPod docks. Some have balconies (€/47). €224

Hôtel d'Albion 15 rue de Penthièvre, 8e ☎ 01 42 65 84 15, ⓦ hotelalbion.net; ⓜ Miromesnil; map p.64. A small family-run hotel in a nineteenth-century townhouse, set around a quiet courtyard garden. Just a 10min walk from the Champs-Elysées, it's not fancy, but it's clean, comfortable and excellent value for the area. Many of the rooms have a view over the garden. €113

BOOKING A HOTEL ROOM

France's **star system** provides some clues as to the pretensions of a hotel, but little else – a two-star hotel might have lovely rooms but fail to be awarded a third star because its staff don't speak enough languages, or its foyer is small. As a rule of thumb, a double room in an old-fashioned two-star will cost between €70 and €150, depending on season and location, though don't expect much in the way of decor at the lower end of the scale. For something with a bit more class – whether that means a touch of design flair, slick service or in-room tech – you'll pay in the region of €150–250, again depending on location/season. At the luxury end of the scale the sky's the limit, with prices above €400 not uncommon – though online and off-season deals can chop a dramatic amount off the official price. It is possible to find a double room in a central location for as little as €60–70, though at this level you might have to do with just a sink (*lavabo*) and a shared bathroom on the landing (*dans le palier*).

Within one hotel, **rooms** can vary hugely, and it's well worth asking what's available. Rooms on the street (*côté rue*) tend to be larger and lighter than those at the back, but noise can be a problem if there is no double-glazing. Certain standard terms recur: *douche/WC* and *bain/WC* mean that you have a shower or bath as well as toilet in the room. A room with a *grand lit* (double bed) is usually cheaper than one with *deux lits* (two separate beds). Many hotels offer *de luxe* or *supérieure* rooms as well as those in a *standard* or *classique* class; a superior room in a less expensive hotel can often be better value than a standard one in a pricier establishment.

19

TOP 10 HOTELS FOR €100 OR LESS

Although Paris is expensive, there are still places where you don't have to spend a fortune. At the following hotels you should be able to find a room for under €100 – and in some cases, less. Do bear in mind, though, that these represent the lowest prices in town – and in some cases for rooms with shared bathrooms – so be sure to keep your expectations realistic.

Hôtel Arioso 7 rue d'Argenson, 8ᵉ ☎ 01 53 05 95 00, Ⓦ arioso-hotel.com; Ⓜ Miromesnil; map p.64. About a 15min walk from the Champs-Elysées, this is a charming, comfy four-star boutique hotel set in a solid Haussmann-era block, run by courteous and helpful staff. The 28 rooms are small, especially the cheaper ones, and some pick up a bit of street noise, but all are cosily decorated with quality furnishings and decorative fabrics. Some of the more expensive rooms have jasmine-strewn balconies looking onto a pretty little tiled interior courtyard, and all bathrooms are stocked with Occitane products. €190

Le Bristol 112 rue du Faubourg St-Honoré, 8ᵉ ☎ 01 53 43 43 00, Ⓦ lebristolparis.com; Ⓜ Miromesnil; map p.64. Among the city's most iconic hotels, *Le Bristol* opened in 1925 and has maintained its reputation for discreet luxury with superb service. The 188-odd rooms, all very spacious, come with authentic antiques – including Gobelins tapestries – and some have private roof gardens (€7500). There's also a spa, swimming pool and three gourmet restaurants. €950

Hôtel Ekta 52 rue Galilée, 8ᵉ ☎ 01 53 76 09 05, Ⓦ hotelekta.com; Ⓜ George V; map p.64. On a quiet side street, just off the Champs Elysées, a former office block houses this stylish new hotel, run by young and welcoming staff. A mirrored staircase takes you up to the striking reception and 25 rooms, sporting a decor of graphic black-and-white checks and zigzags with a shot of yellow, inspired by 60s and 70s fashion design. The rooms range from the small "Classic" to the larger balconied rooms on the top floor; all have phone chargers and Nespresso machines. €190

Hôtel Lancaster 7 rue de Berri, 8ᵉ ☎ 01 40 76 40 76, Ⓦ hotel-lancaster.com; Ⓜ George V; map p.64. The 45 rooms and 11 suites in this elegantly restored nineteenth-century townhouse – the pied-à-terre for the likes of

Garbo, Dietrich and Sir Alec Guinness – retain original features and are chock-full of Louis XVI and Rococo antiques, but with a touch of contemporary chic. A small interior Zen-style garden and impeccable service make for a relaxing stay, and there's an excellent Michelin-starred restaurant, too. €530

Hôtel Le Lavoisier 21 rue Lavoisier, 8ᵉ ☎ 01 53 30 06 06, Ⓦ hotellavoisier.com; Ⓜ St-Augustin; map p.64. A boutique hotel in a Haussmann-era townhouse, on a quiet side street around 15min walk from the Champs-Elysées. Rooms vary in size and style; some are decorated in neutral tones, with a comfortable, gentlemen's club kind of feel, while others are brighter and more decorative; those at the front have Juliet balconies. The comfortable reception area with sofas is a nice place to linger. €150

Le Pavillon des Lettres 12 rue des Saussaies, 8ᵉ ☎ 01 49 24 26 26, Ⓦ pavillondeslettres.com; Ⓜ Champs-Elysées Clémenceau; map p.64. On a quiet road, yet very centrally located, this is an elegant, well-run four-star boutique hotel with a literary theme. Each of the 26 rooms is dedicated to a writer, from Andersen (Hans Christian) to Zola (Emile), with literary quotations decorating the walls; they're pretty small, but comfy and nicely furnished in soothing colours, with bigger-than-average bathrooms. €198

Hôtel de Sers 41 av Pierre 1er de Serbie, 8ᵉ ☎ 01 53 23 75 75, Ⓦ hoteldesers-paris.fr; Ⓜ George V; map p.64. This chic hotel, just off the Champs-Elysées, offers swish rooms with Italian-marble bathrooms, sleek decor and flashes of quirky colour; facilities include iPads and huge TVs. Some of the suites (from €1349) on the top floor have fabulous panoramic terraces with views of the Eiffel Tower. Excellent offers and online deals can bring the rates right down. €449

THE TUILERIES AND LOUVRE

Hôtel Brighton 218 rue de Rivoli, 1ᵉʳ ☎ 01 47 03 61 61, Ⓦ paris-hotel-brighton.com; Ⓜ Tuileries; map p.76. Location is key at this venerable hotel, dating back to the late nineteenth century, with airy, high-ceilinged rooms. There is a range of options: "classic" rooms, which look over the courtyard, are fine if nothing special, while the "Tuileries" and "club" rooms, though small, have views of the gardens or the rue de Rivoli; the larger "deluxe" rooms

TOP 5 GARDENS

(€365) are the best, particularly those on the upper floors, with magnificent vistas of the Tuileries gardens. €264

Le Relais Saint-Honoré 308 rue St-Honoré, 1er ☎ 01 42 96 06 06, ⓦ hotel-relais-saint-honore.com; ⓜ Tuileries; map p.76. A charming little hotel set in a stylishly renovated seventeenth-century townhouse on one of Paris's main fashion streets. The fifteen neat, tastefully furnished rooms are colourful and cheery, some with painted wooden beams and pretty floral fabrics; some are smaller than the others, while others have mezzanine areas. There's a suite suitable for families. €225

★ **Hôtel Thérèse** 5–7 rue Thérèse, 1er ☎ 01 42 96 10 01, ⓦ hoteltherese.com; ⓜ Palais Royal Musée du Louvre; map p.76. Very attractive boutique hotel, run by exceptionally helpful and courteous staff, on a quiet street within easy walking distance of the Louvre. Rooms are small and stylish, with luxury fabrics and cool furnishings; some of them overlook the leafy courtyard. Book in advance, as it's very popular, especially during the fashion shows. €280

THE GRANDS BOULEVARDS AND PASSAGES

Hôtel Chopin 46 passage Jouffroy, 9e; entrance on bd Montmartre, near rue du Faubourg-Montmartre ☎ 01 47 70 58 10, ⓦ hotelchopin paris-opera.com; ⓜ Grands Boulevards; map p.76. A quiet and old-fashioned hotel set in an atmospheric period building at the end of a picturesque 1840s *passage*. The 36 rooms are decorated with *toile de Jouy* fabrics and are clean and spruce; they're good for the price, though the cheaper ones are on the small side and a little dark. €106

Hôtel Crayon 25 rue de Bouloi, 1er ☎ 01 42 36 54 19, ⓦ hotelcrayon.com; ⓜ Louvre Rivoli; map p.76. Colourful, artist-owned hotel with a guesthouse feel. The 26 funky rooms are all different, with vibrant colour blocking and scattered with mismatched vintage and retro furniture. Check online for good deals. *Hôtel Crayon Rouge*, 150m away at 42 rue Croix des Petits Champs, is similar. €169

★ **Hôtel Edgar** 31 rue d'Alexandrie, 2e ☎ 01 40 41 05 19, ⓦ edgarparis.com; ⓜ Sentier; map p.76. Hotels don't get much more designer than this, with twelve small rooms conceived by artists, stylists, film-makers and creatives of every stripe. Everything is presented with great *joie de vivre*, and whether you want the soft greys of "Cocoon", the boudoir chic of "Ma Nuit" or the kooky kiddy kitsch of "Dream", you'll find a niche. It's not all style over substance, either – the staff are friendly, rooms are comfy, with good bathrooms, and it's on a small, quiet square. The hotel also has its own bar-restaurant, specializing in seafood. €170

★ **Hôtel Tiquetonne** 6 rue Tiquetonne, 2e ☎ 01 42 36 94 58, ⓦ hoteltiquetonne.fr; ⓜ Etienne Marcel; map p.76. Located on a pedestrianized street a block away from lively rue Montorgueil, this excellent-value budget hotel in a 1920s building offers old-fashioned charm. Rooms have retro furnishings and are clean and well maintained: many are quite spacious, with larger-than-average bathrooms, though walls are thin. Non-en-suite rooms come with a sink and bidet, with use of a shower on the landing (en suites cost €80). €65

Hôtel Vivienne 40 rue Vivienne, 2e ☎ 01 42 33 13 26, ⓦ hotel-vivienne.com; ⓜ Grands Boulevards/Bourse; map p.76. A 10min walk from the Louvre, this family-run place does the essentials well: the 44 rooms are clean, well sized and come with modern facilities; the cheapest are less impressive, though OK for the price, and have bathrooms down the hall. The more expensive rooms (€176) have a little roof terrace. €90

BEAUBOURG AND LES HALLES

★ **Hôtel du Cygne** 3–5 rue du Cygne, 1er ☎ 01 42 60 14 16, ⓦ hotelducygne.fr; ⓜ Etienne Marcel; map p.88. This friendly hotel, harbouring twenty small, cheerily decorated rooms, some of them with beamed ceilings, occupies a four-storey seventeenth-century townhouse with a dash of charm and a cosy communal lounge – there's no lift, just a narrow twisty staircase (staff will help with bags). It's on a lively pedestrianized street in the heart of the Les Halles district, so can get a little noisy at night. Five singles are available for €62/night in high season, and there are good online deals available. €125

Relais du Louvre 19 rue des Prêtres St-Germain l'Auxerrois, 1er ☎ 01 40 41 96 42, ⓦ relaisdulouvre.com, ⓜ Pont-Neuf/Louvre Rivoli; map p.88. An intimate hotel with 22 rooms set on a quiet backstreet opposite the church of St-Germain l'Auxerrois; you can admire the church's flying buttresses from the front-facing rooms. The rooms have rich fabrics, old prints, period furniture and paintings. There are also three comfy suites sleeping up to four (from €308). The relaxed atmosphere and charming service attract a repeat clientele. €230

Hôtel de Roubaix 6 rue de Greneta, 3e ☎ 01 42 72 89 91, ⓦ hdroubaix.fr; ⓜ Réaumur Sebastopol; map p.88. This family-run budget hotel has been around for years (and started to look like it), but it's just been given a complete lift with a bright new refurb: vintage furniture and chandeliers are still dotted about the 53 small rooms, but the overall look is contemporary with a playful touch lent by comic-book art on the walls. The staff are very welcoming and the location is pretty quiet, yet close to all the Marais action and the Centre Pompidou. €113

TOP 5 COOL STAYS

Hôtel Crayon See opposite
Hôtel Edgar See opposite
Jules et Jim See p.258
Pigalle See p.262
Providence See p.262

19

THE MARAIS

★**Hôtel Bourg Tibourg** 19 rue du Bourg-Tibourg, 4ᵉ ☎01 42 78 47 39, ⓦbourgtibourg.com; ⓜHôtel-de-Ville; map p.99. Oriental meets medieval meets bordello, with a dash of Second Empire, at this stylishly designed little hotel. Rooms are small, but cosseted with rich velvets, silks and drapes; some have their own mini balconies. With well-chosen books, classic movies and even a hotel playlist, this is a hip little romantic hideaway. **€261**

Hôtel de la Bretonnerie 22 rue Ste-Croix de la Bretonnerie, 4ᵉ ☎01 48 87 77 63, ⓦhotelparismarais bretonnerie.com; ⓜHôtel-de-Ville; map p.99. A charming, if slightly tired in places, hotel with 29 individually designed rooms, all decorated with quality fabrics, oak furniture and, in some cases, four-poster beds. The beamed attic rooms, and the split-level or dual-bathroom suites (from €203), are particularly appealing. The location's perfect for exploring the Marais, though front-facing rooms may suffer from street noise at night. **€168**

Caron de Beaumarchais 12 rue Vieille-du-Temple, 4ᵉ ☎01 42 72 34 12, ⓦcarondebeaumarchais.com; ⓜHôtel de Ville; map p.99. Pretty hotel named after the eighteenth-century French playwright, who would have felt quite at home here: all the furnishings – the original engravings and Louis XVI furniture, not to mention the piano in the foyer – evoke the refined tastes of high-society pre-Revolution Paris. There are nineteen rooms; those overlooking the narrow courtyard are petite, while those on the street are more spacious, some with a small balcony, chandeliers and beams. **€145**

Hôtel Ecole Centrale 3 rue Bailly, 3ᵉ ☎01 48 04 77 76, ⓦparis-marais-hotel.fr; ⓜArts et Métiers; map p.96. Very friendly hotel in a Marais townhouse on a quiet cul-de-sac. Though rather garishly decorated, the rooms aren't a bad size, and those on the first and second floors – though they're the most basic – retain original features, including wooden beams. The more expensive deluxe rooms (€216) in the attic have espresso makers, and two have jacuzzis. Various online discounts available, including last-minute and three-night offers, plus special weekend rates that include breakfast. **€165**

Hôtel Jeanne d'Arc 3 rue de Jarente, 4ᵉ ☎01 48 87 62 11, ⓦhoteljeannedarc.com; ⓜSt-Paul; map p.99. This popular and charming old hotel, just off the lovely place du Marché Ste-Catherine, has recently been upgraded, but still remains a good-value choice, considering its central Marais location. The small rooms are elegant and modern, with wooden floors, some retaining original features such as exposed brick walls. The triple at the top has nice views over the rooftops, and corner rooms have more light. Staff are friendly and helpful. **€152**

Jules et Jim 11 rue des Gravilliers, 3ᵉ ☎01 44 54 13 13, ⓦhoteljuteetjim.com; ⓜArts et Métiers; map p.96. Cool, contemporary hotel with lots of hip design features

– check out the reception desk made of books – and 23 quiet, swish rooms, some with balconies. There's a good bar opening onto the cobbled courtyard (it closes at 11pm, to avoid noise disturbing guests in courtyard rooms), and really welcoming staff. **€240**

★**Hôtel de Nice** 42bis rue de Rivoli, 4ᵉ ☎01 42 78 55 29, ⓦhoteldenice.com; ⓜHôtel de Ville; map p.99. A well-run, cosy little establishment, with old-world charm and lots of quirky style: the 23 colourful rooms have Indian-cotton bedspreads, carved wooden wardrobes, elaborate wallpaper and gilded mirrors. The rue de Rivoli is very busy, though double glazing helps to block out most of the traffic noise. **€172**

Hôtel Paris France 72 rue de Turbigo, 3ᵉ ☎01 42 78 00 04, ⓦparis-france-hotel.com; ⓜTemple; map p.96. Welcoming hotel offering sizeable, comfortable rooms, with air-con, in a very convenient location, handy for the canal and the Louvre. The decor is understated and tasteful, with good bathrooms and great Eiffel Tower views from the upper floors. **€128**

★**Hôtel du Petit Moulin** 29–31 rue de Poitou, 3ᵉ ☎01 42 74 10 10, ⓦhoteldupetitmoulin.com; ⓜSt-Sébastien-Froissart/Filles du Calvaire; map p.99. Inside a former bakery – the lovely old exterior remains intact – this luxurious Christian Lacroix-designed boutique hotel is infused with the designer's hallmark *joie de vivre*. The seventeen rooms are a bold fusion of different styles, from elegant Baroque to Sixties kitsch via raunchy bordello; shocking pinks and lime greens give way to *toile de Jouy* prints, while pod chairs rub up alongside antique dressing tables and standalone bathtubs. **€235**

Hôtel de la Place des Vosges 12 rue de Birague, 4ᵉ ☎01 42 72 60 46, ⓦhotelplacedesvosges.com; ⓜBastille; map p.99. A charming, well-priced hotel, run by very helpful staff, in a glorious building dating back to 1605, just near the *place*. Rooms are contemporary in style, and small, but some have wooden floors, stone walls and wooden beams. **€140**

Hôtel St-Louis Marais 1 rue Charles-V, 4ᵉ ☎01 48 87 87 04, ⓦsaintlouismarais.com; ⓜSully Morland; map p.99. Formerly part of the seventeenth-century Célestins Convent, this characterful place retains its period feel, with stone walls, exposed beams and tiled floors. Some of the fifteen rooms are small, but the bathrooms are large and relatively luxurious. A major plus is the location, on a very quiet road, just a short walk from the Marais action, with the Left Bank easily accessible too. Avoid the less appealing annexe rooms. **€150**

BASTILLE AND AROUND

★**Auberge Flora** 44 bd Richard-Lenoir, 11ᵉ ☎01 47 00 52 77, ⓦaubergeflora.fr; ⓜBréguet-Sabin; map p.112. A cute boutique hotel with 21 rooms from singles to "gourmande" options and suites, decorated on a loose theme according to which floor they're on (bohemia, vegetable plot or nature). The cheapest are tiny, but a good

TOP 5 VIEWS

Hôtel Brighton See p.256
Le Citizen Hotel See p.263
Hôtel Esmeralda See p.259
Hôtel Paris France See p.258
Terrass Hôtel See p.262

price, and all are colourful and comfortable, with lots of individual touches. Flora herself is also the chef at the restaurant below, offering deceptively simple, seasonal and delicious Mediterranean-influenced food. **€122**

Hôtel Marais Bastille 36 bd Richard-Lenoir, 11ᵉ ☎01 48 05 75 00, ⓦmaraisbastille.com; ⓜBréguet-Sabin; map p.112. Part of the *Best Western* chain and handily located for both the Marais and Bastille, this warm and friendly 37-room hotel has a swish, contemporary interior. The public spaces are a bit overdesigned, but the rooms, while small, are comfy and clean, done out in soothing hues with splashes of paintbox-bright colour and modern bathrooms. Good online deals available. **€165**

Hôtel Paris Bastille Boutet 22–24 rue Faidherbe, 11ᵉ ☎01 40 24 65 65, ⓦsofitel.com; ⓜCharonne; map p.112. The first five-star hotel in eastern Paris opened in 2016 in a lovely old Art Deco building, a former joinery workshop and chocolate factory. It's been stylishly restored to provide eighty sleek rooms in muted colours, including eight rooftop suites (€375) with pretty terraces. An added attraction is the spa, hammam and beautiful indoor pool with its blue-and-white glazed tiles. **€230**

★**Hôtel de la Porte Dorée** 273 av Daumesnil, 12ᵉ ☎01 43 07 56 97, ⓦhoteldelaportedoree.com; ⓜPorte Dorée; map p.118. This welcoming hotel is not as central as some offerings in its price range but it's very close to the Bois de Vincennes, right next to the métro, and Bastille is just 7min away by métro or a pleasant 20min stroll along the Promenade Plantée. Tastefully refurbished by an American-French family, the contemporary rooms, each with a private shower or bath, TV and comfy beds, have traditional features including ceiling mouldings and fireplaces, plus some antique furnishings. Regular online deals offer significant reductions. **€137**

QUARTIER LATIN

Hôtel Design de la Sorbonne 6 rue Victor Cousin, 5ᵉ ☎01 43 54 58 08, ⓦhotelsorbonne.com; ⓜCluny La Sorbonne; map p.124. Brilliantly situated hotel with designer decor, eye-popping colour schemes and iMacs in each room. Above all, though, the rooms are cosy, comfortable and well equipped, the staff are friendly and prices are very good for this standard and location. **€180**

Hôtel Esmeralda 4 rue St-Julien-le-Pauvre, 5ᵉ ☎01 43 54 19 20, ⓦhotel-esmeralda.fr; ⓜSt-Michel/Maubert Mutualité; map p.124. In an ancient house on square Viviani, this quirky old hotel (no lift) offers a deeply nostalgic feel, with sixteen eccentrically decorated, simple en-suite rooms – a few of them with unrivalled views of Notre Dame. The wallpaper can occasionally be alarming, and there are plenty of worn corners and few mod-cons – but the staff are very helpful and the location is incomparable. **€125**

Familia Hôtel 11 rue des Ecoles, 5ᵉ ☎01 43 54 55 27, ⓦfamiliahotel.com; ⓜCardinal Lemoine/Maubert Mutualité/Jussieu; map p.124. Friendly hotel in the heart of the *quartier*. It's not luxurious, but it has charm – the small rooms are full of old-fashioned character, variously boasting stone walls, beams or pretty murals; some have their own small balcony and some have views of nearby Notre-Dame. **€135**

★**Hôtel des Grandes Ecoles** 75 rue du Cardinal Lemoine, 5ᵉ ☎01 43 26 79 23, ⓦhotel-grandes-ecoles .com; ⓜCardinal Lemoine/Place Monge; map p.124. A cobbled lane leads through to a big surprise: a homely country house-style hotel with a large, gorgeous garden, right in the heart of the Quartier Latin. The rooms are pretty in a chintzy way, with floral wallpaper and old-fashioned furnishings, and the welcome is sincere. Reserve well in advance; it fills up fast. **€165**

Hôtel des Grands Hommes 17 place du Panthéon, 5ᵉ ☎01 46 34 19 60, ⓦhoteldesgrandshommes.com; ⓜMaubert Mutualité/RER Luxembourg; map p.124. There's a certain grandeur in this eighteenth-century townhouse hotel: a number of the rooms look out over the Panthéon and the French Empire-style decor and styling is distinctly luxurious. At heart, though, it's a friendly place, with lovely service. **€190**

★**La Lanterne** 12 Rue de la Montagne Ste-Geneviève, 5ᵉ ☎01 53 19 88 39, ⓦhotel-la-lanterne.com; ⓜMaubert Mutualité; map p.124. Gorgeous boutique hotel in a classy location, with soothing decor brightened by splashes of eye-popping colour. The chic rooms are plush and welcoming, each with their own bedside lanterns and lovely bathrooms; the real star, though, is the little spa – swimming pool, aromatherapy shower and steam room – hidden away in a vaulted stone cellar. Guests receive a smartphone for the length of their stay. **€280**

★**Hôtel Marignan** 13 rue du Sommerard, 5ᵉ ☎01 43 54 63 81, ⓦhotel-marignan.com; ⓜMaubert Mutualité; map p.124. This friendly, welcoming budget hotel is a real find – they're totally sympathetic to the needs of rucksack-toting foreigners, offering free laundry, free breakfast and a basic self-catering kitchen. The rooms are clean and comfortable, with options for up to five people; the cheapest have shared bathrooms. One of the best deals in town. No lift. **€91**

Hôtel Résidence Henri IV 50 rue des Bernardins, 5ᵉ ☎01 44 41 31 81, ⓦresidencehenri4.com; ⓜMaubert Mutualité; map p.124. Set back from busy rue des Ecoles on a quiet cul-de-sac, this hotel is discreet and elegant, with great service. There are eight standard doubles, as well as five larger suites with separate lounging areas (€280). All are classically styled – some have original fireplaces – and all have modern bathrooms and miniature kitchenettes. Good online deals. **€230**

Hôtel St-Jacques 35 rue des Ecoles, 5ᵉ ☎ 01 44 07 45 45, ⓦ paris-hotel-stjacques.com; ⓜ Maubert Mutualité map p.124. This pretty, painting-strewn hotel in the heart of the district combines original nineteenth-century features – check out the decorative ceiling mouldings – with modern comforts. The 36 belle époque-styled rooms are all different; some have balconies and lovely views. There's a bar, too. Book online well in advance for the best deals. **€223**

Select Hôtel 1 place de la Sorbonne, 5ᵉ ☎ 01 46 34 14 80, ⓦ selecthotel.fr; ⓜ Cluny La Sorbonne; map p.124. Situated right on the *place*, this fairly large (65-room), modern four-star hotel has a stylish feel, matching original beams and exposed stone walls with designer furnishings – standard rooms are comfortable, if pretty tiny, with Nespresso machines. Larger rooms with views onto the square are twice the price (€325). The airy public spaces, dotted with contemporary art, include a bar, lounge and library. **€175**

ST-GERMAIN

Hôtel de l'Abbaye 10 rue Cassette, 6ᵉ ☎ 01 45 44 38 11, ⓦ hotelabbayeparis.com; ⓜ St-Sulpice; map p.138. An atmosphere of calm presides over this elegant, prettily decorated four-star hotel, set back from the quiet road. The 44 tasteful rooms have a sumptuous feel – swathes of floral fabric, thick carpets – but best of all is the verdant courtyard garden and conservatory, where you can enjoy breakfast (sometimes included in the rates, otherwise €18–23) or an evening *apéritif* from the little hotel bar. **€290**

La Belle Juliette 92 rue du Cherche-Midi, 6ᵉ ☎ 01 42 22 97 40, ⓦ labellejuliette.com; ⓜ Vaneau; map p.138. Many of the rooms in this chichi four-star boutique hotel look out onto one of the most charming roads on the Left Bank, populated with bijou cafés and shops. The decor brings high-concept arty touches to classic, late eighteenth-century elegance, with poppy colours and plush fabrics. All rooms have iMacs and there's a spa with a tiny pool, café-bar and garden. **€250**

L'Hôtel 13 rue des Beaux-Arts, 6ᵉ ☎ 01 44 41 99 00, ⓦ l-hotel.com; ⓜ Mabillon/St-Germain-des-Prés; map p.138. A boutique hotel epitomizing louche Left Bank opulence, with twenty liberal rooms – the cheapest are small, but gorgeous – accessed by a spiral staircase. There's a tiny steam room/pool in the basement (you need to book), a Michelin-starred restaurant (*Le Restaurant*) and a stylish little bar. Oscar Wilde died here, "fighting a duel" with his wallpaper, and he's now remembered in a room with a "Wilde" theme. **€325**

Hôtel du Danube 58 rue Jacob, 6ᵉ ☎ 01 42 60 34 70, ⓦ hoteldanube.fr; ⓜ St-Germain-des-Prés; map p.138.

This elegant, generally quiet hotel is right in the heart of things. The teeny standard rooms are fine, but the *supérieures* (€185) are the ones to go for, if you can: unusually spacious, with handsome, tall windows. It's popular, especially with Americans, so book well in advance. **€170**

Hôtel Louis II 2 rue St-Sulpice, 6ᵉ ☎ 01 46 33 13 80, ⓦ hotel-louis2.com; ⓜ Odéon; map p.138. Friendly, efficient boutique hotel with a fabulous central location. Standard rooms are small but comfy and clean, with exposed beams and period furnishings; some are looking dated, but overall this is a great choice. **€215**

Hôtel Michelet Odéon 6 place de l'Odéon, 6ᵉ ☎ 01 53 10 05 60, ⓦ hotelmicheletodeon.com; ⓜ Odéon; map p.138. A clean, comfortable choice with a dash of style – a real bargain so close to the Jardin du Luxembourg. There are around forty rooms, some of which face onto the *place*, with good-value triple and family options (€130/€180). Excellent online promotions. **€129**

Hôtel de Nesle 7 rue de Nesle, 6ᵉ ☎ 01 43 54 62 41, ⓦ hoteldenesleparis.com; ⓜ St-Michel; map p.138. Bohemian old hotel with lots of character in its eighteen themed rooms (some with shared facilities and others decorated with love-'em-or-hate-'em murals) and its overgrown courtyard garden. Prices are low for the area, and the owner is a delight. Ideally, phone to reserve (it's best to have a little French). No lift. **€150**

Le Petit Chomel 15 rue Chomel, 7ᵉ ☎ 01 45 48 55 52, ⓦ lepetitchomel.com; ⓜ Sevres–Babylone; ,map p.138. A pretty little boutique hotel filled with quirky and vintage furnishings (it's owned by an interior designer). The 23 rooms are as homely and cosy as they are stylish, with soothing colour schemes; some have tiny balconies overlooking the street. **€199**

Relais Saint-Sulpice 3 rue Garancière, 6ᵉ ☎ 01 46 33 99 00, ⓦ relais-saint-sulpice.com; ⓜ St-Sulpice/ St-Germain-des-Prés; map p.138. Wonderfully located in an aristocratic eighteenth-century townhouse on a side street immediately behind St-Sulpice, this is a discreetly classy hotel with lots of interesting antiques and well-furnished rooms – all are different, but many overlook the leafy courtyard or the church's apse. The cosy lounge, with courtesy bar, is a nice place to relax. **€210**

★ Hôtel de Sèvres 22 rue de l'Abbé Grégoire, 6ᵉ ☎ 01 45 48 84 07, ⓦ hoteldesevres.com; ⓜ Rennes; map p.138. You get very good value for the neighbourhood in this appealing contemporary hotel. The small rooms are comfortable and perfectly adequate, and service is great; nice extra touches include a small spa and a little patio where you can drink a glass of wine or a coffee. **€115**

Hôtel Verneuil 8 rue de Verneuil, 7ᵉ ☎ 01 42 60 82 14, ⓦ hotel verneuil-saint-germain.com; ⓜ St-Germain-des-Prés; map p.138. Ideally situated in a quiet street between St-Germain, the Louvre and the Musée d'Orsay, this boutique hotel exudes understated style and offers impeccable service – including a free smartphone for all guests. The smallest doubles are tiny but they're comfy and luxurious; many retain period features, such as exposed beams. **€246**

THE EIFFEL TOWER QUARTER

★**Hôtel du Champ-de-Mars** 7 rue du Champ-de-Mars, 7ᵉ ☎01 45 51 52 30, ⓦhotelduchampdemars.com; ⓜEcole Militaire; map p.152. In a handsome area just off the rue Cler market, this good-value, quiet hotel has a comforting neighbourhood feel. The rooms are small but cosy, clean and colourful; a couple of them overlook pretty courtyards. Great service and good value. **€155**

Hôtel du Palais Bourbon 49 rue de Bourgogne, 7ᵉ ☎01 44 11 30 70, ⓦbourbon-paris-hotel.com; ⓜVarenne; map p.152. This substantial, handsome old three-star in the hushed, posh district near the Musée Rodin offers comfortable rooms and heaps of old-fashioned charm. Family rooms are available (€235), as well as a few miniature singles (€100). **€150**

MONTPARNASSE AND THE 14ᵉ

Apostrophe Hotel 3 rue de Chevreuse, 6ᵉ ☎01 56 54 31 31, ⓦapostrophe-hotel.com; ⓜVavin; map p.164. Stylish hotel on the edge of Montparnasse, with each (small) room designed to the hilt on a different literary or artistic theme, from "Shéhérazade" to "Calligraphie". Some bathrooms have "chromotherapy" jacuzzi baths (with lights that change colour to stimulate different moods), and others have illuminated, hydromassaging rainshowers. The staff are great. **€150**

Hôtel Delambre 35 rue Delambre, 14ᵉ ☎01 43 20 66 31, ⓦdelambre-paris-hotel.com; ⓜEdgar Quinet; map p.164. Beyond the turquoise exterior you'll find a dependable, friendly hotel on the northern edge of Montparnasse towards St-Germain. Rooms are plain and a little old-fashioned, but comfortable and clean, and some have little balconies. **€119**

★**Solar Hôtel** 22 rue Boulard, 14ᵉ ☎01 43 21 08 20, ⓦsolarhotel.fr; ⓜDenfert Rochereau; map p.164. This modern budget hotel maintains a determinedly ecological spirit, from its waste disposal to its cleaning products. The rooms are unfussy, colourful and comfortable, a little like an upmarket hostel, each with private bathroom; some have minuscule balconies. Rates include a simple organic breakfast, which you can eat in the small garden, and you also get access to a kitchen. Free bikes are available for guests; wi-fi only available in the breakfast room. **€89**

THE 15ᵉ

Hôtel de l'Avre 21 rue de l'Avre, 15ᵉ ☎01 45 75 31 03, ⓦhoteldelavre.com; ⓜLa Motte-Picquet Grenelle; map p.172. Within striking distance of the Eiffel Tower, this good-value hotel lies just off the rue du Commerce – but with its pretty decor you could be forgiven for thinking you

were in the provinces. Some of the rooms – which do vary, so ask to see another if you don't like yours – overlook the sweet courtyard garden. **€135**

Splendid Hotel 54 rue Fondary, 15ᵉ ☎01 45 75 17 73, ⓦsplendid-hotel-paris.com; ⓜLa Motte-Picquet Grenelle; map p.172. You won't get luxury or design flair at this unfussy hotel, set in a nineteenth-century townhouse on a quiet street, but it's a reliable budget choice. It's a 15min walk from the Eiffel Tower – some rooms have views (€120). **€100**

THE 13ᵉ AND AROUND

★**Hôtel Henriette Rive Gauche** 9 rue des Gobelins, 13ᵉ ☎01 47 07 26 90, ⓦhotelhenriette.com; ⓜLes Gobelins; map p.176. Gorgeous boutique hotel with an airy contemporary feel and impeccable attention to detail courtesy of the owner's experience in fashion styling – a bit Scandi, a little Midcentury Modern, a dash of shabby chic. The 32 small rooms are each different, and all lovely – bonuses include the cute walled patio, the quiet location and the warm, friendly staff. **€140**

La Manufacture 8 rue Philippe de Champagne, 13ᵉ ☎01 45 35 45 25, ⓦhotel-la-manufacture.com; ⓜPlace d'Italie; map p.176. Even the smallest rooms of the sixty-odd choices at this comfortable, welcoming budget hotel are attractive, with soothing colour palettes; some have large bathrooms, some have balconies (€75), and others look onto the handsome mairie. **€120**

OFF Paris Seine 86 Quai d'Austerlitz, 13ᵉ ☎01 44 06 62 65, ⓦoffparisseine.com; ⓜGare d'Austerlitz; map p.176. Expect urban cool, rather than idyllic tranquillity, from this designer party hotel, floating on the Seine near the Les Docks complex and opposite the all-night *Concrete* club (see p.176). It's a place to be seen, and can be noisy, with a cocktail bar, outdoor deck and tiny swimming pool, but there is an irresistible lure in sleeping on the water. Teeny cabin-like rooms – at water level or on the top deck – overlook the dock or (more expensive) the Seine (which can be noisy on club nights). **€180**

Port-Royal Hôtel 8 bd Port-Royal, 5ᵉ ☎01 43 31 70 06, ⓦport-royal-hotel.fr; ⓜLes Gobelins; map p.176. At the edge of the 5ᵉ arrondissement, at the rue Mouffetard end of the boulevard, near the métro, this excellent budget hotel has been in the same family since the 1930s. The whole place is clean, comfy and well-cared for, if perhaps a little tired, with a tiny leafy courtyard; the cheapest rooms have shared bathroom facilities (€2.50/timed shower) while en-suite double rooms (from €95) are relatively spacious. No credit cards. **€68**

★ **Le Vert-Galant** 43 rue de Croulebarbe, 13ᵉ ☎01 44 08 83 50, ⓦvertgalant.com; ⓜLes Gobelins; map p.176. On a quiet backwater opposite the verdant square René-le-Gall, this peaceful family-run hotel seems to belong to a provincial French town rather than Paris – it

19

has a garden, and in the evening you can eat at their attached Basque restaurant, *Auberge Etchegorry*. The seventeen plain rooms are clean and comfortable; most of them overlook the garden, and some (€130) have French windows leading directly into it. €130

MONTMARTRE AND THE 9ᵉ

9Hotel Opéra 14 rue Papillon, 9ᵉ ☎ 01 47 70 78 34, Ⓦ 9-hotel-opera-paris.fr; Ⓜ Poissonnière/Cadet/Gare du Nord; map p.182. The small rooms are pretty minimalist but this boutique hotel offers style, comfort and a friendly, personal service. A good option if you need somewhere close to the Gare du Nord yet within easy reach of the charming *passages* and the big department stores. Great online discounts. €170

★ **Hôtel des Arts** 5 rue Tholozé, 18ᵉ ☎ 01 46 06 30 52, Ⓦ arts-hotel-paris.com; Ⓜ Abbesses/Blanche; map p.182. A rare combination of homeliness and efficiency, with courteous, helpful staff and welcoming accommodation. Rooms, each named after a French artist, vary hugely (the cheapest have no a/c), but all are well maintained, quiet and very comfortable, with dashes of colour and style – some have Eiffel Tower views, and the "romantic double" (€168) boasts a lovely little balcony. The location – in the heart of Abbesses, opposite the classic Studio 28 art cinema (see p.314) – is fantastic. €160

Hôtel Bonséjour Montmartre 11 rue Burq, 18ᵉ ☎ 01 42 54 22 53, Ⓦ hotel-bonsejour-montmartre.fr; Ⓜ Abbesses; map p.182. Public spaces in this family-owned budget hotel are bare and a little scruffy – the whole place was undergoing an interminable refit at the time of writing, transforming it from old-fashioned Parisian cheapie to a more contemporary style – but the rooms, clean and relatively spacious, offer a good deal. Standard simple doubles have just a sink (the shared showers and toilets are clean, with no extra charge to use them); some rooms come with private shower but toilet along the hall (€66) and some are full en suites (€95). The corner rooms have charming little balconies. €56

Hôtel Langlois 63 rue St-Lazare, 9ᵉ ☎ 01 48 74 78 24, Ⓦ hotel-langlois.com; Ⓜ Trinité d'Estienne d'Orves; map p.182. This genteel hotel feels as if it has scarcely changed in the last century, though it has all the facilities you'd expect of a three-star, plus excellent service. Each of the rooms is different, but they're all larger than average and handsome, in an old-fashioned way, with high ceilings, fireplaces, the odd antique and en-suite bathrooms, some of which are huge. Excellent online discounts. €120

★ **Hôtel du Moulin** 3 rue Aristide Bruant, 18ᵉ ☎ 01 42 64 33 33, Ⓦ hotelmoulin.com; Ⓜ Abbesses/Blanche; map p.182. A terrific budget hotel in a superb Abbesses location, run by lovely people. Some rooms are looking a little tired, but all are a reasonable size, with good bathrooms, plenty of storage space and comfortable beds; those around the pretty

little decked garden are at a premium. €79

★ **Hôtel Palm** 30 rue de Maubeuge, 9ᵉ ☎ 01 42 85 07 61, Ⓦ astotel.com/hotel/hotel-palm-opera; Ⓜ Cadet; map p.182. Fresh, upbeat hotel typical of the excellent *Astotel* group – all poppy colours and retro styling – with nicely designed, quiet and contemporary rooms as well as good bathrooms. Some have balconies and Eiffel Tower views. Delightful, welcoming staff, plus free snacks and drinks, and a family-friendly atmosphere. Rates include breakfast. €136

★ **Pigalle** 9 rue Frochot, 9ᵉ ☎ 01 48 78 37 14, Ⓦ lepigalle .paris/en; Ⓜ Pigalle; map p.182. In the heart of the cool SoPi nightlife district, this artsy hotel has impeccable hipster credentials – and a good, late-opening restaurant/bar on the ground floor. It's friendly and rooms are plush and very comfortable. The smallest have bunk beds (€166), while the largest come with vinyl and a turntable – but all are kitted out with vintage cool, with quirky art and photos on the walls and iPads loaded with music. €196

Terrass Hôtel 12–14 rue Joseph de Maistre, 18ᵉ ☎ 01 46 06 72 85, Ⓦ terrass-hotel.com; Ⓜ Blanche; map p.182. Designer hotel with colourful contemporary rooms, a gym and a library – there's even a "play zone" with pool table, a retro arcade game, chess boards and a photobooth. The big pull here, though, is the rooftop restaurant/bar with its outdoor terrace offering jaw-dropping views over the city. €250

THE 10ᵉ

District République 4 rue Lucien Sampaix, 10ᵉ ☎ 01 42 08 20 09, Ⓦ hoteldistrictrepublique.com; Ⓜ Jacques-Bonsergent; map p.192. Nothing extraordinary here, just a solid, reasonably priced option on the edge of the 10ᵉ, towards the canal. The 33 rooms are small but contemporary, comfortable and well equipped, with coffee- and tea-making facilities, and the staff are super-helpful. €109

Providence 90 rue René Boulanger, 10ᵉ ☎ 01 46 34 34 04, Ⓦ hotelprovidenceparis.com; Ⓜ Strasbourg St-Denis; map p.192. With a good location on a quiet street, convenient for the Gare du Nord and the Canal St-Martin, this romantic boutique hotel, in a grand nineteenth-century building, offers eighteen beautifully styled rooms – lots of vintage luxe and bohemian quirks – above a cool restaurant and cocktail bar of the same name. Each room, from the bijou "minis" to the penthouse suite (€370), comes with an iMac, cocktail bar and smartphone, and some have balconies. €250

BATIGNOLLES

★ **Hôtel Eldorado** 18 rue des Dames, 17ᵉ ☎ 01 45 22 35 21, Ⓦ eldoradohotel.fr; Ⓜ Place de Clichy; map p.195. Idiosyncratic and enjoyable, this characterful 33-room hotel on a lively street has its own little restaurant, *Bistrot des Dames* (see p.292), and a sweet, flower-filled courtyard garden. The small rooms – some en suite, others with a sink and shared toilet/bathroom facilities – are worn in places but charmingly decorated, with bright colours offsetting flea market furnishings and the old hotel fittings that are fast disappearing from Paris. En-suite doubles are a bargain at €90 – book direct through the website. No lift. **€60**

Idol Hotel 16 rue d'Edimbourg, 8ᵉ ☎ 01 45 22 14 31, ⓦ idolhotel-paris.com; ⓜ Europe; map p.195. Groovy music-themed boutique hotel, near St-Lazare in an area filled with musical-instrument stores. The comfortable rooms have a glam retro vibe, and all come with a Bluetooth music system and Nespresso machine. There's a pretty, secluded courtyard garden, too, where you can enjoy a drink from the honesty bar. **€230**

CANAL ST-MARTIN

Hôtel Beaumarchais 3 rue Oberkampf, 11ᵉ ☎ 01 53 36 86 86, ⓦ hotelbeaumarchais.com; ⓜ Filles du Calvaire/Oberkampf; map p.198. Brightly decorated, with a little indoor garden for relaxing, this hotel's location on buzzy rue Oberkampf, right on the edge of the Marais and near the canal, means it's ideally situated for some of the most vibrant parts of the city. Rooms are small but functional. **€128**

★ **Le Citizen Hotel** 96 quai de Jemmapes, 10ᵉ ☎ 01 83 62 55 50, ⓦ lecitizenhotel.com; ⓜ Jacques-Bonsergent; map p.198. With a perfect setting on the banks of the Canal St-Martin, the *Citizen* is an ecofriendly, beautifully designed hotel with just twelve rooms, including one suite (€250) and one apartment (€380). The soothing decor – light wood, clean lines and predominantly white, blue and grey tones – makes for nice airy rooms, all of which have great views of the canal. The cheaper rooms are compact; the more expensive are twice as big. Rooms come with iPads, a home-made buffet breakfast is included and staff are lovely. It's worth checking the website for last-minute special deals. **€150**

Hôtel Gabriel 25 rue du Grand-Prieuré, 11ᵉ ☎ 01 47 00 13 38, ⓦ hotelgabrielparis.com; ⓜ Oberkampf; map p.198. Beyond the unremarkable exterior is an elegant and tranquil hotel that combines an old-fashioned feel with modern design. Rooms are tiny, but very swish, with lots of cool contemporary furnishings and good bathrooms. Rates include breakfast, which you can eat in your room. **€159**

Le Général Hôtel 5–7 rue Rampon, 11ᵉ ☎ 01 47 00 41 57, ⓦ legeneralhotel.com; ⓜ République; map p.198. This cool boutique hotel, run by young staff and located on a peaceful road near the canal, has bright, airy, compact rooms with spotless bathrooms (complete with rubber ducks). Facilities include a sauna and fitness centre, espresso machines and iPod docks in the rooms; the breakfast area turns into a bar in the evenings. Book early for the lowest rates. **€162**

★ **Hôtel du Nord** 47 rue Albert Thomas, 10ᵉ ☎ 01 42 01 66 00, ⓦ hoteldunord-leparivelo.com; ⓜ Jacques-Bonsergent/République; map p.198. A pretty ivy-strewn

entrance leads into a cosy reception and 24 rooms, each of them different and all tastefully, if simply, decorated. The cheaper ones look onto the courtyard and tend to be a little smaller and darker. Four have a bath, the rest have showers, and a family room is available for €125. The friendly staff can lend out bikes. A genuinely charming budget choice. **€86**

BELLEVILLE AND MÉNILMONTANT

Cosmos Hôtel 35 rue Jean-Pierre-Timbaud, 11ᵉ ☎ 01 43 57 25 88, ⓦ cosmos-hotel-paris.com; ⓜ Parmentier; map p.207. Contemporary budget hotel, excellently located for the bars and cafés of Oberkampf, offering clean, minimalist en-suite rooms. The styling is a little bland, the fittings occasionally a bit rough around the edges, and the bathrooms are minuscule – but beds are super-comfortable and it's a welcoming base (there's even a sleepy hotel cat padding around reception). The larger doubles (€82) are worth the extra for a longer stay, and the four-person room (€98) is a bargain. **€72**

★ **Hôtel Fabric** 31 rue de la Folie Méricourt, 11ᵉ ☎ 01 43 57 27 00, ⓦ hotelfabric.com; ⓜ Sainte-Ambroise/Oberkampf; map p.207. A former fabric mill is the setting for this exceptionally welcoming and delightful contemporary hotel, with vibrant modern decor, high ceilings and exposed brick walls. Nice touches include complimentary coffee and cake and an honesty bar. **€198**

Hôtel des Metallos 50 rue de la Folie Méricourt, 11ᵉ ☎ 01 43 38 73 63, ⓦ hoteldesmetallos.com; ⓜ Oberkampf; map p.207. The uncluttered, colourful decor of this modern establishment is simple and appealing. There's an eco slant, too – energy-saving lightbulbs, water-saving taps and environmentally friendly furniture. **€119**

BAGNOLET

★ **Mama Shelter** 109 rue de Bagnolet, 20ᵉ ☎ 01 43 48 48 48, ⓦ mamashelter.com; ⓜ Alexandre-Dumas; map p.210. The endless focus on hip and cool branding – "Mama says" this, "Mama says" that – can be a bit wearing, but the youthful *Mama Shelter*, owned by *Club Med* founders and designed by Philippe Starck, actually offers surprisingly good rates and can be a lot of fun. Free in-room movies, microwaves and iMacs are standard, while a bar-restaurant (live music at weekends), sun terrace and top-notch service complete the package. The cheapest deals come via the website. **€99**

AUTEUIL AND PASSY

Hameau de Passy 48 rue de Passy, 16ᵉ ☎ 01 42 88 47 55, ⓦ hameaudepassy.com; ⓜ La Muette/Passy; map p.215. Peaceful, modern hotel, around a 10min walk from the Eiffel Tower, set back from the main street, with a little garden area to one side. While the rooms are on the small side, they get lots of natural light and are attractively decorated. Rates include breakfast. Look out for good online deals. **€145**

19

Hôtel Sezz 6 av Frémiet, 16e ☎01 56 75 26 26, ⓦhotelsezz.com; ⓜPassy; map p.215. A sleek boutique hotel hidden behind a nineteenth-century facade on a quiet street near the parc de Passy. Rooms are minimal, veering on the austere, but splashes of colour provide a touch of warmth. The accommodation here is spacious by Paris standards; suites (from €267) come with huge bathtubs big enough for two, and all rooms have iPod docks, coffee machines and CD/DVD players. **€247**

APARTMENTS AND BED & BREAKFASTS

If you're staying for more than a few days, renting an **apartment** can transform a stay in Paris and make you feel that little bit like a local. **Apartment-hotels** – a hotel made up of mini-apartments each with its own self-contained kitchen – may be useful alternatives for families or visitors on an extended stay. Staying on a **bed and breakfast** basis in a private house is also worth considering if you want to get away from the more impersonal set-up of a hotel, and is a reasonably priced option. **Prices** for the following places are quoted per night, unless specified otherwise, and represent a **typical estimate** for two people staying in high season – rates will vary as new places appear on the lists, and in some cases may be much cheaper than quoted here.

Airbnb ⓦairbnb.com. Given the price of hotels in the city, it's not surprising that Paris is one of the top Airbnb destinations – there are thousands of "hosts" in the city, many of them offering rooms (or whole apartments) in trendier areas of town. **€80**

Alcôve & Agapes ⓦbed-and-breakfast-in-paris.com. Personally run bed-and-breakfast organization with a good selection of private rooms on its books. Most accommodate couples, but some are able to welcome families, and some offer extras, such as French conversation, wine tasting or cookery classes. Minimum two or three nights. **€100**

Citadines ⓦcitadines.com. Apartment-hotel chain covering Europe and Asia. Most of its sixteen Paris establishments are centrally located and offer high-standard, comfortable accommodation in compact self-contained studios and apartments, with well-equipped kitchens and bathrooms. They sometimes have special offers and lower rates for long stays. **€145**

France Lodge 2 rue Meissonier, 17e ☎01 56 33 85 80, ⓦfrancelodge.fr. Bed-and-breakfast rooms and apartments (sleeping up to four; €800/week) throughout Paris. Reserve well in advance to be sure of something particularly special. Apartment prices drop dramatically the longer you stay. **€110**

House Trip ⓦhousetrip.com. Very user-friendly site listing hundreds of Parisian apartments, many of them rather stylish, available per night, with guest reviews and some gratifyingly low prices. **€75**

Lodgis ☎01 70 39 11 11, ⓦlodgis.com. A well-run Parisian estate agent that has around one thousand furnished studios and flats for rent by the week. Per week **€350**

Only Apartments ⓦonly-apartments.com. More than one thousand apartments in Paris, searchable by area, amenities and price, with user reviews and easy booking. Most places prefer a booking of more than one night. **€80**

HOSTELS

The best **hostels** in Paris offer fantastic, central locations at prices that only a handful of budget hotels can match. The cleaner, quieter places tend to be run by institutions, and are often aimed at groups – these may have lockouts, with rooms closed for hours in the middle of the day. The funkier, livelier hostels are usually the independents, which are generally open 24hr, but they can be noisy, and standards and cleanliness can suffer in the face of the relentless party vibe. As a rule, double rooms in a hostel aren't a good deal, except in the newer places, where clean private rooms compare with those in the nicest budget hotels.

GROUP AND INSTITUTIONAL HOSTELS

BVJ Opéra 1 rue de la Tour des Dames, 9e ☎01 42 36 88 18, ⓦbvjhostelparis.com; ⓜSt-Georges; map p.183. The well-run *BVJ Opéra* near SoPi is just about the best in the BVJ group (they also have hostels in the Latin Quarter, near the Louvre and in the 17e), attracting a young student crowd from around the world. The historic building is attractive, and though the clean ten-bed dorms (mixed and single sex; shared facilities) have a somewhat institutional feel, the atmosphere is pretty peaceful. No curfew. Breakfast included. Wi-fi costs extra. Dorms **€30**

Le Fauconnier 11 rue du Fauconnier, 4e ☎01 42 74 23 45, ⓦmije.com; ⓜSt-Paul/Pont Marie; map p.99. One of three hostels run by MIJE (Maisons Internationales de la Jeunesse et des Etudiants), all in the Marais. *Le Fauconnier* is in a superbly renovated seventeenth-century building with a courtyard. Dorms (single sex, with en-suite shower) sleep four to eight, and there are also some single (€60) and double rooms with showers; breakfast is included. Silence requested after 10pm. Dorms **€33.50**, doubles **€82**

Le Fourcy 6 rue de Fourcy, 4e ☎01 42 74 23 45; ⓜSt-Paul; map p.99. Another good MIJE hostel, with the same rates as *Le Fauconnier* (see above), including breakfast. Housed in a beautiful mansion, this one has a small garden and an inexpensive restaurant. All the same rules apply as at *Le Fauconnier*. Dorms **€33.50**, doubles **€82**

Foyer International d'Accueil de Paris Jean Monnet
30 rue Cabanis, 14ᵉ ☎ 01 43 13 17 00, ⓦ fiap.paris;
ⓜ Glacière; map p.164. Huge (480-bed), efficient hostel in a
fairly sedate area a couple of métro stops south of the Quartier
Latin. Offers singles (€73), doubles and single-sex en-suite
dorms sleeping up to six. Facilities include a bar and cafeteria;
rates include breakfast. No curfew. Dorms €38, doubles €78

Maubuisson 12 rue des Barres, 4ᵉ ☎ 01 42 74 23 45,
ⓦ mije.com; ⓜ Pont Marie/Hôtel de Ville; map p.99. A
MIJE hostel in the same group as *Le Fauconnier* and nearby
Le Fourcy (see opposite) in a magnificent medieval building
on a quiet street. The same conditions apply as at *Le
Fauconnier*. Dorms only. Dorms €33.50

INDEPENDENT HOSTELS

3 Ducks Hostel 6 place Etienne Pernet, 15ᵉ ☎ 01 48 42
04 05, ⓦ 3ducks.fr; ⓜ Commerce; map p.172. Lively,
long-established and popular hostel in an eighteenth-
century building, offering homely and colourful mixed and
female-only en-suite dorms (four to eight beds), and some
en-suite twins/doubles. Interior decor is quite cool, and the
terrace and lively streetside bar are nice places to hang out.
Rates include breakfast and there's a kitchen for guests' use.
Dorms €40, doubles €125

Beautiful City Hostel 12 rue de l'Atlas, 19ᵉ ☎ 01 44 52
80 65, ⓦ beautifulcity.fr; ⓜ Belleville; map p.207. There
are around thirty bright, clean rooms (all en suite) in this
colourful, relatively quiet Belleville hostel, with clean three-
to six-bed mixed dorms as well as single, twin and double
rooms. Rates include breakfast, and there's a simple kitchen
with microwave for guests' use. Dorms €40, doubles €108

Generator Hostel 9–11 place du Colonel Fabien, 10ᵉ
☎ 01 70 98 84 00, ⓦ generatorhostels.com; ⓜ Colonel
Fabien; map p.198. Well-run and friendly party hostel
with spotless dorms (eight- to ten-bed; one women-only
dorm), some with private bathrooms. As to be expected
from the Europe-wide Generator group, facilities are
generally very good, with a handy café, a rooftop bar and a
cellar club. There are private doubles and quads (€190),
some with en-suite showers. Dorms €39, doubles €140

Oops 50 av des Gobelins, 13ᵉ ☎ 01 47 07 47 00, ⓦ oops-
paris.com; ⓜ Les Gobelins; map p.176. This early "design

hostel", opened in 2007, is decorated in bright colours and
funky patterns. They have two- and four-bed dorms, all en
suite, plus en-suite doubles, and a guest kitchen. Breakfast
included. Cash only (although reservations can be made by
card). Dorms €43, doubles €116

★**Les Piaules** 59 bd de Belleville, 11ᵉ ☎ 01 43 55 09
97, ⓦ lespiaules.com; ⓜ Belleville; map p.207. Very cool
and laidback hostel with a great bar serving good food –
charcuterie, pâté, quiches and the like – and excellent
coffee, with colourful communal spaces and a rooftop
terrace. The dorms (four- to eight-bed, most with shared
bathrooms) feature excellent bunks with blackout curtains,
reading lights, storage space and power plugs, while the
doubles are as hip as any in the city's new breed of designer
hotels. Dorms €34, doubles €130

★**St Christopher's Canal** 159 rue de Crimée, 19ᵉ
☎ 01 40 34 34 40, ⓦ st-christophers.co.uk/paris-hostels/
canal; ⓜ Crimée/Laumière; map p.200. Massive, slick
hostel in an eye-catching, renovated former boat hangar
overlooking the Bassin de la Villette – a great spot, but some
way from the centre. Four- to twelve-bed dorms (including
some women-only) feature curtained-off pod beds, and
there's a lively bar, inexpensive restaurant, waterfront terrace,
book exchange and dozens of activities on offer; prices
fluctuate daily, but always include breakfast. There's another
good *St Christopher's* hostel near Gare du Nord. Some en-suite
doubles (€157), too. Dorms €38, doubles €137

Smart Place 28 Rue de Dunkerque, 10ᵉ ☎ 01 48 78 25
15, ⓦ smartplaceparis.com; ⓜ Gare du Nord; map
p.192. This homely hostel, conveniently located near the
Gare du Nord, offers clean, comfy dorms (three- to six- and
ten-bed, with one female-only four-bedder), all with
private bathrooms, plus twins (€95) and doubles. There's a
guest kitchen and a small bar, but it's definitely not a party
hostel. Dorms €30, doubles €90

Le Village Hostel 20 rue d'Orsel, 18ᵉ ☎ 01 42 64 22 02,
ⓦ villagehostel.fr; ⓜ Anvers; map p.183. Reliable,
friendly hostel in an attractively renovated nineteenth-
century building with a view of Sacré-Coeur from the
terrace. All dorms (some female only) and rooms (with
phones) are en suite. There's a bar and a guest kitchen.
Dorms €30, doubles €77

CAMPING

There's just one **campsite** anywhere near the centre of Paris; the others are way out of town. For a full list, contact the
tourist office (see p.40). The prices listed below are based on two people sharing.

Camping Indigo Paris Bois de Boulogne 2 Allée du
Bord-de-l'Eau, 16ᵉ ☎ 01 45 24 30 00, ⓦ campingparis
.fr; ⓜ Porte Maillot then bus #244 to "Moulins
Camping"; the bus doesn't run in the evening, but a
shuttle bus is laid on in summer; map p.217. The most
central campsite, next to the Seine in the Bois de
Boulogne, with hundreds of pitches, spaces for

campervans (€63), glamping tents (€114), *roulottes*
(shepherd-hut style trailers; €160) and "cottages"
(chalets, effectively; €172); it's usually booked out in
summer. The ground is pebbly, but the site is well
equipped, with a café and food truck, a playground and a
communal living room with outdoor terrace; wi-fi is
available near reception. Camping €45

Eating

The French seldom separate the major pleasures of eating and drinking, and there are thousands of establishments in Paris where you can do both or either, as you wish. A restaurant may call itself a brasserie, *bistrot*, café or indeed restaurant; equally, a café can be a place to eat, drink, listen to music, dance or even watch theatre. To simplify matters, we've split our listings for each geographical area into two parts: under Cafés and wine bars, you'll find venues we recommend primarily for relaxed eating, with perhaps a snack, a sharing plate or light meal and drinks; under Restaurants, you'll find any establishment that focuses on serving full meals. Most cafés and wine bars remain open until fairly late and are perfect for a beer, glass of wine or *digestif*; if you're looking for cocktails, pints or full-on nightlife, however, you'll need to head for the city's bars and clubs (see p.296).

Though many cafés are contemporary affairs – the kinds of cosmopolitan places you find in cities all over the world – happily the traditional Paris **café**, with zinc bar, tobacco-stained ceiling and globe lighting, still exists. Indeed, this type of place is a mainstay of Parisian society, where people come to gossip and discuss, pose and people-watch, or simply read a newspaper or a book. In addition to drinks, most cafés also serve **food**, from the simple pastries, *tartines* (open sandwiches) and toasted sandwiches often available in more basic places, to the dishes and full meals served in the larger cafés and **café-brasseries** – usually salads, *plats du jour* (daily specials), and perhaps a simple, limited- or no-choice two- or three-course *formule* menu. If you've a nostalgic hankering for the **café society** of old, head for boulevards Montparnasse and St-Germain, on the Left Bank, where the famed *Select, Coupole, Closerie des Lilas, Deux Magots* and *Café de Flore* – erstwhile hangouts of Apollinaire, Picasso, Hemingway, Sartre, de Beauvoir et al – still have a place in the hearts of many Parisians (and probably even more tourists). Although they're pricier than other places, it's hard not to be seduced by their historic charm.

Alongside cafés, we've listed **wine bars** or *bistrots à vin*. The most traditional of these offer simple platters of cheeses, charcuterie and regional dishes to go with their fine – but generally inexpensive – wines, while a more recent wave of places focuses on organic or natural wines and creative food that is among the best in the city, usually served in sharing plate style. Also included in this category you'll find **salons de thé** (tearooms), typically serving tea, pastries and light meals, and the best of the city's artisan **coffee houses**, which have brought relief to the many visitors who have traditionally been shocked to find that those wonderful Parisian brasseries don't, as a rule, serve good coffee. Populated with the kind of hipster crowd you'd find in Shoreditch, Melbourne or Brooklyn, these coffee pit stops don't feel terribly Parisian, but if you're craving an expertly sourced and lovingly made brew they're useful to know about.

Many visitors come to Paris with a big appetite and high expectations. This is, after all, the city that invented the **restaurant**, and indeed fine dining. Certainly, Paris can still boast an abundance of Michelin-starred venues that cater for those in search of *haute gastronomie* and classic French cuisine, but the city is also responding to a change in trends. The so-called **bistronomy** movement, spearheaded in the 1990s by chefs such as Yves Camdeborde of *La Régalade* (see p.288), rejected the astronomical prices, stuffy atmosphere and overfussy food of Michelin-starred cooking in favour of more experimental haute cuisine, focusing on zingy, fresh flavours (and even, shockingly, giving a starring role to vegetables), served in (relatively) casual settings. A new generation of committed restaurateurs and passionate chefs swiftly jumped on board, and today many of Paris's most talked about restaurants are the so-called **neo-bistros** where the focus is very much on the food, not on finer points of service or on ostentatious decor. These offer some of the most exciting cooking in town and are generally more affordable than the Old Guard places – that said, though you can keep costs down by picking your way through a menu of sharing plates, prices are rising as the scene gets more and more creative. New-generation **chefs** to watch for include self-trained Basque maverick Inaki Aizpitarte of *Le Châteaubriand* (see p.293) and *Dauphin* (see p.292); American Daniel Rose, who updates French classics at *Spring* (see p.277), *La Bourse et la Vie* (see p.274) and *Chez la Vieille*; Sven Chartier, who creates

---

WAITERS, THE BILL AND TIPPING

Waiters in Paris are considered to be professionals, and are paid as such, so **tipping** is a matter of leaving a few coins, perhaps €3 or so, depending on the service. Many speak English and are eager to practise and/or show off, so try not to be offended if they shrug off your attempts in French. And never call a waiter *garçon*, whatever you were taught in school – *Monsieur, Madame/Mademoiselle* or *s'il vous plaît* or *excusez-moi* are. To ask for **the bill**, the phrase is *l'addition, s'il vous plaît*.

dishes of exquisite simplicity at *Saturne* (see p.276) and *Clown Bar* (see p.294); Katsuaki Okiyama, one of a number of Japanese chefs taking the city by storm at his hole in the wall *Abri* (see p.290), and "Frenchie" Grégory Marchand, colonizing a street in the 2ᵉ with his New York/London/Paris fusion (see p.275).

Meanwhile, the cuisine at the **average Parisian restaurant** or simpler, more **local bistrot** can be surprisingly, and not unappealingly, conservative. Here you'll find *cuisine bourgeoise*, not *gastronomique* – homely meats in sauces, for the most part, with a fine chocolate mousse or perfect apple tart for dessert. Being comfortingly *correcte* is often judged as more important than gourmet flair in these places; some old-time brasseries and historic restaurants have become Parisian **institutions** whose owners and chefs rarely dare to meddle with a decor – or indeed a style of cooking – that has been enjoyed by locals and visitors for generations.

ESSENTIALS

Prices Prices will usually vary for consuming at the bar (*au comptoir*; the cheapest option), sitting down (*la salle*), or on the terrace (*la terrasse*; generally most expensive). Addresses in the smarter or more touristy arrondissements set costs soaring and you'll generally pay more on main squares and boulevards than on backstreets. At almost all cafés and bars, you're presented with a bill along with your drinks, which you settle when you leave. At most decent restaurants you may spend as much as €45 or more on a three-course meal, though the set *menus* (see below) cut costs. House wines are usually inexpensive, but a bottle of something interesting will generally add at least €25 to the bill, and potentially much more for a good bottle in a smart place. A fifteen percent service charge is legally included in your bill at all restaurants, bars and cafés, but you may want to leave an optional tip (see box, p.267).

Fixed-price menus The cheapest way to go is to opt for a fixed-price menu (simply called *le menu* in French, or often *formule* at lunchtime – the French word for "menu" in the English sense is *la carte*), though the choice is accordingly limited. Eating *à la carte* gives you access to everything on offer, though you'll pay a fair bit more; if you just want a main course it's worth looking out for the *plat du jour* (chef's daily special), which tends to be good value. Lunchtime *menus* are typically priced at less than €25 even at quite classy restaurants, and as little as €15 for two courses at good inexpensive places. Fine dining restaurants,

too, typically offer a lunch *menu* for roughly half the price of the full evening experience, while the *menu dégustation* – a "tasting" menu – will be expensive but well worth trying for a splurge.

Opening hours Late-night eating is not common in Parisian restaurants – generally the latest time at which you can walk in and order is about 9.30 or 10pm. Brasseries serve speedier meals, and at most hours of the day, often till midnight or 1am. Note that some restaurants may close for some of – or even all of – August, especially the smaller, family-run places. If you have an establishment in mind to visit during that month and haven't booked, it's always worth calling in advance to check they're open.

Reservations For the more upmarket or fashionable places, and at weekends, it's wise to reserve. Generally you will only need to do this a day or so in advance, but the most renowned places may require booking up to several weeks (or in some cases, months) before you wish to dine.

FOOD AND DRINK

Vegetarians and vegans Traditionally, Paris's gastronomic reputation was largely lost on vegetarians, who had to subsist on salads, omelettes and cheese. Nowadays, however, even the most traditional places will often offer at least one or two non-meaty dishes, while a new breed of gourmet restaurants is turning its attention to the fresh flavours and possibilities of vegetables – Michelin-starred *Arpège* (see p.285) is heaven on earth for veggie diners with cash to splash. There are a number of exclusively veggie restaurants (see p.285), along with *salons de thé* offering lighter dishes such as soups and quiches or flans (*tartes*); neo-bistros and hipper restaurants, and most places serving world cuisine, are also a good bet. If you're not sure, try *Je suis végétarien(ne)* ("I'm a vegetarian") and *Il y a quelques plats sans viande?* ("Are there any non-meat dishes?"). The picture isn't too bad for vegans, either, with a few exclusively vegan places popping up in some of the cooler neighbourhoods, with a particular concentration in the Marais. "I'm a vegan" translates as *Je suis végétalien(ne)*.

Coffee and tea Historically, coffee in Paris has been hit and miss – sometimes good; often bland or burned. We've reviewed a few of the best of the city's newer generation of coffee houses, often helmed by expats hankering after the quality of brews they were used to at home, and listing flat whites and long blacks on their menus. In the traditional French cafés *un café* or *un express* is an espresso, *une noisette* an espresso with a dash of milk (similar to a macchiato), *un café au lait* an espresso with hot milk, and *un crème* a traditional French filter coffee with hot milk (you can get either a *grand crème* or a smaller, *petit crème*) – for a black coffee, simply ask for an Americano. *Un déca* (decaffeinated coffee) and *chocolat chaud* (hot chocolate) are widely available. Drinkers of tea (*thé*) may have to settle for Lipton's teabags, served black; for a good, proper cuppa you'll need to head to the *salons à thé*. You can have a slice of lemon (*citron*) with it, or ask for milk, "*un peu de lait frais*". *Tisanes* or *infusions* are the generic terms for herbal teas. Common varieties include *verveine* (verbena), *tilleul* (lime blossom), *menthe* (mint) and *camomille*.

Soft drinks At cafés, bottled fruit juices and soft drinks are expensive. Better value, and far more French, is a freshly squeezed *citron pressé*: lemon juice served in the bottom of a long, ice-filled glass, with a jug of water and a sugar bowl. Even more French are the various *sirops*, diluted with water to make cool, eye-catching drinks with traffic-light colours, such as *menthe* (peppermint) and *grenadine* (pomegranate). Bottles of mineral water (*eau minérale*) are widely drunk:

ask for *eau gazeuse* for sparkling, *eau plate* (pronounced "platt") for still. In most places, tap water will be brought free to your table if you ask for *une carafe d'eau du robinet*.

Wine Still the thing to drink in Paris, wine is certainly a lot cheaper than the alternatives. The current vogue is for *vins du pays* (country wines), with a blossoming interest in natural and organic (*bio*) wines – but you'll find the top-quality AOC (Appellation d'Origine Contrôlée) bottles on most menus. The annual release of the new red wine from the Beaujolais on November 15 is a much-heralded event – "*le Beaujolais Nouveau est arrivé*". A glass of house wine may also be included as part of a set-price meal – and on the most expensive tasting menus you may get different wines matched with each course. In less expensive restaurants you can usually get a fairly good house wine by the *pichet* (carafe) – ask for *un quart* or *un demi*, a quarter- or half-litre.

Beers While Belgian, German and Alsatian lagers are still in the majority, young Parisians are increasingly taking to craft brews, which are often to be found in the cooler bars (check ⓦ hoppyparis.com for a good rundown of the scene). Most locals simply order *une pression*, or a glass of draught beer, but to be precise you could ask for *un demi* (25cl).

Apéritifs, brandies and liqueurs A *kir*, a white wine with a dash of *cassis* (blackcurrant liqueur), is a popular *apéritif*, sometimes with champagne instead of white wine – *un kir royal*. Another characteristically French *apéritif* is the aniseed-flavoured *pastis* – Pernod and Ricard are the most common

GOURMET RESTAURANTS

While bistronomy and wine bar eating has shaken up the city's dining scene, the gourmet chefs continue to pull in diners eager to splash out on a quintessentially Parisian haute cuisine experience. Perhaps best known is **Alain Ducasse**, who swept through the world of French gastronomy in the early 1990s to become the chef with the most Michelin stars in the world; his headline restaurants include the two-starred *Le Meurice* (see p.274); *Le Jules Verne* (see p.286), halfway up the Eiffel Tower; and another at the *Plaza-Athénée* hotel, where the brave decision – brave in the world of traditional haute cuisine, that is – to focus on contemporary dishes using fish and organic veg won him three Michelin stars. Other gourmet chefs who currently hold three Michelin stars include **Pascal Barbot** at *L'Astrance* (see p.285), known for his bold and innovative cuisine; **Alain Passard**, whose remarkable *L'Arpège* (see p.285) eschews most meat in favour of fish and vegetable dishes; **Pierre Gagnaire**, who has extended his molecular cuisine beyond his titular flagship (see p.272) into a number of restaurants around the world; **Guy Savoy** (see p.141), mentor to Gordon Ramsay; **Yannick Alléno** at the *Pavillon Ledoyen*; and Breton **Christian Le Squer** at *Le Cinq*. In addition, it's worth checking out **Jean-François Piège**'s innovative creations at *Le Grand Restaurant* (see p.290); **Hélène Darroze** (see p.284), who also has a Michelin-starred restaurant in London; and **Adeline Grattard**, who combines French and Chinese cuisine at *yam'Tcha* (see p.277).

In the evening, prices at such places can average about €200, and there's no limit on the amount you can pay for top wines. To **cut costs**, book for a weekday lunch *menu* – it will still be pricey, but at least puts the food within reach of many. In addition, some of the star chefs have made their fine cuisine more accessible by opening less expensive, more **informal**, but still high-quality establishments. Alain Ducasse, for example, also runs *Allard* (see p.284) and *Aux Lyonnais* (see p.275); Hélène Darroze has her tapas-style *Salon d'Hélène* (see p.284); Jean-François Piège runs a *bistrot*, *Clover*, in the 6e; and Guy Savoy has his rôtisserie, *L'Atelier Maître Albert* (see p.282).

20

LE SNACKING, TAKEAWAYS AND PICNICS

Paris is the perfect place for a picnic, and the city has plenty of places to sate "le snacking" demand. Even the simplest **boulangeries** (see p.335) are a good source of traditional takeaway food – most sell savoury quiches and tarts as well as breads and cakes – while you can compose a seriously gourmet picnic from the city's swankier food shops and delis (see p.337). Although specializing in cooked meats like hams and pâtés, most **charcuteries** also stock a range of dressed salads and side dishes. You buy by weight, by the slice (*tranche*) or by the carton (*barquette*).

For **takeaway** hot food, many **crêperie stands** sell *galettes* (savoury buckwheat pancakes) and *gaufres* (waffles) as well as sweet crêpes, while Middle Eastern **falafel** with salad is a great bet in the Jewish quarter of the Marais. Also worth checking out are the ubiquitous Chinese *traiteurs* and Turkish or North African **kebab shops**, the latter also serving couscous, which you can choose to have with *merguez* (spicy sausage), chicken or lamb, or *royale* – with all three.

TOP 5 TAKEAWAYS

Falafels at **L'As du Fallafel** See p.278
Bao buns at **yam'Tcha** See p.277
Deli salads at **Chezaline** See p.280
Foie gras baguettes at **Le Comptoir de la Gastronomie** See p.337
Lobster rolls at **Frenchie to Go** See p.274

brands – which turns cloudy when diluted with water and ice cubes (*glaçons*). As for the harder stuff, there are dozens of *eaux de vie* (brandies distilled from fruit) and liqueurs, in addition to the classic Cognacs or Armagnacs. Measures are generous, but they don't come cheap; the same applies for imported spirits like whisky, usually referred to as *scotch*.

THE ISLANDS

CAFÉS AND WINE BARS

Berthillon 31 rue St-Louis-en-l'Ile, Ile St-Louis, 4ᵉ ☎01 43 54 31 61, ⓦberthillon.fr; ⓜPont Marie; map p.44. *Berthillon* serves some of the best ice cream and sorbets in Paris, in seventy tempting flavours – salted butter caramel ice cream and wild strawberry sorbet are just two of the highlights (€2.50 to take away; €4.50 in the pretty attached *salon de thé*). If there's a queue and you can't face the wait, you could always check out the ice creams at newly opened *Senoble* (daily noon–midnight) just down the road at no. 69. Wed–Sun 10am–8pm; closed Aug.

★**Café Saint-Régis** 6 rue Jean du Bellay, Ile St-Louis, 4ᵉ ☎01 43 54 59 41, ⓦcafesaintregisparis .com; ⓜPont Marie; map p.44. A characterful café-restaurant, nicely designed to pay homage to traditional old bistros – all gleaming white ceramic tiles, mirrored walls, dark wood, zinc bar and leather banquettes, with bustling waiters and a neighbourhood vibe. They serve a simple but tasty selection of French and American snacks and dishes all day – try a breakfast of Poîlane toast, butter and coffee, or a Sunday brunch, or drop by for the good-value happy hour (7–9pm), when it gets particularly lively. Daily 7am–2am.

Taverne Henri IV 13 place du Pont-Neuf, Ile de la Cité, 1ᵉʳ ☎01 43 54 27 90; ⓜPont-Neuf; map p.44. With a comfortable, old-fashioned atmosphere, this traditional wine bar is at its buzziest at lunchtime, when it's full of quaffing lawyers and workers from the nearby Palais de Justice. You can get meat and cheese platters (from around €15), as well as *tartines* (open sandwiches) with a choice of cheeses, hams, pâté and *saucisson*, plus traditional *plats* (around €16) such as *choux farci* (stuffed cabbage) or *coq au vin*. Mon–Sat noon–10.30pm.

RESTAURANT

L'Auberge de la Reine Blanche 30 rue St-Louis-en-l'Ile, 4ᵉ ☎01 46 33 07 87; ⓜPont Marie; map p.44. Located on Ile St-Louis's main street, this long-established little restaurant creates a homely atmosphere with its warm welcome, bistro-style chairs and tables, and copper pans hanging from the wood-beamed ceiling. The cuisine tends towards classics such as soupe à l'oignon, *coq au vin* and *tarte tatin*, as well as more creative dishes – perhaps honey-spiced duck – on the regularly-changing menu. Main courses around €17. Mon, Tues & Thurs–Sun noon–2.30pm & 6.15–10pm.

THE CHAMPS-ELYSEES

CAFÉS AND WINE BARS

Le Café Jacquemart-André 158 bd Haussmann, 8ᵉ ⓦmusee-jacquemart-andre.com;

ⓜSt-Philippe-du-Roule/Miromesnil; map p.64. Within the Musée Jacquemart-André (see p.69) but with independent access, this is among the city's most sumptuously appointed *salons de thé*. Huge tapestries adorn the walls, Louis XV consoles display posh pâtisserie, and ladies with parasols and gents in ruffs look down over a trompe l'oeil balustrade from a wonderful ceiling fresco by Tiepolo. It's best to come for tea and a cake (€11.50) or Sunday brunch (€29.50); the quality of the lunch dishes (around €16) is more uneven. Daily 11.45am–5.30pm.

Le Fouquet's 99 av des Champs-Elysées, 8ᵉ ☎01 40 69 60 50, ⊕lucienbarriere.com; ⊕George V; map p.64. Dating from 1899 and fresh out of a lavish refurb, iconic *Le Fouquet's* (you pronounce the "t") is the favourite venue for celebrations after the annual César film awards and is such a well-established celebs' watering hole that it's been classified a Monument Historique. You can sit out on the *terrasse*, a prime spot for people-watching, or sink into a red velvet banquette in the café-brasserie. Coffee from €8 (€10 on the *terrasse*), mains around €30. Daily 8am–2am.

Wine by One 27 rue de Marignan, 8ᵉ ☎01 45 63 18 98, ⊕winebyone.com; ⊕Franklin-D.-Roosevelt; map p.64. This novel wine bar is a fun way to try out lots of different wines without spending a fortune. The walls are lined with around a hundred different wine bottles in self-service glass cabinets; you pay upfront for a "wine credit card" and then use this in the self-service machines to sample any amount of wine (from a small taste to a full glass) that takes your fancy, with prices ranging from €2 to €8 (happy hour 5–8pm). There's a wide choice, from small producers to the more mainstream, as well as world wines, champagne and sparkling, and you can buy a bottle to take away if you find something you really like. The food is also good and a bargain for the area – €13 for two courses at lunch. A second branch has popped up at 9 rue des Capucines, 1ᵉʳ. Tues–Sat noon–11pm.

RESTAURANTS

Graindorge 15 rue de l'Arc de Triomphe, 17ᵉ ☎01 47 54 00 28, ⊕le-graindorge.fr; ⊕Ternes; map p.64. Tucked away on a side street and frequented largely by locals, the "Barley grain" is a dependable, long-established *bistrot* with a simple 1930s Art Deco interior. The menu features French staples and Belgian specialities, such as *potjevleesch* (a terrine made of four kinds of meat), reflecting the chef's Flemish origins. It's no surprise to find a wide choice of craft Belgian beers on offer, as well as fine French wines. At €36

for the three-course menu, it's hard to find better value in this location. Mon noon–2pm, Tues–Fri noon–2pm & 7–10pm, Sat 7–10pm.

Le Grand Restaurant 7 rue d'Aguesseau, 8ᵉ ☎01 53 05 00 00, ⊕jeanfrancoispiege.com; ⊕Concorde/Madeleine; map p.64. Book a few weeks in advance for one of the 25 covers at much-fêted Jean-Francois Piège's gastronomic restaurant, opened in 2015. Piège is known for his reworkings of classic French dishes, often involving long, slow cooking to concentrate the flavours. Dishes might include *gâteau de foie blond* (chicken livers) with shrimp sauce, lobster cooked in blackcurrant leaves with foie gras, or Challans duck slow-cooked with olives. The creativity in the cuisine is echoed by the striking decor and glass roof, designed by Icelandic-American architect Gulla Jonsdottir. For this level of cuisine the €85 lunch menu is pretty good value; at dinner, menus range from €195 to €560 (the latter including wine pairings). Mon–Fri 12.30–2pm & 7.30–9pm.

La Maison de l'Aubrac 37 rue Marbeuf, 8ᵉ ☎01 43 59 05 14, ⊕maison-aubrac.com; ⊕Franklin-D.-Roosevelt; map p.64. If you're hankering after a really good steak, this all-night establishment is the place. The meat is sourced from the restaurant's own farm in the Auvergne. While the fillet is tender, the flavour in the cheaper, more traditional French cuts such as *onglet* or *bavette* is fuller and richer, and the burger truly is a cut above. Choose from hearty dishes such as *pot-au-feu* or the *trilogie de viande* (*brochette*, steak *tartare* and a small burger). Mains €20–35. Daily 24hr.

Mini Palais Av Winston Churchill, 8ᵉ ☎01 42 56 42 42, ⊕minipalais.com; ⊕Champs-Elysées-Clemenceau; map p.64. The Grand Palais' restaurant lives up to its name with a large, sleek dining room and a stately colonnaded *terrasse* with fabulous views. Triple-Michelin-starred chef Eric Fréchon oversees the seasonal menu, a mix of French classics and international dishes such as tempura prawns or fettuccine with pesto, pine nuts and cockles; you can also just come for a snack (cheese platters €13), or a drink at the bar. Mains €18–40. Daily 10am–2am.

Miss Kô 49–51 av George V, 8ᵉ ☎01 53 67 84 60, ⊕miss-ko.com; ⊕George V; map p.64. This Philippe Starck-designed fusion restaurant evokes a futuristic, pop-art Manga-esque world, with video screens flashing Asian

---

BREAKFAST AND BRUNCH

Given that most hotels typically charge around €7–15 for a pretty ordinary **breakfast**, heading out to a café or a brasserie is usually a far cheaper, and more satisfying, way to start your day. Even if they don't offer formal **petit déjeuner** as such, most cafés advertise **snacks** or *casse-croûtes* (quick bites), and **brasseries** serve coffee, *tartines* (baguettes and butter) and croissants. Meanwhile, **le brunch** has become a Sunday institution in gentrified and *bobo* (bourgeois-bohemian) areas such as the Marais, Bastille, Montmartre and eastern Paris; most places serve it from around noon to 4 or 5pm.

0

TOP 5 HISTORIC CAFÉS

Angélina See below
Café de Flore See p.283
Café de la Paix See p.274
Ladurée See p.274
Le Select See p.286

TV channels up at you under a glass counter and neon lights recalling a Korean or Japanese food street. While the extensive Asian-French menu can be hit and miss (foie gras lollipops, anyone?), it's reasonably priced for the area – and notwithstanding the rock'n'roll vibe, kids love the place, so during the day it's a good family-friendly option. Mains, such as salmon burgers and Vietnamese bo bun, are €19.50–37, while sizeable sushi platters can cost as little as €12.50, plus there's a great choice of inventive cocktails. Daily noon–2am.

Pierre Gagnaire Hôtel Balzac, 6 rue Balzac, 8ᵉ ☎ 01 58 36 12 50, ⓦ pierre-gagnaire.com; Ⓜ George V; map p.64. Eating at the highly acclaimed, three-Michelin-starred *Pierre Gagnaire* is a gastronomic adventure. The seven-course *menu dégustation* (€310) of modern French food might feature such dishes as oyster with cuttlefish, sailor clams and mussels in Kientzheim butter with crunchy fennel and black garlic (and that's just one course); the

desserts are amazing. *A la carte* will set you back around €360 at dinner, €155 at lunch, with wine extra. Closed two weeks in Aug. Mon–Fri noon–1.30pm & 7.30–9.30pm.

Le Relais de l'Entrecôte 15 rue Marbeuf, 8ᵉ ☎ 01 49 52 07 17, ⓦ relaisentrecote.fr; Ⓜ Franklin-D.-Roosevelt; map p.64. The only dish served at this old-fashioned restaurant is *steak frites*, with a delicious, secret-recipe sauce. The set price of €26.50 includes a salad starter – and seconds; desserts, from a long list, including profiteroles and *crème brûlée*, are around €6–9 extra. No reservations, so you may have to queue, or arrive early – it's popular. There are two more branches: one in St-Germain and another near the Jardin du Luxembourg. Daily noon–2.30pm & 7–11.30pm.

Taillevent 15 rue Lamennais, 8ᵉ ☎ 01 44 95 15 01, ⓦ taillevent.com; Ⓜ George V; map p.64. Alain Solivérès' Provençal-influenced cuisine places the emphasis on the classic rather than the experimental; sample dishes on the rarely changing menu include steamed sea bass with leek, champagne and caviar sauce, and spiced roast duckling with verbena-scented fruit and vegetables. The decor is soothing and unobtrusive, and waiters are supremely charming. Eating *à la carte*, count on around €200; the tasting menus cost €198–275, and there's a set lunch for €88. Wine from around €30 a bottle up to €2000. Closed Aug. Mon–Fri 12.30–2pm & 7.30–11pm.

LES TUILERIES

CAFÉS AND WINE BARS

Angélina 226 rue de Rivoli, 1ᵉʳ ☎ 01 42 60 82 00, ⓦ angelina-paris.fr; Ⓜ Tuileries; map p.76. This fabulously grand pâtisserie/*salon de thé*, dating from 1903 and still boasting its murals, gilded stuccowork and leather armchairs, does the best hot chocolate in town – one generous jugful with whipped cream on the side is enough for two (€8.20). The other speciality is the Mont Blanc, a chestnut cream, meringue and whipped cream dessert (€9.30). You could also treat yourself to breakfast (*à la carte*, or *menus* €20–29.50) or brunch (€39.50). There are further branches in town, but this is the original and best. You may have to queue, but you don't usually have to wait long (or you can make an online booking for lunch). Mon–Thurs 7.30am–7pm, Fri 7.30am–7.30pm, Sat & Sun 8.30am–7.30pm.

Maison Maison 16 quai du Louvre, 1ᵉʳ Ⓜ bit.ly/maisonm; Ⓜ Pont Neuf/Louvre-Rivoli; map p.64. Located on the Right Bank of the Parc Rives de Seine, this outdoor restaurant is the perfect place to sip a glass of rosé or craft beer in a deckchair while watching the sun set over the river. The food is really good too: a daily changing menu of charcuterie, cheeses and more substantial dishes. There's even a stand where you can get a takeaway beer for strolling along the *quai*. Check the website above for opening times, but generally daily noon–11.45pm.

RESTAURANTS

L'Ardoise 28 rue du Mont Thabor, 1ᵉʳ ☎ 01 42 96 28 18, ⓦ lardoise-paris.com; Ⓜ Tuileries; map p.76. A neo-bistro with a friendly atmosphere (the chef frequently pops out of the kitchen to greet diners) and a fresh take on the classics: think crab cakes with avocado purée or grilled lamb with celeriac *mousseline* and herb salad. With a three-course *menu* at €38, this is a good-value, reliable choice. Mon–Sat noon–2.30pm & 6.30–11pm, Sun 6.30–11pm.

Loulou Musée des Arts Décoratifs, 107 rue de Rivoli, 1ᵉʳ ☎ 01 42 60 41 96, ⓦ loulou-paris.com; Ⓜ Tuileries/Concorde; map p.50. The Musée des Arts Décoratifs' smart new restaurant, opened in 2016, enjoys a splendid setting, overlooking the Tuileries gardens and the Louvre; in warmer weather you can sit out on the lovely *terrasse* and soak up the views. The elegant interior is attractive too, with its stylish black-and-white "tulip" chairs, marble floor and wicker panelling. On the menu you'll find a mix of French and Italian food, such as pasta and pistachio sauce, truffle pizza and peppered steak; the desserts, such as tiramisu and pavlova, in particular, stand out. Mains cost €25–35, three-course menu €35. It's open all day, so you can also come just for a snack in the afternoon, an *apéritif*, or a late-night drink at the bar. Mon–Fri noon–11pm, Sat & Sun noon–2am.

> **TOP 5 SALONS DE THÉ**
> **Le Barbouquin** See p.294
> **Le Café Jacquemart-André** See p.270
> **La Fourmi Ailée** See p.282
> **Halle St-Pierre** See p.289
> **L'Heure Gourmande** See p.283

20

Le Meurice Hôtel Meurice, 228 rue de Rivoli, 1er ☏ 01 44 58 10 55, ⓦ lemeurice.com; ⓜ Tuileries/Concorde; map p.76. This sumptuous historic restaurant, decorated in Louis XVI style with a few flashes of modern flair from Philippe Starck, is one of the most beautiful dining rooms in Paris. It is also highly sought-after, with two Michelin stars and Alain Ducasse at the helm presenting flawless contemporary French cuisine using seasonal, organic ingredients. The menu might not give away much, offering the likes of "vegetables and fruits"; "sea bream, beetroots, caviar"; "farm hen, black truffle"; even "hazelnuts, chestnuts" – but you can trust that whatever you choose will be exquisite. Lunch *menus* €85–130, *menu dégustation* €380, Sunday brunch €120. Mon–Fri 12.30–2.30pm & 7.30–10pm, Sun noon–2pm.

GRANDS BOULEVARDS

CAFÉS AND WINE BARS

Café de la Paix 5 place de l'Opéra, 9e ☏ 01 40 07 36 36, ⓦ cafedelapaix.fr; ⓜ Opéra; map p.76. The last survivor of the great nineteenth-century cafés that once lined the Grands Boulevards, this counts Zola, Maupassant, Tchaikovsky and Oscar Wilde among its former habitués. You pay a premium to sit in the sumptuously gilded, frescoed dining room, but you can just opt for a table in the adjoining brasserie area which does more affordable light meals, such as croque monsieur (€20) and a fine *soupe à l'oignon* (€21), or in nice weather take an *apéritif* on the *terrasse* with its prime views of the Opéra Garnier – either way, it's a place for a special, quintessentially Parisian treat. Drinks start from €6 for an espresso, €8 for a glass of wine. Daily 7am–midnight.

Ladurée 16 rue Royale, 8e ☏ 01 42 60 21 79, ⓦ laduree.com; ⓜ Madeleine/Concorde; map p.76. This beautiful tearoom's melt-in-your-mouth *macarons* are legendary, but the light-as-air meringues and *millefeuilles* are just as good. When you're done with the pâtisserie, sit back and enjoy the luxurious interior of gilt-edged mirrors and ceiling frescoes. Tea and two *macarons* will set you back around €16. There are other, equally grand branches throughout Paris. Mon–Sat 8am–8pm, Sun 9am–7pm.

Legrand Filles et Fils 7–11 Galerie Vivienne, 2e ☏ 01 42 60 07 12, ⓦ caves-legrand.com; ⓜ Bourse; map p.76. Attached to the classy wine and food emporium of the same name and with tables spilling out into the lovely Galerie Vivienne, *Legrand* attracts a sober-suited, mature crowd with its reserved atmosphere and impressive selection of wines by the glass. Excellent cheese and charcuterie platters and other light bites (from around €19) available too. Mon 11am–7pm, Tues–Sat 10am–7.30pm.

RESTAURANT

Drouant 16–18 place Gaillon, 2e ☏ 01 42 65 15 16, ⓦ drouant.com; ⓜ Opéra; map p.76. Run by famed chef Antoine Westermann, *Drouant* has historic clout (it has been the headquarters of the Goncourt and Renaudot literary prizes since 1914) but offers an updated take on bourgeois cuisine. There's a good choice of seafood dishes, as well as some appetizing vegetarian choices (eg fricassée of seasonal vegetables in pistou sauce with aubergine caviar); and if you can't decide which starters or desserts to have (or you feel like sharing), you can opt for four different ones in bite-size portions. In the warmer months, try and bag a table on the terrace giving onto the pretty place Gaillon. Starters €28, mains plus sides from €33, weekday lunch *menu* €45. Daily noon–2.30pm & 7pm–midnight.

PASSAGES AND PALAIS-ROYAL

CAFÉS AND WINE BARS

Floquifil 17 rue de Montyon, 9e ☏ 01 42 46 11 19; ⓜ Grands Boulevards; map p.76. There are no affectations in this good-looking, relaxed neighbourhood *bistrot à vins* – just excellent wines and country food with the odd contemporary twist. It's easy to linger a while, and difficult not to be charmed. Mains €15–25, lunchtime *plat* plus glass of wine and coffee €16. Mon–Fri 11am–midnight, Sat 6pm–midnight.

Frenchie Bar à Vins/Frenchie to Go 6 rue du Nil, 2e ☏ 01 40 39 96 19, ⓦ frenchie-restaurant.com/home-bar-fr; Frenchie to Go 9 rue du Nil, 2e ☏ 01 40 26 23 43, ⓦ frenchietogo.com; ⓜ Sentier; map p.76. Join the crowds of anglophone foodies enjoying interesting wines and snacking on sharing platters at Grégory Marchand's wine bar annexe – it's best to arrive early (or much later on, as the locals do). During the day you can pick up lobster rolls (€22) and fish and chips (€14) at *Frenchie To Go*, the tiny coffee-shop-cum-deli a few doors down, which also offers a brunchy breakfast – granola (€6), bacon sandwiches on English muffins (€7.50), eggs Benedict (€12) and the like. Frenchie Bar à Vins daily 6.30–11pm; Frenchie To Go Mon–Fri 8.30am–4.30pm, Sat & Sun 9.30am–5.30pm.

Le Nemours 2 place Colette, 1er ☏ 01 42 61 34 14, ⓦ lenemours.paris; ⓜ Palais Royal Musée du Louvre;

map p.76. Popular with actors from the Comédie Française on the other side of the square, this elegant café makes an ideal stop for a light lunch of croque monsieur (€10) or quiche lorraine (€14) after a visit to the Louvre. It's also perfect for a tranquil morning coffee or an evening glass of wine accompanied by a plate of rillettes or pâté de campagne. The interior recently had a makeover, but it's the heated colonnaded terrace that's most coveted, a prime spot for people-watching. Mon–Fri 7am–midnight, Sat 8am–midnight, Sun 8am–9pm.

Racines 8 passage des Panoramas, 2ᵉ ☎ 01 40 13 06 41, ⓦ racinesparis.com; ⓜ Grands Boulevards/Bourse; map p.76. This pretty old *passage* (see p.82) has become quite the foodie hotspot – *Le Coinstot Vino* is another good option along here, but *Racines* has the edge: a cosy, neighbourhood, elbow-to-elbow *bistrot à vins* in a lovely old tile-floored wine shop. The short daily-changing menu offers a simple selection of home-cooked food – the likes of scallops, razor clams, charcuterie, pigeon, and always an excellent cheese platter – which they will pair with natural wines from the store. The desserts are delicious – go for the Mont Blanc if it's on offer. Starters €11–16, mains from €25. There's a second branch (*Racines 2*) at 39 rue de l'Arbre Sec in the 1ᵉʳ. Mon–Fri noon–2.30pm & 7.30–10.30pm.

Verlet 256 rue St-Honoré, 1ᵉʳ ☎ 01 42 60 67 39, ⓦ cafesverlet.com; ⓜ Palais Royal Musée du Louvre; map p.76. The intoxicating aroma of more than thirty types of coffee from all over the world greets you inside this long-established coffee merchant's and café, with its wood furnishings, leather benches and caddy-lined wall. If you're having trouble deciding, opt for one of the rich and smoky house blends; there's a good selection of teas and snacks – including quiches – too. Mon–Sat 9.30am–6.30pm.

RESTAURANTS

Aux Lyonnais 32 rue St-Marc, 2ᵉ ☎ 01 58 00 22 06, ⓦ auxlyonnais.com; ⓜ Bourse/Richelieu-Drouot; map p.76. This gorgeous old *bistrot*, with its *belle époque* tiles, globe lights and mirrored walls, preserves a lovely old-fashioned ambience and serves classic Lyonnais cuisine under the direction of haute cuisine chef Alain Ducasse. Specialities include *quenelles* (delicate fish dumplings), the house black pudding and the delicious Fin Gras du Mézenc beef, a rare find in Paris. Three-course lunch/dinner *menus* €34/€35. Tues–Fri noon–2pm & 7.30–10pm, Sat 7–10pm.

★ **Bistrot des Victoires** 6 rue de la Vrillière, 1ᵉʳ ☎ 01 42 61 43 78; ⓜ Bourse; map p.76. Just behind the chic place des Victoires, but very reasonably priced for the area, this charming, old-fashioned *bistrot* with zinc bar, mustard-coloured walls, globe lamps and velvet banquettes serves good standbys such as *confit de canard* and *poulet rôti* for around €11, as well as huge salads and *tartines* (€9) – try the *savoyarde* (with bacon, potatoes and Emmental). Daily 9am–11pm.

La Bourse et la Vie 12 rue Vivienne, 2ᵉ ☎ 01 42 60 08 83, ⓦ labourselavie.com; ⓜ Bourse; map p.76. Celebrated chef Daniel Rose, best known for his restaurant *Spring* (see p.277), also runs this upmarket *bistrot* specializing in refined traditional cuisine. His hearty *pot-au-feu* and *steak-frites* are regularly proclaimed by food critics to be the best in Paris. Starters might include artichoke hearts with foie gras, and for dessert you might opt for a satisfyingly creamy chocolate mousse or crème caramel. Count on around €55 a head, without drinks. Winning similarly rave reviews is Rose's recently opened *Chez la Vieille*, a revamped old *bistrot* in the Les Halles quarter (ⓦ chezlavieille.com). Mon–Fri 12.30–2pm & 7–9.30pm.

L'Epi d'Or 25 rue Jean-Jacques Rousseau, 1ᵉʳ ☎ 01 42 36 38 12, ⓦ faget-benard.com/jojo/epidor; ⓜ Louvre-Rivoli; map p.76. Christian Louboutin is a fan of this perfect locals' *bistrot* that dishes up comforting, homely standards – from lentils with bacon or *escargots* to steaks and *tarte tatin*, not to mention the seven-hours'-cooked lamb – in an Art Deco dining room. Mains around €25. Mon–Fri noon–2pm & 8–11pm, Sat 8–11pm.

Frenchie 5 rue du Nil, 2ᵉ ☎ 01 40 39 96 19, ⓦ frenchie-restaurant.com; ⓜ Sentier; map p.76. When Grégory Marchand, who worked in New York and with Jamie Oliver at *Fifteen* in London (where he was known, predictably, as "Frenchie"), set up his tiny, simple eponymous restaurant, it quickly became the talk of the town. Using only the freshest ingredients, the menu features French classics with a twist, such as roasted lamb with chickpeas, zaatar and harissa (lunch menu €45, dinner €74). The cheese plates, incongruously, focus on British cheeses from Neal's Yard Dairy. If you can't get a reservation (call well in advance) try and bag a table at his *Bar à Vins* (see opposite) opposite, which doesn't take reservations. Mon–Wed 6.30–10.30pm, Thurs & Fri noon–2pm & 6.30–10.30pm.

Gallopin 40 rue Notre-Dame des Victoires, 2ᵉ ☎ 01 42 36 45 38, ⓦ gallopin.com; ⓜ Bourse; map p.76. Endearing nineteenth-century brasserie, with all its original brass and mahogany fittings and beautiful painted glass. It's a popular, and not expensive, choice for classic French dishes including *escargots*, beef *tartare* and especially the foie gras *maison*, all of which are well above par. Weekday lunch *formule* €22, lunch and evening *menu* €29. Daily noon–3pm & 7–11.30pm.

Higuma 32bis rue Ste-Anne, 1ᵉʳ ☎ 01 47 03 38 59, ⓦ higuma.fr; ⓜ Pyramides; map p.76. One of the best of the many basic Japanese canteens along and near this street, *Higuma* serves cheap and filling staples such as pork *katsu* curry and *gyozas* (meat and cabbage fried dumplings) and *ramen* (noodle soup). Settle at the counter and watch the chefs at work, or sit in one of the two dining rooms. It's very popular; you may have to queue at lunchtime. From €9. Daily 11.30am–10pm.

20

TOP 5 BISTROTS À VIN

Le 5ème Cru See p.281
Au Passage See p.293
La Cave des Abbesses See p.289
Le Garde-Robe See below
Le Verre Volé See p.294

Kunitoraya 5 rue Villedo, 2ᵉ ☎ 01 47 03 07 74, ⓦ kunitoraya.com; ⓜ Pyramides; map p.76. You may have to wait for a table at this casual, authentic Japanese diner, where customers are squashed in at long, narrow tables, but it's worth it for the flavoursome ramen soups (around €10–24) and tempura. Gypsy jazz gets things swinging on Sundays 4.30–7.30pm. Tues–Sat 12.15–2.30pm & 7.30–10.30pm, Sun 12.15–7.30pm.

Saturne 17 rue Notre-Dame des Victoires, 2ᵉ ☎ 01 42 60 31 90, ⓦ saturne-paris.fr; ⓜ Bourse; map p.76. At this highly popular neo-bistro, done out in Scandi-style blonde-wood furnishings and glass ceiling, up-and-coming young chef Sven Chartier reworks traditional French cuisine, marrying interesting flavours and textures. The emphasis is on market-fresh ingredients, accompanied by an extensive list of natural wines. A typical main course

might be lamb with artichokes, citronella, onion compote and smoked mozzarella. At lunch opt for the three-course *menu* (€45) or multi-course fixed menu (€85); the latter is available in the evening, also with wine pairings (€150) – worth considering given the expertise of the restaurant's renowned sommelier, Ewen Lemoigne. Mon–Fri noon–2pm & 8–10.30pm.

Verjus 52 rue de Richelieu, 1ᵉʳ; wine bar 47 rue Montpensier, 1ᵉʳ; ⓜ Pyramides/Palais Royal Musée du Louvre; ☎ 01 42 97 54 40, ⓦ verjusparis.com; map p.76. This pretty, relaxed, American-owned dining room, tucked away above rue Montpensier, offers Modern European food on a six-course *menu dégustation* (€68) that features such dishes as lamb with wild garlic and snails, or pigeon with kale, cabbage, whey, apple and pumpkin seed. If you haven't booked, or want to spend less, pop down the steps and around the corner to the postage-stamp-sized wine bar in the cellar at the back (no reservations), where you can perch on stools and tuck into sharing plates of buttermilk-fried chicken, courgette fritters and the like. Surrounded almost exclusively by American and British foodies, with a cool playlist from Sinatra to New Orleans R&B, it's easy to forget you're actually in Paris, but the food (€6–12) is flawless. Restaurant Mon–Fri 7–11pm; wine bar Mon–Fri 6–11pm, food from 7pm.

BEAUBOURG AND LES HALLES

CAFÉS AND WINE BARS

Dame Tartine 2 rue Brisemiche, 4ᵉ ☎ 01 42 77 32 22; ⓜ Rambuteau/Hôtel de Ville; map p.88. Overlooking the Stravinsky fountain, with outdoor seating under shady plane trees, this popular café is a handy pit stop in a heavily touristed area, offering cheap and tasty, open toasted sandwiches and soups, and a *menu* for children. Daily noon–11.30pm.

★ **Le Garde-Robe** 41 rue de l'Arbre Sec, 1ᵉʳ ☎ 01 49 26 90 60, ⓦ bit.ly/le-garde-robe; ⓜ Louvre-Rivoli; map p.88. Animated, cosy *bistrot à vins* that – with its bare-board floors, retro wallpaper and globe lights – manages to feel effortlessly stylish. Though the wines are superb, with mostly biodynamic and natural choices (around €6 per glass), part of the draw is the food, which you can eat at the counter or at a few tables at the back. A couple of simple and unusual lunchtime *menus* (€12–20) focus on organic ingredients, with tasty veggie choices; in the evenings the likes of cheese and charcuterie plates, *croques* and foie gras take over. Mon–Fri 11am–3pm & 6.30pm–midnight, Sat 6.30pm–midnight.

RESTAURANTS

Au Pied de Cochon 6 rue Coquillière, 1ᵉʳ ☎ 01 40 13 77 00, ⓦ aupieddecochon.com; ⓜ/RER Châtelet-Les Halles; map p.88. Since opening its doors in 1946, *Au Pied de Cochon* has become a Les Halles institution – and it knows it. Still, this big old brasserie is worth a visit for extravagant middle-of-the-night pork chops, fresh lobster,

seafood platters and, of course, pigs' trotters. Mains around €25. Daily 24hr.

Champeaux La Canopée – Forum des Halles, 1ᵉʳ ☎ 01 53 45 84 50, ⓦ alain-ducasse.com; ⓜ Etienne Marcel/Châtelet; map p.88. Installed under the new Les Halles Canopée, this contemporary brasserie run by Alain Ducasse cuts a dash with its long cocktail bar, marble-topped tables, black leather banquettes and huge glass windows. In a novel touch, large departure boards of the kind you see at train stations flick up the menu at regular intervals and add to the general air of hum and bustle (or can make you feel a bit jumpy if you actually have a train to catch at the nearby Châtelet-Les Halles interchange). Best value on the menu are the signature soufflés (from €14), both savoury and sweet (eg cheese, lobster, or pistachio and salted caramel); otherwise count on around €22–40 for brasserie staples such as *filet de boeuf*, duck or pan-fried foie gras. Mon–Wed & Sun 8am–midnight, Thurs–Sat 8am–1am.

★ **Le Comptoir de la Gastronomie** 34 rue Montmartre, 1ᵉʳ ☎ 01 42 33 31 32, ⓦ comptoirdelagastronomie.com; ⓜ Les Halles/Etienne Marcel; map p.88. Gloriously old-fashioned deli (see p.337) serving fabulous baguettes – foie gras with fig chutney; smoked duck; house *terrines* – to take away; perfect for picnics. Alternatively, sit down to a simple, beautifully executed, traditional *plat*, such as roast duck (€17), cassoulet or onion soup (€9.50), in the traditional dining room attached. Deli Mon–Sat 8am–8pm; restaurant Mon–Thurs noon–11pm, Fri & Sat noon–10.15pm.

La Régalade Saint Honoré 123 rue St-Honoré, 1er ☎ 01 42 21 92 40, ⓦ laregalade.paris; ⓜ Louvre-Rivoli/ Les Halles; map p.88. Tourists and locals flock to this pared-back, sober restaurant for Bruno Doucet's accomplished bistronomy cooking: the €39 three-course *menu* offers some of the city's best value, with dishes such as cod poached in chicken broth with beetroot and curried crème fraiche followed by Mont Blanc with green apple. Booking essential. Mon–Sat noon–1.45pm & 7.15–10.45pm, Sun noon–2pm & 7.15–9pm.

Spring 6 rue Bailleul, 1er ☎ 01 45 96 05 72, ⓦ springparis.fr; ⓜ Louvre-Rivoli; map p.88. A leading exponent of the bistronomy movement, Chicago-born Daniel Rose offers a multi-course, fixed tasting menu (€85) at his small, highly sought-after restaurant, where food is prepared at an open kitchen. You might start with poached trout, followed by turbot with saffron and fennel and pigeon breast cooked in red wine, topped off with cherry clafoutis. The short wine list is impeccably chosen. Book well in advance. Tues–Sat 6.30–10pm.

★**La Tour de Montlhéry (Chez Denise)** 5 rue des Prouvaires, 1er ☎ 01 42 36 21 82; ⓜ Louvre-Rivoli/ Châtelet; map p.88. An old-style, late-night, market *bistrot*, packed with regulars sitting elbow to elbow and tucking into rich, substantial French dishes, such as *daube* of beef, bone marrow, *tête de veau* or skate with *frites*, along with Loire wines from the barrel, in a convivial, unforgettable atmosphere. Mains around €25. Mon–Fri noon–3pm & 7.30pm–5am.

★**yam'Tcha** 121 rue St-Honoré, 1er ☎ 01 40 26 08 07, ⓦ yamtcha.com; ⓜ Louvre-Rivoli; map p.88. Having grown out of its original site (see p.337), which now sells tea and serves *bao* buns to take away, *yam'Tcha*'s Chinese-French fusion restaurant moved to larger premises in 2015. The delicate, Michelin-starred food continues to dazzle and surprise – *menus découvertes* (€65/€135) might include roast duck breast with Szechuan-style aubergines, followed by melting meringue with moscatel grapes and lychee with shiso (similar to mint) sorbet. Each course can be paired with either tea or wine. Book well – at least a month – in advance. Wed–Sat noon–1.30pm & 8–9.30pm.

THE MARAIS

CAFÉS AND WINE BARS

Boot Café 19 rue du Pont aux Choux, 3e ☎ 06 26 41 10 66; ⓜ St-Sébastien-Froissart; map p.96. Coffee shops don't get tinier than this cool Aussie-run hole-in-the-wall (a picturesque old cordonnerie, or cobbler's shop), where they serve expert brews – and the odd unusual bite, including various takes on *congee* (Cantonese rice porridge). Grab a coffee to go – or bag one of the few chairs and prepare to be sociable. Daily 10am–6pm.

Café Charlot 38 rue de Bretagne, 3e ☎ 01 44 54 03 30, ⓦ cafecharlotparis.com; ⓜ Filles du Calvaire; map p.96. You'll need to fight for a seat on the *terrasse* of this white-tiled retro café (a former *boulangerie*), which bursts at the seams on weekends with locals and in-the-know tourists. The food – a mix of French and American standards – is not that special, but it's a great place for a drink and a spot of people-watching. Daily 7am–2am.

Café Pinson 6 rue du Forez, 3e ☎ 09 83 82 53 53, ⓦ cafepinson.fr; ⓜ Filles du Calvaire; map p.96. One of a growing number of healthy-eating outlets that have recently popped up in the Haut Marais, *Café Pinson* is a vegan café turning out "cuisine haute vitalité". This translates into dishes such as blanquette de légumes with quinoa and Chinese-style rice with tofu, ginger and tamari sauce. You can sit in the attractive airy dining area, with its light-wood tables, potted plants and open kitchen, or sink into a slouchy sofa and just have a coffee or a fresh juice of the day (carrot, clementine, ginger and apple, say; €6). Two-course lunch €17.50. Mon–Fri 9am–10pm, Sat 10am–10pm, Sun noon–6pm.

Loustic 40 rue Chapon, 3e ☎ 09 80 31 07 06, ⓦ cafeloustic.com; ⓜ Arts et Métiers; map p.96. Just off rue Beaubourg on the Marais borders, this is one of the city's more established expat-run coffee houses, the realm of a friendly Londoner. With the emphasis on expertly made, high-quality brews rather than on hipster style, it's a welcoming place, with a cosy Moroccan-style back room and a few small tables at the front where people relax and chat. Mon–Fri 8am–6pm, Sat 9am–7pm, Sun 10am–6pm.

Le Mary Celeste 1 rue Commines, 3e ⓦ lemaryceleste .com; ⓜ Filles du Calvaire; map p.96. With its high stools, exposed brick walls and cool vibe, this slick corner bar feels more New York than Paris, and it's where bobo (bourgeois-bohemian) Parisians and expats flock in their droves. A daily changing menu of inventive sharing plates (around €10), such as steamed oysters with chilli, black vinegar and crispy shallots or foie gras tostada with blue cheese, radicchio and pickled plums, offers surprising and genuinely exciting food; the cocktails (specials around €12) and natural wines are great, too. It's best to arrive early, as it tends to get busy later. Daily 6pm–2am.

★**Merci** 111 bd Beaumarchais, 3e ☎ 01 42 77 79 28, ⓦ merci-merci.com; ⓜ St-Sébastien-Froissart; map p.96. There are three desirable eating options at this cool concept store (see p.340). The snug *Used Book Café* on the ground floor lets you curl up in a leather armchair with a good read – there are thousands of titles lining the walls – while sipping tea and tucking into pastries; the lower-floor *La Cantine de Merci*, with a little garden, is a family-friendly option that serves healthy, fresh light lunches; and the retro *Cinéma Café*, on street level, with a definite whiff of Parisian cool in its perfectly judged movie theming, offers simple charcuterie, salads and soup. *Used Book Café*

& Cinéma Café Mon–Sat 10am–6.30pm; La Cantine de Merci Mon–Sat noon–6pm.

Le Progrès 1 rue de Bretagne, 3ᵉ 📞 01 42 72 01 44; Ⓜ Filles du Calvaire; map p.96. Locals prop up the zinc bar or bag the *terrasse* tables at this popular corner café, with its traditional mustard-coloured walls and mosaic floor. It's especially popular at *apéritif* time, but also makes a good spot for breakfast or steak frites at lunch. Closed three weeks in Aug. Mon–Sat 8am–2am.

RESTAURANTS

Ambassade d'Auvergne 22 rue de Grenier St-Lazare, 3ᵉ 📞 01 42 72 31 22, Ⓦ ambassade-auvergne.com; Ⓜ Rambuteau; map p.96. Tourists love it, and for good reason: this is tasty, hearty Auvergnat cuisine that would have made Vercingétorix proud, served in a cosy, traditional dining room. The starter of warm lentils and bacon could be a meal in itself, but for the ultimate in comfort food try the *saucisse* and *aligot* (creamy, cheesy potato; €18); the waiter brings the *aligot* to your table in a copper pan and demonstrates its gloriously silky texture by drawing it up high in the air on a spoon. Treats for afters include a vast help-yourself bowl of chocolate mousse and a fabulous cheese plate that includes the region's pungent Cantal. Daily 12.30–2pm & 7.30–10pm.

★ **Chez Janou** 2 rue Roger Verlomme, 3ᵉ 📞 01 42 72 28 21, Ⓦ chezjanou.com; Ⓜ Chemin Vert; map p.96. Fiercely popular Provençal restaurant that serves generous portions of traditional southern food – rabbit, risotto, *daube*, duck (mains from €17) – and more than eighty types of *pastis* in its warm, traditional dining room. Save room for dessert; the house chocolate mousse is legendary, served in a cavernous bowl from which you help yourself. Tables are crammed in, so unless you can bag one on the sunny *terrasse* you'll be getting cosy with your neighbours. Daily noon–3pm & 7pm–midnight.

Chez Omar 47 rue de Bretagne, 3ᵉ 📞 01 42 72 36 26, Ⓦ chez-omar.com; Ⓜ Arts et Métiers; map p.96. You can't reserve at this perennially popular North African couscous restaurant, but it's no hardship to wait for a table at the bar, taking in the handsome old brasserie decor and brisk, spirited atmosphere. It's not gourmet food, but portions are copious and the couscous light and fluffy. The *merguez* (spicy sausage) variety costs €16, the *royale* (with three kinds of lamb) €29 – though if you go for the latter don't expect to have room for the sticky cakes afterwards. No credit cards. Mon–Sat noon–2.30pm & 7–11.30pm, Sun 7–11.30pm.

Pramil 9 rue Vertbois, 3ᵉ 📞 01 42 72 03 60, Ⓦ pramil.fr; Ⓜ Temple/Arts et Métiers; map p.96. Elegant, petite restaurant with simple decor, serving an appetizing menu of classic and more unusual French dishes – cream of pumpkin and chestnut with foie gras "ice cream"; cauliflower cake; chocolate brownie with edamame – to foodie tourists. The wine list (from €24) is small but well chosen, and the set *menus* (dinner €33; lunch €24) are good value. At the end of the night the chef will usually come out and chat to diners, which gives the place a friendly feel. Tues–Sat noon–2.30pm & 7–10.30pm, Sun 7–10.30pm.

CENTRAL MARAIS

CAFÉS AND WINE BARS

L'As du Fallafel 34 rue des Rosiers, 4ᵉ 📞 01 48 87 63 60; Ⓜ St-Paul; map p.99. The sign above the doorway of this falafel shop in the Jewish quarter reads *Toujours imité, jamais égalé* ("always copied, but never equalled"), a boast that few would challenge, given the queues outside. (It also says it's recommended by Lenny Kravitz, but that's another matter.) Falafels to take away start at €3 for ten, €6 in pitta with salad – you could eat them in the peaceful Jardin des Rosiers-Joseph Migneret, hidden away behind the street at no.10. Mon–Thurs & Sun noon–11.30pm, Fri noon–3pm.

La Caféothèque 52 rue de l'Hôtel de Ville, 4ᵉ 📞 01 53 01 83 84, Ⓦ lacafeotheque.com; Ⓜ Pont Marie/ Ⓜ Saint-Paul; map p.99. This arty, aromatic third-wave coffee house, in a sunny spot by the Seine, provides the perfect setting to relax on plump, hessian-covered seating over a brew and make use of the free wi-fi. Coffee is taken seriously here, with daily specials and a three-cup *dégustation* option in addition to espressos, flat whites and the like. Cappuccino €5, café gourmand (espresso and three small cakes) €10. You can buy beans to go, too. Mon–Sat 10am–7pm, Sun noon–7pm.

L'Ebouillanté 6 rue des Barres, 4ᵉ 📞 01 42 71 00 69; Ⓜ Hôtel de Ville; map p.99. In nice weather, this colourful, two-storey café spills onto a peaceful, cobbled street behind the church of St-Gervais. You can choose from an extensive choice of drinks, including home-made hot chocolate, as well as salads and crêpes (€9–17) – the food isn't amazing, but it's a pretty spot and a Marais classic on a sunny evening. Tues–Sun noon–10pm, till 7pm in winter.

Le Loir dans la Théière 3 rue des Rosiers, 4ᵉ 📞 01 42 72 90 61, Ⓦ leloirdanslatheiere.com; Ⓜ St-Paul; map p.99. A much-loved *salon de thé* decorated with arty posters and whimsical *Alice in Wonderland* murals (the name translates as "the dormouse in the teapot"). It's a popular place, nearly always full, and there are a couple of

---

TOP 5 NEO-BISTROS

Le Châteaubriand See p.293
Le Galopin See p.295
Richer See p.291
Semilla See p.285
Le Square Gardette See p.293

comfy leather armchairs for lounging. The enormous (and delicious) home-made cakes are the thing to order (around €11 for tea and cake), but you can also get light meals; come early for the brunch on Sunday (€22.50), or be prepared to queue. Daily 9am–7pm.

Marché des Enfants Rouges 39 rue de Bretagne, 3ᵉ; Ⓜ Filles du Calvaire; map p.99. A great picnic option: in addition to fresh fruit, veg and cheese, this venerable food market (see p.341) is the place to come for street food – rôtisserie, Japanese, couscous, crêpes, Lebanese, Italian, Creole – which you can eat at communal picnic tables. Tues, Wed & Thurs 8.30am–1pm & 4–7.30pm, Fri & Sat 8.30am–1pm & 4–8pm, Sun 8.30am–2pm.

Les Philosophes 28 rue Vieille du Temple, 4ᵉ ⓣ01 48 87 49 64, ⓦ cafeine.com/philosophes; Ⓜ Hôtel de Ville; map p.99. One of a number of *bistrots* on this stretch run by the same people, *Les Philosophes* has a corner *terrasse* brilliantly placed for people-watching, plus tasty, reasonably priced food – snacks and *plats* – matched by decent wines. It's a good spot for a cooked or continental breakfast, too. Daily 9am–2am.

Pozzetto 39 rue du Roi de Sicile, 4ᵉ ⓣ01 42 77 08 64, ⓦ bit.ly/pozzettoparis; Ⓜ Hôtel de Ville; map p.99. Hugely popular ice-cream parlour, serving proper Italian *gelato* – try the moreish Sicilian pistachio flavour – made fresh every day; if you're having trouble choosing, ask for a free taster. You can get authentic Italian coffee here too. There's a newer branch around the corner at 16 rue Vieille du Temple, which also serves salads (open from 9am). Mon–Thurs 12.15–11pm, Fri & Sat 12.15pm–12.15am, Sun 12.15–10.45pm.

RESTAURANTS

Breizh Café 109 rue Vieille du Temple, 3ᵉ ⓣ01 42 72 13 77, ⓦ breizhcafe.com; Ⓜ St-Paul; map p.99. A Breton restaurant serving delicious *galettes* (savoury buckwheat pancakes) and crêpes. Traditional fillings include ham and cheese, but this is a smartish place, so you can get more elaborate options such as salt cod or the Savoyarde, with Reblochon cheese and potatoes. Wash it all down with one of their many ciders and leave room for a sweet crêpe – Valrhona chocolate, perhaps, or ginger and salted caramel. Booking advised. Mains around €9. There's a second branch at 1 rue de l'Odéon, 6ᵉ. Closed three weeks in Aug. Tues–Sat 11.30am–11pm, Sun 11.30am–10pm.

Chez Hanna 54 rue des Rosiers, 4ᵉ ⓣ01 42 74 74 99, ⓦ chezhanna-restaurant.fr; Ⓜ St-Paul; map p.99. This simple restaurant is always packed with locals and in-the-know tourists for its reasonably priced Middle Eastern and Jewish delicacies – the falafel special, with super-fresh, warm falafel, sauce, hummus, fried aubergines and salad, is huge, filling, delicious and a steal at €13.50; the *shawarma* (€17), made with tasty, spiced turkey, is also popular. Takeaway falafel starts at €5.50. Tues–Sun 11.30am–midnight.

★ **Grand Coeur** 41 rue du Temple, 4ᵉ ⓣ01 58 28 18 90, ⓦ grandcoeur.paris; Ⓜ St-Paul; map p.99. Secreted away on an attractive cobbled courtyard is this chic modern brasserie, opened in 2015 by Michelin-starred chef Mauro Colagreco. The food is suitably refined, with dishes such as veal, white asparagus, rhubarb and hibiscus, as well as some appealing vegetarian options, including Sicilian-style aubergine with scamorza cheese. Sit out on the lovely courtyard terrace or in the wood-beamed dining room (a former coaching inn). Lunch *menus* €23/€30, dinner around €55 à la carte. Tues–Sat noon–10.30pm, Sun noon–6pm.

★ **Métropolitain** 8 rue de Jouy, 4ᵉ ⓣ09 81 20 37 38, ⓦ www.metroresto.fr; Ⓜ St-Paul; map p.99. Top Chef finalist Paul-Arthur Berlan is behind the adventurous cuisine at this appealing contemporary *bistrot*, decorated with vintage metro posters. From the limited-choice menu you might choose a starter of French asparagus, Corsican brocciu, lemon confit and wild sorrel, followed by spicy stuffed squid with black rice or Challans duck with ginger-flavoured carrots and kale. Lunch *menu* from €20, dinner from €36. Mon–Fri noon–2pm & 7.30–10pm, Sat 7.30–10pm.

La Petite Maison dans la Cour 9 rue St-Paul, 4ᵉ ⓣ06 89 32 00 10, ⓦ bit.ly/lapetitemaisondelacour; Ⓜ St-Paul; map p.99. Hidden away in a courtyard (part of the Village St-Paul; see p.107) off the main road, this attractive restaurant-salon de thé, with its pretty *terrasse*, is a tranquil spot for lunch or an afternoon cup of one of the best hot chocolates in town, made with Madagascar chocolate and organic milk. The menu is short, but everything is locally sourced and home-made, including savouries such as split-pea and bacon broth, quiches and herbed chicken with black rice. Mains around €12–16. Wed–Fri noon–4pm, Sat & Sun noon–8pm.

Pink Flamingo 105 rue Vieille du Temple, 3ᵉ ⓣ01 42 71 28 20, ⓦ pinkflamingopizza.com; Ⓜ St-Sébastien-Froissart; map p.99. The inventive, tasty pizzas (from €11.50) at the tiny Marais branch of this funky mini-chain – all graffitied walls and retro banquettes – include the Gandhi (*sag paneer*, *baba ganoush* and mozzarella) and the Obama (bacon and pineapple). A fun, friendly budget option, with three other branches around town. Tues–Fri noon–3pm & 7–11.30pm, Sat & Sun noon–4pm & 7–11.30pm.

Le Potager du Marais 24 rue Rambuteau, 3ᵉ ⓣ01 57 40 98 57, ⓦ lepotagerdumarais.fr; Ⓜ Rambuteau; map p.99. A small, welcoming vegan restaurant, rustically styled and with a menu featuring organic and gluten-free options. Dishes might include goat's cheese with honey, "crusty" quinoa burger or seitan Bourguignon, and there are scrumptious desserts (*crème brûlée* with ginger, anyone?). Mains from €17. Wed–Sun noon–3pm & 7–11pm.

BASTILLE AND EAST

CAFÉS AND WINE BARS

★ **Le Baron Rouge** 1 rue Théophile-Roussel, 12ᵉ ☎ 01 43 43 14 32, ⓦ lebaronrouge.net; Ⓜ Ledru-Rollin; map p.114. Stallholders and shoppers from the nearby Marché Aligre gather at this glorious old spit-and-sawdust *bar à vins* for a light lunch or an *apéritif* during the day, especially on Sundays. If it's crowded, join the locals outside standing around the wine barrels and lunching on simple platters of *saucisson*, cheese or five different sizes of fresh oysters; try a half-dozen Cap Ferrat oysters washed down with a glass of Muscadet. Not to be missed. Mon 5–10pm, Tues–Fri 10am–2pm & 5–10pm, Sat 10am–10pm, Sun 10.30am–3.30pm.

Café des Anges 66 rue de la Roquette, 11ᵉ ☎ 01 47 00 00 63, ⓦ cafedesangesparis.com; Ⓜ Bastille; map p.114. This friendly corner café pulls a young, lively, hip crowd, filling up on good-value contemporary French dishes (from around €12) – gourmet burgers (including a tasty duck confit version with onion chutney, Cantal and rocket), fish and chips, veggie lasagne, salads and quiches. It's popular for evening drinks. Daily 7.30am–2am.

★ **Café de l'Industrie** 16 rue St-Sabin, 11ᵉ ☎ 01 47 00 13 53, ⓦ cafedelindustrieparis.fr; Ⓜ Bastille; map p.114. The relaxed atmosphere and shabby neo-colonial/boho glamour – softly polished wood, huge potted plants, retro movie star photos and gypsy jazz soundtrack – attract a mixed crowd at this Bastille institution (there's another branch opposite, but this one has the edge). It's particularly popular at weekends when there's a good-value set brunch (until 5pm) for €18. The menu ranges from generous plates of pasta to more traditional French *bistrot* dishes, and while the food is not outstanding, it's reasonably priced (mains €11–19; weekday lunch *formule* €13). Daily 9am–2am.

Chezaline 85 rue de la Roquette, 11ᵉ ☎ 01 43 71 90 75; Ⓜ Voltaire; map p.114. This gourmet deli has stirred up quite a buzz with its inexpensive, creative take on picnic food – eat in (if you're lucky enough to win one of the few tables) or take out baguettes (ham, artichoke and pesto; roasted cod with tapenade), deli salads and daily changing specials, all from €6. Mon–Fri 11am–7pm.

Pause Café 41 rue de Charonne, corner of rue Keller, 11ᵉ ☎ 01 48 06 80 33; Ⓜ Ledru-Rollin; map p.114. Or maybe "Pose Café" – given the popularity of this cool and colourful café-*bistrot* with the *quartier*'s young crowd, who pack out the pavement tables at lunch and *apéritif* time. Service is predictably insouciant but there's a good atmosphere and an enviable location. The food won't win any prizes, but you can fill up on *plats du jour* including burgers and pasta (around €15). Mon–Sat 8am–2am, Sun 9am–8pm (brunch noon–3pm).

La Ruche à Miel 19 rue d'Aligre, 12ᵉ ☎ 01 43 41 27 10; Ⓜ Ledru-Rollin; map p.114. The mouthwatering array of pistachio, almond, walnut and honey cakes at the entrance to this little Algerian teashop, on the rue d'Aligre market street, entices in many a passer-by. The best accompaniment to the cakes is the sugary fresh mint tea, served in the traditional way, on low brass tables. Around €10 for tea and two cakes; also couscous and tagines (around €12–17), plus hot breads. Tues–Thurs & Sun 9.30am–7.30pm, Fri & Sat 9.30am–11pm.

RESTAURANTS

★ **A la Biche au Bois** 45 av Ledru-Rollin, 11ᵉ ☎ 01 43 43 34 38, ⓦ bit.ly/alabicheaubois; Ⓜ Gare de Lyon; map p.114. The queues leading out of the door tell you all you need to know about this traditional restaurant, which mixes charming service with keenly priced, well-produced food served in generous quantities. This is a carnivore's dream: don't miss the game dishes, the terrines, the wild duck and the huge, rich *coq au vin*. Four-course *menu* (including a fabulous array of cheeses) €33. Mon 7–11pm, Tues–Fri noon–2pm & 7–11pm.

Amarante 4 rue Biscornet, 12ᵉ ☎ 09 50 80 93 80, ⓦ amarante.paris; Ⓜ Bastille; map p.114. Though nothing much to look at, with its plain *bistrot*-style interior, this place is consistently packed out with fans of chef Christophe Philippe's no-fuss, authentic French cuisine, using well-sourced ingredients from the Dordogne, Limousin and other regions. The menu leans heavily towards meat, featuring dishes such as foie gras, veal kidneys, snails and duck. The lunchtime three-course menu is a steal at €22, while at dinner you'll pay around €50 à la carte. Mon, Tues & Fri–Sun 12.30–2pm & 7.30–10pm.

Bistrot Paul Bert 18 rue Paul Bert, 11ᵉ ☎ 01 43 72 24 01; Ⓜ Faidherbe-Chaligny; map p.114. This *bistrot* looks right, with its chalkboard menu, little tables, tiled floor and marbled mirrors, and it feels right, with a genuine neighbourhood buzz. Saturday lunchtime is a delight, with lively groups of friends and family taking their time over the seasonal food, from fried eggs with truffles via steak *au poivre* with crispy *frites*. Save room for dessert, such as the *Paris-Brest* puff pastry oozing hazelnut cream or the Grand Marnier soufflé. Three-course dinner *menu* €39. Reservations advised. Tues–Sat noon–2pm & 7.30–11pm.

Le Bistrot du Peintre 116 av Ledru-Rollin, 11ᵉ ☎ 01 47 00 34 39, ⓦ bistrotdupeintre.com; Ⓜ Ledru-Rollin; map p.114. It's difficult to resist this charming, traditional, rather shabby-chic old *bistrot*, where small tables are jammed together beneath faded Art Nouveau frescoes, undulating mirrors and decorative panelling. There is a wide selection of cheese and charcuterie, with meaty *plats* from €13. Daily 7am–2am.

Bofinger 7 rue de la Bastille, 4ᵉ ☎ 01 42 72 87 82, ⓦ bofingerparis.com; Ⓜ Bastille; map p.114. This big and bustling fin-de-siècle Alsatian brasserie, with its splendid, perfectly preserved coloured-glass dome, is a favourite of opera-goers and tourists. Specialities are seafood and steaming dishes of sauerkraut; don't miss the delicious profiteroles for dessert. *Menus* from €33. Daily noon–3pm & 6.30pm–midnight (Sun till 11pm).

Chez Paul 13 rue de Charonne, corner of rue de Lappe, 11ᵉ ☎ 01 47 00 34 57, ⓦ chezpaul.com; ⓜ Bastille; map p.114. Housed in a wonky, dilapidated corner site, *Chez Paul* is a throwback to an older Bastille, with a long, handwritten menu, faded furnishings, black-and-white floor tiles and a mix of customers. Food is traditional (*pot-au-feu*, steak *au poivre*, *coq au vin* and so on, with a particularly good *boeuf bourguignon*) and affordable, and the ambience very congenial. Mains from €18; weekday lunch *menus* €18 and €21. Mon–Fri noon–3.30pm & 7pm–12.30am, Sat & Sun noon–12.30am.

L'Encrier 55 rue Traversière, 12ᵉ ☎ 01 44 68 08 16, ⓦ lencrierrestaurant.com; ⓜ Ledru-Rollin; map p.114. The simple interior of exposed brick walls and timber beams complements the good-value, homely food served by pleasant staff in this small restaurant near the Viaduc des Arts. A good spot for well-executed dishes with a slight southwestern influence – *andouillette* (tripe sausage) with shallot chutney, say, or steak and morel mushrooms. *Menus* from €13.50 (lunch) or €21.50–36 (evening). Mon–Fri noon–2.15pm & 7.30–11pm, Sat 7.30–11pm.

★ **Les Marcheurs de Planète** 73 rue de la Roquette, 11ᵉ ☎ 01 43 48 90 98, ⓦ lesmarcheursdeplanete.com; ⓜ Voltaire; map p.114. Great restaurant/bar with a good old-fashioned Parisian atmosphere: chess tables; books and graphic novels to read; musical instruments dotted about; posters covering the walls (and ceiling); and a friendly, wild-haired owner. More than 150 wines are on offer, plus top-notch cheeses and charcuterie, and rustic French food including *pot-au-feu* or steak, all at reasonable prices. Live music on Thursdays from around 10pm. Tues–Sun 5.30pm–2am; food served 7.30pm–midnight.

Paris-Hanoï 74 rue de Charonne, 11ᵉ ☎ 01 47 00 47 59, ⓦ parishanoi.fr; ⓜ Charonne; map p.114. A perennially popular, cheap Vietnamese café that sees queues down the street at weekend lunchtimes for the inexpensive stir-fries, noodles and soups – try the *bun cha*, a noodle dish with veg, meatballs and caramelized peanuts. Around €20 a head for a full meal. No credit cards. Daily noon–2.30pm & 7–10.30pm; closed Aug.

Septime/Clamato 80 rue de Charonne, 11ᵉ ☎ 01 43 67 38 29, ⓦ septime-charonne.fr; ⓜ Charonne; map p.114. A star in the city's neo-bistro firmament, *Septime* turns out inventive, delicate food – steamed cod with pickled turnips and *yuzu* sauce, for example, or courgette

TOP 5 BUDGET EATS

Chez Imogène See p.293
Oh Africa! See p.291
Le Pavillon des Canaux See p.293
La Pointe du Grouin See p.291
Wine by One See p.271

with goat's cheese and rhubarb – on *dégustation* menus (lunch menu €32.50; six-course tasting menu €60 for lunch, €70 for dinner). You'll need to reserve at least three weeks in advance, but the adjoining tapas bar, *Clamato*, which serves fish and seafood small plates, accepts walk-ins only (arrive early). Septime Mon 7.30–10pm, Tues–Fri 12.15–2pm & 7.30–10pm; Clamato Wed–Fri 7–11pm, Sat & Sun noon–11pm.

★ **Le Square Trousseau** 1 rue Antoine Vollon, 12ᵉ ☎ 01 43 43 06 00, ⓦ squaretrousseau.com; ⓜ Ledru-Rollin; map p.114. At once elegant – cream leather banquettes, marble columns, decorative ceiling – and cheerful, this brasserie, opposite a park and playground near the Marché Aligré, is as convenient for hungry families (chalk is supplied for decorating the paper tablecloths) as it is for a relaxed lunch. The menu features both traditional and modern French dishes, from chestnut and cep soup and frogs' legs to cheeseburgers or lobster with *frites*. Finish with *tarte tatin* or profiteroles. Mains €20–38. Daily 8am–2am.

Le Train Bleu Gare de Lyon, 12ᵉ ☎ 01 43 43 09 06, ⓦ le-train-bleu.com; ⓜ Gare de Lyon; map p.114. The jaw-dropping decor at *Le Train Bleu* – everything dripping with gilt, chandeliers hanging from lofty ceilings frescoed with scenes from the Paris–Lyon–Marseille train route – is from a bygone golden age, and to add to the spectacle, huge windows give onto the arriving and departing trains below. The traditional French cuisine has a hard time living up to all this, but is acceptable, if pricey (three-course *menu* €65, including a glass of wine). If you just want a glimpse, you could go for coffee (€6) or a drink and snack in the comfy bar (which also serves breakfast). Daily 7.30am–10pm.

Waly Fay 6 rue Godefroy-Cavaignac, 11ᵉ ☎ 01 40 24 17 79; ⓜ Charonne/Faidherbe-Chaligny; map p.114. This West African restaurant has a cosy, stylish atmosphere, the dim lighting, white stone walls and dark timber beams creating an intimate ambience. Smart young Parisians come here to dine on fragrant, richly spiced stews, plantain fritters, jumbo prawns and other delicacies (mains around €20). Daily 7pm–2am.

THE QUARTIER LATIN

CAFÉS AND WINE BARS

★ **Le 5ème Cru** 7 rue du Cardinal Lemoine, 5ᵉ ☎ 01 40 46 86 34, ⓦ 5ecru.com; ⓜ Cardinal Lemoine; map p.124. The shelves at this welcoming *bistrot à vins* are piled high with bottles from French artisan winemakers. Let the friendly staff advise you, then join the locals in the cosy dining area and order plates of excellent charcuterie, cheese and pâté (around €7–10). Mon–Fri noon–3pm & 7pm–midnight, Sat 7pm–midnight.

Bonvivant 7 rue des Écoles, 5ᵉ ☎01 43 26 51 34, 🌐bonvivant.paris; Ⓜ Cardinal Lemoine; map p.124. This friendly wine bar, with biodynamic wines from €6 a glass, serves sharing platters (around €16) and pâtés, hummus or *rillettes* to nibble – and expands at the back into an elegant restaurant, referencing classic French movies, classic French tipples and classic French style. Dishes range from gluten-free options – Thai broth with steamed veg and soba, perhaps – to perfect takes on old French favourites. Mains from €15. Daily 9am–2am.

Café de la Mosquée 39 rue Geoffroy-St-Hilaire, 5ᵉ ☎01 43 31 38 20, 🌐restaurantauxportesdelorient .com; Ⓜ Censier–Daubenton; map p.124. The *salon* at the Paris mosque has a lovely Arabic interior, and a courtyard where tajines and couscous are served (€11–16), but it's the tiled *terrasse* with its fig trees that's the real draw – the perfect spot to refuel with a glass of sweet mint tea and a honey-drenched cake. Watch out for lunchtimes, though, when it's packed and rather chaotic. Female visitors can try a hammam-massage-meal option for €63 (see p.344). Daily 9am–midnight.

★**Café de la Nouvelle Mairie** 19 rue des Fossés-St-Jacques, 5ᵉ ☎01 44 07 04 41; Ⓜ Cluny La Sorbonne/RER Luxembourg; map p.124. Set on a narrow, tree-shaded street near the Panthéon, this contemporary bistro-wine bar has a convivial atmosphere. The daily changing menu (€8–18) features simple small plates, sharing *assiettes* of cheese or charcuterie, and bigger mains such as grilled lamb chops, spinach quiche or cod with red cabbage and wasabi cream are typical. There's also a fine selection of natural wines. Mon–Fri 8am–midnight.

La Fourmi Ailée 8 rue du Fouarre, 5ᵉ ☎01 43 29 40 99; Ⓜ Maubert Mutualité; map p.124. This high-ceilinged *salon de thé*, with its background jazz and colourful decor – mosaic facade, cloudy sky trompe l'oeil, yellow banquettes, book-lined walls – is a welcome stop for locals and tourists. You'll pay around €13–18 for a home-made *plat* – including Provençal specialities and a handful of veggie options – or could simply plump for a large slice of quiche (€10.50) or home-made cake (€6.50) and a *tisane*. Daily noon–midnight.

Nossa 1 rue de l'Ecole Polytechnique, 5ᵉ ☎09 53 67 93 86, 🌐nossa-paris.com; Ⓜ Maubert Mutualité/Cardinal

Lemoine; map p.124. Join the ravenous students tucking into rotisserie chicken and flavoursome sauces in this buzzy little *churrasqueria* – mains start at €6.50, with daily specials including salt cod and Portuguese steak. It's packed at weekday lunchtimes, when the *formule* gets you a quarter chicken, a Portuguese toastie and a side dish for €8. Tues–Sat noon–3pm & 7–10pm, Sun noon–4pm.

Les Pipos 2 rue de l'Ecole Polytechnique, 5ᵉ ☎01 43 54 11 40; Ⓜ Maubert Mutualité/Cardinal Lemoine; map p.124–000. This old corner bar – named for the first-year students at the nearby *école* – is an unreconstructed Latin Quarter institution, full of *bons viveurs* and happy tourists enjoying natural wines by the glass and simple Auvergnat food. Two-course lunch *formule* (Mon–Fri) €14.50. Mon–Sat 9am–1am.

★**Le Verre à Pied** 118bis rue Mouffetard, 5ᵉ ☎01 43 31 15 72; Ⓜ Censier–Daubenton; map p.124. An old-fashioned, charming and very authentic market bar where traders take their morning glass of wine at the bar and engage in lively conversation, or sit down to eat a simple *plat du jour* – steak hâché, *saucisson*, *entrecôte* – for around €12. Lunch *formule* €15. Tues–Sat 9am–9pm, Sun 9.30am–4pm.

RESTAURANTS

L'Atelier Maître Albert 1 rue Maître Albert, 5ᵉ ☎01 56 81 30 01, 🌐ateliermaitrealbert.com; Ⓜ Maubert Mutualité; map p.124. One of Michelin-starred Guy Savoy's more affordable restaurants, this modern rôtisserie specializes in big plates of spit-roast meats – chicken, veal, duck, pork or beef – with lighter dishes including grilled fish or casseroles. *Menus* €28/€35 (lunch) or €35 (dinner). Mon–Fri noon–2.30pm & 6.30–11.30pm, Sat & Sun 6.30–11.30pm.

Le Jardin des Pâtes 4 rue Lacépède, 5ᵉ ☎01 43 31 50 71, 🌐restaurant-lejardindespates.fr; Ⓜ Jussieu; map p.124. In this pretty, plant-filled space you can eat delicious pasta, home-made with freshly ground organic grains and served with gourmet sauces. Try the chestnut pasta with duck, nutmeg and mushrooms, or rice pasta with sautéed veg, soy sauce, ginger and tofu. Mains €12.50–15. Daily noon–2.30pm & 7–11pm.

Le Reminet 3 rue des Grands-Degrés, 5ᵉ ☎01 85 15 27 89, 🌐www.lereminet.fr; Ⓜ Maubert Mutualité; map p.124. This teeny *bistrot* is a special-occasion place, all snowy-white tablecloths, time-blotched mirrors and mini-chandeliers, with French windows opening onto a leafy square. Dinner is wildly overpriced, so come for lunch, when they offer a good-value, tasty three-course *menu* (€16.90) – split pea soup followed by Morteau sausage and then cheese, for example. Daily noon–2.30pm & 7–10.30pm.

Tashi Delek 4 rue des Fossés-St-Jacques, 5ᵉ ☎01 43 26 55 55; RER Luxembourg; map p.124. Unfussy, popular

---

TOP 5 TAPAS AND SHARING

L'Avant Comptoir See p.283
Dauphin See p.292
Hélène Darroze See p.284
Le Mary Céleste See p.277
Verjus See p.276

Tibetan restaurant serving Himalayan dishes ranging from robust, warming noodle soups to the addictive, ravioli-like beef *momok* and a salty, soupy yak-butter tea. It's good value, with evening *menus* at €18.50/€24 and lunch for around €12. Mon–Sat noon–2.30pm & 7–11pm.

★**Les Trublions** 34 rue de La Montagne Sainte-Geneviève, 5ᵉ ☎01 42 02 87 83, ⓦlestrublions.fr; ⓜMaubert Mutualité/Cluny La Sorbonne; map p.124.

ST-GERMAIN

CAFÉS AND WINE BARS

Au Chai de l'Abbaye 26 rue de Buci, 6ᵉ ☎01 43 26 68 26, ⓦauchaidelabbaye.fr/en; ⓜMabillon; map p.138. A bustling old café in the heart of St-Germain. Sink into a red leather banquette and tuck into a *tartine* made with Poilâne bread (from €6). They also offer hefty salads (€12) and charcuterie (from €6). Mon–Sat 8am–11.30pm, Sun 11am–11pm.

★**L'Avant Comptoir/L'Avant Comptoir de la Mer** 3 carrefour de l'Odéon, 6ᵉ ☎01 42 38 47 55, ⓦhotel-paris-relais-saint-germain.com; ⓜOdéon; map p.138. With standing room only, Yves Camdeborde's (see p.267) buzzy wine/tapas bar *L'Avant Comptoir* offers his innovative cooking at affordable prices (tapas from €4). The food, from the oxtail *croque* to the chocolate pot, is outstanding, as are the natural wines – help yourself to fresh crusty bread, butter and pickles from the bar. If you can't get in, console yourself with a takeout crêpe or sandwich from the stall at the front. *L'Avant Comptoir de la Mer*, next door, focuses on fish and seafood tapas (from €5) – Basque hake confit; squid with quinoa, lemon, mint and olives – with a takeout oyster bar at the front. No reservations at either. Both daily noon–11pm.

Café de Flore 172 bd St-Germain, 6ᵉ ☎01 45 48 55 26, ⓦcafedeflore.fr; ⓜSt-Germain-des-Prés; map p.138. One of the city's iconic old literary brasseries, *Flore* is the great rival and immediate neighbour of the even more touristy *Les Deux Magots*. Sartre, de Beauvoir, Camus et al used to hang out here – and there's still the odd reading and debate. It's undeniably fun, but expect to pay (omelettes from €12, salads €19 – even an espresso will set you back €4.60) for the privilege of soaking up all that evocative history. Daily 7.30am–1.30am.

Café de la Mairie 8 place St-Sulpice, 6ᵉ ☎01 43 26 67 82; ⓜSt-Sulpice; map p.138. Popular, old-school café on the sunny north side of the square, opposite St-Sulpice church and with lots of outside tables. The food isn't amazing, and a bit pricey (*croques*, salads, sandwiches and cheese/charcuterie platters €10.50–17), but it's perfect for basking with a coffee or an *apéritif*. Mon–Fri 7am–2am, Sat 8am–2am, Sun 9am–9pm.

Coutume 47 rue de Babylone, 7ᵉ ☎01 45 51 50 47, ⓦcoutumecafe.com; ⓜSt-François Xavier; map p.138. Quintessential hipster coffee shop – all peeling walls and science-lab chic, with an on-site roastery – from an Aussie/

This smart little *bistrot* is a friendly local favourite, delivering bright, creative food made with market-fresh ingredients in a soothingly contemporary dining room. It's particularly good for lunch, when the two-/three-course *menus* offer exceptional value at €14.90/€18.50 – goat cheese wrapped in leek, say, or meltingly tender duckling thigh with sweet onions and mushrooms. Tues–Sat noon–3pm & 7.30–11pm.

French team. The devotion to the bean borders on the obsessive here, which is, of course, how the coffee fiends who pack the place out like it. There's a short menu, too – Bircher muesli, salads, poached eggs, pâtisserie and the like (€5–16). Mon–Fri 8.30am–5.30pm, Sat & Sun 9am–6pm; kitchen daily 9am–3.45pm.

Eggs & Co 11 rue Bernard Palissy, 6ᵉ ☎01 45 44 02 52, ⓦeggsandco.fr; ⓜSt-Germain-des-Prés; map p.138. Much beloved of bloggers and brunchers, this good-natured café packs in a young crowd at a tiny zinc counter and mezzanine dining room, serving eggs in dozens of ways – omelettes, soft-boiled with soldiers, Benedicts, you name it – with decent coffee. It's a set-up more often seen in London or New York, and is usually buzzing with tourists, but the exuberant staff give it a quirky Gallic buzz. Boiled egg €5; brunch €22–31. Mon, Tues, Thurs & Fri 10am–5pm, Sat & Sun 10am–6pm.

L'Heure Gourmande 22 passage Dauphine, 6ᵉ ☎01 46 34 00 40, ⓦbit.ly/hgourmande; ⓜOdéon; map p.138. Hidden away in a cobbled and tree-shaded *passage* between rue Mazarine and rue Dauphine, this *salon de thé* is best on warm days when you can sit on the peaceful vine-draped *terrasse*, quietly enjoying a *coupe* of Berthillon ice cream (see p.270), a fresh juice or a slab of home-made cake (from €5). Mon 11.30am–3pm, Tues–Sun 11.30am–7pm.

Mamie Gâteaux 66 rue du Cherche-Midi, 6ᵉ ☎01 42 22 32 15, ⓦmamie-gateaux.com; ⓜSt-Placide; map p.138. With its cream-painted dressers, Provençal bric-a-brac and vintage crockery, some of which is for sale, this is a *salon à thé* with a hint of country charm. Simple home-made soups, salads and quiches (€6–12) are served for lunch (until 3pm), with pâtisserie, scones (from €4) and fancy teas available in the afternoon. Tues–Sat 11.30am–6pm.

La Palette 43 rue de Seine, 6ᵉ ☎01 43 26 68 15, ⓦcafelapaletteparis.com; ⓜOdéon; map p.138. This former Beaux Arts student café-bar remains a place to be seen – the odd celebrity pops by – but the atmosphere is relaxed. Venerable oil paintings and palettes add to the charm of the interior, and there's an appealing *terrasse* lively with diners. The menu ranges from *croques* (€11) and quiches (€13) to *plats* (€16–24) and sharing platters (mozzarella, maybe, or grilled sardines; €10–27). Daily 8am–2am.

RESTAURANTS

Allard 41 rue St-André-des-Arts, 6ᵉ ☎01 58 00 23 42, Ⓦrestaurant-allard.fr; ⓂOdéon; map p.138. The menu at this proudly unreconstructed Parisian restaurant, opened in the 1930s and now part of the Alain Ducasse empire, is meat-heavy, comforting and traditionally French – ox cheeks, foie gras, frogs' legs, sole meunière – rather than experimental, and the atmosphere is unimpeachably and unironically retro. Mains from €34; good-value three-course lunch *menu* €34. Daily noon–2pm & 7.30–10pm.

Bouillon Racine 3 rue Racine, 6ᵉ ☎01 44 32 15 60, Ⓦbouillonracine.com; ⓂCluny La Sorbonne; map p.138. The bourgeois French cuisine isn't bad – nor is it outrageously expensive, especially if you go for the €16.95 weekday lunch *formule* – but it's the extravagant Art Nouveau decor that's the real pull here, in one of just a few surviving *bouillons* (broth and steak restaurants) that studded Paris in the early 1900s. They serve drinks and tea and cake in the afternoon (3–7pm), so you can enjoy the ambience without having a full meal. Daily noon–11pm.

Café de la Tourelle 5 rue Hautefeuille, 6ᵉ ☎01 46 33 12 47; ⓂSt-Michel; map p.138. An old-fashioned *bistrot*, named after the stone *échauguette* tower outside, that is packed into a low-ceilinged, intimate room. The short menu of meaty cuisine (mains €17) is simple and traditional, if by no means gourmet, listing such dishes as calves' liver and duck *confit*. The *menus* are good value (€19/€23). Mon–Fri noon–1.45pm & 7–9.45pm, Sat 7–9.45pm.

Le Comptoir du Relais 9 carrefour de l'Odéon, 6ᵉ ☎01 44 27 07 97, Ⓦhotel-paris-relais-saint-germain.com; ⓂOdéon; map p.138. Yves Camdeborde blazed the trail in introducing bistronomy to Paris (see p.267); today his flagship restaurant offers a lively *bistrot* ambience during the day and at the weekends (no reservations), when you might choose octopus with buckwheat pasta, squid ink and mint (€20) or thyme-roasted rack of lamb with beans, shallots and sherry (€26) and watch St-Germain's finest sashay by. It's a more formal gourmet experience on weekday evenings, when there's a €60 tasting menu (reservations only). Daily noon–11pm.

L'Epi Dupin 11 rue Dupin, 6ᵉ ☎01 42 22 64 56, Ⓦepidupin.com; ⓂSèvres–Babylone; map p.138. This friendly modern *bistrot* in an untouristy corner is a great find, serving high-quality, seasonal food with imaginative touches and a refreshing focus on fresh veg: roast salsify with mullet and seaweed butter, for example, or pan-fried cabbage and dried apricot with caramelized duck. The decor is simple and relaxed, and the dining room usually full with locals. *Menus* €39/€52; €28 at lunch. Mon 7–11pm, Tues–Fri noon–3pm & 7–11pm.

L'Epigramme 9 rue de l'Eperon, 6ᵉ ☎01 85 15 23 76, Ⓦwww.lepigrammeparis.fr; ⓂOdéon; map p.138. The emphasis in this tiny restaurant – with whitewashed stone walls, a beamed ceiling and soothing cream decor – is on contemporary French cuisine (try the guinea fowl with kumquats or the millefeuille with chestnut, passionfruit and ginger). When it's warm they throw the windows open to a peaceful courtyard, and it can be difficult to drag yourself away. *Menus* €24/€28 at lunch, €38 at dinner. Tues–Sat noon–3pm & 7–10.30pm.

Ferrandaise 8 rue de Vaugirard, 6ᵉ ☎01 43 26 36 36, Ⓦlaferrandaise.com; ⓂOdéon; map p.138. This largely Auvergnat *bistrot*, in a stone-walled dining room near the Jardin du Luxembourg, is famed for its organic beef. Fish-lovers will be happy, too: you could choose a beef cheek confit with lentil and mustard, but the monthly changing menu also lists such dishes as roasted scallops with broccoli purée and chorizo. *Menus* €16/€37 lunch, €37 dinner. Mon 7.30–10pm, Tues–Thurs noon–2pm & 7.30–10pm, Fri noon–2pm & 7.30pm–midnight, Sat 7.30pm–midnight.

La Grande Crèmerie 8 rue Grégoire de Tours, 6ᵉ ☎01 43 26 09 09, Ⓦlagrandecremerie.fr; ⓂOdéon; map p.138. They keep it simple at this contemporary-rustic spot, serving the best produce – white Italian ham with truffles (€24), black pudding with toast (€16), a Mason jar filled with a tasty mackerel and seaweed combination (€17) – alongside natural and organic wines. The quality of the food, the friendly staff and the warm space – all rough whitewashed stone, burnished copper, tin café chairs and distressed zinc – make it a godsend on this crowded stretch. Costs can mount, but the €18 lunch *menu* (a *plat* and a coffee) is worth it. Tues–Fri noon–2pm & 6–11pm, Sat 6–11pm, Sun 6–9.30pm.

Hélène Darroze 4 rue d'Assas, 6ᵉ ☎01 42 22 00 11, Ⓦhelenedarroze.com; ⓂSt-Sulpice/Sèvres–Babylone; map p.138. Darroze divides her time between here and her London restaurant, but the robust food at this Michelin-starred Paris flagship, drawing on Darroze's native Basque cuisine and on international influences and suppliers, continues to impress. There are two dining rooms: the *Salle à Manger* (lunch *menu* €58; lunch and dinner tasting menus from €98) – where typical offerings include wild salmon with clover, crème fraiche and matcha – and the less formal *Salon d'Hélène*, which offers tapas such as octopus with chickpeas, peppers and salsa verde (tapas €7–25; lunch *menus* €30/€49). Tues–Sat 12.30–2.30pm & 7.30–10.30pm.

★ Kitchen Galerie Bis 25 rue des Grands-Augustins, 6ᵉ ☎01 46 33 00 85, Ⓦzekitchengalerie.fr; ⓂSt-Michel; map p.138. This sleek restaurant, lined with splashy modern art, serves innovative and accomplished Mediterranean/Asian fusion food: you might see confit pigeon with cashew nuts and hibiscus or cod with cabbage, Buddha's hand, yuzu kosho and seaweed butter. The €55/€66 *menus découvertes* are not bad value in this neighbourhood (weekday lunch *menus* €29/€36/€49). Tues–Sat noon–2.15pm & 7.15–10.30pm.

Maison de l'Amérique Latine 217 bd St-Germain, 7ᵉ ☎01 49 54 75 10, Ⓦmal217.org; ⓂSolférino; map p.138. Although it's part of the Latin American cultural institute, there's not much Latino about this restaurant – instead you'll discover superior French cooking such as baked cod with truffle ravioli and aged parmesan or guinea fowl with asparagus, thyme and lemon. It is at its best in summer, when you can dine on the romantic outdoor terrace amid beautiful eighteenth-century gardens, which are candlelit in the evening – note, though, that this is one of the places in Paris that closes for some time in August, so check in advance. Set menus only (lunch €40/€51/€59; dinner €59). Mon–Fri noon–2pm & 7–10pm.

THE EIFFEL TOWER QUARTER

CAFÉ AND WINE BAR

★**Rosa Bonheur sur Seine** Near Pont Alexandre III, 7ᵉ ⑩ rosabonheur.fr/rosa-seine; ⑩ Invalides; map p.152. The ever-popular *Rosa Bonheur* (see p.294) continues its warm-hearted formula in this offshoot café-bar, set on a large floating barge, with huge windows and deck seating, by the Berges de Seine. Dotted with colourful lanterns, vintage table football and a pink flamingo, this is the most casual of the Berges eating options, and by far the best – whether you're after a quick coffee or *apéritif*, want to pick at tapas (from €3.50) or feast on oysters (€13 for six), *Rosa* has pulled it off again, with a relaxed, something-for-everyone vibe. There's quayside seating in summer for landlubbers. Wed–Sun noon–1.30am, but hours may change according to season and weather.

RESTAURANTS

★**L'Arpège** 84 rue de Varenne, 7ᵉ ☎01 47 05 09 06, ⑩ alain-passard.com; ⑩ Varenne; map p.152. Alain Passard gives vegetables (all from his own organic *potager*) the spotlight in this chic three-Michelin-starred restaurant, which lacks the snootiness of many of its kind. He can turn a simple beetroot or tomato into a culinary symphony, singing with clean, sophisticated flavours, while dishes such as asparagus sushi with green tea, sweetbread with licorice root, or leek with oysters and sorrel, are astounding. *Menus* €145 (lunch) and €320/€390 (dinner). Reservations essential. Mon–Fri noon–2.30pm & 7–10.30pm.

L'Astrance 4 rue Beethoven, 16ᵉ ☎01 40 50 84 40, ⑩ astrancerestaurant.com; ⑩ Passy; map p.152. Triple-Michelin-starred chef Pascal Barbot's *L'Astrance* produces some of the city's most exciting *nouvelle cuisine* in a non-stuffy atmosphere. The no-choice set menus change daily, but dishes might include foie gras and mushroom *millefeuille* with lemon *confit* and hazelnut oil, or a jasmine-infused custard served in eggshells. The contemporary dining room is small, and bookings are notoriously hard to get. Lunch *menus* €70/€150 (€120/€230 with wine pairings), dinner €230 (€350 with wine pairings). Tues–Fri 12.15–3pm & 8.15–9.30pm.

Au Bon Accueil 14 rue de Monttessuy, 7ᵉ ☎01 47 05 46 11, ⑩ aubonaccueilparis.com; ⑩ École Militaire; map p.152. Huddled in the shadow of the Eiffel Tower, in an otherwise slightly dull area, this relaxed *bistrot* turns out well-executed French dishes – you could choose velouté of red onion and vanilla followed by a perfectly cooked ox cheek braised in red wine. Mains €19; lunch *menu* €36. Mon–Fri noon–2pm & 6.30–10.30pm.

★**Le Cassenoix** 56 rue de la Fédération, 15ᵉ ☎01 45 66 09 01, ⑩ le-cassenoix.fr; ⑩ Dupleix; map p.152. Cosy and friendly neighbourhood *bistrot*, conveniently near the Eiffel Tower, serving sizeable portions of well-executed French food. Dishes are both modern and traditional – *gambas a la plancha* with basil risotto; quail with foie gras – but always seasonal, with a good selection of wines by the glass. It's prix fixe, with a three-course *menu* at €34 (lunch and dinner). Mon–Fri noon–2.30pm & 7–10.30pm.

Les Cocottes 135 rue St-Dominique, 7ᵉ ⑩ maisonconstant.com; ⑩ École Militaire; map p.152. This buzzy contemporary place is one of the more casual restaurants in southwestern chef Christian Constant's mini-empire. The menu focuses on little terrines and *cocottes* (cast-iron casseroles) of hearty, country food – potatoes stuffed with pig's trotters and caramelized, for example. Daily specials are often lighter, spotlighting veg and seafood. It's better as a lunch option than for a romantic dinner. Two-/three-course weekday *formules* €23/€28; *cocotte* of the day €16. Daily noon–11pm.

David Toutain 29 rue Surcouf, 7ᵉ ☎01 45 50 11 10, ⑩ davidtoutain.com; ⑩ Invalides; map p.152. Innovative Michelin-starred food, focusing on seasonal, perfectly judged flavours with lots of farm-fresh veg and delicate fish – typical offerings include beetroot rolls, scallops in Jerusalem artichoke *bouillon*, or smoked eel with black sesame sauce – in a light, modern-rustic space. Tasting

★**Semilla** 54 rue de Seine, 6ᵉ ☎01 43 54 34 50; ⑩ Mabillon; map p.138. The fabulous food at this modern *bistrot* – a light, airy space with an open kitchen – focuses as much on veg and fish as on meat; grilled squid with Jerusalem artichoke, say, or whiting with hazelnut butter, cabbage and saffron cream. Two-course lunch *menu* €29; otherwise mains €23–42, with a six-course tasting menu for €65. Bookings are taken up to 8.30pm; later on you might be able to wait at the bar for a table. Mon–Sat 12.30–2.30pm & 7–11pm, Sun 12.30–2.30pm & 7–10pm.

20

TOP 5 VEGGIE RESTAURANTS

42 Degrés See p.291
Café Pinson See p.277
Le Potager du Marais See p.279
Soul Kitchen See p.290
Soya See p.293

20

menus only – €55/€80/€110 (lunch) and €110 (dinner). Booking essential. Mon–Fri noon–2.30pm & 8–10.30pm.

La Fontaine de Mars 129 rue St-Dominique, 7ᵉ ☎ 01 47 05 46 44, ⊕ fontainedemars.com; Ⓜ La Tour-Maubourg; map p.152. Heavy, pink-checked tablecloths, leather banquettes, attentive service: this restaurant, tucked under a colonnade with outdoor seating opposite an old stone fountain, feels comfortingly French. The food is reliable, meaty and southwestern: think snails, *confit de canard* and delicious Basque *boudin* sausages. Starters €9–21, plats €17–38, plats du jour €22. Mon–Sat noon–3pm & 7.30–11pm, Sun 7.15–11pm.

Les Grands Verres Palais de Tokyo, 16ᵉ ☎ 01 85 53 03 61, ⊕ quixotic-projects.com/venue/les-grands-verres; Ⓜ léna/Alma–Marceau; map p.152. Helmed by a team best known for their super-cool bars – *Candelaria* (see p.298) and *Glass* (see p.301) among them – *Les Grands Verres* has a prime spot within the Palais de Tokyo (see p.160). All stone, wood and brushed metal, with a glass roof at the back, it provides a hipper alternative to the Palais' other restaurant, *Monsieur Bleu* (see opposite); the Eiffel Tower views are equally amazing. The menu (mains €16–25) ticks all the food trend boxes, running the gamut from fried chicken hearts with salt-cured grapes to clam spiralini with whey butter; unsurprisingly, there's a very cool cocktail bar, too (see p.299). Mon–Fri noon–3pm & 7–11pm, Sat & Sun 11am–4pm & 7–11pm.

Le Jules Verne Pilier Sud, Eiffel Tower, 7ᵉ ⊕ lejulesverne-paris.com; Ⓜ Bir-Hakeim; map p.152. Dining halfway up the Eiffel Tower is a draw in itself, but luckily the smart decor and Alain Ducasse's Michelin-starred French food – warm Provençal asparagus with truffled mousseline; steamed turbot with herb pesto – live up to the setting. It's best at dinner (€190/€230 for five/six dishes), but cheaper for a weekday lunch (a mere €105 for three courses). Reserve well in advance (online only), dress

★ **Les Marches** 5 rue de la Manutention, 16ᵉ ☎ 01 47 23 52 80, ⊕ lesmarches-restaurant.com/en; Ⓜ léna; map p.152. This cheerfully old-fashioned *bistrot* opposite the side wall of the Palais de Tokyo makes a perfect lunch stop. It couldn't be more French, with its checked tablecloths, walls lined with classic Parisian menus and assured list of tasty *plats* (€15–19) – you might choose fish soup or lentil and sausage salad followed by steak *tartare* or (at the weekend) a delicious *poulet rôti*. Daily noon–2.30pm & 7.30–10.30pm.

Monsieur Bleu Palais de Tokyo, 16ᵉ ☎ 01 47 20 90 47, ⊕ monsieurbleu.com; Ⓜ léna/Alma–Marceau; map p.152. Within the Palais de Tokyo (see p.160), chic *Monsieur Bleu* is more an experience than anything else – it's all about the stunning Art Deco room, with its views over the Seine and Eiffel Tower. The food – contemporary brasserie dishes (€18–39), from langoustines to lobster ravioli, roast lamb to black cod – is pricey but tasty. Daily noon–2am.

★ **Pottoka** 4 rue de l'Exposition, 7ᵉ ☎ 01 45 51 88 38, ⊕ pottoka.fr; Ⓜ Ecole Militaire; map p.152. Contemporary Basque cuisine, combining punchy flavours (pig's cheeks, squid, red peppers) with elegant refinement (foams, gels) in exciting ways, in a smart but unpretentious dining room. Don't miss the Basque cake for dessert. Mains €22; two-/three-course weekday lunch *menus* €23/€28; dinner *menus* €37/€65. Daily 12.30–2.30pm & 7–11pm.

Le P'tit Troquet 28 rue de l'Exposition, 7ᵉ ☎ 01 47 05 80 39; Ⓜ Ecole Militaire; map p.152. This tiny *bistrot* has a discreetly nostalgic feel, with its marble tables and ornate zinc bar. The cuisine, served to the diplomats of the *quartier* and lots of contented tourists, focuses on traditional meaty dishes (lamb shank, boeuf bourguignon, steak) served with flair. Three-course *menu* €35, plats €21. Reservations recommended. Daily noon–2pm & 6.30–10pm.

MONTPARNASSE AND THE 14ᵉ

CAFÉS AND WINE BARS

L'Entrepôt 7 rue Francis-de-Pressensé, 14ᵉ ☎ 01 45 40 60 70, ⊕ lentrepot.fr; Ⓜ Pernety; map p.164. Arts cinema (see p.311) café with a courtyard and garden where you can enjoy lunchtime *menus* of tasty home-cooked food (€17.50 and €22), Sunday brunch (€31) and *plats du jour* – poulet fermier, scallops, beef *tartare* and the like – for under €20. Frequent evening gigs, but it's best on a sunny day. Mon–Sat noon–2.30pm & 7–11pm, Sun 11.45am–2.45pm & 7–11pm.

Le Select 99 bd du Montparnasse, 6ᵉ ☎ 01 85 15 25 15, ⊕ leselectmontparnasse.fr; Ⓜ Vavin; map p.164. If you want to visit one of the great historic Montparnasse cafés – as frequented by Picasso, Matisse, Henry Miller, Hemingway, Fitzgerald et al – make it this one. Prices are

high, so it's best for a coffee, but *Select* has kept a lot of traditional atmosphere, with little marble tables and an old tiled floor. The brasserie food isn't bad – the €22 lunchtime *menu* gets you a main course, glass of wine and coffee. Mon–Thurs & Sun 7am–2am, Fri & Sat 7am–3am.

RESTAURANTS

★ **L'Assiette** 181 rue du Château, 14ᵉ ☎ 01 43 22 64 86, ⊕ restaurant-lassiette.paris; Ⓜ Pernety; map p.164. Bijou brasserie where David Rathgeber, previously head chef for Alain Ducasse, brings his gastronomic skills to a neighbourhood setting, serving simple but spectacular country classics – the cassoulet is a house special – and fresh, creative creations such as blue prawn tartare. Mains from €27; the two-course lunch *menu* (not Sun) is a

bargain at €23. Reservations essential. Wed–Sun noon–2.30pm & 7.30–10.30pm.

La Cantine du Troquet 89 rue Daguerre, 14ᵉ ☎01 43 20 20 09, ⊛lacantinedutroquet.com; ⓜGaité; map p.164. Friendly little place that brings a youthful energy to the traditional *bistrot* aesthetic – tiled floor, banquettes, mirrors – and produces delicious Basque dishes. Food is punchy and flavourful – razor clams *a la plancha*, jugged hare, winter veg casserole with ham and the like. Mains from €17. There are three more *Cantines* – another in the 14ᵉ, and in the 15ᵉ and 6ᵉ. Mon–Fri noon–2.45pm & 7–11pm, Sat 7–11pm.

Crêperie de Josselin 67 rue du Montparnasse, 14ᵉ ☎01 43 20 93 50; ⓜEdgar-Quinet/Montparnasse Bienvenüe; map p.164. Montparnasse is traditionally the Breton quarter of Paris (the station is on the direct line to northern France) and, with its heavy wood furniture, lace curtains and rustic porcelain, this crêperie couldn't be any more traditionally Breton. The savoury and sweet crêpes (€5–11), with jugs of cider to wash them down, are among the best in the city, so it's always crowded – if you don't get in, choose from the many crêperies lining this street and rue Odessa to the west. No reservations; no cards. Tues–Fri noon–3pm & 6–11pm, Sat & Sun noon–11pm.

La Régalade 49 av Jean-Moulin, 14ᵉ ☎01 45 45 68 58, ⊛laregalade.paris; ⓜAlésia; map p.164. This branch of the famed *Régalade* trio – gastronomic *bistrots* established by Yves Camdeborde and passed on to Bruno Doucet – has, since April 2017, been helmed by English chef Ollie Clarke. Clarke may make some changes, but he's not going to mess with the basic *Régalade* principles and it looks set to maintain its status as one of Paris's finest kitchens. The three-course €37 *prix fixe* is good value – try Puy lentils with roast snails and garlic, perhaps, followed by a beautifully composed meat or fish dish and rounded off with a Grand Marnier soufflé. Doucet himself is still in charge of the other two *Régalades*, in the 1ᵉ and the 9ᵉ. Mon 7–11pm, Tues–Fri noon–2.30pm & 7–11pm.

Le Timbre 3 rue Ste-Beuve, 6ᵉ ☎01 45 49 10 40, ⊛restaurantletimbre.com; ⓜVavin/Notre-Dame-des-Champs; map p.164. "The Postage Stamp" deserves its name: operating from one minuscule corner of a tiny dining room, chef Charles Danet produces modern and light French food on no-choice *prix fixe* menus. You might have marinated tuna with parsley root and citrus vinaigrette or cauliflower velouté with haddock, followed by a perfect lamb sweetbread with parmesan crust – and finish with a poached pear with chocolate mousse. *Menus* €28 at lunch, €36/€45 at dinner. Reservations advised. Tues–Sat noon–3pm & 7.30–11pm.

THE 15ᵉ

RESTAURANTS

Le Café du Commerce 51 rue du Commerce, 15ᵉ ☎01 45 75 03 27, ⊛lecafeducommerce.com; ⓜAvenue Emile Zola; map p.172. This popular brasserie, which opened as a *bouillon* restaurant in 1921, is pricier today, but remains a Paris classic – buzzy and characterful, with two storeys of galleries around a central patio and waiters in waistcoats and bow ties. Honest, high-quality meat and fresh seafood is the speciality; mains €14–23; two-course weekday lunch *menu* €17.50. Daily noon–3pm & 7pm–midnight.

Le Grand Pan 20 rue Rosenwald, 15ᵉ ☎01 42 50 02 50, ⊛legrandpan.fr; ⓜPlaisance; map p.172. Convenient for Parc Georges-Brassens, this classy but convivial *bistrot* puts the focus on seasonal meat, sourced from the Southwest, plus Brittany blue lobster and scallops in season. From the charcuterie to the steaks everything is beautifully prepared and presented, and relished by its neighbourhood crowd. Mains around €14; lunch *menu* €31. Their sister restaurant, *Le Petit Pan*, at 18 rue Rosenwald, serves sandwiches, takeaway and light lunches during the day and sharing plates in the evening (⊛lepetitpan.fr; Tues–Sat noon–2.30pm & 7–11.30pm). Mon–Fri noon–2pm & 7.30–11pm.

★**La Véraison** 64 rue de la Croix Nivert, 15ᵉ ☎01 45 32 39 39, ⊛laveraison.com; ⓜCambronne; map p.172. The open kitchen at this terrific neighbourhood *bistrot* turns out exquisite modern French food – the likes of foie gras and cherry ravioli or asparagus gazpacho with truffle oil – in a laidback space packed with happy locals. Mains €20–26. Reservations advised. Tues–Sat 7–10.30pm.

THE 13ᵉ AND AROUND

CAFÉ

Chefs du Quartier 12 rue du Jura, 13ᵉ ☎09 50 71 47 78, ⊛facebook.com/chefsduquartier; ⓜLes Gobelins; map p.176. This warm-hearted deli-café is a great spot for a cheap-as-chips, no-fuss lunch, either in the tiny dining room or to take away. The short menu is simplicity itself – and focuses on a different cuisine daily, so you're as likely to be offered tabbouleh, veggie curry or quesadillas, all home-made with pride. *Plat du jour* €7 (takeaway €6), three-course *menu* €13 (takeaway €10). Mon–Fri 9am–8pm, Sat noon–3.30pm.

RESTAURANTS

L'Avant Goût 26 rue Bobillot, 13ᵉ ☎01 53 80 24 00, ⊛lavantgout.com; ⓜPlace d'Italie; map p.176. Unassuming but classy Butte-aux-Cailles restaurant with a big reputation for traditional French cuisine – try the rich, spicy *pot-au-feu* – and wines to match. *Menu* €38. Mon–Sat noon–2.30pm & 7.30–10pm.

Coco de Mer 34 bd St-Marcel, 5ᵉ ☎06 20 26 77 67, ⊛cocodemer.fr; ⓜSt-Marcel; map p.176. On the 13ᵉ/5ᵉ border, this leisurely Seychellois restaurant offers something different – Indian Ocean food, including ceviche, curdled octopus and coconut chicken, that you eat beach-shack style, sitting at rough-hewn tables and wriggling your toes in a carpet of real sand. Mains €11–17. Mon 7–11pm, Tues–Sat noon–2pm & 7–11pm.

Lao Lane Xang 2 102 av d'Ivry, 13e ☎ 01 58 89 00 00; Ⓜ Tolbiac; map p.176. Bustling Chinatown restaurant offering fresh, reasonably priced Thai, Vietnamese and Lao cuisine. Try the popular toasted rice salad, served in a lettuce leaf, the garlic frog or the *panaché* of Lao specialities (€24), including delicious pork sausage and red chicken curry. Mon, Tues & Thurs noon–3pm & 7–11pm, Fri noon–3pm & 7–11.30pm, Sat & Sun noon–4pm & 7–11.30pm.

Simone 33 bd Arago, 13e ☎ 01 43 37 82 70, Ⓦ simoneparis.com; Ⓜ Les Gobelins; p.176. A minuscule, homely neo-bistro – all red walls, warm wood and shabby-chic *terrasse* chairs – dominated by its open kitchen. Food is contemporary, with lots of fresh veg – pollack with asparagus, beetroot and fennel for example. Lunchtime *plats du jour* cost €14, with *menus* at €18 and €22; dinner mains start at €23, with a four-course tasting menu at €49. The same people run the *Simone La Cave* wine bar nearby at 48 bd Arago, specializing in natural wines (Tues–Sat 5–11pm). Tues–Fri noon–2pm & 7–10pm, Sat 7–10.30pm.

Le Temps des Cerises 18–20 rue de la Butte-aux-Cailles, 13e ☎ 01 45 89 69 48, Ⓦ letempsdescerisescoop.com; Ⓜ Place d'Italie/Corvisart; map p.176. Unpretentious, unreconstructed locals' place – it's been run as a workers' co-op since 1976 – with elbow-to-elbow seating (some of it on a long communal bench) and a daily choice of French dishes from *cassoulet* to quiche. Drinks include organic coffee and Breton cola. *Plats du jour* €9.50, *menus* €20/€25, lunchtime *formule* €13.50. Food served Mon–Sat 11.45am–2.30pm & 7–11.45pm; coffee and bar food between meal times.

MONTMARTRE AND THE 9e

CAFÉS AND WINE BARS

Blackburn Coffee 34 rue Richer, 9e ☎ 01 40 22 01 71, Ⓦ blackburn-paris.com; Ⓜ Cadet; map p.182. You couldn't get much more minimal than this little spot, but the welcome is warm and it's an airy, restful place for a break. The coffee (from €2.50), including Aeropress and Chemex, is superb, as are the fresh juices (€5) – try the spicy mix of ginger, carrot, beetroot and apple. Snacks and *tartines* are served in the evening (€3–8). It's on the border with the 10e; there's another branch nearby at 52 rue du Faubourg Martin. Tues–Sat 10am–9pm.

Café des Deux Moulins 15 rue Lepic, 18e ☎ 01 42 54 90 50, Ⓦ cafedesdeuxmoulins.fr; Ⓜ Blanche; map p.182. Though still proudly sporting its *Amélie* poster (she waited tables here in the film), and welcoming a stream of movie fans, this café-bar remains a down-to-earth neighbourhood hangout with a gorgeous authentic 1950s interior, suffused in rose and bronze light. The French food, from beef tartare to *blanquette de veau* (veal ragout), is not bad but not outstanding – it's best for breakfast or a drink and perhaps a simple plate of cheese (€11). *Plats* €15–19, lunch *menus* €14.90/€17.50. Mon–Fri 7.30am–2am, Sat 8am–2am.

★**La Cave des Abbesses** 43 rue des Abbesses, 18e ☎ 01 42 52 81 54, Ⓦ cavesbourdin.fr/abbesses; Ⓜ Abbesses; map p.182. This humble neighbourhood wine shop, with a couple of streetfront tables, hides a secret dining room – seating 24 at a pinch – at the back. Squeeze in among the mixed neighbourhood crowd tucking into sharing platters of charcuterie and cheese – fresh oysters and foie gras are also on offer, along with fabulous wines. The decor is no-nonsense at best, but the atmosphere is exuberant, the food is delicious, and the prices are low – a *Grande Mixte* gets you a feast of cheeses, terrines, *rillettes* and ham, with endless supplies of fresh bread, for just €14. No reservations, so arrive early and try your luck. Tues–Fri 5–10.30pm, Sat & Sun noon–10.30pm; last entry 9.30pm.

Cuillier 19 rue Yvonne le Tac, 18e Ⓦ cuillier.fr; Ⓜ Abbesses; map p.182. The cool-coffee-bar aesthetic is a hit familiar, with its pale wood and artfully displayed coffee-related books, but you can't argue with the quality of the drinks – they're more concerned with creating a perfect espresso than checking your hipster credentials. The food menu (mains around €7) is short but on point, listing avocado on toast, fancy sandwiches and salads. If you tire of the laptops, head to the tables at the back – it's a computer-free zone. There are more branches in the 7e and the 2e. Mon–Fri 8am–6pm, Sat & Sun 9am–6pm.

★**Halle St-Pierre** 2 rue Ronsard, 18e ☎ 01 42 58 72 89, Ⓦ hallesaintpierre.org; Ⓜ Anvers/Abbesses; map p.182. Relax surrounded by artworks in the peaceful, light-filled *salon de thé* of this unusual gallery (see p.187), housed in an old market building at the foot of Sacré-Coeur. Speciality teas, coffee and delicious cakes (from €4) are on offer, along with a big, and daily changing, selection of quiches (from €10). Mon–Fri 11am–6pm, Sat 11am–7pm, Sun noon–6pm.

Le Progrès 1 rue Yvonne Le Tac, 18e ☎ 01 42 64 07 37; Ⓜ Abbesses/Anvers; map p.182. A simple, relaxed old café-bar with generous picture windows overlooking a bustling crossroads at the heart of Abbesses. They serve reasonably priced classic French dishes, burgers and salads (€12–23); the whole place transforms into a lively bar at night (cocktails €9). Daily 9am–2am.

Relais de la Butte 12 rue Ravignan, 18e ☎ 01 42 23 24 34; Ⓜ Abbesses; map p.182. On a quiet spot halfway up the butte, this otherwise unremarkable restaurant-bar has

20

20

one of the best *terrasses* in the city, clustered on a tiny tree-shaded, cobbled *place* with lovely views down over Paris. The drinks aren't too expensive when you consider the buzz of sitting out here (glass of wine €5.50), and if you choose a simple salad or cheese plate you can eat reasonably well. Daily noon–midnight.

Le Village 36 rue des Abbesses, 18e ☎01 42 54 99 59, ⓦbistrotlevillage.com; ⓂAbbesses; map p.182. This non-sceney little bar-café knocks the posier sidewalk places on Abbesses into a cocked hat. The *terrasse* is teeny but the interior is a retro delight, with gleaming ceramic wall tiles, high stools, huge mirrors and a zinc bar held up by local *habitués*. Equally good for a morning coffee, a quick lunch (€8–18) – *croques*, salads, omelettes – or a late-night Cognac, and perfect for watching the world go by. Daily 7am–2am.

RESTAURANTS

Le Bistrot de la Galette 102ter rue Lepic, 18e ☎01 46 06 19 65, ⓦbistrotdelagalette.fr; ⓂAbbesses/Lamarck Caulaincourt; map p.182. The old-time ambience is picture-perfect in this neighbourhood *bistrot* headed by *pâtissier* Gilles Marchal. It's a welcoming setting for perfectly executed rustic French staples – steak in peppercorn sauce; roast chicken with trompette mushrooms; duck with fondant potatoes – all served within a flaky pastry lid and base, or *galette* (giant *vol-aux-vents*, effectively). Mains €16–18. Tues–Sun 11am–11pm.

Le Coq Rico 98 rue Lepic, 18e ☎01 42 59 82 89, ⓦlecoqrico.com; ⓂAbbesses/Blanche; map p.182. It's all about the birds at Antoine Westermann's chic, relatively formal Montmartre outfit, from the huge rôtisserie that turns out moist whole grilled chickens, to the duck *rillettes*, roast pigeon, *poule-au-pot* and poultry soups; even the desserts showcase organic eggs. Mains €22–42; lunchtime *plats* €15. Daily noon–2.30pm & 7–11pm.

★ Le Grand 8 8 rue Lamarck, 18e ☎01 42 55 04 55, ⓦrestaurant-legrandhuit.com; ⓂAnvers; map p.182. It's hard to believe that you're just footsteps away from the Sacré-Coeur scrum at this friendly, pared-down *bistrot*, which serves simple food done just right, using market-fresh produce (courgette velouté with egg and parmesan, for example, or Aveyron lamb with seasonal veg) with a light touch. Mains €18–26. Book in advance for a table by the back window, and savour the view over the city. Wed–Sun noon–2pm & 7–11pm.

Miroir 94 rue des Martyrs, 18e ☎01 46 06 50 73; ⓂAbbesses; map p.182. This unfussy brasserie-cum-wine

bar serves quality coffee, speciality teas and craft beers during the day, but its short, seasonal menu comes into its own in the evening. It's all very easy-going: you can pick at a charcuterie plate (€9) or a couple of starters (€5–10) – fish beignets, perhaps, or beetroot with goat cheese – if that suits you better than a full meal. Hungrier diners could choose cod with octopus followed by an all-you-can-eat cheese platter (€18). Mains €12–25. Tues–Fri 8am–10pm, Sat 9am–10pm, Sun 9am–4pm.

Le Mono 40 rue Véron, 18e ☎01 46 06 99 20; ⓂAbbesses; map p.182. Welcoming, casual, family-owned Togolese restaurant with *soukous* on the playlist and African art on the orange walls. Hearty mains (€13–18.50) focus on grilled fish or meat with hot sauces and rice or cassava. The selection starter plate (€15.50) gets you a tasty array including stuffed crab; for dessert, think rum-flambéed bananas. Mon, Tues & Thurs–Sun 7pm–midnight.

★ Le Refuge 72 rue Lamarck, 18e ☎01 42 62 01 62; ⓂLamarck Caulaincourt; map p.182. If you're shocked by the tourist crowds of Montmartre, this classic café, right by the Lamarck-Caulaincourt métro, will indeed feel like a refuge. The decor hasn't changed much in a hundred years, and the clientele is resolutely local. Simple, reasonably priced dishes include *tartines* made with Poilane bread (€10.50), roast chicken with chips (€14.50) and a cheese-laden onion soup for €7. Two-course lunch *formule* €13.90. Daily 11am–11pm.

★ Les Rillettes 33 rue de Navarin, 9e ☎01 48 74 02 90; ⓂSt-Georges/Pigalle; map p.182. The husband-and-wife team create a wonderful, warm-hearted atmosphere in this charming small restaurant – she front of house, he producing amazing food from their tiny open kitchen. As the name suggests, this is meaty cooking, with a short menu of simple, beautifully executed country dishes, such as sausage cooked in a hay pot or pork tenderloin with white beans. The "trillettes" starter – *rillettes* of pork, chicken and sardines – is a must. Mains €19–34. Tues–Sat 7–11pm.

★ Soul Kitchen 33 rue Lamarck, 18e ☎01 71 37 99 95, ⓦfacebook.com/pg/soulkitchenparis; ⓂLamarck Caulaincourt; map p.182. Cosy, rustic veggie restaurant, offering good vegan options, in a pretty room filled with the aroma of baking. Along with fresh salads and savoury tarts, there's a daily changing €13.90 lunch *menu* listing such dishes as a mac'n'cheese *raclette* with butternut squash and roasted onion, or a veg-packed "geisha bowl" in a miso/yuzu broth. It's perpetually full, so come early. Mon–Fri 8.45am–6pm.

THE 10e AND GOUTTE D'OR

CAFÉS AND WINE BARS

Café A 148 rue du Faubourg-St-Martin, 10e ☎09 81 29 83 38; ⓦcafea.fr; ⓂGare de l'Est; map p.192. Arty café

with a picturesque setting in the old Récollets convent (see p.193). The high-ceilinged interior is striking, with its exposed brick walls and distressed concrete columns, but the real draw is the lovely walled garden, shaded with mature trees (open till 11pm). Mains (around €16) include French and international dishes (salmon with wasabi and soy sauce, for example). There are good cocktails, too, with frequent live bands and DJs. Mon–Sat 10am–2am, Sun 11am–1am.

Oh Africa! Marché St-Quentin, 85bis bd de Magenta, 10ᵉ ☎01 72 60 43 15, ⓦfacebook.com/OhAfricaRestaurant; Ⓜ Gare de l'Est; map p.192. Sitdown diner in a busy food market, usually packed with in-the-know locals tucking into tasty home-made African food. The three lunch dishes change regularly (€9) – yassa, perhaps (a chicken, onion and lime dish with rice and plantain), or maffe (chicken or beef with peanut sauce and plantain). You can also try Creole/African tapas (from €4), fresh juices and rum cocktails (€7). Tues–Sat 10am–8pm, Sun 10am–1pm.

Le Petit Château d'Eau 34 rue du Château d'Eau, 10ᵉ ☎01 42 08 72 81; Ⓜ Jacques-Bonsergent; map p.192. Lovely, peaceful old café-bar with zinc bar, gorgeous ceramic tiles on the walls, fresh flowers on the tables and a local crowd enjoying coffee, wine and cheese/charcuterie platters (€14) or classic French plats for around €10. Mon–Fri 8am–midnight, Sat 9am–midnight.

★**La Pointe du Grouin** 8 rue de Belzunce, 10ᵉ ☎01 48 78 28 80, ⓦlapointedugrouin.com; Ⓜ Gare du Nord; map p.192. This high-spirited wine bar-tavern, on a small square near the Gare du Nord, has a strong Breton accent. There's a €10 minimum spend, you need to convert your euros into "grouin" tokens in a vending machine in order to pay, and you order at the bar. Once you've got the hang of it, it's a treat – delicious, inexpensive food, Breton cider and natural wines are served with no fuss at the pub-like tables. Breton cakes and small plates (€4–12) – octopus with tapenade; Breton artichoke with vinaigrette; moules; galettes – are served all day, along with cheese and charcuterie platters (€8–14). The overstuffed lunchtime sandwiches (€4), made from home-baked bread, are a bargain – try the grilled pork with mustard and salad. Things get lively at night. The chef here effectively owns the rue de Belzunce eating scene, with a deliciously retro local bistrot, Chez Casimir, at no. 6, and the pricier, excellent Chez Michel at no. 10. Mon–Fri 11am–3pm & 6pm–midnight, Sat 6pm–midnight.

★**Vivant** 43 rue des Petites-Ecuries, 10ᵉ ☎01 42 46 43 55, ⓦvivantparis.com/vivant; Ⓜ Bonne Nouvelle/Château d'Eau; map p.192. You can drink superb natural wines at this tiny restaurant à vins (most of which is taken up by its counter and open kitchen) and enjoy a short, daily changing grazing menu (€12–28) of impeccably sourced, seasonal produce – roasted cabbage, white asparagus, scallops, pot-au-feu and the like – served with contemporary flair. Mon–Fri 7pm–1am.

RESTAURANTS

42 Degrés 109 rue du Faubourg Poissonnière, 9ᵉ ☎09 73 65 77 88, ⓦ42degres.com; Ⓜ Possonière; map p.192. One of the stars on Paris's vegan bistronomy scene, turning out beautiful organic raw food with creativity and panache – dishes like chia caviar with vegetable charcoal and buckwheat blinis, or celery spaghetti with paprika, goji berries and asparagus tips, are a real adventure. The dining room, with its retro tiled floor and stone walls, is as elegant as the food. Mains around €18. Weekday lunch formules €16/€20; menus €36/€45/€90. Mon–Sat noon–2.30pm & 7–10.30pm, Sun noon–4pm.

★**Abri** 92 rue du Faubourg-Poissonnière, 10ᵉ ☎01 83 97 00 00; Ⓜ Poissonnière; map p.192. Don't be misled by the workaday City Café sign above this hole in the wall – Abri is one of Paris's classiest places to eat, with chef Katsuaki Okiyama turning out elegant French-Asian fusion from the tiny open kitchen. Reserve weeks in advance for the dégustation menus (€26 for four courses at lunch, €49 for six courses at dinner), or come on Sat lunchtime for the gourmet toasted sandwiches (€13 including a drink; arrive early). They also have a soba place, Abri Soba, around the corner at 10 rue Saulnier. Tues–Fri 12.30–2pm & 7.30–10pm, Sat 12.30–3pm & 7.30–10pm.

Flo 7 cour des Petites-Ecuries, 10ᵉ ☎01 47 70 13 59, ⓦbrasserieflo-paris.com; Ⓜ Château d'Eau; map p.192. Hidden down what was once Louis XIV's stableyard, this opulent Alsatian brasserie is so handsome that even the crammed-in tourist and business crowds can't spoil the experience. Serving rich meat dishes and elegant seafood, including oysters, it's not cheap, but you're paying for the setting and the history – and if you go for the menus (from €29; lunchtime formule €18) you won't feel cheated. Mon & Sun 8.30am–11pm, Tues–Sat 8.30am–midnight.

Little Mana 72 rue du Faubourg-Poissonnière, 10ᵉ ☎01 42 46 30 53, ⓦlittlemana.com; Ⓜ Poissonnière; map p.192. Warm-hearted brasserie offering food infused with the sunny flavours of the Med, and natural wines to go with it. Meze (€6) might include labneh with mint oil and cucumber, or a plate of salty feta cheese, while sharing plates (€7–12) range from octopus with orange and sesame vinaigrette to cod roe on toast; mains (€15–22) feature heartier options such as chicken with sumac, yoghurt and bulgur. Two-course lunch formule €18. Mon–Fri noon–2.30pm & 7.30–11pm, Sat 7.30–11pm.

★**Richer** 2 rue Richer, 9ᵉ ⓦlericher.com; Ⓜ Poissonnière/Bonne Nouvelle; map p.192. This light, bright dining room, a fresh update on the traditional all-day Parisian brasserie, is welcoming to business people, bons viveurs and tourists alike. They offer coffee, wine and tapas all day, along with simple breakfasts – but it's the short, seasonal menu that knocks your socks off, using fresh ingredients in innovative ways. Starters (€9–10) might

20

20

include egg yolk with a risotto of celery and Granny Smith apples, served with pancetta, while typical mains (€19–20) include seabass with cauliflower cream, roast cabbage and squid ink. No reservations. *L'Office*, a more intimate

place a few doors down on rue Richer, and *52*, nearby at 52 rue du Faubourg St-Denis, both of which are run by the same people, are also worth checking out. Daily 8am–1am; full meals noon–2.30pm & 7.30–10.30pm.

BATIGNOLLES

RESTAURANTS

Le Bistrot des Dames 18 rue des Dames, 17ᵉ ☎ 01 45 22 13 42, ⓦ eldoradohotel.fr; Ⓜ Place de Clichy; map p.195. The food at this bric-a-brac-strewn *bistrot* is largely French and meat-focused. You'll find interesting Mediterranean and Asian touches in dishes like chicken tajine with olives or Thai salad with marinated beef, but the main draw is the cosy conviviality and the pretty courtyard garden. Starters €7–16, mains €16–24. Mon–Fri noon–2.30pm & 7–11pm, Sat & Sun noon–11pm.

Coretta 151 bis Rue Cardinet, 17ᵉ ☎ 01 42 26 55 55, ⓦ restaurantcoretta.com; Ⓜ Brochant; map p.195. Superb contemporary neo-bistro, where you can eat artistic and accomplished French cuisine, zinging with

delicate flavours, in a sunny, Scandi/retro dining room. Don't miss the crab royale and the veal sweetbreads, if they're on offer. Two-/three-course *menus* €25/€30 at weekday lunchtimes, €35/€41 all day Sun. Reservations essential. Daily 12.30–2pm & 7.30–10pm.

★ **Strobi** 12 rue Biot, 17ᵉ ☎ 01 72 38 59 86, ⓦ facebook .com/lestrobi; Ⓜ Place de Clichy; map p.195. Batignolles is getting a name for its contemporary neighbourhood *bistrots*, typified by *Strobi*, near place de Clichy. Dishes are colourful and pretty, ranging from chilled pea velouté to duck *tartare* with dried fruit and *frites* – and in an inspired move are offered in gourmet (smaller; €9–12) and gourmand (larger; €16–20) portions. The prices are good for the quality on offer. Mon–Sat noon–2.30pm & 7–11pm.

CANAL ST-MARTIN AND AROUND

CAFÉS AND WINE BARS

L'Atmosphère 49 rue Lucien Sampaix, 10ᵉ ☎ 01 40 38 09 21, ⓦ latmosphere.fr; Ⓜ Gare de l'Est; map p.198. Laidback, vaguely boho bar-restaurant with decent, good-value *plats* (onion soup; gorgonzola and goat cheese ravioli with peas; sea bream stuffed with lime) for €8–20. On a pleasant corner beside the Canal St-Martin, it's equally appealing in summer, when tables spill out onto the towpath, and winter, when it's a haven of cosy corners and mulled wine. Mon–Sat 9.30am–2am, Sun 9.30am–midnight.

Café Fluctuat 18 place de la République, 10ᵉ ☎ 01 42 06 42 81, ⓦ fluctuat-cafe.paris; Ⓜ République; map p.198. The city's Latin motto ("It is tossed about but does not sink") became a sort of rallying cry of resistance after the November 2015 attacks (see p.377) and it feels like a fitting name for this lively café, which opened shortly afterwards in the square that saw huge crowds gather in mourning. In keeping with this spirit of solidarity, the café hosts a varied programme of public debates, as well as screenings of sports events, and live music performances – which often spread out onto the large terrace, a great place for people-watching. The food is reasonably priced (€10.90 for the plat du jour, *boeuf bourguignon* for €12.90). It's also a good place for breakfast or an evening cocktail (around €8.40), ranging from classic mojitos to the café's own concoctions: try the Rivolette, a mix of lillet, champagne and grapefruit juice. Mon–Fri 8am–1am, Sat & Sun 9am–1am.

★ **Chez Prune** 36 rue Beaurepaire, 10ᵉ ☎ 01 42 41 30 47; Ⓜ Jacques-Bonsergent; map p.198. Named after the owner's grandmother (a bust of whom is inside), this funky, relaxed café-bar is the quintessential canalside haunt,

gently buzzing with an artsy crowd enjoying everything from a morning coffee to a lazy Sunday brunch (noon–4pm) or a charcuterie platter (€12) and glass of wine at night when full meals aren't served. International lunchtime dishes (lasagne, tandoori, etc) around €15. Mon–Sat 8am–2am, Sun 10am–2am.

Dauphin 131 av Parmentier, 11ᵉ ☎ 01 55 28 78 88, ⓦ restaurantledauphin.net; Ⓜ Goncourt; map p.198. Behind an unassuming shop front, this hot destination is all cool simplicity with its white marble counters and tabletops, dark-wood chairs, mirrors and twinkling candles. If you can't afford a meal at *Châteaubriand* (see p.283) – or even if you can – this is a great and gratifyingly unpretentious spot to enjoy the food of stellar chef Inaki Aizpitarte in tapas portions at €7–13 each, from duck charcuterie or oysters with watercress and chilli to scallops with parsley butter and blood orange. Eat in the bar (no reservations), with a quick glass of wine, or at one of the few tables at the back (reservations taken). Tues–Sat 5.30pm–2am.

Holybelly 19 rue Lucien Sampaix, 10ᵉ ⓦ holybel.ly; Ⓜ Jacques-Bonsergent; map p.198. Get your flat white or long black fix at this third-wave coffee house, which has a definite whiff of Melbourne with its airy ceramic-tiled interior, its short but on-point coffee list, its pancakes and its eggy brunches – plus a few seasonal French lunch dishes for good measure. A new branch was opening at the time of writing just a few doors down at no. 5. Mon, Thurs & Fri 9am–5pm (food till 2.15pm), Sat & Sun 10am–5pm (food till 3.15pm).

★ **La Patache** 60 rue de Lancry, 10ᵉ ☎ 01 42 08 40 51; Ⓜ Jacques-Bonsergent; map p.198. A cosy vibe, low lighting and sharing boards of top-quality regional produce make this bar-restaurant an atmospheric stop for a drink and a bite to eat. Its candlelit corners really come into their own in the colder months, when you can hole up and nurse a well-priced bottle of wine with a comforting *plat* of sausage and lentils or roast lamb (dishes around €16). Mon–Fri 5pm–2am, Sat & Sun 3pm–2am.

Le Pavillon des Canaux 39 quai de la Loire, 19e ☏ 01 73 71 82 90, ⓦ pavillondescanaux.com; ⓜ Laumière; map p.200. A great canalside lunchtime spot, where you can tuck into copious salads (quinoa, prawns, avocado, roquette and orange in a lemon vinaigrette, say; €9) or sample one of their delicious home-made pastries. Either sit out on the *terrasse* or in one of the *Pavillon*'s quirkily decorated rooms full of retro furnishings and knick-knacks. There's plenty going on here, including debates, workshops and music soirées. Mon–Wed 10am–midnight, Thurs–Sat 10am–1am, Sun 10am–10pm.

Péniche Antipode 55 quai de La Seine, 19e ☏ 06 69 09 55 10, ⓦ penicheantipode.fr; ⓜ Riquet; map p.200. This barge moored on the Bassin de la Villette makes a lovely waterside setting for a leisurely lunch or evening drinks and it's very reasonably priced too, with most dishes under €10 (order at the bar). Their speciality is tostadas; try perhaps the Antiponade, made with sheep's cheese, artichokes, pine nuts, coriander and honey. It's wise to reserve for lunch a day or so in advance on weekends, and be sure to check out their programme of live music (see p.306). Mon–Fri noon–2.30pm & 7–11pm, Sat & Sun noon–4pm & 7–11pm.

RESTAURANTS

★ **Au Passage** 1bis passage St-Sebastien, 11e ☏ 01 43 55 07 52, ⓦ restaurant-aupassage.fr; ⓜ St-Sébastien-Froissart; map p.198. Quiet, subtle, market-fresh food served in a bright, noisy, bare-bones dining room – part tapas/wine bar, part restaurant. Small plates (€7–18) focus on seasonal ingredients in simple, contemporary dishes, with lots of fish and veg – asparagus with goat's cheese, for example, or cod with aioli. Larger *plats* from €25. Reservations recommended; walk-ins after 9.30pm. Mon–Sat 7pm–1.30am.

L'Auberge Pyrénées Cévennes 106 rue de la Folie Méricourt, 11e ☏ 01 43 57 33 78; ⓜ République; map p.198. Make sure you come hungry to this cosy, family-run place, serving enormous portions of hearty country cuisine. Highly recommended are the garlicky moules for starters, the boar stew and the *cassoulet*. Three-course *menu* €31.50. Mon–Fri noon–2pm & 7–11pm, Sat 7–11pm.

★ **Le Châteaubriand** 129 av Parmentier, 11e ☏ 01 43 57 45 95, ⓦ lechateaubriand.net; ⓜ Goncourt; map

p.198. In 2006, Basque chef Inaki Aizpitarte helped change the face of the Paris dining scene with this innovative *bistrot*, which remains one of the city's finest addresses and one of the most highly regarded restaurants in the world (though it has yet to snag a Michelin star, apparently because the cuisine is too "unpredictable"). The daily changing menu features amazing ceviches and concoctions such as squid salad with sea asparagus, onions, redcurrants and wakame powder or oyster soup with red fruits and beetroot. It's not obscenely expensive, either: the five-course *menu dégustation* costs €70. Reservations are essential (up to a month in advance); if you don't manage to bag a place, head to Aizpitarte's tapas bar, *Dauphin*, next door (see opposite). The incongruously traditional name, incidentally, is simply carried over from the establishment that existed here before Aizpitarte moved in. Tues–Sat 7–11pm.

Chez Imogène Corner rue Jean-Pierre-Timbaud and rue du Grand-Prieuré, 11e ☏ 01 48 07 14 59, ⓦ creperie-imogene.fr; ⓜ Oberkampf; map p.198. A great crêperie in a beamed dining room: you could start with a home-made blini and smoked salmon, followed by a *savoyarde* crêpe (filled with two cheeses, potato, onion and ham), and finish with a sweet crêpe, perhaps *fromage blanc* with apple. Drinks include Breton cider and a small selection of wines. Menus from €10.50 at lunch, €19 at dinner, with a good kids' *menu* at €8.80. Mon 7–11pm, Tues–Sat noon–2.30pm & 7–11pm.

Le Clown Bar 114 rue Amelot, 11e ☏ 01 43 55 87 35, ⓦ clown-bar-paris.com; ⓜ Oberkampf; map p.198. This buzzy, extremely popular wine *bistrot* – an old belle époque bar, its beautifully tiled interior depicting the antics of clowns – has been given a new lease of life by the formidable team who run *Saturne* (see p.276). A long list of natural wines, many available by the glass, complements the short, seasonal menu of delicacies such as duck and foie gras in puff pastry, succulent pigeon breast with raspberries, or turbot with clams, asparagus and rhubarb. The lunch menu costs €32, at dinner reckon on around €50 à la carte. Book well in advance. Wed–Sun 8am–1.30am (food served noon–2.30pm & 7–10.30pm).

Soya 20 rue de la Pierre Levée, 11e ☏ 01 48 06 33 02; ⓦ Goncourt/Parmentier; map p.198. A cool loft-style converted warehouse housing an inventive organic vegetarian restaurant. The creative fusion cuisine, which is predominantly vegan and gluten-free, ranges from Asian seaweed pâté to tasty couscous and Lebanese stew (mains from €17) – the fresh juices are delicious, too. Mon–Fri noon–3.30pm & 7–11pm, Sat 11.30am–11pm, Sun 11.30am–4pm.

★ **Le Square Gardette** 24 rue Saint Ambroise, 11e ☏ 01 85 15 22 84, ⓦ squaregardette.fr; ⓜ Rue St-Maur/St-Ambroise; map p.198. There's a relaxed,

20

20

arty vibe about this welcoming neo-bistro, a favourite with local literati such as writer Delphine de Vigan. A zinc bar, book-lined shelves and rugs lend the interior a cosy feel, while the stuffed deer heads on the walls add a somewhat eccentric touch. The waiting staff are charming and happy to talk you through the short menu, which usually features a vegetarian choice or two and often some unusual ingredients. Starters might include gorgonzola arancini (stuffed rice ball) or white bean hummus with savory, mains rascasse (scorpionfish), jerusalem artichokes, kumquats, tamarind and Thai basil; or tandoori-style roast cauliflower with pistacchio and pomegranate. The desserts – an impossibly light chocolate mousse, say – are not to be missed either. Reckon on around €45 a head for dinner, without drinks; there are reasonably priced *plats* and a "sandwich du jour" at lunch. Mon–Fri 8am–1am, Sat 9am–1am, Sun 9am–11pm (food served noon–2.30pm & 7.30–10.30pm).

★ **Le Verre Volé** 67 rue de Lancry, 10ᵉ ☎ 01 48 03 17 34, ⓦ leverrevole.fr; ⓜ Jacques-Bonsergent; map p.198. This wine shop doubles as a simple, cool venue for amazing food, with an appreciative local crowd filling the formica tables crammed into the small space. The short menu lists beautifully executed modern and traditional dishes (from €27) along with cheaper, simpler offerings such as black pudding or sausage with lentils (€17), and delicious desserts. The three-course lunch is great value at €22. Their wine selection is impeccable, of course, focusing on natural and biodynamic varieties – staff can select one for you, depending on your tastes and your meal – you pay the over-the-counter price plus €7 corkage fee. Reservations recommended. Restaurant daily 12.30–2pm & 7.30–10.30pm.

BELLEVILLE AND MÉNILMONTANT

CAFÉS AND WINE BARS

L'Autre Café 62 rue Jean-Pierre-Timbaud, 11ᵉ ☎ 01 40 21 03 07, ⓦ lautrecafe.com; ⓜ Parmentier; map p.207. Amid the throng of bars on this popular nightlife stretch, this attractive fin-de-siècle café-bar-restaurant offers something slightly different, welcoming all-comers and giving off an easy, effortless vibe. It's spacious, with high ceilings, a long zinc bar and comfy leather banquettes, drinks are reasonably priced, and the food isn't bad either, especially if you stick to the blackboard specials, which might include *boeuf bourguignon* (around €10). A great place to enjoy a lazy breakfast or to while away time browsing the newspapers or taking advantage of the free wi-fi. Daily 8am–2am.

Aux Deux Amis 45 rue Oberkampf, 11ᵉ ☎ 01 58 30 38 13; ⓜ Oberkampf; map p.207. You'd never guess it from the outside, but this ordinary-looking neighbourhood café on the lower stretch of the rue Oberkampf is one of the area's hot tickets – it packs out quickly so it's best to get there by 7pm and be prepared to elbow your way to the bar. Everyone is here for the fresh and inventive small plates (from around €10; typical dishes might include veal *tartare* with anchovy mayonnaise or an earthy braised squid) and Spanish tapas, all of which can be paired with the fine selection of natural wines. Prices are reasonable, and the vibe fun and boisterous. Tues–Sat noon–2am.

Le Barbouquin 1 rue Denoyez, 20ᵉ ☎ 09 84 32 13 21; ⓜ Belleville; map p.207. Sitting on the corner of rue Denoyez, a graffiti-emblazoned backstreet, this relaxed café is a soothing way-station for a coffee, a fresh mint and ginger tea or a juice. Light food includes savoury tarts and wraps, while the soundtrack wanders from *chanson* to rap. The weekend brunch, including pancakes, goats' cheese and eggs, is good value at €20. Pluck a book from the shelves, settle in an armchair and relax. Tues noon–6pm, Wed–Fri 10am–6pm, Sat & Sun 10.30am–6pm.

La Mère Lachaise 78 bd Ménilmontant, 20ᵉ ☎ 01 73 20 24 44, ⓦ lamerelachaise.fr; ⓜ Père-Lachaise; map p.207. The sunny *terrasse* of this bar-restaurant, popular with students and bobos (bourgeois-bohemians), makes a good place for a drink after a visit to Père-Lachaise, or check out the cosy interior bar with its retro-chic decor. The restaurant serves classic dishes and cheeseburgers (menus from €15). Mon–Sat 8am–2am, Sun 11am–1am.

Rosa Bonheur Parc des Buttes-Chaumont, 2 allée de la Cascade, 19ᵉ ☎ 01 42 00 00 45, ⓦ rosabonheur.fr; ⓜ Botzaris/Jourdain; map p.207. Set inside a former *guinguette* – an open-air café or dance hall – this popular bar (see p.302) is also a nice place for a relaxing drink and snack or light meal – deli dishes and tapas from €4 – during the day. Thurs & Fri noon–midnight, Sat & Sun 10am–midnight.

RESTAURANTS

Astier 44 rue Jean-Pierre-Timbaud, 11ᵉ ☎ 01 43 57 16 35, ⓦ restaurant-astier.com; ⓜ Parmentier; map p.207. This lovely old *bistrot* is a stalwart in this gentrifying area, turning out reliable classics – including roast duck, rabbit and a fabulous foie gras *royale* – in a pleasingly old-fashioned dining room. The cheese board is legendary, so leave space if you can. Three-course *menu* €35, or €45 including cheese. Mon–Fri 12.15–2pm & 7–10.30pm, Sat 12.15–2pm & 7–11pm, Sun 12.30–2.30pm & 7–10.30pm.

★ **Le Baratin** 3 rue Jouye-Rouve, 20ᵉ ☎ 01 43 49 39 70; ⓜ Pyrénées/Belleville; map p.207. At first glance there's not much to distinguish *Le Baratin* from any Parisian *bistrot à vins*: the chalkboard menu, tiled floor and black-and-white photos are all in place. But the genuine neighbourhood feel, the stellar cooking and the fine organic wines – matched with your meal by the waiter – elevate it above the competition. The €25 three-course lunch *menu* changes daily but might include a thick bean soup, melt-in-the-mouth veal cheeks and a quivering crème caramel; in the evenings, count on around €45 a head, without drinks. It's best to book. Tues–Fri noon–2.30pm & 7.30pm–1am, Sat 7.30pm–1am.

★ **Le Galopin** 34 rue Sainte-Marthe, 10ᵉ ☎ 01 47 06 05 03, ⓦ le-galopin.com; ⓜ Belleville/Goncourt; map p.207. With its bare brick walls, stone floor and simple wooden chairs, this pared-down neighbourhood place epitomizes the neo-bistro scene, offering a seven-course dinner *menu* of small, delicate plates (€54). The relaxed atmosphere belies the skill behind Romain Tischenko's innovative cooking: mains might include cauliflower soup with salmon roe, squid with peppers and pork *jus* or sea bass with celery and butternut squash. Book ahead. Mon–Fri 7.30–10.30pm.

Jambo 23 rue Sainte-Marthe, 10ᵉ ☎ 01 42 45 46 55; ⓜ Colonel Fabian; map p.207. With a sunshine-yellow frontage and cosy interior filled with African art, this pan-African restaurant goes out of its way to make you welcome. €28 gets you three courses; dishes range from a sour-sharp Masai soup to samosas from Zanzibar and Rwandan beef stew. Tues–Sat 7.30–10.30pm.

La Sardine 32 rue Sainte-Marthe, 10ᵉ ☎ 01 42 49 19 46, ⓦ barlasardine.com; ⓜ Colonel Fabien/Goncourt; map p.207. Colourful, contemporary café-restaurant in a foodie corner of Belleville. The *terrasse* is a draw on sunny days, and the short menu of home-made food is gratifyingly inexpensive. Weekly lunchtime *plats* (salt cod, chilli, steak *tartare*, burgers) are good value at €11.50–16); they also offer a popular weekend brunch at €20 and Spanish-style tapas (Serrano ham, roasted peppers and the like) from €3.50. Mon–Fri 9am–2am, Sat & Sun 10am–2am.

AUTEUIL AND PASSY

RESTAURANTS

La Gare 19 chaussée de la Muette, 16ᵉ ☎ 01 42 15 15 31, ⓦ restaurantlagare.com; ⓜ La Muette; map p.215. This former Passy train station has been turned into an elegant restaurant bar, which boasts a huge, sunny dining room and an attractive *terrasse*. It's best at lunchtime, when it offers modern French/Mediterranean food – goat cheese and chorizo tart; grilled prawns with polenta – on good-value weekday *menus* (€28). Daily noon–11.30pm.

Hugo Desnoyer 28 rue du Docteur Blanche, 16ᵉ ☎ 01 46 47 83 00, ⓦ hugodesnoyer.fr; ⓜ Jasmin/Ranelagh; map p.215. A carnivore's dream – a few tables in this renowned butcher's shop (supplier to the city's top chefs), where you can dine on the finest cuts – mainly veal and beef, prepared simply and to perfection. It's not cheap, though – reckon on around €65 a head. Tues–Sat 8.30am–7.30pm; food served 11am–3pm.

La Table Lauriston 129 rue Lauriston, 16ᵉ ☎ 01 47 27 00 07, ⓦ latablelauriston.com; ⓜ Trocadéro; map p.215. The staid, well-heeled crowd in this relaxed neighbourhood restaurant enjoys well-executed *cuisine bourgeoise*: Burgundy snails, Basque octopus salad and Chateaubriand with morels are typical. There's a lunch menu for €28, while at dinner you'll easily spend €50–60 per person. Closed Aug. Mon–Sat noon–2.30pm & 7–10.30pm.

20

Drinking and nightlife

Paris's fame as the quintessential home of decadent, hedonistic nightlife has endured for centuries, and there remain plenty of places to drink and to dance, whatever your tastes. Bars run the gamut from genuinely bohemian dives to swanky posers' paradises; added to the mix is a newer breed of hipster cocktail bars with a speakeasy vibe. Following some years of stagnation, the club scene is currently lively, with a variety of cool promoters offering eclectic, mixed programmes in venues from superclubs to refitted old theatres and riverboats. Where the city truly excels, however, is in its array of live music, from world music and rock to jazz and *chanson*.

The city has no rival in Europe for the variety of **world music** to be discovered: Algerian, West and Central African, Caribbean and Latin American sounds are represented in force, along with hip-hop, both imported and domestic. **Jazz** fans are in for a treat, too, with all styles from New Orleans to avant-garde filling venues almost nightly; **gypsy jazz** (*jazz manouche*), pioneered by Django Reinhardt, is also in vogue. French **chanson**, meanwhile – a tradition long associated with Paris, particularly during the war years through cabaret artists like Edith Piaf, Maurice Chevalier and Charles Trenet, and in the 1960s with poet-musicians as diverse as Georges Brassens, Jacques Brel and Serge Gainsbourg – remains as cool, and as popular, as ever. For something entirely different, a truly nostalgic taste of the entertainments of the past, you could head out of town altogether, and make for one of the old suburban eating-drinking-dancing venues known as **guinguettes**.

ESSENTIALS

Information To find out what's on, get hold of one of the city's listings magazines (see p.40). The online Ⓦlylo.fr offers a pretty good rundown of gigs in the city, searchable by genre, but if you want more in-depth coverage, try Ⓦparisbouge.com and the arts and music magazine *Nova* (Ⓦnovaplanet.com). You can also pick up flyers in the city's trendier shops, music stores, bars and cafés.

Tickets Concert tickets, whether rock, jazz or *chanson* (or indeed classical), can be bought at the venues themselves, online, or through agents such as Fnac (see p.334). It can also be worth checking Ⓦbilletreduc.com for cut-price tickets at the more mainstream venues.

BARS

The following listings review the city's livelier venues for night-time drinking, places that stay open late and maybe have DJs or occasional live music. Also included are the more vibrant, late-opening cafés, Alsatian/German-type beer cellars and a scattering of modish speakeasy-style cocktail bars. You'll find lower-key and more relaxed cafés and *bars à vins*, geared more to eating than nightlife, listed in the "Eating" chapter (see p.266), while full-on nightclubs, with entry fees and proper sound systems, are reviewed separately under "Clubs" (see p.302).

THE CHAMPS-ELYSÉES AND AROUND

Blaine 65 rue Pierre Charron, 8ᵉ ☎06 60 97 01 35; ⓂGeorge V; map p.64. Admission to this speakeasy-style bar is by password only (you'll find it on the bar's Facebook page). Once past the plain black door, you descend stairs to basement level, walk down an unlikely-looking corridor and finally emerge into the bar, an alluring, candle-lit room, with velvet chairs, gilt-edged mirrors and framed pictures on the walls. Live jazz completes the 1930s Chicago vibe (with DJs taking over later in the evening). From the extensive cocktail menu (€12–18) try perhaps the Byzantin, made of rum, passion fruit, mint, lemon and pineapple juice. Wed–Sun 7pm–5am.

Pershing Lounge Pershing Hall Hotel, 49 rue Pierre Charron, 8ᵉ ☎01 58 36 58 36, Ⓦpershinghall.com; ⓂGeorge V; map p.64. The swanky *Pershing Hall Hotel*'s lounge bar is an upscale retreat from the bustle of the city, with its 30m-high vertical garden, planted with exotic vegetation. Cocktails are priced to match the setting (€20 and upwards). Daily 6pm–2am.

GRANDS BOULEVARDS AND AROUND

Bar 228 Hôtel Le Meurice, 228 rue de Rivoli, 1ᵉʳ ☎01 44 58 10 10; ⓂConcorde/Palais Royal Musée du Louvre; map p.76. Secreted away inside the luxury *Hôtel Meurice*, the recently renovated *Bar 228*, with its glorious belle époque frescoes, mahogany wood panelling and leather armchairs, is the place to treat yourself to a special pre-dinner drink. Barman William Oliveri, who has been here over thirty years, mixes some mean champagne cocktails (€30). Daily noon–1am.

Bar Costes Hôtel Costes, 239 rue St-Honoré, 1ᵉʳ ☎01 42 44 50 00, Ⓦhotelcostes.com; ⓂConcorde/Tuileries; map p.76. Though its star is waning a little, this hotel bar – haunt of fashionistas, movie stars and media folk – is still a decadently romantic place for an *apéritif* or late-night drinks amid the sexy red velvet, swags and columns, set around an Italianate courtyard draped in ivy and atmospherically lit at night. Dress up, and be prepared for the too-cool-for-school staff. Cocktails from around €20; DJs get going at around 9pm. Daily 5pm–2am.

Delaville Café 34 bd de la Bonne Nouvelle, 10ᵉ ☎01 48 24 48 09, Ⓦdelavillecafe.com; ⓂBonne Nouvelle; map p.76. The grand staircase, gilded mosaics and marble columns hint at this bar's former incarnation as a bordello. It draws in crowds of pre-clubbers, who sling back a mojito or two before moving on to one of the area's clubs. High-profile DJ nights Thurs–Sun. Daily 9am–2am.

Lockwood 73 rue d'Aboukir, 2ᵉ ⓂSentier/Grands Boulevards; Ⓦlockwoodparis.com; map p.76. Ticking all the hipster boxes, and part of a group that includes a number of cool Sydney bars, this artisan café/coffee house transforms into a cocktail bar after dark, its candlelit

21

brick-walled cellar filled with cool young expats and locals quaffing creative whisky cocktails and chatting over the retro playlist. Mon–Sat 9am–2am.

Le Truskel 12 rue Feydeau, 2ᵉ ☎01 40 26 59 97, ⓦtruskel.com; Ⓜ Bourse; map p.76. "In rock we trusk" is this pub-cum-club's motto, so you won't be too surprised to find rock music heavily on the agenda here: there are often live gigs in the early part of the evening, followed by a DJ and dancing from around 10pm. It's also the place to catch live football match screenings. Drinks are not too pricey at €6 for a pint, €8 for a cocktail. Check the website for reduced opening hours in summer. Tues–Sat 7pm–5am.

BEAUBOURG AND LES HALLES

Au Trappiste 4 rue St-Denis, 1ᵉʳ ☎01 42 33 08 50; Ⓜ Châtelet; map p.88. Proudly announcing itself as the "royaume de la bière", this is a temple for beer lovers. More than 140 draught beers, mainly from Belgium, include Belgian Blanche Riva; Jenlain, France's best-known *bière de garde*; and Kriek from the Mort Subite (Sudden Death) brewery – ask for a taster if you can't decide – plus *moules frites*, bistro food and *tartines* to soak it all up. Mon–Thurs & Sun 11am–2am, Fri & Sat 11am–4am.

Le Fumoir 6 rue de l'Amiral de Coligny, 1ᵉʳ ☎01 42 92 00 24, ⓦlefumoir.com; Ⓜ Louvre-Rivoli; map p.88. Sedate, long-established cocktail bar where chatter from the thirty-something crowd rises above the mellow jazz soundtrack and the genteel clatter of cocktail shakers. There's a book-lined dining area, and you can browse the international press. Cocktails around €13 (€8 during the 6–8pm happy hour). Daily 11am–2am.

THE MARAIS

La Belle Hortense 31 rue Vieille du Temple, 4ᵉ ☎01 42 74 59 70, ⓦcafeine.com/belle-hortense; Ⓜ St-Paul; map p.99. You can sip a glass while reading or chatting in this friendly little wine/champagne bar/bookshop with book-lined walls and a zinc bar. There's a snug room with sofas at the back, though you'll be lucky to get a seat there later on. Daily 5pm–2am.

★**Candelaria** 52 rue de Saintonge, 3ᵉ ⓦquixotic -projects.com; Ⓜ Filles du Calvaire; map p.96. An atmospheric, clandestine cocktail bar, set behind an unassuming-looking taqueria; just walk straight to the back and push open what looks like a broom-cupboard door and you'll find yourself in a small, stone-walled, dimly lit bar. You might be lucky to snag one of the low tables, otherwise you'll have to squeeze in around the bar where you can watch the expert staff mix up some exotic concoctions (€13/14); if you can't decide, spin the arrow on the menu or try the classic La Guêpe Verte, made of pepper-infused tequila, lime, agave syrup and coriander. Daily 6pm–2am.

Little Red Door 60 rue Charlot, 3ᵉ ☎01 42 71 19 32, ⓦrdparis.com; Ⓜ Filles du Calvaire/Temple; map p.96. A discreet cocktail bar with a snug candlelit interior. Settle into a velvet sofa and have fun choosing one of the original, award-winning cocktails (€13) – each drink on the menu is illustrated by an artist, the ingredients only revealed when you pull out a tab. It soon gets very crowded, so either arrive early or be prepared to negotiate with the doorman. Thurs–Sat 6pm–3am, Sun–Wed 6pm–2am.

Les Nautes 1 quai des Célestins, 4ᵉ ☎01 42 74 59 53, ⓦlesnautes-paris.com; Ⓜ Pont Marie/Sully Morland; map p.96. Occupying an idyllic spot on the riverbank opposite the Île Saint-Louis, the extensive *terrasse* of *Les Nautes* is the perfect place for chilling out on a warm evening – perhaps with one of their home-made cocktails (€11); the building itself, a fine old stone building (formerly a watering hole for horses), is the venue for live music, such as rock, reggae and jazz, and hosts regular DJ nights. Wed– Fri 5pm–2am, Sat 2pm–2am, Sun 2pm–midnight; occasionally open Mon & Tues.

La Perle 78 rue Vieille du Temple, 3ᵉ ☎01 42 72 69 93, ⓦcafelaperle.com; Ⓜ St-Paul; map p.99. A casually retro and often noisy café-bar that maintains a *très cool* reputation and is popular with an arty, bobo (bourgeois-bohemian) crowd knocking back a pint of beer (around €6.50) or excellent rosé and spilling onto the pavement in the warmer months. Daily 8am–2am.

★**Sherry Butt** 20 rue Beautreillis, 4ᵉ ☎09 83 38 47 80, ⓦsherrybuttparis.com; Ⓜ St-Paul/Bastille; map p.96. Much less pretentious than some of its fashionable equivalents on the Left Bank, this New York-style cocktail bar is nevertheless a shrine to all things cool. The cocktail menu is innovative, listing drinks such as the Sassy Green (Scotch, pistachio and wasabi syrup, lime juice and sage leaves) – they're pricey at around €13, but many of the ingredients are home-made, and staff will also create drinks based on your tastes. Dark leather sofas and low lighting provide a laidback, intimate and relaxing atmosphere. Mon & Sun 8pm–2am, Tues–Sat 6pm–2am.

Stolly's 16 rue Cloche-Percé, 4ᵉ ☎01 42 76 06 76, ⓦcheapblonde.com/stollys.html; Ⓜ St-Paul; map p.99. The antithesis of Parisian cool, this rowdy no-nonsense, Anglo bar is an institution. You can watch broadcasts of major sporting events while enjoying pints of Guinness, Newcastle Brown Ale and "Cheapblonde" beer or a wide selection of spirits and cocktails (€8–9). Happy hour 5–8pm. Daily 5pm–1.30am.

BASTILLE AND AROUND

Le Lèche-Vin 13 rue Daval, 11ᵉ ☎01 43 55 06 70; Ⓜ Bastille; map p.112. An appealing, rough around the edges little bar, dotted with kitschy religious decor. The statue of Mary with a cross in the window sets the tongue-in-cheek scene; the pics in the toilet, on the other hand, are far from pious. It gets packed very quickly at night with a young, cosmopolitan crowd knocking back cheap beers and cocktails (around €5). Daily 6pm–2am.

Moonshiner 5 rue Sedaine, 11e ☎ 09 50 73 12 99; Ⓜ Bréguet-Sabin; map p.112. Deliciously hidden away behind the cold room in an otherwise unremarkable pizzeria, this speakeasy-style bar is a good spot to snuggle down on a leather sofa with a well-mixed gin, vodka or (especially) whisky cocktail. Try if you dare the "Back to Basil" gin fizz with olive oil and basil. Daily 6pm–2am.

QUARTIER LATIN

Le Bateau Ivre 40 rue Descartes, 5e ☎ 07 50 32 51 15, Ⓦ le-bateau-ivre-paris.fr; Ⓜ Cardinal Lemoine; map p.124. Small, dark and ancient, this studenty dive bar is just clear of the Mouffetard scrum, though it attracts a fair number of young tourists in the evenings for its lively vibe and good prices (cocktails from €8). Happy hour daily 5–9.30pm. Daily 6pm–2am.

Little Bastards 5 rue Blainville, 5e ☎ 01 43 54 28 33, Ⓦ facebook.com/lilbastards; Ⓜ Place Monge; map p.124. This sleek little place, a short hop away from rue Mouffetard, is a welcome halt for innovative cocktails – from the Lady Bastard (rum, cachaça, cherry syrup and champagne) to the Toudoux, a lethal concoction of mezcal, absinthe, lime, cucumber and egg white – crafted by friendly mixologists. Good prices, too – from around €8. Mon–Thurs 6pm–2am, Fri & Sat 6pm–4am.

Le Piano Vache 8 rue Laplace, 5e ☎ 01 46 33 75 03, Ⓦ lepianovache.fr; Ⓜ Cardinal Lemoine; map p.124. Venerable, easy-going *boîte* with poster-lined walls and dim lighting, its rickety chairs and old sofas crammed with students setting the world to rights. Live gypsy jazz on Mon, DJs on Fri and Sat, and occasional rock and Goth gigs. Happy hour (soft drinks and beer) 6–9pm. Mon–Sat 6pm–2am.

Le Reflet 6 rue Champollion, 5e ☎ 01 43 29 97 27; Ⓜ Cluny La Sorbonne; map p.124. Cool without trying, this bar-café has a nostalgic flavour of the *Nouvelle Vague* with its scruffy black decor, lights rigged up on a gantry, dog-eared movie posters and Dylan, Coltrane and Cohen LP sleeves adorning the walls. Perfect for a drink before or after a movie at one of the many arts cinemas on this street. Mon–Sat 11am–2am, Sun 3pm–midnight.

ST-GERMAIN

Bar du Marché 75 rue de Seine, 6e ☎ 01 43 26 55 15; Ⓜ Mabillon; map p.138. Perennially crowded retro café-bar near the Buci market, where the *serveurs* are cutely kitted out in flat caps and market trader dungarees. It's a place for animated conversation rather than banging techno, beer and *kir* rather than cocktails. Daily 8am–2am.

Castor Club 14 rue Hautefeuille, 6e ☎ 09 50 64 99 38, Ⓦ facebook.com/Castor-Club-131753693594498;

Ⓜ Odéon; map p.138. An excellent cocktail bar that pulls in the cool set with its secretive no-name frontage and speakeasy-cum-hunting-lodge decor. Come for the daily changing choice of well-crafted cocktails (from €13) – perhaps a Turkish Delight, made with chartreuse, pisco, pistachio cream and cardamom – and playlist of retro Americana. Tues & Wed 7pm–2am, Thurs–Sat 7pm–4am.

★**Chez Georges** 11 rue des Canettes, 6e ☎ 01 43 26 79 15, Ⓦ facebook.com/barchezgeorges; Ⓜ Mabillon; map p.138. This spirited wine bar – all chipped walls and mosaic-tiled floor – is a neighbourhood institution. The predominantly (but not entirely) young, largely local crowd keeps things lively, and it gets good-naturedly rowdy later on in its vaulted cellar bar, where you can sob to *chanson* or dance like a demon to gypsy jazz. Happy hour Mon–Thurs & Sun 7–9pm. Mon & Sun 6pm–1am, Tues–Fri 6pm–2am, Sat 3pm–2am.

Compagnie des Vins Surnaturels 7 rue Lobineau, 6e ☎ 09 54 90 20 20, Ⓦ compagniedesvinssurnaturels .com; Ⓜ Odéon; map p.138. Backed by the team credited with introducing Paris to the creative cocktail scene, this romantic wine bar, with its stone walls, twinkling tea lights, plush sofas and low tables, is a lovely spot to hunker down with a long list of wines by the glass (from €6) or the bottle. The on-trend bar snacks are a bit pricey. Daily 6pm–2am.

La Palette 43 rue de Seine, 6e ☎ 01 43 26 68 15, Ⓦ cafelapaletteparis.com; Ⓜ Odéon; map p.138. A traditional café-bar (see p.283) that brims with a chatty crowd till late, and has a terrific outdoor *terrasse*. Quintessentially Parisian, and great for a relaxed *apéro* or two. Mon–Sat 8am–2am.

Prescription 23 rue Mazarine, 6e ☎ 09 50 35 72 87, Ⓦ prescriptioncocktailclub.com; Ⓜ Odéon; map p.138. A stalwart on the cool cocktail scene, this tiny bar has a swish interior behind its artfully blank facade and creative cocktails (around €14) on its retro-style menu. Chic and restrained earlier in the evening, but pretty lively later on. Mon–Thurs 7pm–2am, Fri & Sat 7pm–4am, Sun 8pm–2am.

★**Tiger** 13 rue Princesse, 6e ☎ 01 84 05 81 74, Ⓦ tiger-paris.com; Ⓜ Mabillon; map p.138. Paris's favourite gin bar is a bright, contemporary spot, decked out in Scandi wood, retro mosaics, bare bulbs and pot plants. A laidback young crowd comes for G&Ts, martinis and other gin cocktails (from €12), with a few rum, mezcal and sake concoctions for good measure. DJs start up as the night proceeds. Mon–Sat 6pm–2am, Sun 7pm–2am.

THE EIFFEL TOWER QUARTER

Les Grands Verres Palais de Tokyo, 16e ☎ 01 01 85 53 03 61, Ⓦ quixotic-projects.com/venue/les-grands-verres; Ⓜ Iéna/Alma–Marceau; map p.152. In a superb

21

21

location within the Palais de Tokyo (see p.260), this swish bar – and restaurant (see p.286) – comes from the same stable as the wildly popular cocktail bars *Candelaria* (see p.298) and *Glass* (see opposite). The atmosphere gives an on-trend twist to rustic chic, with lots of wood and stone – the 13m bar is made of impacted earth, and they grow their own edible flowers – and the cocktails, naturally, are top-notch (from €14). Try the piña colada with goat's milk and white nectarine, or the Tchicki Boum, a creation of calvados, mint, sorrel and caramel. Occasional DJ sets after dark on the terrace, which offers unbeatable Eiffel Tower views. Daily noon–3pm & 7pm–2am.

★ **Rosa Bonheur sur Seine** Near Pont Alexandre III, 7ᵉ ⓦ rosabonheur.fr/rosa-seine; Ⓜ Invalides; map p.152. The riverside sibling of the iconic *Rosa Bonheur* (see p.302), this colourful, friendly café-bar on a barge is the best spot for a relaxed drink on this stretch of the river, offering wine (from €4), beer, cocktails (from €8.50), *apéros* and food (see p.285) to a laidback, mixed crowd. Great live sets too – from disco and DJ nights to *chanson* and flamenco. Wed–Sun noon–1.30am; hours may change according to season and weather.

THE 13ᵉ

★ **La Folie en Tête** 33 rue de la Butte-aux-Cailles, 13ᵉ ⓣ 01 45 80 65 99, ⓦ facebook.com/Lafolieentete; Ⓜ Corvisart; map p.172. This vibrant, alternative Butte-aux-Cailles bar, littered with bric-a-brac, is a classic of the *quartier*, with a playlist of world music, underground beats or *chanson*. A neighbourhood gem. Happy hour 5–8pm. Mon–Sat 5pm–2am.

Le Merle Moqueur 11 rue de la Butte-aux-Cailles, 13ᵉ; Ⓜ Place d'Italie/Corvisart; map p.172. Classic little shop-front-style Butte-aux-Cailles bar, which saw the Paris debut of Manu Chao. Nowadays, it chiefly serves up French rock music and home-made flavoured rums to a merry crowd of young Parisians. Daily 5pm–2am.

MONTMARTRE AND NORTHERN PARIS

Artisan 14 rue Bochart de Saron, 9ᵉ ⓣ 01 48 74 65 38, ⓦ artisan-bar.fr; Ⓜ Anvers; map p.182. It may not feel particularly Parisian, but this SoPi bar – airy and contemporary, but with a distressed/rustic edge to stop it feeling too glacial – is famed citywide for its creative cocktails. They start at €12, or you could splash out on a Green Beast to share (absinthe, lime juice, cucumber; €45). French bar food – *boudin*, charcuterie, *croques* – from €7. Mon–Sat 7pm–2am.

★ **L'Atelier** 6 rue Burq, 18ᵉ ⓣ 01 42 51 32 27, ⓦ facebook.com/ateliermontmartre18; Ⓜ Abbesses; map p.182. Arty, welcoming and on the cool side of scruffy, this bar has the feel of an artist's studio – or a boho living room – mixing and matching flea-market furniture and fresh flowers, bric-a-brac and board games, old

paintings and new art. Exhibitions and performances are staged in the tiny space, but above all it's a relaxed spot for a drink (cocktails €7.50, wine €4.50). The bar food (€4–19) is good, too. Happy hour daily 6–8.30pm. Daily 4pm–2am.

Au Clair de la Lune 1 rue Ramey, 18ᵉ ⓣ 01 46 06 93 61, ⓦ clairdeluneparis.fr/en; Ⓜ Château Rouge; map p.182. Shabbily hip neighbourhood café-bar on the fringes of the Goutte d'Or. The authentic 1950s decor – neon signs, table football, movie posters, copper-edged bar – is fabulous, while the picture windows let you watch the world go by on busy rue Clignancourt. Cocktails around €6; cheese/charcuterie platter €14; happy hour (beer and cocktails only) daily 6–10pm. Daily 7am–11.30pm.

★ **Chez Camille** 8 rue Ravignan, 18ᵉ ⓣ 01 42 57 75 62, ⓦ facebook.com/Chez-Camille-112695022123953; Ⓜ Abbesses; map p.182. Charming little neighbourhood bar on the slopes of the Butte. With a simple list of drinks and unaffected, retro vibe – classic movie posters, ceiling fans, old mirrors, mismatched school tables – it pulls a local crowd of all ages who could as easily be enjoying a quiet chat and a glass of wine (from €3.80) as spontaneously dancing to anything from Elvis or rockabilly to raï. Mon–Sat 6pm–1.30am, Sun 6pm–midnight.

Chez Jeannette 47 rue du Faubourg St-Denis, 10ᵉ ⓣ 01 47 70 30 89, ⓦ chez-jeannette.zenchef.com; Ⓜ Château d'Eau; map p.192. A cool-without-trying corner café-bar that acts as a night-time nexus for the bobos of the 10ᵉ without losing its mixed neighbourhood atmosphere. The space itself is genuine prewar vintage – high ceilings, red lamps, mirrored pillars – with a friendly feel and good, simple food (*menus* from €15). Mon–Sat 8am–11.30pm, Sun 8am–10pm.

★ **Cyrano** 3 rue Biot, 17ᵉ ⓣ 01 45 22 53 34; Ⓜ Place de Clichy; map p.195. This tiny café-bar is a Clichy institution with its superb *belle époque* gold mosaics, giant mirrors and Cyrano de Bergerac paintngs. It's a friendly local during the day; after dark a lively neighbourhood crowd of theatrical types settles in both here and at *L'Entracte*, two doors along. Mon–Fri 9am–1.30am, Sat 10am–1.30am, Sun 10am–1am.

Le Fantôme 36 rue de Paradis, 10ᵉ ⓣ 09 66 87 11 20, ⓦ lefantome.fr; Ⓜ Poissonière; map p.192. Combining retro arcade games, table football, formica and bright poppy trimmings with carefully crafted cocktails (€10–12) and pizza, this place attracts an animated, youthful throng most evenings. Regular DJ nights. Mon–Fri 11am–2am, Sat 6.30pm–2am.

La Fourmi 74 rue des Martyrs, 18ᵉ ⓣ 01 42 64 70 35; Ⓜ Pigalle/Abbesses; map p.182. The long, undulating bar, tall windows and artfully distressed high-ceilinged room here create a warm and welcoming space for a lively, trendy Parisian crowd. Be prepared to fight your way to the bar, and don't expect to be served quickly, but it's worth the wait to enjoy cheap drinks (beer from €3, wine from €3.80), a buzzy vibe and eclectic music. Bar snacks from €3; *plats du jour* €10. Mon–Thurs 8am–2am, Fri & Sat 8am–4am, Sun 9am–2am.

★**Glass** 7 rue Frochot, 9ᵉ ☎ 09 80 72 98 83, ⓦ quixoticprojects.com/venue/glass; ⓜ Pigalle; map p.182. Next to a sex shop and opposite the *Dirty Dick* pub (actually a cool tiki bar), *Glass*, with its knowing take on hipster Americana, is a major player on the SoPi scene. The whisky cocktails (€11–12), hot dogs and craft beers hit the spot with the young, up-for-it crowd – including lots of Americans and Brits – while DJs spin anything from Balearic beats to Krautrock. Occasional live music, too. Mon–Thurs & Sun 7pm–4am, Fri & Sat 7pm–5am.

Lulu White 12 rue Frochot, 9ᵉ ☎ 09 83 58 93 32, ⓦ luluwhite.bar; ⓜ Pigalle; map p.182. They've gone the whole hog with the speakeasy vibe here: pass through the Art Nouveau door to find an opulent paean to Lulu, one of New Orleans's most famous Madams. Melding the glamorous sleaze of Old New Orleans and Old Pigalle, it offers absinthe, of course, along with excellent classic cocktails (from €11). Live jazz and blues on Tues. Mon–Thurs 7pm–2am, Fri & Sat 7pm–4am.

CANAL ST-MARTIN, OBERKAMPF AND AROUND

★**Bar Ourcq** 68 quai de la Loire, 19ᵉ ☎ 01 42 40 12 16, ⓦ barourcq.free.fr; ⓜ Laumière; map p.200. With its sky-blue facade and windows looking out onto the *quai*, this canalside bar really comes into its own in the warmer months when you can sit out on the quayside, or borrow the bar's set of pétanques. It's cosy inside, too, with sofas and cushions. DJ sets early evenings Thurs–Sun plus late Fri & Sat. Tues–Thurs 3pm–midnight, Fri & Sat 3pm–2am, Sun 3–10pm.

Café Charbon 109 rue Oberkampf, 11ᵉ ☎ 01 43 57 55 13; ⓜ Rue St-Maur/Parmentier; map p.207. The place that pioneered the rise of the Oberkampf bar scene is still going strong and continues to draw in a young, fashionable, mixed crowd day and night for its attractively restored *belle époque* decor – all high ceilings, huge mirrors, comfy booths and dangling lights – and the long happy hour (daily 4.30–8pm). Food is served, too. Fri & Sat 9am–4am, Sun–Thurs 9am–2am.

★**Le Comptoir Général** 80 quai de Jemmapes, 10ᵉ ☎ 01 44 88 24 48, ⓦ lecomptoirgeneral.com; ⓜ République/Goncourt; map p.198. Tucked away like a secret off a lane behind the canal, this rambling space is a "ghetto museum" during the day (see p.198), while at night, the whole place transforms into a supercool garage-style bar. The two bars, huge space, friendly staff and impeccably cool playlist – from Velvet Underground to soukous – keep the lively, mixed crowd happy. Occasional live African music, too. Donation for entry requested. Daily 11am–2am.

TOP 10 BARS: DJS AND DANCEFLOORS
Le 9b See below
Café Chéri(e) See below
Chez Georges See p.299
Le Comptoir Général See below
La Féline See p.302
Glass See above
Les Nautes See p.298
Nüba See p.303
Panic Room See below
Le Truskel See p.298

Le Kitch 10 rue Oberkampf, 11ᵉ ☎ 01 40 21 94 41; ⓜ Filles du Calvaire/Oberkampf; map p.198. Living up to its name, this little bar brims with eclectic jumble – a ceramic Bambi here, a garden gnome there. Punters pile in for the excellent-value happy hour (5.30–9pm), when cocktails are €6 (go with tradition and order the minty green Shrek) – it's crowded, noisy and fun. Tues–Sun 5.30pm–2am.

Panic Room 101 rue Amelot, 11ᵉ ☎ 01 58 30 93 43, ⓦ www.panicroomparis.com; ⓜ Filles du Calvaire; map p.198. Wildly popular DJ bar with a cool young set knocking back cocktails – €10–12 (€7 during happy hour 6.30–9pm) and dancing to electronica. You can bring your own snacks. Mon–Sat 6.30pm–2am.

★**Point Ephémère** 200 quai de Valmy, 10ᵉ ☎ 01 40 34 02 48, ⓦ pointephemere.org; ⓜ Jaurès; map p.198. Housed in a former boathouse on the banks of the canal, this young, creative space, run by an arts collective, showcases music (see p.306), dance and visual arts. There's always interesting multi-lingual conversation going on around the bar, and you can get decent street food in the restaurant looking out onto the canal. Mon–Sat noon–2am, Sun noon–9pm (later if there's a concert).

BELLEVILLE AND MÉNILMONTANT

Le 9b 68 bd de la Villette, 19ᵉ ☎ 01 40 18 08 10, ⓦ le9b.com; ⓜ Belleville/Colonel-Fabien; map p.207. A convivial, no-frills bar with a highly prized *terrasse* where a young crowd comes for cheap drinks or a bite to eat – maybe a burger and *frites* or couscous – before heading on down to the basement club to dance the night away to electro, hip-hop and rock. Mon–Sat 9am–2am.

Aux Folies 8 rue de Belleville, 20ᵉ ☎ 06 28 55 89 40, ⓦ aux-folies-belleville.fr; ⓜ Belleville; map p.207. Once a café-théâtre hosting the likes of Edith Piaf and Maurice Chevalier, the charmingly shabby *Aux Folies* offers a slice of old Belleville life; its *terrasse* and brass bar, with mirrored tiles and neon lights, are packed with a mixed, cosmopolitan crowd enjoying cheap beer, cocktails and mint tea. Occasional live music. Daily 7am–2am.

Café Chéri(e) 44 bd de la Villette, 19ᵉ ☎ 01 42 02 02 05;

Ⓜ Belleville; map p.207. This shabby-cool DJ bar, with a scruffy red interior and popular terrace, is where local hipsters sit at their laptops during the day, or drop in for drinks after work and stay long into the night. Drinks are reasonably priced. Music, from hip-hop to indie, Thurs–Sat nights. Daily 11am–2am.

Joséphine - Caves Parisiennes 25 rue Moret, 11ᵉ ☎ 01 48 07 16 70, Ⓦ cafejosephine.fr; Ⓜ Ménilmontant; map p.207. Just off the top end of rue Oberkampf, this sophisticated little speakeasy-type bar serves wine, whiskies, champagne and cocktails (€10–15), plus platters of cheese and charcuterie and interesting offerings including tuna *rillettes* with wasabi (€6–11). Mon–Wed 6pm–3am, Thurs–Sat 6pm–4.30am.

La Féline 6 rue Victor Letalle, 20ᵉ Ⓦ lafelinebar.com; Ⓜ Ménilmontant; map p.207. Ménilmontant dive bar packed with a high-spirited mix of rockabilly kids, wild-eyed punks, old rockers and hip tourists. There's live music – garage rock, punk, ska – plus burlesque and DJ nights, but above all this is a deliciously unpretentious place to hang out and have a really good time. Tues–Sat 6pm–2am.

★ **Lou Pascalou** 14 rue des Panoyaux, 20ᵉ ☎ 01 46 36 78 10, Ⓦ cafe-loupascalou.com; Ⓜ Ménilmontant; map p.207. A friendly, relaxed place with a zinc bar and sunny terrace. Be sure to try their delicious mint tea – over a game of chess if you fancy. You can also choose from a wide range of reasonably priced beers, bottled and on tap. Good music, too, including gypsy jazz, Latin singers and *chanson*. Happy hour 5–8pm. Daily 9am–2am.

Le Perchoir 14 rue Crespin du Gast, 11ᵉ ☎ 01 48 06 18 48, Ⓦ leperchoir.tv; Ⓜ Ménilmontant; map p.207. The drinks may be pricey for the neighbourhood (cocktails €12), and you may have to queue to get in, but this popular seventh-floor cocktail bar has real pulling power – in summer you can languish on the huge rooftop terrace, enjoying amazing city views. Mon–Wed 6pm–2am, Thurs & Fri 4pm–2am, Sat & Sun noon–2am.

★ **Rosa Bonheur** Parc des Buttes-Chaumont, 2 av des Cascades, 19ᵉ ☎ 01 42 00 00 45, Ⓦ rosabonheur.fr; Ⓜ Botzaris/Jourdain; map p.207. Tucked away in the Parc des Buttes-Chaumont, the pretty *Rosa Bonheur* is set inside a former *guinguette* – an open-air café or dance hall. A very mixed crowd of Parisians of all ages comes to drink, dance and nibble on tapas here in a relaxed setting amid the birds and the trees. It gets packed in summer. Entrance to the park after closing is exclusively via 7 rue Botzaris. Thurs & Fri noon–1am, Sat & Sun 10am–1am.

CLUBS

Once awash with wall-to-wall techno, the **club scene** in Paris today is dominated by edgier, esoteric programmes put on at smaller venues, and where deep house once ruled, you can find hip-hop, r'n'b, electro-lounge, rock, reggae and more. The clubs listed below are among the most popular, but the music and the general vibe really depend on who's running the "soirée" on a particular night. Some clubs showcase occasional live acts, too. It's also worth checking the listings for **live music** venues (see p.304), which tend to hold DJ sessions after hours, and the **LGBT+** club listings (see p.357). Note that lots of **bars** (see p.297) bring in DJs, especially on weekend nights. Venues rarely warm up before 1am or 2am, whatever their opening hours.

CHAMPS-ELYSÉES AND AROUND

Zig Zag Club 32 rue Marbeuf, 8ᵉ ☎ 06 35 25 03 61, Ⓦ zigzagclub.fr; Ⓜ Franklin-D-Roosevelt; map p.64. One of the city's newer electronica clubs, with a fantastic Funktion One sound system and big-name and underground DJs filling the huge dancefloor with a wild crowd (capacity 1200). Entry from around €12. Fri & Sat 11.30pm–7am.

GRANDS BOULEVARDS AND PASSAGES

Rex Club 5 bd Poissonnière, 2ᵉ ☎ 01 42 36 10 96, Ⓦ rexclub.com; Ⓜ Bonne Nouvelle; map p.76. The iconic *Rex* is the clubbers' club: spacious and serious about music,

which is strictly electronic, notably techno, played through a top-of-the-line sound system. Refreshingly unpretentious, with big-name DJs. Entry up to €20. Thurs–Sat 11.30pm–7am.

Silencio 142 rue Montmartre, 2ᵉ ☎ 01 40 13 12 33, Ⓦ silencio-club.com; Ⓜ Bourse; map p.76. Styling itself as a place of artistic exchange, this chic club (with cinema, stage and library), set in a basement and reached via six flights of stairs, was opened in 2011 by director David Lynch, who designed everything – from the 1950s-style furniture to the striking gold-leaf walls – taking his inspiration from the club in his film *Mulholland Drive*. Up until midnight it's members only; after that, doors open to the public, and DJs play house techno till the early hours. Drinks are on the pricey side (€18 for a cocktail). Free entry. Tues–Thurs 6pm–4am, Fri & Sat 6pm–6am.

BEAUBOURG AND LES HALLES

Chacha 47 rue Berger, 1ᵉʳ ☎ 01 40 13 12 12, Ⓦ chachaclub.fr; Ⓜ Louvre-Rivoli; map p.88. A

TOP 5 COCKTAIL BARS

Little Bastards See p.299
Candelaria See p.298
Little Red Door See p.298
Tiger See p.299
Sherry Butt See p.298

restaurant (Wed–Sat 8pm–midnight), bar and club, but it's the club that's the real draw, set over several levels and comprising a number of rooms and cosy corners, all beautifully decorated in 1930s style. The music varies from Eighties sounds to house and hip-hop. Drinks from around €10. Free entry. Wed–Sat 8pm–6am.

BASTILLE AND AROUND

Badaboum 2bis rue des Taillandiers, 11ᵉ ☎ 01 48 06 50 70, ⓦ badaboum.paris; ⓜ Bastille; map p.112. Relatively intimate club, concert venue and cocktail bar/ street-food restaurant rolled into one, in a converted warehouse. Music focuses on digital EDM, but can stray as far as zouk and hip-hop, with live bands earlier on. Entry €12–15. Cocktail bar Wed–Sat 7pm–2am; club hours vary according to event, but roughly Mon–Wed & Sun 7.30pm–midnight, Thurs 7pm–5am, Fri & Sat 7.30pm–6.30am.

★**Concrete** 69 Port de la Rapée, 12ᵉ ⓦ concreteparis.fr; ⓜ Gare de Lyon; map p.116. Moored on a boat on the Seine, out near the Gare de Lyon and the first place in Paris to be granted a 24hr licence, this is one of the hottest spots on the clubbing scene, putting on all-night and all-day techno parties and featuring the biggest-name DJs. Entry is usally €10–20. Fri–Sun often nonstop, but check online first.

EASTERN PARIS

Glazart 7–15 av de la Porte de la Villette, 19ᵉ ☎ 01 40 36 55 65, ⓦ glazart.com; ⓜ Porte de la Villette; map p.202. Artsy, alternative-leaning venue that's serious about its music – a hugely eclectic range of club nights and live acts covering everything from pagan metal to dub. It's spacious, and in summer (June–Sept) there's a glorious outdoor "beach". Entry varies, but around €10–20. Wed–Sun; times vary, but club nights Thurs–Sat usually 11pm–5am.

Le Nouveau Casino 109 rue Oberkampf, 11ᵉ ☎ 01 43 57 57 40, ⓦ nouveaucasino.net; ⓜ Parmentier; map p.207. Next to *Café Charbon* (see p.301), this excellent venue puts on an interesting line-up of live gigs that makes way for a relaxed, dancey crowd later on, with music ranging from electro-pop or techno to funk. There's a good sound system and ventilation, but not much space. Entry €9–15, depending on whether you reserve online and when you arrive. Fri & Sat midnight–5am.

ST-GERMAIN

Le Rive Gauche 1 rue du Sabot, 6ᵉ ☎ 01 42 22 51 70, ⓦ rive-gauche.paris; ⓜ St-Germain-des-Prés; map p.138. A stylish set flocks to this plush little place for its club nights – funk, electro, groove, disco and pop. It's been around since the 1970s and still has some of its gold mirror-mosaic decor. Contact them via the website for password and free entry. Club nights 11pm–6am.

EIFFEL TOWER QUARTER

YOYO Palais de Tokyo, 13 av du Président-Wilson, 16ᵉ ☎ 01 84 79 11 70, ⓦ yoyo-paris.com; ⓜ léna; map p.152. Housed in the huge basement of the Palais de Tokyo, this is one of the city's top dance clubs, serving up rap, techno, house anthems and electro to massive crowds. Entry price varies. Days vary, 11pm–6am.

THE 13ᵉ

★**Batofar** Opposite 11 quai François Mauriac, 13ᵉ ☎ 01 53 60 17 00, ⓦ batofar.fr; ⓜ Quai de la Gare; map p.172. Though you're spoiled for choice for cool nightlife spots along this stretch of the river – other excellent floating options here include *Le Petit Bain*, a modernist bar/ performance space with an eclectic schedule (ⓦ petitbain .org); *La Dame de Canton* (ⓦ damedecanton.com/en), a world music venue on a beautiful Chinese junk; and *El Alamein* (ⓦ bateauelalamein.com), a dilapidated barge putting on great *chanson* and jazz – this is one of the originals and still one of the best. An old lighthouse boat moored at the foot of the Bibliothèque Nationale, it offers a club, live music space and restaurant, with a broad playlist of alternative electro, folk, hip-hop, whatever – and the odd experimental funk night thrown in. Entry generally from €10. Opening times vary.

Nüba 34 quai d'Austerlitz, 13ᵉ ⓦ nuba-paris.fr; ⓜ Gare d'Austerlitz; map p.172. On the top floor of the Cité de la Mode et du Design (see p.178), this waterside restaurant-bar-club comes into its own in good weather when the rooftop deck opens up. It's a great place to be on sunny evenings, sipping a cocktail looking out over the Seine while a DJ plays an electro or dance set. Entry price for club nights varies. Tues–Sat 6pm–5am, Sun noon–2am, plus daytime events.

MONTMARTRE AND THE 9ᵉ

★**Chez Moune** 54 rue Jean-Baptiste Pigalle, 9ᵉ ☎ 09 67 50 28 44, ⓦ facebook.com/chezmouneofficiel; ⓜ Pigalle; map p.182. Behind the gorgeous Art Nouveau door is a happening little club, all tatty opulence, that pulls in a young crowd for its eclectic dance nights – mainly underground electro but with some surprises. Entry varies, and is often free. Thurs 11pm–5am, Fri & Sat 11pm–6am.

Kabukicho 14 rue Frochot, 9ᵉ ☎ 09 67 48 91 19, ⓦ kabukicho.fr/en/le-club; ⓜ Pigalle; map p.182. On one of SoPi's hottest nightlife streets, this sleek micro-club – basically a bar where you can dance – has DJ sets from around 10pm. It's named after Tokyo's red-light district, and the vibe is very Japanese-cool, with sake and Japanese beers available. DJs spin anything from house, techno and disco to Afrobeat, rap and funk. Cocktails from €10. Free entry. Wed–Sun 8pm–2am.

★**La Machine du Moulin Rouge** 90 bd de Clichy, 18ᵉ ☎ 01 53 41 88 89, ⓦ lamachinedumoulinrouge.com;

2

Ⓜ Blanche; map p.182. Next to the fabled *Moulin Rouge*, this club/live music venue has a concert space hosting international names – from Moodymann to Fuck Buttons – plus a basement club/music venue known as "La Chaufferie" and a funky bar with a garden. EDM is the order of the day here, but a touch of hedonism lifts it above the usual monster club. Entry €10–22. Club nights generally Fri & Sat midnight–6am, often with gigs beforehand; days and times of live music and other events vary.

★ **Pigalle Country Club** 59 Rue Jean-Baptiste Pigalle, 9e, Ⓦ pigallecountryclub.com; Ⓜ Pigalle; map p.182. A breath of fresh air on Paris's clubbing scene, with DJ sets spanning the range from new wave to glam rock plus retro gaming nights – Street Fighter II, Street of Rage and the like – open mics, movies and even occasional tarot sessions. Entry varies, and is often free. Mon–Wed 6pm–3am, Thurs–Sat 6pm–5am.

ROCK AND WORLD MUSIC

Paris is a fantastic place to see **world music**, with artists from throughout Africa, in particular, making regular appearances. Most of the **venues** listed here are primarily devoted to live acts, though some double up as clubs on certain nights or after hours. A few will have live music all week, but the majority host bands on just a couple of nights. Note that the most interesting **clubs** (see p.302) tend to host gigs earlier on, and that some bars (see p.297) have occasional live music, too. It's also worth checking the **jazz venues** (see p.306), as these often branch out into other genres such as world music and folk – *New Morning* (see p.308) is a classic example.

BASTILLE

Café de la Danse 5 passage Louis-Philippe, 11e ☎ 01 47 00 57 59, Ⓦ cafedeladanse.com; Ⓜ Bastille; map p.112. Reliable, unpretentious venue for the best contemporary rock, world, folk and jazz music played in an intimate space with dancing room and a bar. Entry €20–30. Opening times vary, but usually Tues–Sun.

Café de la Plage 59 rue de Charonne, 11e ☎ 06 68 17 56 78, Ⓦ lecafedelaplage-paris.com; Ⓜ Ledru-Rollin; map p.112. This friendly bar stages a wide variety of live music and club nights. The emphasis is on Latin, but you could also catch ska gigs, Indonesian concerts or New Orleans funk. Shows start 9 or 10pm. Tues–Sat 6pm–2am.

Supersonic 9 rue Biscornet, 12e Ⓦ supersonic-club.fr; Ⓜ Bastille; map p.112. Set in a former warehouse done up New York-loft-style, *Supersonic* takes off most evenings at 8pm with a free live gig – usually pop, rock or indie, and including well-known names as well as bands on the up. A "food truck" serves street food, such as burgers, and the drinks are reasonably priced. On Fri and Sat the place turns into a club at midnight. Mon–Thurs, Fri & Sat 6.30pm–6am, Sun 6.30pm–midnight.

MONTMARTRE

★ **La Cigale** 120 bd de Rochechouart, 18e ☎ 01 49 25 89 99, Ⓦ lacigale.fr; Ⓜ Pigalle; map p.182. Opened in 1887 and formerly playing host to the likes of Mistinguett and Maurice Chevalier, this gorgeous 1400-seater Pigalle theatre has become a leading venue for world music and French and continental European bands. The occasional big name plays here, from Toots and the Maytals to Macy Gray. *La Boule Noir* (Ⓦ laboule-noire.fr), in the same building, is smaller, with a more indie vibe. Entry varies. Opening times vary.

Divan du Monde 75 rue des Martyrs, 18e ☎ 01 40 05 08 10, Ⓦ dlvandumonde.com; Ⓜ Pigalle; map p.182. Housed in one of Montmartre's many historic cabarets, this venue offers a vibrant programme of live Francophone music and cool club nights; *Madame Arthur*, in the same building (same website), hosts transvestite *chanson* evenings with a twist. Entrance fee varies. Wed–Sat 8pm–6am.

★ **Elysée Montmartre** 72 bd de Rochechouart, 18e ☎ 01 44 92 78 00, Ⓦ elysee-montmartre.com; Ⓜ Anvers; map p.182. Iconic concert hall – it's hosted everyone from Toulouse-Lautrec (in the audience) to David Bowie (on the stage) – with a roster of high-profile rock acts running the gamut from French artist Talisco to Jesus and Mary Chain and Future Islands. Entrance fee varies. Opening times vary.

EASTERN PARIS

Le 104 5 rue Curial, 19e ☎ 01 53 35 50 00, Ⓦ 104.fr; Ⓜ Riquet; map p.200. It's always worth checking out the schedule at this innovative arts centre (see p.194) to find pop gigs, indie rock, *chanson* sets and contemporary *bals de danse*. Tues–Sun; opening times vary.

★ **L'Alimentation Générale** 64 rue Jean-Pierre-Timbaud, 11e ☎ 01 43 55 42 50, Ⓦ alimentation-generale. net; Ⓜ Parmentier; map p.207. Despite its name, this is not the local grocer's shop – confusingly, there is a real *alimentation générale*, further up the road, with the same street number, so don't be deterred – but one of Oberkampf's most popular nightlife spots, with a global line-up of live music ranging from Afro rock to Balkan beats and trance. A DJ usually takes over later and there's some room for dancing. There's often a cover charge of €5–10 that includes that first drink, but it tends to be free before 11pm. Food – tapas, burgers, cheese plates – is available. Daily 6pm–2am.

★ **La Bellevilloise** 19–21 rue Boyer, 20e ☎ 01 46 36 07 07, Ⓦ labellevilloise.com; Ⓜ Gambetta/Ménilmontant; map p.207. There's always something interesting going on

at this former workers' co-operative, dating back to 1877, now a dynamic bar, club, concert venue and exhibition space. It also hosts film festivals, community events and vintage and organic markets. Its cool bar-restaurant, *La Halle aux Oliviers*, with real olive trees dotted about beneath a glass roof, makes an attractive place for a drink, dinner (from €16 for mains such as spinach and ricotta ravioli or steak and chips), or jazz brunch on Sunday (€29). The excellent basement club and live music venue hosts bands, playing anything from Afro jazz to Balkan beats, *chanson* to swing. Opening times vary, but generally: Wed & Thurs 7pm–1am, Fri 7pm–2am, Sat 6pm–2am, Sun 11.30am–midnight.

★**L'International** 5 rue Moret, 11ᵉ ☎01 42 02 02 05, ⓦl.international.fr; ⓜMénilmontant; map p.207. With two stages and at least two free gigs a night (usually 9 & 11pm), this friendly *café-concert*, related to the record shop opposite (see p.335), is a staple on the Oberkampf scene, showcasing the best new, indie and edgy acts – mostly French, but not exclusively – in all genres, from rap to electro. DJs take over later on. Happy hour daily 6–9pm. Daily 6pm–2am.

Maroquinerie 23 rue Boyer, 20ᵉ ☎01 40 33 35 05, ⓦlamaroquinerie.fr; ⓜGambetta; map p.207. Cool arts

centre with a smallish concert venue downstairs. The line-up encompasses anything from folk and jazz to metal and hip-hop, with international names and a good selection of French musicians. A classy restaurant (daily 7–11pm) offers a small menu of modern food (from chestnut gnocchi to pulled pork in focaccia with kimchee) from €14. Opening times vary.

Péniche Antipode 55 quai de La Seine, 19ᵉ ☎01 42 03 39 07, ⓦpenicheantipode.fr; ⓜRiquet; map p.200. This popular venue, a barge moored on the Bassin de la Villette, puts on a lively programme of music (as well as plays, comedy nights and much else), including gypsy jazz, rock, reggae and *chanson*. It's also a lovely place to come for a drink or a meal (see p.293). Nearby *Péniche Anako* (ⓦpenicheanako.org) is also worth checking out for its world music gigs. No credit cards. Daily noon–2am.

★**Point Ephémère** 200 quai de Valmy, 10ᵉ ☎01 40 34 02 48, ⓦpointephemere.org; ⓜJaurès/Louis Blanc; map p.198. Run by an arts collective in a disused boat-house, this superbly dilapidated cultural venue (see p.301) is a nexus for alternative and underground performers of all kinds. There are gigs most nights, covering anything from electro to Afro jazz via folk rock. Mon–Sat noon–2am, Sun noon–9pm (later if there's a concert).

JAZZ AND CHANSON

Traditional French **chanson** is alive and well in Paris, as is **jazz**, with clubs plying all styles from Dixieland to avant-garde. **Gypsy jazz** (*jazz manouche*), pioneered by Django Reinhardt, remains in vogue; carrying on the tradition are musicians such as Romane and the Ferré brothers. Other jazz names to look out for are saxophonist Didier Malherbe; violinist Didier Lockwood; British-born but long-time France resident, guitarist John McLaughlin; pianist Alain Jean-Marie; clarinettist Louis Sclavis; and accordionist Richard Galliano, who updates the French *musette* style. *Bistrots* and bars can be a good place to catch gypsy jazz, as well as *chanson*; look out for flyers and posters in the venues themselves. In addition to the places listed here, it's also worth checking out the world and rock venues listed above for occasional *chanson* or jazz concerts.

GRANDS BOULEVARDS AND PASSAGES

★**Au Limonaire** 18 Cité Bergère, 9ᵉ ☎01 45 23 33 33, ⓦlimonaire.free.fr; ⓜGrands Boulevards; map p.76. Tiny, cosy backstreet wine bar/"*bistro chantant*", perfect for Parisian *chanson* nights, showcasing young singers, zany music/poetry performances and boozy singalongs. Reserving a table for dinner guarantees a seat for the show at 10pm (Sun 7pm); otherwise you'll be crammed up against the bar, if you can get in at all. Daily 6pm–midnight.

JAZZ IN PARIS

Jazz has long enjoyed an appreciative audience in France, especially since the end of World War II, when the intellectual rigour and agonized musings of bebop struck an immediate chord of sympathy in the existentialist hearts of the *après-guerre*. Charlie Parker, Dizzy Gillespie, Miles Davis – all were being listened to in the 1950s, when in Britain their names were known only to a tiny coterie of fans.

Gypsy guitarist **Django Reinhardt** and his partner, violinist Stéphane Grappelli, whose work represents the distinctive and undisputed French contribution to the jazz canon, had much to do with the genre's popularity. But it was also greatly enhanced by the presence of many front-rank black American musicians, for whom Paris was a haven of freedom after the racial prejudice of the States. Among them were the soprano sax player **Sidney Bechet**, who set up a legendary partnership with French clarinettist Claude Luter, and Bud Powell, whose turbulent exile partly inspired the tenor man played by Dexter Gordon in the film *Round Midnight*.

GUINGUETTES

Though Paris has a number of contemporary riverside bars and venues, for the ultimate retro experience you need to head out of the centre to a traditional riverbank **guinguette**. You can usually eat homely French food at these places, but the real draw is the band. Depending on the venue you'll find families, older couples and trendy young things from the city swaying with varying degrees of skill to foxtrots, tangos and lots of well-loved accordion numbers – especially nice on a Sunday afternoon.

Chalet du Lac Facing the Lac de St-Mandé, Bois de Vincennes, 12e ⓣ 01 43 28 09 89, ⓦ chaletdulac.fr; Ⓜ St-Mandé-Tourelles. Tango tea dances in the afternoons (Mon & Thurs 2–8pm, Sat 1–6.30pm; €8) and occasionally other types of dance, such as Latin and swing (check the programme for listings). It turns into a club on Fri & Sat at 10pm. The restaurant (Fri & Sat 8–11pm, Sun 11.30am–3pm) serves brasserie classics.

Chez Gégène 162bis quai de Polangis, Joinville-le-Pont ⓣ 01 48 83 29 43, ⓦ chez-gegene.fr; RER Joinville-le-Pont. Just the other side of the Bois de Vincennes from the *Chalet du Lac* (see above), this is a genuine *guinguette* established in the 1900s, though today the band mixes in pop anthems with the accordion tunes. There's a decent restaurant, but the time to come is on Saturday nights (9pm–2am) and Sunday afternoons (2.30–6.30pm), when a live band plays ballroom music and traditional French numbers (booking in advance is required). Entry €12 for non-diners, €45 with a meal. April–Dec.

Guinguette de l'Ile du Martin-Pêcheur 41 quai Victor-Hugo, Champigny-sur-Marne ⓣ 01 49 83 03 02, ⓦ guinguette.fr; RER A2 to Champigny-sur-Marne. Traditional and charming rural *guinguette* situated on a shady island in the River Marne. Entry free, dinner around €30. March–May, Sept & Oct Sat 7.30pm–1.30am, Sun noon–6pm; June–Aug Fri 7.30pm–midnight, Sat 7.30pm–1.30am, Sun noon–6pm; Nov & Dec Sat 7.30pm–1.30am.

LES HALLES

Le Baiser Salé 58 rue des Lombards, 1er ⓣ 01 42 33 37 71, ⓦ lebaisersale.com; Ⓜ Châtelet; map p.88. The "salty kiss" is a small, crowded, upstairs room with live music every night – usually jazz, but also world music, funk, flamenco and soul (from €12). There are free jazz jam sessions on Mon, and the downstairs bar is great for chilling out. Most sets start at 7 & 9.30pm. Daily 5.30pm–6am.

Duc des Lombards 42 rue des Lombards, 1er ⓣ 01 42 33 22 88, ⓦ ducdeslombards.com; Ⓜ Châtelet/Les Halles; map p.88. This modern venue is a high-profile place to hear jazz piano, blues and fusion, with big names from Ahmad Jamal to Jamie Cullum. Admission varies but is usually around €30. Shows 7.30 & 9.30pm; free jam sessions Fri & Sat 11.30pm. Daily 7pm–3am.

Le Sunset/Le Sunside 60 rue des Lombards, 1er ⓣ 01 40 26 46 60, ⓦ sunset-sunside.com; Ⓜ/RER Châtelet-Les Halles; map p.88. Two clubs in one: *Le Sunside* on the ground floor features mostly traditional, acoustic jazz, whereas the *Sunset* cellar is a venue for electric and fusion. Both usually host two shows per night. Performers have been as diverse as Benny Golson, Didier Lockwood, Brad Mehdau, Kenny Barron and Avishai Cohen. If you're travelling with young children check out the teatime jazz sessions on Sun at 4pm. Entry €15–30. Daily 8pm–2.30am.

THE MARAIS

Péniche Le Marcounet Moored on the quai de l'Hôtel de Ville by the Pont Marie, 4e ⓣ 06 60 47 38 52, ⓦ peniche-marcounet.fr; Ⓜ Pont Marie; map p.99. A romantic and quirky way to experience live jazz, swing, blues and flamenco – on a canal boat. Enjoy an *apéritif* on deck then head below to the concert area. Entry free–€12. Tues–Sat 6pm–midnight, Sun 11am–4pm (concerts Tues–Thurs, plus sometimes Fri & Sat; musical brunch Sun from noon).

QUARTIER LATIN

Aux Trois Mailletz 56 rue Galande, 5e ⓣ 01 43 25 96 86, ⓦ lestroismailletz.fr; Ⓜ St-Michel; map p.124. This corner café-restaurant, which has hosted greats from Sidney Bechet to Nina Simone, transforms into a convivial piano bar (after 6pm); even later (after 8.30pm) a good jazz/cabaret bar sets up in the basement, featuring *chanson*, jazz and some world music, with lots of dancing. Mon–Thurs & Sun €20, Fri & Sat €25. Daily 6pm–5am.

Caveau de la Huchette 5 rue de la Huchette, 5e ⓣ 01 43 26 65 05, ⓦ caveaudelahuchette.fr; Ⓜ St-Michel; map p.124. An atmospheric, historic old cellar bar – self-styled "*temple du swing*" – that offers a wonderful slice of old Parisian life in this touristy area. The live Dixieland, boogie woogie, big band and swing is often joined by energetic dancing from the enthusiastic crowd. Mon–Thurs & Sun €13, Fri & Sat €15. Mon–Thurs & Sun 9pm–2.30am, Fri & Sat 9pm–4am.

MONTPARNASSE

Au Magique 42 rue de Gergovie, 14e ⓣ 01 45 42 26 10, ⓦ aumagique.com; Ⓜ Pernety; map p.164. Unpretentious restaurant-bar and "*chanson* cellar" with traditional performances from local performers. Entry around €6; drinks are reasonably priced. Wed–Sun 8pm–2am.

MONTMARTRE AND THE 10ᵉ

★ **Au Lapin Agile** 22 rue des Saules, 18ᵉ ☎ 01 46 06 85 87, Ⓦ au-lapin-agile.com; Ⓜ Lamarck Caulaincourt; map p.182. A legendary cabaret bar famously painted and patronized by Picasso, Utrillo and other leading lights of the early twentieth-century Montmartre scene, the "nimble rabbit" – in an adorable shuttered building with a pretty garden – is now an intimate club much beloved by tourists. Visitors sit packed in the old back room, listening – and occasionally joining in with – *chanson*, cabaret and poetry. €28 including one drink, students under 26 €20 (except Sat.) Tues–Sun 9pm–1am.

Au Petit Théatre du Bonheur 6 rue Drevet, 18ᵉ ☎ 09 54 48 44 83, Ⓦ petittheatredubonheur.com/le-theatre; Ⓜ Abbesses; map p.182. Hidden away in Montmartre, set halfway up a steep flight of steps, this adorable mini-theatre – with space for just twenty – stages *chanson*, comic songs, cabaret, poetry and monologues. Free entry Thurs 7–8pm, when Les Jetés d'Encre play their world-music-tinged *chanson* for tips. Days and times vary.

Autour de Midi...et Minuit 11 rue Lepic, 18ᵉ ☎ 01 55 79 16 48, Ⓦ autourdemidi.fr; Ⓜ Blanche; map p.182. Its prime Montmartre location means it is inevitably touristy, but this cosy cellar jazz club is an amiable place to sit back and enjoy a variety of acts, from swing via bebop to gypsy jazz. Jam sessions Tues and Wed. Entrance fee varies. Tues–Sat; hours vary.

★ **New Morning** 7–9 rue des Petites-Ecuries, 10ᵉ Ⓦ newmorning.com; Ⓜ Château d'Eau; map p.192. Although relatively understated, this famed venue, housed in a former printing press, pulls big international jazz names and a very knowledgeable crowd – it's usually packed. Excellent blues, funk and world music, too. Entry prices vary. Days and concert times vary.

Les Trois Baudets 64 bd de Clichy, 18ᵉ ☎ 01 42 62 33 33, Ⓦ lestroisbaudets.com; Ⓜ Blanche/Pigalle; map p.182. This refitted 1940s theatre is now an intimate space specializing in developing young, upcoming French singer-songwriters of all stripes, so concerts are something of a lucky dip. There's a lively bar/restaurant, too. Entrance fee varies. Concert nights 7pm–midnight.

FURTHER AFIELD

Instants Chavirés 7 rue Richard-Lenoir, Montreuil ☎ 01 42 87 25 91, Ⓦ instantschavires.com; Ⓜ Robespierre. Highly respected avant-garde, experimental and improvised jazz joint close to the Porte de Montreuil. A place where musicians go to hear each other play. Entry €11.50–17. Concerts 8 or 8.30pm.

CINÉMATHÈQUE

Film, theatre and dance

Cinema-lovers in Paris have a choice of hundreds of film screenings in any one week, taking in contemporary French movies, classics, world cinema and mainstream hits. The city also has vibrant theatre and dance scenes, with innovative, cutting-edge domestic productions jostling with the best shows touring or transferring from across Europe. The famous cabarets – places such as the *Lido* and *Moulin Rouge* – thrive off group bookings for an expensive dinner-and-show formula, and while they have a certain camp charm they retain little of the bohemian edge depicted in Toulouse-Lautrec's sketches or Baz Luhrmann's film. Listings for all films and stage productions are detailed in *L'Officiel de Spectacles* and other weeklies (see p.40).

FILM

Paris is truly a cinephile's city – one of the few capitals in the world where you can enjoy not only entertainment but also a wonderful film education from the programmes of regular (never mind specialist) cinemas. **Independent movie houses**, especially in the Latin Quarter, continue to hold their own against the popcorn-touting clout of the big **chains** – UGC, Gaumont and MK2 – by screening classic and contemporary films, retrospectives, seasons and all-nighters. Most indie places show their movies in **v.o.** (*version originale*). The unappealing alternative, **v.f.** (*version française*) – which means the film has been dubbed into French – is mostly used for blockbusters screened in the big chains.

PROGRAMMES AND TICKETS

Séances (programmes) run throughout the day, sometimes as early as 10am, and can continue until 10.30pm or so. Tickets (*billets*) rarely need to be bought in advance, and they're not expensive by European standards – many cinemas also offer discounts for senior travellers and students. We've quoted standard prices below, which usually start at around €9; the cheapest tickets are at the smaller, independent venues. If you're in town in March, watch out for Printemps du Cinéma (ⓦ printempsducinema .com), when, for three days, cinemas across the city charge a flat rate of €4.

CINÉMATHÈQUES AND CULTURAL INSTITUTIONS

Cultural institutions and embassies often have their own cinema programmes: the Centre Pompidou (see p.87) runs particularly good seasons, focusing on anything from documentaries to retrospectives (ⓦ centrepompidou.fr). In addition, some of the city's foreign institutes host occasional screenings, so if your favourite director is a Hungarian, a Swede or a Korean, check what's on at those countries' cultural centres.

★**Cinémathèque Française** 51 rue de Bercy, 12ᵉ ☎01 71 19 33 33, ⓦ cinematheque.fr; Ⓜ Bercy. This is the best venue in Paris for movie buffs. Along with a museum of cinema (see p.117), you get a choice of around thirty different films every week, including retrospectives,

shorts and silents, from all around the world; many are rarely shown commercially. All this in an incredible building designed by Frank Gehry. Closed Tues. Tickets €6.50.

Forum des Images 2 rue du Cinéma, Porte St-Eustache, Forum des Halles, 1ᵉʳ ☎01 44 76 63 00, ⓦ forumdesimages.fr; Ⓜ/RER Châtelet-Les Halles/ Châtelet. Five screens devoted to classic movies, themed seasons, director-led events and festivals. The Salle des Collections (see p.92) offers individual terminals with digital access to the (huge) archive and some wonderfully obscure titles. Tickets (€6) include a screening and 2hr in the Salle des Collections.

CINEMAS

L'Arlequin 76 rue de Rennes, 6ᵉ ☎01 45 44 28 80, ⓦ lesecransdeparis.fr; Ⓜ St-Sulpice. Owned by Jacques Tati in the 1950s, then by the Soviet Union as the Cosmos cinema until 1990, L'Arlequin is a Left Bank temple to film, showing indie movies, world classics and underground works. Tickets €9.60.

★**Le Champo** 51 rue des Ecoles, 5ᵉ ☎01 43 54 51 60, ⓦ lechampo.com; Ⓜ Cluny La Sorbonne/Odéon. Boho little Latin Quarter cinema at the foot of rue Champollion, beloved by film buffs since 1938; the gorgeous restored interior features a Jacques Tati silhouette and lots of Art Deco styling. A beautifully selected choice of movie classics, plus themed *v.o.* seasons over a week or more, featuring Oshima, perhaps, or Ingmar Bergman. Tickets €9.

HOME-GROWN FILM

Cinemas and film foundations all over Paris help promote and support the French film industry. The **Fondation Jérôme Seydoux-Pathé** has its headquarters in a Renzo Piano-directed renovation of the old Cinéma Rodin – whose facade was sculpted by Rodin, no less – at 73 av des Gobelins, 13ᵉ (Ⓜ Place de Italie/Les Gobelins; Tues–Fri 1–7pm, Sat 10am–7pm; ☎01 83 79 18 96, ⓦ fondation-jeromesey doux-pathe.com). It is primarily a research centre, but also has an exhibition space for temporary shows of posters, stills, programmes and the like, a small gallery of cinematographic equipment from 1896 onwards and a screening room showing silent movies with live accompaniment. Meanwhile, in 2012 the director Luc Besson opened the **Cité du Cinéma** studio in a former power plant at 20 rue Ampère in the suburb of St-Denis (Ⓜ Carrefour Pleyel/RER Saint-Denis; ☎01 49 15 98 98, ⓦ citeducinema.org). As a studio complex where film-makers can, if necessary, produce an entire movie without having to move off site, the aim, much like at Pinewood Studios in the UK, is to support the work of the French film industry both creatively and financially. Movies produced here include François Ozon's *Une Nouvelle Amie* (2014) and Oscar-nominated *Jackie* (2016). The studio stages exhibitions, events and **backstage tours** (1hr 45min; €14.90; book in advance on ⓦ cultival.fr).

FILM FESTIVALS

March is a good month for film festivals in Paris. In the southeastern suburb of Créteil, the mac arts centre (see p.235) hosts **Films de Femmes** (Ⓦ filmsdefemmes.com; Ⓜ Créteil-Préfecture), a ten-day extravaganza of international women's cinema, while in Bobigny, northeast of the city, Magic Cinéma runs **Bande(s) à Part** (Ⓦ bandesapart.fr; Ⓜ Bobigny/Pablo-Picasso), focusing on movies for and about young people. In the city itself, **Cinéma du Réel** (Ⓦ cinemadureel.org) is a well-regarded international event, screening a fortnight's worth of documentary movies in a number of venues including the Pompidou Centre.

Summer sees the **Festival de Cinéma en Plein Air** (end July to end Aug; Ⓦ cinema.arbo .com), when free, classic and independent movies, in their original language, are screened outdoors at the Parc de la Villette (Ⓜ Porte de Pantin) – unless it's raining. Entry is free, but you have to pay €7 if you want to rent a deckchair; most people arrive early, with a bottle and blanket, and hang out until the sun goes down. Things get a little more obscure at the **Paris Independent Film Festival** (Ⓦ filmfestival.paris), held over five days in November, when a couple of indie cinemas present low-budget work and new directors from around the world.

Other movie events worth looking into include **Quinzaine des Réalisateurs** in May (see p.322) and the **Fête du Cinéma** in June/July (see p.322).

Christine 21 4 rue Christine, 6ᵉ Ⓣ 01 43 25 85 78, Ⓦ christine21.cine.allocine.fr; Ⓜ Odéon/St-Michel. World classics from Miyazaki via de Sica to Hitchcock, and anything from Hollywood musicals to rediscovered cult movies. Tickets €8.

Cinéma des Cinéastes 7 av de Clichy, 17ᵉ Ⓣ 08 92 68 97 17, Ⓦ cinema-des-cineastes.fr; Ⓜ Place de Clichy. Three-screen cinema in an old cabaret building with a decidedly retro feel, showing world cinema and French movies, with themed evenings, retrospectives, cult classics and good programming for kids. Tickets €9.50.

Cinéma du Panthéon 13 rue Victor-Cousin, 5ᵉ Ⓣ 01 40 46 01 21, Ⓦ facebook.com/cinemadupantheonparis; Ⓜ Odéon. Open since 1907, this lovely indie cinema shows the best new world releases and cult hits, with director talks and themed nights, and a good tea room/restaurant – designed in part by Catherine Deneuve – for post-movie debates. Tickets €8.50.

Le Desperado 23 rue des Ecoles, 5ᵉ Ⓣ 01 43 25 72 07, Ⓦ desperado.cine.allocine.fr; Ⓜ Jussieu/Maubert Mutualité. Rediscovered classics and cult Hollywood movies, with a good scattering of French golden oldies. Tickets €8.

★ **L'Entrepôt** 7 rue Francis-de-Pressensé, 14ᵉ Ⓣ 01 45 40 07 50, Ⓦ lentrepot.fr; Ⓜ Pernety. This alternative cinema has been keeping Montparnasse ciné-addicts happy for years with its three screens dedicated to the obscure, the subversive and the brilliant, as well as events and seasons ("Cinema and philosophy", for example). There's a nice garden bar-restaurant, too. Tickets €8.

L'Escurial 11 bd de Port-Royal, 13ᵉ Ⓣ 01 47 07 28 04, Ⓦ lesecransdeparis.fr; Ⓜ Les Gobelins. Combining plush seats, two screens – one of them huge – and more art than commerce in its programming policy, this cinema, first established in 1911, shows anything from French classics to the latest big-name offerings from around the world. Tickets €9.

Espace Saint-Michel 7 place St-Michel, 5ᵉ Ⓣ 01 44 07 20 49, Ⓦ espacesaintmichel.free.fr; Ⓜ St-Michel. Open as a movie house since 1911, this cinema (which now has two screens) is in the heart of the 5ᵉ, focusing on world movies and underground films, with lots of director/actor Q&A sessions. Tickets €8.

★ **La Filmothèque du Quartier Latin** 9 rue Champollion, 5ᵉ Ⓣ 01 43 26 70 38, Ⓦ lafilmotheque.fr; Ⓜ Cluny La Sorbonne. Art-house cinema specializing in creative and thoughtful retrospectives, themed seasons and lectures; though it digs out some wonderful French titles, it has a particular love affair with classic and rediscovered Hollywood movies – the small screening rooms (97 and 60 seats) are named after Audrey Hepburn and Marilyn Monroe. Tickets €9.

Grand Action 5 rue des Ecoles, 5ᵉ Ⓣ 01 43 54 47 62, Ⓦ legrandaction.com; Ⓜ Cardinal Lemoine/Maubert Mutualité. New prints of old classics, cult movies and contemporary films from around the world, with themed seasons on subjects such as female destiny or cult Italian movies. Tickets €9.50.

Le Grand Rex 1 bd Poissonnière, 2ᵉ Ⓣ 01 45 08 93 89, Ⓦ legrandrex.com; Ⓜ Bonne Nouvelle. This glamorous 1930s movie house, with an Art Deco facade, is the largest cinema in Europe, specializing in the biggest blockbusters – dubbed, if the film is from overseas. There are eight screens, including the colossal (2650-seater), three-storey Grande Salle, which has a ceiling of glowing stars and a kitsch, Hollywood-meets-Baroque cityscape backdrop – it's also used for major concerts. Tickets €9 (€11 for the Grande Salle).

★ **Le Louxor** 170 bd de Magenta, 10ᵉ Ⓣ 01 44 63 96 96, Ⓦ www.cinemalouxor.fr; Ⓜ Barbès Rochechouart.

PARIS ON FILM

Parisians have had a passionate love affair with cinema since the day the **Lumière** brothers projected their "Cinematograph" at the Parisian *Grand Café du Boulevard des Capucines* in 1895. The 1930s were the golden age of French cinema, with stars of musicals and theatres being showcased in casually censored film vehicles that helped create the French reputation for naughtiness, and *auteurs* scripting, directing and producing moody classics with a gritty, humanist edge. **Jean Renoir**, son of the Impressionist painter Auguste, was among them; check out his *Le Crime de Monsieur Lange* (1935), an affecting Socialist romance set in a print shop in the then-crumbling Marais. The movement known as Poetic Realism grew up around Renoir and the director Marcel Carné, who made the Canal St-Martin area famous in *Hôtel du Nord* (1938), a film that starred Arletty, a great populist actress of the 1930s and 40s. Arletty and Poetic Realism reached their apogee in Carné's wonderful *Les Enfants du Paradis* (1945), set in the theatrical world of nineteenth-century Paris, with a script by the poet Jacques Prévert.

Postwar, Renoir continued to make great films: his *French CanCan* (1955) is *the* film about the *Moulin Rouge* and the heyday of Montmartre. Like the vast majority of prewar films, however, even those with a Parisian setting, it was shot in the studio. An exception to this was Claude Autant-Lara's wartime comedy *La Traversée de Paris* (1956), which follows Jean Gabin smuggling black-market goods across the city. From 1959, however, the directors of the revolutionary **Nouvelle Vague** ("New Wave") took their new, lightweight cameras out onto the streets, abandoning the big studio set pieces in favour of a fluid, avant-garde style in real-life locations. Among seminal works, **Les Quatre Cents Coups** (1959), by François Truffaut, and **A Bout de Souffle** (1959), by Jean-Luc Godard, showcase the city streets to thrilling, kinetic effect. Other key Nouvelle Vague Paris movies include *Paris Vu Par* (*Six in Paris*; 1965), a collection of shorts by the key figures of the genre; and the quirky *Zazie dans le Métro* (1961), which is only outdone for its Parisian locations by Agnès Varda's *Cléo de 5 à 7* (1962), which depicts two hours in the life of a singer as she moves through the city – mainly around Montparnasse.

Following the success of Claude Berri's *Jean de Florette* (1986), French cinema concentrated on "heritage" movies. Few did Paris any favours, although there were a couple of exceptions: Jean-Pierre Jeunet's *Un long dimanche de fiançailles* (2004) re-created the city – including the market pavilions of Les Halles – during World War I, while Bernardo Bertolucci's *Innocents*, or *The Dreamers* (2003), was set in the radical Paris of 1968. In contrast, the **Cinéma du Look** movement captured a cool, image-conscious version of Paris in films like Léos Carax's *Les Amants du Pont-Neuf* (1991), though its bridge was actually

a set in the south of France; Jean-Jacques Beineix's *Diva* (1981), which takes in the Bouffes du Nord theatre (18e); Luc Besson's *Nikita* (1990), with its classic scene in the railway restaurant *Le Train Bleu* (12e); and Besson's *Subway* (1985), filmed largely in the Auber métro station (15e).

In the **1990s**, Paris was depicted in a more meditative and less frenetic style. Krzysztof Kieslowski's *Three Colours: Blue* (1993) featured Juliette Binoche as the quintessential melancholy Parisian – and had her swimming in the Pontoise pool (5e). The premise of Cédric Klapisch's *Chacun cherche son chat* (1995) – *When the Cat's Away* – was the perfect excuse to explore the Bastille quarter in its full, mid-1990s swing. Far edgier is Mathieu Kassovitz's **La Haine** (1996), a savage portrayal of exclusion and racism in the *banlieu*. In the **new millennium**, Kassovitz also had international hits as an actor in the Jeunet-directed *Amélie* (2001) – which relaunched Montmartre as an international tourist destination – and in Gaspar Noé's shocking *Irréversible* (2002), which follows two bourgeois-bohemian Parisians drawn into a nightmare underworld. Equally dark is *Caché* (2005), Austrian director Michael Haneke's haunting story of voyeurism, race and murder set in the Butte-aux-Cailles (13e), while Cédric Klapisch's *Paris* (2008), a touching ensemble piece seen largely from Romain Duris's Montmartre balcony window, is lighter in tone. Pawel Pawlikowski's psychological thriller *The Woman in the Fifth* (2011), meanwhile, depicts a lonely, empty city in two contrasting locations – a seedy hotel and an elegant Left Bank apartment – but it's back to the suburbs again for Celine Sciamma's *Girlhood* (2014), which, with its almost exclusively black cast and focus on female characters, takes a long-overdue, fresh take on the coming-of-age-in-the-*banlieu* genre.

For **non-French films** with Paris locations, look no further than Vincente Minnelli's musical *An American in Paris* (1951), featuring Gene Kelly and Leslie Caron dancing on the *quais* of the Seine – a scene hilariously homaged in Woody Allen's *Everyone Says I Love You* (1996). Other gems include Billy Wilder's *Love in the Afternoon* (1957); Stanley Donen's musical *Funny Face* (1957) and his comic thriller *Charade* (1963), both starring Audrey Hepburn; Roman Polanski's nightmarish *Frantic* (1988); Richard Linklater's romantic sequel to *Before Sunrise* (1995), *Before Sunset* (2004), featuring Ethan Hawke and Julie Delpy living out a one-night Parisian fantasy; Doug Liman's upmarket thriller *The Bourne Identity* (2002); Woody Allen's sweetly romantic *Midnight in Paris* (2011), whose protagonist roams through a nostalgic dreamworld of 1920s Paris; and, equally bittersweet, Martin Scorsese's love letter to the city, and to cinema itself, *Hugo* (2011). The darkly funny British *Le Week-End* (2013), meanwhile, scripted by Hanif Kureishi, turned the romantic dream upside down in its account of two jaded spouses struggling to rekindle their love in the City of Light.

Standing in the heart of the Barbès hustle and bustle, this legendary 1920s moviehouse was restored to its former glory in 2013. Three screens show art-house and mainstream films, as well as hosting festivals and special events – the imposing neo-Egyptian architecture in the largest *salle* is a real treat. There's a lovely cinema bar, too. Tickets €9.50.

Lucernaire 53 rue Notre-Dame-des-Champs, 6ᵉ ☎ 01 45 44 57 34, 🖰 lucernaire.fr; 🚇 Notre-Dame-des-Champs/Vavin. Arts complex with three screening rooms, theatres, an art gallery, bookshop, bar and restaurant. Shows art movies and undubbed contemporary releases from around the world. Tickets €9.

Luminor Hôtel de Ville 20 rue du Temple, 4ᵉ ☎ 01 42 78 47 86, 🖰 luminor-hoteldeville.com; 🚇 Hôtel de Ville. The only cinema in the 4ᵉ, putting on a varied programme of art-house movies, documentaries, premieres and festivals in a restored and reconditioned 1912 movie house. Tickets €9.

Max Linder Panorama 24 bd Poissonnière, 9ᵉ ☎ 01 48 24 00 47, 🖰 maxlinder.com; 🚇 Grands Boulevards. This Art Deco cinema, with a huge, curved screen – and three tiers of seating – always shows films in the original language and has surround sound. It offers a mixed programme of mainstream and artier offerings. Tickets €10.30.

MK2 Bibliothèque 128–162 av de France, 13ᵉ ☎ 08 92 98 44 84, 🖰 mk2.com; 🚇 Bibliothèque François Mitterrand/Quai de la Gare. Behind the Bibliothèque Nationale, this member of the excellent, citywide MK2 chain is an architecturally cutting-edge cinema with a cool café and sixteen screens showing *v.o.* movies and a range of French films – mostly new – along with retrospectives and seasons. Tickets €11.20.

MK2 Odéon 113 bd St-Germain, 6ᵉ ☎ 08 92 69 84 84, 🖰 mk2.com; 🚇 Odéon. This branch of the MK2 is in an excellent St-Germain location, showing big mainstream releases plus the edgier new releases. Tickets €11.20.

MK2 Quai de Seine 14 quai de la Seine, 19ᵉ ☎ 08 92 69 84 84, 🖰 mk2.com; 🚇 Jaurès/Stalingrad. You could come to this cinema for the location alone. It's on the banks of the Canal de l'Ourcq, across the water from another MK2 cinema (the Quai de Loire) – both offer a mixed programme that appeals to art-house lovers as well as blockbuster fans. Tickets €11.20.

★**Nouvel Odéon** 6 rue de l'Ecole de Médecine, 6ᵉ ☎ 01 46 33 43 71, 🖰 nouvelodeon.com; 🚇 Odéon/Cluny La Sorbonne. A minimalist treat for anyone who loves old movies, with an enticing art-house programme that includes some splendid little-known gems from French and international cinema. Tickets €9.50.

★**Reflet Médicis** 3 rue Champollion, 5ᵉ ☎ 01 43 54 42 34, 🖰 lesecransdeparis.fr; 🚇 Cluny La Sorbonne. Three screens showing rare movies and classics, including frequent retrospectives covering directors, both French and international, and world cinema (always *v.o.*). Tickets €9.30.

★**Studio 28** 10 rue Tholozé, 18ᵉ ☎ 01 46 06 36 07, 🖰 cinemastudio28.com; 🚇 Blanche/Abbesses. In its early days, after one of the first showings of Buñuel's *L'Age d'Or*, this cinema was done over by extreme right-wing Catholics who destroyed the screen and the paintings by Dalí and Ernst in the foyer. It still hosts avant-garde premieres, followed occasionally by discussions with the director, though nowadays it focuses mainly on the best new releases from France and overseas. There's a courtyard bar/café tucked away at the back. Tickets €9.

THEATRE

Looking at the scores of métro posters in Paris, you might think bourgeois farces starring gurning celebs form the backbone of French theatre. To an extent, that's true, though the classics – Molière, Corneille and Racine – are also regularly performed, and well worth a try if your French is up to it. You can get by with quite basic French at one of the plays by the postwar generation of Francophone dramatists, such as Anouilh, Genet, Camus, Ionesco and Samuel Beckett. For non-French-speakers, the most rewarding theatre in Paris is likely to be the genre-busting, radical kind best represented by **Ariane Mnouchkine** and her **Théâtre du Soleil**, based at the Cartoucherie in Vincennes. The best time of all for theatre-lovers to come to Paris is for the **Festival d'Automne** from mid-September to late December (see p.323), an international celebration of all the performing arts, which attracts high-calibre stage directors from around the world. For a useful rundown of the city's theatre scene, including listings, check out the free monthly arts journal **La Terrasse**, available from venues and bars and online at 🖰 journal-laterrasse.fr. Note that some theatres are closed during August.

BUYING TICKETS

Booking well in advance is essential for the big new productions. Prices are mostly in the range of €20–40, but you may well find cheaper seats than that; inexpensive previews are advertised in the listings magazines, and some venues offer student and senior discounts. The easiest place to get tickets to see a stage performance in Paris is from one of the Fnac shops (see p.334) or online at 🖰 fnac.com, 🖰 theatreonline.com or 🖰 billetreduc.com (which offers discounts). Same-day tickets with a fifty percent discount (minus €3.50 commission) are available from half-price ticket kiosks (🖰 kiosqueculture.com) on place de la Madeleine, 8ᵉ and at place Raoul Dautry next to the Tour Montparnasse, 15ᵉ (both Tues–Sat 12.30–7.30pm,

CAFÉ-THEATRE

Café-théâtre, a revue, monologue or mini-play performed in a place where you can drink, and sometimes eat, is in reality probably less accessible to non-Parisians than a Racine tragedy at the Comédie Française – the humour or dirty jokes, wordplay, and allusions to current fads, phobias and politicians can leave even a fluent French-speaker in the dark. If you want to give it a try, head for one of the main venues in the Marais. The spaces are small, though you have a good chance of getting in on the night during the week, and tickets are likely to be cheaper than at standard theatres.

Blancs Manteaux 15 rue des Blancs-Manteaux, 4ᵉ ☎ 01 48 87 15 84, ⓦ blancsmanteaux.fr; Ⓜ Hôtel de Ville/Rambuteau. Revues, plays, stand-up comedy and *chanson*. As well as hosting established names, it encourages new talent and has launched a number of French stars. Tickets €20.

Café de la Gare 41 rue du Temple, 4ᵉ ☎ 01 42 78 52 51, ⓦ cdlg.org; Ⓜ Hôtel de Ville/Rambuteau. Founded in 1969, this place retains a reputation for

novelty and specializes in stand-up comedy and comic plays. Tickets €20–26.

Point Virgule 7 rue Ste-Croix-de-la-Bretonnerie, 4ᵉ ☎ 01 42 78 67 03, ⓦ lepointvirgule.com; Ⓜ Hôtel de Ville/St-Paul. With a policy of giving new and up-and-coming performers a chance to shine, this popular venue also offers an eclectic variety of comic acts. Tickets €10–20.

Sun 12.30–3.45pm; closed July & Aug); and on the place des Ternes, 17ᵉ (Tues–Sat 12.30–2.30pm & 3–7.30pm). Queues can be long, however.

VENUES

★ **Bouffes du Nord** 37bis bd de la Chapelle, 10ᵉ ☎ 01 46 07 34 50, ⓦ bouffesdunord.com; Ⓜ La Chapelle/Gare du Nord. Ground-breaking theatre director Peter Brook resurrected the derelict Bouffes du Nord in 1974 and was based here until 2010, mounting experimental works, most famously his nine-hour *Mahabharata* in 1985. The gorgeous old theatre's two current French directors, Olivier Mantei and Olivier Poubelle, are continuing Brook's innovative approach.

Le Bout 6 rue Frochot, 9ᵉ ☎ 01 42 85 11 88, ⓦ lebout .com; Ⓜ Pigalle. Set on one of SoPi's cool nightlife streets, this is a quirky little spot. The eye-catching retro exterior – scarlet with Art Nouveau flourishes – opens directly onto a tiny fifty-seater space, staging polished comic theatre, standup and improv, and good kids' shows.

★ **Cartoucherie** Rte du Champ-de-Manœuvre, 12ᵉ ⓦ cartoucherie.fr; Ⓜ Château de Vincennes. This ex-army barracks is home to several cutting-edge theatre companies: the Théâtre du Soleil (☎ 01 43 74 24 08, ⓦ theatre-du-soleil.fr); the French-Spanish troupe Théâtre de l'Epée de Bois (☎ 01 48 08 39 74, ⓦ epeedebois.com); the Théâtre de la Tempête (☎ 01 43 28 36 36, ⓦ la-tempete.fr); and the Théâtre de l'Aquarium (☎ 01 43 74 72 74, ⓦ theatredelaquarium.net).

Ciné 13 Théatre 1 av Junot, 18ᵉ ☎ 01 42 54 15 12, ⓦ cine13-theatre.com; Ⓜ Abbesses. Tucked away on one of the swishest streets on the Butte, near the old windmills, this neighbourhood gem is a lovely small venue – with just one hundred seats – for everything from political theatre and comedy to *chanson*.

★ **Comédie Française** Place Colette, 1ᵉʳ ☎ 01 44 58 15 15, ⓦ comedie-francaise.fr; Ⓜ Palais Royal Musée du Louvre. This venerable national theatre is *the* venue for the French classics, with a regular roster of tragedies and comedies from the likes of Molière, Feydeau and Rostand, but it also extends its remit to embrace writers as varied as Bertolt Brecht or Colm Toibin. There are three sites: the Théâtre du Vieux-Colombier, 21 rue du Vieux-Colombier, 6ᵉ; the mini Studio-Théâtre, under the Louvre, accessed via the Carrousel, 1ᵉʳ; and the headquarters, next to the Palais Royal on place Colette, 1ᵉʳ – the Salle Richelieu or "Maison de Molière", as it's dubbed.

Maison des Arts de Créteil (mac) Place Salvador-Allende, Créteil ☎ 01 45 13 19 19, ⓦ maccreteil.com; Ⓜ Créteil–Préfecture. As well as hosting the Films de Femmes festival (see box, p.322), mac also serves as a lively suburban theatre with a good variety of shows, including for kids.

MC93 9 bd Lénine, Bobigny ☎ 01 41 60 72 72, ⓦ mc93 .com; Ⓜ Bobigny Pablo Picasso. In the Bobigny suburb, MC93 – Maison de la Culture de Seine-St-Denis – is a highly regarded contemporary theatre that specializes in thoughtful, challenging productions, and regularly features foreign directors.

Ménagerie du Verre 12/14 rue Léchevin, 11ᵉ ☎ 01 43 38 33 44, ⓦ menagerie-de-verre.org; Ⓜ Parmentier. Multi-disciplinary studio devoted to experimental theatre, performance art and contemporary dance; their annual festival, Etrange Cargo (March/April), is always worth a look.

Odéon Théâtre de l'Europe Place de l' Odéon, 6ᵉ ☎ 01 44 85 40 40, ⓦ theatre-odeon.eu; Ⓜ Odéon. This Neoclassical state-funded theatre puts on only European and American plays – mainly contemporary, although there are some modern interpretations of the classics

– occasionally in their *version originale*. During May 1968, the theatre was occupied by students and became an open parliament with the backing of its directors.

Le Tarmac 159 av Gambetta, 20ᵉ ☎01 43 64 80 80, ⓦletarmac.fr; Ⓜ St-Fargeau/Gambetta. Specializing in works from the Francophone world, this passionate and innovative theatre stages contemporary works from countries as varied as Burkina Faso and Canada.

Théâtre des Amandiers 7 av Pablo-Picasso, Nanterre ☎01 46 14 70 00, ⓦnanterre-amandiers.com; RER Nanterre-Préfecture and free theatre shuttle bus. Renowned for innovative, challenging and avant-garde productions of classic and contemporary theatre and dance, including many plays performed in *v.o.*

Théâtre de l'Atelier 1 place Charles Dullin, 18ᵉ ☎01 46 06 49 24, ⓦtheatre-atelier.com; Ⓜ Anvers/Pigalle. Small, historic theatre on a pretty little square below the Montmartre Butte. The great mime Jean-Louis Barrault – who played the celebrated real-life mime artist Baptiste in the 1945 movie *Les Enfants du Paradis* – made his debut here; today it puts on well-regarded contemporary and literary works, often with a philosophical or political slant.

Théâtre de la Bastille 76 rue de la Roquette, 11ᵉ ☎01 43 57 42 14, ⓦtheatre-bastille.com; Ⓜ Bastille. One of the best venues for new work and fringe productions – in both theatre and dance.

Théâtre de la Cité Internationale 17 bd Jourdan, 14ᵉ ☎01 43 13 50 50, ⓦtheatredelacite.com; RER Cité Universitaire. Three spaces staging an innovative and sometimes provocative programme of theatre, music, circus and some dance.

Théâtre de la Huchette 23 rue de la Huchette, 5ᵉ ☎01 43 26 38 99, ⓦtheatre-huchette.com; Ⓜ St-Michel. Some sixty years on, this intimate theatre, seating ninety, is still showing Ionesco's *La Cantatrice Chauve* (*The Bald Prima Donna*; 7pm) and *La Leçon* (8pm), two classics of the Theatre of the Absurd (Tues–Sat).

Théâtre National de la Colline 15 rue Malte Brun, 20ᵉ ☎01 44 62 52 52, ⓦcolline.fr; Ⓜ Gambetta. Dedicated to supporting emerging writers, and known for its modern and cutting-edge productions. Each season sees between a dozen and twenty shows.

Théâtre Paris Villette 211 av Jean-Jaurès, 19ᵉ ☎01 40 03 72 23, ⓦtheatre-paris-villette.fr; Ⓜ Porte de Pantin. Occupying a grand Neoclassical former abattoir in the creative hub of La Villette, this exciting venue has two stages featuring challenging and fresh new work for children and adults.

Théâtre de l'Opprimé 78 rue du Charolais, 12ᵉ ☎01 43 40 44 44, ⓦtheatredelopprime.com; Ⓜ Reuilly–Diderot. Located in an old furniture store, the "Theatre of the Oppressed" – inspired by the ideas of 1970s Brazilian director Augusto Boal, who used drama to give oppressed people a voice – puts on challenging and lively productions that deal with complex political issues.

DANCE

Paris is a key player in the nation's dance scene and regularly hosts the best **contemporary** practitioners. Names worth looking out for include Compagnie Maguy Marin and troupes from Régine Chopinot, Jean-Claude Gallotta, Catherine Diverrès and Angelin Preljocaj. As for **ballet**, the principal stage is at the Opéra Garnier, home to the Ballet de l'Opéra National. It still bears the influence of Rudolf Nureyev, its charismatic, controversial director from 1983 to 1989, and frequently revives his productions. Plenty of space and critical attention are also given to **tap**, **tango**, **folk** and **jazz dancing**, and to international traditional dance troupes. The free monthly arts journal **La Terrasse** (ⓦjournal-laterrasse.fr), available at bars, cafés and arts venues, is a good resource for dance news and events. **Prices** vary wildly, starting as low as €7 but increasing for the big shows; it's possible to buy tickets online at ⓦtheatreonline.com, and you may be able to find reductions on some dance performances at the city's three half-price ticket kiosks (see p.314).

DANCE VENUES

Centre Mandapa 6 rue Wurtz, 13ᵉ ☎01 45 89 99 00, ⓦcentre-mandapa.fr; Ⓜ Glacière. Mainly stages (and gives lessons in) classical Indian dance, but also showcases other music and dance traditions, from Asia and around the world.

★**Centre National de la Danse** 1 rue Victor Hugo, Pantin ☎01 41 83 98 98, ⓦcnd.fr; Ⓜ Hoche/RER Pantin. Converted from a disused 1970s monolith in the suburb of Pantin into an airy, high-tech space, the national centre for dance promotes the art through training, workshops and exhibitions. They also offer performances, masterclasses, dance movies and a huge archive/multi-media library.

Maison des Arts de Créteil (mac) Place Salvador-Allende, Créteil ☎01 45 13 19 19, ⓦwww.maccreteil.com; Ⓜ Créteil–Préfecture. This always interesting theatre/arts venue stages occasional dance and physical theatre shows.

Ménagerie du Verre 12/14 rue Léchevin, 11ᵉ ☎01 43 38 33 44, ⓦmenagerie-de-verre.org; Ⓜ Parmentier. Creative multi-disciplinary studio/performance space encouraging innovation in conceptual dance and physical theatre, with regular shows and a well-regarded annual festival, Etrange Cargo, in March/April.

★**Opéra Bastille** Place de la Bastille, 12ᵉ Ⓜ Bastille; **Opéra Garnier** Place de l'Opéra, Ⓜ Opéra; ⓦoperadeparis.fr. Two very different opera houses (see

DANCE FESTIVALS

Major dance festivals – many of which incorporate theatre, mime and experimental and classical music – include **Faits d'Hiver** in January (Ⓦfaitsdhiver.com); **Etrange Cargo** at the Ménagerie du Verre (see opposite), usually held in March or April (Ⓦmenagerie-de-verre.org); **Les Etés de la Danse** in July (Ⓦwww.lesetesdeladanse.com), held in various venues; **Paris l'Eté** from mid-July to early August (Ⓦquartierdete.com), which sometimes takes to the streets; and the mighty **Festival d'Automne**, which fills the city with dance fans from mid-September to December (Ⓦfestival-automne.com).

p.74) – Bastille modern, Garnier extravagent and ornate – putting on high-profile ballet and dance. The Garnier, the main home of the Ballet de l'Opéra National, puts on a strong programme of classic ballet; dance shows at the Bastille are often more contemporary.

Pompidou Centre Entrance rue Beaubourg, 4ᵉ ☎01 44 78 12 33, Ⓦcentrepompidou.fr; ⓂRambuteau. A consistently interesting programme of contemporary performances by visiting companies.

Regard du Cygne 210 rue de Belleville, 20ᵉ ☎01 43 58 55 93, Ⓦleregarducygne.com; ⓂPlace des Fêtes/Jourdain. A studio promoting innovative dance in all styles. One of the centre's best-known events is its series of "Sauvages", in which virtually anyone can perform and exchange ideas with other artists and professional dancers.

Théâtre des Abbesses 31 rue des Abbesses, 18ᵉ ☎01 42 74 22 77, Ⓦtheatredelaville-paris.com; ⓂAbbesses. Sister company to the Théâtre de la Ville (see below), with a slightly more offbeat programme, including international dance.

Théâtre de la Bastille 76 rue de la Roquette, 11ᵉ ☎01 43 57 42 14, Ⓦtheatre-bastille.com; ⓂBastille. As well

as new and traditional theatre, this venue also hosts dance and mime performances by young dancers and choreographers.

Théâtre des Champs-Elysées 15 av Montaigne, 8ᵉ ☎01 49 52 50 50, Ⓦtheatrechampselysees.fr; ⓂAlma–Marceau. This prestigious venue regularly hosts major foreign troupes and stars from around the world.

★**Théâtre National de la Danse Chaillot** Palais de Chaillot, place du Trocadéro, 16ᵉ ☎01 53 65 30 00, Ⓦtheatre-chaillot.fr; ⓂTrocadéro. With a beautiful interior and a lobby looking out on to one of the most famous vistas in the world, the Chaillot theatre is worth a trip for the venue alone. Dance from some of France's leading choreographers, as well as regular slots by foreign ballet companies, all adds up to a varied and imaginative programme.

★**Théâtre de la Ville** 2 place du Châtelet, 4ᵉ ☎01 42 74 22 77, Ⓦtheatredelaville-paris.com; ⓂChâtelet. The biggest contemporary dance venue in the city, specializing in mainstream and avant-garde productions by French companies as well as working with some of Europe's best choreographers.

PHILHARMONIE DE PARIS

Classical music and opera

Classical music, as you might expect in this Neoclassical city, is alive and flourishing. Since 2015, not just one but two state-of-the-art concert halls have opened in the capital: Jean Nouvel's Philharmonie de Paris auditorium in La Villette and the Seine Musicale to the west of Paris. Their eclectic programming and location away from the city centre are drawing in a more diverse audience and helping to shake up the classical music scene. The Paris Opéra, meanwhile, with its two homes, puts on a fine selection of opera and ballet, from core repertoire to new commissions. There's an energetic contemporary music scene, too, with a major point of focus at IRCAM, near the Pompidou Centre, and smaller venues elsewhere. The city also hosts a good number of music festivals; the Chopin and St-Denis festivals, the Fête de la Musique and Paris Quartier d'Eté (see p.321) are particularly worthwhile.

ESSENTIALS

Tickets Ticket prices for classical concerts depend on the seat, venue and event; opera, ballet and celebrity performers attract higher prices, while churches and museums tend to be relatively inexpensive. You might pay anything from €5 for a recital in a small church, or a restricted-view seat in a big venue, to €150 for a stalls ticket in a big-name opera, but most seats cost €30–90. Tickets can almost always be bought online; for big names you may find overnight queues at the actual box office.

Listings and information Listings mag *L'Officiel des Spectacles* (ⓦoffi.fr), *Pariscope* (ⓦpariscope.fr), excellent monthly magazine *Diapason* (ⓦdiapasonmag .fr), devoted to the music scene, and *Opéra* (ⓦopera-magazine.com), with its emphasis, as the name suggests, on opera, can be bought at *tabacs* or browsed online. Listings can also be found in the free arts mag *La Terrasse* (ⓦwww.journal-laterrasse.fr), or online at ⓦconcertclassic.com.

CLASSICAL MUSIC

Besides the **Orchestre de Paris**, Paris's other main orchestra is the **Orchestre National de France**, under the baton of Emmanuel Krivine. **Early music** has a dedicated following; the most respected Baroque ensemble is William Christie's Les Arts Florissants (ⓦarts-florissants.com), renowned for exciting renditions of Rameau's operas and choral works by Lully and Charpentier. **Contemporary** and **electronic** work flourishes, too. Regular concerts are given at IRCAM, a vast laboratory of acoustics and "digital signal processing", headed for many years by renowned composer Pierre Boulez, who died in 2016. The acclaimed Ensemble Intercontemporain (ⓦensembleinter.com), which was formed by Boulez and is based at the Philharmonie de Paris, still bears its creator's stamp and is committed to performing new work. The following venues host regular concerts, but many other museums and churches – including Notre-Dame cathedral (see p.46) – put on occasional events, including gospel concerts; check *Pariscope* (see p.40).

AUDITORIUMS AND THEATRES

Bouffes du Nord 37bis bd de la Chapelle, 10ᵉ ☎01 46 07 34 50, ⓦbouffesdunord.com; Ⓜ La Chapelle/Gare du Nord; map p.192. This excellent and rather beautiful theatre, famously brought back to life by Peter Brook (see p.315), is also known for its superb chamber music recitals. Tickets €25.

Conservatoire National Supérieur de Musique et de Danse de Paris 209 av Jean-Jaurès, 19ᵉ ☎01 40 40 46 47, ⓦconservatoiredeparis.fr; Ⓜ Porte de Pantin; map p.202. Debates, masterclasses and free performances from the Conservatoire's students, based in the Parc de la Villette.

IRCAM (Institut de Recherche et Coordination Acoustique/Musique) 1 place Igor-Stravinsky, 4ᵉ ☎01 44 78 48 43, ⓦwww.ircam.fr; Ⓜ Hôtel de Ville; map p.88. IRCAM hosts regular experimental concerts on-site and also in the nearby Pompidou Centre and at the Théâtre des Bouffes du Nord.

Maison de Radio France 116 av-du-Président-Kennedy, 16ᵉ ☎01 56 40 15 16, ⓦradiofrance.fr; Ⓜ Passy; map p.215. The radio station France Musique schedules an excellent range of classical music, plus operas and contemporary music, on-site (at both the renovated Salle 104 and a new 1461-seat auditorium) and at venues around town – some are free.

Philharmonie 2 221 av Jean-Jaurès, 19ᵉ ☎01 44 84 44 84, ⓦphilharmoniedeparis.fr; Ⓜ Porte de Pantin; map p.202. The old Cité de la Musique concert hall, renamed and now rather in the shadow of the adjacent Philharmonie de Paris, still stages concerts in its two auditoriums (capacity 900 and 250), covering anything from traditional Korean music to the Ensemble Intercontemporain, with the occasional airing of instruments from the on-site Musée de la Musique (see p.204). Tickets from around €26.

★**Philharmonie de Paris** 221 av Jean-Jaurès, 19ᵉ ☎01 44 84 44 84, ⓦphilharmoniedeparis.fr; Ⓜ Porte de Pantin; map p.202. Designed by celebrated architect Jean Nouvel, the city's long-awaited new concert hall finally opened in 2015. The state-of-the-art structure – a massive (capacity 2400), aluminium-clad angular building, with a zigzagging ramp leading up to the roof – has been likened by some to a huge spaceship. If the exterior seems forbidding by day, at night it looks more inviting, lit up and sparkling, drawing concert-goers up a long elevator to the main entrance. The interior is creamy-warm and soft, with curved balconies dipping down towards the stage; acoustics are excellent and the ambience is intimate. The resident Orchestre de Paris, under conductor Daniel Harding, and the Ensemble Intercontemporain put on an exciting programme of music-making, and the many workshops and extra activities, as well as the relatively affordable tickets (many around €10–30), seem to have brought in a broader audience than at the more traditional city-centre venues.

Salle Gaveau 45 rue la Boétie, 8ᵉ ☎01 49 53 05 07, ⓦsallegaveau.com; Ⓜ Miromesnil; map p.64. This atmospheric concert hall, built in 1907, is a major venue for piano recitals by world-class players, and also stages chamber music recitals and full-scale orchestral works.

La Seine Musicale Ile Seguin, Boulogne-Billancourt ☎01 74 34 54 00, ⓦlaseinemusicale.com; Ⓜ Pont de Sèvres. Hot on the heels of the Philharmonie (see above) comes this spectacular new concert venue on an island in the Seine to the west of Paris. Built on the old Renault car factory site, the new building, opened in 2017 and designed by Japanese architect Shigeru Ban and Frenchman Jean de Gastines, is a striking spherical structure, around which a

23

solar "sail" covered in photovoltaic panels moves on rails, maximising exposure to the sun during the day. Facilities include a 6000-seat multi-purpose hall and a 1150-seat classical music auditorium, the new home of the Insula Orchestra, which plays on period instruments. The centre's director, Jean-Luc Choplin, who shook things up at the Théâtre du Châtelet, promises an eclectic line-up of classical and contemporary repertoire, musicals, ballets, pop and rock concerts. Tickets from €20.

★ **Théâtre des Champs-Elysées** 15 av Montaigne, 8ᵉ ☎01 49 52 50 50, ⓦ theatrechampselysees.fr; Ⓜ Alma–Marceau; map p.64. Two-thousand-seater Modernist theatre, seeping history, with sculptures by Bourdelle and paintings by Vuillard. Opened in 1913, it was the location of the premiere of Stravinsky's *Rite of Spring*, whose modernity scandalized Paris. Now home to the Orchestre National de France and Orchestre de Chambre de Paris (ⓦ www.orchestredechambredeparis.com), it also hosts international orchestras, superstar conductors and ballet troupes, and has a vigorous operatic programme. Tickets for seats with no view at all are a bargain, but you can pay up to €150 or so for star performers.

Théâtre du Châtelet 1 place du Châtelet, 1ᵉʳ ☎01 40 28 28 40, ⓦ chatelet-theatre.com; Ⓜ Châtelet; map p.88. This prestigious concert hall (see p.93), which puts on a varied programme of operas, concerts and musicals, was closed for renovation at the time of writing until the end of 2019.

CHURCHES AND MUSEUMS

Auditorium du Louvre Musée du Louvre (Pyramide entrance), 1ᵉʳ ☎01 40 20 55 00, ⓦ louvre.fr;

Ⓜ Louvre-Rivoli/Palais Royal Musée du Louvre; map p.50. Lunchtime and evening concerts of chamber music, contemporary works and young artists. Tickets from €15.

Eglise de la Madeleine Place de la Madeleine, 8ᵉ ☎01 42 50 96 18, ⓦ eglise-lamadeleine.com; Ⓜ Madeleine; map p.64. Organ recitals, chamber concerts and choral performances; some free, some ticketed, with prices at around €30.

Musée National du Moyen Age 6 place Paul Painlevé, 5ᵉ ☎01 53 73 78 16, ⓦ musee-moyenage.fr; Ⓜ Cluny-La-Sorbonne; map p.124. Regular concerts of little-known medieval music (tickets €16), as well as short choral concerts Sun at 4pm and Mon at 12.30pm (from €6).

Musée d'Orsay 1 rue de Bellechasse, 7ᵉ ☎01 40 49 47 50, ⓦ musee-orsay.fr; Ⓜ Solférino/RER Musée d'Orsay; map p.135. The Musée d'Orsay puts on a varied and high-quality programme of recitals and concerts, often themed to link with temporary exhibitions. Tickets €16–40.

St-Eustache 2 impasse Saint-Eustache, 1ᵉʳ ☎01 42 36 31 05, ⓦ saint-eustache.org; Ⓜ Les Halles; map p.88. This beautiful Gothic church is known for its music, and offers a consistently good programme of chamber music, choral pieces and awe-inspiring (free) organ recitals.

St-Séverin 3–4 rue des Prêtres St-Séverin, 5ᵉ ☎01 48 24 16 97, ⓦ saint-severin.com; Ⓜ Cluny-La-Sorbonne; map p.124. Atmospheric fifteenth-century church offering varied programmes, usually with free entry.

Sainte-Chapelle 8 bd du Palais, 1ᵉʳ ☎01 42 77 65 65, ⓦ sainte-chapelle.fr; Ⓜ Cité; map p.44. A fabulous setting for mainly Mozart, Bach and Vivaldi classics. Tickets €38–50, available in advance on the door or online at ⓦ www2.classictic.com.

OPERA

The venerable Opéra National de Paris has two homes: the **Opéra Garnier** and the less appealing **Opéra Bastille**. The more popular productions sell out within days of **tickets** (€5–231) becoming available – note that they go online first. For last-minute tickets, join the queue early at the venues – they go on sale at 11.30am Mon–Sat and one hour before the performance on Sundays and public holidays. Unfilled seats are also sold at a discount to people under the age of 28 and over 65 30min before the curtain goes up. In addition, at the Opéra Bastille 32 standing-room tickets are sold for €5 from the ticket machines in the foyer roughly 90min before each show, while at the Opéra Garnier some seats at €10 with restricted or no view are available on the day of the performance. In recent years, the smaller **Opéra Comique** has staged a comeback into the world of opera and puts on an interesting programme of lesser-known repertoire. Major multi-purpose **performance venues** such as the Olympia rock venue (ⓦ olympiahall.com) and even the Stade de France stadium (ⓦ stadefrance.fr) occasionally stage large-scale opera and musical events – these are usually well advertised.

VENUES

Opéra Bastille Place de la Bastille, 12ᵉ ⓦ operadeparis .fr; Ⓜ Bastille; map p.112. Opened in 1989, Paris's main opera house hasn't been entirely successful. The design is unlovable and opinions differ over the acoustics. The stage, at least, is well designed and allows the auditorium uninterrupted views, prices are generally a little lower than at the Palais, and there's no doubting the high calibre of the performers and orchestra.

Opéra Comique 5 rue Favart, 2ᵉ ☎08 25 01 01 23,

ⓦ opera-comique.com; Ⓜ Richelieu-Drouot; map p.76. The renovated Opéra Comique, under its dynamic director Olivier Mantei, offers a richly varied repertoire, including forgotten works of the French opera genre "*opéra comique*" and obscure operas by well-known composers.

Opéra Garnier Place de l'Opéra, 9ᵉ ⓦ operadeparis.fr; Ⓜ Opéra; map p.76. An evening in this opulent nineteenth-century opera house, used for ballets and smaller-scale opera productions, is unforgettable. While views from some of the side seats can be poor, the acoustics are excellent.

NUIT BLANCHE

Festivals and events

Paris hosts an impressive roster of festivals. The city's biggest jamborees are
Bastille Day, on July 14, and the summer-long Paris Plages, but there's
invariably something on throughout the year – if it's not one of the major
exhibitions, it'll be an arts event subsidized by the ever-active town hall or
culture ministry. Neighbourhood events can be even more fun: many
quartiers such as Belleville, Ménilmontant and Montmartre have open-door
weeks when artists' studios are open to the public, for example. The tourist
office can give details of the mainstream happenings; otherwise check
listings in Paris magazines (see p.40) and keep an eye open for posters and
flyers. For a few more festivals dedicated to movies and dance, take a look at
our "Film, theatre and dance" chapter (see p.311 & p.317).

JANUARY

Paris Face Cachée (end Jan/early Feb) Three days of one-off events all over the city, allowing you to experience places that are usually closed to the public or to revisit familiar spaces from unusual angles – from meeting the city's gilders to discovering hidden treasures in the métro (🕸 parisfacecachee.fr).

FEBRUARY

Chinese New Year (mid-Feb) Celebrations in different neighbourhoods; the main parade weaves through the heart of Chinatown around av d'Ivry in the 13e (🕸 parisinfo.com).

Carnaval de Paris/Carnival des Femmes (Sun before Shrove Tues) The pre-Lenten, Mardi Gras-style Carnaval de Paris parade starts in the 20e and ends at Place de la République (see p.197), with brass bands, giant puppets and carnival groups from around the world; the associated Carnival des Femmes – or Fête des Blanchisseuses – is a raucous mid-Lenten parade (also held on a Sun) of women, and men dressed as women, that circuits the Marais (🕸 carnaval-paris.org and 🕸 carnaval-des-femmes.org).

MARCH

Banlieues Bleues (throughout March) International festival of jazz and roots music in the *communes* of Seine-St-Denis, northeast of central Paris – including Montreuil, Bagnolet, Pantin and St-Ouen (🕸 banlieuesbleues.org).

Films de Femmes (mid-March) Major women's international film festival (see p.311) held over ten days at Créteil, in the southeastern suburbs (🕸 filmsdefemmes.com).

100% Afrique (end March) This ambitious ten-day celebration of creativity from Africa and the diaspora – from dance and fashion to cinema and art – has featured British grime stars, Johannesburg township dancers, Malian singers and Congolese playwrights (🕸 lavillette.com).

APRIL

Marathon International de Paris (early/mid-April) The Paris Marathon (see box, p.344) departs from the Champs-Elysées and arrives, via the Bois de Vincennes and the Bois de Boulogne, on the av Foch just over 42km later. There's also a half-marathon in March and a 20km run in Oct, starting and ending at the Eiffel Tower (🕸 parismarathon .com; 🕸 semideparis.com; 🕸 20kmparis.com).

MAY

Festival Jazz à St-Germain (mid-May) Ten days of big jazz names and new talent from around the world performing in all manner of St-Germain venues (🕸 festivaljazzsaintgermainparis.com).

Printemps des Rues (mid-May) A weekend festival of free street theatre and experimental performances in the 18e and around the Canal St-Martin in the 10e (🕸 leprintempsdesrues.com).

Quinzaine des Réalisateurs (mid-/late May) The Forum des Images hosts a fortnight of screenings from the alternative Cannes film festival (🕸 quinzaine-realisateurs.com).

Nuit des Musées (usually third Sat in May) Most of Paris's museums stay open till around midnight, many putting on workshops, talks and concerts (🕸 nuitdesmusees.culture.fr).

Villette Sonique (last week of May) The venues, and the grounds, of the Parc de la Villette are taken over by underground, innovative and experimental musicians from around the world (🕸 villettesonique.com).

Internationaux de France de Tennis (three weeks from late May to early June) The French Open tennis championships (see p.347), on the clay courts of Stade Roland Garros (🕸 rolandgarros.com).

JUNE

Festival de St-Denis (throughout June) Classical and world music festival with many performances in the Gothic St-Denis basilica (🕸 festival-saint-denis.com).

Fête du Vélo (early June) Cyclists unite, taking to the streets for mass bike rides, picnics and festivities during this France-wide weekend celebration (🕸 feteduvelo.fr).

Festival de Chopin (mid-June to mid-July) Chopin recitals, some by candlelight, held in the Orangerie de Bagatelle, in the Bois de Boulogne (🕸 frederic-chopin.com).

Paris Jazz Festival (mid-June to late July) Big-name jazz and world music in the Parc Floral at the Bois de Vincennes (🕸 parisjazzfestival.fr).

Fête de la Musique (June 21) Summer solstice festival with concerts in open and public spaces throughout the city; orchestras play in courtyards, buskers take to the streets and the big music venues stage free concerts (🕸 fetedelamusique.culture.fr).

LGBT Pride (last Sat of June) France's biggest LGBT Pride march – aka Marche des Fiertés – sees hundreds of thousands of people hit the streets (🕸 gaypride.fr).

Fête du Cinéma (late June) Five days of screenings, from classics to the cutting-edge in French and foreign cinema, throughout the city. All tickets cost just €4 (🕸 feteducinema .com).

La Goutte d'Or en Fête (late June to early July) Music festival that embraces all kinds of music from around Africa and the diaspora, with local and international performers, arts events, food stalls, parades and dances in the Goutte d'Or district (🕸 gouttedorenfete.org).

JULY

Bastille Day (July 14 and evening before) The 1789 surrender of the Bastille is celebrated with a military parade along the Champs-Elysées, fireworks and concerts. On the evenings of the 13th and 14th, live bands play, people dance in the streets around Bastille, and riotous "Bals des Pompiers" parties rage inside the city's fire stations – rue Blanche and rue du Jour are known to be among the best.

Paris l'Eté (mid-July to early Aug) A broad range of cinema, dance, music, circus and theatre events around the city, in formal venues and public spaces (🖥parislete.fr).

Paris Plages (mid-/late July to mid-/late Aug or early Sept) Wildly popular scheme in which 3km of the Seine *quais* – roughly from the Pont des Arts to Pont de Sully – are transformed into beaches, complete with sand, parasols and deckchairs, with free activities from t'ai chi to salsa. There's also a "beach" at the Bassin de la Villette, where you can muck about in kayaks and pedal boats or simply relax and enjoy a drink, and another in front of the Hôtel de Ville in the 4ᵉ (🖥en.parisinfo.com).

Arrivée du Tour de France (third or fourth Sun in July) The biggest event of the French sporting calendar (see box, p.347): the Tour de France cyclists cross the finishing line on the Champs-Elysées (🖥letour.fr).

Festival de Cinéma en Plein Air (end July to end Aug) Free alfresco movie festival (see p.311) in the Parc de la Villette (🖥cinema.arbo.com).

AUGUST

Rock en Seine (late Aug) Major three-day music festival – artists have included PJ Harvey, Chemical Brothers and the Libertines – in a lovely Seine-side park on the western edge of the city (🖥rockenseine.com).

SEPTEMBER

Jazz à la Villette (early to mid-Sept) Two-week festival with legendary greats, big contemporary names and local conservatory students performing in the Parc de la Villette venues, and smaller gigs in Belleville and Ménilmontant (🖥jazzalavillette.com).

Festival d'Automne (mid-Sept to late Dec) Major festival of international contemporary theatre, music, dance and avant-garde arts, held throughout the city and its surrounds (🖥festival-automne.com).

Fête de l'Humanité (mid-Sept) Sponsored by the French Communist Party and *L'Humanité* newspaper, this huge three-day event, north of Paris at La Courneuve, mixes French and international music – from Joan Baez to the Prodigy – with political and cultural debates, plus food stalls, fairground attractions and kids' activities (🖥fete.humanite.fr).

Technoparade (mid-Sept) Marking the end of Paris Electronic Week, which celebrates electronic music in all its forms, this parade attracts hundreds of thousands. The route changes each year, culminating in a major afterparty with dozens of DJs (🖥technoparade.fr and 🖥pariselectronicweek.fr).

Journées du Patrimoine (third weekend in Sept) France-wide "heritage weekend" where normally off-limits buildings are opened to the public (🖥journeesdupatrimoine .culture.fr).

OCTOBER

Festival de l'Imaginaire (Oct–Dec) Musical performances, screenings and workshops throughout the city, showcasing traditional cultures from around the world (🖥festivaldelimaginaire.com).

Weather Festival (early Oct) House and techno festival with mainstream and underground artists, a 24hr party over the weekend and various afterparties on the Mon (🖥weatherfestival.fr).

Nuit Blanche (first Sat in Oct) Citywide event, from dusk to dawn, that brings together musicians, artists, circus acts and all sorts to create an unforgettable night – underwater dancers in vertical tanks, a giant crescent moon hoisted onto the St-Eustache church, spooky street parades – of dreamlike spectacles (🖥facebook .com/NBParis).

Fêtes des Vendanges (early or mid-Oct) Lively five-day festival in Montmartre, celebrating the grape harvest of the local vineyard with exhibitions, concerts, tastings, artisan food stalls and literary events (🖥fetedesvendangesdemontmartre.com).

Foire Internationale d'Art Contemporain (FIAC) (third week in Oct) International contemporary art fair taking place over four days at the Grand and Petit Palais and outdoor spaces such as the Jardin des Tuileries and Place Vendôme (🖥fiac.com).

NOVEMBER

Paris Photo (mid-Nov) Held at the Grand Palais, this four-day event is one of the world's largest photography exhibitions, showing international work from early images to modern masterpieces (🖥parisphoto.com).

Beaujolais Nouveau Day (third Thurs of Nov) Oenophiles flock to the city's bars and cafés to taste the first Beaujolais nouveau *vin de primeur*, released for sale on this day.

DECEMBER

Noël (Dec 24–25) Christmas Eve is a huge affair, much more important than the following day. Notre-Dame, the Eglise de la Madeleine and the Basilique du Sacré-Coeur hold midnight Mass services.

Le Nouvel An (Dec 31) New Year's Eve means dense crowds of out-of-towners on the Champs-Elysées and super-elevated restaurant prices everywhere.

24

AGNÈS B.

Shopping

Paris is almost as fabled for shopping as it is for gastronomy and romance. From the flagship "concept stores" of Europe's glitziest couture houses to the humblest of neighbourhood bakeries, you'll find throughout the city an obsession with quality and style, and a fierce pride in detail. Supermarkets and chains have made small advances in the city, but Parisians, for the most part, remain loyal to local traders and independently owned shops. Whether you can afford to buy or not, some of the most entertaining experiences of a trip to Paris are to be had for free just browsing in small boutiques, their owners proudly displaying their cache of offbeat items, particular passions and mouthwatering treats.

ESSENTIALS

Opening hours Many shops in Paris stay open all day Monday to Saturday. Most tend to close comparatively late – 7 or 8pm as often as not. Some smaller businesses close for up to two hours at lunchtime, somewhere between noon and 3pm.

Sunday trading Sunday trading laws are becoming ever more relaxed, and over the next few years a growing number of shops are likely to open on a Sunday. At the time of writing, however, most are closed on Sunday and some on Monday as well. An exception is made for the shops in the major tourist zones, which gives these areas – some of which are also

pedestrianized on that day – a pleasant, relaxed buzz. Sunday zones include the Butte Montmartre, around Abbesses (18e); the Marais, between place des Vosges and rue des Francs-Bourgeois (3e–4e); the Viaduc des Arts (12e); Bercy Village (12e); rue d'Arcole, on the Ile de la Cité (4e); boulevard St-Germain (6e); rue de Rivoli (1er); and the Champs-Elysées (8e). The big department stores and shopping malls (see p.326) also open on a Sunday, and many food shops, especially boulangeries, open in the morning.

VAT It's worth researching VAT reimbursement for non-EU citizens (see p.39).

CLOTHES, SHOES AND ACCESSORIES

Milan, New York and London are fierce contenders, but Paris remains the world capital of **fashion**. As a tourist, you may not be able to get into the haute couture shows, but there's nothing to prevent you trying on fabulously expensive creations – as long as you can brave the intimidatingly chic assistants and the awesome chill of the marble portals. But if it's actual shopping you're interested in, there are plenty of good areas to browse and affordable, interesting shops to discover. **Sales** are held twice a year, generally beginning in early January and the end of June/beginning of July and lasting about six weeks, while ends of lines and old stock from the couturiers are sold year-round in "stock" **discount** shops (see p.329), or at La Vallée, inside the frontiers of Disneyland (see p.329).

25

DEPARTMENT STORES

Le BHV Marais 52–64 rue de Rivoli, 4e ☎01 42 74 96 79, ⓦ bhv.fr; Ⓜ Hôtel de Ville; map p.99. Just two years younger than Le Bon Marché (see p.99), the *BHV* is noted for its homewares, DIY department and artists' materials, with the womenswear and shoe departments in particular worth a look. There's a good-value self-service restaurant with nice views on the top floor and a very popular panoramic bar, *Le Perchoir du Marais*, on the seventh floor.

The store used to be seen as more downmarket than its rivals, but it's been busy giving itself a makeover over the last few years and expanding its range. A number of offshoots have sprung up in the surrounding streets, including a *BHV Homme* (36 rue de la Verrerie), set over four floors and offering a wide selection of accessories and clothing for men, as well as a popular alfresco dining area, *La Cour Bleue*, with various street-food stalls; there's even a *BHV Niche* (42 rue de la Verrerie), which has everything for

---

WHERE TO SHOP IN PARIS

The smartly renovated nineteenth-century covered **arcades**, or *passages*, in the **2e** and **9e** **arrondissements**, offer distinctive and unusual shopping possibilities, from toyshops to independent designers to antique book stores and wine cellars. On the streets proper, the square kilometre around **place St-Germain-des-Prés** is hard to beat – for window-shopping at least; to the north of the square, the narrow streets are lined with antique shops and arts and interior design stores, while to the south, and in particular along **rue du Cherche Midi**, are designer clothing brands and the famed Le Bon Marché department store (see p.326). St-Germain is also good for classy food outlets. The other major department stores, Galeries Lafayette (see p.326) and Printemps (see p.326), are on **Boulevard Haussmann**, which also boasts some good independent shops and concept stores in the surrounding streets.

The **Marais**, especially the Haut Marais (focused on rues Vieille du Temple, Poitou and Charlot), and the hip **Canal St-Martin** *quartier* have filled up with dinky little boutiques, arty interior design stores, specialist shops and galleries, many of them quite pricey. **Montmartre** (in particular around Abbesses and rue des Martyrs) is a good hunting ground for independent fashion and upmarket food; for Parisian **haute couture**, the traditional bastions are avenue Montaigne, rue François-1er, and the upper end of **rue du Faubourg-St-Honoré** in the 8e, while **Les Halles** is good for high-street fashion.

Place de la Madeleine is the place to head for seriously luxury **food** stores, such as Fauchon (see p.337), while the Latin Quarter is bookshop and graphic novel terrain. Last-minute or convenience shopping is probably best done at shopping malls, the big department stores (for high-quality merchandise) and Monoprix (for basics).

the pampered dog or cat in your life. Mon–Sat 10am–8pm, Sun 11am–7pm.

★ **Le Bon Marché** 24 rue de Sèvres, 7ᵉ ☎ 01 44 39 81 81, ⊛ 24sevres.com; Ⓜ Sèvres-Babylone; map p.138. The world's oldest department store, founded in 1852 and now run by the luxury goods empire LVMH. It's smaller, calmer and classier than Galeries Lafayette and Printemps, and has an excellent kids' department and a legendary food hall (see p.337). Mon–Wed, Fri & Sat 10am–8pm, Thurs 10am–8.45pm, Sun 11am–8pm.

Galeries Lafayette 40 bd Haussmann, 9ᵉ ☎ 01 42 82 34 56, ⊛ haussmann.galerieslafayette.com; Ⓜ Havre-Caumartin; map p.76. This store's forte is high fashion, with two floors given over to the latest creations by leading designers; the fourth floor has a huge selection of lingerie, the basement is dedicated to shoes, and there's a large children's clothes section on the fifth floor. Then there's a host of big names in men's and women's accessories, a huge *parfumerie* and a branch of *Angélina salon de thé*, all under a superb 1912 dome. Just down the road at no. 35 is Lafayette Maison/Gourmet, its five floors split between quality kitchenware, linens and furniture, and luxury food and wine. Galeries Mon–Sat 9.30am–8.30pm, Sun 11am–7pm; Maison/Gourmet Mon–Sat 8.30am–9.30pm, Sun 11am–7pm.

★ **Printemps** 64 bd Haussmann, 9ᵉ; Ⓜ Havre-Caumartin; Carrousel du Louvre, 99 rue de Rivoli, 1ᵉʳ; Ⓜ Louvre-Rivoli; ☎ 01 42 82 50 00, ⊛ departmentstoreparis.printemps .com; map p.76. The beautiful *belle époque* store on boulevard Haussmann is in a glorious building full of decorative flourishes; Printemps' iconic sixth-floor brasserie sits right underneath the stunning stained-glass dome. The women's store is devoted to an extensive collection of fashion, shoes and accessories, while the men's store was totally revamped and expanded in 2017, as was the cosmetics department, now taking up three floors. The beauty/home store, which includes children's gear and food, sports a rooftop terrace restaurant with panoramic views. The branch in the Carrousel du Louvre (see below) focuses on leather goods, make-up, jewellery and watches. Mon–Sat 9.35am–8pm, Thurs 9.35am–8.45pm, Sun 11am–7pm.

SHOPPING MALLS

Bercy Village Cour St-Emilion, 12ᵉ ☎ 08 25 16 60 75, ⊛ bercyvillage.com; Ⓜ Cour St-Emilion; map p.116. A good place to come for some leisurely shopping, especially on a Sunday when everything remains open. You'll find a range of homeware and design stores, popular French fashion brands Sandro and Maje, a Sephora beauty store, plus plenty of restaurants – all attractively set in old wine warehouses. Daily 11am–9pm.

Centre Commercial Beaugrenelle 12 rue Linois, 15ᵉ ☎ 01 53 95 24 00, ⊛ beaugrenelle-paris.com; Ⓜ Javel–André Citroën/Charles Michels/RER Javel; map p.172. A smart, glass-roofed mall, one of the largest in Paris, with all the major brand names, as well as some not usually found in shopping centres, such as Guerlain and Michael Kors. You could arrive here by batobus, one stop down from the Eiffel Tower. Mon–Sat 10am–8.30pm, Sun 11am–7pm.

Carrousel du Louvre 99 rue de Rivoli, 1ᵉʳ ☎ 01 43 16 47 10, ⊛ carrouseldulouvre.com; Ⓜ Palais Royal Musée du Louvre; map p.76. This underground complex concentrates mostly on lifestyle and gift shops rather than fashion; its thirty-plus boutiques include an Apple Store, Occitane, a Printemps (see above) and a Musée City selling scarves, mugs, jewellery etc inspired by artworks in Paris museums. Daily 10am–8pm.

Forum des Halles 101 Porte Berger, 1ᵉʳ ☎ 01 44 76 87 08, ⊛ forumdeshalles.com; map p.88. The recent revamp of Les Halles (see p.92) has made this underground shopping and leisure complex much more inviting. It houses mostly high-street fashion, plus a good Fnac bookshop (see p.334) and a new Lego flagship store. Mon–Sat 10am–8pm, Sun 11am–7pm.

HIGH FASHION AND FRENCH CHIC

agnès b. 6 rue du Vieux Colombier, 6ᵉ ☎ 01 44 39 02 60; Ⓜ St-Sulpice; map p.138; 3, 4 & 6 rue du Jour, 1ᵉʳ Ⓜ /RER Châtelet-Les Halles; map p.88; ⊛ europe.agnesb .com. Born in Versailles, this queen of understatement (it's pronounced "ann-yes bay") favours cool, simple staples – matelot shirts, straw hats and the like. While the line has expanded into watches, sunglasses and cosmetics, her clothing for men, women and kids remains chic, timeless and relatively affordable. 6 rue du Vieux Colombier (plus a men's store at no. 10) Mon–Sat 10am–7.30pm; 3 & 6 rue du Jour Oct–April Mon–Sat 10am–7pm; May–Sept Mon–Fri 10.30am–7.30pm, Sat 10am–7.30pm; 4 rue du Jour Oct–April Mon–Sat 10am–7pm; May–Sept Mon–Sat 10.30am–7.30pm.

Ba&sh 22 rue des Francs-Bourgeois, 3ᵉ ☎ 01 42 78 55 10, ⊛ ba-sh.com; Ⓜ St-Paul; map p.99. Barbara Boccara and Sharon Krief produce modern, chic and easy-to-wear women's clothes in quality materials such as silk and cashmere. Their hallmarks are slouchy tops and short tunic dresses, with most items in the €140–200 range. There are other branches at 215 St Honoré and 21 rue Etienne Marcel (both 1ᵉʳ), 59 rue Bonaparte (6ᵉ) and 81 rue St Dominique (7ᵉ). Mon–Sat 10.30am–7.30pm, Sun 11.30am–7.30pm.

Chanel 31 rue Cambon, 1ᵉʳ ☎ 01 44 50 66 00, ⊛ chanel .com; Ⓜ Madeleine/Opéra; map p.76. Karl Lagerfeld is currently at the helm of the iconic brand, which retains the elegance and classic style of Coco's conception while continuing to offer new, modern interpretations of the classic suits and little black dresses. Mon–Sat 10am–7pm.

Isabel Marant 16 rue de Charonne, 11ᵉ ☎ 01 49 29 71 55, ⊛ isabelmarant.com; Ⓜ Bastille/Ledru-Rollin; map p.122. Parisian Marant has an international reputation for her feminine and flattering clothes, including elegantly tapered trousers, wedged trainers and ruffled, floaty tops and dresses, as well as her more affordable line, Etoile. There are other branches at 1 rue Jacob (6e), 47 rue de Saintonge (3e) and 151 av Victor Hugo (16e). Mon 11am–7pm, Tues–Sat 10.30am–7.30pm.

Lanvin 22 rue du Faubourg-St-Honoré, 8e ⓣ01 44 71 31 73, ⓦlanvin.com; ⓜConcorde; map p.64. One of the first French fashion houses, Lanvin epitomizes classic French elegance, although the designs of the originally Breton label often incorporate idiosyncrasies such as taffeta trench coats, satin capes, and removable cuffs and collars. There's a men's store a few doors down at no. 15. Mon–Sat 10.30am–7pm.

Lemaire 28 rue de Poitou, 3e ⓣ01 44 78 00 09, ⓦlemaire.fr; ⓜSaint Sebastien Froissart/Filles du Calvaire; map p.99. A coolly converted former pharmacy is the setting for designer Christophe Lemaire's collection of beautiful men's and women's clothes, distinguished by their long flowing lines, the odd ruffle or pleat and a certain understated elegance. From around €300. Mon 1–7pm, Tues–Sat 11am–7.30pm.

Maison Fabre Jardin du Palais Royal, 128–129 Galerie de Valois, 1er ⓣ01 42 60 75 88, ⓦmaisonfabre.com; ⓜPalais Royal Musée du Louvre; map p.76. Gloves to die for, from another era: butter-soft leather, with a classic chic that could only be French. Prices start at around €90; for a special treat you could order a bespoke pair. Mon–Sat 11am–7pm.

L'Eclaireur 40 rue de Sévigné, 3e ⓣ01 48 87 10 22, ⓦleclaireur.com; ⓜChemin Vert; map p.99. Paris's pioneering first concept store is still going strong and now has a number of outlets; the rue de Sévigné is the most recent and striking, styling itself as an experience rather than a shop, with clothes hidden behind screens and sliding panels. Discover well-known and also more off-beat designers, as well as perfumes, books and accessories for both men and women. Mon–Sat 11am–7pm, Sun 2–7pm.

★**Maje** 49 rue Vieille du Temple, 4e ⓣ01 42 74 63 77, ⓦmaje.com; ⓜSt-Paul; map p.99. This Paris-based but now international brand offers utterly Parisian clothes: relaxed, slightly bohemian, cool and always elegant. This is a sizeable store, offering a good choice, with many other branches around town. Mon–Sat 10.30am–7.30pm, Sun 1–7pm.

★**Paul & Joe** 62–64 rue des Sts-Pères, 7e ⓣ01 42 22 47 01, ⓦpaulandjoe.com; ⓜSèvres-Babylone; map p.138. The clothes here are quintessentially French: quirky but not overly showy, playful but not overly radical – for men and women alike. As long as you've got a slim, French-style figure to match, Paul & Joe will magically transform you into a chic Parisian. There are seven branches in Paris, including Paul & Joe Sister (64 rue des Saints Pères, 7e), the slightly more youthful offshoot. Mon–Sat 10am–7pm.

Saint Laurent 38 rue du Faubourg St Honoré, 8e ⓣ01 42 65 74 59; ⓜConcorde; map p.64; 6 place St-Sulpice 6e ⓣ01 43 29 43 00; ⓜSt-Sulpice/Mabillon; map p.138;

25

CLOTHES SHOPPING IN THE FASHION CAPITAL

For designer prêt-à-porter, the **department stores** Galeries Lafayette (see opposite) and Printemps (see opposite) have unrivalled selections; if you're looking for a one-stop hit of Paris fashion, this is probably the place to come.

For couture and seriously expensive designer wear, head to the wealthy, manicured streets around the **Champs-Elysées**, especially rue François-1er, avenue Montaigne, avenue George V and **rue du Faubourg-St-Honoré**. Younger designers have colonized the lower reaches of the last street, between rue Cambon and rue des Pyramides. In the heart of this area, luxurious **place Vendôme** abounds in top-end jewellery.

A notch or two down in terms of price is the compact area around **St-Sulpice** métro, on the Left Bank. You'll find a host of upscale French clothing brands in **St-Germain** on rues du Vieux Colombier, de Rennes, Madame, de Grenelle and du Cherche-Midi; the chichi department store, Le Bon Marché (see opposite), is a stone's throw away on rue de Sèvres.

On the eastern side of the city, around the **Marais** and **Bastille**, the clothes, like the residents, are younger, cooler and more relaxed. Chic boutiques line the Marais' main shopping street, **rue des Francs-Bourgeois**, and there are good indie options on rues Charlot, de Saintonge, de Turenne and de Poitou. Young, cool designers and some good secondhand outlets congregate on Bastille's **rue de Charonne** and **rue Keller** and on the streets off the trendy **Canal St-Martin** (especially rues Beaurepair, de Marseille, des Vinaigriers and Lucien Sampaix).

At the more alternative end of the spectrum, there's a selection of the hipper high-street names and one-off designer boutiques at the foot of Montmartre spreading down south of Pigalle – try rues des Martyrs, des Trois Frères, de la Vieuville, Houdon and Durantin. **Rue Etienne Marcel** is good for high-end boutiques, while there are plenty of cheaper offerings in the **Forum des Halles** mall (see opposite) and surrounding roads, and a clutch of discount clothes shops in the southern arrondissements.

25

ⓦ ysl.com. Yves Saint Laurent's pioneering designs and brand live on, currently under the direction of Antony Vaccarello. Classic monochrome chic remains the staple for men, while womenswear swings from rock'n'roll to ultra-feminine according to the season. The men's store is at no. 32 rue du Faubourg-St-Honoré (ⓣ 01 53 05 80 80). All branches Mon 11am–7pm, Tues–Sat 10.30am–7.30pm.

Sandro 47 rue des Francs-Bourgeois, 4ᵉ ⓣ 01 49 96 56 55; ⓜ Hôtel de Ville; map p.99; discount "stock" shop 26 rue de Sévigné, 4ᵉ ⓣ 01 42 71 91 59; ⓜ Hôtel de Ville; map p.99; ⓦ sandro-paris.com. With more than forty outlets around the city, most of them in the main shopping areas, you won't need to look far to find this chic French brand, whose stock in trade is classic separates in block colours and feminine shorts, minis and tailored trousers. Their men's gear is a tad more casual. Rue des Francs-Bourgeois daily 10am–8pm; rue de Sévigné Mon–Sat 10.30am–7.30pm, Sun 11am–7pm.

Sonia by Sonia Rykiel 6 rue de Grenelle, 6ᵉ ⓣ 01 49 54 61 00, ⓦ soniaby.com; ⓜ St-Sulpice; map p.138. This less expensive (roughly €120–350) offshoot of the Rykiel brand (see below) is younger, fresher and more everyday in feel, but still features the signature Gallic stripes, flounces and slogan T-shirts and enjoys playful use of colour. Mon–Sat 10.30am–7pm.

Sonia Rykiel 175 bd St-Germain, 6ᵉ ⓣ 01 49 54 60 60; ⓜ St-Germain-des-Prés; map p.138; 70 rue du Faubourg-St-Honoré, 8ᵉ ⓜ Concorde; map p.64; ⓦ soniarykiel .com. Unmistakeably Parisian designer who brought out her first line when the *soixante-huitards* threw Europe into social revolution, and whose early customers included Brigitte Bardot and Audrey Hepburn. Her elegant multi-coloured designs – especially those stripy sweaters – are still all the rage. Both branches Mon–Sat 10.30am–7pm.

★ **Spree** 16 rue de la Vieuville, 18ᵉ ⓣ 01 42 23 41 40, ⓦ spree.fr; ⓜ Abbesses; map p.182. A gallery-like concept store whose hip, feminine clothing collection is led by designers such as Isabel Marant and Christian Wijnants. Often a few vintage pieces, too, plus bigger-brand lines (Comme des Garçons, for instance), accessories, homeware and furniture. Clothing mostly €200–600. Mon & Sun 3–7pm, Tues–Sat 11am–7.30pm.

Vanessa Bruno 25 rue St-Sulpice, 6ᵉ ⓣ 01 43 54 41 04; ⓜ Odéon; map p.138; 100 rue Vieille du Temple, 3ᵉ ⓣ 01 42 77 19 41; ⓜ St-Sébastien-Froissart; map p.99; ⓦ vanessabruno.com. Typically sophisticated, effortlessly beautiful women's fashions from the Parisian model turned designer, with a hint of hippie chic and lots of pretty draped tailoring. Around €260 for a top or skirt. Rue St-Sulpice Mon–Sat 10am–7pm; rue Vieille du Temple Mon 12.30–7.30pm, Tues–Sat 10.30am–7.30pm, Sun 2–7pm.

Zadig & Voltaire 1 rue du Vieux Colombier, 6ᵉ ⓣ 01 43 29 18 29; ⓜ St-Sulpice; map p.138; discount outlet 22 rue du Bourg-Tibourg, 4ᵉ ⓣ 01 44 59 39 62; ⓜ Hôtel de Ville;

map p.99; ⓦ zadig-et-voltaire.com. The women's clothes at this upmarket chain focus on urban chic, with tailored pieces, dark tones, skinny pants and textured fabrics, and sporty and tailored styles for men. Tops from around €130. There are more than twenty branches. Rue du Vieux Colombier Mon–Sat 10.30am–7.30pm; rue du Bourg-Tibourg Mon–Fri 11am–7pm, Sat 11am–7.30pm, Sun 2–7.30pm.

BOUTIQUES

★ **Antoine et Lili** 95 quai de Valmy, 10ᵉ ⓣ 01 40 37 41 55; ⓜ République; map p.198; 51 rue des Francs-Bourgeois, 4ᵉ ⓣ 01 42 72 26 60; ⓜ St-Paul; map p.96; 90 rue des Martyrs, 18ᵉ ⓣ 01 42 58 10 22; ⓜ Abbesses; map p.182; ⓦ antoineetlili.com. Quirky Parisian institution, with a flagship store on Quai de Valmy whose three neighbouring candy-coloured frontages (one for women's clothes, one for kids, and one for homeware) light up the Canal St-Martin. There are several branches across the city, each as colourful. The women's and children's clothes and accessories, influenced by Asian and African styles, have a dose of kitsch and an emphasis on fun. Dresses and trousers start at around €100. Shoes and colourful homeware, too. Quai de Valmy Mon–Fri 10.30am–7.30pm, Sat 10am–8pm, Sun 11am–7pm; rue des Francs-Bourgeois Mon–Fri 10.30am–7.30pm, Sat 10.30am–8pm, Sun 11am–7.30pm; rue des Martyrs Mon 11am–2pm & 3–8pm, Tues–Fri 11am–8pm, Sat 10am–8pm, Sun 11am–1pm & 2–7pm.

★ **APC** 38 rue Madame, 6ᵉ ⓣ 01 42 22 12 77; ⓜ St-Sulpice; map p.138; 3 bd des Filles du Calvaire, 3ᵉ ⓜ St-Sébastien-Froissart; map p.96; APC Surplus 20 rue André del Sarte, 18ᵉ ⓣ 01 42 62 10 88; ⓜ Barbès Rochechouart; map p.182; ⓦ apc.fr. This chain is perfect for young, urban basics. Simple cuts and fabrics create a minimal, Parisian look – with tops from €75. The main shop is on rue Madame, but there are seven branches and counting, with a men's outlet on Filles du Calvaire in the Marais, and APC Surplus selling discounted over-stock items. Rue Madame Mon–Sat 11am–7.30pm; bd des Filles du Calvaire Mon–Sat 11am–7.30pm, Sun 1–7pm; APC Surplus Mon–Sat noon–7.30pm.

Autour du Monde 12 rue des Francs-Bourgeois, 4ᵉ ⓣ 01 42 77 16 18, ⓦ bensimon.com; ⓜ St-Paul; map p.99. Bensimon, known for their cute canvas sneakers in eye-popping colours (from around €30), also sell casual clothes at this bright, youthful store. A second branch at no. 8, a few doors down, extends the brand into homeware. Mon–Sat 11am–7pm, Sun 1.30–7pm.

Le Centre Commercial 2 rue de Marseille, 10ᵉ ⓣ 01 42 02 26 08, ⓦ centrecommercial.cc; ⓜ Jacques-Bonsergent; map p.199. The name may sound unpromising, but venture in and you'll find an interesting concept store dedicated to ecofriendly clothes for men, mostly, including relatively new French labels such as Bleu de Paname and Etudes, as well as accessories, travel and fashion books and furniture. There's a children's shop around the corner on rue Yves Toudic. Mon 1–7.30pm, Tues–Sat 11am–8pm, Sun 2–7pm.

La Fausse Boutique 19 rue des Ecouffes, 4ᵉ ☎ 01 73 74 90 78, ⓦ lafausseboutique.com; Ⓜ St-Paul; map p.99. Unique, edgy and playful one-offs from French and international designers, with separates for men and women, from simple vests to glamorous capes and funky sneakers to statement jewellery, plus gifts. Mon, Wed–Fri noon–7pm, Sat noon–7.30pm, Sun noon–6.30pm.

French Trotters 128 rue Vieille du Temple, 3ᵉ ☎ 01 44 61 00 14, ⓦ frenchtrotters.fr; Ⓜ Filles du Calvaire; map p.99. A well-curated collection of lesser-known fashion labels, as well as the store's own-brand casual-chic clothing for men and women. There's also a good range of homeware and accessories, and a second branch at 30 rue de Charonne, 11ᵉ. Tues–Sat 11.30am–8pm, Sun 2–7pm.

★ **Sessùn** 34 rue de Charonne, 11ᵉ ☎ 01 48 06 55 66, ⓦ sessun.com; Ⓜ Ledru-Rollin; map p.112. The bright and spacious boutique on this trendy shopping street sells all the womenswear you could want, from pretty prints and elegant winter coats to cosy knits and basic T-shirts. Prices start at around €100 – good value, given the quality. Mon–Sat 11am–7.30pm.

Swildens 18 rue du Vieux Colombier, 6ᵉ ☎ 01 42 84 31 84, ⓦ swildens.fr; Ⓜ St-Sulpice; map p.138. Juliette Swildens designs well-cut clothes for women and teens with a hint of vintage styling. Typical are off-the-shoulder smocks, slouchy sweatshirts, tailored blazers and layered knits (prices around €130–300). There are other branches at 16 rue de Turenne (4ᵉ), 9 rue Guichard (6ᵉ) and 16 bd des Filles du Calvaire (11ᵉ). Mon–Fri 10.30am–7pm.

DISCOUNTED DESIGNER FASHION

A number of dedicated "stock" shops (short for *déstockage*) sell end-of-line and last year's collections at thirty- to fifty-percent reductions, while the best of the many consignment stores – *dépôts-ventes* – sell pre-loved couture and designer clothes for hundreds of euros off retail. The best times of year to join the scrums are after the new collections have come out in January and October.

Défilé de Marques 171 rue de Grenelle, 7ᵉ ☎ 01 45 55 63 47, ⓦ mondepotvente.com; Ⓜ La Tour-Maubourg; map p.152. Wide choice of designer clothing for women – last season's lines returned unsold from the big-name boutiques, plus some vintage. Labels from Chanel to YSL via Alexander McQueen and Prada, for around €300–700 for jackets, half that for shoes, or as little as €50 for accessories. Tues–Sat 1–8pm.

Madame de 65 rue Daguerre, 14ᵉ ☎ 01 77 10 59 46, ⓦ madamede.net; Ⓜ Denfert Rochereau; map p.164. There's a good mix in this *dépôt-vente*, from last season's Isabel Marant to some vintage couture, all of it in great nick. Tues–Fri 11am–7.30pm, Sat 11am–6.30pm.

Réciproque 89, 92, 93–97 & 101 rue de la Pompe, 16ᵉ ☎ 01 47 04 30 28, ⓦ reciproque.fr; Rue de la Pompe; map p.215. This *dépôt-vente* spreads along the street, offering pre-owned haute couture from names including Christian Lacroix, Moschino and Manolo Blahnik. There are three womenswear shops – no. 93 concentrates on evening wear; no. 95 couture, casualwear, sportswear and accessories; no. 101 accessories, bags, jewellery and swimsuits. No. 92 is the men's store, and no. 89 sells gifts and jewellery. No. 97 is for deposits. Tues–Fri 11am–7pm, Sat 10.30am–7pm.

La Vallée Inside Disneyland Paris boundary ☎ 01 60 42 35 00, ⓦ lavalleevillage.com; map p.248. Outlet shopping village, best for discounted designer labels, with more than one hundred names including Armani, Burberry, Calvin Klein and the like. Daily 10am–8.30pm.

SECONDHAND AND VINTAGE

The vintage scene is going from strength to strength in Paris, from the *dépôts-ventes* selling last season's clothes to smaller thrift-store-type outlets, often referred to as *friperies*. In addition to the places reviewed here, try the flea markets at Porte de Montreuil (see p.341) and St-Ouen (see p.341).

Casablanca 17 rue Moret, 11ᵉ ☎ 06 64 27 90 15, ⓦ casablanca-vintage.fr; Ⓜ Ménilmontant; map p.207. Cool vintage store – with its own little dog – near Oberkampf, with lots of Thirties, Forties and mid-century gear and a particularly good line in natty men's suits. A visiting barber offers vintage haircuts. Mon–Sat 2–7pm.

Chezel 59 rue Condorcet, 9ᵉ ☎ 01 53 16 47 31; Ⓜ Pigalle; map p.182. One of the best of three or four (the others come and go) little vintage fashion shops on this street. Prices from €30 to easily five times that for a classic – some serious designer-wear finds its way here. Tues–Fri noon–7.30pm, Sat 11.30am–7.30pm.

Chinemachine 100 rue des Martyrs, 18ᵉ ☎ 01 80 50 27 66, ⓦ chinemachinevintage.com; Ⓜ Abbesses; map p.182. A colourful, funky *friperie/depot-vente* run by a New Yorker and stocking a good range of women's and men's clothing. In among the H&M and Zara pieces you may well come across a rare designer find at a knockdown price. There's a second branch at 10 rue des Petites Ecuries, 10ᵉ. Mon–Thurs noon–8pm, Sun 1–8pm.

Free "P" Star 52 rue de la Verrerie, 4ᵉ ☎ 01 42 76 03 72; 61 rue de la Verrerie, 4ᵉ ☎ 01 42 78 00 76; Ⓜ Hôtel de Ville; map p.88; 20 rue de Rivoli, 4ᵉ ☎ 01 42 77 63 43; Ⓜ St-Paul; map p.99; ⓦ freepstar.com. Small chain of very popular vintage clothing shops, with racks of Lacoste polo shirts, 1970s floral dresses, inexpensive Levis, army surplus, 1920s flapper gear, leather jackets and more. Many items €10–30. Mon–Sat 11am–8.30pm, Sun noon–8.30pm.

★ **Kiliwatch** 64 rue Tiquetonne, 2ᵉ ☎ 01 42 21 17 37, ⓦ kiliwatch.paris; Ⓜ Etienne Marcel; map p.76. You'll have no problem coming up with an original outfit in this

25

25

vast store, where vintage duds meet cheap'n'chic streetwear: match cool trainers/sneakers with army surplus, lumberjack shirts, 1970s boho gear and a great selection of vintage women's shoes. It's also *the* place to buy jeans, with loads of brands. Mon 10.30am–7pm, Tues–Sat 10.30am–7.30pm.

Kilo Shop 69–71 rue de la Verrerie, 4ᵉ ☎09 67 13 79 54; ⓂHotel-de-Ville; map p.88; 125 bd St-Germain, 6ᵉ ☎01 43 26 00 36; ⓂMabillon; map p.138; ⓦkilo-shop .com. A popular concept – everything is sold by weight (€20–60/kg) so you can pile up your basket with retro casual gear (Levis, combat jackets, lacy shirts, Eighties sweats) and tot up costs on the scales provided. Rue de la Verrerie Mon 2–7.30pm, Tues–Fri 11am–7.30pm, Sat 11am–7.45pm, Sun 2–7.30pm; bd St-Germain Mon–Sat 11am–7.45pm, Sun 1–7.45pm.

Mamz'Elle Swing 35 bis rue du Roi de Sicile, 4ᵉ ☎01 48 87 04 06, ⓦmamzelleswing.com; ⓂSt-Paul; map p.99. True to its name, this cute little Marais store specializes in 1950s and 1950s-inspired frocks, with a variety of styles from simple cotton daywear to fancy netted cocktail dresses, plus lingerie and accessories. Mon–Sat 2–7pm, Sun 3–7pm.

★Violette & Léonie 114 rue de Turenne, 3ᵉ ☎01 44 59 87 35, ⓦvioletteleonie.com; ⓂFilles du Calvaire/ St-Sébastien-Froissart; map p.96. This secondhand (*dépôt-vente*) shop looks so smart you'd think it was a designer boutique, and its decent range of stock, from high-end labels to H&M and Zara, is in great condition. Mon 1–7.30pm, Tues–Sat 11am–7.30pm, Sun 2–7pm.

SHOES

Streets with a concentration of shoe shops include rue de Grenelle (6ᵉ) and rue Meslay (3ᵉ). In addition to the places reviewed below, don't forget the department stores' huge collections, especially Galeries Lafayettes', and also see Autour du Monde (see p.328) for funky and inexpensive tennis shoes beloved of the city's young bobos (bourgeois bohemians).

Annabel Winship 29 rue du Dragon, 6ᵉ ☎01 71 37 60 46, ⓦwww.annabelwinship-shop.com; ⓂSt-Sulpice; map p.138. Quirky and playful, these feminine women's shoes – emblazoned with flowers, Union Jacks, glam lightning bolts and colourful piping – are designed by an English expat and guaranteed to make you smile. At the time of writing the shop was due to move to new premises, so it's best to check the website for the latest information. Mon–Sat 11am–7pm.

Christian Louboutin 38–40 rue de Grenelle, 7ᵉ ☎01 42 22 33 07, ⓦchristianlouboutin.com; ⓂRue du Bac; map p.138. The iconic red-soled shoes are the object of every female fashionista's desires; according to the designer, men love them too. This sumptuous little

boutique is a shrine to his creations; there are other branches, all on the right bank, including at 17 and 19 rue Jean-Jacques Rousseau (1ᵉʳ) and 68 rue du Faubourg-St-Honoré (8ᵉ). Mon–Sat 10.30am–7pm.

Free Lance 30 rue du Four, 6ᵉ ☎01 45 48 14 78; ⓂMabillon; map p.76; 54 rue Montmartre, 2ᵉ ☎01 40 26 61 00; ⓂSentier; map p.138; ⓦfreelance.fr. From leather to feathers, these very popular, free-spirited shoe shops attract young and funky Parisians, though you can expect to pay from €200 upwards. Both branches Mon–Sat 10.30am–7pm.

K Jacques 16 rue Pavée, 4ᵉ ☎01 40 27 03 57, ⓦkjacques.fr; ⓂSt-Paul; map p.99. This iconic St Tropez brand has been crafting simple strappy leather sandals since the 1930s and still defines quintessential South of France boho chic, as worn by Bardot, Picasso and Kate Moss. April to mid-Aug Mon–Sat 10am–7.30pm, Sun 11–7.30pm; mid-Aug to March Mon–Sat 10am–7am, Sun 1–7pm.

Repetto 22 rue de la Paix, 2ᵉ ☎01 44 71 83 12, ⓦrepetto.fr; ⓂOpéra; map p.76. This long-established supplier of ballet shoes, which has shod dancers from Margot Fonteyn to Sylvie Guillem, also produces attractive ballerina pumps in assorted colours as well as a range of heels, much coveted by the fashion crowd – and at a price. Many branches throughout town. Mon–Sat 9.30am–7.30pm.

Sawa 2 rue de la Ferronnerie, 1ᵉʳ ☎01 76 53 94 06, ⓦsawashoes.com; Ⓜ/RER Châtelet-Les Halles; map p.88. Sawa's stylish, vaguely retro-looking trainers are all made in Ethiopia and come in a variety of appealing colours and styles for men (from €85), women and children. Mon–Sat 11am–7pm.

LINGERIE

It's no cliché to say that lingerie is a national obsession, and Paris offers a dazzling selection of outlets where you can stock up on *sous-vêtements*. For the widest choice you're best off at the department stores, but there are also some standout boutiques.

Aubade 33 rue des Francs-Bourgeois, 3ᵉ ☎01 42 76 96 87, ⓦaubade.com; ⓂSt-Paul; map p.99. Aubade lingerie is traditionally considered the height of refinement, glamour and seduction: lacy and sexy yet discreet and elegant. This store features corsets, basques and other items in addition to perfectly designed bras that cost upwards of €90. Mon 1.30–7.30pm, Tues–Sat 10.30am–7.30pm, Sun noon–7pm.

Cadolle 4 rue Cambon, 1ᵉʳ ☎01 42 60 94 22, ⓦcadolle .fr; ⓂConcorde; map p.76. This family has produced couture lingerie and corsets since 1889 – at this ready-to-wear boutique you can pick up an exquisite bra and camiknickers for a mere €200 or so. Mon & Tues 10.30am–6.30pm, Wed–Sat 11am–7pm.

25

BEST PARISIAN PARFUMERIES

Annick Goutal 12 place St-Sulpice, 6ᵉ ☎ 01 46 33 03 15, ⓦ annickgoutal.com; Ⓜ St-Sulpice; map p.138. Though Goutal has passed on, the business is still in the family, continuing to produce her exquisite perfumes, all made from natural essences and presented in old-fashioned, ribbed-glass bottles. This is the original branch. From €79 for 50ml eau de toilette. Mon–Sat 10am–7pm.

Belle de Jour 7 rue Tardieu, 18ᵉ ☎ 01 46 06 15 28, ⓦ belle-de-jour.fr; Ⓜ Abbesses/Anvers; map p.182. Deeply old-fashioned shop selling perfume bottles, both new and vintage. From €10 for an inexpensive mini gift-bottle to €500 (or more) for the serious antiques – which range from eighteenth-century to desirable Art Nouveau numbers. Tues–Fri 10.30am–1pm & 2–7pm, Sat 10.30am–1pm & 2–6pm.

Editions de Parfums Frédéric Malle 37 rue de Grenelle, 7ᵉ ☎ 01 42 22 76 40, ⓦ fredericmalle.com; Ⓜ Rue du Bac; map p.138. All the perfumes at this deliciously serious boutique are from *créateurs*, which

means professional *parfumeurs* working under their own name through this "publishing house". A 50ml bottle costs more than €100, but you're buying a genuine work of art, and getting seriously expert advice too. A classy new branch, designed by Jakob & MacFarlane, has opened in the Marais at 13 rue des Francs-Bourgeois (4ᵉ). Mon–Sat 11am–7pm.

Officine Universelle Buly 1803 6 rue Bonaparte, 6ᵉ ☎ 01 43 29 02 50, ⓦ buly1803.com; Ⓜ Rue du Bac; map p.138. A revival of a nineteenth-century brand, this apothecary-style perfumery is beautifully decorated with oak cabinets, marble counters and terracotta floors. Lining the shelves are over seven hundred botanical-based soaps, perfumes, salves for every kind of skin condition, powders and scrubs bearing names such as Pommade Virginale and Huile de Noyaux de Prune, all attractively packaged in vintage style. Prices start from around €28. At the time of writing, a second branch was due to open in the Marais, including a café. Mon–Sat 10am–7pm.

Fifi Chachnil 34 rue de Grenelle, 7ᵉ ☎ 01 42 22 08 23, ⓦ fifichachnil.com; Ⓜ Rue du Bac; map p.138. Soft lighting and sumptuous furnishings make this decadent boutique feel more like a boudoir than a shop. Part-fantasy, part-Parisian chic, Chachnil's vintage-inspired, frou-frou creations strike a careful balance between saucy and elegant. Mon–Sat 11am–7pm.

Princesse Tam Tam 4 rue de Sèvres, 6ᵉ ☎ 01 45 48 27 49, ⓦ princessetamtam.com; Ⓜ St-Sulpice; map p.138. In the market since the 1930s, French lingerie brand Princesse Tam Tam offers a reasonably priced (bras from €30), comprehensive range, from vintage-style silk slips to sportier, more contemporary styles. There are many branches in Paris, and in all the main department stores. Mon–Fri 10am–7.30pm, Sat 11am–7pm.

★**Sabbia Rosa** 71–73 rue des Sts-Pères, 6ᵉ ☎ 01 45 48 88 37; Ⓜ St-Germain-des-Prés; map p.138. This gorgeous jewel-box of a store sells supermodel scanties – they all shop here – at supermodel prices. The retro, boudoir-style space is the perfect setting for the beautiful, luxurious lingerie, made in France using natural materials – lots of shimmering silk – in vibrant, bold colours. Mon–Sat 10am–7pm.

ACCESSORIES AND JEWELLERY

Anthony Peto 56 rue Tiquetonne, 2ᵉ ☎ 01 40 26 60 68, ⓦ anthonypeto.com; Ⓜ Etienne Marcel; map p.76. A friendly, largely men's *chapelier*, loaded with fedoras, top hats, panamas and the like in wool and cotton plaid, tweed, velour and fur, all handmade in their Paris atelier.

Most of the fancier hats run at around €100. Mon–Sat 11am–7pm.

Delphine Pariente 19 rue de Turenne, 4ᵉ ☎ 01 44 61 45 39; Ⓜ St-Paul; map p.99; 101 rue de Turenne, 3ᵉ; Ⓜ Filles du Calvaire; map p.96; 10 rue des Filles du Calvaire, 3ᵉ; Ⓜ Filles du Calvaire; map p.96; ⓦ delphinepariente.fr. After working with Jean-Paul Gaultier and Christian Lacroix, Delphine Pariente opened her boutiques in the Marais selling delicate gold- and silver-plated necklaces, bangles, rings and earrings, many engraved or employing a witty use of words. Prices from €50. All branches daily 11am–7pm (rue Filles du Calvaire branch closed Sun & Mon).

★**French Touche** 90 rue Legendre, 17ᵉ ☎ 01 42 63 31 36, ⓦ frenchtouche.com; Ⓜ La Fourche; map p.195. This "galerie d'objets touchants" gathers together an appealing selection of jewellery, bags, scarves, ceramics and much else by young and little-known designers, all beautifully displayed and catering to a wide range of budgets. You might come away with an unusual lacquered and gold bracelet by Pagil Blaja (€39), an embroidery kit by Britney Pompadour (€24) or a paper lantern by Jurianne Matter (€12.50). Tues–Sat 11am–8pm.

Hermès 24 rue du Faubourg-St-Honoré, 8ᵉ ☎ 01 40 17 46 00; Ⓜ Concorde; map p.64; 17 rue de Sèvres, 6ᵉ ☎ 01 42 22 80 83; Ⓜ Sèvres-Babylone; map p.138; ⓦ hermes. com. This superluxe fashion and accessories store is the place to come for an iconic "Birkin" or "Kelly" bag or the ultimate silk scarf – at a price. Check out the rue de Sèvres concept store, housed in an Art Deco swimming pool. Rue du Faubourg-St-Honoré Mon–Sat 10am–6.30pm; rue de Sèvres Mon–Sat 10.30am–7pm.

Hervé Chapelier 1bis rue du Vieux-Colombier, 6ᵉ 📞 01 44 07 06 50; Ⓜ St-Sulpice; map p.76; 390 rue Saint-Honoré, 1ᵉʳ 📞 01 42 96 38 04, Ⓜ Concorde; map p.138; ⓦ hervechapelier.com. Often imitated, rarely matched, these classic nylon bags and purses with their distinctive, bold two-tone colour scheme never go out of fashion. Tote bags from around €60. Mon–Fri 10.15am–1pm & 2–7pm, Sat 10.15am–7.15pm.

Louis Vuitton 101 av des Champs-Elysées, 8ᵉ 📞 01 53 57 52 00, ⓦ louisvuitton.com; Ⓜ George V; map p.76. You'll have to contend with the crowds but this colossal flagship store offers you the best of LV – a "bag bar", jewellery emporium and men's and women's ready-to-wear collections. Mon–Sat 10am–8pm, Sun 11am–7pm.

Matières à Réflexion 19 rue de Poitou, 3ᵉ 📞 01 42 72 16 31, ⓦ matieresareflexion.com; Ⓜ St-Sebastien-Froissart; map p.99. Many of the stylish leather bags in this men's and women's *boutique-atelier* are one-off designs made from upcycled leather jackets and other clothing cast-offs (they can even turn one of your own jackets into a bag for you), with prices starting at around €130. In addition, you'll find a selection of clothes and jewellery by cutting-edge designers. There's another branch at 20 rue Houdon (18ᵉ). Daily noon–7pm.

Marie-Hélène de Taillac 8 rue de Tournon, 6ᵉ 📞 01 44 27 07 07, ⓦ mariehelenedetaillac.com; Ⓜ Odéon; map p.138. Beautiful contemporary jewellery, mixing vivid, bold-coloured precious stones with deep, antique-looking gold in eye-catching designs. Expensive: even a tiny pair of earrings is more than €500. Mon–Sat 11am–7pm.

Marie Mercié 23 rue St-Sulpice, 6ᵉ 📞 01 43 26 45 83, ⓦ mariemercie.com; Ⓜ St-Sulpice; map p.138. This grande dame of *chapellerie* sells a glamorous and whimsical collection of plaid, straw, felt and fur hats for all (fancy) occasions – at €250 and up. Mon–Sat 11am–7pm.

Maroquinerie Saint Honoré 334 rue St-Honoré, 1ᵉʳ 📞 01 42 60 03 28; Ⓜ Pyramides/Tuileries; map p.76. An unexpected find on one of the city's most exclusive shopping streets, this bargain shop sells very stylish French-made leather handbags in a range of colours, with many items under €100. Mon–Sat 10.30am–6.30pm.

Médecine Douce 10 rue de Marseille, 10ᵉ 📞 01 82 83 11 53, ⓦ bijouxmedecinedouce.com; Ⓜ République/Jacques-Bonsergent; map p.198. Marie Montaud's delicate, elegant gold bracelets and pearl necklaces, as well as more unusual pieces made from feathers and enamel, are crafted on-site in this *boutique-atelier* on the hip rue de Marseille. Prices start at around €90. Mon–Sat 11am–7pm.

ART, CRAFTS, STATIONERY AND PHOTOGRAPHY

Dubois 20 rue Soufflot, 5ᵉ 📞 01 44 41 67 50, ⓦ dubois-paris.com; Ⓜ Cluny-La Sorbonne; map p.124. In the same great apothecary-style building since the 1860s, the Dubois family still offers an excellent selection of art supplies, notebooks and pens. Mon 10am–1pm & 2–6.30pm, Tues–Sat 9.30am–6.30pm.

Entrée des Fournisseurs 8 rue des Francs-Bourgeois, 4ᵉ 📞 01 48 87 58 98, ⓦ lamercerieparisienne.com; Ⓜ St-Paul; map p.99. Set back from the main road, this cheery spot has everything you might need to make clothes yourself, including buttons, ribbons, fabrics, patterns and knitting equipment. Mon–Sat 10.30am–7pm.

★**Mélodies Graphiques** 10 rue du Pont-Louis-Philippe, 4ᵉ 📞 01 42 74 57 68; Ⓜ St-Paul; map p.99. A tiny shop selling beautiful writing paper, vintage-style cards, postcards and leather-bound notebooks. It also stocks everything a calligrapher might need, including inks in a range of unusual colours and exquisite glass fountain pens (€20–60), made especially for the shop. Mon & Sun 2–6pm, Tues–Sat 11am–7pm.

Papier Plus 9 rue du Pont-Louis-Philippe, 4ᵉ 📞 01 42 77 70 49, ⓦ papierplus.com; Ⓜ St-Paul; map p.99. Top-quality, colourful stationery, including notebooks, travel journals, photo albums and artists' portfolios, starting from around €12. Mon–Sat noon–7pm.

Papier Tigre 5 rue des Filles du Calvaire, 3ᵉ 📞 01 48 04 00 21, ⓦ papiertigre.fr; Ⓜ Filles du Calvaire; map p.96. Bold, funky graphic designs characterize the notebooks, cards, desk accessories and pens at this Marais stationery shop. Prices are very reasonable – from €5 for a notebook. Mon–Fri 11.30am–7.30pm, Sat 11am–8pm.

Photo Rent 6 bd Beaumarchais, 11ᵉ 📞 01 47 00 66 77, ⓦ photorent.fr; Ⓜ Chemin Vert; map p.112. New and secondhand photographic equipment. If they don't have what you're looking for, you could try the other camera shops on the same street. Mon–Fri 9am–12.30pm & 2–6pm.

Sennelier 3 quai Voltaire, 7ᵉ 📞 01 42 60 72 15, ⓦ magasinsennelier.com; Ⓜ St-Germain-des-Prés; map p.138. Serious, old-fashioned art suppliers, with beautiful and reasonably priced sketchbooks. Other branches at 4bis rue de la Grande Chaumière (6ᵉ) and 6 rue Hallé (14ᵉ). Mon 2–6.30pm, Tues–Sat 10am–12.45pm & 2–6.30pm.

BOOKS

Paris has a gratifying number of bookshops compared to other European cities – the most atmospheric areas for **book shopping** are the Seine *quais*, with their rows of new and secondhand bookstalls perched against the river parapet, and the narrow streets of the Quartier Latin. For a particularly good **LGBT bookshop** in the Marais, try Les Mots à la Bouche (see p.358).

ENGLISH-LANGUAGE BOOKS

Abbey Bookshop 29 rue de la Parcheminerie, 5ᵉ ☎ 01 46 33 16 24, ⊚ abbeybookshop.wordpress.com; ⓜ St-Michel; map p.124. An overstuffed warren of a place, this Canadian bookshop, round the corner from Shakespeare and Company (see below), is packed from ceiling to floor with used British and North American fiction and travel guides. Helpful staff, soothing classical music – and free coffee. Mon–Sat 10am–7pm.

★ **Galignani** 224 rue de Rivoli, 1ᵉʳ ☎ 01 42 60 76 07, ⊚ www.galignani.fr; ⓜ Concorde; map p.76. Reputedly the first English bookshop established on the Continent, opened (on a different site) way back in the early 1800s. Not all the stock is English-language, but what there is is top-notch, including fiction, fine art and children's books. Mon–Sat 10am–7pm.

Shakespeare and Company 37 rue de la Bûcherie, 5ᵉ ☎ 01 43 25 40 93, ⊚ shakespeareandcompany.com; ⓜ St-Michel; map p.124. A cosy and very famous literary haunt (see p.122), run by Americans and staffed by earnest young Hemingway wannabes. They offer the biggest selection of secondhand English-language books in town, and lots of new stock, especially Paris-related – on busy days you may have to wait to get in. There's a reading room upstairs where you can sit for as long as you like, frequent readings and signings (arrive early), and a café in an adjacent building. Daily 10am–11pm.

WH Smith 248 rue de Rivoli, 1ᵉʳ ☎ 01 44 77 88 99, ⊚ whsmith.fr; ⓜ Concorde; map p.76. The Parisian outlet of the British chain stocks a wide range of new books, newspapers, magazines and DVDs (albeit at a price), plus a small selection of gifts. The newly opened upstairs tea room is the place to read your new purchase, perhaps over a Twinings tea and iced cake. Mon–Sat 9.30am–7.30pm, Sun 10.30am–7pm.

FRENCH BOOKS

Fnac Forum des Halles, Niveau 2, Porte Pierre-Lescot, 1ᵉʳ; ⓜ /RER Châtelet-Les Halles; map p.88; 74 av des Champs-Elysées, 8ᵉ; ⓜ Franklin-D.-Roosevelt; map p.64; ☎ 08 25 02 00 20, ⊚ fnac.com. Fnac is France's leading retail chain for books, CDs, games and electronics – as well as for concert and sports events tickets. There are nine branches in Paris. The shops offer supermarket-style discounting, but the range of books and music extends into the higher brow. Lots of comics, guidebooks and maps. Forum des Halles Mon–Sat 10am–8pm, Sun 11am–7pm; Champs-Elysées Mon–Sat 10am–11.30pm, Sun noon–11.30pm.

Gallimard 15 bd Raspail, 7ᵉ ☎ 01 45 48 24 84, ⊚ gallimard.fr; ⓜ Sèvres-Babylone; map p.138. Most French publishers operate their own flagship bookshops, and Gallimard's is one of the greats, with a full selection of their own and other titles – particularly strong on art, literature and travel. Mon–Sat 10am–7.30pm.

Gibert Jeune 6 place St-Michel, 5ᵉ ☎ 09 69 32 05 31, ⊚ gibertjeune.fr; ⓜ St-Michel; map p.138. There's a fair English-language and discounted selection at this branch of the classic Quartier Latin student/academic bookshop. A vast selection of French books can be found in the other seven branches, which are dotted all around the *place*, and easily spotted with their distinctive yellow awnings. A real institution. Mon–Sat 9.30am–7.30pm.

Gibert Joseph 26 bd St-Michel, 6ᵉ ☎ 01 44 41 88 88, ⊚ gibertjoseph.com; ⓜ St-Michel; map p.138. Neighbour and rival of the very similar Gibert Jeune group (see above), with new and secondhand English books in addition. Mon–Sat 10am–8pm.

ART, DESIGN, PHOTOGRAPHY AND FILM BOOKS

Artazart 83 quai de Valmy, 10ᵉ ☎ 01 40 40 24 03, ⊚ artazart.com; ⓜ Jacques-Bonsergent; map p.198. Very cool Canal St-Martin store, with books, magazines and gifts devoted to contemporary graphic art, design and photography, plus regular book signings, exhibitions and events. Mon–Fri 10.30am–7.30pm, Sat 11am–7.30pm, Sun 1–7.30pm.

★ **Artcurial** 7 Rond-Point des Champs-Elysées, 8ᵉ ☎ 01 42 99 16 19, ⊚ librairie.artcurial.com; ⓜ Franklin-D.-Roosevelt; map p.64. In an astonishingly grand townhouse that also houses an auctioneer's, this is a swanky setting for excellent art books, including French and foreign editions. Mon–Fri 9am–7pm, Sat 10.30am–7pm.

La Chambre Claire 14 rue St-Sulpice, 6ᵉ ☎ 01 46 34 04 31, ⊚ la-chambre-claire.fr; ⓜ Odéon; map p.138. Photography specialist selling art titles, style guides and instruction manuals, with coffee-table books and some English-language offerings. Tues–Sat 11am–7pm.

La Hune 18 rue de l'Abbaye, 6ᵉ ☎ 01 42 01 43 55, ⊚ groupe-flammarion.com; ⓜ St-Germain-des-Prés; map p.138. The main selling point of this general French bookshop – apart from its history as a Left Bank arts institution – is the art, design, fashion and photography collection on the mezzanine. Mon–Thurs & Sun 11am–8pm, Fri & Sat 11am–10pm.

★ **La Librairie du Cinéma du Panthéon** 15 rue Victor Cousin, 5ᵉ ☎ 01 42 38 08 26, ⊚ cinelitterature .fr; ⓜ Cluny-La Sorbonne; map p.138. Superb store devoted to cinema, with shelves of books, not all in French – biographies, technical manuals, screenplays, theory, coffee-table titles – plus magazines, posters, cards and DVDs. There are also books on literature, music, psychology and art, plus comics, all with some relationship to cinema. Mon–Fri 1–8pm, Sat 11am–8pm.

Librairie le Moniteur Cité de l'Architecture et du Patrimoine, place du Trocadéro, 16ᵉ ☎ 01 78 09 03 00,

Ⓦ www.librairiedumoniteur.com; Ⓜ Trocadéro; map p.152. Well-curated little store dedicated to architecture books, contemporary and historical, with some in English. Mon, Wed & Fri–Sun 11am–7pm, Thurs 11am–8pm.

COMICS (BANDES DESSINÉES)

Album 8 rue Dante, 5ᵉ Ⓣ 01 43 25 85 19; Ⓜ Maubert -Mutualité; map p.124; 84 bd St-Germain, 5ᵉ Ⓣ 01 43 25 25 68; Ⓜ Cluny-La Sorbonne; map p.138; Ⓦ album.fr. Album offers a good range of indie and mainstream material; the Dante branch in particular (on a street with at least six comics shops) has a serious collection of French *bandes dessinées* (BDs), some of them rare editions with original artwork. Rue Dante Mon–Fri 10.30am–7.30pm, Sat 10am–8pm; bd St-Germain Mon–Sat 10am–8pm, Sun noon–7pm.

Thé-Troc 52 rue Jean-Pierre-Timbaud, 11ᵉ Ⓣ 01 43 55 54 80; Ⓜ Parmentier; map p.207. The friendly owner of this old-school treasure-trove publishes *The Fabulous Furry Freak Brothers* in French and English, and sells underground comic books and memorabilia, secondhand records and assorted junk. The attached *salon de thé* (until 7pm) is comfy, colourful and restful. Mon–Sat 10am–noon & 2–8pm.

TRAVEL BOOKS

★ **Latitude Litteraire** 48 rue Ste-Anne, 2ᵉ Ⓣ 01 42 86 17 38, Ⓦ latitude-litteraire.fr; Ⓜ Pyramides; map p.76. This slick, stylish and sprawling bookshop, offshoot of the travel agency/travel goods store on the same street, is devoted to travel writing, with guides in English and translation, plus travel literature, notebooks, maps and accessories. Mon–Sat 9.30am–7pm.

Librairie Ulysse 26 rue St-Louis-en-l'Ile, 4ᵉ Ⓣ 01 43 25 17 35, Ⓦ ulysse.fr; Ⓜ Pont Marie/Sully-Morland; map p.44. Tiny bookshop, piled from floor to ceiling with thousands of new and secondhand travel writing and run by a friendly English-speaking owner. Tues–Fri 2–8pm, mornings & Sat by appointment.

MUSIC

The 11ᵉ, especially around Bastille, Ménilmontant and the Canal St-Martin, is a good place to look for specialist record shops selling vinyl. For mainstream releases, Fnac (see opposite) usually has the best prices.

Crocodisc/Crocojazz 40–42 rue des Ecoles, 5ᵉ Ⓣ 01 43 54 33 22; 64 rue de la Montagne-Ste-Geneviève, 5ᵉ Ⓣ 01 46 34 78 38; both Ⓜ Maubert-Mutualité; Ⓦ crocodisc .com; map p.124. The rue des Ecoles shop has been selling new and used records at low prices for decades. You'll dig up everything here, except classical – reggae, Latin, punk, film music, gospel, country, you name it, with a particularly good world music selection. Crocojazz, on rue de la Montagne-Ste-Geneviève, focuses on jazz from bebop to crooners. Rue des Ecoles Tues–Sat 11am–7pm; rue de la Montagne-Ste-Geneviève Tues–Sat 11am–1pm & 2–7pm; closed first two weeks in Aug.

International Records 12 rue Moret, 11ᵉ Ⓣ 09 80 57 12 61; Ⓜ Ménilmontant; map p.207. Offshoot of the splendid little live music venue off Oberkampf (see p.306), this store is a great hunting ground for indie music of all stripes – chillwave to krautrock, drone to dub – on vinyl and CD used and new. Mon–Thurs noon–8pm, Fri & Sat noon–10pm.

Patate Records 57 rue de Charonne, 11ᵉ Ⓣ 01 48 06 58 11, Ⓦ patate-records.com; Ⓜ Charonne; map p.112. Jamaican specialist, packed with vinyl, CDs and DVDs covering everything from dancehall to dub and piled high with flyers for reggae and world music gigs. Tues–Sat 1–7pm.

FOOD AND DRINK

Paris has resisted the march of mega-stores with admirable resilience. Almost every *quartier* still has its charcuterie, boulangerie and weekly market, while some **streets**, such as rue Daguerre in the 14ᵉ, rue des Martyrs in the 9ᵉ, rue Cler in the 7ᵉ and rue de Bretagne in the 3ᵉ, are lined with grocers', butchers' shops, delis, pâtisseries, cheese shops and wine merchants. We have reviewed the best of the **specialist food shops** – many of which are fairly expensive – but you should also hit the city's **street markets** (see p.340), where you can pick up gourmet picnic foods for a snip. **Health food** and organic shops are also easy to find; look for the many branches of Naturalia and Biocoop.

BREAD

Du Pain et Des Idées 34 rue Yves Toudic, 10ᵉ Ⓣ 01 42 40 44 52, Ⓦ dupainetdesidees.com; Ⓜ Jacques-Bonsergent; map p.198. Christophe Vasseur, a former fashion-industry sales executive, produces heavenly baguettes, brioches, pastries and the signature *pain des amis*, a nutty sourdough bread, in a store that exudes retro Parisian chic. Don't miss the croissants flavoured with green tea or rosewater. Mon–Fri 6.45am–8pm.

★ **Gontran Cherrier** 22 rue Caulaincourt, 18ᵉ Ⓣ 01 46 06 82 66, Ⓦ gontrancherrierboulanger.com; Ⓜ Abbesses; map p.182. Stunning artisan boulangerie and pâtisserie in a contemporary little corner spot. While the sweet pastries are amazing (just try to resist the green tea and white chocolate scones), the black squid-ink and nigella seed buns filled with jamon and rocket are the real stars. Green (rocket and courgette) and red (paprika) buns are also available. There's some counter seating, and coffee on offer. Mon, Tues & Thurs–Sat 7.30am–8pm, Sun 8am–7.30pm.

★ **Le Grenier à Pain** 38 rue des Abbesses, 18ᵉ ☎ 01 42 23 85 36, ⊛ legrenierapain.com; Ⓜ Abbesses; map p.182. The long queues outside this unassuming Montmartre bakery tell the story – this excellent small chain offers outstanding breads, tarts and pastries at astonishingly low prices. Their baguettes frequently win "Best in Paris" awards, their buttery croissants, fruit tarts and quiches are irresistible, and their nut- or fruit-packed loaves could feed a family for days, but it's the mini *ficelles* and *fougasses* – packed with cheese and olives – that steal the show, for less than a euro. Mon & Thurs–Sun 7.30am–8pm.

Poilâne 8 rue du Cherche-Midi, 6ᵉ ☎ 01 45 48 42 59; Ⓜ Sèvres-Babylone; map p.138; 38 rue Debellyme, 3ᵉ ☎ 01 44 61 83 39; Ⓜ Filles du Calvaire; map p.96; 48 bd de Grenelle, 15ᵉ ☎ 01 45 79 11 49; Ⓜ Dupleix; map p.172; ⊛ poilane.com. A classic, source of the famous "Pain Poilâne" – a sourdough bread baked using traditional methods (albeit ramped up on an industrial scale) as conceived by the late, legendary Monsieur Poilâne himself. The shops also have dining areas serving an interesting selection of *tartines*, pies and salads. Rue du Cherche-Midi Mon–Sat 7am–8.30pm; rue Debellyme Wed–Sun 7am–8.30pm, Sun 7am–4.45pm; bd de Grenelle Tues–Sun 7am–8.30pm.

Sacha Finkelsztajn/Boutique Jaune 27 rue des Rosiers, 4ᵉ ☎ 01 42 72 78 91, ⊛ laboutiquejaune.com; Ⓜ St-Paul/Hôtel de Ville; map p.99. This Ashkenazi family-owned bakery has been here since 1946, producing the best *boreks* and blinis, strudels and *latkes* – plus great *challah* bread and cheesecake – to be found in the Marais. There's a deli counter, too, plus a handful of tables at which to sit. Wed & Thurs 10am–7pm, Fri–Sun 10am–7.30pm.

PÂTISSERIE

La Bague de Kenza 106 rue St-Maur, 11ᵉ ☎ 01 43 14 93 15, ⊛ labaguedekenza.com; Ⓜ Parmentier; map p.112. The window of this Algerian pâtisserie is groaning with enticing little cakes made of dates, oranges, pistachios, figs, almonds and other tasty ingredients plus hot Algerian breads and savoury pastries. There's a *salon de thé* attached. Mon–Thurs, Sat & Sun 9am–9pm, Fri 1.30–9pm.

★ **Des Gâteaux et du Pain** 63 blvd Pasteur, 15ᵉ ☎ 06 98 95 33 18, ⊛ desgateauxetdupain.com; Ⓜ Gare Montparnasse/Falguiere; map p.172. Claire Damon's beautiful creations stand out like jewels against the black decor of this starkly designed *boulangerie/pâtisserie*. The light and fluffy *pains au chocolat* and croissants are regularly rated among the best in the capital, while the gâteaux, such as the strawberry *J'adore la Fraise*, are real works of art. A second branch can be found at 89 rue du Bac (7ᵉ). Blvd Pasteur Mon & Wed–Sat 9am–8pm, Sun 9am–6pm; rue du Bac Mon & Wed–Sat 10am–8pm, Sun 9am–6pm.

Mesdemoiselles Madeleines 37 rue des Martyrs, 9ᵉ ☎ 01 53 16 28 82, ⊛ mllesmadeleines.com; Ⓜ Pigalle; map p.182. Pamper your inner Proust and head to this sleek boutique devoted solely to the little cakes of the author's youth. These are not Madeleines as Marcel would know them, though – try the Faustine, made with fresh fennel and topped with blackcurrant; the Hortense, crowned with a lemon curd dome; or the René, a savoury treat of black olive tapenade, carrots and cumin. Tues–Sun 10.30am–7pm.

Pâtisserie Stohrer 51 rue Montorgueil, 2ᵉ ☎ 01 42 33 38 20, ⊛ stohrer.fr; Ⓜ Sentier; map p.76. Pâtisserie, chocolate and deli delights have been produced in this lovely little shop since 1730. The window display is irresistible: from delectable chocolate eclairs to towering vol-aux-vents and quail stuffed with foie gras. Daily 7.30am–8.30pm.

★ **Pierre Hermé** 72 rue Bonaparte, 6ᵉ ☎ 01 43 54 47 77, ⊛ pierreherme.com; Ⓜ St-Sulpice; map p.138. The *macarons* made by this pastry demigod are widely considered to be the best in Paris, if not France. While the more unusual flavour pairings, such as foie gras and chocolate, may sound risky, Hermé hasn't earned his stellar reputation for nothing. There are various branches around town. Mon–Fri & Sun 10am–7pm, Sat 10am–8pm.

Sébastien Gaudard 22 rue des Martyrs, 9ᵉ; Ⓜ Notre-Dame de Lorette; map p.182; 1 rue des Pyramides, 1ᵉʳ; Ⓜ Tuileries; map p.76; ☎ 01 71 18 24 70, ⊛ sebastiengaudard.fr. Beautiful old pâtisserie whose elegant array of pastries and tarts, from *Paris-Brests* to *vacherin*, harks back to a golden era of classic pâtisserie. The newer, smaller Tuileries branch includes a *salon de thé*. Rue des Martyrs Tues–Fri 10am–8pm, Sat 9am–8pm, Sun 9am–7pm; rue des Pyramides Tues–Sat 10am–7.30pm, Sun 10am–7pm.

CHOCOLATE AND SWEETS

Chocolaterie Jacques Genin 133 rue de Turenne, 3ᵉ ☎ 01 45 77 29 01, ⊛ jacquesgenin.fr; Ⓜ République; map p.96. After years supplying chocolates to Paris's top restaurants, Genin opened his own shop in 2008. You'll find a wonderful selection of chocolates, caramels, nougats and ganaches; flavours include Earl Grey, raspberry and Szechuan pepper. There's a *salon de thé* too for a seriously posh pitstop, and another branch in the 7ᵉ at 27 rue de Varenne. Tues–Fri & Sun 11am–7pm, Sat 11am–7.30pm.

Debauve et Gallais 30 rue des Sts-Pères, 7ᵉ ☎ 01 45 48 54 67, ⊛ debauve-et-gallais.fr; Ⓜ St-Germain-des-Prés/Sèvres-Babylone; map p.138. This beautiful shop specializing in chocolate and elaborate sweets has been around since chocolate was taken as a medicine and an aphrodisiac, and is designated a *Monument Historique*.

There's a smaller branch at 33 rue Vivienne (2e). Mon–Sat 9am–7pm.

Joséphine Vannier 4 rue Pas de la Mule, 4e ☎ 01 44 54 03 09, ⓦ chocolats-vannier.com; Ⓜ Bastille; map p.96. This creative chocolatier sells chocolate shaped into anything from accordions and violins to hiking boots, stilettos, Eiffel Towers and Arcs de Triomphe – exquisite and daft creations, almost too realistic to eat. Tues–Sat 11am–7pm, Sun 11am–1pm.

SPECIALIST GROCERS

Le Comptoir de la Gastronomie 34 rue Montmartre, 1er ☎ 01 42 33 31 32, ⓦ comptoirdelagastronomie.com; Ⓜ Les Halles/Etienne Marcel; map p.88. The walls of this lovely old-fashioned shop are stacked high with foie gras, *saucisses*, hams, *terrines*, preserves, oils and wine. The deli does a fine line in baguettes to take away, and there's also a superb little restaurant (see p.226). Mon 9am–8pm, Tues–Sat 8am–8pm.

Fauchon 26 & 30 place de la Madeleine, 8e ☎ 01 70 39 38 00, ⓦ fauchon.fr; Ⓜ Madeleine; map p.76. The luxury brand's flagship store (no. 26) sells extravagantly beautiful groceries, pâtisserie, charcuterie and wines both French and foreign – at exorbitant prices. The quality is assured by blind testing, which all suppliers have to submit to. Don't miss their sublime éclairs, the brie with truffles, or the *macarons*. No. 30 is perfect for foodie gifts – tea, jam, truffles, chocolates, exotic vinegars, mustards and so forth. No. 26 Mon–Sat 8am–8pm; no. 30 Mon–Sat 8am–9pm.

★ **La Grande Epicerie** 38 rue de Sèvres, 7e ☎ 01 44 39 82 00, ⓦ lagrandeepicerie.com; Ⓜ Sèvres-Babylone; map p.138. This offshoot of the famous Bon Marché department store (see p.326) is a fabulous emporium of fresh and packaged foods, with a focus on what's new and unusual as well as all the traditional favourites. Popular among choosy Parisians, expats (for its country-specific goodies, from Yorkshire tea to Marmite) and foodie tourists alike. Mon–Sat 8.30am–9pm.

CHEESE

Androuet 134 rue Mouffetard, 5e ☎ 01 45 87 85 05, ⓦ androuet.com; Ⓜ Censier-Daubenton; map p.124. One of a selection of fine cheese shops on the rue Mouffetard market street, all offering wonderful selections, beautifully displayed. There are around seven branches of this highly regarded chain in Paris. Tues–Fri 9.30am–1pm & 4–7.30pm, Sat 9.30am–7.30pm, Sun 9.30am–1.30pm.

★ **Barthélémy** 51 rue de Grenelle, 7e ☎ 01 42 22 82 24; Ⓜ Rue du Bac; map p.138. Exquisite, historic store packed to the rafters with carefully ripened and meticulously stored seasonal cheeses. Knowledgeable staff will help you choose. Tues–Thurs 8.30am–1pm & 3.30–7.15pm, Fri & Sat 8.30am–1.30pm & 3–7.15pm.

Fromagerie Alléosse 13 rue Poncelet, 17e ☎ 01 46 22 50 45, ⓦ fromage-alleosse.com; Ⓜ Ternes; map p.64. A connoisseur's selection, including Brie from Champagne, creamy Brillat-Savarin, nutty-flavoured Mont d'Or and an enormous variety of goat's cheeses. Tues–Sat 9am–1pm & 3.30–7pm, Sun 9am–1.45pm.

OIL, SPICES, JAMS AND CONDIMENTS

Les Abeilles 21 rue de la Butte-aux-Cailles, 13e ☎ 01 45 81 43 48, ⓦ lesabeilles.biz; Ⓜ Corvisart/Place d'Italie; map p.172. Honey from all over France and further afield, sold from a barrel by an experienced beekeeper, plus honey-infused oils, vinegars, soaps and cakes. Try the prized – and pricey – Miel de Paris – harvested from beehives across the city. Tues–Sat 11am–7pm.

★ **G. Detou** 58 rue Tiquetonne, 2e ☎ 01 42 36 54 67; Ⓜ Etienne Marcel; map p.76. Friendly neighbourhood-style épicerie that gets packed to the gills on Saturdays. Kilos of spices, nuts and chocolate, plus *confiserie* (confectionery), *marrons glacés*, jars and tins, mustards, *confit*, foie gras and the like. Mon–Sat 8.30am–6.30pm.

Maille 6 place de la Madeleine, 8e ☎ 01 40 15 06 00, ⓦ maille.com; Ⓜ Madeleine; map p.76. Founded in 1747, Maille is best known for its Dijon mustard, but it also makes scores of other varieties, with specials including such flavours as pesto, rocket and white wine, or cocoa and raspberry, plus flavoured vinegars and rustic, hand-painted mustard pots. Mon–Sat 10am–7pm.

COFFEE AND TEA

★ **L'Arbre à Café** 10 rue du Nil, 10e ☎ 01 84 17 41 17, ⓦ larbreacafe.com; Ⓜ Sentier; map p.76. A trailblazer in Paris's much-lauded coffee renaissance, this little shop offers the haute cuisine of beans, with an impeccable selection bought direct from small biodynamic and organic estates – from Ethiopia to Hawaii – and roasted on demand. Tues–Fri 12.30–7.30pm, Sat 10am–7pm.

Mariage Frères 30 rue du Bourg-Tibourg, 4e ☎ 01 42 72 28 11, ⓦ mariagefreres.com; Ⓜ Hôtel de Ville; map p.99. Hundreds of teas, prettily packed in tins, line the floor-to-ceiling shelves of this historic tea emporium that's been trading since 1854. There's also a classy *salon de thé* (serving from 3pm). Also at 32 and 35 rue du Bourg-Tibourg, and other branches throughout the city. Daily 10.30am–7.30pm.

Verlet 256 rue St-Honoré, 1er ☎ 01 42 60 67 39, ⓦ verlet.fr; Ⓜ Palais Royal Musée du Louvre; map p.76. An old-fashioned *torréfacteur* (coffee merchant), selling both familiar and less common varieties of coffee and tea from around the world. There's also a tearoom, perfect for a pick-me-up. Mon–Sat 9.30am–7pm.

yam'Tcha 4 rue Sauval, 1er ☎ 01 40 26 06 06, ⓦ yamtcha.com; Ⓜ Les Halles; map p.88. An offshoot of the famed gourmet restaurant (see p.227), this pocket-sized teahouse sells delicate teas and accessories from China and Taiwan and serves chef Adeline Grattard's delicious steamed *bao* buns to take away. Wed–Sat 11.30am–10pm.

WINE AND BEER

Nicolas, Nysa and Le Repaire de Bacchus are the most reliable of the chains, but it's really worth speaking to the knowledgeable staff in the independent shops reviewed here; you'll be more likely to go home with some gems. As for natural wines, you're spoiled for choice, with an increasing number of places offering a good range of biodynamic, sulphite-free and organic options.

La Cave des Papilles 35 rue Daguerre, 14ᵉ ☎ 01 43 20 05 74, 🖥 lacavedespapilles.com; Ⓜ Denfert Rochereau; map p.164. More than a thousand organic and natural wines, hand-selected from small-scale producers by the charming owners, along with champagnes, whiskies, cognacs, Armagnacs and brandies. Mon 3.30–8.30pm, Tues–Fri 10am–1.30pm & 3.30–8.30pm, Sat 10am–8.30pm, Sun 10am–1.30pm.

Les Caves Augé 116 bd Haussmann, 8ᵉ ☎ 01 45 22 16 97, 🖥 cavesauge.com; Ⓜ St-Augustin; map p.64. This old-fashioned, wood-panelled shop is the oldest *cave* in Paris, dating back to 1850, and sells around six thousand French and foreign wines and champagne, many of them organic or natural. Mon–Sat 10am–7.30pm.

★**La Dernière Goutte** 6 rue Bourbon Le Château, 6ᵉ ☎ 01 43 29 11 62; Ⓜ Mabillon; map p.138. A much-loved neighbourhood wine shop. Owner Juan Sanchez hand-picks a selection of wines from small and mid-sized French producers, mainly organic and biodynamic. They also hold regular wine-tasting sessions in English for €55; you can reserve on their website (🖥 wine-class-in-english.paris). Mon 3.30–8pm, Tues–Sat 10.30am–1.30pm & 3–8pm, Sun 11am–7pm.

Lavinia 3–5 bd de la Madeleine, 8ᵉ ☎ 01 42 97 20 20, 🖥 lavinia.fr; Ⓜ Madeleine; map p.76. Vast wine and spirits store with a modern interior displaying thousands of bottles from more than 43 countries, and a wine cellar that holds some of the rarest bottles in the world. The attached wine library and bar/restaurant allow you to read up, then drink up. Mon–Sat 10am–8.30pm.

De Vinis Illustribus 48 rue de la Montagne-Ste-Geneviève, 5ᵉ ☎ 01 43 36 12 12, 🖥 devinis.fr; Ⓜ Maubert-Mutualité; map p.124. Connoisseur Lionel Michelin set up shop in this ancient wine cellar in 1994. He still specializes in very old and very rare vintages but is just as happy selling you a €9 bottle of Coteaux du Languedoc and orating eloquently on its tannins. Tues–Sat 2–7pm.

HOMEWARE AND KITCHENWARE

In addition to the selection of shops below, it's worth checking out the art and design **museums**, as well as the homeware and **kitchen departments** at Le BHV Marais (see p.325) and Lafayette Maison (see p.326).

A. Simon 48–52 rue Montmartre, 2ᵉ ☎ 01 42 33 71 65; Ⓜ Etienne Marcel; map p.76. A huge collection of anything and everything for professional and home cooks, including a wide range of cast-iron and copper cookware, and fine glassware. Bovida, at no. 36, and MORA, at no. 13, are the big rivals on the street, but this place has the edge. Mon–Sat 8.30am–6.30pm.

★**Astier de Villatte** 173 rue St-Honoré, 1ᵉʳ ☎ 01 42 60 74 13, 🖥 astierdevillatte.com; Ⓜ Palais Royal Musée du Louvre; map p.76. Delightful, unusual shop modelling the arty, shabby elegance of its carefully selected ceramics, homeware, candles and gifts in a beautiful space of parquet floorboards, dark wood cabinets and peeling-plaster walls (pieces from around €35). A second branch has opened at 16 rue de Tournon (6ᵉ). Mon–Sat 11am–7.30pm.

Cire Trudon 78 rue de Seine, 6ᵉ ☎ 01 43 26 46 50, 🖥 trudon.com; Ⓜ Mabillon; map p.138. Reputedly France's oldest candle-maker, dating back to 1643, and renowned for using the highest-quality beeswax. Choose from an assortment of colours as well as 32 different scented candles (€70), such as Carmélite, which supposedly evokes the odour of a convent's mossy walls, and Dada, inspired by the Surrealist movement and emanating a "clever" and "bewildering" scent of vetiver, tea, mint and eucalyptus. You can also buy a candlewax "bust" of Napoleon, Marie Antoinette and other figures. There's an additional branch at 11 rue Ste Croix de la Bretonnerie (4ᵉ). Mon 11am–7pm, Tues–Sat 10am–7pm.

★**CSAO** 9 rue Elzévir, 3ᵉ ☎ 01 42 71 33 17, 🖥 csao.fr; Ⓜ St-Paul; map p.99. They sell everything from recycled plastic bracelets to woven baskets in this stylish and colourful African store/gallery – it stands for Compagnie du Sénégal et de l'Afrique de l'Ouest. A great spot for colourful cushions and fabrics, kitchen goods, lamps, crockery and table linen, most of it from reclaimed, refashioned and upcycled materials. Tues–Sun 11am–7pm.

Dominique Picquier 10 rue Charlot, 3ᵉ ☎ 01 42 72 39 14, 🖥 dominiquepicquier.com; Ⓜ Filles du Calvaire/St-Sébastien-Froissart; map p.99. "A tribute to nature in the city" is how this textile designer describes her beautiful fabrics printed with striking graphic patterns. Picquier also does an attractive range of retro-influenced accessories, including tote bags and purses (from €49), often focusing on city landmarks. Tues–Fri 11am–7.30pm, Sat 2.30–7.30pm.

E. Dehillerin 18–20 rue Coquillière, 1er ☎01 42 36 53 13, ⓦe-dehillerin.fr; Ⓜ/RER Châtelet-Les Halles; map p.88. This nineteenth-century institution, in business since 1820, is laid out like a traditional ironmonger's: narrow aisles, no fancy displays, prices buried in catalogues, but they have a good-quality stock of knives, slicers, peelers, presses and a great selection of copper and pewter pans, many of restaurant quality, at reasonable prices. Mon 9am–12.30pm & 2–6pm, Tues–Sat 9am–6pm.

★**Empreintes** 5 rue de Picardie, 3e ☎01 44 01 08 30, ⓦempreintes-paris.com; ⓂSt-Sébastien-Froissart; map p.96. The first of its kind in France, this arts and crafts concept store occupies an attractive, light-filled space, spread over four floors, and presents a wide-ranging collection of ceramics, jewellery, ornaments, tableware and much else, all hand-crafted in French workshops. There are around one thousand items, including wooden bowls made in the Cévennes, beautiful vases, glass-handled shaving brushes, brass engraved bookmarks and exquisite porcelain sculptures. Some works are expensive one-offs, others part of a more affordable limited edition. Even if you don't buy, it's a nice place to linger, especially as there's also a café and a bookshop. Mon–Sat 11am–7pm.

Gab & Jo 28 rue Jacob, 6e ☎09 84 53 58 43, ⓦgabjo.fr; ⓂSt-Germain-des-Prés; map p.138. Colourful, intriguing and original – everything in this concept store, from soap to furniture to candles to books, is designed and made in France. Mon–Sat 11am–7pm.

★**Merci** 111 bd Beaumarchais, 3e ☎01 42 77 00 33, ⓦmerci-merci.com; ⓂSt-Sébastien-Froissart; map p.96. Flowers, bed linen, throws, kitchenware, fragrances and clothes (some specially created for the store by leading designers such as Stella McCartney) are all available from this hip and original concept store set in an attractively light and airy space (a former wallpaper factory). This stuff is not cheap, but all profits go to charity. There are three good eating options, too (see p.277). Mon–Sat 10am–7pm.

ANTIQUES AND COLLECTIBLES

★**Boîtes à Musique Anna Joliet** Jardin du Palais Royal, 9 rue de Beaujolais, 1er ☎01 49 27 98 60; ⓂPalais Royal Musée du Louvre; map p.76. A delightful, minuscule boutique selling every style of music box, from inexpensive self-winding toy models to grand cabinets costing thousands of euros. Parisians have long loved mechanical instruments, and many of these play old favourites such as *La Vie en Rose* and *Chim Chim Cheree*. Prices from around €50. Mon–Sat noon–7pm.

Deyrolle 46 rue du Bac, 7e ☎01 42 22 30 07, ⓦdeyrolle.com; ⓂRue du Bac; map p.138. Extraordinary, historic palace of taxidermy – as much a sight as a shop (see p.147) – full of quirky treasures. Downstairs offers garden and inexpensive homewares; upstairs you can spend from €10 for a pinned iridescent butterfly or a fossil, or €35 for a vintage pharmacy bottle filled with squid ink to €50,000 for a (naturally deceased) zebra. Mon 10am–1pm & 2–7pm, Tues–Sat 10am–7pm.

Les Drapeaux de France Place Colette, 1er ☎01 40 20 00 11, ⓦlesdrapeauxdefrance.com; ⓂPalais Royal Musée du Louvre; map p.76. The windows and interior of this old-fashioned shop teem with miniature tin soldiers (whole battalions of French hussars, for example), Napoleons, Asterixes, Tintins, circus figures, *Alice in Wonderland* characters and much else – some are antiques, others contemporary, all made and painted by hand (from around €18). Tues–Sat 11am–7.30pm.

Livres et Papiers 6 rue Vivienne, 2e ☎06 03 70 41 65; ⓂBourse; map p.76. Antique engravings and maps, some dating back to the sixteenth century, at a range of prices. You might have to search a bit for what you want, but the friendly assistant is more than happy to help. Mon–Sat 2.30–7pm.

Louvre des Antiquaires 2 place du Palais-Royal, 1er ☎01 42 97 27 27, ⓦlouvre-antiquaires.com; ⓂPalais Royal Musée du Louvre; map p.76. An enormous antiques and furniture hypermarket where you can pick up anything from a Mycenaean seal ring to an Art Nouveau vase – for a price. Tues–Sun 11am–7pm

Lulu Berlu 2 rue du Grand-Prieuré, 11e ☎01 43 55 12 52, ⓦluluberlu.com; ⓂOberkampf; map p.198. This sunshine-yellow store is crammed with twentieth-century toys and curios, most in their original packaging. There's a particularly good collection of 1970–90s favourites, including *Doctor Who*, *Star Wars*, *Planet of the Apes* and *Batman* figures. Mon–Sat 11am–7.30pm.

MARKETS

Paris's **markets** are a grand spectacle. Most of the food markets are resolutely French, their produce forming an enduring tie between the city and that great national obsession: *terroir*, or land/region. But you'll also find ethnic markets: African on the fringes of the 18e arrondissement and in the 11e, for example, and Southeast Asian in the 13e. There are regular food markets in all the arrondissements – a list can be found at ⓦparis.fr (search for "marchés"). Other street markets – among them the **puces de St-Ouen**, covered in our "Suburbs" chapter (see p.222) – are dedicated to secondhand goods (the *marchés aux puces*), clothes and textiles, flowers, birds, books and stamps.

BEST MUSEUM SHOPS
The Louvre See p.49.
Musée des Arts Décoratifs See p.60
Musée Picasso See p.102
Centre Pompidou See p.87
Institut du Monde Arabe See p.133

BOOKS AND STAMPS
Marché du Livre Ancien et d'Occasion 104 rue Brancion, 15e; gippe.org; Porte de Vanves; map p.164. Around fifty stalls selling secondhand and antiquarian books. Best in the morning. Sat & Sun 9am–6pm.

Marché aux Timbres Junction of avs de Marigny and Gabriel, on the north side of place Clemenceau in the 8e; Champs-Elysées-Clemenceau; map p.64. The stamp market in Paris, attracting professional dealers as well as individual sellers. You can also buy postcards and phonecards. Thurs, Sat, Sun & hols 9am–7pm.

CLOTHES AND FLEA MARKETS
Porte de Montreuil Av de Porte de Montreuil, 20e; Porte de Montreuil; map p.112. Cheap new clothes now dominate what used to be the city's best market for secondhand clothes; it's cheapest on Mondays when weekend leftovers are sold off. Also old furniture, household goods and assorted flea market finds. Mon, Sat & Sun 7am–5pm.

★**Puces de St-Ouen** 18e marcheauxpuces-saintouen .com; map p.223. By far the biggest and most visited of Paris's flea markets, situated on the northern outskirts (see p.223). Different markets keep slightly different hours, but as a rule Mon 11am–5pm, Sat & Sun 10am–5.30pm.

Puces de Vanves Av Georges Lafenestre/av Marc Sangnier, 14e pucesdevanves.fr; Porte de Vanves; map p.164. Bric-a-brac and Parisian knick-knacks, with professionals dealing alongside weekend amateurs. Sat & Sun 7am–1pm, or till around 3pm on av Georges Lafenestre.

FOOD MARKETS
★**Marché d'Aligre** Place d'Aligre, 12e; Ledru-Rollin; map p.112. Historic street and covered food market in the square; one of the cheapest and most popular in Paris. Tues–Sat 9am–1pm & 4–7.30pm, Sun 9am–1.30pm.

★**Marché Bastille** Bd Richard-Lenoir, 11e; Richard-Lenoir; map p.112. Huge, authentic Parisian street market, with lots of regional produce. Thurs & Sun 7am–2.30pm.

Marché Belleville Bd de Belleville, 11e; Belleville; map p.207. Lively, noisy neighbourhood market selling a good range of fresh produce, with some ethnic food. Tues & Fri 7am–2.30pm.

Marché Biologique des Batignolles Bd des Batignolles between nos. 27 and 35, 17e; Rome; map p.195. One of the city's main haunts for organic produce. Sat 9am–3pm.

Marché Brancusi Place Brancusi, 14e; Gaîté; map p.164. Excellent organic market. Sat 8am–2pm.

Marché Cler Rue Cler, 7e; La Tour-Maubourg; map p.152. Fancy delis and food stores line the street, joined by gourmet and produce stalls, with antiques and junk at the weekend. Tues–Fri, plus Sat & Sun mornings.

Marché Convention Rue de la Convention, 15e; Convention; map p.172. One of the largest markets in Paris, with a wide selection of fresh produce plus clothing on Thursdays. Tues, Thurs & Sun 7am–2.30pm.

Marché Daumesnil Place Félix Eboué and bd de Reuilly, 12e; Bel Air; map p.112. Large fresh-produce market that also offers clothes and household goods. Tues & Fri 7am–2.30pm.

Marché Dejean Rue Dejean, 18e; Chateau Rouge; map p.182. Predominantly West African foods and household items in the Goutte d'Or. Tues–Sat & Sun morning.

★**Marché Edgar-Quinet** Bd Edgar-Quinet, 14e; Edgar-Quinet; map p.164. Two separate markets: food and arts and crafts. The food market is superb, with a vast range of fresh produce, from seafood and artisan cheese to fresh crêpes and home-made pizza. Food Wed & Sat 7am–2.30pm, art and crafts Sun roughly 10am–dusk.

Marché des Enfants Rouges 39 rue de Bretagne, 3e; Filles du Calvaire; map p.99. Covered food market abounding in eating outlets (see p.279) and fresh produce. Tues, Wed & Thurs 8.30am–1pm & 4–7.30pm, Fri & Sat 8.30am–1pm & 4–8pm, Sun 8.30am–2pm.

Marché Monge Place Monge, 5e; Place Monge; map p.124. Fabulous (and quite pricey) produce set around the pretty Monge fountain; organic stalls on Sun. Wed, Fri & Sun 7am–2.30pm.

Marché Montorgueil Rue Montorgueil, 1er; Etienne Marcel; map p.76. Market stalls, artisan produce and gourmet food stores spread along this foodie street. Tues–Fri, plus Sat & Sun mornings.

Marché Mouffetard Rue Mouffetard, 5e; Place Monge; map p.124. Lively (and extremely touristy) market street with open-air stalls joining permanent food and wine stores. Tues–Sun mornings.

★**Marché Raspail/Marché Bio** Bd Raspail, 6e; Rennes; map p.138. The city's main organic market, also selling herbal remedies and artisan produce. Sun 9am–3pm.

★**Marché Saxe-Breteuil** Av de Saxe, 7e; Ségur; map p.172. Often regarded as the city's most beautiful market, in the shadow of the Eiffel Tower. You'll find fresh produce plus clothing and household goods. Thurs & Sat 7am–2.30pm, Sun 6–11pm.

2

JOSÉPHINE BAKER POOL

Activities and sports

If you've had enough of following crowds through museums or wandering through the city in the blazing sun or pouring rain, then it may be time to do what the Parisians do. There are ice rinks to glide over, green parks to run through and some genuinely beautiful swimming pools for a cooling dip. Hammams, or Turkish baths, are popular, and range from the chichi to the steamily authentic. You could also learn the tricks of the gourmet chef at a cookery school, or simply play a few rounds of boules. There's a world-leading array of spectator sports on offer, too, from football to horse racing, not to mention the triumphal arrival of the Tour de France in July. Information on municipal facilities is available from the Hôtel de Ville (wparis .fr) or at the *mairies* of each arrondissement. For details of sporting events, try the sports paper *L'Equipe* (wlequipe.fr).

BOULES

The classic French game, **boules** (or pétanque), is a common sight on balmy summer evenings in many of the city's parks and gardens. You could search for "Terrain de boules" on ⓦ paris.fr to find a court near you, but you'll certainly see it played at the Arènes de Lutèce (see p.350), Jardin du Luxembourg (see p.114) and the Bois de Vincennes (see p.218). The principle is the same as British bowls but the terrain is always rough – usually gravel or sand, and never grass – and the area much smaller. The metal ball is also smaller than a bowling ball, usually thrown upwards from a distance of about 10m, with a strong backspin in order to stop it skidding away from the wooden marker (*cochonnet*). Though traditionally the social equivalent of darts or perhaps pool, the game is becoming far less male-dominated; there are café or neighbourhood teams and many local championships.

COOKERY COURSES

Paris is, of course, the perfect place to get to grips with French gastronomy and wine. There are a large number of institutions offering **courses**.

L'Atelier des Chefs ⓦ atelierdeschefs.fr. A variety of classes (in French) in the 4ᵉ, 8ᵉ, 9ᵉ and 15ᵉ. One convenient option is the fun 30min session in which you prepare a quick lunch (sea bass with blood orange and herbed potatoes, perhaps, or crispy chicken with tarragon pesto), for €17. With more time, consider the 2hr classes – the regularly changing schedule offers instruction on everything from classic pâtisserie to lobster done four ways (€76). Lots of options for kids and families.

L'Atelier des Sens ⓦ atelier-des-sens.com. This unstuffy school has three kitchens in Paris – in the 3ᵉ, the 9ᵉ and the 11ᵉ – and offers a host of courses (including many on weekday evenings and Sun, and some for children). You can make chocolate eclairs or Breton cakes, or focus on individual French regions, seasonal ingredients or world cuisine. They do run occasional courses in English, but you'll be able to choose from a much wider selection if you can opt for a class in French. Most cost about €68 for 2hr or €92 for 3hr.

Le Cordon Bleu 13–15 quai André Citroën, 15ᵉ ☎ 01 85 65 15 00, ⓦ lcbparis.com; ⓜ Javel. This famed institution offers half- to four-day bilingual workshops on how to prepare French regional cuisine and pâtisserie, with sessions ranging from "cordon vert" vegetarian food to how to cook with foie gras (€85–990).

Les Cours Miss Lunch Première Pression Provence, 3 rue Antoine Vollon, 12ᵉ ☎ 01 53 33 03 59, ⓦ lunchintheloft.com. Based in a fancy olive-oil store near the Marché d'Aligre (see p.341), Miss Lunch creates original, warm-hearted dishes (rabbit prosecco terrine with capers and quails' eggs, say, or a Persian soup with fresh herbs) – based on the freshest produce and inspired by her mixed heritage – from Egypt to South Africa via Pantelleria, an island between Sicily and Tunisia. Morning (4hr) and evening (2hr 30min) lessons from €120.

Ecole de Cuisine Alain Ducasse 64 rue du Ranelagh, 16ᵉ ☎ 01 44 90 91 00, ⓦ ecolecuisine-alainducasse. com; ⓜ Ranelagh. Though Ducasse doesn't actually teach here, many alumni of his kitchens do, making it a superb place to pick up top techniques in preparing bread, pâtisserie, seafood, haute cuisine and bistro classics. English-language classes from €90 for a 2hr session.

Le Foodist 59 Rue du Cardinal Lemoine, 5ᵉ ☎ 06 71 70 95 22, ⓦ lefoodist.com. Lively, informative English-language classes and demonstrations in the Latin Quarter. Prepare and then eat your pâtisserie with a cup of tea or coffee while listening to stories from French food history (3hr; from €99), or start your cooking class with a market visit before making – then eating – a three-course meal (€189). Also wine and cheese pairing lunches (€79).

CYCLING

The French are mad about cycling, and Parisian cyclists are benefiting hugely from the city's commitment to reducing pollution on the streets. The **Vélib'** bike-rental scheme (see p.29) goes from strength to strength, while under the terms of mayor Hidalgo's Plan Vélo (see p.379) there are now around 700km of dedicated **cycle lanes**, with double that planned by 2020. In addition, the **Paris Respire** scheme (see p.30) bans cars from certain roads on Sundays and public holidays year-round, which brings out the cyclists and rollerbladers in force. If you would rather ride in a greener environment, you may prefer the Bois de Boulogne or the Bois de Vincennes, both of which have extensive bike tracks. You can pick up Vélib' bikes by the entrances to all the major parks, which offer bicycles for children too (see p.354). Keen cyclists might also want to visit the city during one of the major **cycling events** (see box, p.347).

GYMS, EXERCISE, YOGA AND DANCE

You'll find any number of aerobics classes, dance workouts and anti-stress fitness programmes in Paris, along with yoga, t'ai chi and martial arts. Many **gyms** organize their activities in courses or require a minimum month's or year's subscription, but if your latest meal has left you feeling the need to shed a few kilos, here are some options.

Ashtanga Yoga Paris 40 av de la République, 11e ☎01 45 80 19 96, ⓦashtangayogaparis.fr; ⓜCouronnes/ Parmentier. A bilingual yoga studio run by a Franco-Canadian couple offering a range of classes, including ashtanga, Mysore and Vinyasa yoga, in two good-sized rooms. A one-hour drop-in class is €22, or it's €50 for a week-long pass, with classes held daily, many in the evening. Mats are available. You can just turn up for a class, but if you're coming before 8am or after 8pm, or at the weekend, call or email first to get the door code.

Centre de Danse du Marais 41 rue du Temple, 4e ☎01 42 77 58 19, ⓦparis-danse.com; ⓜHôtel de Ville. More than forty dance disciplines are on offer here, from rock'n'roll, tap and Bollywood to African, flamenco and twerking – with classes for all levels and one-off visitors welcome. Each session costs €20 (€65 for four), though you must become a member for insurance purposes (€12). Mon–Fri 9am–9pm, Sat 9am–8pm, Sun 9am–7pm.

Gym Suedoise ☎01 45 00 18 22, ⓦgymsuedoise.com.

Hour-long "Swedish gym" classes combine aerobics, stretching and simple dance steps. You don't have to be experienced or hyper-fit (or speak French), and can just show up, without booking (numbers permitting), to any one of the dozens of classes held all over Paris. Check the website for your nearest class. €10/class; no cash – cards only.

Le Quartier Sport 19 rue de Pontoise, 5e ☎01 55 42 77 88, ⓦlequartiersport.fr; ⓜMaubert Mutualité. In addition to the fantastic pool (see p.346) this complex has a gym, exercise classes and squash courts. It's not cheap: you'll pay €21.60 per gym session, €173 for ten sessions or €152 for monthly membership – though this does include access to the pool. Mon–Fri 9am–midnight, Sat & Sun 9.30am–7pm.

Rasa Yoga 21 rue Saint-Jacques, 5e ☎01 43 54 14 59, ⓦrasa-yogarivegauche.com; ⓜCluny La Sorbonne. A welcoming yoga studio on the Left Bank with plenty of classes (€22; three classes for €42) in English. There's a wide range of disciplines on offer, for all levels, plus various massages from €50.

HAMMAMS

Turkish baths, or **hammams**, are one of the unexpected delights of Paris. More luxurious than the standard Swedish sauna, but less soothingly upmarket than a spa, these are places to linger, meet up and chat – some of them can get quite raucous, but that's all part of the fun. You can usually pay extra for a massage and a *gommage* – an exfoliation – followed by mint tea or a cool drink to recover. You're often given a strip of linen and modest towel on entry, and usually some slippers, but bring your own swimsuit for mixed men-and-women sessions.

Hammam Medina Center 43–45 rue Petit, 19e ☎01 42 02 31 05, ⓦhammam-medina.com; ⓜLaumière. This traditional hammam is a bit far from the centre, but it's one of the most popular in the city, attracting locals for its sauna, steam room and pool, and its range of massages. €44 hammam and *gommage*; from €59 with massage. Swimsuit compulsory in all sessions. Women: Mon–Fri 11am–10pm & Sun 9am–7pm; mixed: Sat 10am–9pm.

Hammam de la Mosquée 39 rue Geoffroy-St-Hilaire, 5e ☎01 43 31 14 32, ⓦrestaurantauxportesdelorient .com; ⓜCensier–Daubenton. This lovely mosque (see p.132) includes an old-fashioned public bath, for women only, where locals come to relax and chat. It has an atmospheric, vaulted cooling-off room and a marble-lined steam chamber. Good value at €18, though towels are extra

(€4), and you can also have a reasonably priced massage and brisk *gommage* (€12 for a 10min session of either), or a €43 package, which gets you entrance, traditional Moroccan "black soap", *gommage*, a 10min massage and a mint tea. Leave time to enjoy tea and cakes in the tiled *terrasse* café (see p.282). Daily except Tues 10am–9pm.

O'Kari Hammam 22 rue Dussoubs, 2e ☎01 42 36 94 66, ⓦo-kari.com; ⓜRéaumur Sébastopol. Very soothing (during off-peak hours at least), women-only hammam in a pretty little building. Packages start at €59 for an hour including steam, *gommage*, shampoo and a home-made lemonade. They also have a good range of face and hair masks, all made from natural products. Mon–Wed, Fri & Sat 10am–8pm, Thurs 10am–9pm.

ICE-SKATING

In addition to the permanent rinks, a number of festive, temporary *patinoires* spring up in Paris over the **Christmas** season – including on the Champs-Elysées and the first floor of the Eiffel Tower. Perhaps most stunning of all is the Grand Palais des Glaces in the **Grand Palais** (mid-Dec to early Jan daily 10am–2am; ⓦlegrandpalaisdesglaces.com) – said to be the largest indoor rink in the world.

PERMANENT RINKS

Patinoire de l'AccorHotels Arena 222 quai de Bercy, 12e ☎01 58 70 16 75, ⓦaccorhotelsarena .com/fr/arena/la-patinoire; ⓜBercy. Especially lively on Friday and Saturday nights, when the place practically

transforms into a disco on ice. Admission €4, €6 on Fri and Sat evenings; skate rental €3. Hours vary, but usually Wed 3–6pm, Fri 9.30pm–12.30am, Sat 3–6pm & 9.30pm–12.30am, Sun 10am–noon & 3–6pm.

Patinoire Pailleron 32 rue Edouard Pailleron, 19ᵉ ☎01 40 40 27 70, ⓦpailleron19.com; ⓜBolivar. In the same sports complex as the lovely Art Deco Pailleron swimming pool (see p.346), this rink is particularly popular with families. Admission €4.20; skate rental €3. Mon & Tues noon–1.30pm & 4.15–8.30pm, Wed 2.45–9.30pm, Thurs & Fri noon–1.30pm & 4.15–10.30pm, Sat 12.30–10.30pm, Sun 10am–noon (families only) & noon–6pm; hours are extended during the school holidays, when there are daily family sessions.

ROCK CLIMBING

Mur Mur Pantin 55 rue Cartier Bresson, Pantin ☎01 48 46 11 00, ⓦmurmur.fr; ⓜAubervilliers/RER Pantin. The Paris suburbs lay claim to a huge, superb indoor climbing arena, with walls between 8m and 17m high, as well as a bouldering section for climbing without rope or harness. First visit €20, then €9 on weekday mornings (€15 weekday afternoons and weekends) for return visits. They have a second branch in Issy-les-Moulineaux, in the southwestern suburbs. Mon–Thurs 9.30am–11pm, Fri 9.30am–midnight, Sat 9.30am–8pm, Sun 9.30am–6.30pm.

ROLLERBLADING AND SKATEBOARDING

For many years it has been a tradition for thousands of Parisian **rollerbladers** to meet on Friday nights by the Gare Montparnasse (14ᵉ; ⓜMontparnasse) before setting off on a demanding **three-hour circuit** of the city's streets; check out ⓦpari-roller.com for the latest details. A more sedate outing – and a popular choice for families – takes place on Sunday afternoons; check ⓦrollers-coquillages.org. Popular areas for **rollerblading and skateboarding** include the concourse of the Palais de Chaillot (ⓜTrocadéro) and the flat areas beside the place de la Bastille and place du Palais-Royal; on Sunday, when a number of roads throughout the city are closed to cars as part of the "**Paris Respire**" scheme, rollerbladers come out in force (see ⓦparis.fr for the list of routes, complete with maps). A good place for **information** and to **rent blades** (around €9 for a half-day, including helmet and padding) is Nomades, 37 bd Bourdon, 4ᵉ (Tues–Fri 11am–1.30pm & 2.30–7.30pm, Sat 10am–7pm; ☎01 44 54 07 44, ⓦnomadeshop.com; ⓜBastille).

SQUASH, TABLE TENNIS AND TENNIS

Squash Dedicated squash centres include Squash Montmartre, 14 rue Achille-Martinet, 18ᵉ (Mon–Fri 10am–11pm, Sat & Sun 10am–8pm; ☎01 42 55 38 30, ⓦsquashmontmartre-paris.com; ⓜLamarck-Caulaincourt), which charges €16 for your first visit (40min) and after that around €26/game; book in advance. Alternatively, Le Quartier Sport (see opposite) has squash courts at €31/hr.
Table tennis The Mairie provides outdoor table-tennis tables in many of the smaller parks and outdoor spaces in Paris – search for "Le sport en plein air" on ⓦparis.fr to pull up an arrondissement-by-arrondissement list. It's up to you to bring a racquet and balls.
Tennis Private clubs demand steep membership fees, but most of the city's forty or so municipal courts (Mon–Sat 8am–10pm, Sun 8am–6pm) are in quite good shape. One of the nicest places to play is in the Jardin du Luxembourg, which has open-air asphalt courts (☎01 43 25 79 18; ⓜLuxembourg). You can book city courts online at ⓦtennis.paris.fr, though you'll need to scan in ID to create an account (open-air €9/hr, covered €17/hr); in practice, it's often fine to just turn up with your kit and wait on the spot – usually no more than an hour, except at busy times.

RUNNING

When it comes to **running**, the Jardin du Luxembourg, Tuileries and Champ de Mars are particularly popular with Parisians; all provide decent, varied, though short runs, and are more or less flat. The riverside Parc Rives de Seine (see box, p.91) is also a good bet, though it gets busy with joggers at lunchtime and after work. The "**Paris Respire**" scheme, which bans cars from certain roads on Sundays and public holidays year-round, can make city jogging more pleasant (see p.30). If you want to run for longer distances or tackle hills, head for the Parc des Buttes-Chaumont in the 19ᵉ or Parc Montsouris in the 14ᵉ, or, best of all, the Bois de Boulogne and the Bois de Vincennes, which are the largest open spaces (though both are cut through by a number of roads). And if you fancy keeping fit while sightseeing at the same time, contact **Paris Running Tours**, who provide English-speaking guides to run with you on a variety of customized circuits (from 1hr; from €90 for one person, €75 for two; ⓦparisrunningtour.com).

THE PARIS MARATHON

The **Paris Marathon**, held in early/mid-April, starts at the Champs-Elysées and includes sections in the Bois de Vincennes and the Bois de Boulogne. If you want to join in, check out ⓦparismarathon.com, where you can register to run. A **half-marathon** is held in March (ⓦsemideparis.com), and **"Les 20km de Paris"** takes place in mid-October, beginning and finishing at the Eiffel Tower (ⓦ20kmparis.com).

SWIMMING

Paris is currently embarking on a programme to renovate, modernize and increase in number its **municipal pools**, with new outdoor pools planned, for example, in the bassin de la Villette and on the Seine near Parc André-Citroën – keep track of developments at ⓦ paris.fr/nager. The municipal pools reviewed in the list below are among the most central and convenient options. Their **opening hours** vary, with a complex schedule of early morning, lunchtime and evening sessions, and with longer hours in summer and during the school holidays; check ahead online. For a searchable list and map of Parisian pools, see ⓦ meslieux.paris.fr/piscines.

Les Amiraux 6 rue Hermann-Lachapelle, 18ᵉ ☏ 01 46 06 46 47; ⓜ Simplon. This 33m-long municipal pool is in a handsome 1920s building – as featured in the film *Amélie* – surrounded by tiers of changing cabins. €3; €24 for ten swims. Daily.

Butte-aux-Cailles 5 place Paul-Verlaine, 13ᵉ ☏ 01 45 89 60 05; ⓜ Place d'Italie. Another historic municipal pool, housed in a spruced-up Art Nouveau building with a striking arched ceiling. The main 33m indoor pool is joined in summer by two outdoor pools (25m and 12m). €3; €24 for ten swims. Tues–Sun.

Les Halles Suzanne Berlioux 10 place de la Rotonde, Niveau 3, Porte du Jour, Forum des Halles, 1ᵉʳ ☏ 01 42 36 98 44, ⓦ piscine-berlioux.fr; ⓜ/RER Châtelet/ Châtelet-Les Halles. Very centrally located 50m pool with a huge glass wall looking through to a tropical garden. It stays open conveniently late (till 11pm on Mon and Wed). €4.80; €43 for ten swims. Daily.

Hébert 2 rue des Fillettes, 18ᵉ ☏ 01 55 26 84 90; ⓜ Porte de la Chapelle. With a glass facade that means it is usually bathed in light, this lovely municipal option – one 14m pool, one 25m – has a retractable roof that's opened in summer to let the sunshine flood in. €3; €24 for ten swims. Daily.

Henry-de-Montherlant 30 bd Lannes, 16ᵉ ☏ 01 40 72 28 30; ⓜ Rue de la Pompe. You get two pools at this municipal spot, one 25m and one 15m, plus a terrace for sunbathing – and the Bois de Boulogne is close by. €3; €24 for ten swims. Tues–Sun.

Jean Taris 16 rue Thouin, 5ᵉ ☏ 01 55 42 81 90; ⓜ Cardinal Lemoine. Municipal pool with a 25m and a 15m pool in the centre of the Quartier Latin; a student favourite. €3; €24 for ten swims. Tues–Sun.

Joséphine Baker Quai François-Mauriac, 13ᵉ ☏ 01 56 61 96 50, ⓦ www.piscine-baker.fr; ⓜ Bibliothèque François Mitterrand. A fabulous place to swim outdoors: this floating 25m, four-lane municipal pool is moored on a barge on the Seine, close to the Bibliothèque Nationale (and with a number of cool floating bars and clubs on the river nearby). In winter, a retractable roof transforms it into an indoor space. There's also a jacuzzi, sauna, gym and a large paddling pool for children; it can get crowded. Winter €3.60, summer €6. Daily.

Pailleron 32 rue Edouard Pailleron, 19ᵉ ☏ 01 40 40 27 70, ⓦ pailleron19.com; ⓜ Bolivar. A 1930s Art Deco marvel, 33m long, surrounded by tiers of changing rooms and arched over by a gantry-work roof, this is hugely popular and can get packed, especially during school holidays. The ozone-treated water is relatively gentle on your hair and eyes. €3.60; €29 for ten swims. Daily.

Le Quartier Sport 19 rue de Pontoise, 5ᵉ ☏ 01 55 42 77 88, ⓦ lequartiersport.fr; ⓜ Maubert Mutualité. Its excellent central location, Art Deco architecture, beautiful blue mosaic interior and 33m-long pool make this one of the top draws in the city. Juliette Binoche memorably swam here in the Kieslowski film *Three Colours: Blue*. €4.80/ swim; €38 for ten swims; €11.10/€100 for evening entry with access to gym. Daily.

SPECTATOR SPORTS

Paris St-Germain (PSG), one of France's richest and most powerful **football** teams, is the only major-league club in the city. The capital's teams also retain a special status in the **rugby** and **tennis** worlds, and **horse racing** is a serious pursuit. Probably the biggest deal, however, is **cycling**, with a number of major events to look out for.

BALL GAMES

AccorHotels Arena 8 bd de Bercy, 12ᵉ ☏ 01 58 70 16 00, ⓦ accorhotelsarena.com; ⓜ Bercy. This stadium hosts all manner of sporting events – basketball, handball, hockey, boxing – as well as gigs from the likes of Ed Sheeran and Lady Gaga. It holds twenty thousand people, so you've a fair chance of getting a ticket at the door, championships excepted – otherwise, book ahead online.

Parc des Princes 20 av du Parc des Princes, 16ᵉ ⓦ psg .fr; ⓜ Porte de St-Cloud. The capital's main stadium for domestic football events (*le foot*), and home ground to the first-division PSG. Tickets from €20.

Stade de France 93216 St-Denis ☏ 01 55 93 00 00, ⓦ stadefrance.com; ⓜ St-Denis Porte de Paris. Specially built to host the 1998 World Cup (see p.227) – which France then went on to win – this eighty-thousand-seat stadium out in the suburbs is the venue for international football matches and major rugby union matches (from €20). It's also a regular for the big stadium rockers – U2, Coldplay, Guns N' Roses and such like.

Stade Jean-Bouin 26 av du Général Sarrail, 16ᵉ ⓦ stade.fr/club/stade-jean-bouin; ⓜ Porte de St-Cloud.

CYCLING EVENTS

The biggest event of the French sporting year is the grand finale of the **Tour de France** (Ⓦletour.fr), which ends in a sweep along the Champs-Elysées in the third or fourth week of July with the ceremonial presentation of the coveted *maillot jaune* (the overall winner's yellow jersey). Though exciting, this is largely a ceremonial occasion; only very rarely does Paris witness memorable scenes such as those of 1989, when American Greg Lemond snatched the *maillot jaune* at the last minute on the final day. Other classic long-distance bike races that begin or end in towns near Paris – despite their names they don't usually start within the city – include the week-long **Paris–Nice** event in March, covering more than 1200km (Ⓦletour.fr/paris-nice) and the **Paris–Roubaix** in April, instigated in 1896, which, with its brutally cobbled route, is reputed to be the most exacting one-day race in the world (Ⓦletour.com/paris-roubaix). The 610km **Bordeaux–Paris**, meanwhile, the world's longest single-stage race, held between 1891 and 2014, is now an amateur event (held different times of year; Ⓦbordeauxparis.com).

Major cycling events, including time trials, are held at the **national velodrome**, in the suburbs at Saint-Quentin-en-Yvelines, near Versailles around 25km west of the city (Ⓦvelodrome-national.com).

Twenty-thousand-seater stadium next to the Parc des Princes. It's home to the Stade Français rugby club and hosts most of their home matches. Tickets from €7.

HORSE RACING

Major races The week starting the last Sunday in June sees a variety of big racing events near Paris, at St-Cloud and Chantilly (see p.237), and within the city at Vincennes and Longchamp in the Bois du Boulogne. The last also hosts the biggest horse race in the world, the Qatar Prix de l'Arc de Triomphe (Ⓦprixarcdetriomphe.com), in the first week of October. In May the Great Paris Steeplechase (Ⓦgrandsteeple.com), the poshest of all French equestrian competitions, is held in the Auteuil racecourse, also in the Bois du Boulogne. Auteuil is off the route d'Auteuil (ⓂPorte d'Auteuil), and Longchamp is off the route des Tribunes (ⓂPorte Maillot and then bus #244, or free shuttle buses on Sat and Sun). See *Paris-Turf* (Ⓦparis-turf.com) for details of horse-racing events.

Trotting races These races, with the jockeys in chariots, are held at the Vincennes racecourse in the Bois de Vincennes (RER Joinville-le-Pont, then free shuttles; Ⓦlctrot.com/courses spectacle).

TENNIS

Roland Garros Bd d'Auteuil, 16ᵉ Ⓦrolandgarros.com; ⓂPorte d'Auteuil. The French equivalent of Britain's Wimbledon complex (with clay courts), Roland Garros hosts the French Tennis Open, one of the four major events that together comprise the Grand Slam, in late May and early June. Tickets (€50–230) need to be reserved online months in advance (usually in March, with last-minute offers from mid-May).

Paris for children

The French are welcoming to children on the whole, and Paris's vibrant atmosphere, with its street performers, pavement cafés and merry-go-rounds, is certainly family-friendly. Disneyland aside (see p.246), there are plenty of attractions and activities to keep kids happy, from circuses to rollerblading. Museum-hopping with youngsters in Paris can be as tedious as in any other big city, but remember that while the Louvre and Musée d'Orsay cater to more acquired tastes, the Musée des Arts et Métiers, the Pompidou Centre, Parc de la Villette and some of the other attractions listed here will interest children and adults alike. Travelling with a child also provides the perfect excuse to enjoy some of the simpler pleasures of city life – the playgrounds, ice creams and toyshops that Paris seems to offer in abundance.

ESSENTIALS

Peak times It's worth remembering that the peak times for children's activities are Wednesday afternoons, when primary school children are off, and Saturdays; Wednesdays continue to be child-centred even during the school holidays.

Listings The most useful sources of information for current shows, exhibitions and events are the special sections in the listings magazines: "Enfants" in *Pariscope* and "Pour les jeunes" in *L'Officiel des Spectacles* (W offi.fr). The bimonthly *Paris with Kids*, the English edition of *Paris Mômes* (*môme* being French for "kid"), provides the lowdown on current festivals, concerts, films and other activities for children up to age 12; it's available for free from the tourist office, or look up the website, W parismomes.fr. The tourist office also has ideas for family outings on its website W parisinfo .com. It's worth checking the festivals calendar (see p.320) for annual events such as Paris Plage, Bastille Day, the Tour de France and the Fête de la Musique.

Discounts Many cafés, bars or restaurants offer *menus enfants* (special children's set menus) or are often willing to cook simpler food on request, and hotels tack on only a small supplement for an additional bed or cot. Throughout the city the RATP (Paris Transport) charges half-fares for 4–10s; under-4s travel free on public transport.

Babysitting Many hotels can organize babysitting; just check when you book. Otherwise, reliable babysitting agencies include Baby Sitting Services, 1 place Paul Verlaine, Boulogne Billancourt 92100 (T 01 46 21 33 16, W babysittingservices.fr). You can also try individual notices at the American Church, 65 quai d'Orsay, 6e (M Invalides; W acparis.org), the Alliance Française, 101 bd Raspail, 6e (M St-Placide; W alliancefr.org), or CIDJ, 101 quai Branly, 15e (M Bir-Hakeim; T 01 44 49 12 00, W cidj.com).

PARKS, GARDENS AND ZOOS

Younger kids in particular are well catered for by the parks and gardens within the city. Although there aren't, on the whole, any open spaces for spontaneous games of football, baseball or cricket, most parks have an enclosed playground with swings, climbing frames and a sandpit, while there's usually a netted enclosure for older children to play casual **ball games**. The most standard forms of entertainment in parks and gardens are puppet shows and **Guignol**, the French equivalent of Punch and Judy, these usually last about 45 minutes, cost around €3 and take place on Wednesday, Saturday and Sunday afternoons (more frequently during school holidays). Children under 8 seem to appreciate these shows most, with the puppeteers eliciting an enthusiastic verbal response from them; even though it's all in French, the excitement is contagious and the stories are easy enough to follow. For more information on any of Paris's parks, visit the municipal website W meslieuxparis.fr and type in the park's name.

MAJOR PARKS

Jardin d'Acclimation Bois de Boulogne, by Porte des Sablons T 01 40 67 90 82, W jardindacclimatation.fr; M Les Sablons/Porte Maillot; map p.219. The Jardin d'Acclimation, dating back to 1860, is a cross between a funfair, playground, farm and amusement park, with temptations including bumper cars, merry-go-rounds, pony and camel rides, distorting mirrors, adventure playgrounds, a paddling pool and a fine puppet theatre installed in a renovated Second Empire stable block. The Jardin was created by Napoléon III in 1860 and has an appealing old-fashioned charm; some of its rides, such as the magical mini-canal ride ("*la rivière enchantée*"), date back to the park's beginnings, as does the little train with open-air carriages that you can take to get here; it departs from near M Porte Maillot – cross over the *boulevard périphérique* (every 15min: Mon, Tues, Thurs & Fri noon–6pm, from 10am Wed, Sat & Sun and during hols; €6.40 return, includes admission). Attractions for older children include a zip wire and an adventure course, but note that these are only open on Wed, Sat, Sun & hols noon–5pm; the same is true of the pony and camel rides and the puppet shows. Entry to the park for adults and children €3.50, under-3s free; rides and attractions €2.90, or buy a carnet of ten tickets for €30. Daily: May–Sept 10am–7pm; Oct–April 10am–6pm.

Parc de la Villette Av Jean-Jaurès, 19e T 01 40 03 75 75, W lavillette.com; M Porte de Pantin/Porte de la Villette; map p.200. The Parc de la Villette boasts the Cité des Enfants (see p.354), wide-open spaces to run around or picnic in, and a series of ten themed gardens, some specially designed for kids. All are linked by a walkway called the Promenade des Jardins, indicated on the park's free map. Most popular with children are the Jardin du dragon, with its huge slide in the shape of a dragon, and the Jardin des dunes et des vents (April–Oct daily 10am–8pm; Nov–March Wed, Sat, Sun & school hols 10am till dusk; under-13s only and their accompanying adults), with sandpits, large air-filled cushions that roll like waves and are great for bouncing on, climbing frames, zip wires and tunnels. The park also holds regular workshops and activities for children, such as music, baking and gardening. Full details are given on the website or at the information centre at the Porte de Pantin entrance. Admission free. Daily 6am–1am.

Parc Floral Bois de Vincennes, Esplanade du Château de Vincennes T 01 49 57 24 81, W parcfloraldeparisjeux .com; M Château-de-Vincennes, then bus #112 or a 10min walk past the Château de Vincennes ; map p.118. The excellent playground at the Parc Floral has a treetop adventure park (Evasion Verte; see below), as well as slides, swings, ping-pong, quadricycles, mini-golf

27

modelled on Paris monuments (adults €12, children €8), an electric car circuit, and a little train touring all the gardens (April–Oct daily 1–5pm). Tickets for the paying activities are sold at the playground between 2 and 5.30pm weekdays and until 7pm at weekends; activities stop fifteen minutes later. Note that many of these activities are available only in the afternoon from March/April to Sept on Wed and weekends, daily during the school holidays. Also in the park is a children's theatre, the Théâtre Astral, which has mime, clowns and other not-too-verbal shows for small children aged 3 to 8 – it's best to book ahead online for these, as they're popular with school groups (usually Wed & Sun 3pm, school hols Mon–Fri & Sun 3pm; €8, free Nov–April; ⓦ theatreastral.com). There is also a series of pavilions with child-friendly educational exhibitions (free), which look at nature in Paris; the best is the butterfly garden (mid-May to mid-Oct Mon–Fri 1.30–5.15pm, Sat & Sun 1.30–6pm). Parc Floral is free except June–Sept Wed, Sat & Sun when entry is €5.50, €2.75 for 7–26-year-olds (under-7s are always free). Daily: April to mid-Sept 9.30am–8pm; mid-Sept to mid-Oct 9.30am–7pm; mid-Oct to March 9.30am–5/6pm.

Evasion Verte Parc Floral ⓦ evasion-verte.fr. The Parc Floral's "Green Escape" attraction allows you to explore the treetops by walking along rope bridges, swinging on ropes from tree to tree and suchlike. There are four walkways of varying height and difficulty. All children have to be accompanied by an adult. Children aged 6 and under 1.30m in height €16, adults and children over 1.30m in height €21; ticket valid for 2hr. Generally, open Wednesdays, weekends and school holidays in the afternoon, but check online for the latest opening times.

OTHER PARKS, SQUARES AND GARDENS

Arènes de Lutèce Rue des Arènes, 5ᵉ; ⓜ Place Monge; map p.124. This great public park, built on what used to be a Roman theatre, has a fountain, sandpit and jungle gyms (also see p.129). Daily 7.30 or 8am till dusk.

Buttes-Chaumont 19ᵉ; ⓜ Buttes-Chaumont/Botzaris; map p.207. Built on a former quarry, these grassy slopes are perfect for rolling down and offer fantastic views. Unusually for Paris there are no "keep off the grass" signs. You'll also find several playgrounds, a lake, waterfall, pony rides (Wed & Sat 3–6pm) and Guignol shows (see p.349). Daily 7.30 or 8am till dusk.

Champ de Mars 7ᵉ; ⓜ Ecole-Militaire; map p.152. Large playground, merry-go-round and pedal cars. Puppet shows Wed, Sat & Sun at 3.15pm & 4.15pm.

Jardin du Luxembourg 6ᵉ ⓦ senat.fr/visite/jardin; ⓜ St-Placide/Notre-Dame-des-Champs/RER Luxembourg; map p.138. Within the elegant Jardin du Luxembourg (see p.138) are a large playground for under-12s and one for under-6s, an old-fashioned merry-go-round and swing boats, sandpits, pony rides and toy-boat rental (Wed & Sun). A 45min marionette show takes place Wed at 3.15pm & 4.30pm, Sat & Sun at 11am & 3.30pm. Daily 7.30 or 8am till dusk.

Jardin des Plantes 57 rue Cuvier, 5ᵉ ⓦ jardindesplantes .net; ⓜ Jussieu/Monge; map p.124. The wonderful botanical gardens contain a small zoo, called the Ménagerie (April–Sept Mon–Sat 9am–6pm, Sun 9am–6.30pm; Oct–March daily 9am–5pm; €9, under-26s €7, under-4s free), a playground, hothouses and plenty of greenery (see p.130). Daily: April–Aug 7.30am–8pm; Sept–March 8am–dusk.

Jardin du Ranelagh Av Ingres, 16ᵉ; ⓜ Muette; map p.215. Marionettes, playground, sandpits and pony rides (weekends & hols). Daily 7.30 or 8am till dusk.

PARIS WITH BABIES AND TODDLERS

You will have little problem in getting hold of **essentials for babies** in Paris. Familiar brands of baby food are available in the supermarkets, as well as disposable nappies (*couches à jeter*), and the like. After hours, you can get most goods from late-night pharmacies, though they are slightly more expensive.

Getting around with a pushchair poses the same problems as in most big cities. The métro is especially awkward, with its endless flights of stairs (and few escalators). Buses are much easier, with seats near the front for passengers with young children.

Unfortunately, many of the lawns in Parisian **parks** are out of bounds ("*pelouse interdite*"), so sprawling on the grass with toddlers and napping babies is often out of the question. That said, more and more parks are now opening the odd grassy area to the public, and there are two central spaces that offer complete freedom to sit on the grass: place des Vosges and Parc des Buttes-Chaumont.

Finding a place to **change and feed** a baby is especially challenging. While most of the major museums and some department stores have areas within the women's toilets equipped with a shelf and sink for changing a baby, most restaurants do not. Breast-feeding in public, though not especially common among French women, is, for the most part, tolerated if done discreetly. Few restaurants have high chairs available for babies and toddlers.

27

EATING OUT WITH CHILDREN

Restaurants in Paris are usually good at providing small portions or allowing children to share dishes. A number of places listed in the "Eating" chapter (see p.266) offer a **menu enfant**, including *Chez Imogène* (see p.293), *Merci* (see p.277) and *Dame Tartine* (see p.276), which last also has the advantage of outside tables in a traffic-free environment. Other family-friendly options include *Miss Kô* (see p.271), just off the Champs-Elysées, and *Le Square Trousseau* (see p.281), opposite a park and playground in the Bastille area.

Jardin des Tuileries Place de la Concorde/rue de Rivoli, 1er ☎ 01 40 20 90 43; Ⓜ Place de la Concorde/Palais Royal Musée du Louvre; map p.50. Pony rides (Wed, weekends & hols), vintage merry-go-round, marionettes, trampolines, toy sailing boats (Wed & Sun) and funfair in July & Aug (see p.71). Daily 7.30 or 8am till dusk.

Parc de Belleville 20e; Ⓜ Couronnes; map p.207. Built into the slopes of the hilly Belleville park is this fun adventure playground made up of wooden climbing walls, with ropes and slides, aimed at children over 6 years old. Daily 10am until around an hour before dusk.

Parc Georges-Brassens Rue des Morillons, 15e; Ⓜ Convention/Porte de Vanves; map p.170. Access the park at the entrance across from 86 rue Brancion. Climbing rocks, puppets (Ⓦ marionnettes-parc-brassens.fr), artificial river, playground and scented herb gardens (see p.175). Daily dawn till dusk.

Parc Monceau Bd de Courcelles, 17e; Ⓜ Monceau; map p.64. There's a lake where you can feed the ducks, a playground and a rollerblading circuit (see p.68). Daily 7.30 or 8am till dusk.

Parc Montsouris Bd Jourdan, 14e; Ⓜ Glacière/RER Cité-Universitaire; map p.164. Puppet shows by the lake (Wed & Sat 3.30pm & 4.30pm, Sun 11.30am, 3.30pm, 4.30pm & 5.30pm), a number of playgrounds and a waterfall (see p.171). Daily 9am till dusk.

Parc Rives de Seine Ⓜ Invalides; map p.88. This pedestrianized stretch of the river (see box, p.91) has floating gardens, climbing walls and various open-air games for children, such as a giant snakes-and-ladders board painted on the ground.

Parc Zoologique de Paris Junction of av Daumesnil and route de la Ceinture du Lac, 12e ☎ 08 11 22 41 22, Ⓦ parczoologiquedeparis.fr; Ⓜ Porte Dorée; map p.118. Paris's main zoo (see p.119) is sure to appeal with its lions, zebras, giraffes, manatees and enormous tropical hothouse. Admission €22, 3–11 year olds €14, 12–25-year-olds €16.50. Mid-March to mid-Oct Mon–Fri 10am–6pm, Sat, Sun & hols 9.30am–7.30pm; mid-Oct to mid-March daily 10am–5pm.

Place des Vosges 4e; Ⓜ Bastille/Chemin Vert/St-Paul; map p.96. The oldest square in Paris (see p.95) has two popular sandpits, a small playground and plenty of space to run around in. Daily 7.30 or 8am till dusk.

FUNFAIRS, MERRY-GO-ROUNDS AND THEME PARKS

Funfairs Three big funfairs (*fêtes foraines*) are held in Paris each year. The season kicks off in late March with the Foire du Trône in the Bois de Vincennes (running until late May), followed by the funfair in the Tuileries gardens late June to late August, with more than forty rides, including a giant Ferris wheel, and ending up with the Fête à Neu-Neu, held near the Bois de Boulogne from early September to mid-October. Look up "Fêtes Populaires" under "Agendas" in *Pariscope* (see p.40) for details if you're in town at these times.

Merry-go-rounds There's usually a merry-go-round at the Forum des Halles, on place de l'Hôtel de Ville and beneath the Tour St-Jacques at Châtelet, with carousels for smaller children on place de la République, at the Rond-Point des Champs-Elysées by avenue Matignon, at place de la Nation, at the base of the Montmartre funicular in place St-Pierre and at place des Abbesses.

Musée des Arts Forains 53 av des Terroirs de France, 12e ☎ 01 43 40 16 15, Ⓦ arts-forains.com; Ⓜ Cour St-Émilion; see p.116. Located within one of the old Bercy wine warehouses on the edge of the Parc de Bercy, the

privately owned funfair museum has working merry-go-rounds as well as fascinating relics from nineteenth-century fairs. Visits, which consist of a 90min guided tour and cost €16 (children €8), are by advance reservation only, either by phone or online.

PARC ASTÉRIX

Parc Astérix Plailly, 38km north of Paris off the A1 autoroute ☎ 08 26 46 66 26, Ⓦ parcasterix.fr. Disneyland Paris (see p.246) has put all Paris's other theme parks into the shade, though Parc Astérix – better mind-fodder, less crowded and cheaper – is well worth considering. Interesting historical-themed sections including Ancient Greece, Roman Empire, Gallic Village, Middle Ages and Old Paris are sure to spark curiosity in your children. A Via Antiqua shopping street, with buildings from every country in the Roman Empire, leads to a Roman town where gladiators play comic battles and dodgem chariots line up for races. In another area, street scenes of Paris show the city changing from Roman Lutetia to the

SWIMMING, ROLLERBLADING AND OTHER FAMILY ACTIVITIES

One of the most fun things a child can do in Paris – and as enjoyable for the minders – is to have a wet and wild day at **Aquaboulevard**, a giant leisure complex with a landscaped wave pool, slides and a grassy outdoor park. In addition, many municipal **swimming pools** (see p.346) in Paris have dedicated children's pools.

Cycling and **rollerblading** can also be fun for the whole family (see p.343). Sunday is the favoured day to be *en famille* on wheels in Paris, when the central *quais* of the Seine and the Canal St-Martin are closed to traffic. One of the most thrilling wheelie experiences is the **mass rollerblading** (see p.345) that takes place on Friday nights and Sunday afternoons (the Sunday outings tend to be family affairs and the pace is a bit slower). Paris à Vélo C'est Sympa (see p.30) has a good range of kid-sized bikes as well as baby carriers and tandems, and they also offer bicycle tours of Paris. The popular Vélib' scheme extends to children with **P'tit Vélib'**; bikes in four different sizes for 2- to 8-year-olds, including a balance bike for toddlers, can be rented at six locations, such as the Bois de Boulogne and the Parc Rives de Seine, mostly on weekends and Wednesdays only. They're generally free for the first half-hour, then €3 for a subsequent two hours, but check the website ⓦ en.velib .paris.fr for the latest details.

Boules (see p.343) and **billiards** are both popular in Paris and might amuse older kids and teenagers.

present-day capital. All sorts of rides are on offer, including the Trace du Hourra, a bobsled that descends very fast from high above. Dolphins and sea lions perform tricks for the crowds; there are parades and jugglers; restaurants for every budget; and most of the actors speak English. The easiest way to get here is to take the shuttle bus from the Louvre, which runs in the summer and can be booked online; check website for times (€20). Alternatively, take

the half-hourly shuttle bus (9am–6/7pm; €8.50, under-12s €7.50) from RER Roissy-Charles-de-Gaulle (line B). Admission €49 (children aged 3–11 €41, under-3s free), though the website often has special offers. Parking €10. Check the website or phone for opening times, as they vary, but generally April–June daily 10am–6pm; July & Aug daily 10am–7pm; Sept & Oct Sat & Sun 10am–6pm; also closed for several days in May.

CIRCUSES, THEATRE, MAGIC AND CINEMA

Language being less of a barrier for smaller children, the younger your kids, the more likely they are to appreciate Paris's many special **theatre** shows and **films**. There's also **mime** and the **circus**, which need no translation.

CIRCUS (CIRQUE)

Unlike funfairs, **circuses** are taken seriously in France, coming under the heading of culture as performance art (and there are no qualms about performing animals). Some circuses have permanent venues, of which the most beautiful in Paris is the nineteenth-century Cirque d'Hiver Bouglione (see below). You'll find details of the seasonal ones under "Cirques" in the "Pour les Jeunes" section of *L'Officiel des Spectacles* and under the same heading in the "Enfants" section of *Pariscope*, and there may well be visiting circuses from Warsaw or Moscow.

Cirque Diana Moreno-Bormann 1 place Skanderbeg, 19ᵉ ☎ 01 41 61 45 90, ⓦ cirque-diana-moreno.com; bus #65 (direction Mairie d'Aubervilliers). A traditional circus, with lion-tamers, camels, zebras, acrobats, jugglers, trapeze artists – the lot. From €10, children under 4 free. Shows Wed, Sat & Sun 3pm.

Cirque d'Hiver Bouglione 110 rue Amelot, 11ᵉ ☎ 01 47 00 28 81, ⓦ cirquehiver.com; ⓜ Filles du Calvaire.

From mid-October to early March, this splendid Second Empire building, decorated with pilasters, bas-reliefs and sculpted panels, is the setting for dazzling acrobatic feats, juggling, lion-taming and much more – the Christmas shows are extremely popular. (It hosts TV and fashion shows the rest of the year.) Tickets from €10. See website for show times.

Cirque Micheletty 115 bd Charles-de-Gaulle, Villeneuve-La-Garenne ☎ 01 47 99 40 40, ⓦ journee -au-cirque.com; RER Les Grésillons then bus #177. This dream day out allows you to spend an entire day at the circus (from €37, including show and lunch). In the morning you are initiated into the arts of juggling, walking the tightrope, clowning and make-up. You have lunch in the ring with your artist tutors, then join the spectators for the show, after which you might be taken round to meet the animals. You can, if you prefer, just attend the show at 2pm (from €15, under-12s €10), but you'd better not let the kids know what they've missed.

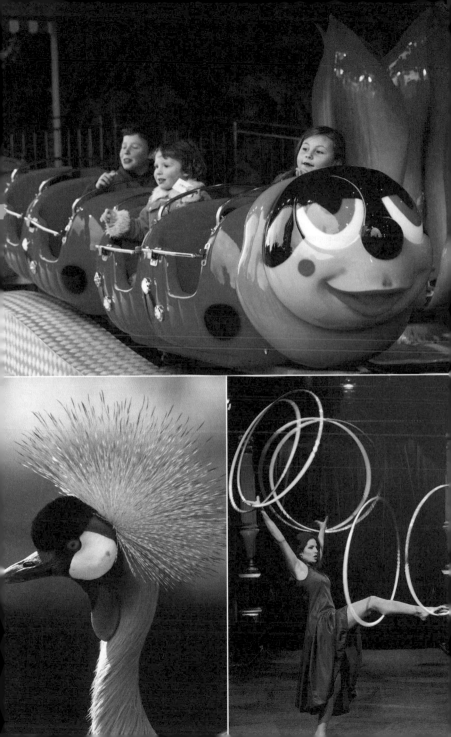

27

Jan–June, Sept & Oct 10am–5pm on varying days (see website).

Cirque Pinder Pelouse Reuilly Bois de Vincennes, 12ᵉ ☎ 01 45 90 21 25, ⓦ cirquepinder.com; ⓜ Porte de Charenton/Porte Dorée. This travelling circus has been entertaining French audiences since 1854 with acts featuring performing lions, elephants and camels, clowns and trapeze artists. From €11. Early Nov to early Jan.

THEATRE AND MAGIC

The "Spectacles" section under "Enfants" in *Pariscope* lists details of magic, mime, dance and music shows. Several theatres, in addition to the Théâtre Astral in the Parc Floral (see p.118), specialize in shows for children, and a few occasionally have shows in English. Le Point Virgule, 7 rue Ste-Croix-de-la-Bretonnerie, 4ᵉ ☎ 01 42 78 67 03, ⓦ lepointvirgule.com; ⓜ Hôtel de Ville), in the Marais, has an excellent reputation for occasional programming for kids, while Théâtre Dunois, 7 rue Louise Weiss, 13ᵉ ☎ 01 45 84 72 00, ⓦ theatredunois.org), and Théâtre

Paris-Villette, 211 av Jean-Jaurès, 19ᵉ (☎ 01 40 03 74 20, ⓦ theatre-paris-villette.fr), are dedicated almost solely to children's theatre. If your kids are really into magic they should visit the Musée de la Magie (see p.108), where a magician performs throughout the day.

Le Double-Fond 1 place du Marché Ste-Catherine, 4ᵉ ☎ 01 42 71 40 20, ⓦ www.doublefond.com; ⓜ St-Paul; map p.99. The magicians' venue hosts a special children's magic show (€12), though there's a lot of chat in French along with the sleight of hand. Sat 2.30pm & 4.30pm, Sun 4.30pm.

CINEMA

There are many cinemas (see p.310) showing cartoons and children's films, but if they're foreign they are usually dubbed into French. The Cinémathèque Française (see p.310) screens films for children on Wednesday and Sunday afternoons, and the Forum des Images (see p.310) shows films on Wednesday and Saturday, followed by an afternoon tea. At La Villette (see p.200), the Géode IMAX cinema will appeal to most children.

MUSEUMS

Cité des Enfants Cité des Sciences, Parc de la Villette, 30 av Corentin-Cariou, 19ᵉ ☎ 08 92 69 70 72, ⓦ cite-sciences.fr; ⓜ Porte de la Villette; map p.200. The Cité des Enfants, the Cité des Science's special section for children, with sessions for 2–7s and 5–12s, is totally engaging. Kids can touch, smell and feel inside things, play about with water (it's best to bring a change of clothes), construct buildings on a miniature site (complete with cranes, hard hats and barrows), experiment with sound and light, manipulate robots, race their own shadows, and superimpose their image on a landscape. They can listen to different languages by inserting telephones into the appropriate country on a globe, and put together their own television news. Everything, including the butterfly park, is on an appropriate scale, and the whole area is beautifully organized and managed (if you haven't got a child, it's worth borrowing one just to get in here). The rest of the museum is also pretty good for kids, particularly the planetarium, the various film shows, the Argonaute

submarine and the frequent temporary exhibitions designed for the young. In the Parc de la Villette, there's lots of wide-open green space and a number of playgrounds. Admission to the Cité des Enfants costs €9 (€12 for over-25s); as sessions are very popular, advance booking online is recommended, or you can book a place (for weekday sessions only) by phone. Tues–Sun; sessions last 1hr 30min; check online for times.

Le Musée en Herbe 21 rue Hérold, 1ᵉʳ ☎ 01 40 67 97 66, ⓦ museeenherbe.com; ⓜ Les Halles/Palais Royal Musée du Louvre; map p.88. Fun, interactive art exhibitions, using jigsaws, dressing-up clothes and the like, designed for children from as young as 2; recent exhibitions have included the world of Tintin and the works of street artist Invader. They also run popular art workshops (from €9) that chime in with the exhibitions – some are for toddlers (aged 2 and a half to 4), others for children aged from 5 to 12. General admission €6. Daily 10am–7pm, Thurs till 9pm.

CHILDREN'S WORKSHOPS

Many museums organize children's **workshops** on Wednesdays, Saturdays and daily throughout the school holidays. The **Musée d'Art Moderne de la Ville de Paris** (see p.160) has special exhibitions and workshops in its children's section (entrance 14 av de New-York). Other museums with sessions for kids include the **Musée d'Orsay** (see p.135), **Musée des Arts Décoratifs** (see p.60), **Institut du Monde Arabe** (see p.133), **Musée du Quai Branly** (see p.151) and the **Petit Palais** (see p.67). For the current programme of workshops, look under "Animations" in the "Pour les Jeunes" section of *L'Officiel des Spectacles*.

TOP TEN CHILD-FRIENDLY PARIS SIGHTS

One of the best treats for children of every age from 2 upwards is probably the Cité des Enfants (see p.201) within the Cité des Sciences, and the Cité des Sciences museum itself, in the Parc de la Villette. However, lots of Paris's main attractions, although not exclusively aimed at children, have much to offer young visitors; here are our top ten recommendations.

Les Arts Décoratifs The collections of cutting-edge furniture and temporary fashion and design exhibitions here may well appeal to style-conscious teenagers. See p.60

Catacombs Older children may relish the creepiness of the catacombs, stacked with millions of bones from the city's old charnel houses and cemeteries. See p.167

Cinéaqua An impressive aquarium in the Jardins du Trocadéro, with thousands of exotic fish – and sharks too – in giant fish tanks. See p.159

Eiffel Tower Children love the drama of this magnificent structure; try and book tickets well in advance, or join the shorter queue for the ascent on foot – children from around age 5/6 should manage the steps up. See p.149

Grande Galerie de l'Evolution in the Jardin des Plantes Includes a children's discovery room, the Galerie des Enfants, on the first floor with child-level microscopes, glass cases with live caterpillars and moths, and a burrow of Mongolian rodents. See p.130

Jardin d'Acclimatation Children could easily spend a whole day in this enchanting playpark in the Bois de Boulogne. See p.349

Musée de la Magie Lots of hands-on fun on offer here – operate quirky automata, experiment with optical illusions and enjoy a magic show. See p.108

Musée de la Musique A wonderful way to introduce children to musical instruments from the past and present, helped by audioguides with English-language commentary (and excerpts of music) specially for kids. There are regular free workshops and concerts for children, too. See p.204

Centre Pompidou Children will enjoy ascending the escalator and seeing what's on at the Galerie des Enfants. See p.87

Sewers Entered through a large square manhole, and some 500m down, *les égouts* are dank, damp, dripping, claustrophobic and filled with echoes. It's a fascinating way to explore the city. See p.151

SHOPS

The fact that Paris is filled with beautiful, enticing, delicious and expensive things all artfully displayed is not lost on most children. Toys, gadgets and clothing are all bright, colourful and appealing, while the sheer amount of ice cream, chocolate, biscuits and sweets of all shapes and sizes is almost overwhelming. The only goodies here are safe from are high-tech toys, of which France seems to offer a particularly poor range. A worthwhile place to head is **rue Vavin**, just north of boulevard Montparnasse, in the St-Germain district, which has a good concentration of children's shops.

ENGLISH-LANGUAGE BOOKS

★**Chantelivre** 13 rue de Sèvres, 6ᵉ ☎01 45 48 87 90, ⓦ chantelivre.com; ⓜ Sèvres-Babylone; map p.138. A huge selection of everything to do with and for children, including great picture books for the younger ones, an English section, and a play area. Mon 1–7.30pm, Tues–Sat 10.30am–7.30pm.

Galignani 224 rue de Rivoli, 1ᵉʳ ☎01 42 60 76 07, ⓦ galignani.com; ⓜ Tuileries; map p.76. This long-established English bookshop (see p.334) stocks a decent range of children's books. Mon–Sat 10am–7pm.

Shakespeare and Company 37 rue de la Boucherie, 5ᵉ ⓦ shakespeareandcompany.com; ⓜ Maubert-Mutualité; map p.124. There's a children's classics area at this famous bookshop (see p.122). Daily 10am–11pm.

WH Smith 248 rue de Rivoli, 1ᵉʳ ⓦ whsmith.fr; ⓜ Concorde; map p.76. This British bookseller has a very good children's section (and a nice tea room, too). Mon–Sat 9am–7pm, Sun 12.30–7pm.

TOYS AND GAMES

In addition to the shops below, be sure to check out the superb selection of toys at Le Bon Marché department store (see p.326).

Amuzilo 34 rue Dauphine, 6ᵉ ☎01 43 54 12 70; ⓜ Odéon; map p.138. Small, friendly toyshop with a nice selection of wooden toys (some handcrafted in France) for toddlers; marionettes, dolls' house furniture and games for primary-school-aged children. Mon 3–7.30pm, Tues–Sat 11am–7.30pm, Sun 2–6pm.

Le Bonhomme de Bois 141 rue d'Alésia, 14ᵉ ☎01 40 44 58 20, ⓦ bonhommedebois.com; ⓜ Alésia;

map p.164. Perfect little shop with classic wooden cars and dolls, and plush, colourful, floppy-eared stuffed animals. Mon–Sat 10.30am–7pm.

Le Ciel Est à Tout le Monde 10 rue Gay-Lussac, 5ᵉ ☎ 01 46 33 53 91; RER Luxembourg; map p.124. Once a kite shop, now specializing in traditional wooden toys, mobiles, kids' cutlery and other accessories, mostly aimed at babies and young children. Mon 1–7pm, Tues–Sat 10.30am–7pm.

Clair de Rêve 35 rue Saint-Louis-en-L'Ile, 4ᵉ ☎ 01 43 29 81 06, ⊕ clairedereve.com/boutique; ⓜ Pont-Marie; map p.44. A small shop, part of a specialist puppetry and automata company, housed in an old building on the Ile St-Louis. Browse beautiful handmade puppets (from around €200), wind-up toys and more affordable music boxes, plus French-made watches. Mon–Sat 11am–1pm & 2–7pm.

Les Cousins d'Alice 36 rue Daguerre, 14ᵉ ☎ 01 43 20 24 86; ⓜ Gaîté/Edgar-Quinet; map p.164. *Alice in Wonderland* decorations, toys, games, puzzles and mobiles, plus a general range of books. Tues–Sat 10am–7.30pm.

★ **Pain d'Epices** 29 passage Jouffroy, 9ᵉ ☎ 01 47 70 08 68, ⊕ paindepices.fr; ⓜ Grands Boulevards; map p.76. Fabulous dolls' house necessities from furniture to wine glasses. Mon 12.30–7pm, Tues–Sat 10am–7pm.

Puzzles Michèle Wilson 116 rue du Château, 14ᵉ ☎ 01 42 22 28 73, ⊕ puzzles-et-jeux.com; ⓜ Pernety; map p.164. Beautiful wooden jigsaw puzzles of paintings and Paris scenes, with workshop on the premises. Tues–Sat 10.30am–1pm & 2–7pm.

★ **Si Tu Veux** 68 galerie Vivienne, 2ᵉ ☎ 01 42 60 59 97, ⊕ situveuxjouer.com; ⓜ Bourse; map p.76. Well-made traditional toys plus toy-making kits and ready-made costumes. Mon–Sat 10.30am–7pm.

Tout s'arrange 27 rue Delambre, 14ᵉ ☎ 01 43 26 44 68, ⊕ toutsarrange.fr; ⓜ Vavin; map p.164. A delightfully idiosyncratic miniature boutique selling inexpensive tiny treasures (jewellery, decorations, micro-dollies) handmade using objects found or recycled by the owner, who also makes toys and bags. Tues–Sat 10.30am–7pm.

Vilac Galerie 9 rue de Beaujolais, Palais Royal, 1ᵉʳ ☎ 01 42 60 08 22; ⓜ Bourse/Pyramides; map p.76. A toyshop in the Palais Royal gardens selling good-quality wooden toys by traditional French brand Vilac, jigsaw puzzles of the Eiffel Tower and other Paris monuments, and appealingly old-fashioned dolls by Petitcollin. Mon–Sat 10.30am–7pm.

CLOTHES

Besides the specialist shops listed here, most of the big department and discount stores have children's sections (see p.325). Monoprix offers reasonable prices and quality.

Alice à Paris 9 rue de l'Odéon, 6ᵉ ☎ 01 42 22 53 89, ⊕ aliceaparis.com; ⓜ Odéon; map p.138. Beautiful, chic clothes to make your children perfect little Parisians. From babies upward, but best for toddlers and older children. Tops and skirts from around €25. Mon 2–7pm, Tues–Sat 11am–7pm.

Bonpoint 50 rue Etienne Marcel, 2ᵉ ☎ 01 40 26 20 90, ⊕ bonpoint.com; ⓜ Etienne Marcel; map p.76. Insanely expensive but utterly elegant outfits for the 0- to 6- to going-on-24-year-old. These are stylish, well-designed clothes mixing traditional children's outfitting with contemporary touches. Prices in the €50–100 range. A half-dozen other branches around the city, and available at Le Bon Marché (see p.326). Mon–Sat 10am–7pm.

★ **Du Pareil au Même** 122 rue du Faubourg-St-Antoine, 12ᵉ ☎ 01 43 44 67 46, ⊕ dpam.com; ⓜ Ledru-Rollin; map p.112. Beautiful kids' clothing at attractive prices. Gorgeous floral dresses, cute jogging suits and brightly coloured basics. Branches all over Paris. Mon–Sat 10am–7pm.

★ **Petit Pan** 37 rue François Miron, 4ᵉ ☎ 09 80 44 85 51, ⊕ petitpan.com; ⓜ St-Paul; map p.99. Covetable accessories and clothes for babies and toddlers including quilts (€60), backpacks (€30), cushions (€12) and padded jackets (€50), all made of colourful printed cotton fabric. A couple of doors down at no. 39 is a branch selling fabrics, tiles, bedding and other homeware. Mon & Sun–10.30am–1pm & 2–7.30pm, Tues–Sat 10.30am–7.30pm.

Les P'tits Bo'Bo 7 rue Clauzel, 9ᵉ ☎ 01 45 26 61 91; ⓜ St-Georges; map p.182. A treasure trove of secondhand but top-quality children's clothing for newborns to 12-year-olds, stocking leading "bourgeois-bohemian" brands like Bonpoint, Bonton, IKKS and Luco, plus internationals Burberry and Finger in the Nose. Also sells used toys and accessories. Tues–Sat 11am–2 & 3–7pm.

GAY PRIDE MARCH

LGBT+ Paris

Paris has long had a strong gay presence – boosted in recent times by the fact that the city's mayor for thirteen years, Bertrand Delanoë, was openly gay. The focal point of the scene over the past few decades has traditionally been the Marais – its central street, rue Ste-Croix-de-la-Bretonnerie, may be filling up with sleek chain stores, but still has many visibly gay-oriented businesses. That said, there are other LGBT-friendly pockets scattered throughout the city and gay travellers will feel comfortable in mixed/bohemian neighbourhoods such as Canal St-Martin or SoPi. The community is well catered for by rights and support organizations and an active press; the high spot on the calendar is the annual LGBT Pride parade, which takes place on the last Saturday in June (ⓦgaypride.fr).

ESSENTIALS

USEFUL CONTACTS

★**Centre LGBT de Paris** 63 rue Beaubourg, 3e Ⓦ centrelgbtparis.org; Ⓜ Arts et Métiers/Rambuteau. The first port of call for information and advice – legal, social, psychological and medical – plus a friendly bar, classes and social events. The website has links to many other useful LGBT+ organizations. Mon–Fri 3.30–8pm, Sat 1–7pm.

Inter-LGBT Ⓣ 01 72 70 39 22, Ⓦ inter-lgbt.org. Actively campaigns for gay rights and is the driving force behind the annual Pride march (see p.322) along with other public events; the site has a wealth of LGBT+ links.

MAG 106 rue de Montreuil, 11^e Ⓣ 01 43 73 31 63, Ⓦ mag-jeunes.com; Ⓜ Nation. Aimed at people under 26 years old, the Mouvement d'Affirmation des Jeunes Gais et Lesbiennes, Bi et Trans organizes a drop-in welcome service for young LGBT+ people (Wed 6–8pm, Fri 6–10pm, Sat 4–9pm).

Paris Gay Village Ⓦ parisgayvillage.com. Voluntary association that acts as an alternative tourist office, with a free one-to-one, one-hour welcome-to-gay-Paris service, inexpensive monthly guided walks and museum visits (covering the Moreau Museum, for example, or a lesbian walk from place du Châtelet to place de la Concorde).

PRINT AND ONLINE MEDIA

Barbieturix Ⓦ barbieturix.com. Excellent online lesbian magazine, with news, reviews, interviews and articles, plus good club and bar listings.

Citegay Ⓦ citegay.fr. Newsy website packed with features, interviews and some listings.

Les Mots à la Bouche 6 rue Ste-Croix-de-la-Bretonnerie, 4e Ⓣ 01 42 78 88 30, Ⓦ motsbouche.com; Ⓜ Hôtel de Ville; map p.99. The city's main gay and lesbian bookshop, with exhibition space and a good selection of titles, from graphic novels to biographies and art books, and some literature in English. There are lots of free listings, maps and club flyers to pick up, too. Mon 11am–8pm, Tues–Sat 11am–11pm, Sun 1–9pm.

Têtu Ⓦ tetu.com. Geared mostly towards a male readership, *Têtu* – the name means "headstrong" – is the glossiest and most readable of France's gay online monthlies, with news stories, lifestyle articles, listings (in Paris and beyond) and reviews.

NIGHTLIFE

In terms of **nightlife**, Paris's "gay village" is the Marais, centred on rue Ste-Croix-de-la-Bretonnerie, rue des Archives and spreading up past the Pompidou Centre towards métro Etienne Marcel. There are also a few gay bars and clubs on **rue Sainte-Anne** in the 1er and clustered around the **Bonne Nouvelle** métro on rue Poissonnière in the 2e. **Straights** are welcome in some gay establishments, especially when in gay company, but not necessarily – women, in particular, may be denied entry to some of the heavier male clubs. The city is not over-stocked with **lesbian bars**, but the ones that do exist are generally welcoming; in addition to those listed below, check the *Rosa Bonheur* bars (see p.300 & p.302) – which, although mixed, have a strong lesbian following – and the links on Ⓦ barbieturix.com. We've listed the main **clubs** below, but bear in mind, too, that many mainstream clubs run gay *soirées* – check websites, keep an eye on flyers and ask around in the LGBT+ bars. **Entry prices** vary widely, so you should expect to pay anything from €10 to €25, depending on the size of the venue and the popularity of the individual *soirée*.

BARS – MAINLY WOMEN

3W-Kafé 8 rue des Ecouffes, 4e Ⓣ 01 48 87 39 26, Ⓦ bit .ly/2nuVsmL; Ⓜ Hôtel de Ville; map p.99. Lipstick-lesbian lounge-café that warms up considerably at weekends, when the cellar dancefloor gets rowdy. Drinks are pricey. 3W stands for "women with women", incidentally. Wed & Sun 7pm–3am, Thurs 7pm–4am, Fri & Sat 7pm–6.30am.

La Champmeslé 4 rue Chabanais, 2e Ⓣ 01 42 96 85 20, Ⓦ lachampmesle.fr; Ⓜ Pyramides; map p.76. Long-established lesbian address, particularly popular among thirty-somethings, though it packs everyone in for occasional cabaret nights. A good place to begin exploring the scene. Mon–Sat 4pm–4am.

★ **Mutinerie** 176–178 rue St-Martin, 3e Ⓣ 01 42 72 70 59, Ⓦ lamutinerie.eu; Ⓜ Rambuteau; map p.88. It's not all about partying at this welcoming, left-wing "QueerFéministeTransLesbien" bar: yes, there's a pool table, karaoke and regular club nights, but the queer/trans collective that runs it also offers free workshops, talks and exhibitions, all with a view to inclusivity and political awareness. Friendly and fun. Daily 5pm–2am.

Le So What 30 rue du Roi de Sicile, 4e Ⓣ 01 42 71 24 59, Ⓦ facebook.com/LeSoWhat; Ⓜ St-Paul; map p.99. A lesbian bar/club aimed at a more mature crowd. Friendly ambience, with good DJ sets, and club nights at the weekend. Check the Facebook page for listings. Thurs 8pm–2am, Fri & Sat 11pm–5am.

BARS – MAINLY MEN

Café Cox 15 rue des Archives, 4e Ⓣ 01 42 72 08 00, Ⓦ cox.fr; Ⓜ Hôtel de Ville; map p.99. Muscular types, up for a seriously good time, pack out the terrace of this loud, well-established bar – an essential fixture on the Marais circuit. There's an extended happy hour (Mon–Sat 6–10pm, Sun 6pm–2am) and regular DJ nights focusing on house music. Daily 5.30pm–2am.

★ **Le Duplex** 25 rue Michel-le-Comte, 3ᵉ ☎01 42 72 80 86, ⓦbit.ly/leduplex; Ⓜ Rambuteau; map p.99. Said to be the oldest gay bar in the Marais, this place is popular with intellectual and media types for its relaxed and chatty atmosphere. Friendly rather than cruisey, with regular art exhibitions. Mon–Thurs & Sun 8pm–2am, Fri & Sat 8pm–4am.

Le Free DJ 35 rue Ste-Croix de la Bretonnerie, 4ᵉ ☎01 48 04 95 14, ⓦfreedj.fr; Ⓜ Hôtel de Ville; map p.99. This stylish DJ bar draws a youngish crowd of beautiful types; it's friendly, though, and features some big sounds (house, disco-funk) in the basement club (Fri–Sun). Daily 6pm–4am.

L'Open Café 17 rue des Archives, 4ᵉ ⓦopencafe.fr; Ⓜ Hôtel de Ville; map p.99. *L'Open*, on a busy Marais crossroads, is perhaps the most famous gay bar in Paris. As such, it's quite touristy, but good fun, with not-bad café food and lots of *terrasse* seating. An essential stop on the circuit. Mon–Thurs & Sun 11am–2am, Fri & Sat 11am–3am.

Le Raidd 23 rue du Temple, 4ᵉ ☎01 42 77 04 88, ⓦfacebook.com/RaiddBar; Ⓜ Hôtel de Ville; map p.99. One of the city's glossiest bars, famous for its beautiful staff, topless waiters and go-go boys' raunchy (and sudsy) shower shows. Mon–Thurs & Sun 6pm–4am, Fri & Sat 6pm–5am.

★ **Les Souffleurs** 7 rue de la Verrerie, 4ᵉ ☎01 44 78 04 92, ⓦfacebook.com/lessouffleurs; Ⓜ Hôtel de Ville; map p.99. Managing to be both stylish and unintimidating, this is a laidback gay bar that specializes in rum cocktails

and offers regular DJ sets from some pretty big names. Happy hour daily 6–9pm. Daily 6pm–2am.

CLUBS

CUD 12 rue des Haudriettes, 3ᵉ ☎01 42 77 44 12, ⓦfacebook.com/cudbar; Ⓜ Rambuteau; map p.99. The "Classic Up and Down" is just that: bar upstairs, club below. The dancefloor is tiny, and it can get packed, but there are no queues or door policies – and it keeps going all night. Daily 11pm–7am.

Gibus 18 rue du Faubourg du Temple, 11ᵉ ☎01 47 00 78 88, ⓦgibusclub.fr; Ⓜ Republique; map p.198. Hugely popular club/live music venue putting on some of the city's biggest gay nights, including Crazyvores and Power Pouf. The up-for-it crowd looks good and is generally friendly. Club nights (generally Fri–Sun) from 11pm.

★ **Le Tango/La Boîte à Frissons** 13 rue au Maire, 3ᵉ ☎01 48 87 25 71, ⓦboite-a-frissons.fr; Ⓜ Arts et Métiers; map p.96. Unpretentious, inclusive (and inexpensive) LGBT+ club in a retro 1930s dance hall, with a traditional Sun-afternoon tea dance/*bal* from 6pm, featuring slow dances as well as anything from tango to camp disco classics. Fri and Sat nights also begin with couples of all sexual orientation dancing every kind of traditional *danse à deux*, until the legendary "Madison" line dance at 12.30am, after which it's pure fetish costume and disco – and no techno allowed. Themed and singles nights, too. Entry €6–9. Fri & Sat 10pm–5am, Sun 6–11pm.

VIEW FROM ARC DE TRIOMPHE TO LA DEFENSE

Contexts

History

Early humans – and for many millennia their Neanderthal cousins alongside them – first lived in the Paris region some 600,000 years ago, when deer, boar, bear and aurochs roamed the banks of a half-kilometre-wide river. The waters slowly shifted southward before settling in the current bed of the Seine in around 30,000 BC (leaving behind today's Marais or "marsh"). The discovery of 14,000-year-old reindeer-hunter campsites at Pincevent, Verberie and Etiolles, in the Paris basin, suggests that modern humans arrived relatively recently. The oldest encampment yet uncovered, dating back to about 7600 BC, was found by the river in the southwest corner of the modern 15^e arrondissement; it seems to have been a site for sorting flint pebbles. At Bercy, several well-preserved dugout canoes probably date from a marshy fishing and hunting settlement of around 4500 BC.

The Parisii

Mud and water were clearly still major features of the area when the **Gauls** or **Celts** began to settle, probably in the third century BC, as the Roman rendition of their name for the city, **Lutetia** or Lucotetia, is drawn from *luco*, a Celtic root word for "marshland". The local Quarisii or **Parisii** tribe built an oppidum or Iron Age fort on the eastern part of what is now the Ile de la Cité. The island was originally part of a miniature archipelago of five islets, with two further islets lying to its east (these became the modern Ile St-Louis; another, easternmost island was only joined to the Right Bank at boulevard Morland in 1843). The fort of the Parisii commanded a perfect site: defensible and astride the most practicable north–south crossing point of an eminently navigable river.

Roman Paris

When Julius Caesar's conquering armies arrived in 52 BC, they found a thriving and populous settlement – the Parisii had managed to send a contingent of some eight thousand men to stiffen the Gallic chieftain Vercingétorix's doomed resistance to the invaders. Romanized Lutetia prospered, thanks to its commanding position on the Seine trade route, the river's *nautes*, or boatmen – remembered in the carved pillar now in the Musée du Moyen Age (see p.123) – occupying an important position in civic society. And yet the town was fairly insignificant by **Roman** or even Gaulish standards, with a population no larger than the Parisii's original eight-thousand-strong war band; other Gallo-Roman cities, by contrast, had populations of twenty to thirty thousand. The Romans established their basilica on the Ile de la Cité, but the town lay almost

Third century BC	52 BC	Around 275
A tribe known as the Parisii begins to settle on the Ile de la Cité.	When Julius Caesar's conquering armies arrive they find a thriving settlement of some eight thousand people.	St-Denis brings Christianity to Paris. He is martyred for his beliefs at Montmartre.

entirely on the Left Bank, on the slopes of the Montagne Ste-Geneviève. Though no monuments of their presence remain today, except the baths by the Hôtel de Cluny and the amphitheatre in rue Monge, their street plan, still visible in the north–south axes of rue St-Martin and rue St-Jacques, determined the future growth of the city.

Roman rule in Gaul disintegrated under the impact of **Germanic invasions** around 275 AD, at about the same time St-Denis (see box, p.227) established **Christianity** in the Paris region. Roman Lutetia itself, however, or "Paris", as it was beginning to be called, held out for almost two hundred years. The Emperor Julian was headquartered in the city for three years from 358, during his campaign against the German and Frankish tribes – the latter so-called after the Latin word for "ferocious" – making Paris the de facto capital of the Western Empire. Julian found the climate agreeable, with mild winters and soft breezes carrying the warmth of the ocean, and noted that the water of the Seine was "very clear to the eye".

Franks and Capetians

The marauding bands of **Attila the Hun** were repulsed in 451, supposedly thanks to the prayerful intervention of Geneviève, who became the city's patron saint. (Popular legend has it that Attila had massacred eleven thousand virgins in Cologne, on his way to Paris, and that there weren't enough virgins in the city to make it worth his while.) In any case, the city finally fell to **Clovis the Frank** in 486, the leader of a group of Germanic tribes who traced their ancestors back to Merowech, the son of a legendary sea monster – hence the name of the **Merovingian** dynasty Clovis founded. (This sea-monster story has, if anything, more respectable historical roots than the conspiratorial theory that the Merovingians were the descendants of Jesus and Mary Magdalene.) It was the first but by no means the last time the city would fall to German troops.

Clovis's own conversion to Christianity hastened the Christianization of the whole country. In 511 Clovis's son Childebert commissioned the cathedral of St-Etienne, whose foundations can be seen in the Crypte Archéologique under the square in front of Notre-Dame. He also imported the relics of St Vincent to a shrine on the Left Bank. The site slowly grew to become the great monastery at St-Germain-des-Prés, while St-Denis, to the north of the city, became the burial site of the Merovingians from Dagobert I onwards, in the early seventh century.

The endlessly warring, fratricidally minded Merovingians were gradually supplanted by the hereditary Mayors of the Palace, the process finally confirmed by the coronation of Pépin III, "the Short", in St-Denis, in 754. Pépin's heir, Carolus Magnus or "**Charlemagne**", who gave his name to the new Carolingian dynasty, conquered half of Europe and sparked a mini-Renaissance in the early ninth century. Unfortunately for Paris, he chose to live far from the city. Paris's fortunes further plummeted after the break-up of Charlemagne's empire, being repeatedly sacked and pillaged by the **Vikings** from the mid-840s onwards. Finally, in the 880s, **Eudes**, the Comte de Paris, built strong fortifications on the Ile de la Cité, and the Vikings were definitively repulsed. Yet Paris lay largely in ruins, a provincial backwater without power, influence or even a significant population. Only the Right Bank, which lacked the wealthy monasteries of the main city, had escaped the Vikings' depredations. It was to emerge as the heart of a reborn city.

486	768	845–85
The city falls to Clovis the Frank. His dynasty, the feuding Merovingians, governs Paris for the next two hundred years or so.	Charlemagne is proclaimed king at St-Denis. Over the next forty years he conquers half of Europe – but spends little time in Paris.	Vikings repeatedly sack Paris.

The medieval heyday

In 987, Eudes' descendant Hugues Capet was crowned king, but the early rulers of the new **Capetian dynasty** rarely chose to live in Paris, despite the association of the monarchy with the city. Regrowth, therefore, was slow, and by 1100, the city's population was only around three thousand. One hundred years later, however, Paris had become the largest city in the Christian world (which it would remain until overtaken by London in the eighteenth century), as well as its intellectual and cultural hub. By the **1320s**, the city's population had swollen again, to around a quarter of a million. This unparalleled success rested on the city's valuable river-borne trade and the associated expansion of the **merchant classes**, coupled with thriving **agriculture** in the wider Paris region. Vines and cereals grew to the south, while swathes of rich woodland lay to the east and west, and in the north, between the city and the hill of Montmartre. The economic boom was matched by the growth of the city's university, and protected by the novelty of a relatively strong – and largely Paris-based – monarchy, which gradually brought the surrounding regions under its overlordship. Between them, Louis VI, Louis VII and Philippe-Auguste ruled with confidence for almost all the twelfth century.

Walls and Watermen

To protect his burgeoning city, **Philippe-Auguste** (1180–1223) built the **Louvre fortress** whose excavated remains are now on display beneath the Louvre museum. He also constructed a vast **city wall**, which swung north and east to encompass the Marais, and south to enclose the Montagne Ste-Geneviève – a line roughly traced by the inner ring of modern Paris's 1er–6e arrondissements (though the abbey at St-Germain-des-Prés remained *extra muros*). European contemporaries saw the fortifications as a wonder of the world (even if by Rabelais' time "a cow's fart" would have brought down the walls on the Left Bank), a vital guarantee of the city's security and a convincing proof of the monarchy's long-term ambitions to construct an imperial capital. Famously appalled by the stench of the city's mud as a young man, Philippe-Auguste even began to pave some of the city's streets, though most remained filthy, hopelessly rutted and crowded with people and animals – Louis VI's heir had even been killed when de-horsed by a runaway pig in 1131.

LEFT AND RIGHT: A TALE OF TWO RIVERBANKS

During the medieval era, the city's commercial activity naturally centred on the place where goods came in to the city – a trade monopolized by the powerful Watermen's guild of Paris. The chief landing place was the place de Grève, a strip of marshy ground which lay where the Hôtel de Ville now stands, on the Right Bank. The Left Bank's intellectual associations were formed equally early, as students came to study at the two great monasteries of Ste-Geneviève and St-Germain-des-Prés. Europe's pre-eminent scholar, Peter Abélard – famously the lover of Héloïse and the victim of violent castration – taught in Paris in the early twelfth century, and in 1215 a papal licence allowed the official formation of what gradually became the renowned University of Paris, eventually to be known as the **Sorbonne**, after Robert de Sorbon, founder of a college for poor scholars in 1257. By 1300 there were around three thousand students on the Left Bank of the city, protected by ecclesiastical rather than city law. At this time, the Latin used both inside and outside the schools gave the student district its name of the "Latin Quarter".

987	1200s	1330s to 1430s
Hugues Capet, one of the counts of Paris, is elected king of Francia and makes Paris his capital.	Paris experiences an economic boom, its university becomes the centre of European learning and King Philippe-Auguste constructs a vast city wall.	The French and English nobility struggle for power in the Hundred Years' War. One year in four is a plague year and Paris's population falls by half.

The administration of the city remained in the hands of the monarchy until 1260, when **Louis IX** (St Louis) ceded a measure of responsibility to the *échevins* or leaders of the Paris Watermen's guild (see box, p.363). The city's government, when it has been allowed one, has been conducted ever since from the place de Grève/place de l'Hôtel de Ville, and the guild's motto, *fluctuat nec mergitur* (it is tossed but does not sink), was later adopted by the city itself.

A city adrift

From the **mid-fourteenth** to **mid-fifteenth centuries**, Paris shared the same unhappy fate as the rest of France, embroiled in the long and destructive **Hundred Years' War**, which pitted the French and English nobilities against each other in a power struggle whose results were misery for the French peasant classes, and penury for Paris. A break in the Capetian line led to the accession of Philippe VI, the first of the **Valois dynasty**, but the legitimacy of his claim on the throne was contested by Edward III of England. Harried by war, the Valois monarchs spent much of their troubled reigns outside their capital, whose loyalty was often questionable. Infuriated by the lack of political representation for merchant classes, the city mayor, or Prévôt des Marchands, **Etienne Marcel**, even let the enemy into Paris in 1357.

Charles V, who ruled from 1364, tried to emulate Philippe-Auguste by constructing a new Louvre and a new city wall that increased Paris's area by more than half again (roughly incorporating what are now the modern 9ᵉ–11ᵉ arrondissements, on the Right Bank), but the population within his walls was plummeting due to disease and a harsh climate in Europe generally, as well as warfare and political instability. The **Black Death**, which arrived in the summer of 1348, killed some eight hundred Parisians a day, and over the next 140 years one year in four was a plague year. In the fourteenth century, the state and populace alike easily found scapegoats for such ills. Leading knights of the wealthy Templar order were burnt at the stake on the tip of the Ile de la Cité in 1314, and they were followed to their deaths by hundreds of **Jews** falsely accused of poisoning the city's wells. France's Jews were definitively expelled from the kingdom in 1394. Paris had lost two of its most economically productive minorities. Harvests repeatedly failed – icebergs even floated on the Seine in 1407 – and politically, things were no better. Taxes were ruinous, trade almost impossible and government insecure.

In 1422 the Duke of Bedford based his overlordship of northern France in Paris. **Joan of Arc** made an unsuccessful attempt to drive the English out in 1429, but was wounded in the process at the Porte St-Honoré, and the following year the English king, Henry VI, had the cheek to have himself crowned king of France in Notre-Dame. Meanwhile, the Valois kings fled the city altogether for a life of pleasure-seeking irrelevance in the gentle Loire Valley, a few days' ride to the southwest.

Renaissance

During the hundred years leading up to the mid-fifteenth century, Paris's population more than halved. It was only when the English were expelled – from Paris in 1437 and from France in 1453 – that the economy had the chance to recover from decades

1429

Joan of Arc attempts to drive the English out of Paris. It is not until 1437 that Charles VII regains control of his capital.

1528

François I transfers the royal court from the Loire to his new palace at the Louvre.

of devastation. Even so, it was many more years before the Valois monarchs felt able to quit their châteaux and hunting grounds in the Loire and return to the city. Finally, in 1528, **François I** decided to bring back the royal court to Paris, aiming, like Philippe-Auguste before him, to establish a new Rome. Work began on reconstructing the Louvre and building the Tuileries palace for **Catherine de Médicis**, and on transforming Fontainebleau and other country residences into sumptuous Renaissance palaces. An economic boom brought peasants in from the countryside in their thousands, and the city's population surpassed its medieval peak by the 1560s. Centralized planning coughed into life to cope with the influx; royal edicts banned overhanging eaves on houses, and a number of gates were removed from Charles V's walls to improve street congestion. But Paris remained, as Henri II put it, a city of "mire, muck and filth".

The wars of religion

In the second half of the century, war interrupted the early efforts at civic improvement – this time **civil war** between Catholics and Protestants. Paris, which swung fanatically behind the Catholic cause – calls for the establishment of a new Jerusalem quickly replaced the old Roman ideals – was the scene of one of the worst atrocities ever committed against French Protestants. Some three thousand of them were gathered in Paris on August 18, 1572 for the wedding of Henri III's daughter, Marguerite, to Henri, the Protestant king of Navarre. On August 25, 1572, **St Bartholomew's Day**, the majority of these Protestants were massacred at the instigation of the noble "ultra-Catholic" Guise family. When, through this marriage, Henri of Navarre became heir to the French throne in 1584, the Guises drove his father-in-law, Henri III, out of Paris. Forced into alliance, the two Henris laid siege to the city in May 1590 – Henri III claiming to love the city more than he loved his own wife (which, given he was a notorious philanderer among both men and women, was almost certainly true). Parisians were quickly reduced – and it wasn't to be for the last time – to eating donkeys, dogs and rats. Five years later, after Henri III had been assassinated and some forty thousand Parisians had died of disease or starvation, Henri of Navarre entered the city as king **Henri IV**. "Paris is worth a Mass", he is reputed to have said, to justify renouncing his Protestantism in order to soothe Catholic sensibilities.

Henri's inheritance

The Paris that Henri IV inherited was not a very salubrious place. It was **overcrowded**: no domestic building had been permitted beyond the limits of Philippe-Auguste's twelfth-century walls because of the guilds' resentment of the unfair advantage enjoyed by craftsmen living outside the jurisdiction of the city's tax regulations. The swollen population had caused an **acute housing shortage** and a terrible strain on the rudimentary water supply and drainage system. It is said that the first workmen who went to clean out the city's cesspools in 1633 fell dead from the fumes. It took seven months to clean out 6420 cartloads of filth that had been accumulating for two centuries. The overflow ran into the Seine, whence Parisians drew their drinking water.

1572	**1607**	**1661–1715**
On St Bartholomew's Day, August 25, some three thousand Protestants gathered in Paris are massacred at the instigation of the ultra-Catholic Guise family.	The triumphant monarch Henri IV builds the Pont-Neuf and sets about creating a worthy capital.	Louis XIV transfers the court to Versailles, but this doesn't stop the city growing in size, wealth and prestige.

> ## BOULEVARDS AND AVENUES
>
> Aside from his grand palace at Versailles, just outside Paris (see p.231), Louis XIV's most significant architectural legacy was perhaps the demolition of Charles X's old fortifications to make way for the new **boulevards** – which took their name from the bulwarks, or giant earthen ramparts, that they replaced – and the creation of long, tree-lined **avenues** such as the Champs-Elysées, which was laid out in 1667 by the landscape designer Le Nôtre. Avenues and boulevards were to become the defining feature of Paris's unique cityscape.

Planning and expansion

As the **seventeenth century** began, Henri IV's government set to work in Paris, regulating street lines and facades, and laying out the splendidly harmonious place Royale (later renamed the place des Vosges) and place Dauphine. Most emblematic of all the new construction work, however, was the **Pont-Neuf**, the first of the Paris bridges not to be cluttered with medieval houses. It was a potent symbol of Paris's renewal and architectural daring. After Henri IV was assassinated in 1610 – while caught in his carriage in a seventeenth-century traffic jam on rue de la Ferronrie – his widow built the **Palais du Luxembourg**, the first step in the city's colonization of the western Left Bank – previously the province of abbeys and churches.

The tradition of grandiose public building initiated by Henri IV perfectly symbolized the bureaucratic, centralized power of the newly self-confident state. The process reached its apogee in the seventeenth century under **Louis XIV**, whose director of architecture promised to fill the city "with so many magnificent buildings that the whole world will look on in wonder". Under the unifying design principles of grace and **Classicism**, the places Vendôme and Victoire were built, along with the sublime Cour Carrée of the Louvre, and half a dozen Italianate Baroque domes.

Grandiose building projects were commissioned as often without royal patronage as with it. The aristocratic *hôtels*, or private mansions, of the **Marais** were largely erected during the seventeenth century, to be superseded early in the **eighteenth century** by the **Faubourg St-Germain** as the fashionable quarter of the rich and powerful. Despite the absence of the court, Paris only grew in size, wealth and prestige, until the writer Marivaux could claim, with some truth, in 1734 that "Paris is the world, and the rest of the earth nothing but its suburbs". By the 1770s and 1780s, conversational *salons*, Masonic lodges, coffee houses or "cafés" and newspapers had opened by the hundreds to serve the needs of the burgeoning **bourgeoisie**, while the Palais Royal became the hub of fashionably decadent Europe – a gambling den, brothel, mall and society venue combined. In 1671, however, Louis repaired with his entire court to a new and suitably vast palace at **Versailles**, declaring it was "the spot where I can most be myself". The monarchy would not return until Louis' grandson, Louis XVI, was brought back at pike-point in 1789.

The poor

Meanwhile, the centre of the city remained a densely packed and unsanitary warren of **medieval lanes and tenements**. And it was only in the years immediately preceding the 1789 Revolution that any attempt was made to clean it up – the buildings crowding the bridges were dismantled as late as 1786. Pavements were introduced for the first

1789	1793	1799
Long-standing tensions explode into revolution. Ordinary Parisians, the "sans-culottes", storm the Bastille prison on July 14.	The revolutionaries banish the monarchy and execute Louis XVI. A dictatorship is set up, headed by the ruthless Robespierre.	Army general Napoleon Bonaparte seizes control in a coup and, in 1804, crowns himself emperor in Notre-Dame.

time and attempts were made to improve the drainage. A further source of pestilential infection was removed with the emptying of the overcrowded cemeteries into the catacombs. One gravedigger alone claimed to have buried more than ninety thousand people in thirty years, stacked "like slices of bacon" in the charnel house of the Innocents, which had been receiving the dead of 22 parishes for eight hundred years.

In 1786 Paris received its penultimate ring of fortifications, the so-called **wall of the Fermiers Généraux**, which roughly followed the line of modern Paris's inner and outer ring of arrondissements. The wall had 57 *barrières* or toll gates (one of which survives in the middle of place Stalingrad), where a tax was levied on all goods entering the city. At its outer edge, beyond the customs tolls, new houses of entertainment sprang up, encouraging a long tradition of Parisians crossing the boundaries of the city proper in search of drink, dancing and other kinds of transgression. It was a tradition that would culminate – and largely die – with the early twentieth-century artistic boom-towns of Montmartre and Montparnasse.

The Revolution

The **Revolution of 1789** was provoked by a financial crisis. Louis XVI had poured money into costly wars and the only way to increase revenue was to tax the clergy and nobility. He couldn't easily impose his will despotically, so, for the first time since 1614, he recalled the **Estates General** – a kind of tax-raising parliament made up of representatives of the country's three "estates", or orders: the clergy (the First Estate), the nobility (the Second) and the rest (the Third). In May 1789 each of the three orders presented its grievances to the Crown; the bourgeois delegates representing the Third Estate were particularly resentful and outspoken. Responding to rising tension, Louis XVI began posting troops around Versailles and Paris, as though preparing for a coup to reverse his actions.

Fear of attack by royal troops propelled the Parisian people from the sidelines into the heart of the action. The Parisian electoral assembly entered the Hôtel de Ville, declared itself the municipal government or **Commune**, and set up a bourgeois militia, later to become known as the National Guard. It was supposed to keep order in an agitated city, but actually joined in when a band of ordinary Parisians stormed the **Bastille** prison on July 14. The Parisian working classes, known as the **sans-culottes**, literally "the people without breeches", now became major players in the unfolding drama. As the king gathered troops at Versailles, the deputies of the Third Estate proclaimed themselves the **National Assembly** and threatened to unleash a popular explosion in Paris. The king was forced to recognize the new parliament which, in August 1789, passed the **Declaration of the Rights of Man**, sweeping away the feudal privileges of the old order. Rumours were rife of counter-revolutionary intrigues at the court in **Versailles** and, in October, a group of Parisians marched on Versailles and forced the king to return to Paris with them; they installed him in the Tuileries, where he was basically kept prisoner. In 1791 he attempted to flee abroad, but was stopped at Varennes and humiliatingly brought back to Paris.

As France was drawn into a succession of wars with neighbouring states, radical clamours for the overthrow of the king grew. The National Assembly was divided, but in August 1792 the *sans-culottes* rose up again, imprisoned the king and set up an

1820s	**1830**	**1848**
Paris acquires gas lighting and its first omnibus.	After three days of fighting, known as les trois glorieuses, Louis-Philippe is elected constitutional monarch.	In June, revolution erupts once again. Louis Napoléon Bonaparte, Napoleon's nephew, is elected president. In 1851 he declares himself Emperor Napoléon III.

insurrectionary **Commune** at the Hôtel de Ville. Under pressure from the Commune, the Assembly agreed to disband and order elections for a new **Convention** to draw up a new, republican, constitution. Later that month the Convention abolished the monarchy, set up a republic and convicted the king of treason. He was guillotined on place de la Révolution (now place de la Concorde) in January 1793. Europe was in uproar.

The Terror

The Convention, under the radical **Jacobin** faction, set up a war dictatorship. The Committee of Public Safety, headed by the chillingly ruthless Maximilien **Robespierre**, began the extermination of "enemies of the people", a period known as the *Grande Terreur*. Among the first casualties was **Marie Antoinette**, who went with calm dignity to the guillotine in October 1793. Over the next few months some further 2600 individuals were executed, including many of the more moderate revolutionaries such as **Georges Danton** whose last words as he went to his death were typical of his proud spirit: "Above all, don't forget to show my head to the people; it's well worth having a look at." **The Terror** finally ended in July 1794 when Robespierre, now widely perceived as a tyrant, was himself arrested by members of the Convention; he suffered the fate he had meted out to so many.

Power was thereafter put into the hands of a more temperate – but fatally weak – five-man **Directory**. The longed-for strong leader quickly emerged in the form of the celebrated General **Napoleon Bonaparte**, who had put down a Royalist insurrection in Paris in October 1795 with the minimum of fuss. In November 1799 he overthrew the Directory in a **coup d'état**. He appointed himself first consul for life in 1802 and **emperor** in 1804.

Napoleon

Napoleon is best known for his incessant **warmongering**, but he also upheld the fundamental reforms of the Revolution. His rights-based Code Civil, or Code Napoléon, long outlasted his empire and has been a major influence on legal systems in many other countries. He established the system of education which still endures today, and created an efficient **bureaucracy** that put Paris in still firmer control of the rest of the country. He wanted to make Paris the "capital of capitals", but focused more on public works than monuments: he lined the Seine with 4km of stone *quais*, built three bridges and created canals and reservoirs, providing Paris with its modern water supply. He also built the arcs de Triomphe and Carrousel, extended the Louvre, and drew up plans for a temple to the Grande Armée – which later became the Eglise de la Madeleine. He laid out the long and straight rue de Rivoli and rue de la Paix and devised new street-numbering (still in place) – odd on one side, even on the other; where streets ran parallel to the Seine, the numbering followed the flow of the river; in other streets, numbering started at the end nearest the river.

By 1809 Napoleon's conquered territory stretched from southern Italy to the Baltic, an empire much greater than that achieved by Louis XIV or even Charlemagne, but the **invasion of Russia** in 1812 was a colossal disaster. Out of four hundred thousand men (half of whom were conscripts from Napoleon's empire), barely twenty thousand made it back home. In March 1814 an army of Russians, Prussians and Austrians marched

1850s and 1860	**1863**	**1870**
Baron Haussmann literally bulldozes the city into the modern age, creating long, straight boulevards and squares. The poor are driven out to the suburbs.	At the Salon des Refusés, Manet's proto-Impressionist painting *Le déjeuner sur l'herbe* scandalizes all of Paris.	Hundreds die of starvation as the city is besieged by the Prussians.

into Paris – the first time foreign troops had invaded the city since the English in 1420. Napoleon was forced to abdicate and **Louis XVIII**, brother of the decapitated Louis XVI, was installed as king. In a last desperate attempt to regain power, Napoleon escaped from exile on the Italian island of Elba and reorganized his armies, only to meet final defeat at **Waterloo** on June 18, 1815. Louis XVIII was restored to power.

Restoration and barricades

For the rest of the **nineteenth century** after Napoleon's demise, France was occupied fighting out the contradictions and unfinished business left behind by the Revolution of 1789. Aside from the actual conflicts on the streets of the capital, there was a tussle between the class that had risen to wealth and power as a direct result of the destruction of the monarchy and the survivors of the old order, who sought to make a comeback in the 1820s under the **restored monarchy** of Louis XVIII and Charles X. This conflict was finally resolved in favour of the new bourgeoisie. When Charles X refused to accept the result of the 1830 National Assembly elections, **Adolphe Thiers** – who was to become the veteran conservative politician of the nineteenth century – led the opposition in revolt. Barricades were erected in Paris and there followed three days of bitter street fighting, known as **les trois glorieuses**, in which 1800 people were killed (they are commemorated by the column on place de la Bastille). The outcome of this **July Revolution** was parliament's election of **Louis-Philippe** in August 1830 as constitutional monarch, or *le roi bourgeois*, and the introduction of a few liberalizing reforms, most either cosmetic or serving merely to consolidate the power of the wealthiest stratum of the population.

As the demands of the disenfranchised poor continued to go unheeded, so their radicalism increased, exacerbated by **deteriorating living and working conditions** in the large towns, especially Paris, as the **Industrial Revolution** got under way. There were, for example, twenty thousand deaths from cholera in Paris in 1832, and 65 percent of the population in 1848 were too poor to be liable for tax. Eruptions of discontent invariably occurred in the capital, with insurrections in 1832 and 1834. When Thiers ringed Paris and its suburbs with a defensive wall (thus defining the limits of the modern city), his efforts soon appeared misdirected. In 1848, the lid blew off the pot. Barricades went up in February, and the **Second Republic** was quickly proclaimed. It looked for a time as if working-class demands might be at least partly met, but in the face of agitation in the streets, the more conservative Republicans lost their nerve, and the nation showed its feelings by returning a spanking reactionary majority in the April elections.

Revolution appeared the only alternative for Paris's radical poor. On June 23, 1848, working-class Paris – Poissonnière, Temple, St-Antoine, the Marais, Quartier Latin, Montmartre – rose in revolt. In what became known as the **1848 Revolution**, men, women and children fought side by side against fifty thousand troops. In three days of fighting, nine hundred soldiers were killed. No-one knows how many of the *insurgés* – the insurgents – died. Fifteen thousand people were arrested and four thousand sentenced to prison terms. **Louis Napoléon Bonaparte**, the nephew of Napoleon I, was elected president in November 1848, but within three years he brought the tottering republic to an end by announcing a coup d'état. Twelve months later, he had himself crowned Emperor **Napoléon III**.

1871

Paris surrenders in March, but the Prussians withdraw after just three days. In the aftermath, workers rise up and proclaim the Paris Commune. It is speedily and bloodily suppressed by French troops.

1889

The all-new Eiffel Tower steals the show at the Exposition Universelle, or "Great Exhibition".

Baron Haussmann

The nearly twenty years of the **Second Empire** brought rapid **economic growth** alongside virulent repression designed to hold the potentially revolutionary underclasses in check. It also brought **Baron Haussmann**, who undertook a total **transformation of the city**. In love with the straight line and grand vista, he drove 135km of broad new streets through the cramped quarters of the medieval city, linking the interior and exterior boulevards, and creating long, straight north–south and east–west cross-routes.

In 1859, all the land up to Thiers' wall of 1840 was incorporated into the city of Paris. A contemporary journalist railed "they have sewn rags onto the dress of a queen", but it was a brave and possibly brilliant decision – and a move that subsequent governments have consistently failed to emulate, leaving Paris's future suburbs to swell energetically but chaotically, then wallow in unregulated and unadorned semi-squalor. Between 1860 and the outbreak of World War I, the population of Paris "beyond the walls", or the **banlieue** as it became known, tripled in size, becoming the home of 1.5 million almost-Parisians. (The city proper had been surpassed in population by London in the eighteenth century; after 1900 it was overtaken by New York too, with Berlin, Vienna and St Petersburg catching up fast.)

The dark side

Haussmann's demolitions were at least in part aimed at keeping workers and the poor in their place. Barracks were located at strategic points – like the place du Château-d'Eau, now République, controlling the turbulent eastern districts – and the broad boulevards were intended to facilitate cavalry manoeuvres and artillery fire, with angled intersections that would allow troops to outflank any barricades. In other ways, however, **the poor** within the city were largely left to fend for themselves. Some 350,000 Parisians were displaced. The prosperous classes moved into the new western arrondissements, abandoning the decaying older properties. These were divided and

---

HAUSSMANN'S HARMONIOUS CITY

In half a century, from 1853, much of Paris was rebuilt, transforming an overgrown and insanitary medieval capital into an **urban utopia**. Napoléon III's government provided the force, while banks and private speculators provided the cash. The poor, meanwhile, were either used for labour or cleared out to the suburban badlands.

The presiding genius was the emperor's chief of works, **Baron Haussmann**. In his brave new city, every apartment building was seven storeys high. Every facade was built in creamy limestone, often quarried from under the city itself, with **Neoclassical details** sculpted around the windows. Every second and fifth floor had its wrought-iron balcony and every lead roof sloped back from the street-front at precisely 45 degrees. It would all have been inhumanly regular if it hadn't been for the ground-floor shops, which have provided Paris's streets with a more varied face ever since.

The basic Haussmann design proved astonishingly resilient. In the Art Nouveau period, sinuous curves and contours crept across the faces of apartment buildings, and Art Deco and Modernism provided their own, stripped-down, facelifts, but still, underneath the new styles, many Parisian buildings followed the basic Haussmann pattern. The result is a city of rare and enduring harmony.

1895	1900	1914
Parisians are the first people anywhere in the world to see the jerky cinematic documentaries of the Lumière brothers.	The Métropolitain underground railway, or "métro", is unveiled.	War with Germany calls time on the *belle époque*. In September, the Kaiser's armies are just about held off by French troops shuttled from Paris to the front line, only 24km away.

subdivided into ever-smaller units as landlords sought to maximize their rents. Sanitation was nonexistent. Water standpipes were available only in the street. Migrant workers from the provinces, sucked into the city to supply the vast labour requirements, crammed into the old villages of Belleville and Ménilmontant. Many, too poor to buy furniture, lived in barely furnished digs or *demi-lits*, where several tenants shared the same bed on a shift basis. Cholera and TB were rife. Until 1870, refuse was thrown into the streets at night to be collected the following morning. When in 1884 the Prefect of the day required landlords to provide proper containers, they retorted by calling the containers by his name, Poubelle – and the name has stuck as the French word for "dustbin".

The Siege and the Commune

In September 1870, Napoléon III surrendered to Bismarck at the border town of Sedan, less than two months after France had declared war on the well-prepared and superior forces of the **Prussian** state. The humiliation was enough for a Republican government to be instantly proclaimed in Paris. The Prussians advanced and by September 19 were laying **siege** to the capital. Minister of the Interior Léon Gambetta was flown out by hot-air balloon to rally the provincial troops, but further balloon messengers ended up in Norway or the Atlantic. The few attempts at military sorties from Paris turned into yet more blundering failures. Meanwhile, the city's restaurants were forced to change menus to fried dog, roast rat or peculiar delicacies from the zoos, and death from disease or starvation became an ever more common fate.

The government's half-hearted defence of the city – more afraid of revolution within than of the Prussians – angered Parisians, who clamoured for the creation of a 1789-style Commune. The Prussians, meanwhile, were demanding a proper government to negotiate with. In January 1871, those in power agreed to hold elections for a new National Assembly with the authority to surrender officially to the Prussians. A large monarchist majority, with the conservative Adolphe Thiers at its head, was returned, and on March 1, Prussian troops marched down the Champs-Elysées and garrisoned the city for three days while the populace remained behind closed doors in silent protest. On March 18, amid growing resentment from all classes of Parisians, Thiers' attempt to take possession of the National Guard's artillery in Montmartre (see box, p.186) set the barrel alight. The **Commune** was proclaimed from the Hôtel de Ville and Paris was promptly subjected to a second siege by Thiers' government, which had fled to Versailles, followed by the remaining Parisian bourgeoisie.

The Commune lasted just 72 days, and implemented no lasting reforms. It succumbed to Thiers' army on May 28, 1871, after a week of street-by-street warfare – the so-called *semaine sanglante*, or "Bloody Week" – in which some 25,000 men, women and children were killed, including thousands in random revenge shootings by government troops.

The belle époque

The Commune left great landmarks such as the Tuileries palace and Hôtel de Ville as smoking ruins, but within six or seven years few signs of the fighting remained.

1920s	1940
In the aftermath of war, the decadent années folles (or "mad years") of the 1920s rescue Paris's international reputation for hedonism.	In May and June, the government flees Paris, and Nazi soldiers are soon marching down the Champs-Elysées. Four years of largely collaborative fascist rule ensue.

Visitors remarked admiringly on the teeming streets, the expensive shops and energetic nightlife. Charles Garnier's Opéra was opened in 1875. Aptly described as the "triumph of moulded pastry", it was a suitable image of the frivolity and materialism of what the British called the "naughty" Eighties and Nineties, and the French called the **belle époque**, or "Age of Beauty". In 1889 the **Eiffel Tower** stole the show at the great Exposition Universelle. For the 1900 repeat, the Métropolitain or "**métro**" was unveiled.

The years up to World War I were marked by the unstable but thoroughly conservative governments of the **Third Republic**. On the extreme right, fascism began to make its ugly appearance with Charles Maurras' proto-Brownshirt organization, the Camelots du Roi. Despite – or maybe in some way because of – the political tensions, Paris emerged as the supremely inspiring environment for artists and writers – the so-called bohemians – both French and foreign. It was a constellation of talents such as Western culture has rarely seen. **Impressionism**, **Fauvism** and **Cubism** were all born in Paris in this period, while French **poets** like Guillaume Apollinaire, Jules Laforgue, Max Jacob, Blaise Cendrars and André Breton were preparing the way for Surrealism, concrete poetry and Symbolism. **Cinema**, too, first saw the light in Paris, with the documentaries of the Lumière brothers and George Méliès' fantastical features both appearing in the mid-1890s.

War and Depression

As a city, Paris escaped **World War I** relatively lightly, with only a brief Zeppelin bombardment in 1916, and heavy shelling from the Germans' monstrous, long-range "Big Bertha" cannon mercifully restricted to the early part of 1918. The human cost was rather higher: one in ten Parisian conscripts failed to return. But Paris remained the world's art – and party – capital after the war, with an injection of foreign blood and a shift of venue from Montmartre to Montparnasse. Indeed, the **années folles** (or "mad years") of the 1920s were among Paris's most decadent and scintillating, consolidating a long-standing international reputation for hedonistic, often erotic, abandon that has sustained its tourism industry for the best part of a century. Meanwhile, work on the dismantling of Thiers' outmoded fortifications progressed with aching slowness from 1919 until 1932 – after which the cleared space languished as a wilderness of shantytowns, or *bidonvilles*, until the construction of the *boulevard périphérique* ring road in the 1960s.

As **Depression** deepened in the 1930s and Nazi power across the Rhine became more menacing, however, the mood changed. Politicized thuggery grew rife in Paris, and the Left united behind the banner of the Popular Front, winning the **1936 elections** with a handsome majority. Frightened by the apparently revolutionary situation, the major employers signed the Matignon Agreement with Socialist Prime Minister Léon Blum. It provided for wage increases, nationalization of the armaments industry, a forty-hour week, paid annual leave and collective bargaining on wages. These reforms were pushed through Parliament, but when Blum tried to introduce exchange controls to check the flight of capital, the Senate threw the proposal out and he resigned. The Left returned to opposition, where it remained, with the exception of coalition governments, until 1981.

1942	1944	1961
Parisian Jews are rounded up – by other Frenchmen – and shipped off to Auschwitz.	Liberation arrives on August 25, with General de Gaulle motoring up the Champs-Elysées to the roar of a vast crowd.	As France's brutal repression of its Algerian colony reaches its peak, at least two hundred Algerians are murdered by police during a civil rights demonstration.

Fascism and Resistance

The outbreak of war was followed with stunning swiftness by the **Fall of France**. After sweeping across the low countries, the German army broke across the Somme in early June. The French government fled south to Bordeaux, declaring Paris an "open city" in an attempt to save it from a destructive siege. By June 14, Nazi troops were parading down the Champs-Elysées. During the **occupation** of Paris in **World War II**, the Germans found some sections of Parisian society, as well as the minions of the Vichy government, only too happy to hobnob with them. For four years the city suffered fascist rule with curfews, German garrisons and a Gestapo HQ. Parisian Jews were forced to wear the Star of David and in 1942 were rounded up – by other Frenchmen – and shipped off to Auschwitz.

The **Resistance** was very active in the city, gathering people of all political persuasions into its ranks, but with Communists and Socialists, especially of East European Jewish origin, well to the fore. The job of torturing them when they fell into Nazi hands – often as a result of betrayals – was left to their fellow citizens in the fascist militia. Those who were condemned to death – rather than the concentration camps – were shot against the wall below the old fort of Mont Valérien above St-Cloud.

As Allied forces drew near to the city in 1944, the FFI (armed Resistance units) called their troops onto the streets. Alarmed at the prospect of the Left seizing power in his absence, the free French leader, **Général de Gaulle**, urged the Allies to let him press on towards the capital. To their credit, the Paris police also joined in the uprising, holding their Ile de la Cité HQ for three days against German attacks. On August 23, Hitler famously gave orders that Paris should be physically destroyed, but the city's commander, Von Cholitz, delayed just long enough. **Liberation** arrived on August 25 in the shape of General Leclerc's tanks, motoring up the Champs-Elysées to the roar of a vast crowd.

Revolts and demonstrations

Postwar Paris has remained no stranger to political battles in its streets. Violent demonstrations accompanied the Communist withdrawal from the coalition government in 1947. In the Fifties, the Left took to the streets again in protest against the colonial wars in Indochina and Algeria. And, in 1961, in one of the most shameful episodes in modern French history, some two hundred Algerians were killed by the police during a civil rights demonstration – a "**secret massacre**", which remained covered by a veil of total official silence until the 1990s.

In the extraordinary month of **May 1968**, a radical, libertarian, leftist movement gathered momentum in the Paris universities. Students began by occupying university buildings in protest against old-fashioned and hierarchical university structures (see box, p.126), but the extreme reaction of the police and government helped the movement to spread until it represented a mass revolt against institutional stagnation that ended up with the occupation of hundreds of factories across the country and a general strike by nine million workers.

Yet this was no revolution. The vicious battles with the paramilitary CRS (Compagnies Républicaines de Sécurité) police on the streets of Paris shook large sectors of the population – France's silent majority – to the core. Right-wing and

1968	1969	1973
In May, left-wing students occupying university buildings are supported by millions of striking and marching workers.	President de Gaulle loses a referendum, and retires, wounded, to his country house.	Paris's first skyscraper, the Tour Montparnasse, tops out at 56 hideous storeys. The périphérique ring road is completed in April.

"nationalist" demonstrations – orchestrated by de Gaulle – left public opinion craving stability and peace, and a great many workers were satisfied with a new system for wage agreements. Elections called in June returned the Right to power, the occupied buildings emptied and the barricades in the Latin Quarter came down. For those who thought they were experiencing The Revolution, the defeat was catastrophic.

But French institutions and French society had changed – de Gaulle didn't survive a referendum in 1969. His successor, **Georges Pompidou**, only survived long enough to begin the construction of the giant Les Halles development, and the expressways along the *quais* of the Seine. In 1974, he was succeeded by the conservative **Valéry Giscard d'Estaing**, who appointed one Jacques Chirac as his prime minister. In 1976, Chirac resigned, but made a speedy recovery as Mayor of Paris less than a year later.

Corruption and cohabitation

When **François Mitterrand** became president in 1981, hopes and expectations were initially high. By 1984, however, the flight of capital, inflation and budget deficits had forced a complete volte-face, and the Right won parliamentary elections in 1986, with **Chirac** beginning his second term as prime minister, while also continuing as Paris's mayor (he occupied the latter office continuously from 1977 to 1995). This was France's first period of "cohabitation": the head of state and head of government belonging to opposite sides of the political fence. Paris, meanwhile, pursued its own course, with the town halls of all twenty of the city's arrondissements remaining under right-wing control through much of the 1980s. It was a period of widespread corruption, but it didn't stop the city's mayor, **Jacques Chirac**, winning the election as **president** and taking office in May 1995.

That summer, **bombs** thought to have been planted by an extremist Algerian Islamic group exploded across Paris. There were further bomb threats throughout the autumn. The tense atmosphere was compounded by widespread discontent and a wave of massive strikes protesting against Prime Minister Alain Juppé's proposed sweeping **economic liberalization**, seen by many as a threat to the founding values of the French republic. Chirac and his successors would face similar protests again and again, ultimately frustrating every attempt to alter the course of the French economy.

Cataclysms, demonstrations and heat waves

When France won the football **World Cup** in July 1998, change seemed to be in the air. The victory at the new Stade de France in the ethnically mixed Paris suburb of St-Denis, with a multi-ethnic team, prompted a wave of popular patriotism. For once, support for "les bleus" seemed to override all other colour distinctions, and some even thought that Parisians might start being interested in football. Both notions, however, would soon be proved ephemeral.

After the smooth **introduction of the euro** on January 1, 2002, came the shocking success of the far-Right candidate **Jean-Marie Le Pen** in the first round of the presidential election of spring 2002. On May 1, some 800,000 people packed the boulevards of Paris in the biggest **demonstration** the capital had seen since the student protests of 1968. Two weeks later, in the run-off, Chirac duly triumphed, winning 90 percent of the vote in Paris.

1998

2001

In July, a multi-racial French team wins the football World Cup at the new Stade de France, in the suburb of St-Denis.

Unassuming Socialist candidate, Bertrand Delanoë, is elected Mayor of Paris in March.

THE MODERN FACE OF PARIS

Paris changed little up to the late 1960s – all the action took place out in the suburbs. Even the 1970s brown-glass skyscraper of the **Tour Montparnasse** only led to a law limiting buildings taller than 37m in the city centre. And the demolition of the ironwork marketplace of Les Halles resulted in a conservationist outcry – though it didn't prevent the construction of its replacement, the ugly curved-glass pit of the **Forum des Halles** shopping centre, itself recently revamped and covered over with a less-than-inspiring giant glass roof, the so-called Canopée (see p.91). The only postmodern success was the **Centre Pompidou**. Critics called it a giant petrol refinery, but Parisians were soon happily referring to it as Beaubourg – or "Prettytown" – after the name of the ancient district in which it was built.

Owing largely to the **Grands Projets** of Socialist president François Mitterrand, Paris changed more in the 1980s and 1990s than it had since the era of Gustave Eiffel, with I.M. Pei's glass **Pyramide** in the Louvre's courtyard, Jean Nouvel's **Institut du Monde Arabe** and the **Cité de la Musique** at La Villette all becoming well-loved classics. However, there were also some less successful projects: the **Bibliothèque Nationale** was deemed woefully inadequate for its purpose, while the **Grande Arche de la Défense** feels overweening rather than triumphal. As for the unhappy **Opéra Bastille**, it has been compared to a hospital, an elephant and even, according to Parisophile Edmund White, "a cow palace in Fort Worth".

The twenty-first century has seen the construction of fewer landmark buildings. The two most recent structures couldn't be more different. Jean Nouvel's huge, aluminium-clad **Philharmonie** concert hall in La Villette (see p.203), which feels like a leftover from the Grands Projets era, is brooding, dark and angular, while Frank Gehry's **Fondation Louis Vuitton** in the 16ᵉ (see p.219) is a light, airy, deconstructed glass building that looks as though it might float off (or possibly collapse) at any moment.

Paris's **skyline** could undergo a much more radical shift in future: in 2011 the city council changed the law so that buildings of up to 180m can be built, and the go-ahead was given for the construction of a number of skyscrapers, albeit on the city's periphery. At the time of writing, the **Tour Triangle** was taking (triangular) shape at the Porte de Versailles in the 15ᵉ, while in the 17ᵉ, at the Porte de Clichy, a 160m tower of steel and glass boxes, designed by Renzo Piano (who built the Pompidou Centre), will become the new home of the Palais de Justice in 2018. In the 13ᵉ, construction has started on the Tours DUO, a pair of tower blocks, 180m and 120m tall, which will house shops, offices and co-working spaces. Even **high-rise flats** have been given the go-ahead; two tower blocks, 50m tall, were erected in 2015, also in the 13ᵉ. Given that the mayor, Anne Hidalgo, is against a "heritage vision" of Paris and all in favour of a "living, dynamic" city, it seems likely that many more such structures will see the light of day.

Building high is not the only concern of the city authorities; there are also plans to go underground and give new life to some of the métro's "**ghost stations**"; in all, there are sixteen métro stops which have been disused for seventy years or so. As part of a new initiative called "**Reinvent Paris**", architects are being invited to take part in an international competition to put forward ideas for how three of these stations might be developed for cultural or economic use, with the results to be announced in late 2018. In the past, there have been proposals to turn abandoned stations into swimming pools, nightclubs and bars.

With such a mandate, Chirac and his reformed and renamed UMP party decided to take on the public sector: first pensions and unemployment benefits, then worker-friendly hiring and firing rights, and finally the world-leading health service. Again, hundreds of thousands came out onto the streets in protest. More trouble came when Chirac declared

2002

Parisians find themselves paying a little extra for their coffees and baguettes with the introduction of the euro, on January 1.

2002

On April 21, far-Right candidate Jean-Marie Le Pen knocks Socialist Lionel Jospin into third place in the first round of presidential elections. Incumbent president Jacques Chirac wins the second round.

in March 2003 that he would veto any UN resolution that contained an ultimatum leading to **war in Iraq**. The cherished but often fragile Franco-American relationship collapsed, catastrophically, and American tourists seemed to vanish from the capital. That **summer** was as heated in reality as politically. Parisian temperatures in the first half of August regularly topped 40°C (104°F) – more than 10°C above the average maximum for the time of year – and **climate change** finally forced its way onto the mainstream agenda.

Delanoë and the greening of Paris

Climate change and green issues were major priorities for the new mayor of Paris, **Bertrand Delanoë**, who was elected in 2001. (Incidentally, the fact that this was the first time the Left had won control of the capital since the bloody uprising of the Paris Commune in 1871 was far more of a shock to most Parisians than the fact that he was openly gay.) Delanoë tackled traffic congestion and created **bus lanes, cycle lanes and pedestrianized areas** (including a 2km stretch of the Seine). He also introduced the tremendously popular hop-on, hop-off community bicycles, **Vélib'** ("free bike"), and **Autolib'**, electric rental cars; all-new **tramway lines** began threading through the suburbs and encircling the ring road. His other popular measures, **Paris Plage** ("Paris Beach"), in which large stretches of the riverbank roads are turned into a public beach each summer, and **Nuit Blanche** ("Sleepless Night"), a city-wide all-night party of live music and performance art in October, are now established events on the city's calendar.

"Sarko"

In 2004, a new political force emerged in the hyperenergetic if diminutive shape of **Nicolas Sarkozy** – a kind of Margaret Thatcher meets JFK, bent on giving France a dose of neoliberal or "Anglo-Saxon" capitalism. In 2005 and again in 2006 – when students once again occupied the Sorbonne – waves of passionate strikers flooded the city streets, but the more dramatic **civil unrest** began after two teenagers died fleeing what they thought was police pursuit in Clichy-sous-Bois, a run-down area in the Paris banlieue. Local **car-burnings** and confrontations with police quickly spread to other Parisian suburbs and then beyond. Night after night, for three weeks, youths across France torched cars, buses, schools, and police and power stations – anything associated with the state. As Interior Minister, "Sarko" demanded that the neighbourhoods were cleaned with power-hoses.

Such right-wing posturing seemed to pay off, and, on May 16, 2007, Nicolas Sarkozy became President. Then came the **global financial crisis** of 2008–09. Suddenly, the "Anglo-Saxon" form of market-led, laissez-faire capitalism seemed exactly what French socialists had always said it was: a debt-fuelled castle built on sand. In response, Sarkozy performed an astonishing political about-turn, pledging to wield the power of the state to ensure stability. Strong-state *dirigisme* was back. National reform, again, would have to wait.

The Republic under attack

Seduced by promises of budgetary rigour and social justice, and somewhat disenchanted with the brash bling of Sarkozy, in 2012 voters chose Socialist candidate **François Hollande** as their new president. Hollande's inept handling of the economy,

2002	2003
Mayor Bertrand Delanoë launches Paris's new image by turning 3km of riverbank expressway into a summer beach: "Paris Plage" is an immense success.	Following Chirac's spat with George W. Bush over Iraq, US tourists temporarily vanish from the capital. In the summer, temperatures soar above 40°C (100°F).

however, and rising unemployment levels saw his ratings tumble dramatically from 65 to 13 percent in a couple of years, making him the least popular president since the start of the Fifth Republic in 1958. The country seemed to be in the grip of a general malaise, from which it was brutally shaken in 2015 by two devastating terror attacks. The first occurred on January 7, when French-born jihadi gunmen shot dead seventeen people at the offices of the satirical magazine **Charlie Hebdo** and at a kosher supermarket. The victims included cartoonists Jean Cabut and Georges Wolinski, well-loved, household names, known for their cartoons satirizing religion, including Islam. The attack seemed to be an outright assault on cherished Republican values and freedom of speech, and provoked a huge outpouring of grief and protest; on January 11, up to two million people, including forty world leaders, took to the streets in a "**unity rally**" and marched through Paris, congregating at the place de la République. People expressed their solidarity with the victims with cries of *Je suis Charlie, je suis Ahmed* (a Muslim police officer shot dead as he lay wounded on the ground) and *Je suis juif*, and ordinary French citizens reaffirmed their identity and support for the Republican ideals of "Liberté, Egalité and Fraternité".

Later that year, huge crowds again turned out in shock and mourning after a second horrific wave of attacks. On November 15, Islamic State terrorists stormed the Bataclan concert hall, in the 11ᵉ, killing people indiscriminately and also targeting a number of bars and restaurants in the area, as well as the Stade de France. A total of 130 were left dead and many more injured. Despite a general mood of defiance among Parisians, these attacks inevitably took their toll on the city. A state of emergency was declared; the sight of soldiers on the streets became familiar, security was tightened at major tourist sights, and visitor numbers declined.

The city took another knock in June 2016 when, after the wettest spring in Paris since records began 150 years ago, the Seine burst its banks and river levels rose dangerously high, prompting the closure of several parks and museums, while the Louvre was forced to relocate priceless artworks from its basement. Although not as severe as the last great flood, in 1910, when thousands of Parisians had to be evacuated from their homes, it was a reminder of how vulnerable Paris is to rising water levels, especially as climate change makes extreme weather more likely in future.

Macron

The year 2017 saw the meteoric rise of a new force in French politics in the shape of relative newcomer Emmanuel Macron, an ex-investment banker and leader of the En Marche! "radical centrist" party, formed only a year previously. In a dramatic presidential election, neither the Socialiste nor the Républicain candidate made it through to the second round for the first time since the period after World War II, upstaged instead by Marine Le Pen of the extreme right Front National (FN) and Macron. Fifteen years earlier, in 2002, when Le Pen *père*, Jean-Marie, made it through to the second round, there had been widespread shock and massive demonstrations on the streets of Paris, but this time only a small number of marchers, mostly students and far-left radicals, came out onto the streets. It was a sign of how much more accepted the FN had become in mainstream politics. In 2002, the Left and Right had rallied round Chirac in order to block Jean-Marie Le Pen, but in 2017, there was no such

2005	2007
In late October, disaffected youths riot in the impoverished Paris suburb of Clichy-sous-Bois. Right-wing interior minister, Nicolas Sarkozy, declares a state of emergency.	As Nicolas Sarkozy becomes president, Mayor Delanoë continues his greening of Paris: bus and cycle lanes appear everywhere, as do the new Vélib' rental bikes. Smokers are banished from cafés and restaurants.

THE NEW GREATER PARIS: THE FUTURE METROPOLIS

While France has long lavished money on its capital, adorning the city centre with grand buildings and cultural institutions, the banlieue, or suburbs, have festered as they have grown, kept at arm's length from the centre by the administrative and physical barricade of the *périphérique* ring road. Currently, a large part of the suburban population, including many immigrants and their families, living in troubled *cités* (housing estates), is effectively excluded from the city centre. The high-paying, white-collar jobs of the shopping, banking and governmental districts just don't seem to be available to black youths from the "9–3" – as the depressed *département* of Seine St-Denis, officially numbered 93, is known.

In an attempt to break down these barriers, the government has created a new city authority, the **Métropole du Grand Paris (MGP)**, which came into effect in 2016–17. It includes the three administrative *départements* of the Petite Couronne ("Little Crown"), the suburban districts immediately encircling Paris, containing some four million people – twice as many as Paris proper. This plan to expand Paris beyond its current boundaries arose from an earlier initiative, the "Grand Paris", launched in 2009. Central to the plan and the creation of a greater Paris is the construction of a new high-speed suburban transport network, **Grand Paris Express**, with 200km of new lines and 72 new stations, linking key suburbs and airports. Billions of euros more will be spent on improving and extending existing métro lines.

Another key concern of the "Grand Paris" is housing. Rising house prices, together with desirable new towns to the south and west of the city, are sucking away Paris's lifeblood: its **population**. There are now 2.2 million people living "intra-muros", or in Paris proper, down from 2.8 million in the late 1950s. Retirees make up fifteen percent of the population, while twenty percent of flats in the historic centre are second homes. Parisians are regularly alarmed by horrifying statistics such as the fact that the city has lost roughly a quarter of its small food stores in the last decade, or that bakeries are nowhere to be found near the Champs-Elysées. (They may be comforted to learn, however, that a city with "only" 159 cheese shops is not yet facing a crisis.) Intent on preventing the "museumification" of Paris, the Mairie has bought up private apartment buildings in the historic centre, to be rented out as **social housing**, while the suburbs have been promised thousands of new and affordable flats and houses.

Whether these plans to erase the boundaries between the rich centre and its poorer suburbs will go far enough to create a more up-to-date **metropolis** on the lines of New York or London remains to be seen. What is clear is that, with climate change, social unrest and economic disturbances all lapping at the city's walls, Paris cannot remain an island forever.

united front, with many voters claiming they would abstain, unable to vote for either a "fascist or a banker". Even so, there was no real doubt about the outcome, and despite a high abstention rate, Macron won by a decisive 66 to Le Pen's 34 percent. Whether Macron, at 39, the youngest head of state since Napoleon, can fulfil his promise to introduce radical economic reforms remains to be seen, but he has certainly shaken up the political establishment and brought a new mood of hope and optimism to a country that has deep social divisions and fractures.

Madame la maire

Born to Spanish migrants and brought up on a housing estate outside Lyon, Socialist Anne Hidalgo was elected as Paris's first female mayor in 2015. *Madame la maire*, as Hidalgo insists on being called, much to the annoyance of French grammarians (the

2009

Paris contemplates its future with an exhibition of architectural visions for the green mega-city to come, dubbed "Le Grand Paris".

2012

Disenchanted with Sarkozy, French voters elect Socialist François Hollande as president, but rue their choice when Hollande fails to tackle the country's economic woes.

correct spelling is *le maire*), has continued her predecessor Bertrand Delanoë's policies of making Paris greener and has shown a steely determination to push through controversial policies, for example, the pedestrianization of a section of the Right Bank of the Seine (see p.90) and the closure of the Champs-Elysées to traffic every first Sunday of the month. Other plans to "reconquer the public space" for pedestrians and cyclists include many more cycle lanes (dubbed the "Plan Vélo"), the pedestrianization of large squares, such as the place de la Bastille, and a new east–west electric tram-bus, which has been dubbed the "Olympic tramway" as part of the city's bid to host the Olympic Games in 2024. If the city does win the bid (as looked likely at the time of writing), it could open up all kinds of exciting new prospects for visitors to the city, not least the possibility of swimming in the Seine.

2015

Paris is rocked by two major terror attacks: in January, jihadist militants kill seventeen people, and in November, Islamic State terrorists kill 130 people.

2017

Newcomer Emmanuel Macron of the centrist En Marche! movement comes from nowhere to become the youngest head of state since Napoleon.

Books

Countless books have been written about Paris. Here is just a selection of our favourites; those marked with a ★ symbol are particularly recommended. Most of these books are in print; any that are not should be easy to find on sites such as ⑩abebooks.co.uk.

HISTORY AND POLITICS

Anthony Beevor and Artemis Cooper *Paris After the Liberation: 1944–1949*. Gripping account of a crucial era in Parisian history, featuring de Gaulle, the Communists, the St-Germain scene and Dior's New Look. Five strange, intense years that set the tone for the next fifty.

Larry Collins and Dominique Lapierre *Is Paris Burning?* A classic history-as-thriller account of the race to save Paris from the destruction threatened by the retreating Nazis.

Alistair Horne *The Fall of Paris* and *Seven Ages of Paris*. Highly regarded historian Alistair Horne's *The Fall of Paris* is a very readable and humane account of the extraordinary period of the Prussian siege of Paris in 1870 and the ensuing struggles of the Commune. His *Seven Ages of Paris* is a compelling (if rather old-fashionedly fruity) account of significant episodes in the city's history.

★**Andrew Hussey** *Paris, The Secret History*. Delves into some fascinating and little-known aspects of Paris's history, including occultism, freemasonry and the seedy underside of the city. Hussey is concerned above all with ordinary Parisians, and their frequent clashes with authority. His more recent book, *The French Intifada: The Long War between France and Its Arabs*, is indispensable reading for an understanding of the background to the simmering tensions between France and its Arab population.

★**Colin Jones** *Paris: Biography of a City*. Jones focuses tightly on the actual life and growth of the city, from the Neolithic past to the future. Five hundred pages flow by easily, punctuated by thoughtful but accessible boxes on characters, streets and buildings whose lives were especially bound up with Paris's, from the Roman *arènes* to Zazie's métro. The best single book on the city's history.

Peter Lennon *Foreign Correspondent: Paris in the Sixties* (out of print). Irish journalist Peter Lennon went to Paris in the early 1960s unable to speak a word of French. He

became a close friend of Samuel Beckett and was a witness to the May 1968 events.

Lucy Moore *Liberty: The Lives and Times of Six Women in Revolutionary France*. Follows the fervid lives of six influential women through the Revolution, taking in everything from sexual scandal to revolutionary radicalism.

Orest A. Ranum *Paris in the Age of Absolutism*. A truly great work of city biography, revealing how and why seventeenth-century Paris rose from medieval obscurity to become the foremost city in Europe under Louis XIV.

★**Graham Robb** *Parisians*. This playful, joyfully readable but magnificently researched book tells the story of Paris from 1750 to today, through the eyes of the people who have played key roles in its turbulent life. Among other scenes, Robb shows us Marie Antoinette fleeing the Tuileries, Napoleon losing his virginity in the Palais Royal, Hitler's day-trip conqueror's tour, and the nasty build-up to the suburban riots of 2005.

Duc de Saint-Simon *Memoirs*. Written by an insider, this compelling memoir of life at Versailles under Louis XIV is packed with fascinating, gossipy anecdotes.

Anne Sebba *Les Parisiennes: Resistance, Collaboration, and the Women of Paris under Nazi Occupation*. This compelling, pacy account of life during the German occupation of Paris throws light on the terrible dilemmas faced by many ordinary women during this period, and looks at what made some, such as Coco Chanel, choose to collaborate and others, including Général de Gaulle's niece, Geneviève de Gaulle, resist.

Gillian Tindall *Footprints in Paris*. In this beautifully written and personal micro-history of the Quartier Latin, Tindall reconstructs the intimate lives of a handful of the quarter's residents, both celebrated and obscure, creating an evocative portrait of the city in the nineteenth and twentieth centuries.

CULTURE AND SOCIETY

★**Marc Augé** *In the Metro*. A philosophically minded anthropologist descends deep into métro culture and his own memories of life in Paris. A brief, brilliant essay in the spirit of Roland Barthes.

Walter Benjamin *The Arcades Project*. An all-encompassing portrait of Paris covering 1830–70, in which the *passages* are used as a lens through which to view

Parisian society. Never completed, Benjamin's magnum opus is a kaleidoscopic assemblage of essays, notes and quotations, gathered under such headings as "Baudelaire", "Prostitution", "Mirrors" and "Idleness".

James Campbell *Paris Interzone*. The feuds, passions and destructive lifestyles of Left Bank writers in 1946–60 are evoked here. The cast includes Samuel Beckett,

Boris Vian, Alexander Trocchi, Eugène Ionesco, Jean-Paul Sartre, Simone de Beauvoir, Vladimir Nabokov and Allen Ginsberg.

Rupert Christiansen *Paris Babylon: Grandeur, Decadence and Revolution 1869–1875*. Written with verve and dash, Christiansen's account of Paris at the time of the Siege and the Commune is exuberant and original. Worth reading for its evocative and insightfully chosen contemporary quotations alone – it begins with a delightful 1869 guidebook to "Paris Partout!"

Richard Cobb *Paris and Elsewhere*. Selected writings on postwar Paris by the acclaimed historian of the Revolution, with a personal and meditative tone.

Adam Gopnik *Paris to the Moon*. Intimate and acutely observed essays from the Paris correspondent of the *New Yorker* on society, politics, family life and shopping. Probably the most thoughtful and enjoyable book by an expat in Paris.

★**Julien Green** *Paris*. Born in Paris in 1900, Green became one of the city's defining writers. This bilingual edition presents twenty-odd short, meditative and highly personal essays on different aspects and *quartiers* of Paris, from Notre-Dame and the 16ᵉ to "stairways and steps" and the lost cries of the city's hawkers. Proust meets travel writing.

★**Eric Hazan** *The Invention of Paris*. Utterly compelling psycho-geographical account of the city, picking over its history *quartier* by *quartier* in a thousand *aperçus* and anecdotes. It's a weighty book, but a zesty, lefty bias nicely brings out the passions behind the rebellions and revolutions.

J.K. Huysmans *Parisian Sketches*. Published in 1880, Huysmans' fantastical, intense prose pieces on contemporary Paris drip with decadence, and cruelly acute observation. Rhapsodies on "Landscapes" and "Parisian characters" are matched by an exhilaratingly vivid account of the Folies Bergère. If Manet had been a novelist, he might have produced this.

Ian Littlewood *A Literary Companion to Paris* (out of print). A thorough account of which literary figures went where, and what they had to say about it.

★**Elaine Sciolino** *The Only Street in Paris: Life on the Rue des Martyrs*. Sciolino, a former Paris bureau chief for the *NY Times*, turns her gift for digging out people's life stories to the many and varied inhabitants of this ancient shopping street, from cheesemongers and boulangers to the last repairer of antique barometers in the city and the eighty-year-old who runs a drag club. It's a fascinating portrait of what the London *Sunday Times* magazine once described as the best shopping street in Paris, known for its villagey atmosphere and independent, traditional businesses in the same family for generations.

Gertrude Stein *The Autobiography of Alice B. Toklas*. The most accessible of Stein's works, written from the point of view of her long-time lover, is an amusing account of the artistic and literary scene of Paris in the 1910s and 1920s.

Tad Szulc *Chopin in Paris: The Life and Times of the Romantic Composer*. Not much on music, but explores Chopin's relationship with his friends – Balzac, Hugo, Liszt among them – and his lover, George Sand, and their shared life in Paris.

Judith Thurman *Colette: Secrets of the Flesh*. An intelligent and entertaining biography of Colette (1873–1954), highly successful novelist, vaudeville artist, libertine and flamboyant *bon viveur*.

Edmund White *The Flâneur*. An American expat novelist muses over Parisian themes and places as diverse as the Moreau museum, gay cruising and the history of immigration, as well as the art of being a good *flâneur* – a thoughtful urban wanderer.

William Wiser *The Twilight Years: Paris in the 1930s*. Breathless account of the crazy decade before the war, all jazz nights, scandals, and the social lives of expat poets and painters.

ART AND ARCHITECTURE

André Chastel *French Art*. The great French art historian tries to define what is distinctively French about French art in this insightful and superbly illustrated three-volume work.

Ross King *The Judgement of Paris: The Revolutionary Decade That Gave the World Impressionism*. High-octane account of the fierce battles in the 1860s and 1870s between the "finishers", the Classical painters of the academic Salons, and the upstart "sketchers" who tried to supplant them with their impressionistic canvases. Focuses

on the culture and political atmosphere of the times as much as the art.

Sue Roe *In Montmartre*. A vivid, intimate portrait of the intertwined lives and rivalries of the young Picasso, Matisse, Derain, Vlaminck and Modigliani in the seedy Montmartre of 1900–10.

Anthony Sutcliffe *Paris – An Architectural History*. Excellent overview of Paris's changing cityscape, as dictated by fashion, social structure and political power.

CHILDREN'S BOOKS

Miroslav Sasek *This is Paris*. A kind of illustrated child's travel guide, with enticing facts about the city and beautiful, quirky watercolours and drawings. First

published in 1959, but still a brilliant companion (or preparation) for a trip with children.

FICTION

IN ENGLISH

Helen Constantine (ed) *Paris Tales*. Twenty-two (very) short stories and essays, each chosen for their evocation of a particular place in Paris. From Balzac in the Palais Royal and Colette in Montmartre cemetery, to Perec on the Champs-Elysées and Jacques Réda on the rue du Commerce. In a similar vein, Constantine's *Paris Metro Tales* is a literary tour of Paris by underground – literally – with a map provided to take you to the correct métro station and the next story's location.

Charles Dickens *A Tale of Two Cities*. Paris and London during the 1789 Revolution and before. The plot is pure, breathtaking Hollywood, but the streets and the social backdrop are very much for real.

Ernest Hemingway *A Moveable Feast*. Hemingway's memoirs of his life as a young man in Paris in the 1920s. Includes fascinating accounts of meetings with literary celebrities Ezra Pound, F. Scott Fitzgerald and Gertrude Stein, among others.

Henry Miller *Tropic of Cancer; Quiet Days in Clichy*. Semi-autobiographical, rage- and sex-fuelled roar through the 1930s Parisian demi-monde; or, "a gob of spit in the face of Art", as the narrator puts it.

George Orwell *Down and Out in Paris and London*. Documentary account of breadline living in the 1930s – Orwell at his best.

Jean Rhys *Quartet*. A beautiful and evocative story of a lonely young woman's existence on the fringes of 1920s Montparnasse society. In the same vein are the subsequent *After Leaving Mr Mackenzie* and *Good Morning, Midnight*, both exploring sexual politics and isolation in the atmospheric streets, shabby hotel rooms and smoky bars of interwar Paris, all in Rhys's spare, dream-like style.

FRENCH (IN TRANSLATION)

★**Honoré de Balzac** *The Père Goriot*. Biting exposé of cruelty and selfishness in the contrasting worlds of the fashionable faubourg St-Germain and a down-at-heel but genteel boarding-house in the Quartier Latin. Balzac's equally brilliant *Wild Ass's Skin* is a strange moralistic tale of an ambitious young man's fall from grace in early nineteenth-century Paris.

Muriel Barbery *The Elegance of the Hedgehog*. This whimsical, philosophically minded novel, set among the eccentric characters of a Parisian apartment block, sold over a million copies in France. Deftly exposes the pretensions and aspirations of the upper middle classes.

André Breton *Nadja*. First published in 1928, *Nadja* is widely considered the most important and influential novel to spring from the Surrealist movement. Largely autobiographical, it portrays the complex relationship between the narrator and a young woman in Paris.

Louis-Ferdinand Céline *Death on Credit*. Disturbing, semi-autobiographical novel recounting working-class Paris through the eyes of an adolescent at the beginning of the twentieth century. Much of it takes place in the passage Choiseul, and its claustrophobic atmosphere is vividly evoked.

Blaise Cendrars *To the End of the World*. An outrageous, bawdy tale of a randy septuagenarian Parisian actress, having an affair with a deserter from the Foreign Legion.

Colette *Chéri*. Considered Colette's finest novel, *Chéri* brilliantly evokes the world of a demi-monde Parisian courtesan who has a doomed love affair with a man at least half her age.

Didier Daeninckx *Murder in Memoriam*. A thriller involving two murders: one of a Frenchman during the massacre of the Algerians in Paris in 1961, the other of his son twenty years later. The investigation by an honest detective lays bare dirty tricks, corruption, racism and the cover-up of the massacre.

★**Gustave Flaubert** *Sentimental Education*. A lively, detailed 1869 reconstruction of the life, manners, characters and politics of Parisians in the 1840s, including the 1848 Revolution.

Victor Hugo *Les Misérables*. A long but eminently readable novel by the master. Set among the Parisian poor and low-life in the first half of the nineteenth century, it's probably the greatest treatment of Paris in fiction – unless that title goes to Hugo's haunting (and shorter) *Notre-Dame de Paris*, a novel better known in English as *The Hunchback of Notre-Dame*.

Claude Izner *Murder on the Eiffel Tower*. 1889: a young bookseller falls in love and investigates a series of curious murders. One of the best of a series of detective stories from the team of bookish sisters known as "Claude Izner".

François Maspero *Cat's Grin* (out of print). Moving and revealing, semi-autobiographical novel about a young teenager living in Paris during World War II, with an adored elder brother in the Resistance.

★**Guy de Maupassant** *Bel-Ami*. Maupassant's *chef-d'oeuvre* is a brilliant and utterly sensual account of corrupt Parisian high society during the *belle époque*. Traces the rake's progress of the fascinating journalist and seducer, Georges Duroy.

Karim Miské *Arab Jazz*. Set in the multi-cultural 19e arrondissement, this brilliant debut crime thriller from a French-Mauritian film-maker explores the theme of fundamentalism – Islamic, Jewish and Christian – with a light and humorous touch and a colourful cast of characters.

Daniel Pennac *Monsieur Malaussène*. The last in the "Belleville Quintet" of quasi-detective novels set in the working-class east of Paris is possibly the most disturbing, centred on a series of macabre killings. Witty, experimental and chaotic, somewhat in the mode of Thomas Pynchon.

Georges Perec *Life: A User's Manual*. An extraordinary literary jigsaw puzzle of life, past and present, human, animal and mineral, extracted from the residents of an imaginary apartment block in the 17^e arrondissement.

Jean-Paul Sartre *The Age of Reason*. The first in Sartre's *Roads to Freedom* trilogy is probably his most accessible work. A philosophy teacher in wartime Paris's Montparnasse struggles to find both the money for his girlfriend's abortion and the answers to his obsession with freedom.

Georges Simenon *Maigret at the Crossroads* – or any other of the Maigret crime thrillers. The Montmartre and seedy criminal locations are unbeatable. If you don't like crime fiction, go for *The Little Saint*, the story of a young boy growing up in the rue Mouffetard when it was a down-at-heel market street.

★ **Emile Zola** *Nana*. The rise and fall of a courtesan in the decadent times of the Second Empire. As the quintessential realist, Zola is *the* novelist for bringing the seedy, seething reality of nineteenth-century Paris alive. Paris is also the setting for Zola's *L'Assommoir*, *The Masterpiece*, *Money*, *Thérèse Raquin*, *The Debacle* and *The Ladies' Paradise*.

French

There's probably nowhere harder to speak or learn French than Paris. Like people from most capital cities, many Parisians speak a kind of hurried slang. Worse still, many speak fairly good English – which they may assume is better than your French. Generations of keen visitors have been offended by being replied to in English after they've carefully enunciated a well-honed question or menu order. Then there are the complex codes of politeness and formality – knowing when to add Madame/Monsieur is only the start of it. Despite this, the essentials are not difficult to master and can make all the difference. Even just saying "Bonjour Madame/Monsieur" and then gesticulating will usually get you a smile and helpful service, even if your efforts to speak French come to nothing. The *Rough Guide Phrasebook: French* and the *Rough Guide Audio Phrasebook and Dictionary: French* (ebook) give more detail.

Pronunciation

One easy rule to remember is that consonants at the end of words are usually silent. Pas plus tard (not later) is thus pronounced "pa-plu-tarr". But when the following word begins with a vowel, you run the two together: pas après (not after) becomes "pazapray".

Vowels are the hardest sounds to get right. Roughly:

a/à as in hat	**u** as in a pursed-lip, clipped version of toot
â as in father	
e as in get	
é between get and gate	More awkward are the combinations in/im, en/em, on/om, un/um at the end of words, or followed by consonants other than n or m. Again, roughly:
è like the ai in pair	
eu like the u in hurt	**in/im** like the "an" in anxious
i as in machine	**an/am, en/em** like "on" said with a nasal accent
o as in hot	**on/om** like "on" said by someone with a heavy cold
ô/au as in over	**un/um** like the "u" in understand
ou as in food	

Consonants are much as in English, except that ch is always sh, h is silent, th is the same as t, ll is sometimes pronounced like the y in "yes" when preceded by the letter "i" as in "fille" and "tilleul" and r is growled (or rolled).

WORDS AND PHRASES

THE TOP TWELVE

yes	oui	**hello**	bonjour
no	non	**goodbye**	au revoir
please	s'il vous plaît	**good morning/afternoon**	bonjour
thank you	merci	**good evening**	bonsoir
excuse me	pardon/excusez-moi	**OK/agreed**	d'accord
sorry	pardon, Madame/ Monsieur	**I (don't) understand**	Je (ne) comprends (pas)

KEY WORDS AND PHRASES

French nouns are divided into masculine and feminine. This causes difficulties with adjectives, whose endings have to change to suit the gender of the nouns they qualify. If in doubt, stick to the masculine form, which is the simplest – it's what we have done in the glossary below.

today	aujourd'hui
yesterday	hier
tomorrow	demain
in the morning	le matin
in the afternoon	l'après-midi
in the evening	le soir
now	maintenant
later	plus tard
at one o'clock	à une heure
at three o'clock	à trois heures
at ten-thirty	à dix heures et demi
at a quarter to two	à deux heures moins le quart
at a quarter past four	à quartre heures et quart
at midday/midnight	à midi/minuit
man	un homme
woman	une femme
here	ici
there	là
this one	ceci
that one	cela
open	ouvert
closed	fermé
big	grand
small	petit
more	plus
less	moins
a little	un peu
a lot	beaucoup
half	la moitié
cheap	bon marché/pas cher
expensive	cher
good	bon
bad	mauvais
hot	chaud
cold	froid
with	avec
without	sans

TALKING TO PEOPLE

When addressing people, you should always use Monsieur for a man, Madame for a woman and Mademoiselle for a girl – plain "bonjour" by itself is not enough. This isn't as formal as it seems, and it has its uses when you've forgotten someone's name or want to attract someone's attention. "Bonjour" can be used well into the afternoon, and people may start saying "bonsoir" surprisingly early in the evening, or as a way of saying goodbye.

How are you?	Comment allez-vous?/ Ça va?
Fine, thanks	Très bien, merci
I don't know	Je ne sais pas
I see!	Ah bon!
Do you speak English?	Vous parlez anglais?
How do you say... in French?	Comment dit-on... en français?
What's your name?	Comment vous appelez-vous?
My name is...	Je m'appelle...
I'm English/	Je suis anglais(e)/
Irish/	irlandais(e)/
Scottish/	écossais(e)/
Welsh/	gallois(e)/
American/	américain(e)/
Australian/	australien(ne)/
Canadian/	canadien(ne)/
a New Zealander	néo-zélandais(e)
Can you speak more slowly?	S'il vous plaît, parlez moins vite?
Let's go	Allons-y
See you tomorrow	A demain
See you soon	A bientôt
goodnight	bonne nuit

EMERGENCIES

Leave me alone	Laissez-moi tranquille
Please help me	Aidez-moi, s'il vous plait
Help!	Au secours!

QUESTIONS AND REQUESTS

The simplest way of asking a question is to start with "s'il vous plaît" (please), then name the thing you want in an interrogative tone of voice. For example:

Where is there a bakery?	S'il vous plaît, la boulangerie?
Which way is it to the Eiffel Tower?	S'il vous plaît, pour aller à la Tour Eiffel?
We'd like a room for two	S'il vous plaît, une chambre pour deux?
Can I have a kilo of oranges?	S'il vous plaît, un kilo d'oranges?
where?	où?
how?	comment?
how many?	combien?
how much is it?	c'est combien?
when?	quand?
why?	pourquoi?
at what time?	à quelle heure?
what is/which is?	quel est?

GETTING AROUND AND DIRECTIONS

metro/subway station	métro
Where is the nearest metro?	Où est le métro le plus proche?
bus	bus
bus (coach)	car
bus station	gare routière
bus stop	arrêt
car	voiture
train/taxi/ferry	train/taxi/ferry
boat	bateau
plane	avion
railway station	gare
platform	quai
What time does it leave /arrive?	Il part/arrive à quelle heure?
a ticket to…	un billet pour…
single ticket	aller simple
return ticket	aller retour
validate your ticket	compostez votre billet
valid for	valable pour
ticket office	vente de billets/billetterie
how many kilometres?	combien de kilomètres?
how many hours?	combien d'heures?
on foot	à pied
Where are you going?	Vous allez où?
I'm going to…	Je vais à…
I want to get off at…	Je voudrais descendre à…
the road to…	la route pour…
near	près/pas loin
far	loin
left	à gauche
right	à droite
straight on	tout droit
on the other side of	de l'autre côté de
on the corner of	à l'angle de
next to	à côté de
behind	derrière
in front of	devant
before	avant
after	après
under	sous
to cross	traverser
bridge	pont
to park the car	garer la voiture
car park	un parking
no parking	défense de stationner/ stationnement interdit
petrol station	poste d'essence

ACCOMMODATION

a room for one /two people	une chambre pour une personne/deux personnes
with a double bed	avec un grand lit
a room with a shower	une chambre avec douche
a room with a bath	une chambre avec baignoire
for one/two/three night(s)	pour une/deux/trois nuit(s)
Can I see it?	Je peux la voir?
a room in the courtyard	une chambre sur la cour
a room over the street	une chambre sur la rue
first floor	premier étage
second floor	deuxième étage
with a view	avec vue
key	clé
to iron	repasser
do laundry	faire la lessive
sheets	draps
blankets	couvertures
quiet	calme
noisy	bruyant
hot water	eau chaude
cold water	eau froide
Is breakfast included?	Est-ce que le petit déjeuner est compris?
I would like breakfast	Je voudrais prendre le petit déjeuner
I don't want breakfast	Je ne veux pas le petit déjeuner
youth hostel	auberge de jeunesse

MONTHS, DAYS AND DATES

January	janvier
February	février
March	mars
April	avril
May	mai
June	juin
July	juillet
August	août
September	septembre
October	octobre
November	novembre
December	décembre
Monday	lundi
Tuesday	mardi
Wednesday	mercredi
Thursday	jeudi
Friday	vendredi
Saturday	samedi
Sunday	dimanche
August 1	le premier août
March 2	le deux mars
July 14	le quatorze juillet
November 23, 2014	le vingt-trois novembre, deux mille quatorze

NUMBERS

1	un	19	dix-neuf
2	deux	20	vingt
3	trois	21	vingt-et-un
4	quatre	22	vingt-deux
5	cinq	30	trente
6	six	40	quarante
7	sept	50	cinquante
8	huit	60	soixante
9	neuf	70	soixante-dix
10	dix	75	soixante-quinze
11	onze	80	quatre-vingts
12	douze	90	quatre-vingt-dix
13	treize	95	quatre-vingt-quinze
14	quatorze	100	cent
15	quinze	101	cent un
16	seize	200	deux cents
17	dix-sept	1000	mille
18	dix-huit	2000	deux mille
		1,000,000	un million

FOOD AND DRINK TERMS

BASICS

déjeuner	lunch
dîner	dinner
menu	set menu
carte	menu
à la carte	individually priced dishes
entrées	starters
les plats	main courses
une carafe d'eau/de vin	a carafe of tap water/wine
eau minérale	mineral water
eau gazeuse	fizzy water
eau plate	still water
carte des vins	wine list
un quart/demi de rouge /blanc	a quarter/half-litre of red/ white house wine
un (verre de) rouge/blanc	a glass of red/white wine
Je voudrais réserver une table pour deux personnes, à vingt heures et demie	I'd like to reserve a table, for two at 8.30pm
Je prendrai le menu à trente euros	I'm having the €30 menu
Monsieur/Madame!	Waiter! (never say "garçon")
l'addition, s'il vous plaît	the bill, please
une pression	a glass of beer
un café	coffee (espresso)
un café americain	black coffee
un crème	white coffee
un café au lait	big bowl of milky breakfast coffee
un cappuccino	cappuccino
une noisette	an espresso with a dash of hot milk

COOKING TERMS

chauffé	heated
cuit	cooked
cru	raw
emballé	wrapped
à emporter	takeaway
fumé	smoked
salé	salted/savoury
sucré	sweet

ESSENTIALS

beurre	butter
bio	organic
bouteille	bottle
couteau	knife
cuillère	spoon
fourchette	fork
huile	oil
lait	milk
oeufs	eggs
pain	bread
poivre	pepper
sel	salt
sucre	sugar
verre	glass
vinaigre	vinegar

SNACKS

crêpe	pancake (sweet)
...au citron	...with lemon
...à la confiture	...with jam
...au miel	...with honey
...aux œufs	...with eggs
...au sucre	...with sugar
galette	buckwheat (savoury) pancake
un sandwich/une baguette	sandwich
...jambon	ham sandwich
...fromage	cheese sandwich
...mixte	ham and cheese sandwich
croque-monsieur	grilled cheese and ham sandwich
croque-madame	croque-monsieur with an egg on top
oeufs	eggs
...au plat	fried eggs
...à la coque	boiled eggs
...durs	hard-boiled eggs
...brouillés	scrambled eggs
omelette	omelette
...nature	plain omelette
...aux fines herbes	omelette with herbs
...au fromage	cheese omelette

SOUPS (SOUPES)

bisque	shellfish soup
bouillabaisse	Marseillais fish soup
bourride	thick fish soup
potage	thick vegetable soup
velouté	thick soup, usually with fish or poultry

STARTERS (ENTRÉES, OR HORS D'OEUVRES)

assiette de charcuterie	plate of cold meats
crudités	raw vegetables with dressings
hors d'œuvres variés	combination of the above

FISH (POISSON), SEAFOOD (FRUITS DE MER) AND SHELLFISH (CRUSTACES OR COQUILLAGES)

anchois	anchovies
anguilles	eels
bar	sea bass
barbue	brill
brème	bream
brochet	pike
cabillaud	cod
calmar	squid
carrelet	plaice
claire	type of oyster
colin	hake
coquilles St-Jacques	scallops
crabe	crab
crevettes grises	shrimps
crevettes roses	prawns
daurade	sea bream
flétan	halibut
friture	whitebait
gambas	king prawns
hareng	herring
homard	lobster
huîtres	oysters
langouste	spiny lobster
langoustines	saltwater crayfish (scampi)
limande	lemon sole
lotte de mer	monkfish
loup de mer	sea bass
louvine, loubine	similar to sea bass
maquereau	mackerel
merlan	whiting
morue	dried, salted cod
moules (marinière)	mussels (with shallots in white wine sauce)
raie	skate
rouget	red mullet
sandre	pike-perch
saumon	salmon
seiche	squid
sole	sole
thon	tuna
truite	trout
turbot	turbot

FISH: DISHES AND RELATED TERMS

aïoli	garlic mayonnaise served with salt cod and other fish
béarnaise	sauce made with egg yolks, white wine, shallots and vinegar
beignets	fritters
la douzaine	a dozen
frit	fried
fumet	fish stock
gigot de mer	large fish baked whole
hollandaise	butter & vinegar sauce
à la meunière	in a butter, lemon and parsley sauce
mousse/mousseline	mousse
quenelles	light dumplings

MEAT (VIANDE) AND POULTRY (VOLAILLE)

agneau (de pré-salé)	lamb (grazed on salt marshes)
andouille, andouillette	tripe sausage
bavette	beef flank steak
boeuf	beef
boudin blanc	sausage of white meats
boudin noir	black pudding
caille	quail
canard	duck
caneton	duckling
contrefilet	sirloin roast
coquelet	cockerel
dinde	turkey
entrecôte	rib steak
faux filet	sirloin steak
foie	liver
foie gras	fattened (duck/goose) liver
gigot (d'agneau)	leg (of lamb)
grillade	grilled meat
hachis	chopped meat or mince hamburger
langue	tongue
lapin, lapereau	rabbit, young rabbit
lard, lardons	bacon, diced bacon
lièvre	hare
merguez	spicy, red sausage
mouton	mutton
museau de veau	calf's muzzle
oie	goose
onglet	cut of beef
os	bone
pièce de boeuf	steak
porc	pork
poulet	chicken
poussin	baby chicken
ris	sweetbreads
rognons	kidneys
rognons blancs	testicles
sanglier	wild boar
tête de veau	calf's head (in jelly)
tournedos	thick slices of fillet
tripes	tripe
veau	veal
venaison	venison

MEAT AND POULTRY: DISHES AND RELATED TERMS

aile	wing
blanquette de veau	veal in cream and mushroom sauce
boeuf bourguignon	beef stew with red wine, onions and mushrooms
canard à l'orange	roast duck with orange and wine sauce
carré	best end of neck, chop or cutlet
cassoulet	casserole of beans and meat
choucroute garnie	sauerkraut served with sausages or cured ham
civet	game stew
confit	meat preserve
coq au vin	chicken with wine, onions and mushrooms, cooked till it falls off the bone
côte	chop, cutlet or rib
cou	neck
cuisse	thigh or leg
cuisses de grenouille	frog legs
daube, estouffade, hochepot, navarin and ragout	stews of different kinds
en croûte	in pastry
epaule	shoulder
escargots	snails
farci	stuffed
au feu de bois	cooked over a wood fire
au four	baked
garni	with vegetables
gésier	gizzard
grillé	grilled
magret de canard	duck breast
marmite	casserole
médaillon	round piece
mijoté	stewed
museau	muzzle
pavé	thick slice
rôti	roast
sauté	lightly cooked in butter
steak au poivre (vert/rouge)	steak in a black (green/red) peppercorn sauce
steak tartare	raw chopped beef, topped with a raw egg yolk

FOR STEAKS

bleu	almost raw
saignant	rare
à point	medium
bien cuit	well done
très bien cuit	very well cooked
brochette	kebab

GARNISHES AND SAUCES

beurre blanc	sauce of white wine and shallots, with butter

chasseur	white wine, mushrooms and shallots
diable	strong mustard seasoning
forestière	with bacon and mushroom
fricassée	rich, creamy sauce
mornay	cheese sauce
pays d'Auge	cream and cider
piquante	gherkins or capers, vinegar and shallots
Provençale	tomatoes, garlic, olive oil and herbs

VEGETABLES (LEGUMES), HERBS (HERBES) AND SPICES (EPICES)

ail	garlic
algue	seaweed
anis	aniseed
artichaut	artichoke
asperges	asparagus
avocat	avocado
basilic	basil
betterave	beetroot
carotte	carrot
céleri	celery
champignons, cèpes, chanterelles	mushrooms of various kinds
chou (rouge)	(red) cabbage
chou-fleur	cauliflower
ciboulette	chives
concombre	cucumber
cornichon	gherkin
echalotes	shallots
endive	chicory
epinards	spinach
estragon	tarragon
fenouil	fennel
flageolets	white beans
gingembre	ginger
haricots	beans
…verts	string/French beans
…rouges	kidney beans
…beurres	butter beans
laurier	bay leaf
lentilles	lentils
maïs	corn
menthe	mint
moutarde	mustard
oignon	onion
pâtes	pasta
persil	parsley
petits pois	peas
pignons	pine nuts
piment	pimento
poireau	leek

pois chiche	chickpeas
pois mange-tout	snow peas
poivron (vert, rouge)	sweet pepper (green, red)
pommes (de terre)	potatoes
primeurs	spring vegetables
radis	radishes
riz	rice
safran	saffron
salade verte	green salad
sarrasin	buckwheat
tomate	tomato
topinambour	Jerusalem artichoke
truffes	truffles

VEGETABLES: DISHES AND RELATED TERMS

beignet	fritter
farci	stuffed
forestière	with mushrooms
gratiné/au gratin /gratin de	browned with cheese or butter
jardinière	with mixed diced vegetables
à la parisienne	sautéed in butter (potatoes); with white wine sauce and shallots
parmentier	with potatoes
sauté	lightly fried in butter
à la vapeur	steamed

FRUITS (FRUITS) AND NUTS (NOIX)

abricot	apricot
amandes	almonds
ananas	pineapple
banane	banana
brugnon	nectarine
cacahouète	peanut
cassis	blackcurrants
cerises	cherries
citron	lemon
citron vert	lime
figues	figs
fraises (des bois)	strawberries (wild)
framboises	raspberries
fruit de la passion	passion fruit
groseilles	redcurrants and gooseberries
mangue	mango
marrons	chestnuts
melon	melon
myrtilles	bilberries
noisette	hazelnut
noix	nuts
orange	orange
pamplemousse	grapefruit

pêche (blanche)	(white) peach
pistache	pistachio
poire	pear
pomme	apple
prune	plum
pruneau	prune
raisins	grapes

FRUIT: RELATED TERMS

beignets	fritters
compote de…	stewed…
coulis	sauce
flambé	set aflame in alcohol
frappé	iced

DESSERTS (DESSERTS) AND PASTRIES (PÂTISSERIE)

bavarois	mousse or custard – the term refers to the mould
bombe	ice cream dessert, moulded
brioche	sweet, high-yeast breakfast roll
charlotte	custard and fruit in lining of almond fingers
coupe	serving of ice cream
crème Chantilly	vanilla-flavoured and sweetened whipped cream
crème fraîche	sour cream
crème pâtissière	thick, eggy pastry filling
crêpe	pancake

crêpe suzette	thin pancake with caramelized butter and sugar, orange juice and liqueur
financier	almond cake
glace	ice cream
île flottante/oeufs à la neige	soft meringues floating on custard
macarons	macaroons
madeleine	small sponge cake
Mont-Blanc aux marrons	chestnut purée and cream on a rum-soaked sponge cake
mousse au chocolat	chocolate mousse
palmiers	caramelized puff pastries
parfait	frozen mousse, some times ice cream
petit suisse	smooth mixture of cream and curds
petits fours	bite-sized cakes/pastries
sablé	shortbread biscuit
savarin	filled, ring-shaped cake
tarte	tart
tartelette	small tart
truffes	truffles, chocolate or liqueur variety
yaourt, yogourt	yoghurt

CHEESE (FROMAGE)

There are more than four hundred types of French cheese, most of them named after their place of origin. *Chèvre* is goat's cheese and *brebis* is cheese made from sheep's milk. *Le plateau de fromages* is the cheeseboard, and bread – but not butter – is served with it.

Glossary

arrondissement one of any of the twenty districts of Paris
banlieue suburb
berge riverside
biologique or bio organic
chemin path
consigne left-luggage office
défense de… It is forbidden to…
dégustation tasting (wine or food)
fermeture closing period
gare station; "routière" – bus station; "SNCF" – train station
hôtel hotel, but also a townhouse or mansion
jours fériés public holidays
marché market
navette shuttle
nocturne late-night opening

place square
plan city map; "du métro" – métro map
porte gateway or door
poste post office
quartier district
rez-de-chaussée ground floor
roman Romanesque (as opposed to "romain", which means "Roman")
soldes sales
sortie exit
tabac bar or shop selling stamps, cigarettes, etc
tarif price of admission; **tarif réduit** reduced price (for children, students etc)
villa a small residential street
zone bleue restricted parking
zone piétonne pedestrian zone

Small print and index

A ROUGH GUIDE TO ROUGH GUIDES

Published in 1982, the first Rough Guide – to Greece – was a student scheme that became a publishing phenomenon. Mark Ellingham, a recent graduate in English from Bristol University, had been travelling in Greece the previous summer and couldn't find the right guidebook. With a small group of friends he wrote his own guide, combining a contemporary, journalistic style with a thoroughly practical approach to travellers' needs.

The immediate success of the book spawned a series that rapidly covered dozens of destinations. And, in addition to impecunious backpackers, Rough Guides soon acquired a much broader readership that relished the guides' wit and inquisitiveness as much as their enthusiastic, critical approach and value-for-money ethos. These days, Rough Guides include recommendations from budget to luxury and cover more than 120 destinations around the globe, from Amsterdam to Zanzibar, all regularly updated by our team of roaming writers.

Browse all our latest guides, read inspirational features and book your trip at **roughguides.com**.

Rough Guide credits

Editor: Freya Godfrey
Layout: Ankur Guha
Cartography: Rajesh Mishra
Picture editor: Michelle Bhatia
Proofreader: Jan McCann
Managing editor: Monica Woods
Assistant editor: Shasya Goel

Production: Jimmy Lao
Cover photo research: Mark Thomas
Photographer: Lydia Evans
Editorial assistant: Aimee White
Senior DTP coordinator: Dan May
Programme manager: Gareth Lowe
Publishing director: Georgina Dee

Publishing information

This sixteenth edition published January 2018 by
Rough Guides Ltd,
80 Strand, London WC2R 0RL
11, Community Centre, Panchsheel Park,
New Delhi 110017, India
Distributed by Penguin Random House
Penguin Books Ltd, 80 Strand, London WC2R 0RL
Penguin Group (USA), 345 Hudson Street, NY 10014, USA
Penguin Group (Australia), 250 Camberwell Road,
Camberwell, Victoria 3124, Australia
Penguin Group (NZ), 67 Apollo Drive, Mairangi Bay,
Auckland 1310, New Zealand
Penguin Group (South Africa), Block D, Rosebank Office
Park, 181 Jan Smuts Avenue, Parktown North, Gauteng,
South Africa 2193
Rough Guides is represented in Canada by DK Canada, 320
Front Street West, Suite 1400, Toronto, Ontario M5V 3B6
Printed in Singapore
© Rough Guides, 2018
Maps © Rough Guides

416pp includes index
A catalogue record for this book is available from the
British Library
ISBN: 978-0-24130-607-9
The publishers and authors have done their best to
ensure the accuracy and currency of all the information
in **The Rough Guide to Paris**, however, they can accept
no responsibility for any loss, injury, or inconvenience
sustained by any traveller as a result of information or
advice contained in the guide.
1 3 5 7 9 8 6 4 2

Help us update

We've gone to a lot of effort to ensure that the sixteenth
edition of **The Rough Guide to Paris** is accurate and up-
to-date. However, things change – places get "discovered",
opening hours are notoriously fickle, restaurants and
rooms raise prices or lower standards. If you feel we've got
it wrong or left something out, we'd like to know, and if
you can remember the address, the price, the hours, the
phone number, so much the better.

Please send your comments with the subject line
"**Rough Guide Paris Update**" to mail@uk.roughguides.
com. We'll credit all contributions and send a copy of the
next edition (or any other Rough Guide if you prefer) for
the very best emails.

ABOUT THE AUTHORS

Ruth Blackmore is a freelance editor and writer, and longstanding contributor to the Rough Guides to Paris and France. She grew up in South Wales and lives in Dorset with her young family.

Samantha Cook is a London-based writer and editor who has been nipping across the Channel to Paris on a regular basis since the age of seven. Her other books as author include Rough Guides to London; Vintage London; Kent, Sussex & Surrey; Budget Accommodation in Britain; New Orleans; and Chick Flicks.

Acknowledgements

Ruth Blackmore would like to thank Freya Godfrey for her thorough, sharp-eyed editing; Sam Cook for being a joy to work with; Philippa Chadwick for her company and spirit of adventure; Luce Herriou for her insights and tips; Léonard Klein for invaluable recommendations; and Dylan, Hannah and Rosa for their constant support and generosity.

Samantha Cook Many thanks to Ruth and Freya, both of whom made working on this guide a total pleasure, and to Greg, for everything.

Readers' updates

Thanks to all the readers who have taken the time to write in with comments and suggestions (and apologies if we've inadvertently omitted or misspelt anyone's name):

Martin Allen; Steve Harris; Justin Wigoder.

Photo credits

All photos © Rough Guides, except the following:
(Key: t-top; c-centre; b-bottom; l-left; r-right)

1 4Corners: Tim Draper
2 4Corners: Massimo Ripani
4 Alamy Stock Photo: imageimage
7 Alamy Stock Photo: Garden Photo World (tl). **Getty Images:** Peter Phipp (b)
9 Corbis: Bertrand Gardel (t). **Robert Harding Picture Library:** Andrea Innocenti (c)
10 Corbis: Bertrand Rieger
11 Corbis: Owen Franken (t). **Getty Images:** Fernand Ivaldi (b)
12 4Corners: Cogoli Franco (t)
14 Robert Harding Picture Library: Godong (tr). **SuperStock:** Thomas Craig (tl)
15 Alamy Stock Photo: Hemis (c). **Corbis:** Tuul & Bruno Morandi (b). **Getty Images:** Mehdi Fedouach (t)
16 Glass: Guillaume Belvèze (t)
17 Fabien Campoverde: Fabien Campoverde (tr). **Corbis:** Benjamin Leterrier (tl)
20 Corbis: Neil Farrin
42 SuperStock: Tristan Deschamps
49 Dreamstime.com: Dennis Dolkens
59 Robert Harding Picture Library: Stuart Dee (b)
62 Alamy Stock Photo: Horizon Images / Motion
81 Robert Harding Picture Library: Bernard Jaubert (t)
86 Alamy Stock Photo: Nathaniel Noir
94 Alamy Stock Photo: Hemis
103 Alamy Stock Photo: Hemis (b). **Fabien Campoverde:** Fabien Campoverde (tl)
120 Corbis: Ben Johnson
131 Corbis: Arnaud Chicurel (b)
134 Dreamstime.com: Nikonaft

145 Alamy Stock Photo: David Coleman (tl); Godong (tr); Hemis (bl)
148 Corbis: Massimo Borchi
161 Corbis: Sylvain Sonnet
169 Alamy Stock Photo: Roger Coulam (t); John Kellerman (b)
189 Alamy Stock Photo: Hemis (t); Brian Jannsen (b)
196 Alamy Stock Photo: Hideo Kurihara
207 Alamy Stock Photo: Hemis
213 Corbis: Huften and Crow
221 Alamy Stock Photo: John Kellerman
229 Alamy Stock Photo: John Kellerman
236 Getty Images: Maremagnum
246 Alamy Stock Photo: Howard Sayer
273 Alamy Stock Photo: Per Karlsson – BKWine.com (tl)
287 Alamy Stock Photo: Glenn Harper (tl); Hemis (br). **Hotel Eldorado, Paris** (tr)
305 Alamy Stock Photo: LOOK Die Bildagentur der Fotografen GmbH (tl). **Le Comptoir Général** (b)
312 Corbis: Swim Ink 2, LLC (tl). **Etoile Cinémas:** (tr)
313 Alamy Stock Photo: AF archive (tl). **Corbis:** John Springer Collection (tr)
318 Corbis: Charles Platiau
331 Alamy Stock Photo: Sueddeutsche Zeitung Photo (tl). **Corbis:** Alistair Philip Wiper (bl)
342 SuperStock: Maurizio Borgese
353 Corbis: Horacio Villalobos (bl). **Getty Images:** Bertrand Guay / AFP (br)
357 Alamy Stock Photo: Lucas Dolega / epa
360 Corbis: John Harper

Cover: *Close-up detail of the Eiffel Tower* **4Corners:** Massimo Ripani

Index

Maps are marked in grey

Moulin, Jean 165, 244
movies 312
Moyen Age, Musée National du
....123
Mur des Fédérés 212
Musée de – see proper name: eg
   Musée d'Orsay is listed under O
museum passes 35
museums for children............354
music venues................ 304–306
   104, Le....................................304
   Alimentation Générale, L'........304
   Au Lapin Agile............................308
   Au Limonaire...............................306
   Au Magique...................................307
   Au Petit Théâtre du Bonheur.......308
   Autour de Midi…et Minuit.........308
   Aux Trois Mailletz........................307
   Baiser Salé, Le...............................307
   Bellevilloise, La.............................304
   Café de la Danse............................304
   Café de la Plage............................304
   Caveau de la Huchette.................307
   Chateau du Lac...............................307
   Chez Gégène...................................307
   Cigale, La..304
   Divan du Monde 304
   Duc des Lombards..........................307
   Elysée Montmartre.........................304
   Guinguette de l'Ile du
      Martin-Pecheur.........................307
   Instants Chavirés............................308
   International, L'................................306
   Maroquinerie....................................306
   New Morning 308
   Péniche Antipode............................306
   Péniche Le Marcounet.....................307
   Point Ephémère...............................306
   Sunset/Le Sunside, Le 307
   Supersonic..304
   Trois Baudets, Les............................308
Musique, Musée de la.............204

N

Napoleon.................46, 51, 57, 63,
   72, 78, 79, 80, 82, 84, 105, 110,
   143, 149, 150, 154, 155, 196,
   222, 230, 233, 237, 241, 368
Napoléon III 43, 50, 54, 57, 72,
   74, 91, 143, 186, 242, 349, 369
Napoleon's tomb 155
national war museum..............154
natural history museums 132
Navigo pass 28
New Year 323
newspapers 31
Nissim de Camondo, Musée
....69
Notre-Dame de la Médaille
   Miraculeuse 147
Notre-Dame de Lorette...........191

Notre-Dame du Travail 170
Notre-Dame, Cathédrale de 46
Nôtre, Le 71
Nouvel An, Le.............................323
Nouvel, Jean ...133, 151, 167, 203
Nouvelle Athènes 190
Nuit Blanche 323, 376
Nuit des Musées 322

O

Observatoire de Paris..............170
occupation.................................373
Odéon quarter...........................143
Olympiades, Les........................178
opening hours........................... 38
opera..320
Opéra, Bibliothèque-Musée del'
.... 75
Opéra Bastille................... 110, 375
Opéra Garnier..............................74
Orangerie (Jardin du
   Luxembourg) 146
Orangerie, Musée de l'.............. 72
Orly airport 25
Orsay, Musée d'........... 135–140

P

P'tit Vélib....................................352
Pagode, La..................................157
Palais Brongniart........................ 82
Palais de Chaillot 158
Palais de Justice 43
Palais de la Découverte............. 66
Palais de Luxembourg..............144
Palais de Tokyo 160
Palais de Tokyo Site de Création
   Contemporaine 159
Palais des Tuileries..................... 72
Palais Galliera 159
Palais Royal.................................80
Panthéon 127
Parc André-Citroën 174
Parc Astérix 351
Parc de Bagatelle 220
Parc de Belleville 208, 351
Parc de Bercy 116
Parc de la Villette 349
Parc de la Villette 202
Parc des Buttes-Chaumont....208
Parc Floral 118, 349
Parc Georges-Brassens
....175, 351
Parc Monceau 68, 351
Parc Montsouris 171, 351

Parc Rives de Seine
.... 6, 91, 154, 351
Parc Zoologique de Paris
.... 119, 351
Parfum, Grande Musée du 67
Parfum Fragonard, Musée du
.... 75
parfumeries 332
Paris Carte 28
Paris Face Cachée 322
Paris Jazz Festival.....................322
Paris l'Eté 323
Paris Marathon 345
Paris Mosque 132
Paris Museum pass 35
Paris Photo 323
Paris Plages 6, 199, 323, 376
Paris Rive Gauche 178
Paris Visites pass 28
Parisii, the 361
parking...................................... 28
parks 349–351
passage Brady..........................193
passage Choiseul....................... 82
passage des Panoramas............ 82
passage des Princes................... 84
passage du Caire 84
passage du Grand-Cerf............. 85
passage Jouffroy........................ 84
passage Molière 90
passage Verdeau........................ 84
passages.......................80–85
Passerelle Debilly......................160
Passerelle Simone de Beauvoir
....178
Passy and Auteil........... 214–221
Passy and Auteil 215
Pavillon Amont...........................140
Pavillon de l'Arsenal.................108
Père-Lachaise cemetery
.... 209–212
Père-Lachaise cemetery 210
Pernety quarter.........................170
pet cemetery.............................195
Petit Palais 67
Petite Ceinture..........................217
Petits-Pères, place des 81
pharmacies 37
Philharmonie 2..........................204
Philharmonie de Paris... 203, 375
phones....................................... 39
Piaf, Edith....................111, 206, 211
Picasso, Musée..........................102
Picasso, Pablo ...72, 89, 102–104,
   122, 136, 140, 146, 150, 160,
   163, 166, 167, 184, 186, 267
picnic food................................270
Pigalle 188
Piscine Josephine Baker..........178
place d'Italie..............................175

Map index

Listings key

- ■ Accommodation
- ● Eating
- ■ Drinking/Nightlife
- ● Shopping

City plan

The **city plan** on the pages that follow is divided as shown:

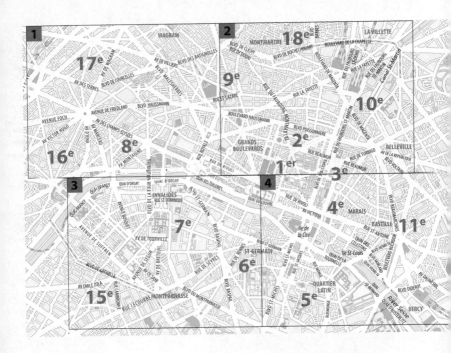

Map symbols

– – – Chapter division boundary	✈ Airport	✡ Synagogue
Motorway	Ⓜ Métro	⛪ Basilica
Major road	Ⓡ RER Paris	⛪ Cathedral
Minor road	Ⓣ Tram stop	◆ Place of interest
Pedestrian road	🚢 Boats	Building
Steps	P Parking	Church
Railway	✉ Post office	Stadium
– – Ferry route	ⓘ Tourist information	Cemetery
– – – Footpath	⊞ Hospital	Park
River	⊙ Statue	
⋊ Bridge	🏰 Château	

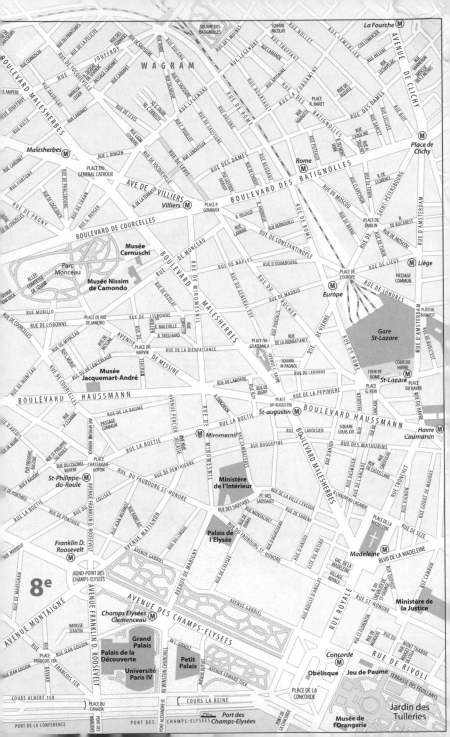

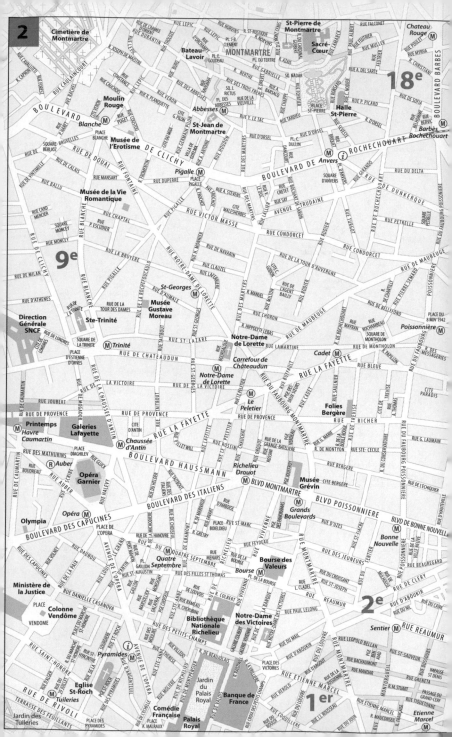

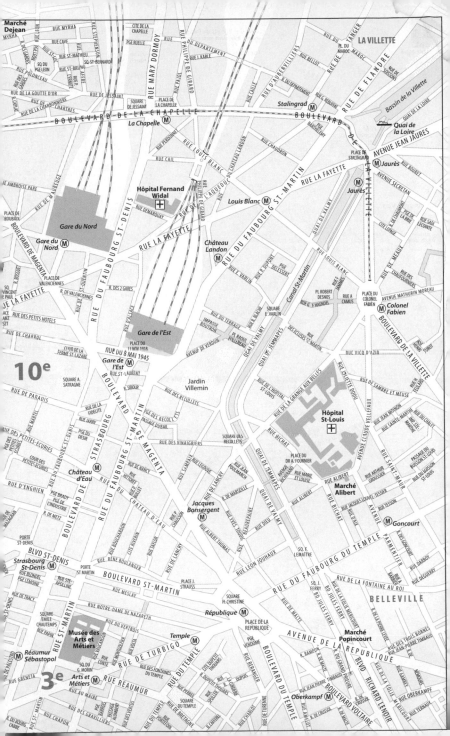

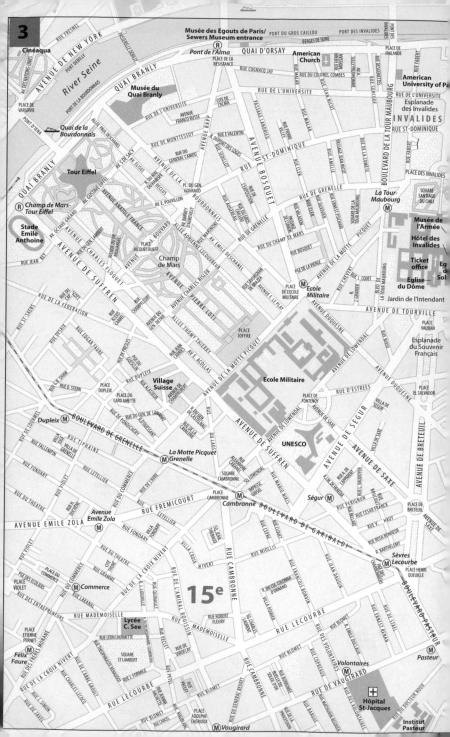

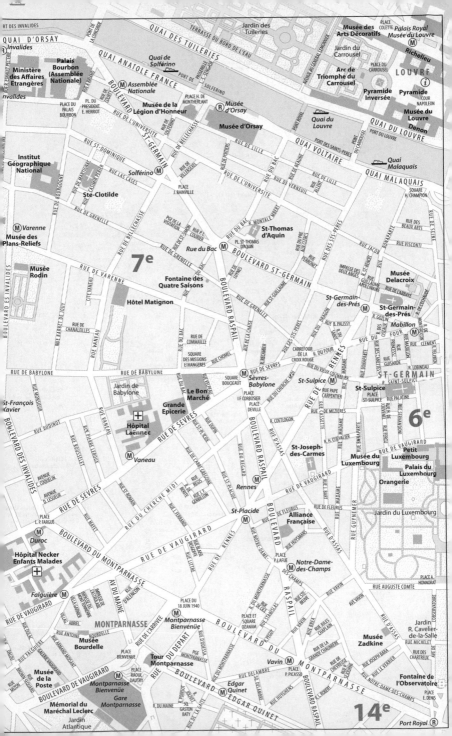

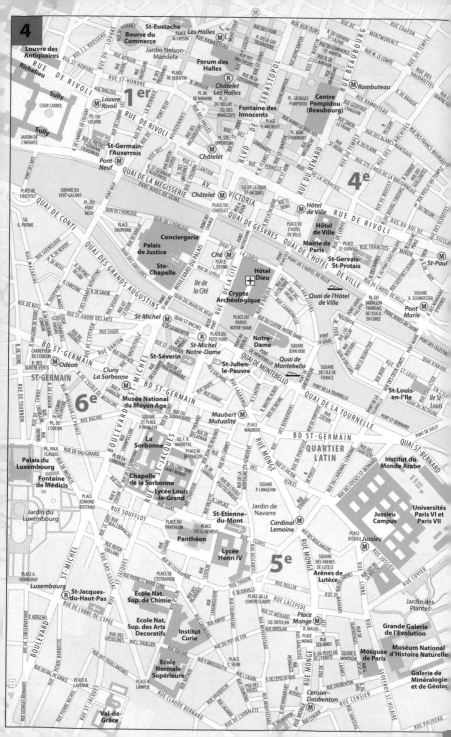

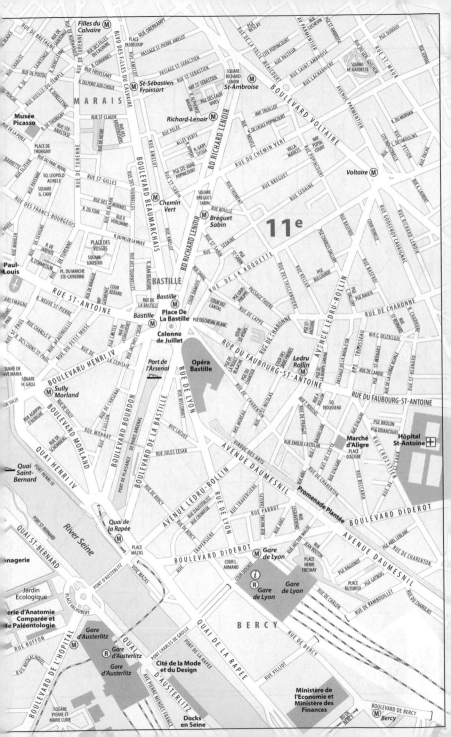

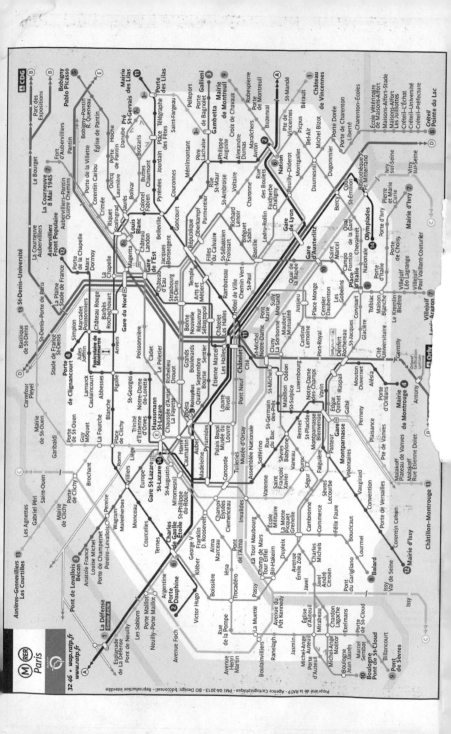